Modern Spain

Recent Title in Understanding Modern Nations

Modern China
Xiaobing Li

MODERN SPAIN

Understanding Modern Nations

Enrique Ávila López

 ABC-CLIO™

An Imprint of ABC-CLIO, LLC
Santa Barbara, California • Denver, Colorado

Copyright © 2016 by ABC-CLIO, LLC

Library of Congress Cataloging-in-Publication Data

Ávila López, Enrique.
   Modern Spain / Enrique Ávila López.
     pages cm.—(Understanding modern nations)
   Includes bibliographical references and index.
   ISBN 978-1-61069-600-5 (alk. paper)—ISBN 978-1-61069-601-2 (ebook)   1. Spain–Description and travel.   I. Title.
     DP43.2.A95   2016
    946–dc23   2015023737

ISBN: 978-1-61069-600-5
EISBN: 978-1-61069-601-2

20 19 18 17 16   1 2 3 4 5

This book is also available on the World Wide Web as an eBook.
Visit www.abc-clio.com for details.

ABC-CLIO
An Imprint of ABC-CLIO, LLC

ABC-CLIO, LLC
130 Cremona Drive, P.O. Box 1911
Santa Barbara, California 93116-1911

This book is printed on acid-free paper ∞

Manufactured in the United States of America

CONTENTS

SERIES FOREWORD

We live in an evolving world, a world that is becoming increasingly globalized by the minute. Cultures collide and blend, leading to new customs and practices that exist alongside long-standing traditions. Advancing technologies connect lives across the globe, affecting those from densely populated urban areas to those who dwell in the most remote locations in the world. Governments are changing, leading to war and violence but also to new opportunities for those who have been oppressed. The *Understanding Modern Nations* series seeks to answer questions about cultures, societies, and customs in various countries around the world.

Understanding Modern Nations is geared toward readers wanting to expand their knowledge of the world, ideal for high school students researching specific countries, undergraduates preparing for studies abroad, and general readers interested in learning more about the world around them. Each volume in the series focuses on a single country, with coverage on Africa, the Americas, Asia and the Pacific, and Europe.

Each country volume contains 16 chapters focusing on various aspects of culture and society in each country. The chapters begin with an Overview, which is followed by short entries on key topics, concepts, ideas, and biographies pertaining to the chapter's theme. In a way, these volumes serve as "thematic encyclopedias," with entries organized for the reader's benefit. Following a general Preface and Introduction, each volume contains chapters on the following themes:

- Geography
- History
- Government and Politics
- Economy
- Religion and Thought
- Social Classes and Ethnicity
- Gender, Marriage, and Sexuality
- Education
- Language
- Etiquette
- Literature and Drama
- Art and Architecture

- Music and Dance
- Food
- Leisure and Sports
- Media and Popular Culture

Each entry concludes with a list of cross references and Further Readings, pointing readers to additional print and electronic resources that might prove useful.

Following the chapters are appendices, including "A Day in the Life" feature, which depicts "typical" days in the lives of people living in that country, from students to farmers to factory workers to stay-at-home and working mothers. A Glossary, Facts and Figures section, and Holidays chart round out the appendices. Volumes include a Selected Bibliography, as well as sidebars that are scattered throughout the text.

The volumes in the *Understanding Modern Nations* series are not intended to be comprehensive compendiums about every nation of the world, but instead are meant to serve as introductory texts for readers, examining key topics from major countries studied in the high school curriculum as well as important transitioning countries that make headlines daily. It is our hope that readers will gain an understanding and appreciation for cultures and histories outside of their own.

PREFACE

The idea of writing this type of book started in the 1990s when I moved to England, where I finished my studies and pursued my career teaching Spanish culture. Since then, Spanish culture has been a constant topic of my classes. Once in Canada in 2004, I also noticed the need for these particular books, written in English, for courses such as Romance Studies and Spanish Culture, which are staples in the Arts as well as in the International programs of most North American universities.

The main philosophy in writing *Modern Spain* has been to find a conciliatory voice, which subsequently has also become my most difficult challenge. That is to say, my major goal has been to conciliate different voices about Spain as the principal topic. On one hand, I incorporate what Spaniards have written on different subjects (i.e., history, religion, politics, and the economy). This task alone adds an extra difficulty to the job at hand due to the fact that Spaniards tend to disagree with each other and have their own views on the same subject. For instance, there are multiple versions of the beginning of Spain as a country. On the other hand, since part of my background is Canadian, I have also tried to add what English thinkers have written about Spain. As a result, I obtained a more comprehensive knowledge of Spain, because the country is seen from multiple perspectives rather than from a single ethnocentric point of view. In doing so, I try to avoid Eurocentrism as well as Americentrism.

This book is organized into 16 chapters plus a final section entitled "A Day in the Life," in which four different people provide their daily routines of living a normal day in Spain. In terms of language and translation, I have tried to keep it original. For instance, most place names keep their local Spanish version such as Sevilla or Catalunya instead of the Anglicized ones (Seville or Catalonia). Most of the translations, if not indicated, are mine, and I take full responsibility if there are any errors.

The breadth of the book focuses not only on history, politics, the economy, literature, and cinema, which are usually the main topics analyzed often as a single theme by English publications. It also includes other important subjects such as religion, gender, education, language, etiquette, art, architecture, music, food, sport, geography, media, and popular culture. Because of the interdisciplinary nature of its contents, this book differs from the typical English manual, which very rarely covers in depth the whole array of interesting issues that define Spain in the 21st century.

I would like to thank numerous people whose collaboration has been essential on many levels. First, I would like to thank my parents for their incalculable support including not only many days of free, all-inclusive accommodation in the sunny south of Spain (as part of the traditional Spanish culture), but also for showing me Spain on many memorable trips, as well as keeping me in the know with regard to the latest news from Spain.

Second, I am particularly grateful for the help and enthusiasm shown by many of my family members, friends, and former students including Joan, Santi, Esmeralda, Belén, and James. Also I would like to thank my publisher ABC-CLIO and, in particular, its team of editors including Kaitlin Ciarmiello, Erin Ryan, Nicholle Lutz, and Karen Woerner.

Third, I want to thank my institution, Mount Royal University, whose continuous financial assistance has facilitated my research. Their funding has been invaluable. As we say in Spain, *mil gracias*. I am also especially thankful to my dean Dr. Jeff Keshen and my colleagues Dr. José Gordillo and Dr. Karim Dharamsi.

Finally, I am always in debt to my wife, Lisa Bush, who provides me with tremendous support and guidance. In fact, this book simply would not have seen the light of day without her.

To our daughter Catherine Marisa, this book is for you—don't eat it. ☺

INTRODUCTION

Spain still constitutes an enigma and faces numerous problems in the 21st century. For instance, who are the Spaniards? Is there only one way of being Spanish? Is el Greco, who was born in Crete but lived in Spain, a Spanish artist? And what about Pablo Picasso, who was born in Málaga, but spent an extensive period of his life abroad—is he too Spanish? Yet if place of birth, place of residence, ethnicity, religion, political ideologies, or geographical borders do not define a Spaniard, then what in fact does?

Is the film *Vicky Cristina Barcelona* (2008) directed by the American Woody Allen a Spanish movie? Based on the fact that Spain or Spanish-ness (*españolidad*) is one of the main topics of the film, and due to the nationality of some of the characters (Javier Bardem, Penélope Cruz) as well as the fact that part of the budget was provided by the country itself, the answer is clear: *maybe*.

Popular Spanish television series have also been dealing with Spanish identity as a main subject. For instance, *Cuéntame como pasó* (TVE1: 2001–2014, *Tell Me How It Happened*) and *El ministerio del tiempo* (TVE1: 2015–present, *The Ministry of Time*) both recreate different episodes of Spanish history. Yet two other series have become very popular recently, although they use different approaches with regard to the representation of Spain. On the one hand, *Isabel* (TVE1: 2012–2014) portrays Queen Isabel as the principal character whose identity is strongly defined, reflecting all the intricacies of her time. On the other hand, *Sin identidad* (Antena 3: 2014–) depicts the story of a millennial female citizen whose identity is unknown (hence its title, which means "Without Identity") as she tries to discover her origins.

For some, Spain is still an anomaly in many spheres of Western society (i.e., economically, politically, institutionally, and even religiously). For others, however, the particular label of Spanish singularity (i.e., promoted in the 1960s by the old motto "Spain is different") has been consigned to the past.

And then there is the question, what is Spain exactly? Though historically the origin of the country had been attributed to the union of Isabel and Ferdinand, the people of the Iberian Peninsula at the time were multiethnic, with varying religious and political loyalties, including the iconic figure of *El Cid*. And if the country is to be considered as starting with Isabel and Ferdinand, then what about the Muslims that ruled for almost eight centuries previously? Should the Mosque of Córdoba or the Alhambra Palace not be considered Spanish? Certainly they are. Spain has been under the rule of various kings from different countries whose origins include Austria, France, and Italy. And a political definition of Spain continues to be tricky. In the 20th century alone Spain has been ruled by two kings (Alfonso XIII and Juan Carlos I), one republic (second in Spain's history, 1931–1939), two dictators (Miguel Primo de Rivera and Francisco Franco), multiple coup d'états including the Spanish Civil War (1936–1939), and four presidents who led Spain as a democracy (Adolfo Suárez, Leopoldo Calvo Sotelo, Felipe González, and José María Aznar).

The selection of entries attempts to reflect Spain's multifaceted historical past but also constitutes a reflection toward Spain's future. Some topics, however, have proven to be difficult to write about (i.e., Etiquette, *Marca España*, Diaspora), because of the sensitivity surrounding those particular subjects but also due to the limited amount of information available in either Spanish or English, which have been the two main languages used for sources.

I have made a conscious effort for my sources to reflect my intent, have collected my information from current Spanish popular media and ancient Spanish philosophers, English journalists as well as other European writers and sources, and North American theologians and art historians, to name a few. Sometimes the information may appear to be contradictory, but often the identity of a Spaniard is in conflict, based on who is being examined and through what lens.

This volume was not meant to be all-compassing but is rather an attempt to provide a solid overview of important topics, events and people, and geographical information about Spain.

Spain's land is astonishingly diverse. It consists of some of the largest and most untouched areas of wilderness in Europe. Geographical features include semi-arid land, snowcapped mountains, rolling green hills, rivers, volcanoes, lakes shrouded in mist, caves, beaches, and rocky cliffs overlooking the sea. Spain introduced the concept of national parks to Europe for the first time in 1918 with the Covadonga and Ordesa Park. Doñana Park constitutes the largest ecological reserve in Europe. Spain had 557 (in 2015) blue flag beaches, indicating it is safe to swim—the most in the EU. Spain has 8,000 species of plants and 60,000 species of animals. It ranks second worldwide in biosphere reserves on the UNESCO list. More than 80 percent of the species in Europe are found in Spain. Overall, Spain is home to 27 out of 425 biosphere reserves around the world.

The Spanish economy currently occupies an awkward position within the global economy. In fact, it has been described as an anomaly, different, unique. Although Spain does not belong to the G-8, the Spanish economy was the world's eighth largest in 2008, surpassing Canada's in 2006 (Encarnación 2008). From 2005 to 2007 Spain's economy grew more than any other country in the EU, and even more than some countries of the G-8. However, Spain does not have a significant voice within the 28 European Union countries, despite the fact that it is the eurozone's fifth-largest economy. Spain has gone through its worst economic crisis in recent history (2008–2014), and once again it seems to be growing more than any EU country in 2015.

The troubled economy is a strong component of Spain's social attitudes. On the one hand, many politicians have been caught in fraud and tax evasion, including members of the Spanish monarchy. At the same time, a percentage of Spaniards also embrace the idea of having more than one job, something that they coined as *pluriempleo* (multiple jobs), which does not necessarily present Spain as a higher employment rate. For instance, the lowest unemployment rate that Spain has ever achieved in its history was in 2006 with 8.26 percent (which any economist would consider still very high) while 2012 recorded Spain's highest unemployment rate with 25.77 percent, which simply is unacceptable and unsustainable. So, why are the Spanish citizens not protesting in the streets incessantly?

Overall, Spaniards are very resilient people and the role of the family has played a crucial part during the financial crisis. However, some Spaniards, regardless of whether they already have a job or not, unethically claim unemployment benefits. This corruption has been frequent since the 1990s, and it has been particularly pronounced in Andalucía, which is Spain's region with the highest level of unemployment. More recently, there has been the scandalous ERE case of 2011 on which Spain still awaits a final verdict, where 721 million euros of public money were allegedly channeled into private projects and some citizens received money for jobs they never did. Also, it is very common among Spaniards to partake in the custom of doing seasonal jobs (colloquially called *chapuzas*), which are paid in cash only (*en metálico* or *en negro*) in order to avoid taxes.

On the other hand, Spain still has the *indignados* movement 15-M which began in 2011, and has been seeking, among other demands, a decent wage. This request was in response to many Spaniards being paid less than 1,000 euros per month, who are popularly known as *mileuristas* (people who earn around a thousand euros monthly). The indignados as well as the mileuristas strongly criticize politicians who publicly occupy two or more official positions earning well over the salary of the average Spanish citizen. They denounce the malpractice of those Spanish politicians and authorities who since the 1990s have been engaging in the so called *cultura del pelotazo*, a term that refers to the idea of becoming rich quickly.

Spain is a secular country according to its 1978 Constitution; however, in 2014, 69 percent of Spaniards identified themselves as Catholics and many Spanish families still spend more than €2,000 on a child's first Holy Communion. Yet between 2000 and 2005 Spain's divorce rate rose to 277 percent, going from one of the lowest rates in the EU (2000) to the highest rate in 2007. Furthermore, in 2007 Spain developed one of the most pro-LGTB agendas in the world. Domestic violence, however, is still a huge issue in the country; for instance, in 2013, 22 percent of Spanish women acknowledged experiencing gender-specific violence. Also, Spain's recent history has been a violent one. For example, in the 20th century alone, three presidents were assassinated (Canalejas 1912; Dato 1921; and Carrero Blanco 1973), and Spain experienced two dictatorships, which, apart from their intolerance toward dissent of any form, involved rigidity that reached a level of absurdity in many social venues including even in the area of gastronomy. For example, during Franco's time the popular Spanish dish *ensaladilla rusa* was officially renamed *ensaladilla imperial*, avoiding the name of Russia because it was a country that supported Spain's republic.

Like Spanish cuisine, Spanish music is also full of flavor and tremendously varied. In fact, every region in Spain has its own distinctive heritage with its own regional music and dance. For instance, in Catalunya the dance is the *sardana*; in the Basque Country it is the *zortzicos*; and in Aragón it is the *jota*. In Galicia and Asturias they play the *muñeiras, alboradas, saudades,* and *pandeiradas* while in the two regions of Castilla they dance the *jota segoviana* (of Segovia), apart from being the home of the *seguidillas, las canciones de Ronda, los pasacalles,* and *la rueda.* Other popular dances are: *el fandango, el chotis, el pasodoble, el paloteo* or *ball de bastons, las pardicas, la charrada, el contrapás, las habas verdes, la isa canaria, la revolada, los verdiales,* and *la rumba.* Although the last is originally from Cuba, different Spanish groups have been able to adapt it into distinctive Spanish songs. Musicians such as Peret, and El Pescaílla and bands like The Gipsy Kings, Los Manolos, Estopa, and more recently Melendi have achieved huge success with this particular fusion sound, in which they manage to mix rumba, flamenco, and pop successfully.

A fusion of different elements is perhaps what defines Spain at its best on many levels including the Spanish landmark, which has been developed a step further in the new millennium. Nowadays, for instance, a single building incorporates a national as well as an international flair, mainly due to the collaboration of Spanish professionals working in conjunction with other international experts. Like the mega soccer teams of Real Madrid, and F. C. Barcelona, which successfully integrate national and international players, the result of other multicultural collaborations can be seen, for example, in the new terminal 4 at Barajas Airport (2006) in Madrid, designed by a Spaniard, Antonio Lamela, and an Englishman, Richard Rogers. More significantly, the airport was renamed Adolfo Suárez Madrid-Barajas in March 2014 in homage to Spain's first democratic president elected in 1979. He was a politician who embodied the transition of Spain from dictatorship to democracy.

Spain is currently undergoing a transition; yet transition is something the country is familiar with. My hope is that these entries adequately capture the complexity, the history, and the future possibilities of this dynamic country and its people.

SPAIN

Bay of Biscay

France

Santander

Oviedo•

•Bilbao

Santiago

Cordillera Cantabrica

•Vigo

Pyrenees

•Pamplona

Ebro

Duero

•Zaragoza

Barcelona•

Salamanca.

S p a i n

Mediterranean
Sea

Madrid★

Tajo

•Toledo

Valencia◄

Portugal

•Ibiza

Canary
Islands

Morocco

Alicante•

Guadalquivir

•Cordoba

Cartagena◄

Algeria

•Sevilla

Granada

Sierra Nevada

Canary Islands

North
Atlantic
Ocean

Cadiz•

Malaga•

Lanzarote•

La Palma

Strait of
Gibraltar

Tenerife

Fuerteventura

•Ceuta

La Gomera

•Mt. Teide

•Melilla

El Hierro

Gran Canaria

M o r o c c o

CHAPTER 1

GEOGRAPHY

OVERVIEW

Spain is the second largest country in the European Union (EU) and contains a rich natural diversity. Spain occupies 195,364 square miles (505,991 square kilometers), of which one-sixth lies at over 3,280 feet. Spain is second only to Switzerland in Europe for average land height (650 meters; 2,132 feet).

Spain borders Andorra and France to the north; the towering Pyrenees Mountains also construct Spain's northern boundary. Spain is bordered by Portugal in the west. The southern tip of Spain runs along the small region of Gibraltar, a land mass that Great Britain took over in 1713 at the end of the War of the Spanish Succession. At its southernmost point Spain is a mere eight miles away from the northern coast of Africa.

Spain boasts a vast shoreline, one that exceeds 3,107 miles (5,000 kilometers). More than half of its coast runs along the Atlantic sea. Spain borders the tranquil waters of the Mediterranean Sea to the southeast and east.

In addition to the mainland, Spain also consists of two chains of islands and two colonies in North Africa. The Canary Islands are a chain of seven geographically unique islands located in the Atlantic Ocean 620 miles south of the Iberian Peninsula and 67 miles from the northwest African mainland. The Balearic Islands consist of five islands located in the western Mediterranean Sea. The group of islands is located 50 to 190 miles east of the Iberian Peninsula. Ceuta, located on the north coast of Morocco, and Melilla, which is farther east on the Moroccan coast, are two colonies that have been governed by Spain for centuries.

The geography of the Iberian Peninsula is home to multiple rivers and mountain ranges that dominate the landscape of Spain. The country is dissected by five large rivers: the Tajo, the Ebro, the Duero, the Guadiana, and the Guadalquivir. The Tajo (626 miles), Ebro (565 miles), and Duero (556 miles) are among Europe's longest rivers. In addition to the Pyrenees Mountains in the north, major mountain ranges include Cordillera Cantábrica, the Cordillera Central located in Spain's interior, as well as Cordillera Bética and Sierra Nevada in the south of Spain. The mountains of the Canary Islands are also significant, with Teide Peak on Tenerife boasting the highest point in the country at 12,198 feet. Central Spain consists of a plateau or *meseta* that rises half a mile above sea level.

The mountain ranges and rivers not only shape Spain's geographical landscape, they also played a key role in establishing Spain's early political kingdoms. To date, geography is the main reason for Spain maintaining its regional traditions and diversity due to the fact that isolated pockets of communities were far removed from the rapidly changing culture of the cities.

Spain's land is astonishingly diverse. It consists of some of the largest and most untouched areas of wilderness in Europe. Geographical features include snowcapped mountains, rolling green hills, rivers, volcanoes, lakes shrouded in mist, caves, beaches, and rocky cliffs overlooking the sea. The landscape is one of the factors that makes Spain a popular tourist destination, and the country has gone to great lengths to conserve its land, sea, and coastline. Over 14 million hectares of land have been protected as well as 1 million hectares of sea. Spain's coastline varies considerably and currently consists of cliffs (20%); rocky coast (21%); flood plains (28%); and beaches (18%). The remaining 13 percent of coastline has been altered by humans. In recent years there is a tension between man-made developments and land conservation. Spain continues to strive to protect its natural habitat, most notably through the park system.

Spain introduced the concept of national parks to Europe for the first time in 1918 with the Covadonga and Ordesa Park. Doñana Park constitutes the largest ecological reserve in Europe. In 2015 Spain had 577 blue flag beaches, indicating it is safe to swim—the most in the EU. The history of Spain's commitment to conserving the environment can be dated to the 18th century. However, the Ministry of Environment was not created until 1996.

Spain has 8,000 species of plants and 60,000 species of animals. Spain ranks second worldwide in biosphere reserves on the UNESCO list. More than 80 percent of the species in Europe are found in Spain. Overall, Spain is home to 27 out of 425 biosphere reserves around the world.

Much of Spain's land had been cultivated for agricultural purposes. Spain has the most planted vineyards in the world with 1,032 billion hectares, becoming the second largest wine exporter behind only Italy. Spain is a world leader in organic farming, and it is the largest exporter of olive oil in the world at 1,100,000 tons per year. Spain is the number one producer and exporter of table olives in the world; number one producer of pine nuts in the world; number one exporter of citrus fruits; Europe's top producer of fruit preserves, honey, and fish from fish farms; the world's second biggest producer and exporter of almonds, fish preserves, and shellfish; and the world's second largest producer of saffron, artichokes and mussels.

Table 1.1   FOREST AREA (2010)

EU—Out of 27 members at the time	Thousands of hectares
Sweden	28,203
Finland	22,157
Spain	18,173
France	15,954
Germany	11,076

Source: Eurostat.

Spain is one of the world leaders in desalination of sea water, brackish water, and the use of renewable energy. For instance, the company Acciona Agua is a world leader in reverse osmosis desalination technology, and is participating in the construction of the world's largest desalination plant in Saudi Arabia. Spain is ranked fourth in the world in desalinated water (3 million cubic meters per day).

Spaniards consume 36.5 kilograms of fish per capita a year, making it the world's second largest per capita consumer of seafood (behind Japan). Spain leads the EU in landing fish, fleet tonnage, and number of fishermen. The Calvo Company is one of the five largest canned food companies in the world. In 2010, Spain was first in total fish production in the EU, and in particular, in aquaculture (or the farming of organisms in aquatic plants), where it accounted for 20.1 percent of all aquaculture in the EU. Although Spanish waters produce thousands of tons of seafood each year, it is not nearly enough to feed the Spanish appetite for fish. Spain, largely through importers in San Sebastián, buys from Norway, France, South Africa, and even South America.

The dry climate of parts of Spain can make the land susceptible to forest fires. In 2012, there was a surge of forest fires in Spain—both natural and man-made. For instance, there were 38 large fires in 2012 alone, which contrasts with the average of 28 that occurred in the past decade.

Spain's greenhouse gas emissions were 7.5 percent of the total of the EU in 2010. Most of the emissions were caused by transport (25.7%) and energy industries (20.3%). With regards to temperature, the year 2012 was warmer than usual. In fact, it reached an estimated average of 59.4°F, which was over the normal average figure of 33.26°F. In terms of precipitation, 2012 was also unusual in the sense that it was drier than normal. The northwest Atlantic coast is the main area of rain in Spain, "but most of all on the village of Grazalema, high in the mountains between Málaga and Cádiz" (Oldale 2012).

There are two very distinct types of vegetation in Spain due to its warmer and wetter areas. On one hand, the north is a wet range where there is plenty of green vegetation such as the common oak, lime trees, chestnut trees, elm trees, ash trees, maple trees, and hazelnut trees. The second largest area of vegetation in Spain is located in the south, which is characterized by a dry, summer climate. Dominant species are the evergreen oak and cork oak forests plus the distinctive olive trees as a common feature in the region of Andalucía. The southern city of Jaén has more olive trees than any other place in the world.

Spain is home to a vast assortment of animal species originating from European, African, and Mediterranean habitats. Some of the animals associated with the country include the wolf, Iberian lynx, Spanish ibex, and wild boar. Spain also contains numerous bird species such as eagles, hawks, bearded vultures, and goshawks. In addition, Spain serves as a stop for migratory birds traveling between Europe and Africa such as ducks and flamingos. Spain is known for its freshwater rivers and lakes, which are home to a variety of fish such as barbell and trout.

Spain's economy is the fifth largest of the EU which, according to a recent study (Tukker et al. 2014), subsequently generates a high environmental footprint. For example, the carbon, land, and material footprints of Spain are higher than the world average. Also, partly due to its dry climate, Spain has one of the highest water footprints per capita (sixth position) in the world. Spain occupied the 15th position in 2012 in "the Global Significance Rank (alternatively 'Google Search Rank'), which gauges each country's contemporary prominence in the eyes of the world by measuring its internet footprint as a proxy" (Oldale 2012).

Further Reading

Farino, Teresa, and Mike Lockwood. *Travellers' Nature Guides: Spain*. Oxford: Oxford University Press, 2003.

Knowles, Laura. *Countries around the World: Spain*. Chicago: Charlotte Guillain, 2012.

Oldale, John. *A World of Curiosities*. New York: Plume, 2012.

Tukker, Arnold, et al. *The Global Resource Footprint of Nations. Carbon, Water, Land and Materials Embodied in Trade and Final Consumption*. Delft: Leiden University, 2014.

Archaeological Artifacts

Approximately one million years ago numerous cultures began to occupy the Iberian Peninsula. Some of these civilizations are still visible through monuments throughout Spain. Others have been studied through artifacts. One fact, however, remains: every single village in Spain contains facets of Spanish heritage. Canadian archaeologist James M. Anderson describes Spain as "a great museum" (Anderson 1997).

More recently, on December 4, 2013, a group of Spanish anthropologists decoded the oldest-known human DNA in the world, extracted from a 400,000-year-old thigh bone found in the Sima de los Huesos (Pit of Bones), preserved by a deep subterranean chill in Spain's northern Sierra de Atapuerca highlands (Gruber 2013). According to Juan Luis Arsuaga, Bermúdez de Castro, and Eudald Carbonell, this new finding poses an intriguing and complex pattern of evolution in the origin of modern humans. While this important discovery is being analyzed, however, another relevant fact about Spain remains: the Iberian Peninsula constitutes a key site for humanity where different cultures thrived.

Following Anderson's thesis, initially cave cultures occupied what is known as Spain today. However, the main influences came first from Europe and secondly from the eastern part of the Mediterranean Sea—hence the legacy of the Celts. The heritage of other foreign cultures can also be felt in Spain today, including the Phoenician, the Carthaginian, and the Greek, followed by the Roman legacy, and subsequently the Visigoth legacy. Later on, the north of Africa also played a vital role in the development of Spain as the last major influential culture that shaped Spain in such a way that makes it different from the rest of Europe. Modern Spain, like many other nations, is the consequence of different events in which foreign cultural elements became an integral part of the local societies in order to form one multifaceted civilization.

Between 1000 BCE and 200 BCE the Iberians, Celts, Phoenicians, Greeks, and Carthaginians came in succession to the Iberian Peninsula. There were also many Jews among the early settlers. The Romans controlled the Peninsula between 201 BCE and the early years of the fifth century CE. At the beginning of the fifth century several Germanic tribes, including the Visigoths (*godos*), conquered the Roman forces and maintained control of the Peninsula until the Muslim invasion in 711. Christian kings regained control of the Peninsula by 1492. Muslims living under Christian rule were called *mudéjares*. Their artistic and architectural work is called *mudéjar* art. Many mudéjares settled in the New World, where their crafts flourished in places such as Mexico, Colombia, Ecuador, and Peru. However, cultural diversity has also been a long-standing source of conflict in Spain. The Basque and Catalonian separatist movements, for example, are not only political phenomena, but also cultural ones.

Archaeological artifacts can be seen throughout Spain. The following are examples of different cultural trips:

- Caves in Álava and Burgos
- Dolmens of Antequera
- Talayot in the Balearic Islands of Majorca and Minorca
- Pre-Roman churches in Asturias
- Celtic, Roman, and Visigoth vestiges in the cities of León and Lugo
- Dolmens in Álava and Logroño
- Megaliths, Roman, and Jewish artifacts in Girona
- Greek, Iberian, and Roman artifacts in Girona
- Iberian, Roman, and Arab artifacts in Jaén
- Iberian settlements and rural paintings in Castelló and Tarragona
- Phoenician and Roman artifacts in Málaga and Granada
- Roman and Visigoth artifacts in Guadalajara and Cuenca
- Engravings on rocks in Pontevedra
- Roman and Arab artifacts in Cádiz and Málaga
- Phoenician, Roman, Arab, and rural paintings in Málaga
- Roman mausoleums in Zaragoza
- Roman villas with tiles in Palencia
- Old churches in Burgos, Palencia, and Cantabria

See also: Chapter 1: Overview; Natural Resources and Environment; Regions of Spain; World Heritage. Chapter 2: Overview; Timeline; Adriano; Séneca. Chapter 3: Overview. Chapter 5: Overview. Chapter 9: Overview; Chapter 11: Overview. Chapter 12: Overview. Chapter 14: Overview.

Further Reading

Anderson, James M. *Guía arqueológica de España*. Madrid: Alianza Editorial, 1997.

Gruber, Karl. "Discovery of Oldest DNA Scrambles Human Origins Picture." *National Geographic,* December 4, 2013. http://news.nationalgeographic.com/news/2013/12/131204-human-fossil-dna-spain-denisovan-cave/

Bodies of Water: Tajo, Ebro, Sanabria, Covadonga

The Tajo River is Spain's longest river (1,038 km; 645 miles). It arises in the Sierra de Albarracín in the region of Aragón, and runs westward across Spain to empty in Portugal into the Atlantic Ocean near Lisbon. The central city of Toledo is surrounded by the Tajo River, which irrigates most of the nearby area as well as enhances the splendor of the city of Toledo, which was designated a World Heritage Site by UNESCO in 1986 for being a multicultural hub of Spain. The film *El río que nos lleva* (1989, *The River That Takes Us*) has been declared a film of cultural interest by UNESCO for its contribution to the preservation of the cultural and ecological values of the Tajo River. Although the plot is the story of the *gancheros*—a group of loggers that disappeared in the mid-1940s while transporting tree trunks from the upper reaches (Alto Tajo) down river to the collecting mills at Aranjuez—the movie becomes a lesson that deeply explores the meaning of *Spanishness* during the middle of the 20th century.

The Ebro River is Spain's largest river (930 km; 578 miles). The Ebro originates in the Cantabria region of northern Spain and ends in Amposta in the region of Catalunya. It travels through many villages and towns. For example, the city of Zaragoza enjoys the glory of its waters. The Ebro River flows into a delta that has been declared a protected space—the Delta del Ebro Natural Park. The Ebro Delta has become a niche in Europe for bird watchers, since it is possible to spot up to 300 species of birds.

Nestled in a landscape formed 100,000 years ago, Sanabria Lake Nature Reserve has amazing views and landscape. Sanabria Lake is found in the northeast in the town of Zamora, and the mountainous area is characterized by an abundance of glacier lagoons. The Sanabria Lagoon is the most significant one, which is a magnificent glacier with ice that stretches more than 20 kilometers. Today its 318 hectares of land, and depth of up to 51 meters, make it the largest lake on the Iberian Peninsula. Sanabria Lake constitutes a good research location for studying glaciers, and there are numerous foot trails.

The Covadonga Lakes (or *Picos de Europa*) are the most visited lakes in Spain. They can be found in the heart of the oldest National Park in Spain, separated by the fell of the Picota, Enol, and Ercina. They are located within the Picos de Europa National Park and can be found 27 kilometers from the town of Cangas de Onís (Asturias). Sailors coming from America to Europe named it Picos de Europa because it was the first mountain they could see when navigating to Europe. This impressive area occupies three Spanish regions: Asturias, Cantabria, and León. Its beauty is captivating at all times of the year. Beginning at the Covadonga sanctuary, access to the lakes is an equally remarkable experience. The road to the lakes has 12 kilometers of twisting bends and curves that slowly reveal the marvelous natural landscape. Beech and oak forests are the habitat of the marten (*marta*, or *Martes martes*) and the local duck (*ánade real* or *Anas platyrhynchos*). Halfway to the lakes is the Mirador de la Reina with fantastic views of the area.

Lake Enol is at a height of 1,070 meters above sea level. Cows, horses, and sheep graze calmly on the endless green pastures around the lake, taking no notice of the visitors. Ercina Lake is at a height of 1,108 meters above sea level with a spectacular range of colors.

Due to the plants in the water and the changes in light, the waters of the lake change color, going from light green to dark green with, on occasion, splashes of yellow or red.

See also: Chapter 1: Overview; Mountain Ranges: Teide, Sierra Nevada, and the Pyrenees; National Parks; Natural Resources and Environment; Regions of Spain; World Heritage.

Further Reading

Copons, Elisenda. *Montañas de España. Rutas, paseos y aventuras*. Barcelona: ElCobre Ediciones, 2006.

Dunlop, Fiona. *National Geographic Traveler: Spain*. Washington: National Geographic Society, 2012.

Real, Antonio del, Dir. *El río que nos lleva*. Madrid: Producciones Dulcinea and TVE, 1989.

Cities: Barcelona, Madrid, Sevilla, Valencia

The contemporary, bustling city of Barcelona is located in the northeast region of Spain. It is situated between the Pyrenees Mountains and the Mediterranean Sea. It has a Mediterranean climate, which consists of mild wet winters and hot summers. Barcelona is the second largest city in Spain with a population of approximately 1.6 million. Barcelona is well-connected with Europe and also within Spain, being served by the high speed train AVE as well as a very efficient tramway system, which is divided into two subsystems: the *Trambaix*, which serves the western part of the city and the *Trambesòs*, which serves the eastern side.

Barcelona is the capital of the region of Catalunya, and the city has one of the highest annual salaries in comparison with the national average. According to Instituto Nacional de Estadística (INE: National Institute of Statistics), in 2010 in Barcelona the average salary was €26,635, which is roughly €2,220 monthly (about $3,050).

Barcelona is also well-known for its avant-garde *modernsite* architecture and its international cuisine. The famous architect Antoni Gaudí transformed the city, creating a magical architecture inspired mainly by natural and religious elements. For example, the Sagrada Familia, Parc Güell, and Casa Milà (also known as La Pedrera) are great examples of Gaudí's whimsical style. Other 19th-century masterpieces of Barcelona are Domènech i Montaner's Casa Lleó Morera and the conservatory called Palau de la Música Catalana—both examples of a modernist style. More recently, the Museu Picasso and the MACBA (Museu d'Art Contemporani de Barcelona) are two prestigious museums recognized worldwide.

Eating in Barcelona, like in the rest of the region of Catalunya, is a pleasure that has been acknowledged nationally and internationally. The names of Ferran Adrià, the Roca Brothers, and Carme Ruscalleda, just to name a few, have already received global attention for the originality and creativity of their cuisine. The Nou Camp, which is the largest football stadium in Europe; the food market, la Boqueria; and the Liceu, Barcelona's opera house, are also three major local institutions that make Barcelona inhabitants proud.

Madrid is located in the middle of Spain and was made its capital in 1561 by King Philip II, who in his time was the most powerful person in the world. As a result, "Madrid is unique among European capitals for having been founded with disregard for comfort or convenience" (Oldale 2012). Madrid is the largest city of Spain with 3.2 million people, and the third largest in the European Union (after London and Berlin). It has continental weather, which usually consists of a dry, cold climate during the winter season and hot summers. Madrid is the second highest capital city in Europe (after Andorra la Vella at 1,123 meters = 2,684 ft) with an elevation of 646 meters or 2,120 feet. The skyline of Madrid has recently become taller. Currently, Madrid has several tall buildings such as Torre de Cristal (249 m = 817 ft), Torre Bankia (248.3 m = 814 ft), Torre PwC (236 m = 774 ft), and Torre Espacio (224.15 m = 735 ft).

Madrid is also a very well connected city nationally and internationally by road, train, and air. Madrid's metro is one of the longest subways in the EU. According to Instituto Nacional de Estadística (INE: National Institute of Statistics), in 2010 Madrid's average salary was €29,578, which is roughly €2,465 monthly (about $3,386). Madrid is relatively cheap in comparison with many other cities within the EU.

Madrid houses monuments from the 17th and 18th centuries such as the Town Hall, Plaza Mayor, Royal Palace, and Puerta de Alcalá. Madrid is also a pivotal center for cultural arts and home to three major international museums: Prado, Reina Sofía, and the Thyssen-Bornemisza. The latter contains one of the largest private collections of paintings in the world. Soccer is the main sport of Spain, so much so that Madrid

A view of the Madrid skyline includes emblematic buildings such as Kio Towers, October 17, 2011. (Victor Torres/Dreamstime.com)

acquired the title of "The Soccer Capital" in 2014, when two local teams from the same city (Real Madrid and Atlético de Madrid) played the UEFA Champions League Final for the first time in the history of the game in Europe.

Sevilla is located southwest of Madrid. It is the capital of the region of Andalucía with a population of less than a million (just over 700,000). The city enjoys good, sunny weather most of the year, although it can also be unpleasantly hot during the summer. After hosting the Universal Exposition in 1992, the urban landscape inherited a great infrastructure such as the theme park of Isla Mágica, the American Garden (in La Cartuja), and the Parque del Alamillo–San Jerónimo, which is the largest park in Andalucía. Sevilla was one of the first cities to connect with Madrid through the high speed train or AVE. According to Instituto Nacional de Estadística (INE: National Institute of Statistics), in 2010, the average salary was €18,345, which is roughly €1,529 monthly (about $2,100).

In the 17th century, due to Spanish colonization, Sevilla was the largest city in Europe with 140,000 people, just behind London, Paris, and Napoli. Philip II did not move his Crown to Sevilla because he was afraid it was too cosmopolitan for his strong religious background. Instead he chose Madrid, which was located in the middle of nowhere at the time. As an old city, Sevilla offers many historic monuments, such as the Cathedral, Alcázar, Archives of the Indies, the Maestranza bullring, the Teatro de la Maestranza concert hall, Parque de María Luisa, Plaza de América, Plaza de España, and Torre de Oro, to name a few. More recently, Sevilla also has seen the construction of many modern buildings such as the Metropol Parasol, which opened in 2011 and is "currently the world's largest wood structure" (Schoenfeld 2015).

Valencia is located in the east central part of Spain. The town of Valencia is also the capital of the region Comunitat Valenciana. The city has a population of approximately 800,000 people. It enjoys mild Mediterranean weather with moderate temperatures throughout the year. Due to its privileged position near the Mediterranean Sea, Valencia is not only well connected by sea, but also by road, train, and air. Because of its consistently good climate, Valencia possesses some of the most fertile land in Europe, and is "the most densely populated agricultural region outside Egypt and India" (Morris 2008). For instance, the cultivation of rice, oranges, and almonds are quintessential products of the region. Valencia is also rich in history, and two well-known examples are the celebration of the *Fallas* and the *Fiesta de Moros y Cristianos*. Both festivities consist of a re-enactment of different episodes in the history of Valencia.

According to Instituto Nacional de Estadística (INE: National Institute of Statistics), in 2010, the average salary in Valencia was €21,251, which is roughly €1,771 monthly (about $2,433). As an old city Valencia retains several historical buildings including the Cathedral; the Lonja de los Mercaderes, also known as *Lonja de la Seda* (the Silk Exchange); and the Palacio del Marqués de Dos Aguas, which houses the *Museo Nacional de Cerámica* (National Museum of Ceramics). In recent years Valencia has gained a modern look thanks in particular to the famous local architect Santiago Calatrava, who designed the so-called "City of Arts and Sciences" (*Ciutat de les Arts i les Ciències*), a large complex devoted to scientific and cultural dissemination. Valencia also offers a modern art museum known as the Institut Valencià d'Art Modern (IVAM), and the Mercat Central, which is one of Europe's oldest markets.

See also: Chapter 1: Overview; Population and Demography; Transportation. Chapter 2: Timeline. Chapter 6: Overview; Nationalism. Chapter 12: Museums. Chapter 14: Overview; Chefs and Restaurants. Chapter 15: Soccer.

Further Reading

Hughes, Robert. *Barcelona: The Great Enchantress*. Washington, D.C.: National Geographic, 2004.

Morris, Jan. *Spain*. London: Faber & Faber, 2008.

Nash, Elizabeth. *Seville, Córdoba, and Granada: A Cultural History*. Oxford: Oxford University Press, 2005.

Nash, Elizabeth. *Madrid: A Cultural History*. Northampton: Interlink Books, 2012.

Oldale, John. *A World of Curiosities*. New York: Plume, 2012.

Schoenfeld, Bruce. "The Sizzle of Seville." *National Geographic Traveler,* February/March 2015: 30–40.

Climate and Water Conservation

Spain's climate is diverse because of the large size of the country and the fact that it is a peninsula containing many mountains. Hence, the weather in Spain varies depending on the altitude and the distance from the sea. Overall, Spain's climate is categorized into four major types: a) Atlantic or oceanic climate; b) Mediterranean climate; c) mountain climate; and d) arid subtropical climate of the Canary Islands.

The Mediterranean area is usually characterized by mild winters as opposed to the northern Atlantic coast, which experiences much colder winters like those in the mountains. The north is the wet area of Spain, generally known for being the green part of the Iberian Peninsula because of its regular rains. Conversely, the south of Spain is well-known for being hotter and drier. Some areas like Murcia and Almería have a semiarid climate, where precipitation is less than 300 millimeters per year.

Due to the scarce rainfall in some parts of the country, and more recently because of the high volume of tourists (i.e., Spain received over 65 million visitors in 2014 alone, which is a number greater than the country's total population of 47 million), Spaniards have been building dams and reservoirs for thousands of years. Reservoirs, or *pantanos* in Spanish, are man-made lakes that are especially common in the southern part of the country. Apart from supplying drinkable water, other purposes include hydropower production, irrigation, and flood protection. Perhaps it is not surprising to learn that Spain, with approximately 1,200, has the largest number of reservoirs in Europe.

Another way of producing drinkable water is by desalination. Spain is one of the biggest producers in the world of reverse osmosis in conjunction with Saudi Arabia and the United Arab Emirates. However, the Torrevieja desalination plant near Alicante in southeastern Spain has already generated global controversy. Despite costing €300 million ($438 million) and being Europe's largest facility for transforming seawater into freshwater and the second biggest desalination plant in the world, it became worldwide news that this massive infrastructure has lain idle since 2011, due to its vast amount of electricity consumption and environmental risks. However, according to José Luis Sánchez, professor of marine sciences at Alicante University, "the costs and environmental risks of reverse osmosis have been exaggerated by the Popular Party" (Barr 2011). Interestingly, *The New York Times* wrote a special report in 2013 on Torrevieja's massive desalination plant, and one of the main conclusions is that the problem of water in Spain "is more political than economic" (Cala 2013). More recently, a group of Spanish researchers published an academic article ("Environmental Impact"), in which they conclude that "desalination is clearly the highest pollutant alternative, but large water transport infrastructures also contributed to the environmental impact of the water supply, especially when they are partly operated" (Uche 2015). To give an idea, every deslination plant needs 6,000 watts of electricity to purify 229,545 cubic feet of water every 24 hours (Kohen 2003) while the average consumption of watts per person in Spain was 645 watts in 2011.

See also: Chapter 1: Overview; Bodies of Water: Tajo, Ebro, Sanabria, Covadonga; Mountain Ranges: Teide, Sierra Nevada, and the Pyrenees; Natural Resources and Environment; Population and Demography. Chapter 4: Production of Energy; Tourism.

Further Reading

Atlas Climático Ibérico / Iberian Climate Atlas. Agencia Estatal de Meteorología (España); Ministerio de Medio Ambiente y Medio Rural y Marino (España). Instituto de Meteorología de Portugal. 2011.

Barr, Caelainn. "EU Waste: Massive Spanish Desalination Plant Lies Idle." *The Bureau of Investigative Journalism,* April 27, 2011. https://www.thebureauinvestigates.com/2011/04/27/eu-waste-massive-spanish-desalination-plant-lies-idle/

Cala, Andrés. "Spain's Desalination Ambitions Unravel." *The New York Times,* October 9, 2013. http://www.nytimes.com/2013/10/10/business/energy-environment/spains-desalination-ambitions-unravel.html?pagewanted=all

Kohen, Elizabeth, and Marie Louise Elias. *Cultures of the World: Spain.* 2nd ed. New York: Marshall Cavendish, 2003.

Uche, Javier, Amaya Martínez-Gracia, Fernando Círez, and Uriel Carmona. "Environmental Impact of Water Supply and Water Use in a Mediterranean Water Stressed Region." *Journal of Cleaner Production* 88 (February) 2015: 196–204.

Mountain Ranges: Teide, Sierra Nevada, and the Pyrenees

After Switzerland, Spain is the second most mountainous country in Europe. The 10 tallest mountains in Spain are listed in Table 1.2.

Teide Volcano is on the island of Tenerife. In the old local language of *guanche*, *Tenerife* means "snow mountain," and it is the largest of the Canary Islands. A range of mountains divides Tenerife into two clear parts: the north, which is humid and green and

Table 1.2 SPAIN'S HIGHEST MOUNTAINS

Peak's name	Location	Altitude
Teide	Tenerife	3,718 m
Mulhacén	Granada–Sierra Nevada	3,481 m
Aneto	Huesca–Pyrenees	3,404 m
Veleta	Granada–Sierra Nevada	3,396 m
Posets	Huesca–Pyrenees	3,375 m
Alcazaba	Granada–Sierra Nevada	3,365 m
Monte Perdido	Huesca–Pyrenees	3,355 m
Cilindro	Huesca–Pyrenees	3,328 m
Perdiguero	Huesca–Pyrenees	3,321 m
Maladeta	Huesca–Pyrenees	3,309 m

famous for its banana plantations; and the south, which is dry and receives hardly any rain. The flora is among the most unique in the world. Tenerife's flora contains 140 species of different ecosystems: Mediterranean, tropical, and desert. The dragon tree is typical of the Canary Islands. The fauna of Tenerife is mainly in the form of birds, reptiles, and invertebrates. The lizard (*Gallotia galloti* or *lagarto tizón)* is one of the endemic reptiles of the area.

Geologically, Tenerife is fascinating due to the different formations of rocks and plants, which create a spectacular landscape that ends in the Teide. Teide is an enormous volcano that emerges from a crater, Las Cañadas, located in the center of the island. At 16 kilometers (52,493 ft) in diameter, it is one of the largest craters in the world. Teide was formed by an accumulation of the materials erupted by the volcano. The National Park of Las Cañadas in the Teide is, without a doubt, the most spectacular of 43 parks in the Canary Islands. It occupies 18,990 hectares and the visit seems like a journey to the moon. It is possible to walk all over the park by the different hiking

---

MULHACÉN

Mulhacén or Muley Hacén was the name of the penultimate Nazari king of Granada. According to legend, when he died on October 28, 1485, his wife Zoraya ordered that his body be deposited in the highest spot in the Sierra Nevada to make sure that nobody, including his Christian enemies, could desecrate it. Sierra Nevada is Spain's largest national park, occupying 86,208 hectares. *Las Alpujarras* is a distinctive area of Sierra Nevada located between Granada and Almería, which has Arabic origins. The Moors found refuge in those charming white Andalusian villages, where Arab heritage can still be found, for instance, in the sophisticated method of transporting water for agricultural purposes to the *bancales* (terraces) of the *barranco de Poqueira* (Poqueira ravine). The British writer Gerald Brenan established his second residence there, and gradually thousands of ex-pats followed his path.

routes. Near Teide is Pico Viejo, one of the craters, which is 800 meters (2,624 ft) in diameter and 3,100 meters (10,170 ft) in altitude.

As a national park, the Sierra Nevada Mountain range is the largest one in Spain (86,208 hectares), lying also within a *parque natural* of 171,985 hectares, occupying the areas of Marquesado del Zenete, Valley of Lecrín, parts of Almería and La Alpujarra. Mulhacén is the highest summit in the peninsula with impressive views. On a clear day it is possible to see La Mancha and Morocco. Despite being considerably elevated, there is no need to be an expert hiker to climb to the top. It is highly recommended to do the route between July and September, where there is little snow. There are many routes to hike in Sierra Nevada. Among them, the Estrella route follows the old tram line to the mountain.

Apart from fauna characterized by the *cabra montés* (*Capra Pyrenaica*) and the golden eagle, the Appolo butterfly or *pavón diurno* constitutes one of the most distinctive animals of the area. With among 1,700 botanical species identified, Sierra Nevada is home to 66 unique plants on the mountain. One is the *manzanilla real* (*Artemisia granatensis*), which is used in medical applications and is in serious danger of extinction. Quite recently a local man was sentenced with a heavy penalty for taking this plant for his personal use.

The Pyrenees are a combination of spectacular high peaks, deep green valleys, and wild beauty that range from France to northern Spain. The Moors called these mountains *El Hadjiz* (the barricade), which is effectively what they are, isolating Spain from the rest of Europe. Pico de Aneto at 11,168 feet (3,404 meters) is the highest summit to

The Spanish Pyrenees offer a wonderland to walkers versus alpinists. (Alberto Raso Bautista/ Dreamstime.com)

be found on the Spanish side of the border, in the region of Aragón (Huesca). The melting waters of the small Aneto glacier pass underground in the cave called Forau de *Aiguallut* (*Trou de Toro*). In order to climb the Aneto, it is necessary to carry proper equipment such as a *piolet* and crampons in winter. The Vall d´Aran, close to Pico de Aneto, is a botanical paradise at any time of year. Within the 33,000 hectares in the area of Aragón only, in the natural park of Posets-Maladeta it is possible to find vestiges of 13 glaciers and 95 lakes of glacier origin. In Ballibierna there is a black pine tree forest, which is the highest in Europe. Among flora, dog tooth violets often appear in the footsteps of the retreating snow along with many gentians. Large birds such as golden and Bonelli's eagles as well as several varieties of vultures can be identified. But perhaps the two most distinctive flora and fauna are the Serbal (*Sorbus aria*) tree, which does not grow tall due to the extreme weather conditions; and the *Mirlo capiblanco* (*Turdus torquatus*), a small bird of about 24 centimeters, which probably survived the glacier period in Europe. Baños de Benasque is about nine kilometers from Benasque, where there is spring water close to the Maladeta Mountain.

See also: Chapter 1: Overview; National Parks. Chapter 15: Overview; Family Outings and Vacations.

Further Reading

Copons, Elisenda. *Montañas de España. Rutas, paseos y aventuras*. Barcelona: ElCobre Ediciones, 2006.

Dunlop, Fiona. *National Geographic Traveler: Spain*. 2nd ed. Washington, D.C.: National Geographic, 2005.

Farino, Teresa, and Mike Lockwood. *Travelers' Nature Guides: Spain*. Oxford: Oxford University Press, 2003.

Lucia, Paul. *Through the Spanish Pyrenees. GR11: A Long Distance Footpath*. 2nd ed. Milnthorpe: Cicerone Press, 2000.

National Parks

Ordesa y Monte Perdido (Huesca) was established as a National Park on August 16, 1918. It was declared a World Heritage site in 1997 by UNESCO. It consists of four main valleys and has a wide variety of ecosystems with both an Atlantic and Mediterranean influence. The diverse habitat of the park produces a rich and varied flora and fauna; for example, the park is home to over 131 species of butterflies. Forests make up 28 percent of the park and include pine, beech, and fir trees. Fauna include *Bucardo* (*Capra pyrenaica*), *rebeco* (*Rupicapra*), *quebrantahuesos* (osprey), *águila real* (Golden Eagle), *marmota* (marmot), and *nutria* (beaver). The rest of the park is made up of rock or green pasture spotted with wildflowers during the summer months.

Teide (Santa Cruz de Tenerife) is known for containing the largest volcano in Spain. Teide is also the highest point in the country, surpassing even the famous Sierra Nevada

Table 1.3 SPAIN'S NATIONAL PARKS

National Park	Region / State	City / Cities	Total surface in hectares
Aigüestortes I Estany de Sant Maurici	Catalunya	Lleida	14,119
Archipiélago de Cabrera	Illes Balears	Cabrera	10,021
Cabañeros	Castilla-La Mancha	Ciudad Real, Toledo	40,856
Caldera de Taburiente	Canarias	La Palma, Tenerife	4,690
Doñana	Andalucía	Huelva, Sevilla	54,252
Garajonay	Canarias	La Gomera, Tenerife	3,986
Islas Atlánticas de Galicia	Galicia	Pontevedra, A Coruña	8,480
Monfragüe	Extremadura	Cáceres	18,396
Ordesa y Monte Perdido	Aragón	Huesca	15,608
Picos de Europa	Asturias, Castilla y León, Cantabria	Sotres, Posada de Valdeón, Liébana	64,660
Sierra de Guadarrama	Castilla-La Mancha, Madrid	Segovia, Ávila, Madrid	33,960
Sierra Nevada	Andalucía	Granada, Almería	86,208
Tablas de Daimiel	Castilla-La Mancha	Ciudad Real	1,928
Teide	Canarias	Tenerife	18,990
Timanfaya	Canarias	Lanzarote	5,107

Mountains in Granada. Teide is not only visually stunning but also of biological significance. Rare species of plants and animals can be found in this natural park including the purple flower (*violeta del Teide*), which grows at over 2,000 meters of altitude and the local lizard (*lagarto tizón*), both species being unique in the world and in extinction. It is the second most visited national park in the world after Japan's Mount Fuji.

Caldera de Taburiente (Santa Cruz de Tenerife) was established on October 6, 1954. It is an immense crater surrounded by the highest peaks on the island of Tenerife: El Roque de los Muchachos (2,426 m; 7,959 ft), Pico de la Cruz (2,351 m; 7,713 ft), Piedra Llana (2,321 m; 7,614 ft), Pico de la Nieve (2,236 m; 7,336 ft), and Punta de los Roques (2,085 m; 6,840 ft), among others. From here, the terrain drops steeply into the crater in almost vertical cliff faces over 800 meters high until a height of 430 meters above sea level, with a difference of altitude around 2,000 meters. The mountains of the Canary Islands are so high that they surpass the clouds.

Aigüestortes i Estany de Sant Maurici (Lleida) was established on October 21, 1955. As Catalunya's only national park, it offers the highest concentration of lakes on the Iberian Peninsula with a total of 272 lakes. The rugged granite terrain is home to a variety of landscapes including glacial lakes or *estanys*, waterfalls, rocky slopes, and rugged peaks. It also contains silver-fir, pine, and birch forest where many interesting alpine and northern plants and animals live.

Doñana (Huelva and Sevilla) was established on October 16, 1969. It was declared a UNESCO Biosphere Reserve in 1980. It is considered the most important wetland in Spain. The landscape lies on the right bank of the powerful Guadalquivir River and stretches to the Atlantic Ocean. It is formed by a set of ecosystems from stabilized sand dunes, known as *cotos*, and marshes or *marisma*. The park is an essential refuge for numerous migratory birds from Europe and Africa and approximately 378 species of birds have been sighted here. It is the habitat of unique species like the Spanish Imperial Eagle and the Iberian lynx (*Lynx pardina*), a carnivore indigenous to the Iberian Peninsula that has become the park's emblem.

Tablas de Daimiel (Ciudad Real) was established on June 28, 1973. It was declared a wetland of international importance by the Ramsar Agreement. The park is a unique and special ecosystem, with shallow wetlands formed by the rivers overflowing in their middle sections, causing flooding. In 1986, this park's future was in question when the springs that fed the park dried up for the first time in recorded history. This change in ecosystem was due to overuse of the underground reservoir that fed the springs (Aquifer 23) by the surrounding agricultural land. Since then, in part due to wetter winters and in part due to channeling water from the Tajo-Segura canal, Tablas de Daimiel has partially recovered. However, the wetlands today cover a mere 20 square kilometers as opposed to the 150 square kilometers that they covered a few decades earlier. The highest ecological value is the presence of birds that come to spend the winter and nest here, creating an area full of water birds.

Timanfaya (Lanzarote) was established on August 9, 1974. The main interest is the abrupt landscapes where black and dark red shades are abundant in conjunction with dark basaltic lava. From the summit of Montaña Rajada, one can view the impressive sight of rolling hills of lava that extend to the Atlantic coastline. Since it was formed, the people living on the island have had to learn how to coexist with this unusual landscape, and they even grow dry land crops such as melons, onions, tomatoes, and vineyards in the area of La Geria.

Garajonay (La Gomera) was established on March 1981. It was declared a World Heritage site by UNESCO in 1986. Located in the Canary Islands, Garajonay hosts some of the most pristine and untouched vegetation of Spain's parks. The humid forest is often clouded in mist and is known for its horizontal rain. The volcanic landscape contains numerous streams and springs, further adding to the lush vegetation.

Cabrera Archipiélago (Palma de Mallorca) was established on April 25, 1991. It is an important stop for over 150 migratory birds as well as the home of 200 species of fish and numerous invertebrates. The marine ecosystem stands out in this cluster of calcareous islands and islets, with meadows of *Posidonia oceanica*, which favor the proliferation of a large number of species of marine fauna. It is one of the best-conserved sea beds on the Spanish coast. There are also many endemic plants and important bird colonies. For these reasons it was declared a Land and Sea-based National Park in 1991.

Picos de Europa (Asturias, León, and Cantabria) was established on May 30, 1995. It was declared a World Heritage site by UNESCO in 2002. The Picos de Europa Mountains consist of three important mountain massifs that together create the Cordillera Cantábrica: Andara massif is in the east; Urrieles massif in the center; and Cornión massif in the west. The highest peak is Torrecerredo (2,646 m or 8,606 ft), which is located in the central mountain system, the most dramatic of the three with its steep inclines and vertical drops. This natural barrier runs parallel to Spain's northern coast, which contributes to its humid and rainy climate. Meadows and forests, streams and rivers are common features in the landscape. The famous Covadonga Lakes are nestled in the peaks of this park. This is home to many rare species such as the Iberian brown bear, the Golden Eagle, Griffon vultures, and *urogallo* (*Capercaillie*).

Cabañeros (Ciudad Real and Toledo) was established on November 20, 1995. The landscape is formed by pastures, bushes, and Mediterranean forests with a special abundance of cork trees and holm oak trees. This park is refuge to exclusive species such as the salamander and the *jara común* or *princosa,* which refers to a particular flower that has become the symbol of the area. Located between the cities of Ciudad Real and Toledo in the middle of Spain, Cabañeros Park provides shelter to a variety of animals near extinction, including the Iberian lynx, eagles, and black vultures. It is also home to wildlife such as deer, roe deer, and wild boar.

Sierra Nevada (Granada and Almería) was established on January 11, 1999. It was declared a Biosphere Reserve by UNESCO in 1986. It is the highest mountain system in Western Europe after the Alps. The Mulhacén and the Veleta are the two highest peaks in the peninsula. The mountains were formed by glaciers leaving behind glacier lakes. In contrast with the heat of Andalucía during summer time, however, it is not uncommon for Sierra Nevada to have snow all year around. Fifteen of its peaks are over 3,000 meters (9,842 ft) high. Its landscape includes forest and natural mineral springs.

Illas Atlánticas de Galicia (A Coruña and Pontevedra) was established in July 1, 2002. The park covers four clusters of rocky islands, with cliffs on the western side, facing the Atlantic Ocean, and beautiful beaches and dunes on the eastern side, facing the estuaries. The most important and spectacular colonies of sea birds on the Spanish coast live on these islands, and many other underwater animal species can also be seen. They are popularly known as the islands of sea birds.

Monfragüe (Cáceres) was established in 1997. It was declared a Biosphere Reserve by UNESCO in 2003. It is home to the Tajo River, gentle slopes, forests, and meadows. It was created to protect the rare wildlife and vegetation of the region, and today is considered a sanctuary for bird watching. Black storks, rare imperial eagles, and numerous vultures can be found in the area. According to some experts, Monfragüe is "probably the world's largest breeding nuclei of black vultures and Spanish imperial eagles" (Farino and Lockwood 2003).

Sierra de Guadarrama (Segovia, Ávila, and Madrid) was established on June 26, 2013, and is the fifth largest in Spain's National Parks system. This newly established national park consists of 62 miles of mountain range that cross from East to West through the center of Spain. It is colder and wetter than the surrounding plateau. Its streams and forests provide refuge for biodiversity.

See also: Chapter 1: Overview; Bodies of Water: Tajo, Ebro, Sanabria, Covadonga; Climate and Water Conservation; Mountain Ranges: Teide, Sierra Nevada, and the Pyrenees; Natural Resources and Environment; Regions of Spain; World Heritage. Chapter 15: Family Outings and Vacations.

Further Reading

Dunlop, Fiona. *National Geographic Traveler: Spain*. Washington, D.C.: National Geographic, 2012.

Farino, Teresa, and Mike Lockwood. *Travellers' Nature Guides: Spain*. Oxford: Oxford University Press, 2003.

Harris, Patricia, and David Lyon. *Frommer's Spain*. Frommer Media LLC, 2015.

Natural Resources and Environment

For centuries, Spain has enjoyed the abundance of natural resources that its diverse land and geographical situation offer. However, in recent years, agriculture, fishing, and mining industries have faced numerous challenges both environmental in nature and man-made, namely, the Europe-wide policies that came with Spain joining the EEC (European Economic Community) in 1986.

Though agriculture currently makes up a significant amount of Spain's natural resources, it experienced a substantial decline between 1960–1975. The "economic miracle" of the 1960s was the springboard for major paradigm shifts: agriculture, which accounted for 24 percent of the GDP in 1960, plummeted to a mere 9 percent in 1975 as the economy gravitated toward industry and services. The small scale of Spain's individual farming industry is a current challenge due to lack of knowledge of new farming techniques and lack of modern machinery found on more efficient large scale farms. Compared with other western European countries, Spain invests about one-fifth of the average on advancements to farmland. Spain's attempts to bring additional land under irrigation has also caused environmental concerns, exhausting underground aquifers.

Challenges aside, a significant amount of Spain's natural resources is still comprised of farming. In the dry plains of interior Spain, grains such as barley and wheat thrive; wheat being Spain's principal crop in both 2000 and 2002. Rice is grown in regions along the eastern coast where seasonal flooding occurs, as in Valencia and southern Catalunya. Corn also enjoys success in the north. The Southern regions with a Mediterranean climate use both irrigation and modern green house techniques—which consist of covering large tracts of land in white plastic—in order to produce an abundance of fruits and vegetables. Olives, grapes, fish, citrus fruits, melons, eggplants, zucchini, lettuce, tomatoes, peppers, apples, apricots, bananas, pears, peaches, and plums are all grown in Spain, many of which are exported to countries such as Germany and the United Kingdom. Spain is currently the wold's largest producer of olive oil, which is derived principally from Andalucía. Grapes are also a prominent crop of Spain, as Spain is one of the world's largest producers of wine, know for its Rioja (La Rioja), Ribera del Duero (Castilla y León), and Albariño (Galicia) wines, to name a few. The region of Jerez de la Frontera in Andalucía is the cradle of sherry.

On the plains, sheep are raised for meat, wool, and milk. In the wetter regions of Northern Spain, dairy cattle are prevalent. *Manchego* is sheep's cheese from the region of Castilla–La Mancha that is exported throughout the world. The region of Galicia is also famous for its cheese such as the soft, lesser known *Tetilla*. Pigs are another common type of livestock in Spain and their meat is used to make the well-known Spanish *chorizo*. Pork is the most significant source of meat production in Spain with beef, poultry, and lamb following.

Since Spain is a country with over 5,000 miles of coastline (8,000 km), it is not surprising that the fishing industry in Spain is the largest in the EU. Despite its decline over the past few decades, fishing currently accounts for 1 percent of Spain's GDP. Spain consumes more fish and seafood than any other country in Europe (so much that they have to import fish from other countries) and Spain's fishing fleets are among the largest in the world. Galicia, with its extensive Atlantic coastline, produces more than 50 percent of Spain's seafood, including tuna, sardines, lobster, clams, and crabs. However, in recent years the fishing industry has faced numerous problems due to both environmental factors and EU policy factors. Overfishing off the coasts of Spain has resulted in a depleted supply. Recent EU policy limiting the size of fishing fleets is an additional challenge to Spain's fishing industry. Consequently, Spanish fishermen are moving farther out to sea—sometimes as far as the Pacific and Indian Oceans. This migration has caused conflict between the fishermen and authorities of Ireland, Morocco, and Canada, resulting in numerous arrests for illegal fishing.

Forestry accounts for only a fraction of Spain's agricultural output. Spain's once immense native woodlands have significantly decreased and in some cases disappeared altogether. Under the rule of Franco in the 1940s, reforestation efforts began due to economic concerns (as opposed to environmental concerns). However, instead of replacing the woodlands with native trees, often trees were selected and imported due to their rapid growth. Yet these imported trees, such as the Australian eucalyptus and varying species of pine, while fast growing, also burn easily. So, ironically, the plants selected to aid in reforestation also aid in the rapid spread of forest fires, which have become an increasing cause of concern. Centuries of erosion and clearing of forests for livestock also constitute a threat to Spain's forests. Important forestry products include cork, eucalyptus, oak, pine, and poplar.

Spain has a varied and significant, by Europe's standards, mining industry. For example, Spain's most valuable mineral products consist of coal, lignite, copper, zinc, gold, steel, cement, and alumina, and other natural resources include kaolin, sepiolite, gypsum, fluorspar, uranium, lead, tungsten, iron ore, magnesite, potash, hydropower, and arable land. Globally, Spain is the third largest producer of gypsum; the sixth largest producer of fluorspar, and the eighth largest producer of cement. Metal production is one of Spain's main heavy industries, along with shipbuilding. According to the World Steel Association reports, Spain produced nearly 16.3 metric tons per year of crude steel in 2010 (AZMining Editors). The classic cutlery knife (*navaja*) appeared in Spain at the end of the 16th century. The cities of Toledo and Albacete (aceros-de-hispania.com) played a noteworthy role in the history of Spanish steel production.

Another important natural resource in Spain is cinnabar. The small town of Almadén (Ciudad Real) contains the world's largest reserves of cinnabar, a mineral essential for the extraction of mercury. Cinnabar was initially used for color by the Romans. Later, the mineral was mainly used for medicine by the Muslims. In 2012 UNESCO listed Almadén as World Heritage of Mercury in conjunction with the town of Idrija (Slovenia), where mercury was first found in 1490 CE. In the words of Jean Benoît Nadeau and Julie Barlow, "much of Tartessos's mining wealth came from an area on the river then known as Luxia. Because its water was red and had a very high pH level, the river would later be known as *río Tinto* (Red River). This is the origin of the name of the world's largest mining conglomerate, the Australo-British Rio Tinto plc, which got its start when it purchased the old Tartessian mines in 1873" (Nadeau and Barlow 2013).

The first sedentary communities were established in Catalunya, the Levante, and Andalucía. They subsequently introduced technological advances, including working with pottery, linen, and wool, while lithic equipment was further developed into weapons and tools. Later, the use of copper was gradually incorporated in the middle of the second millennium in the southern regions of the peninsula. Under Muslim rule, the rural economy was steadily upgraded. For instance, if the Romans introduced the aqueducts as the main irrigation system, the Moors upgraded it with the *noria* (water wheel). The region of al-Andalus was a hub of industrial activity, producing all the necessary goods of everyday life, including textiles, ceramics, glassware, metalwork, leather goods, and paper. According to the historian Simon Barton, the cultural center of al-Andalus also brought foreign influences to Cordoban high society, introducing "new fashions in hairstyles, clothes, and cuisine, as well as such innovations as the guitar, toothpaste, and underarm deodorants" (Barton 2004).

Apart from generating hydroelectric power using Spain's rivers, solar energy and wind power are also two clear examples of Spain's current commitment to produce clean and renewable energy. For instance, a solar energy tower near Sevilla collects sunlight reflected by 624 large mirrors, which in 2013 was "expected to provide energy for 180,000 homes in Sevilla" (Knowles 2012). On the other hand, remaining in the southern region of Andalucía, "Spain's famous tourist destination of Costa del Sol (Málaga) has been caustically referred to as the 'Costa Concreta' for the manner in which it has been completely built over with tourist accommodations" (Ostergren 2011). Indeed, there is a need to integrate environmental concerns into economic decisions in many sectors. According to the study "Ruido y Salud 2012" ("Noise and Health"), Spain is the second noisiest country in the world, with Japan in first place.

See also: Chapter 1: Overview; Climate and Water Conservation; National Parks; Population and Demography. Chapter 2: Overview; Franco, Francisco. Chapter 4: Overview; Agriculture and Fishing Industry; Tourism. Chapter 14: Overview; Alcohol: Beer, Brandy, Cava, Sherry, Wine; Cheeses and Jamón; Seafood Dishes.

Further Reading

Barton, Simon. *A History of Spain*. London: Palgrave, 2004.

Knowles, Laura. *Countries around the World: Spain*. Chicago: Charlotte Guillain, 2012.

Nadeau, Jean-Benoît, and Julie Barlow. *The Story of Spanish*. New York: St. Martin's Press, 2013.

Ostergren, Robert C., and Mathias Le Bossé. *The Europeans. A Geography of People, Culture, and Environment*. 2nd ed. New York: The Guildford Press, 2011.

Population and Demography

Spain has a population of approximately 47 million, which is less than .70 percent of the total population of the world. However, Spain consumes 1.6 percent of the total water available on the planet. According to the 2014 study "The Global Resource Footprint of Nations" written by the Dutch research institute TNO which compares 43 countries, Spain ranks sixth worldwide for water consumption (Tukker 2014). Every Spanish citizen consumes 600 cubic meters as opposed to 250 cubic meters, which is the global average. In comparison to other countries, Spain is also far from the world average per capita in material footprint (16th in the world), land footprint (21st), and carbon footprint (24th).

Spain's population is concentrated mainly in cities. According to the latest census by the Instituto Nacional de Estadística (INE: National Institute of Statistics, January 2014), only 20.9 percent of Spaniards live in villages with less than 10,000 inhabitants. By 2014, Spain had a registered population of 46.7 million people, of whom 86.6 percent were born in Spain while 13.4 percent were born abroad; 49.1 percent of the Spanish population were men and 50.9 percent were women. Following the same data provided by INE 2014, in Spain there was 228 villages with a population of foreigners comprising over 25 percent of the total population, and 18 places had over 50.

Multiculturalism started in Spain with the founding of the country. For instance, the Phoenicians founded several cities in the Iberian Peninsula such as Gadir (Cádiz) between the eighth and sixth centuries BCE. Cádiz (Andalucía) is the oldest city in Europe. Similarly, the Greeks also established themselves in strategic places in the sixth century and they founded cities such as Emporio, which today is called Ampurias (Catalunya). Considered equally beautiful is the city of Cartagena (Murcia) founded by the Carthaginians, who also settled themselves in Spain. In 205 BCE the Romans extended their power throughout most of the Iberian Peninsula and built cities such as Itálica (Sevilla, Andalucía); Emerita Augusta (Mérida, Extremadura); Tarraco (Tarragona, Catalunya); Barcino (Barcelona, Catalunya); Astigi (Écija, Andalucía); and Caesar Augusta (Zaragoza, Aragón). The influence of the Arab world in Spain is also majestically evident since their arrival in 711. Examples of the Muslim heritage are the Andalusian cities of Córdoba and Granada. Furthermore, it is worth noting that foreign influences came to Spain first through the south—particularly through the strait of Gibraltar, which is only 11 kilometers (6.8 miles) away from the Spanish land. Since most of the invasions and influences reached Spain from the south, this partly explains why so many Spanish rulers looked with apprehension toward the south. Spain's millennial multiculturalism can be understood as a clash of cultures, on the one hand, or more positively as the end product of centuries of hybridization resulting from multiple cultures intermixing from its foundation.

Based on Spain's 2011 GDP, most Spaniards work in four major sectors: Services (71.6%); Industry and Energy (15.6%); Construction (10.1%); and Agriculture (2.7%). In 2011, Spain's exports were $330,600 million, including automobiles, machinery, and food (i.e., fruits, legumes, meat, drinks, and fish). Spain's imports were $384,600 in 2011. Machinery, transport equipment, energy sources (i.e., petrol and, paradoxically, electricity, despite being one of the countries with a huge potential for generating solar and wind energy), food, and chemicals were imports.

Prior to 1980, Spain was mainly a land of emigration. That status quo began to change with post-Franco democratization after 1975 and membership in the EU in 1986. The 1986–1999 period saw rapidly increasing immigration, particularly from North Africa, which was boosted by economic growth, the large-scale incorporation of Spanish women into the labor market that generated a demand for labor (such as domestic work), and regulation of entry through recruitment and regularizations. After 2000, growth consolidated, Latin American migration was encouraged, and family migration grew in significance. The registered foreign population in Spain grew from 279,000 in 1990 to 1.3 million in 2000. By 2005, it had shot up to 4.1 million, only to increase further to 5.7 million in 2010, which represented 12.4 percent of its total population (Castles et al. 2014).

While entries to some of the earlier main immigration countries—like France, the U.K., Belgium, and the Scandinavian countries—increased considerably over the 2000s, the biggest increases in the number of legal entries occurred in Southern Europe, which peaked in 2007 at 921,000 in Spain and 515,000 in Italy. However, the economic crisis hit Spain particularly hard. It led to rising unemployment among immigrants, especially in sectors such as construction. The unemployment rate of foreigners climbed to 36 percent in 2011. This partly explains the decline in immigration from 958,000 in 2007 to 455,000 in 2010. In parallel, outflows have also increased, although more modestly from 227,000 in 2007 to 371,000 in 2011, although the real emigration figures are likely to be higher due to under-registration. The crisis has also prompted a new Spanish emigration movement, principally toward the U.K., France, Germany, and the U.S., but also to Argentina, Brazil, China, and Australia (Castles et al. 2014).

Based on data from the INE (*Spain in Figures 2013*), Spain's demographics in 2013 are displayed in Table 1.4.

Table 1.4   DEMOGRAPHICS FOR SPAIN (2013)

Place	Number of children	2010 GDP per capita (Euros)	Number of Businesses	Employed (thousands)	Unemployed (%)
Spain	1.36	22,766	3,199,617	17,282	25.0
Andalucía	1.42	17,299	482,334	2,627.8	34.6
Almería	1.54	18,079	41,021	236.4	35.4
Cádiz	1.39	17,107	59,027	361.9	35.9
Córdoba	1.41	16,327	46,601	247.4	34.7
Granada	1.35	16,073	56,243	277.5	35.7
Huelva	1.39	17,250	25,008	163.3	34.7
Jaén	1.37	15,919	34,000	188.2	36.3
Málaga	1.36	17,641	107,385	519.8	34.4
Sevilla	1.49	18,345	113,049	633.3	31.6
Aragón	1.36	25,330	89,116	533.7	18.6

Huesca	1.34	25,413	16,151	99.4	14.7
Teruel	1.34	24,523	9,212	55.6	15.9
Zaragoza	1.37	25,433	63,753	388.7	19.8
Asturias	1.05	21,209	68,967	376.2	21.8
Illes Balears	1.31	24,039	85,372	464.7	23.2
Canarias	1.05	19,494	131,315	750.9	33.0
Las Palmas	1.07	19,559	68,104	379.1	34.6
Santa Cruz de Tenerife	1.02	19,425	63,211	371.8	31.3
Cantabria	1.23	22,160	38,137	229.2	17.7
Castilla y León	1.19	22,001	164,994	943.3	19.7
Ávila	1.26	18,742	10,735	58.9	24.4
Burgos	1.35	26,186	25,196	153.0	17.3
León	1.05	20,640	32,386	159.7	21.8
Palencia	1.10	21,849	10,640	62.4	19.0
Salamanca	1.15	19,008	22,626	128.5	19.7
Segovia	1.32	21,770	11,218	62.4	19.2
Soria	1.21	22,496	5,907	38.5	14.5
Valladolid	1.20	24,751	34,309	221.2	18.8
Zamora	0.96	18,279	11,977	58.6	23.1
Castilla-La Mancha	1.41	19,144	127,632	710.9	29.5
Albacete	1.36	17,990	26,400	127.8	31.7
Ciudad Real	1.36	17,812	30,600	159.8	30.9
Cuenca	1.24	18,071	13,702	70.6	22.6
Guadalajara	1.50	19,613	13,213	100.6	23.0
Toledo	1.50	17,996	43,717	252.2	29.7
Catalunya	1.50	26,635	592,192	2,889.2	22.7
Barcelona	1.50	26,635	446,147	2,101.2	22.6
Girona	1.57	26,745	57,971	293.4	24.6
Lleida	1.53	26,752	34,921	177.4	17.6
Tarragona	1.45	26,470	53,253	317.3	23.6
Comunitat Valenciana	1.30	20,150	342,484	1,904.6	27.7
Alacant	1.20	19,148	129,728	648.9	29.4
Castelló	1.36	21,872	39,748	210.6	28.0
Valencia	1.37	21,251	173,008	945.2	27.1
Extremadura	1.30	15,857	64,671	336.2	33.0
Badajoz	1.35	15,782	39,433	215.9	33.5
Cáceres	1.21	15,982	25,238	120.3	32.1
Galicia	1.07	20,625	194,511	1,039.5	20.7
A Coruña	1.09	22,146	80,408	461.3	19.5
Lugo	0.98	19,264	24,288	128.9	16.5
Ourense	0.95	18,674	22,945	106.4	21.2
Pontevedra	1.12	19,976	66,970	342.8	24.6

(continued)

Table 1.4 DEMOGRAPHICS FOR SPAIN (2013) *(continued)*

Place	Number of children	2010 GDP per capita (Euros)	Number of Businesses	Employed (thousands)	Unemployed (%)
Comunidad de Madrid	1.41	29,578	499,098	2,741.1	19.0
Región de Murcia	1.54	19,003	89,606	535.2	27.9
Comunidad Foral de Navarra	1.49	29,966	41,305	259.5	16.2
País Vasco	1.39	30,156	159,005	875.3	14.9
Araba	1.48	33,112	20,644	133.6	15.5
Bizkaia	1.32	28,914	82,787	286.0	12.2
Gipuzkoa	1.47	30,872	55,574	455.6	16.3
La Rioja	1.40	25,276	22,486	121.6	20.5
Ceuta	2.07	20,237	3,622	21.2	38.5
Melilla	2.72	18,423	3,770	23.0	29.6

See also: Chapter 1: Overview; Archaeological Artifacts; Cities: Barcelona, Madrid, Sevilla, Valencia; Climate and Water Conservation; Natural Resources and Environment. Chapter 2: Overview; Timeline; Adriano; Séneca; Viriato. Chapter 3: Overview; Regional Government and Regionalism. Chapter 4: Overview; Agriculture and Fishing Industry; Automobile Industry; Manufacturing Industry; Production of Energy. Chapter 5: Averroes, Ibn Rushd. Chapter 6: Overview; Immigration; Multiculturalism; Nationalism. Chapter 12: Alhambra Palace.

Further Reading

Castles, Stephen, Hein de Hass, and Mark J. Miller. *The Age of Migration: International Population Movements in the Modern World.* 5th ed. New York: The Guildford Press, 2014.

Tukker, Arnold, et al. *The Global Resource Footprint of Nations. Carbon, Water, Land and Materials Embodied in Trade and Final Consumption.* Delft: Leiden University, 2014.

WWF Living Planet Report: Human Impact, in panda.org/lpr

Regions of Spain

After the Spanish Constitution of 1978, Spain was divided into 17 regions plus the two African colonies of Ceuta and Melilla—two cities located in Morocco that are governed under the region of Andalucía. The most populated regions of Spain by 2013 were Andalucía (8.3 million); Catalunya (7.5 million); Comunidad de Madrid (6.4 million); and Comunidad Valenciana (4.9 million). The least populated regions in Spain were La Rioja (319,000 inhabitants); Cantabria (589,000); and Navarra (640,000). The regions with the largest number of foreigners were the Illes Ballears (18.3%); Murcia

Table 1.5 THE REGIONS OF SPAIN

Region	Capital	Cities	Population (INE 2012)	Land	GDP	Average income (INE 2010)
Andalucía	Sevilla	8	8,499,985	87,596.97 km²	13.4%	17,299€
Aragón	Zaragoza	3	1,349,467	47,720.25 km²	3.2%	25,330€
Asturias	Oviedo	2	1,077,360	10,602.46 km²	2.1%	21,209€
Balearic Islands	Palma de Mallorca	5	1,119,439	4,991.66 km²	2.5%	24,039€
Basque country	Vitoria	3	2,193,093	7,230.33 km²	6.2%	30,156€
Canary Islands	Las Palmas de Gran Canaria	7	2,118,344	7,446.95 km²	3.9%	19,494€
Cantabria	Santander	1	593,861	5,326.54 km²	1.2%	22,160€
Castilla y León	Valladolid	9	2,546,078	94,226.91 km²	5.2%	22,001€
Castilla-La Mancha	Toledo	5	2,121,888	79,461.97 km²	3.4%	18,144€
Catalunya	Barcelona	4	7,570,908	32,090.54 km²	18.9%	26,635€
Comunidad de Madrid	Madrid	1	6,498,560	8,027.69 km²	17.9%	29,578€
Comunidad Foral de Navarra	Pamplona	1	644,566	10,390.36 km²	1.7%	28,866€
Comunitat Valenciana	València	3	5,129.266	23,254.49 km²	9.5%	20,150€
Extremadura	Mérida	2	1,108,130	41,634.50 km²	1.6%	15,857€
Galicia	Santiago de Compostela	4	2,781,498	29,574.69 km²	5.4%	20,625€
La Rioja	Logroño	1	323,609	5,045.25 km²	0.8%	25,276€
Región de Murcia	Murcia	1	1,474,449	11,313.91 km²	2.6%	19,003€
Ceuta			84,018	19.48 km²	0.1%	20,237€
Melilla			80,802	13.41 km²	0.1%	18,423€

(14.7%); and Comunidad Valenciana (14.7%), plus the city of Melilla (15%). Conversely, the regions with the least foreigners were Extremadura (3.4%); Galicia (3.6%); and Asturias (4.2%). By 2013, the only place that increased its number of foreigners was Melilla. However, in the same year, 545,980 foreigners left the country while 141,361 Spaniards returned to Spain after living abroad.

See also: Chapter 1: Overview; Cities: Barcelona, Madrid, Sevilla, Valencia; Population and Demography. Chapter 3: Overview; Regional Government and Regionalism.

Chapter 4: Overview; Agriculture and Fishing Industry. Chapter 6: Overview; Immigration. Chapter 9: Overview; Peninsular Languages. Chapter 14: Regional Dishes and Drinks.

Further Reading

Harris, Patricia, and David Lyon. *Frommer's Spain*. Frommer Media LLC, 2015.

Knowles, Laura. *Countries around the World: Spain*. Chicago: Charlotte Guillain, 2012.

Transportation

Spain's transport networks overall offer good quality road and rail transportation in comparison to any EU country. In fact, most of the investment comes from the EU funding that Spain began to receive after 1986 when it joined the EU in order to improve its transport standards. During the mid-1980s, Spain continually developed its highways, most of which are now efficient. Also, Spain has been investing heavily in a fast rail system called AVE (acronym of Spanish High Speed, which also means 'bird' –*ave*, as appears in the logo), which is becoming increasingly popular among tourists. Furthermore, since the new millennium, Spain has also been expanding airport terminals (i.e., Madrid, Barcelona, Málaga), as well as building new airports to the point that some have been viewed as unnecessary and severely criticized. This is the case with such costly new airports as Castellón and Ciudad Real. The latter is still waiting for its first passengers, and in 2015 was put for sale.

AENA (acronym in Spanish for Spanish Airports and Air Navigation) is a state-owned company that operates most Spanish airports, and one of the largest airport operators in the world. RENFE (acronym of National Network of Spanish Railways) is another state-owned company that drives freight and passenger trains. Apart from introducing the rail system in Spain, RENFE also operates the high-speed train AVE. Currently Spain has the world's fifth longest high-speed railway line, which is the Madrid-Barcelona-French Border (804 km), reaching speeds of 350 kilometers per hour, and taking 2.38 hours to travel from Madrid to Barcelona.

See also: Chapter 1: Overview; Cities: Barcelona, Madrid, Sevilla, Valencia. Chapter 12: Architects; Graphic Design.

Further Reading

Champion, Neil. *Countries of the World: Spain*. New York: Facts On File, 2006.

Pickard, Piers. *The World: A Traveller's Guide to the Planet*. Melbourne: Lonely Planet, 2014.

Villages

Luis Carandell (1929–2002) wrote extensively about Spain and with interesting observations on Spanish villages, which he considered the "jewels" of Spain. Josep Pla

(1897–1981), who also knew Spain well through his personal travel experiences, considered the villages to be the most important social structure of Spain. The sense of locality is very strong in Spanish villages. In fact, every single Spanish village wants to maintain its own distinctive identity, which inevitably generates rivalry among other neighboring villages. Usually, everybody knows each other in the village, and it is very common to invite outsiders to visit the village during the local fiestas, because it is when the village achieves its maximum splendor. Indeed, the local fiestas, which occur for a week or two, have become one of the most distinctive common features of most villages across Spain. The Spanish language has a saying that is very difficult to translate but beautifully encapsulates the charm of these magical places: "echar la casa por la ventana" is what villagers usually do during their local fiestas. It literally means "to throw the house through the window." Translated more loosely, it means to spare no expense, or that money is no object for a party.

Since Spain is divided into 17 regions, Table 1.6 highlights some of the unique, local characteristics of one village in each region, which also explains why the different regions are known all over Spain for their natural beauty and heritage.

See also: Chapter 1: Regions of Spain; Cities: Barcelona, Madrid, Sevilla, Valencia. Chapter 2: Overview. Chapter 12: Overview. Chapter 14: Overview; Alcohol: Beer, Brandy, Cava, Sherry, Wine; Cheeses and Jamón; Regional Dishes and Drinks; Seafood Dishes. Chapter 15: Overview; La Tomatina; Las Fallas; Los Reyes Magos; Moros y Cristianos; San Fermín; Semana Santa.

Further Reading

Carandell, Luis. *Celtiberia Show*. Madrid: Guadiana de Publicaciones, 1971.

Carandell, Luis. *Spain*. Madrid: Incafo, 1980.

Ollé Martín, Albert. *Pueblos de España*. Barcelona: Lunwerg, 2009.

Pla, Josep. *Viaje en Autobús*. Barcelona: Destino, 1942.

Pla, Josep. *Viaje a pie*. Barcelona: Destino, 1949.

Regàs, Rosa. *España: Una nueva mirada*. Barcelona: Lunwerg, 1997.

World Heritage

Spain has 55 sites that have been given World Heritage designation by UNESCO, which makes Spain home to the third-greatest number of protected historical resources in the world. This vast cultural patrimony reflects the variety and cultural richness of Spain, including flamenco, falconry, the mystery play of Elche, the whistled language of Gomera, and the irrigators' tribunal of the Spanish Mediterranean. Monumental buildings and architectural sites exist alongside landscapes, nature areas, routes, and ethnological traditions. Places declared world heritage sites by UNESCO include those in Table 1.7.

Table 1.6 SPAIN'S DIVERSITY: 17 VILLAGES OF SPAIN

Region	Village	City	Landscape	Architecture	Food	Fiesta
Andalucía	**Mojácar**	Almería	White houses	Arab/Jew/Roman	Olla de trigo & migas	Moros y Cristianos in June
Aragón	**Albarracín**	Teruel	Red brick & narrow steep streets	Wood balconies & wrought iron railings	Trout	Encierros de vaquillas Sept. 15–17
Asturias	**Cudillero**		Village & houses are built on a slope on hillsides (escalonada)	Roman	Merluza a la sidra, Fabes, curadillo & los suspiros	L'Amuravela June 29
Balearic Islands	**Ciutadella**	Menorca	Medieval streets	Phoencian/Roman /Arab	Caldereta de langosta & caragols amb cancra	Sant Joan
Basque Country	**Laguardia**	Álava	Medieval historic monuments	Roman	Impressive wineries	San Juan Degollao August 29
Canary Islands	**La Orotava**	Tenerife	Renaissance mansions, churches & *terreras* houses	Route of the water mills	Puchero tradicional de La Florida	Corpus Christi, end of May
Cantabria	**Santillana del mar**	Santander	Medieval religious monuments	Altamira's caves	Cocido montañés, anchovies, Tresviso's cheese & Deer's cecina	San Roque's romería, August 15–16
Castilla-La Mancha	**Sigüenza**	Guadalajara	Medieval village: castle is one of the best *paradores*	Arab/Roman	Roasted goat & pickled quail	San Vicente's fiestas, January 22
Castilla y León	**La Alberca**	Salamanca	Medieval houses with no cathedrals or palaces; only houses	Visigoth/Roman/Arab	Cabrito cuchifrito, asado serrano & cold cuts	Pendón's Day on Monday Easter

Region	Town	Province	Description	Period/Origin	Food	Festival
Catalunya	**Cadaqués**	Girona	Mediterranean village of fishermen's houses Narrow streets	Roman	Anchovies	International festival of music, July 30–August 20
Extremadura	**Trujillo**	Cáceres	Medieval town with mansions, churches & plaza Mayor	Arab/Roman	Goat cheese, Cochifrito de lechón	Cheese Fair, first weekend of May
Galicia	**O Cebreiro**	Lugo	Mountanous town *Pallozas's* houses	Pre-Roman/Celt Rural	Cheese	Cheese Fair end of March
La Rioja	**Santo Domingo de la Calzada**	Logroño	Medieval religious town with cathedral, tower, wall, palace & *parador*	Cistersian monastery & House of Trastamara	Ahorcaditos	Cofradía's fiestas, April 25–May 13
Madrid	**Aranjuez**	Madrid	Royal palace inspired by French influence (Versailles)	18th century	Pheasant during hunting season	Motín's fiesta, Sept. 2
Murcia	**Lorca**	Murcia	Renaissance religious town	Pre-hispania Arab /Roman	Olla gitana = local stew	Holy Easter
Navarra	**Estella**	Pamplona	Medieval collection of Roman churches	Roman/Jew	Chistorra, Pamplona's sausage, Estella's soup	Farmers' Fair, end of Nov.
Valencia	**Peñíscola**	Castellón	Mediterranean town, Blue pottery	Pre-hispania Phoencian/Greek	Rice and *suquets* of fish	Moros y Cristianos, April 29–30

Table 1.7   SPAIN'S WORLD HERITAGE SITES

City	Sites
Andalucía	• Mosque and downtown Córdoba (1984/1994)
	• Alhambra, Generalife and Albayzín of Granada (1984/1994)
	• Cathedral, Alcázar and Archivo de Indias of Sevilla (1987)
	• National Park of Doñana (1994)
	• Úbeda-Baeza Renaissance monuments (2003)
Aragón	• Mudejar architecture of Aragón (1986/2001)
	• National Park of Ordesa & Monte Perdido (Pyrénées) (1997/1999)
Asturias	• Monuments of Oviedo and the Kingdom of Asturias (1985/1998)
Balearic Islands	• Biodiversity and culture of Ibiza (1999)
	• Cultural landscape of the Serra de Tramuntana (Majorca) (2011)
Basque Country	• Vizcaya Bridge (Portugalete) (2006)
Canarias	• National Park of Garajonay (La Gomera) (1986)
	• Colonial architecture of San Cristóbal de la Laguna (Tenerife) (1999)
	• Teide National Park (2007)
Cantabria	• Altamira caves (Santillana del Mar) (1985)
Castilla-La Mancha	• Downtown of Toledo (1986)
	• Downtown of Cuenca (1996)
	• Heritage of Mercury (Almadén) (2012)
Castilla y León	• Burgos Cathedral (1984)
	• Downtown of Ávila, walls and churches (1985)
	• Downtown of Segovia and Aqueduct (1985)
	• Downtown of Salamanca (1988)
	• Auriferous deposit of Las Médulas (León) (1997)
	• Archaeological sites of Atapuerca (Burgos) (2000)
	• Prehistoric Rock-Art Sites in the Côa Valley and Siega Verde (2010)
Catalunya	• Works by Antoni Gaudí (Barcelona) (1984)
	• Monastery of Poblet (Tarragona) (1991)
	• Palau de la Música Catalana and Hospital of St. Pau (Barcelona) (1997)
	• Romanesque churches of Valley of Boí (Lleida) (2000)
	• Archaeological site of Tárraco (Tarragona) (2000)
Comunidad de Madrid	• Monastery and site of the El Escorial (1984)
	• University and historic precinct of Alcalá de Henares (1998)
	• Aranjuez cultural landscape (Aranjuez) (2001)
Comunidad de Valencia	• Lonja de la Seda (Silk Exchange) of Valencia (1996)
	• Palmeral of Elche (Alicante) (2000)
Extremadura	• Downtown Cáceres (1986)
	• Archaeological site of Mérida (Badajoz) (1993)
	• Royal Monastery of Santa María de Guadalupe (Cáceres) (1993)

Galicia	• Downtown of Santiago de Compostela (1985)
	• Roman walls of Lugo (2000)
	• Tower of Hercules (2009)
La Rioja	• Monasteries of San Millán & Suso (Logroño) (1997)
Various communities	• Route of Santiago de Compostela (1993)
	• Rock Art of the Mediterranean Basin (1998)

See also: Chapter 1: Overview; Archaeological Artifacts; Cities: Barcelona, Madrid, Sevilla, Valencia; National Parks. Chapter 2: Overview; Timeline. Chapter 5: Overview; Churches, Mosques, and Synagogues; The Pilgrimage to Santiago de Compostela. Chapter 12: Overview; Alhambra Palace.

Further Reading

Oldale, John. *A World of Curiosities*. New York: Plume, 2012.

UNESCO: World Heritage List. whc.unesco.org

REFERENCES

Anderson, James M. *Guía arqueológica de España*. Madrid: Alianza Editorial, 1997.

Atlas Climático Ibérico / Iberian Climate Atlas. Agencia Estatal de Meteorología (España); Ministerio de Medio Ambiente y Medio Rural y Marino (España). Instituto de Meteorología de Portugal. 2011.

Barton, Simon. *A History of Spain*. London: Palgrave, 2004.

Carandell, Luis. *Celtiberia Show*. Madrid: Guadiana de Publicaciones, 1971.

Carandell, Luis. *Spain*. Madrid: Incafo, 1980.

Castles, Stephen, Hein de Hass, and Mark J. Miller. *The Age of Migration. International Population Movements in the Modern World*. 5th ed. New York: The Guildford Press, 2014.

Copons, Elisenda. *Montañas de España. Rutas, paseos y aventuras*. Barcelona: ElCobre Ediciones, 2006.

Crow, John Armstrong. *Spain: The Root and the Flower: An Interpretation of Spain and the People*. Berkeley: University of California Press, 1985.

Dunlop, Fiona. *National Geographic Traveler: Spain*. 2nd ed. Washington, D.C.: National Geographic, 2005.

Evans, Polly. *It's Not about the Tapas: A Spanish Adventure on Two Wheels*. London: Bantam, 2003.

Farino, Teresa, and Mike Lockwood. *Travellers' Nature Guides: Spain*. Oxford: Oxford University Press, 2003.

Handelsman, Michael H., et al. *La cultura hispana: dentro y fuera de los Estados Unidos*. New York: Random House, 1981.

Hooper, John. *The Spaniards*. London: Viking, 1986.

Hooper, John. *The New Spaniards*. 2nd ed. London: Penguin, 2006.

Kern, Robert W. *The Regions of Spain: A Reference Guide to History and Culture*. Westport: Greenwood Press, 1995.

Knowles, Laura. *Countries around the World: Spain*. Chicago: Charlotte Guillain, 2012.

Lewis, Norman. *Voices of the Old Sea*. New York: Viking, 1985.

Lucia, Paul. *Through the Spanish Pyrenees*. Milnthorpe: Cicerone Press, 2000.

Nadeau, Jean-Benoît, and Julie Barlow. *The Story of Spanish*. New York: St. Martin's Press, 2013.

Ollé Martín, Albert. *Pueblos de España*. Barcelona: Lunwerg, 2009.

Operé, Fernando, and Carrie B. Douglass. *España y los españoles de hoy. Historia, sociedad y cultura*. New Jersey: Pearson, 2008.

O'Reilly, James, et al. *The Best Travel Writing 2008*. Palo Alto: Travelers' Tales, an imprint of Solas House, Inc., 2008.

Ostergren, Robert C., and Mathias Le Bossé. *The Europeans: A Geography of People, Culture, and Environment*. 2nd ed. New York: The Guildford Press, 2011.

Pickard, Piers. *The World: A Traveller's Guide to the Planet*. Melbourne: Lonely Planet, 2014.

Pla, Josep. *Viaje en Autobús*. Barcelona: Destino, 1942.

Pla, Josep. *Viaje a pie*. Barcelona: Destino, 1949.

Real, Antonio del, Dir. *El río que nos lleva*. Madrid: Producciones Dulcinea and TVE, 1989.

Regàs, Rosa. *España. Una nueva mirada*. Barcelona: Lunwerg, 1997.

Richardson, Paul. *Our Lady of the Sewers and Other Adventures in Deep Spain*. London: Little, Brown, 1998.

Schlecht, Neil E. *Spain for Dummies*. 4th ed. Hoboken: Wiley Publishing, Inc., 2007.

Shrady, Nicholas. *Sacred Roads: Adventures from the Pilgrimage Trail*. London: Viking, 1999.

Stewart, Chris. *Driving Over Lemons: An Optimist in Andalucía*. London: Sort of Books, 1999.

Tukker, Arnold, et al. *The Global Resource Footprint of Nations: Carbon, Water, Land and Materials Embodied in Trade and Final Consumption*. Delft: Leiden University, 2014.

Uche, Javier, Amaya Martínez-Gracia, Fernando Círez, and Uriel Carmona. "Environmental Impact of Water Supply and Water Use in a Mediterranean Water Stressed Region." *Journal of Cleaner Production* 88 (February) 2015:196–204.

Van der Kiste, John. *A Divided Kingdom: The Spanish Monarchy from Isabel to Juan Carlos*. Charleston: History Press, 2011.

VV.AA. "Ruido y Salud." *Observatorio salud y medio ambiente* (Numero 3). España: DKV, 2012.

VV.AA. *Recursos naturales. Inventario español de caza y pesca*. Ministerio de Agricultura, Alimentación y Medio Ambiente. 2010.

Websites

Aceros de Hispania. aceros-de-hispania.com

AZoMining Editors. "Spain: Mining, Minerals and Fuel Resources." http://www.azomining.com/Article.aspx?ArticleID=95

Barr, Caelainn. "EU Waste: Massive Spanish Desalination Plant Lies Idle." *The Bureau of Investigative Journalism,* April 27, 2011. https://www.thebureauinvestigates.com/2011/04/27/eu-waste-massive-spanish-desalination-plant-lies-idle/

BBC. "Catalonia's Bullfight Ban Provokes Emotional Response," July 29, 2010. http://www.bbc
.co.uk/news/world-europe-10798210

Cala, Andrés. "Spain's Desalination Ambitions Unravel." *The New York Times,* October 9, 2013.
http://www.nytimes.com/2013/10/10/business/energy-environment/spains-desalination-
ambitions-unravel.html?pagewanted=all

Corral Cortés, Esther. *Spain Today 2013.* Madrid: Ministry of the Presidency, 2013. http://
publicacionesoficiales.boe.es

Eurostat. http://epp.eurostat.ec.europa.eu

Gruber, Karl. "Discovery of Oldest DNA Scrambles Human Origins Picture." *National Geographic,*December4,2013.http://news.nationalgeographic.com/news/2013/12/131204-human-
fossil-dna-spain-denisovan-cave/?rptregcta=reg_free_np&rptregcampaign=20131016_rw
_membership_r1p_intl_ot_w#

INE: Instituto Nacional de Estadística. ine.es

Living Planet Report 2014. panda.org/lpr

Ministerio de Agricultura, Alimentación y Medio Ambiente. http://www.magrama.gob.es/es

Red de Parques Nacionales. http://www.magrama.gob.es/es/red-parques-nacionales/

Spain Info: "Spanish National Parks." http://www.spain.info/en/reportajes/parques_nacionales
_de_espana_ver_para_creer.html

Spain is culture. http://www.spainisculture.com/en/espacios_naturales/parque nacional_de
_sierra_nevada.html

Spain in Figures 2013 (available in INE). ine.es

Spanish Tourism Office. spain.info

UNESCO. unesco.org *UNESCO: World Heritage List.* whc.unesco.org

World Heritage Foundation. worldheritageproject.com

CHAPTER 2

HISTORY

OVERVIEW

The Greek historian Posidonio (135–51 BCE) called the Iberian Peninsula "the house of the Goddesses's richness" in an attempt to visually express the diversity that characterizes the rich geography of Spain, the variety of its products, the curiosities of its history, the plurality and different behavior of its inhabitants and, above all, the peculiarities of its development. While the ethnic origins of the people of the Iberian Peninsula are not fully known, what is certain is that Spain's climate of extremes influenced even its earliest inhabitants. Also, its location between Africa and Europe allowed access to a multitude of human societies, which shaped both Spain's history and its culture.

Apart from the so-called "Hombre de Orce" (Man of Orce) found in Venta Micena (Orce, Granada), which dates to around 1,350,000 BC, excavations in northern Spain in the Sierra de Atapuerca (Burgos) revealed fossils from approximately 1,200,000 BCE. The first fossils (*Homo antecessor*) were discovered in 1976 in Gran Dolina Cave (Burgos). It is possible to conclude that hominids had inhabited the peninsula for the past million years and had survived by hunting species such as rhinoceros, mammoth, and bison, as well as routinely resorting to cannibalism. The *Sima de los Huesos* (Pit of Bones) is the largest collection of hominid bones in the world and is located near the Gran Dolina cave. Over 30 human (*Homo sapiens heidelbergensis*) remains were found that date to 400,000 years ago. As there were signs of injuries and the humans were in their late teens or twenties, this could have been a burial site. Through DNA analysis it has been proven that the lineage of the *Homo neanderthalensis* found in Gibraltar in 1848 was separated from modern man (*Homo sapiens sapiens*) by around 600,000 years.

During the Upper Palaeolithic Period (ca. 40,000–10,000 BCE) Neanderthals, whose remains were found in Gibraltar, the Orce-Man found in Granada, and the *Homo antecessor*, who arrived in northern Spain, coexisted on the Iberian Peninsula. While they were cave dwellers, hunters, fishers, and food gatherers, the *Homo antecessor* left behind some of the oldest cave paintings in the world, including the cave of Altamira near Santander in northern Spain. These paintings are both artistically and culturally significant, depicting animals such as horses, bison, and reindeer. These paintings may have ritualistic significance or practical significance; they were possibly used as an initiation rite for young hunters. A series of cave paintings of animals dating from around

18,500–14,000 years ago can be found in the northern regions of Asturias and Cantabria. Analysis of the oldest DNA of human remains found in Spain shows them to be roughly 400,000 years old, and suggests the complexity and possible mixing of different human groups within the first hominids found in Europe.

Around 5,000 BCE, Neolithic (New Stone Age) people arrived, bringing with them improved tools but also agriculture and animal husbandry. Societies became less transient and the first communities in Andalucía and the eastern coastline were established. The population increased. Two notable Bronze Age groups migrated onto the Iberian Peninsula: the Iberians from North Africa; and the Celts, who arrived around 1000 to 300 BCE via the Pyrenees and settled along the Atlantic coast. Habitations on the peninsula contained no central kingdoms but rather consisted of small cities of villages that practiced herding, agriculture, ceramics, iron weaponry, and mining.

From 1700 to 1200 BCE the main Bronze Age societies were in the southeast and southwest as well as in small concentrations on the plains of La Mancha. New farming villages were established and trade routes grew along the Mediterranean. Iberian copper was in demand. Contact with other Mediterranean communities spread cultural and technological advances. By 850 BCE Bronze Age communities were enjoying a significantly wealthier lifestyle as seen by gold and bronze artifacts discovered along the Iberian Peninsula.

During the first century the peninsula was exposed to a variety of external cultures. Around 800 BCE Phoenicians, and later Greeks and Carthaginians, established trading posts on the peninsula. Iberian metals such as gold, silver, copper, and lead, as well as sea food and timber were in demand. Phoenicians founded the city of Cádiz (1100–800 BCE), making it Western Europe's oldest city. Among other things, the Greeks and Phoenicians brought to the Iberian Peninsula imported plants such as the grapevine and the olive, making Spain a leading producer of wine and olive oil. Around 600 BCE Celtic tribes established themselves in northwest Spain.

The Carthaginians established a colony on Ibiza and moved inland in hopes of a stronger presence on the Iberian Peninsula. In 219 Hannibal Barca launched an attack on the city of Saguntum (Valencia), which the townspeople fought to their death to defend. After the battle Rome launched a full-scale war against Carthage, driving the Carthaginians from Spain in 206 BCE. Full control of the Iberian Peninsula was a slow process lasting approximately 200 years. Rome would have a strong presence in Spain through the fourth century.

For almost six centuries beginning in 206 BCE Spain—or Hispania—became part of the Roman Empire and was one of its richest regions. The peninsula, with its agricultural land and abundance of minerals, was a desirable acquisition for the Romans. Roman rule brought with it a new social, economic, and political structure—a change that was relatively easy to impose on the southern lands where shifts in rulers were more common. However, the more rural areas of central and northern Spain resisted, making the process of Roman domination take over 200 years to accomplish in the last remaining regions of the far north, Cantabria and Asturias. Roman rule largely united Spain—with the exception of the Basque region—during this time, providing the peninsula with a long period of relative peace and prosperity. The Roman language (Latin), legal system, arts, and religion were practiced throughout the peninsula, and their influence has shaped modern

Spain—most notably its language, which has direct Latin roots. Great philosophers and poets such as Séneca, Martial, and Quintilian were born during this time. Mérida, a Roman town founded in 25 BCE, was militarily one of the Roman Empire's most important locations in Hispania; several architectural monuments exist there today.

Around 480 the Visigoths appeared and by 585 had successfully claimed the Iberian Peninsula. In 587, King Reccard converted to Catholicism in an attempt to ally himself with the Catholic clergy and win over his Catholic subjects. Life during Visigoth rule was unstable and characterized by civil wars and general unrest. The peak of Visigoth culture was during the time of Isidore of Sevilla (560–636), who was a scholar, politician, and theologian. By 711 the Visigoths had created a monarchy similar to others in Western Europe, yet it came to an abrupt end due to Muslim forces.

From 711 to 1492, Muslims retained control of various parts of the Iberian Peninsula. Islamic Spain joined the Islamic Kingdom's Golden Age, in contrast to the rest of Western Europe, which was entrenched in the Middle Ages. When the Muslims invaded the Iberian Peninsula in 711, Spain's population already consisted of Christians, Jews, and Arabs. The latter named the territories they conquered al-Andalus, which became a politically independent emirate in 756. It survived until 1492, when the Christian Reconquest was completed. This year also coincided with the discovery of the New World. As a result, Spain had become a major European power by the beginning of the 16th century, possessing linguistic, religious, and political unity.

Spanish language, Christianity, and Catholic monarchs were the official institutions of Spain after 1492. However, other languages including Ladino were spoken in Spain, and other people such as the *conversos* (Jews or Muslims who converted to Catholicism) and the *moriscos* (Muslims who were forced to convert to Christianity) developed tenacious ways to keep their own religion/identity. Also, in terms of government, the kingdom of Castilla and the Crown of Aragón maintained different systems of central and local government, taxation, and constitutional principles (MacKay 2002), despite the fact that both Crowns were united by marriage (Queen Isabel and King Ferdinand, also known as "the Catholic Monarchs"). In other words, early Spanish history suggests that Spain's population since medieval time consisted of a range of different heritages.

MARRIAGE OF ISABEL AND FERDINAND

The Marriage of Isabel to Ferdinand was controversial from the beginning. They married against the wishes of Isabel's half-brother (King Enrique), who had arranged her marriage to King Alfonso V of Portugal. Such a union was unappealing to Isabel both for practical reasons such as his age (he had children that were older than she) and for political reasons (the children from his first marriage meant that Isabel's future children would not inherit the throne to Portugal). Yet Enrique was determined, at one point threatening to imprison Isabel if she refused to marry Alfonso. Despite Enrique's threats, Isabel moved forward with a secret nuptial ceremony while Enrique was traveling in Granada. In 1469, the 18-year-old Isabel, heir to the throne of Castilla, married 19-year-old Ferdinand, the future kind of Aragón.

Explorer Christopher Columbus being received by King Ferdinand and Queen Isabel of Spain after his first expedition to the New World. Columbus waited nearly a decade to obtain permission for his trip and included a promise to spread Christianity in the New World. (Library of Congress)

Upon the death of Isabel, the fate of the peninsula was extremely precarious. Ferdinand remained the king of Aragón, and the title of Queen of Spain was given instead to their daughter, Juana, who was mentally ill and unfit to rule. Juana's husband, Philip I, the Hapsburg son of Maximillian the Holy Roman Emperor, was then named king, but ruled for a short time before dying mysteriously. The throne then passed to Juana and Philip I's son, Carlos I, who, prior to assuming the role of king, had never been to Spain, could not speak the language, and brought with him an entourage of Flemish advisors. Thus began the rule of the Hapsburg dynasty over Spain. Though his rule was met with opposition and an uprising of the Spanish people, it also led to the Golden Age—a period of world culture, power, dominance, and glory. Hapsburg kings Charles I and Philip II followed, in an empire that dominated Europe for some time, but eventually declined with the subsequent Hapsburg kings, Philip III, Philip IV, and Charles II.

Since Charles II died with no heir and no definite individual directly in line for the throne, the War of Succession occurred, bringing years of bloody strife (1702–1714) culminating in the birth of the Bourbon (French) Dynasty in Spain, the line of monarchs that still exists today. Philip V was confirmed as heir to the throne. It was agreed that upon his ascension to the Spanish throne, he would renounce his right to also become king of France. Mirroring Carlos I almost two decades later, Philip V began his rule not speaking the language and surrounded by a group of French advisors. Philip V suffered from "melancholy" and was ill equipped to rule. His rule was followed by deficits including mental instability and debilitating decadence.

The Napoleonic period began in 1808 when Spain suffered a humiliating defeat with Charles IV's abdication of the throne. Two months later, his son Ferdinand did likewise at the hand of Napoleon who then declared his brother, Joseph Bonaparte, the new Spanish king; and the country was occupied by French troops (1808–1813). However, the people of Spain, aided by British troops, expelled the French and restored the throne to Ferdinand VII in December 1813.

Left in tatters, Spain did not enjoy the progress made by the rest of Europe during the 19th century. Political instability dominated. The institution of the Monarchy was being questioned by the Spanish people. During the latter part of the century Spain alternated between republic and monarchy, with tensions that continued into the 20th century. The 1900s began with the dictatorship of General Miguel Primo de Rivera, followed by a Republican-socialist government, and finally culminated in the Spanish Civil War (1936–1939). The war was won by the right-wing nationalist faction led by Francisco Franco, who would go on to be the dictator of Spain until 1975. Under Franco's rule, the nation of Spain was politically unified and forced to be unified ideologically through dictated religious beliefs and political policies. Any voice of dissent was quickly stamped out, and many artists, writers, and intellectuals left the country or faced dire consequences, including work camps or death.

Since Franco's death in 1975, Spain has rapidly grown into a democratic, socially progressive nation. Yet the idea of Spain as a united nation is still an enigma for historians. According to Américo Castro (1885–1972), Spain has to be understood as a hybrid—a multiculturally diverse peninsula that started with the collision of three cultures living in the same space: Christians, Muslims, and Jews (Castro 1948). Claudio Sánchez-Albornoz (1893–1984), on the other hand, postulates that the origin of Spain began with the Romanization of the Iberian Peninsula and not with the Islamic influence (Sánchez-Albornoz 1956). In other words, Spain already existed in legal, political, and economic institutions before the important influence of the Muslims and the Jews in medieval Iberia. Since then, many books have been written about the origin of Spain as a nation. One of the most recent ones was written by Juan Pablo Fusi (1945–), who pointed out in his book *Historia mínima de España* (*Minimum History of Spain*) a clear thesis:"España, muchas historias posibles" (Fusi 2012), meaning that Spain has many possible histories. That is to say, the history of Spain is extremely complex. For instance, one case in point is the Basques. For Mark Kurlansky "they are a mythical people, almost an imagined people" (Kurlansky 1999). The Basques can be considered, as Kurlansky proposes, Europe's oldest nation despite the fact that they have never been a country. More recently, new research has pointed out that the presence of the Basque genome has been found in the ancestry of American admixed populations (Montinaro et al. 2015).

Further Reading

Castro, Américo. *The Meaning of Spanish Civilization: The Inaugural Lecture of Américo Castro*. New Jersey: Princeton University, 1941.

Hill, Fred James. *Spain: An Illustrated History*. New York: Hippocrene Books, 2001.

Kurlansky, Mark. *The Basque History of the World*. New York: Walker, 1999.

MacKay, Angus, et al., eds. *Medieval Spain: Culture, Conflict, and Coexistence*. New York: Palgrave Macmillan, 2002.

Montinaro, Francesco, et al. "Unravelling the Hidden Ancestry of American Admixed Populations." *Nature Communications* 7596 (2015): 1–7.

Phillips, William D., and Carla Rahn Phillips. *A Concise History of Spain*. Cambridge: Cambridge University Press, 2010.

Sánchez-Albornoz, Claudio. *Spain: A Historical Enigma*. Madrid: Fundación Universitaria Española, 1975.

TIMELINE

1,000,000 BCE	First relics of human activity, known as *Hombre de Orce,* discovered in the Guadix-Baza basin of southern Spain near Orce (Granada) in 1982.
800,000 BCE	*Homo antecessor* found in northern Spain in Sierra de Atapuerca in the Gran Dolina Cave near Burgos. The fossils were discovered in 1976 and indicate that this hunting community of hominids were also cannibals.
400,000 BCE	The largest collection of hominid bones in the world was discovered in northern Spain near Gran Dolina (Burgos). Over 30 human remains were found, all in their late teens or twenties with signs of injuries indicating a possible burial site.
100,000 BCE	First adult Neanderthal skull ever found in Iberia (Gibraltar, in 1848).
40,800 BCE	Oldest known cave art in the world discovered in the Cave of El Castillo near Puente Viesgo, Cantabria. These paintings in the form of hand prints could have been created by Neanderthals.
35,000– 11,000 BCE	A series of cave paintings discovered in northern Spain depict animals such as horse, bison, and reindeer that were hunted at the time. One of the best preserved early cave paintings is in the Altamira cave near Santander.
5500 BCE	Residues of agriculture and farming were found, implying that communities were becoming less transient. First communities established in Andalucía, Catalunya, and the Levante.
2000 BCE	Small numbers of Iberians settle in the south of the Iberian Peninsula bringing with them a knowledge of agriculture, mining, metal work, and stonework.
1100 BCE	Attracted by deposits of gold, silver, copper, and tin, the Phoenicians build Gadir (Cádiz), making it Western Europe's oldest city. Phoenicians

	subsequently establish a series of trading posts including Malaca (Málaga) and Onuba (Huelva).
654 BCE	Founding of Ebyssus (Ibiza) and Cartago Nova (Cartagena) by the Carthaginians; Emporion (Empúries—nowadays known as Girona) by the Greeks, and Saguntum (Valencia) by the Romans. Romanization begins (197 BCE–19 CE).
206 BCE	Hispania is a Roman province that belongs to the Roman Empire. Rome divides the peninsula into two regions: Hispania Citerior and Hispania Ulterior. A war with Lusitanian tribes, Celtiberians, and the Vaccaei starts. Reorganization of Hispania into Baetica, Lusitania, and Citerior.
1st century CE	Christianity spreads in Spain. Invasion of the Suebi, Vandals, and Alans. The Visigoths, allies of Rome against the Suebi, settle in the peninsula. Division of Hispania into six regions. Christianity gradually becomes the major religion of Hispania.
476	Disappearance of the Roman Empire in the Western world. The Visigoths settle in Hispania. Toledo is capital of the Visigoth kingdom. Liuvigild (525–586), a Visigoth king, unifies the peninsula. Reccared I renounces Arianism in favor of Catholicism.
711	Muslim Tariq ibn Ziyad's troops land in Gibraltar. Creation of al-Andalus, also known as Moorish or Islamic Iberia, governed by the Umayyad Caliphate (Damascus).
756	The exiled Umayyad prince Abd al-Rahman I (nicknamed *al-Dākhil*, the Immigrant) establishes himself as the Emir of Córdoba, independent from Damascus. Birth of the kingdoms of Asturias, Pamplona, León, and of the counties of Aragón, Sobrarbe, Ribagorza, and Barcelona.
1137	Union of Aragón and Catalunya. Creation of Aragón's Crown. Independence of Portugal. Reunification of al-Andalus by the Almoravids. Independent kingdom of Navarra.
1229	Jaume I conquers the Balearic Islands and Valencia. King Ferdinand III, called "the Saint," unifies the kingdoms of Castilla and León, and conquers Murcia, Córdoba, Jaén, Sevilla, Jeréz, Cádiz, and Niebla. The Nazari Kingdom of Granada is formed (1237).
1252	Alfonso X the Wise establishes himself in Toledo and creates a prestigious cultural center (Toledo's School of Translators). The *Siete Partidas* (seven-part code) is compiled by Alfonso X to establish a uniform body of normative rules for the kingdom.
1450	Navarra, Catalan, and Galician civil wars, which will end, first, with the Treaty of the Bulls of Guisando, and second, with the unification represented by the marriage between Isabel I of Castilla and Ferdinand II of Aragón (1469).
1492	The capitulation of Granada. End of the Christian Reconquest. Christopher Columbus sails to the Americas. Expulsion of the Jews. Antonio

de Nebrija writes the first *Gramática castellana* (Grammar of the Castilian language).

1505   The kingdom of Napoli is attached to Spain. The University of Alcalá de Henares is founded in 1508. The kingdom of Navarra joins the unified kingdom of Spain (1512). Vasco Núñez de Balboa discovers the Pacific Ocean in 1513.

1519   Conquest of Mexico by Hernán Cortés. Charles I and V of the Holy Spanish Empire (Germany, Italy, Netherlands, and Burgundy) rule over extensive domains in Europe, America, and Asia. Revolt of the *Comuneros* (Brotherhoods) in Castilla (1520). Creation of councils of State, Hacienda, War, and Indies.

1521   Wars against France in Italy. Circumnavigation trip by Magallanes-Elcano.

1526–1529   Peace of Cambray after wars against France. The *Compañía de Jesus* is created. Conquest of Peru by Pizarro.

1563   Construction of El Escorial. Uprising against Spain in Flanders (until 1648). Conquest of the Philippines. The Catholic Church promulgates the *Index Librorum Prohibitorum* (list of prohibited books).

1605   The first part of *El ingenioso hidalgo don Quijote de la Mancha* is published by Miguel de Cervantes. Expulsion of the Arabs. Conquest of the African city of Ceuta. Uprising in Catalunya and Portugal (1640).

1702   War of Succession to the Crown of Spain. Centralization and reform of the Spanish territorial administration. Creation of the secretaries of State. End of the Wars of Succession. Spain relinquishes Flanders and their territories in Italy to Austria; Sicily to Savoy; and Gibraltar and Menorca to Great Britain (1714).

1714   The Royal Spanish Academy of Language is created. Creation of the Royal Academy of Fine Arts of San Fernando in 1744.

1756   Seven Years' War. Spain acquires the American state of Louisiana from France. War of Independence of the American colonies against England. Spain recovers Menorca and Florida (1776). Free trade with America (1778). War of the Rosellón, between Spain and France for two years (1793).

1807   Portugal is occupied by Spain and France. Spain authorizes the entry of French troops into its territory.

1808   Mutiny of Aranjuez. The Bayonne Statute. The Second of May Uprising. Ferdinand VII reigns. War of Independence. French José I Bonaparte reigns in Spain (1808–1813).

1810   Some South American governments are recognized by the Spanish king but not by the Spanish or French national governments of the time. Caracas, Buenos Aires, Montevideo, Quito, Santiago, and Asunción claim independence. French occupation of Sevilla. Goya's *Los Desastres de la Guerra* (*The Disasters of War*). Spain's first national sovereign assembly, the *Cortes Generales* (parliament), in refuge in Cádiz during the Peninsular War, signs the Spanish Constitution nicknamed *La Pepa* (1812).

1833   Queen Isabel II abolishes the Salic Law which, as in France, allows only men to reign. First Carlist War (civil war in Spain 1833–1839). Regency of María Cristina de Borbón. Spanish Royal Statute or charter in the constitution. The government of Mendizábal confiscates religious properties (also known as *la Desamortización*) in 1835.

1845   Second Carlist War (1845–1849). First train. General O'Donnell makes a *pronunciamiento* (speech) against the government and is named president of Spain, although for less than three months. Finance Minister Pascual Madoz's *desamortización*: properties owned by municipalities, military orders, hospitals, hospices, and *casas de misericordia* (charity homes) are confiscated and sold to raise funds for the State in 1855.

1859   Spanish-Moroccan War. *La Gloriosa* (Glorious Revoluton), results in the expulsion of Queen Isabel II. Democratic revolution headed by General Prim. Anti-Spanish revolt in Cuba.

1869   Generals Prim and Serrano denounce the government in 1868, resulting in Serrano becoming regent of Spain (June 18, 1869–September 27, 1870) and Prim a progressive liberal president. New constitution. Constitutional monarchy. Male universal suffrage. President Prim is assassinated in 1870. *Asociación Internacional de Trabajadores* (AIT; International Association of Workers) is created.

1873   Amadeo I of Savoy abdicates. First Republic of Spain. Third Carlist War. Martínez Campos leads a coup d'état to restore the throne to Alfonso XII in 1874.

1874   Alfonso XII reigns. New constitution in 1876. Conservative and liberal governments alternate in power. Foundation of *Partido Socialista Obrero Español* (PSOE: Party of the Socialist Workers of Spain). Creation of the *Unión General de Trabajadores* (UGT, The General Union of Workers).

1895   War against Cuba. President Antonio Cánovas, author of Spain's 1876 constitution, is assassinated by an Italian anarchist in 1897. Processes of Montjuich against the anarchists.

1898   War against the United States. Loss of Cuba, Puerto Rico, and the Philippine Islands.

1909   Melilla War. *La Semana Trágica* (Tragic Week) in Barcelona. The *Confederación Nacional del Trabajo* (CNT; National Confederation of Labor) is created. It is a Spanish confederation of anarcho-syndicalist labor unions affiliated with the Asociación Internacional de los Trabajadores.

1921   Founding of *Partido Comunista de España* (PCE: Spanish Communist Party).

1923   Coup d'état by General Miguel Primo de Rivera (dictatorship). Construction of reservoirs. Creation of Campsa (monopoly of the distribution of gasoline) and Iberia (commercial flight company). International exhibitions of Sevilla and Barcelona in 1929.

1932   Statute of autonomy of Catalunya. Approval of the agricultural reform law. Frustrated coup d'état by General Sanjurjo (August).

1933   Anarchist riots in Casas Viejas. Victory of the center and the Catholic right (CEDA) in the general elections (November). Creation of the *Falange Española* (far-right Fascist party).

1934   General strike. Revolutionary uprisings in Asturias and Catalunya. Suspension of the autonomy of Catalunya. Scandals of corruption by the radical government.

1936   Victory of Frente Popular in the general elections. Dismissal of Alcalá-Zamora. Azaña becomes president of the Republic. Serious altercations end in a military uprising (Franco, Mola) against the Republic (July 18). The Spanish Civil War begins on July 18. The International Brigades help the Republican army.

1937   The bombing of Guernica (April). Nationalist General Mola dies in a flight accident.

1939   The Republican army surrenders. End of the Spanish Civil War (April 1). Dictatorship of General Francisco Franco.

1940   Franco-Hitler talks in Hendaye. Creation of *Instituto Nacional de Industria* (INI: National Institute of Industry). Spain is isolated from the international community. Franco returns all Spanish ambassadors.

1953   Franco signs the Concordat with the Vatican in an effort to break Spain's international isolation. Franco makes an agreement with the U.S. to allow military bases in Spain in exchange for economic aid.

1959   Creation of the Basque terrorist group *Euskadi Ta Askatasuna (ETA)*, which makes its first deadly terrorist attack in 1968. Franco chooses Juan Carlos I de Borbón to succeed him as king of Spain (1969) on his death.

1973   ETA kills President Carrero Blanco (June 9, 1973–December 20, 1973).

1975   Execution of members of ETA. International protest against the Spanish regime. The *Marcha verde* (Green March) of Morocco over the Spanish Sahara. Franco dies. Juan Carlos I reigns. A process of democratic transition begins.

1976   Adolfo Suárez, president of the government. Law of Political reform. Legalization of the Communist party. Democratic elections for a constituent parliament. UCD government formed.

1978   New constitution: democratic and constitutional monarchy, and regional state.

1979   Triumph of *Unión de Centro Democrático* (UCD: Union of the Democratic Center) in the general elections. Statutes of autonomy in the Basque country and Catalunya.

1981   After Suárez resigns on January 29, 1981, Leopoldo Calvo Sotelo (UCD) is appointed president (February 25, 1981–December 1, 1982). 23-F is an attempted coup d'état also known as *El Tejerazo* (named after

Colonel Antonio Tejero). King Juan Carlos I reaffirms the Spanish Constitution of 1978. Spain joins NATO. New Law of Divorce.

1982   Spain holds the 1982 FIFA World Cup. Felipe González's PSOE wins the election three times in a row (1986; 1989; 1993). Decriminalization of abortion. Law of university reform. Beginning of the industrial renovation.

1986   Spain joins the European Community and NATO membership is approved in a referendum. ETA detonates a bomb in a supermarket in Barcelona in 1987.

1989   Renovation of the right-wing party: creation of the *Partido Popular* (Popular party). Felipe González becomes president of the European Community.

1992   Spain holds the Olympic Games in Barcelona; Madrid is named the City of Culture by the EU, and Sevilla celebrates the Universal Exhibition. Several scandals of corruption (Filesa, Roldán, Ibercorp).

1996   José María Aznar's PP wins the election twice in a row (1996; 2000). In the 1996 elections, PP forms a government with the support of CiU, PNV, and Coalición Canarias. Spain becomes a member of the European Monetary Union. ETA kills Miguel Ángel Blanco, a PP politician in the Basque country. Mass protests against continued terrorism in the Basque country. The leadership of Basque terrorist group *Herri Batasuna* jailed.

1998   Ex-minister José Barrionuevo and his deputy Rafael Vera from the previous Socialist government are sentenced to jail for approving state terrorism against ETA (known as the GAL affair).

2000   Popular party wins election with overall majority. Batasuna, the political party of ETA becomes illegal in 2002. Tension with Morocco over the little island of Perejil.

2004   On March 11, Madrid train bombings—three days before Spain's general elections—becomes Europe's biggest terrorist attack on Spanish soil. José Luis Rodríguez Zapatero's PSOE wins the elections twice in a row (2004; 2008). Zapatero returns the Spanish troops from Iraq. Wedding of Prince Felipe and Letizia Ortiz. Law allowing same-sex marriage.

2006   Ceasefire of ETA. Negotiations between the government and ETA. Passage of *Ley de igualdad* (Law of Equality). Founding of the political party *Ciudadanos* (Citizens).

2007   Passage of *Ley de Memoria Histórica* (Law of Historic Memory). Foundation of the political party *Unión, Progreso y Democracia* (Union, Progress, and Democracy).

2008   Severe economic crisis. The Spanish economy comes very close to bankruptcy.

2011   ETA announces a complete cessation of violence (October 20). Mariano Rajoy's PP wins the election of November 20. *15-M* (May 15); Spanish protests: *Los indignados* (Indignant movement) holds a series of ongoing demonstrations in Spain.

2012   HM Juan Carlos I unexpectedly appears on national television to apologize in twelve words: "Lo siento mucho. Me he equivocado. Y no volverá a ocurrir. Gracias" (I am very sorry. I made a mistake. It will not happen again. Thank you.). He was photographed by the Spanish media hunting elephants in Botswana while many Spaniards were struggling due to the economic recession.

2014   Spain's President Mariano Rajoy asks for pardon over party corruption scandal. Several scandals of corruptions including Andalucía's ERE, Bankia, Bárcenas, Gürtel, Urdangarin, and Jordi Pujol. Pujol was president of the region of Catalunya (1989–2003), and was stripped of his titles after admitting tax fraud for the past 30 years. Founding of the political party *Podemos* (We can), which obtained five seats in the European Parliament and received the fourth most votes in the election (7.98%).

2015   Regional and general elections in Spain. The power in hands of conservative (PP) or socialist (PSOE) is challenged by refreshing new political parties such as *Ciudadanos* and *Podemos*, breaking up the traditional duopoly (PP and PSOE) in Spain.

Abderramán III (891–961)

At the age of 21, Abderramán III became the Emir and Caliph of Córdoba (912–961) of the Ummayad dynasty in al-Andalus. Although he lost the battle of Simancas (939) against Ramiro II of Asturias, Abderramán managed to impose Arab power against the Christian kingdoms of León, Navarra, and the counts of Barcelona and Castilla, who had to pay him a stipend annually. In 929 he obtained the titles of emir and caliph and, as a result, he defended the religion as well as political independence of al-Andalus against any superior authority coming from Bagdad or Tunisia. Abderramán conquered Melilla, Tangier, and Ceuta and also managed a peaceful kingdom developing the economy, the arts, and culture of his empire. He built several monuments in his native Córdoba like the new residential city for the court: Madinat al-Zahra. However, the heterogeneous population of the time and their inability to integrate within a common nation was an ongoing source of instability.

See also: Chapter 2: Don Pelayo; Don Rodrigo; Jaime I "the Conqueror"; Maimónides.

Further Reading

Bendiner, Elmer. *The Rise and Fall of Paradise: When Arabs and Jews Built a Kingdom in Spain.* New York: Barnes & Noble, 1983.

Fierro Bello, María Isabel. *Abd al-Rahman III: The First Cordoban Caliph.* Oxford: Oneworld, 2005.

Adriano (76–138)

Known in English as Hadrian, Adriano was a Roman Emperor from 117–138. He became ruler of the Roman Empire thanks to the support of Trajan's wife Plotina and the influence of the Spanish sector in the Senate. His rule was characterized by his continuous travels, visits to regions, and founding of new cities, as well as building Hadrian's Wall, which marked the northern limit of Roman Britain. His rule constituted a long period of peace during which he improved the Advisory Board for the Emperor and reformed the bureaucracy, the army, and the territory. Hadrian is also known for major construction projects such as the amphitheater of Nimes (France), the castle of Sant'Angelo, and the bridges over the Tiber in Rome. During the last days of his rule, however, Hadrian was abandoned by his main collaborators and he died before assigning a successor.

See also: Chapter 2: Leovigildo; Séneca; Viriato.

Further Reading

Birley, Anthony. *Hadrian: The Restless Emperor.* New York: Routledge, 1997.

Speller, Elizabeth. *Following Hadrian: A Second-Century Journey through the Roman Empire.* Oxford: Oxford University Press, 2003.

Alcalá Zamora, Niceto (1877–1949)

A conservative republican or liberal politician who declared himself to be anti-monarchist during the Restoration, Niceto Alcalá Zamora served as ceremonial president of the Second Spanish Republic (1931–1936), as head of the provisional government, and then as president of the Second Republic in 1931. Alcalá Zamora resigned as president in October 1931, when the *Cortes* (parliament) enacted legislation to place church financing and religious orders under state control. Manuel Azaña took on the role of president and therefore of the head of government, while Alcalá Zamora became the president, technically the head of state but a largely ceremonial role. According to the Spanish historian Domínguez Ortiz, Alcalá Zamora had the ability to be hated by everyone. After the civil war, he was forced into exile. He died in Argentina.

See also: Chapter 2: Azaña, Manuel; Franco, Francisco; Juan Carlos I of Spain; Largo Caballero, Francisco; Negrín, Juan; Pasionaria, La; Primo de Rivera, Miguel.

Further Reading

Casanova, Julián, and Carlos Gil Andrés. *Twentieth-Century Spain: A History.* Cambridge: Cambridge University Press, 2014.

Azaña, Manuel (1880–1940)

Manuel Azaña was a writer and Republican leader and is considered one of the most important political figures during the Second Republic. He served as the second and last president of the Republic (1936–1939). The Spanish Civil War broke out while he was in power. Born into a rich family, Azaña did little to reform the taxation system to shift the burden of government onto the wealthy. Azaña's extreme anti-clerical program alienated the more moderate Spaniards; he was hostile both toward the monarchy and the Church. Azaña's lack of social sensibility was exemplified when he forbid religious institutions to teach and dissolved the *Compañía de Jesús*. He formed a government with socialists, Catalan and Galician regional politicians, plus a small group of his Acción Republicana political party. He moved to France when the victory of Franco's nationalist army was imminent.

See also: Chapter 2: Alcalá Zamora, Niceto; Franco, Francisco; Juan Carlos I of Spain; Largo Caballero, Francisco; Negrín, Juan; Pasionaria, La; Primo de Rivera, Miguel.

Further Reading

De Rivas Cherif, Cipriano, Paul Stewart, and Enrique de Rivas. *Portrait of an Unknown Man: Manuel Azaña and Modern Spain*. Madison: Fairleigh Dickinson University Press, 1995.

Sedwick, Frank. *The Tragedy of Manuel Azaña and the Fate of the Spanish Republic*. Columbus: Ohio State University Press, 1964.

Cánovas del Castillo, Antonio (1828–1897)

Antonio Cánovas del Castillo was a journalist and a historian before he began to collaborate with General O'Donnell, becoming minister of various cabinets during the kingdom of Isabel II. Cánovas also assumed the functions of the Head of State during the regency of María Cristina. As a conservative politician, he developed a pacific restoration process. Cánovas obtained all powers in 1873 to direct the Spanish monarchy. While he was educating Alfonso XII in England, Cánovas also drafted the *Manifesto of Sandhurst*, in which he explained the guidelines of a modest, parliamentary, and liberal monarchy where Alfonso XII prevailed. At the end he managed to see Alfonso XII (1874–1885) and Alfonso XIII (1886–1931) enthroned as kings of Spain. He was able to strengthen the monarchy to an unprecedented level during a tumultuous period. He is known for incorporating members of the Carlist party into his Conservative party in order to appease the competing militarists. Cánovas is also remembered in Spanish history for declaring that in order to combat separatism Spain would sacrifice "hasta el último hombre y la última peseta" (to the last man and the last *peseta* [an old Spanish currency]). Cánovas was a key figure in the restoration of the Bourbon family to the Spanish Crown as well as being the author of Spain's constitution of 1876.

See also: Chapter 2: de Borbón, María Cristina; Espartero, Baldomero; Prim y Prats, Juan; Sagasta, Práxedes Mateo.

Further Reading

Casanova, Julián, and Carlos Gil Andrés. *Twentieth-Century Spain: A History*. Cambridge: Cambridge University Press, 2014.

Carlos II "the Bewitched" (1661–1700)

Carlos II died at the very young age of 38 and his legacy represents the decline of the Spanish empire. Carlos II was the last Hapsburg ruler of Spain. Due to his weak physical condition since birth, attributed to the long heritage of his family's inbreeding, Carlos did not talk until he was four years old, nor did he walk until he was eight. He was coddled and spoiled until 14 years of age. Even then, his mother managed to legally extend his childhood for two more years in order to avoid the testament, when at the age of 14 he supposedly should have become an adult. Carlos II was married at the age of 18 to 16-year-old Marie Louise d'Orléans (1662–1689), who died at 26 deeply depressed after knowing that her husband was impotent. His second marriage with the 23-year-old Palatine princess María Anna of Neuburg did not produce the much-desired heir either. The Court of Spain, including the government, tried everything possible in order to cure Carlos II's impotency. The European powers were also preoccupied by the question of succession of childless Carlos II of Spain. In fact, the Spanish administration were convinced that he was the victim of a spell and, therefore, they decided to practice exorcism on him. As a result, the monarch died after being the target of an exorcism and suffering terrible pains in his body.

See also: Chapter 2: The Catholic Monarchs; Columbus, Christopher; Cortés, Hernán; Eugenia, Isabel Clara; Philip II.

Further Reading

Langdon-Davies, John. *Carlos the Bewitched: The Last Spanish Hapsburg 1661–1700*. London: Jonathan Cape, 1963.

The Catholic Monarchs (1474–1504)

The Catholic Monarchs is the joint title used in history for Queen Isabel I (1451–1504) of Castilla and King Ferdinand II (1452–1516) of Aragón whose marriage represented the beginning of modern Spain. The union of the peninsula's two largest kingdoms, Castilla and Aragón, plus the repossession of the kingdom of Navarra in conjunction with the conquest of the Kingdom of Granada meant the birth of Spain as a unified country and a European power. The Catholic Monarchs also made a significant contribution to the New World by financing Christopher Columbus's trip to America. In so doing, they laid the foundation for establishing Spain as a New World empire. Although the aristocracy enjoyed economic power, the middle class was supported by the Crown, while the populace cultivated the land. This social calm was disrupted by the expulsion of the Jews in 1492 as well as the creation of the Inquisition as the supreme authority in moral matters. The Catholic Monarchs converted the Alhambra into their military base. It is hard to attribute a key role to one single person within this political marriage.

See also: Chapter 2: Carlos II "the Bewitched"; Columbus, Christopher; Cortés, Hernán; Eugenia, Isabel Clara; Philip II.

Further Reading

Edwards, John. *The Spain of the Catholic Monarchs, 1474–1520*. Malden: Blackwell Publishers, 2000.

Elliott, J. H., ed. *Imperial Spain 1469–1716*. London: Penguin Books, 2003.

Kamen, Henry. *Spain, 1469–1714: A Society of Conflict*. New York: Pearson, 2005.

Columbus, Christopher (1451–1506)

Christopher Columbus was a Genoese sailor who sought funding for a trip to Japan and was turned down by the king of Portugal. Spain's Catholic Monarchs gave the matter some thought. Columbus's idea of sailing due west to reach the Orient was, if not wholly original, still unusual. It took him nearly a decade to get his plan approved, which included a promise to spread Christianity abroad. Finally, mostly thanks to Isabel, Columbus's proposed venture was funded and launched. From Spain, Columbus sailed to the Canary Islands, then west for seven weeks without sighting land, his worried crew growing ever more mutinous. The *Pinta*, the *Niña*, and the *Santa María* sailed toward the West Indies. On October 12, 1492, Columbus's flagship *Santa María* made landfall on the large island of Hispaniola (shared today by Haiti and the Dominican Republic), although for the rest of his life Columbus believed that he had in fact landed on the eastern reaches of Asia. It remained for a later navigator, Italian Amerigo Vespucci, to prove that Columbus had bumped into a new continent. A published version of Vespucci's accounts led to the new land being named "America" in his honor. Columbus died in Valladolid in poverty, despite being the first governor of Hispaniola. He urged kind treatment of the natives, and he and the colony profited from the cotton the Taíno Indians produced and the gold they acquired, mostly through island trade. His accomplishments were overlooked in the mad rush for discovery and colonization.

See also: Chapter 2: Carlos II "the Bewitched"; The Catholic Monarchs; Cortés, Hernán; Eugenia, Isabel Clara; Philip II.

Further Reading

Hyslop, Stephen G., Bob Somerville, and John Thompson. *Eyewitness History from Ancient Times to the Modern Era*. Washington, D.C.: National Geographic, 2011.

Cortés, Hernán (1485–1547)

As a 19-year-old, brash and quarrelsome, Hernán Cortés had sailed to the Caribbean in 1504. After helping colonize Cuba, he was authorized to lead an expedition to Mexico in 1519. Well-schooled in how to dominate native populations, he sailed to the land of the Aztecs with 600 men in 11 ships. Landing in the new port of Veracruz, he burned his ships to impress on his men that there was no turning back. The army marched inland, cannons and horses intimidating locals, who had never seen either. With the help of his mistress and interpreter, Malinche, Cortés befriended Aztec ruler Moctezuma II, who believed at first that the Spaniard was an incarnation of Quetzalcoatl, the feathered serpent god. But Cortés then took the king hostage, and the Aztecs, under Moctezuma's brother, attacked the Spaniards. Moctezuma was mortally wounded and Cortés retreated from the capital of Tenochtitlan. After recruiting some 200,000 Indians who were disaffected by the Aztec demands for tribute and sacrificial victims, Cortés returned the next year. Moctezuma had died, and Cortés found a revolt—and a smallpox epidemic—under way. Following a four-month siege, he took and destroyed the capital in 1521. In its place he founded Mexico City.

Hernán Cortés kneels before Emperor Montezuma. Cortés destroyed the capital of the Aztec civilization in 1521 with a small group of soldiers, smallpox, and the aid of rebellious tribes, one of which included his mistress and interpreter, Malinche. Immediately after, Cortés conquered Mexico and founded Mexico City. (Library of Congress)

See also: Chapter 2: Carlos II "the Bewitched"; The Catholic Monarchs; Columbus, Christopher; Eugenia, Isabel Clara; Philip II.

Further Reading

Hyslop, Stephen G., Bob Somerville, and John Thompson. *Eyewitness History from Ancient Times to the Modern Era*. Washington, D.C.: National Geographic, 2011.

de Borbón, María Cristina (1806–1878)

María Cristina of Bourbon was Queen Consort of Spain (1829–1833), regent of Spain (1833–1840), and princess of the two Sicily's. She became Queen Consort of Spain when she married her uncle Ferdinand VII in 1829. From this marriage were born two girls, the future Queen of Spain (1843–1868) and the infant Luisa Fernanda, who was the Duchess of Montpensier after marrying Antoine, Duke of Montpensier (1824–1890). Due to the influence of María Cristina over her husband, the king decided to abolish the law in 1830 in order to allow his daughter to inherit the Spanish Crown. When he died, María Cristina was named Regent Queen of Spain until her daughter became old enough to reign. This was a politically turbulent period in which she had to deal with differences between liberals and conservatives. Following the death of her husband, María Cristina wed Agustín Fernando Muñoz (1808–1873). Due to his lowly status as an ex-sergeant from the royal guard, their marriage was kept secret. When news of her marriage was known by the public, her already declining popularity plummeted and she renounced her regency and left Spain with her spouse. Years later, Isabel II named Muñoz Duke of Riansares. She managed a considerable fortune, taking advantage of her position, which she invested in Cuba—where she had the largest hacienda on the island and became a major proprietor of slaves for the sugar cane on the island.

See also: Chapter 2: Cánovas del Castillo, Antonio; Espartero, Baldomero; Prim y Prats, Juan; Sagasta, Práxedes Mateo.

Further Reading

Bergamini, John D. *The Spanish Bourbons: The History of a Tenacious Dynasty*. New York: Putnam, 1974.

Marichal, Carlos. *Spain (1834–1844): A New Society*. London: Tamesis Books, 1977.

de Farnesio, Isabel (1692–1766)

Isabel de Farnesio known in English as Elizabeth Farnese, was Queen Consort of Spain who exerted great influence over Spain's foreign policy after marrying Philip V of Bourbon from France. While she limited the pro-French influence to her throne, she managed to bring Cardenal Alberoni and other Italians into relevant positions in the Spanish court. She came from Parma, north of Italy, and was obsessed with placing her children in good positions. Isabel made it possible that America and the Spanish peninsula ended up in the hands of Ferdinand VI, the son of her husband's first marriage, while her sons Charles III (future king of Spain) and Philip inherited the Crowns of Napoli (Charles III), Milan, and Parma (Philip). Her daughter María Teresa married Luis Fernando of France, becoming Queen Consort of France while her other daughter, María Antonia, became Queen Consort of Sardinia when she married Víctor Amadeo III. Isabel de Farnesio spent much of her later days at the palaces of La Granja and Aranjuez.

See also: Chapter 2: de Godoy, Manuel.

Further Reading

Harcourt-Smith, Simon. *Alberoni or the Spanish Conspiracy*. London: Faber & Faber, 1945.

Petrie, Charles. *King Charles III of Spain: An Enlightened Despot*. London: Constable, 1971.

de Godoy, Manuel (1767–1851)

Manuel de Godoy was president of Spain from 1792 to 1797 and from 1801 to 1808, although his major aspiration was to become the future king of Spain, after becoming a favorite of King Carlos IV and Queen María Luisa. Godoy married María Teresa de Borbón, Countess of Chinchón, who hated him. He was in charge of saving the Monarchy and culminating the reforms of the French Enlightenment. However, Godoy was seen by the Spaniards as an outsider who represented the French Enlightenment in a negative way. While he was in power, Spain lost Santo Domingo and Louisiana, and Spain's finances were in ruins after a catastrophic war with Britain. However, Godoy received many titles including Prince of Peace (*Príncipe de la Paz*) and at the age of 22 was named a knight of the Order of Santiago. The English romantic poet and politician Lord Byron mentions Godoy in his *Childe Harold's Pilgrimage* (1812) where a Spanish "lusty muleteer . . . chants *Viva el Rey* / And checks his song to execrate Godoy, / The royal wittol Charles." According to Byron, "It is to this man that the Spaniards universally impute the ruin of their country."

See also: Chapter 2: de Farnesio, Isabel.

Further Reading

Byron, Lord. *Childe Harold's Pilgrimage*. Newcastle: Cambridge Scholars Publishing, 2009.

de Godoy, Manuel. *Memoirs of Don Manuel de Godoy*. Vol. 2: *Prince of the Peace*. Whitefish, Montana: Kessinger, 2008.

Don Pelayo (685–739)

Don Pelayo was a noble Visigoth who became king of Asturias after defeating the Arabs in the battle of Covadonga in 718. He was the founder of the Christian kingdom of Asturias, which turned out to be an important Crown in political, cultural, and religious terms. For example, the Battle of Covadonga marked the beginning of the Christian Reconquista. After the collapse of the Roman Empire, the Goths, a Christian people of Germanic origin, entered Spain in the fifth century. They tried to maintain Roman order through the *Ordo Gothorum*, which essentially stipulated that every territory conquered by the Visigoths would automatically be governed following the laws of the Visigoth dynasty. However, despite Pelayo's early victory, the Christian Reconquista took considerable time. In fact, it began with Pelayo in 718 and ended in 1492 under the Catholic Monarchs. After Pelayo died, he was succeeded by his son Favila. However, he was killed in a hunting accident two years later. Pelayo's son-in-law, Alfonso I, was proclaimed king.

See also: Chapter 2: Abderramán III; Don Rodrigo; Jaime I "the Conqueror"; Maimónides.

Further Reading

Elliot, J. H., ed.. *The Hispanic World: Civilization and Empire, Europe and the Americas, Past and Present*. London: Thames & Hudson, 1991.

Kyle Freyschlag, Elizabeth. *A Consideration of Pelayo in Spanish Literature*. Stanford: Stanford University Press, 1965.

Don Rodrigo (?–711)

Don Rodrigo, known in English as Roderic, was the last Visigoth king of Hispania, reigning for a brief period between 710 and 712. He was defeated in the battle of Guadalete against the Arabs, who began to occupy the Spanish territory. The popular legend paints don Rodrigo as a loser and a sinner king who seduced an aristocrat, Florinda (called "the Prostitute" by the Arabs), whose father, the powerful governor of Ceuta, gave away his territory to the Arabs in revenge. The Iberian Peninsula experienced a further peaceful period as a result of intermarriage. Particularly interesting was the relationship between the Muslim conquerors and leading members of the Visigoth aristocracy, such as Abd Al-'Azīz taking as his wife King Roderic's widow, Egilona.

See also: Chapter 2: Abderramán III; Don Pelayo; Jaime I "the Conqueror"; Maimónides.

Further Reading

Altamira, Rafael. *Spain under the Visigoths*. eBooks: Didactic Press, 2014.

Barton, Simon. *A History of Spain*. London: Palgrave Macmillan, 2004.

Strange, G. Le. *Spanish Ballads*. Cambridge: Cambridge University Press, 2013.

Espartero, Baldomero (1793–1879)

General Espartero became a general, prince of Vergara, and regent of Spain during a turbulent period (1840–1843). He abandoned his religious studies to fight against the rebellions in South America, where he lived between 1815–1824. After his return to Spain, he married a rich landowner's daughter in Logroño, converting it into the most important city of Spain in the 19th century. Espartero was an ardent defender of the right of King Ferdinand VII's daughter, Isabel II, to occupy the Spanish throne, and fought her cause in the Carlist War. During the last three years of the war, Espartero exercised from Logroño a huge influence over Madrid. When he won the war the queen regent and her ministers attempted to reduce the power of Espartero and his followers. However, a *pronunciamiento* (statement) in Madrid essentially honored him with the post of president. His popularity increasingly overshadowed Queen Cristina, who took offense and eventually resigned. Espartero was elected regent and accepted with the intention of remaining regent until Isabel II came of age. Yet his support declined after his unmerciful execution of conspirators, some of whom were popular war heroes, notably General Diego de León. Espartero's hope for a modern Spain through free trade and civil liberties upset both those to the right and left of his political ideology. In 1843, Espartero was exiled to England and General Ramón María Narváez replaced him as advisor to the young queen.

See also: Chapter 2: Cánovas del Castillo, Antonio; de Borbón, María Cristina; Prim y Prats, Juan; Sagasta, Práxedes Mateo.

Further Reading

Fernández, Gilbert Gerald. *The Making of Spain's First Caudillo: The Life and Career of General Baldomero Fernández Espartero through the First Carlist War, 1793–1840*. Tallahassee: Florida State University, 1974.

Sencourt, Robert. *Spain's Ordeal. A Documented Survey of Recent Events*. London: Longmans, Green and Co, 1940.

Eugenia, Isabel Clara (1556–1633)

Isabel Clara Eugenia played an important role in the dynasty of her father, Philip II. After an attempt to make her queen of France since she was Henry II of France's granddaughter, in 1598 her father named her queen and later governor of the Spanish Netherlands. Isabel was the only person whom Philip allowed to help him with his administration, including translating Italian documents into the Spanish language for him. Her father decided to cede the Spanish Netherlands to her on condition that she marry her cousin, Archduke Albert of Austria. They reigned over the Netherlands jointly as duke/count and duchess/countess. After Albert's death Isabel was appointed Governor of the Netherlands on behalf of the king of Spain. Isabel's reign is considered the Golden Age of the Spanish Netherlands. She acted as a patron of the arts and transformed Brussels into one of the foremost political and artistic centers in Europe of that time. On the other hand, her father's support for her becoming queen of Holland terminated the family's good relations with the British. As a result, English pirate attacks on the Spanish navies intensified and later the Spanish Armada was defeated by England.

See also: Chapter 2: Carlos II "the Bewitched"; The Catholic Monarchs; Columbus, Christopher; Cortés, Hernán; Philip II.

Further Reading

Van Wyhe, Cordula. *Isabel Clara Eugenia: Female Sovereignty in the Courts of Madrid and Brussels*. London: Holberton, 2011.

Franco, Francisco (1892–1975)

Francisco Franco was the last dictator of Spain from 1939 until his death in 1975. He came to power during the Spanish Civil War while serving as the *generalísimo* (supreme commander) of the Nationalist faction. Franco initially pursued autarkic development strategies. He was conservative, Catholic, and obsessed with communism and freemasonry. Based on the fascist ideas of the Falange Española, the ideas of the Church, and the authority and discipline of the military, Franco's regime was a personal dictatorship whose main allies between 1945–1950 were Hitler's Germany and Mussolini's Italy. Franco became the youngest general in Spain in 1926; ten years later he became Chief of the General Staff, and soon thereafter he named himself generalísimo of Spain.

To this day, Franco's rule remains entrenched in controversy. In 2006, the European Parliament "firmly" condemned his "multiple and serious violations" of human rights. Even his place of burial at *Valle de los Caídos* (Valley of the Fallen) generates controversy in Spain. This large-scale memorial was built by political prisoners in honor of the Francoist Civil War soldiers who lost their lives in battle. The Council of Ministers of the socialist Spanish government of 2004–2011 approved on July 28, 2006, *Ley de la memoria histórica de España* (Law on the Historical Memory of Spain), described as "a bill to recognize and extend rights and establish measures in support of those who suffered persecution or violence during the Civil War and the Dictatorship." Political rallies in celebration of the former dictator are now banned. This law dictated that "the management organization of the Valley of the Fallen should aim to honor the memory of all of those who died during the civil war and who suffered repression." *Franco's*

Crypt is an erudite book about Spain's historical memory written by the British writer Jeremy Treglown. As he points out, there is already a whole library of books and films about Franco, the war, and "what came after" (Treglown 2013).

See also: Chapter 2: Alcalá Zamora, Niceto; Azaña, Manuel; Juan Carlos I of Spain; Largo Caballero, Francisco; Negrín, Juan; Pasionaria, La; Primo de Rivera, Miguel.

Further Reading

Preston, Paul. *Franco: A Biography*. New York: BasicBooks, 1994.

Rutledge Southworth, Herbert. *Conspiracy and the Spanish Civil War: The Brainwashing of Francisco Franco*. London: Routledge, 2014.

Treglown, Jeremy. *Franco's Crypt: Spanish Culture and Memory since 1936*. New York: Farrrar, 2013.

Jaime I "the Conqueror" (1208–1276)

Jaime I became the king of Aragón at the age of five; he was named Count of Barcelona, and Lord of Montpellier from 1213 to 1276. At an early age, Jaime I was sent to the castle of Monzón (Aragón), where he was entrusted to the care of Guillem de Montredón, the head of the Knights Templar in Spain and Provence. The regency fell to his great uncle Sancho, Count of Roussillon. After the defeat of the Arabs in the battle of Navas de Tolosa (1212), Jaime I expanded the Crown of Aragón and Catalunya in the Mediterranean, conquering Mallorca, Menorca (1231), and Ibiza (1235), as well as the kingdoms of Valencia (1238) and Murcia (1266). The latter he donated to Alfonso X for the treaty of Almizra (1244). With the new territories, he managed to control and establish commercial routes through the Mediterranean Sea. In 1258 he signed the Treaty of Corbeil with Louis IX of France, for which he renounced the northern territories of the Pyrenees (Languedoc and Provence, except Montpellier) in exchange for the county of Barcelona controlled by the French king as a descendant of Charlemagne. When he conquered Valencia, Jaime I established that every official document related to the Crown of Valencia had to be written in *valenciano* (Valencian). The linguistic diversity of Spain was a reality with Latin, Valencian, Basque, Arabic, Hebrew, and, of course, Spanish, which was soon to become the predominant language of what he called "los cinco regnes d'Espanya" (the five kingdoms of Spain).

See also: Chapter 2: Abderramán III; Don Pelayo; Don Rodrigo; Maimónides.

Further Reading

Burns, Robert Ignatius. *The Worlds of Alfonso the Learned and James the Conqueror: Intellect and Force in the Middle Ages*. Princeton: Princeton University Press, 2014.

Burns, Robert Ignatius. *Negotiating Cultures: Bilingual Surrender Treaties in Muslim Crusader Spain under James the Conqueror.* Leiden: Brill, 1999.

Juan Carlos I of Spain (1938–)

King Juan Carlos I of Spain was born in exile and proclaimed king of Spain by the Francoist regime immediately after the dictator died in 1975. In fact, Franco selected him as his successor in 1969. Through the 23-F 1981 coup d'état, Juan Carlos I played what is considered by many historians his most important role during his reign when he impeded the coup d'état. This action subsequently earned him admiration and legitimacy. On May 14, 1962, he married Sofia (Athens, 1938–), who became queen of Spain. They had three children: Elena, Felipe, and Cristina. Although Elena is the eldest, however, according to the Constitution of 1978, the first in the line of succession to the Spanish throne is a male heir.

As a result of several scandals, including being caught by the media hunting elephants in Africa while Spain was in the middle of an economic meltdown or his daughter Cristina being summoned for embezzlement (through her husband Iñaki Urdangarín), King Juan Carlos interestingly began the *casareal.es* website in 2011 with the following remarks: "We are living through very demanding times. Many difficulties await us but we also have the support of the strong values that make us feel proud to be Spanish and the stimulus of our recent history of overcoming difficulties" (Palacio de la Zarzuela, December 24, 2011). As Paul Preston concluded in his biography, "For Juan Carlos at least, 'to live like a king' has meant sacrifice and dedication on a scale that has given the monarchy a legitimacy that was unthinkable in 1931, in 1939, and even in 1975" (Preston 2004). Spanish King Juan Carlos I and Queen Sofía did not officially celebrate their golden wedding anniversary in 2012. On June 2, 2014, King Juan Carlos I abdicated in favor of his son, King Felipe VI.

See also: Chapter 2: Alcalá Zamora, Niceto; Azaña, Manuel; Franco, Francisco; Largo Caballero, Francisco; Negrín, Juan; Pasionaria, La; Primo de Rivera, Miguel.

Further Reading

Powell, Charles T. *Juan Carlos of Spain: Self-Made Monarch.* London: Macmillan, 1996.

Preston, Paul. *Juan Carlos: Steering Spain from Dictatorship to Democracy.* New York: W. W. Norton, 2004.

Largo Caballero, Francisco (1869–1946)

Francisco Largo Caballero was one of the historic leaders of the Spanish Socialist labor union (UGT, Union General de Trabajadores) and president of the Second

Spanish Republic during the Spanish Civil War. He formed a predominantly Socialist government, supporting social revolution as a means to ensure the loyalty of Spanish workers. However, Largo Caballero could not placate workers who, disillusioned with the growing bureaucracy of the UGT, moved to the CNT (Confederación Nacional de Trabajo / National Confederation of Workers)—a group that was more radical and less committed to the government and whose ideology was inclined to use violence, identifying themselves with the FAI (Federación Anarquista Ibérica / Iberian Anarchist Federation). As American historians William and Carla Phillips explain, "Largo Caballero had little choice but to crush the rebellion in Barcelona, alienating most of the Republic's most loyal supporters. Socialists, Communists, and Republicans then united to vote Largo out of power on May 15, with the Communists taking the lead" (Phillips 2010). Largo Caballero fled Spain for the protection of France in 1939 where he was later arrested by German forces and held in the Sachsenhausen-Oranienburg concentration camp until World War II ended. He died in exile living in Paris in 1946.

See also: Chapter 2: Alcalá Zamora, Niceto; Azaña, Manuel; Franco, Francisco; Juan Carlos I of Spain; Negrín, Juan; Pasionaria, La; Primo de Rivera, Miguel.

Further Reading

Durgan, Andrew. *The Spanish Civil War*. New York: Palgrave Macmillan, 2007.

Maiden, Peter. "Image of the Spanish Lenin: The Radicalization of Francisco Largo Caballero." San José: San José State University, 1996. [Thesis].

Phillips, William D., and Carla Rahn Phillips. *A Concise History of Spain*. Cambridge: Cambridge University Press, 2010

Leovigildo, known in English as Liuvigild (525–586)

Leovigildo could be considered the first Spanish monarch (572–586). He attempted to unify the Iberian Peninsula through laws and an agreement between Arianism and Catholicism. However, during his 14 years on the throne, there was only one year of peace. Arianists denied the double nature of God as a human being as well as a divinity, which created an obstacle for the Visigoth kingdom. Despite Liuvigild's efforts to create tolerance between both groups, his goal did not materialize since his son Hermenegild, governor of Sevilla and a newly converted Catholic, initiated a revolt against his father that extended to Extremadura. However, Liuvigild overcame the rebels and his son escaped to Córdoba where he was captured and later killed in Tarragona in 585. Liuvigild's ruthlessness with his own son strengthened his authority over the kingdom by dissuading the nobility from challenging his power. Liuvigild established Toledo as the capital of Spania—a name given by the Visigoths. He also made his own coins, and modified the old *Code of Euric,* creating his own *Codex Revisus.* When he died, most of the peninsula was a Visigoth state, except the Levante area occupied by the Byzantines.

See also: Chapter 2: Adriano; Séneca; Viriato.

Further Reading

Deanesly, Margaret. *A History of Early Medieval Europe from 476 to 911*. New York: Barnes & Noble, 1974.

Wilentz, Sean. *Rites of Power: Symbolism, Ritual, and Politics since the Middle Ages*. Philadelphia: University of Pennsylvania Press, 1999.

Maimónides (1135–1204)

Maimónides was a Jewish philosopher, scientist, astronomer, theologist, and one of the most influential scholars and physicians of the Middle Ages. Due to the persecution against the Jews at the time, he was exiled as a rabbi, physician, and philosopher to Morocco and Egypt. His prestige as a scientist and thinker allowed him to become the spiritual chief of a Jewish minority in Egypt until his death in Cairo. Although his vast work deals with different disciplines, his main research is built upon his desire to blend Jewish theology with Aristotle's philosophy, making him into an intellectual bridge between Western tradition and Oriental knowledge. His *Guide for the Perplexed* is an attempt to reconcile faith and reason. Also, in the field of medicine he translated into Latin Galen's extensive writing, such as *Commentary on the Aphorisms of Hippocrates*, adding his own views, which was an influential reference in the sciences of the time. Currently, several prestigious schools of medicine in the United States bear his name. His birth city also honors him with a statue in the Jewish district. Throughout his life he considered himself a Sephardi—a Jew deeply rooted in the traditional culture of Spanish Hebraism.

See also: Chapter 2: Abderramán III; Don Pelayo; Don Rodrigo; Jaime I "the Conqueror."

Further Reading

Nuland, Sherwin B. *Maimónides*. New York: Nextbook: Schocken, 2008.

Rudavsky, Tamar. *Maimonides*. Malden: Willey-Blackwell, 2010.

Negrín, Juan (1892–1956)

Juan Negrín was a physician and a controversial figure in Spanish politics. He served as finance minister for Francisco Largo Caballero in September 1936. Negrín used terror as one of his main tactics to remain in power. Despite being pro-USSR and pro-Communist, Negrín crushed the revolutionary faction of the UGT and sent Largo Caballero to prison, after ousting him as the head of the union. He became president during the Spanish Civil War from May 17, 1937 to April 1, 1939. When Franco wanted an unconditional surrender, however, Negrín was opposed to any agreement, because he was convinced that a new war was going to ignite in Europe.

See also: Chapter 2: Alcalá Zamora, Niceto; Azaña, Manuel; Franco, Francisco; Juan Carlos I of Spain; Largo Caballero, Francisco; Pasionaria, La; Primo de Rivera, Miguel.

Further Reading

Bolloten, Burnett. *The Spanish Civil War: Revolution and Counterrevolution*. Chapel Hill: The University of North Carolina Press, 2007.

Jackson, Gabriel. *Juan Negrín: Physiologist, Socialist and Spanish Republican Leader*. Brighton: Sussex Academic Press, 2010.

Pasionaria, La (1895–1989)

Dolores Ibárruri, better known as La Pasionaria, was a communist politician from the Basque country, who became an activist during the Spanish Civil War. One of her most famous phrases was *¡No pasarán!* (They shall not pass!), which was addressed to the nationalist troops of Franco. Because of her talent and passion delivering her political speeches, Ibárruri is considered an iconic figure in Spain's 20th-century politics. After the victory of the nationalists, she was exiled first to France and later to the USSR. Even during her exile, Ibárruri carried out her duties within her political party, becoming the president of the Communist party in 1960. In 1961 she received a Doctor Honoris Causa in Historical Sciences from the University of Moscow for her contributions to Marxist theory. In 1977 she returned to Spain, after her Communist party was legalized again. Ibárruri has been an inspiration not only for Spaniards. In 1974 Scottish artist Arthur Dooley sculpted a La Pasionaria statue in Glasgow. She died at the age of 93 of pneumonia in 1989. Her funeral drew international attention and she received the same ceremony as that of the Spanish president.

See also: Chapter 2: Alcalá Zamora, Niceto; Azaña, Manuel; Franco, Francisco; Juan Carlos I of Spain; Largo Caballero, Francisco; Negrín, Juan; Primo de Rivera, Miguel.

Further Reading

Burnet, Andrew. *Chambers Book of Great Speeches*. Edinburgh: Chambers, 2013.

Gioseffi, Daniela. *Women on War: Essential Voices for the Nuclear Age*. New York: Simon & Schuster, 1988.

Low, Robert. *La Pasionaria: The Spanish Firebrand*. London: Hutchinson, 1992.

Philip II (1527–1598)

Philip II was probably the most powerful king who ever reigned in Spain; he ruled over England and Ireland, and his power extended to the Netherlands, Naples, Sicily, Milan, and his namesake, the Philippine Islands. During his time in power, Spain reached the height of its glory; Philip's empire included territories on every continent then known to Europeans. The expression "The Empire on which the sun never sets" was coined during Philip's time to reflect the extent of his possessions. Although he was an enthusiast about parties and gaiety as a young prince, he became prudent as a king, assuming great responsibility in governing the vast expanse of his territories. He moved Spain's capital to Madrid, and built El Escorial palace-monastery, where he increased the Inquisition's activities. When the Calvinists rebelled in Holland, he had their leader beheaded and many of his followers slaughtered, thus cementing his reputation as a religious fanatic and a merciless king. He gave no concessions to particular regional preferences, except serving God and country. King Philip II once said he would prefer not to rule rather than to reign over a nation of heretics. Protestants were killed in spectacular *autos-da-fé's* (trial and execution ceremonies), and anyone "tainted" with Jewish blood was persecuted. He also made the Inquisition hunt out the *moriscos*, Spaniards of Islamic ancestry, many of whom had converted to Christianity during Queen Isabel's rule but were still suspected of adhering to the Muslim faith. Portugal was his only successful war in 1580. In 1588 he sent the Invincible Armanda to invade Protestant England. Instead of the expected victory, the Spanish fleet suffered catastrophic losses and lost international credibility.

See also: Chapter 2: Carlos II "the Bewitched"; The Catholic Monarchs; Columbus, Christopher; Cortés, Hernán; Eugenia, Isabel Clara.

Further Reading

Kamen, Henry. *Philip of Spain*. New Haven: Yale University Press, 1999.

Kelsey, Harry. *Philip of Spain, King of England*: *The Forgotten Sovereign*. London: Tauris, 2012.

Parker, Geoffrey. *The Grand Strategy of Philip II*. New Haven: Yale University Press, 1998.

Prim y Prats, Juan (1814–1870)

Juan Prim y Prats was a general and statesman. The regent María Cristina promoted him to major-general, and made him *conde de Reus* (Count of Reus) and captain-general of Puerto Rico (governor of Puerto Rico) for his service to the Spanish Crown in 1847. However, four years later he was forced to resign for his rigid administration of the Caribbean Island, and for not condemning slavery. He became a member of the Cortes in 1854 and was made lieutenant-general in 1856. Due to his outstanding efforts in the war with Morocco in 1860, Queen Isabel II made him *marqués de los Castillejos* (marquis of Los Castillejos) and *Grande de España* (grandee of Spain). Yet, in 1862 he was forced into exile, since Queen Isabel II became increasingly tyrannical under the influence of the Jesuits and did not allow liberal ideas within the government. From abroad, Prim managed to form an anti-Isabel coalition. On September 19, 1868, he published the manifesto *España con honra* (Spain with Honor), which ignited the Revolution of September. With the triumph of *La Gloriosa* (1868, Glorious Revolution), as the insurrection movement was popularly known, Prim came to Madrid and took control of the Ministry of War during the provisional government. In 1869 he searched the European courts in an attempt to find someone not opposed to being an elected monarch. The search for a monarch by Prim constitutes one of the most embarrassing episodes in Spanish history. Prim chose Amadeo of Savoy, who was elected king of Spain on November 6, 1870. When the new king landed in Spain, he received news that recent President Prim had been assassinated—probably by some furious Republicans.

See also: Chapter 2: Cánovas del Castillo, Antonio; de Borbón, María Cristina; Espartero, Baldomero; Sagasta, Práxedes Mateo.

Further Reading

Carty, Maria D. "Juan Prim y Prats and Democratic Constitutional Monarchy." Cambridge: Harvard University, 1994 [Thesis].

Primo de Rivera, Miguel (1870–1930)

Miguel Primo de Rivera was the president of Spain during Spain's Restoration era (1923–1930). He established his career in military campaigns as an army officer in Cuba, the Philippines, and Morocco. His dictatorship was unlike the military rule practiced by Espartero, Narvaez, or Serrano. Primo de Rivera took office in an attempt to stop the paralysis resulting from the traditional inoperative political parties of the time. Initially it was an interim regime with no political or religious platform, although it supported the legality of the monarchy without insisting on it. King Alfonso XIII named Primo de Rivera head of the *Directorio Militar* (Military Directory).

Alfonso XIII supported the dictatorship of Primo de Rivera during the first three years. However, at the end it cost him the crown. The king was gradually alienated from all the politicians in parliament, including Socialists and intellectuals, while he was busy playing polo and hunting. Until 1927, the dictatorship enjoyed a general consensus with the Spanish population and it was not an anomaly in Europe. Primo de Rivera launched a plan of industrialization and public works, which considerably improved the roads, created reservoirs, and extended the electric power system. He also restored castles and palaces known as *paradores*.

The economic boom lost momentum toward the end of the 1920s, the *peseta* plunged against foreign currencies, inflation was high, and a poor harvest aggravated the insufficient food supply. When Primo de Rivera canvassed the army in 1930 to gauge his support and found that he had lost it, the king did not hesitate in accepting his resignation. Primo de Rivera was responsible for the diminishing support of the monarchy and increasing social discord that would eventually lead to the Spanish Civil War. After the death of Primo de Rivera, his son José Antonio Primo de Rivera (1903–1936) championed the fascist movement in Spain. He was the founder of the fascist group Falange and Franco saw him as a rival. He was shot in 1936 after the Civil War began and became a martyr-hero. Streets were renamed after Civil War generals; the most prominent ones often bore the name of Primo de Rivera.

See also: Chapter 2: Alcalá Zamora, Niceto; Azaña, Manuel; Franco, Francisco; Juan Carlos I of Spain; Largo Caballero, Francisco; Negrín, Juan; Pasionaria, La.

Further Reading

Ben-Ami, Shlomo. *Fascism from Above: The Dictatorship of Primo de Rivera in Spain, 1923–1930*. Oxford: Oxford University Press, 1983.

Carr, Raymond. *Spain, 1808–1939*. Oxford: Clarendon Press, 1975.

Quiroga, Alejandro. *Making Spaniards: Primo de Rivera and the Nationalization of the Masses, 1923–30*. New York: Palgrave Macmillan, 2007.

Sagasta, Práxedes Mateo (1825–1903)

Práxedes Mateo Sagasta was an engineer who served as president of Spain during the Spanish-American War of 1898, during which time Spain lost its remaining colonies. Because of fear of a new Carlist war, and also fear of a revolution promoted by the Republican left parties opposed to a monarchy, the conservative leader Antonio Cánovas, in conjunction with the liberal leader Mateo Sagasta, agreed to alternate the government. The latter was known in Spain as *turno pacífico* or a swing government (*de balancín*). Although this type of government was maintained through most of the regency period, however, it could not stop internal political fights against the Republican parties and several disturbances within the regional political parties. In fact, during one of these uproars, Cánovas del Castillo was assassinated by an anarchist in 1897. There was also a wave of anti-clerical protests, which triggered the fall of the conservatives and, subsequently, the return to power of Sagasta's liberals. The loss of Spain's last colonies (*Desastre del 98*) was the main cause for anti-clerical protest. However, as Sagasta recognized, Spain's dissatisfaction was also provoked by a series of actions taken by the conservative government, including strong religious views expressed by members of the government and the administration maintaining religious subsidies despite making deep cuts in public expenditures. Sagasta, after swearing allegiance to the constitution (an oath or affirmation required by the Spanish Constitution), died at the age of 76, marking the end of a generation.

See also: Chapter 2: Cánovas del Castillo, Antonio; de Borbón, María Cristina; Espartero, Baldomero; Prim y Prats, Juan.

Further Reading

Barnes, Mark R. *The Spanish-American War and Philippine Insurrection, 1898–1902*. New York: Routledge, 2011.

Casanova, Julián, and Carlos Gil Andrés. *Twentieth-Century Spain: A History*. Cambridge: Cambridge University Press, 2014.

Smith, Joseph. *The Spanish-American War 1895–1902: Conflict in the Caribbean and the Pacific*. New York: Routledge, 2013.

Séneca (4–65)

Séneca was one of the main philosophers during the Roman Empire as well as a prestigious lawyer and statesman. He was exiled to Corsica in 41, after being accused of adultery with Emperor Nero's niece. However, eight years later he was called again to Rome to work as a tutor and later as an advisor to Emperor Nero. Séneca retired from public life in 62. In 65, Séneca was allegedly involved in a plot to kill Nero. Although it is unlikely that he conspired, Séneca was ordered by Nero to kill himself. His philosophy deals primarily with his goal of achieving virtue. He wrote about natural sciences, and about the relationship between earthquakes and volcanoes. Séneca wrote nine plays inspired in the Greek tradition as well as a political satire on the Roman emperor Claudius.

See also: Chapter 2: Adriano; Leovigildo; Viriato.

Further Reading

Damschen, Gregor, and Andreas Heil, eds. *Brill's Companion to Seneca: Philosopher and Dramatist*. Leiden: Brill, 2014.

Fitch, John G. *Seneca*. Oxford: Oxford University Press, 2008.

Veyne, Paul. *Seneca: The Life of a Stoic*. New York: Routledge, 2003.

Viriato (?–139 BCE)

Viriato was the main leader who fought against the invasion of the Romans. He successfully occupied part of Spain, in particular, the interior side of the *meseta*, Segóbriga. Following repeated conflicts with the Romans, he managed to sign a peace treaty with the invaders. However, the Romans bribed Viriato's right-hand men and, as a consequence, he was assassinated by his own peers. After Viriato's death, the resistance was weak and Rome was able to consolidate its empire within the Iberian Peninsula.

See also: Chapter 2: Adriano; Leovigildo; Séneca.

Further Reading

Grünewald, Thomas. *Bandits in the Roman Empire: Myth and Reality*. New York: Routledge, 2004.

Silva, Luis. *Viriathus and the Lusitanian Resistance to Rome 155–139 BC*. Barnsley: Pen & Sword Military, 2013.

REFERENCES

Álvarez-Blanco, Palmar, and Toni Dorca, eds. *Contornos de la narrativa española actual (2000–2010)*. Madrid: Iberoamericana, 2011.

Ashford Hodges, Gabrielle. *Franco. A Concise Biography*. London: Weidenfeld & Nicolson, 2000.

Barton, Simon. *A History of Spain*. New York: Palgrave, 2004.

Carr, Raymond, ed. *Spain. A History*. Oxford: Oxford University Press, 2000.

Casanova, Julián, and Carlos Gil Andrés. *Breve historia de España en el siglo XX*. Barcelona: Ariel Quintaesencia, 2012.

Castro, Américo. *España en su historia*. Buenos Aires: Editorial Losada, 1948.

Chislett, William. *Spain. What Everyone Needs to Know*. Oxford: Oxford University Press, 2013.

Domínguez Ortiz, Antonio. *España, tres milenios de historia*. Madrid: Marcial Pons, 2000.

Eslava Galán, Juan. *Historia de España contada para escépticos*. Barcelona: Booket, 2013.

Fusi, Juan Pablo. *Historia mínima de España*. Madrid: Turner, 2012.

García de Cortázar, Fernando, and José Manuel González Vesga. *Breve historia de España: Nueva edición 2013*. Madrid: Alianza Editorial, 2011.

Gomaespuma. *Grandes disgustos de la Historia de España. ¡Pa habernos matao!*. Madrid: Temas de hoy, 2003.

Hermanos Cortijo. *Nunca te acostarás sin saber dos o tres cosas más*. Barcelona: El Aleph, 2005.

Hill, Fred James. *Spain: An Illustrated History*. New York: Hippocrene Books, 2001.

Hooper, John. *The New Spaniards*. 2nd ed. London: Penguin, 2006.

Hyslop, Stephen G., Bob Somerville, and John Thompson. *Eyewitness History from Ancient Times to the Modern Era*. Washington, D.C.: National Geographic, 2011.

Kurlansky, Mark. *The Basque History of the World*. Toronto: Knopf, 1999.

MacKay, Angus, et al., eds. *Medieval Spain: Culture, Conflict, and Coexistence*. New York: Palgrave Macmillan, 2002.

Marco, José María. *Una historia patriótica de España*. Barcelona: Booket, 2013.

Montinaro, Francesco, et al. "Unravelling the Hidden Ancestry of American Admixed Populations." *Nature Communications* 7596 (2015): 1–7.

Phillips, William D., and Carla Rahn Phillips. *A Concise History of Spain*. Cambridge: Cambridge University Press, 2010

Pierson, Peter. *The History of Spain*. Westport: Greenwood Press, 1999.

Powell, Charles. *España en democracia, 1975–2000*. Barcelona: Plaza y Janés, 2001.

Preston, Paul. *Juan Carlos: Steering Spain from Dictatorship to Democracy*. London: W. W. Norton, 2004.

Preston, Paul. *The Spanish Holocaust*. London: W. W. Norton, 2012.

Queralt del Hierro, María Pilar. *Historia de España*. Madrid: Tikal, 2009.

Sánchez-Albornoz, Claudio. *España: un enigma histórico*. Buenos Aires: Ed. Latinoamericana, 1956.

Treglown, Jeremy. *Franco's Crypt. Spanish Culture and Memory since 1936*. New York: Farrar, 2013.

Tremlett, Giles. *Ghosts of Spain*. London: Faber & Faber, 2006.

Veslasco, Pilar. *No nos representan. El manifiesto de los indignados en 25 propuestas*. Madrid: Temas de hoy, 2011.

CHAPTER 3

GOVERNMENT AND POLITICS

OVERVIEW

Spain is geographically distanced from much of Europe and therefore its political path has deviated from the course shared by many Western European countries. Because it is a peninsula and due to its close proximity to Africa, it has sustained multiple invasions that created what Spain is today—an amalgamation of different cultural heritages.

Early Spanish society was formed by various groups including the Carthaginians, Greeks, and Romans. The latter called Spain *Hispania* while the Greeks named it *Iberia*. The Romans (143 BCE–395 CE), the Goths (414–711), and the Arabs (711–1036) ruled the peninsula at intervals and left varying degrees of influence on Spain. The first settlers embraced a basic social structure that included worshipping deities (religion), paying respect to the dead, and practicing hunting techniques (i.e., bison in the Altamira cave at Burgos; goats and horses in the Pileta cave in Málaga). The development of Christianity came from the northern regions of Asturias (722: Christians defeated the Arabs for the first time in the Battle of Covadonga), the Basque homelands, and Catalunya.

Proximity to the Atlantic Ocean also played an important role in Spain's history, especially on a geopolitical level. For instance, Juan Sebastián Elcano was the first person to circumnavigate the globe (1519–1522). Preceding this event, Christopher Columbus discovered new territories in the Americas in 1492, making universal history and, in a political context, establishing Spain as a colonial superpower among competing European states. Columbus's discovery further funded Queen Isabel and King Ferdinand's totalitarian rule in Spain. The period of the *Reconquista* or Reconquest (722–1492) was completed in 1492, and the dominance of the Catholic Monarchs paved the way in unifying Spain. Today, the political boundaries of Spain's territories continue to follow the basic structure mapped out by the Catholic Monarchs, despite separatist forces from some northern regions (Basque and Catalunya regions), the War of Independence (1808–1813), and the First Republic (1873–1874).

After the death of the Catholic Monarchs, their grandson Charles I took over the throne in 1516, launching Spain's Golden Age. During the next two centuries, wealth from the New World was brought to Spain, fostering a cultural renaissance that lasted almost two centuries, ending with the reign of Charles II (1665–1700).

Two major political factors can be highlighted from the Golden Age and both were inspired by the same monarch, Philip II, the son of Charles I. First, Philip II led the Counter-Reformation against Protestants in Europe. In doing so, he tried to invade

Protestant England by sea with his famous fleet known as the *Invincible Armada*, but was defeated. This loss in 1588 marked the beginning of the decline of Spain's empire. Secondly, St. Ignatius of Loyola founded the Society of Jesus in 1540, a Jesuit religious order that ignited the Counter-Reformation, a period of intense Catholic devotion that has dominated Spanish life, including politics, for centuries.

The 18th century began with the War of Spanish Succession (1701–1714). French King Louis XIV occupied Spanish land and placed his grandson, Philip V, on the Spanish throne. This marked the beginning of the dynasty of the Bourbons or French rulers in Spain. They centralized power and turned away from a strong religious orientation. In 1767 the Jesuits were expelled, and the Inquisition, a court used to identify heretics which was established by King Ferdinand II in 1478, was limited in its scope. It was not fully abolished until 1831.

In 1794 Spain served as a French base during France's revolutionary wars. Spaniards' resentment grew toward the Spanish throne and government, which made Spain politically weaker due to internal dissent. The Napoleonic period started in 1808, when Napoleon Bonaparte forced the King of Spain, Charles IV, to abdicate in favor of his brother Joseph Bonaparte. The Spaniards protested the French occupation and were fervent to introduce their own form of government. Despite the drawing up of a democratic constitution, liberals and conservatives disputed the interpretation of its principles for nearly 100 years. Thanks to the British army and Spanish *guerrillas*, the Spanish throne was restored to King Ferdinand VII in 1814, when France was forced to relinquish its power over Spanish land.

While the rest of Europe was rapidly industrializing during the 19th century, Spain was distressed by war and the loss of its colonies in the New World. Political stability was uncertain for decades. Numerous quarrels over succession to the throne of Ferdinand VII led to the Carlist Wars in 1833. Most of the 19th century can be described as a time of troubles (1814–1875) in which the common political feature was the predominance of an unstable government, alternating between monarchy and republic. The first Spanish Republic was declared in 1873, and in 1874 Alfonso XII became king. Antonio Cánovas del Catillo, a conservative political leader, was assassinated in 1897, and in 1898 Spain lost its last three colonies—Cuba, Puerto Rico, and the Philippines—during the Spanish-American War.

The political situation of Spain's 20th century was also tumultuous. At the beginning of the century, Spain was at war in northern Morocco, and social uprisings led to the dictatorship of General Miguel Primo de Rivera from 1923 to 1930, who was later forced to resign mainly due to economic mismanagement and his attacks on liberals. In 1931, after the election of a Republican-socialist government, King Alfonso XIII abdicated and fled the country to avoid a national civil war. The second Spanish Republic lasted for eight years (1931–1939), which resulted in widespread political participation in Spain as well as positive reforms. However, it also divided Spain into two opposing factions: the conservative or right wing, and the liberals or left wing. Eventually, continuous domestic problems and disputes led to the Spanish Civil War (1936–1939). General Francisco Franco championed the right-wing nationalist movement, aided by Italian and German fascists. Franco won the Spanish Civil War in 1939, and ruled the devastated country as a conservative military dictator for the next 36 years.

After Franco's death in 1975, King Juan Carlos I guided Spain toward political liberalization. The first democratic elections in 40 years were held in 1977, and a new Constitution was written in 1978, restoring civil liberties, freedom of the press, and political activity. Under Franco, Spain had a repressed economy and was politically ostracized by most of the world. However, by the end of the 20th century, Spain—with the help of King Juan Carlos—changed from a military regime to a parliamentary, democratic, constitutional monarchy. Due to the massive European funds that Spain regularly received upon joining the European Union in 1986, Spain has experienced rapid progress, both economically and politically.

It is interesting to observe that in only two years, 2012 and 2013, over a dozen books discussing the current political situation of Spain were written by experts in the field. Two fundamental conclusions can be derived from reading these studies: The first is that Spanish politicians are the main culprits in the current financial crisis in which Spain is still immersed; and the second is that urgent political reforms at all levels are desperately needed. The *Centro de Investigaciones Sociológicas* (CIS: Center for Sociological Research) took a survey on December 2013 asking Spaniards to list the main problems of their country. The five most important issues identified were the following: unemployment (77%); corruption (37.6%); the economy (29.7%); the medical system (10.9%); and education (8.4%).

Current System of Government

According to the Constitution of 1978, Spain's current system of government follows the principle of separation of State powers into legislative, executive, and judicial branches.

The Crown

Spain's government is a parliamentary monarchy. The king or queen, as head of State, symbolizes the unity of the State, and is the highest representative of Spain in international relations. The Crown is also commander-in-chief of the armed forces. Royal participation in national affairs must be approved by the *Congreso de los diputados* (the lower house of parliament).

Legislative Power

The legislative power of the State is given to the *Cortes Generales* (parliament), which represents the Spanish people and controls the actions of the government. It is comprised of two houses: the *Congreso de los diputados* (lower house) which is formed by 350 members, elected proportionally depending on the population of each region; and the *Senado* (upper house) consisting of 266 directly elected members. It is, therefore, a two-chamber parliamentary system. Members of both houses are elected every four years. The president of the government may request the early dissolution of the Parliament. However, the Congreso de los diputados has the power to investigate the Spanish president and also to make him/her resign, if necessary. Currently, the role of the Spanish Senate has been questioned as being unnecessary because it has much less power and essentially carries out the same duties as the Congreso de los diputados.

Executive Power

The executive power mainly resides in the figure of the president, who acts as head of the government. After winning the elections, the president of the government is officially named by the king for a period of four years. The cabinet or Council of Ministers is recommended by the president and appointed by the king. They assist the president in running the nation. For example, the government is responsible for drawing up a financial budget. Also, the government oversees domestic and foreign policy, civil and military administration, and defense of the State. The current government (2011–) consists of the President, the vice-president, and twelve ministers.

According to the Spanish constitution (1978), there are also two institutions directly attached to the Parliament that perform specific tasks regarding control of the government. The *Tribunal de cuentas* (Court of Auditors), according to the Constitution, is the maximum regulatory body of the State's accounts and financial management as well as the regulatory body of the public sector. It is attached to the Parliament, and its president is appointed by the king with a mandate of three years. The *Defensor del Pueblo* (ombudsman) is the "high commissioner" of the Parliament and guarantees the defense and protection of fundamental rights of all Spaniards. The Defensor del Pueblo is elected by the Parliament for a period of five years. Each region of Spain also has a Defensor del Pueblo who deals with similar cases.

Judiciary Power

The judicial system of Spain is headed by the *Tribunal Supremo* (Supreme Court), and includes territorial, provincial, regional, and municipal courts. Each region has its own high court, which deals with criminal cases. The president of the Supreme Court is the highest authority in all inquiries of law, except constitutional issues, which the Constitutional Court handles. He is appointed by the king, and presides over the *Consejo General del Poder Judicial* (General Council of the Judiciary), formed by 20 members including magistrates, judges, and attorneys appointed by the parliament. Also, the *Fiscal General del Estado* (the Crown Prosecutor of the State or Attorney General) is appointed by the king at the proposal of the government, after consulting the General Council of the Judiciary. The mission of the Office of the Crown prosecutor is to initiate legal proceedings to protect the rights of citizens and the public interest. It is also responsible for safeguarding the independence of the courts and defending the public interest in court proceedings.

However, the perception of justice by many Spaniards is different. First, the justice system in Spain works very slowly. Second, many Spaniards believe that Spanish justice is not equal for everyone, as certain privileged individuals manage to circumvent prison sentences. For the previously stated reasons, the Spanish justice system needs to improve. Surprisingly, the problem is not a lack of lawyers since Madrid alone has more lawyers than in all of France. In fact, after New York, Madrid seems to be the city with the most lawyers in the world, and four of the biggest European law firms are located in Spain. César Molinas mentions that Spain has 87 justice courts per 100,000 inhabitants while France has 32 and Germany 66. Neither the Spanish judges, nor their personnel, have to sign when entering or leaving work. Hence, there is little documentation or supervision of any sort. There is no clear criteria for why some cases are tried while others are put on hold indefinitely. The Spanish government has been notoriously more interested in controlling the justice system toward their own personal interests than in improving the mechanism and, thereby making it a truly independent institution.

Further Reading

Kern, Robert W. *The Regions of Spain: A Reference Guide to History and Culture.* Westport: Greenwood Press, 1995.

Phillips, William D., and Carla Rahn Phillips. *A Concise History of Spain.* Cambridge: Cambridge University Press, 2010.

Ross, Christopher J. *Contemporary Spain: A Handbook.* 2nd ed. London: Arnold, 2002.

Smith, Ángel. *Historical Dictionary of Spain.* Lanham: Scarecrow Press, 2009.

Army and National Police

The king of Spain, Felipe VI, under the current constitution, is the commander-in-chief of the Armed Forces. He, with the consent of the *Cortes Generales* (parliament), has the power to declare war and make peace. The constitution gives the central government powers of military administration and defense of the realm. It allocates to the Armed Forces—comprised of the Army, the Navy, and the Air Force—the mission of safeguarding the sovereignty and independence of Spain and defending its territorial integrity and constitutional order. The minister for defense designs and executes military policy and is the head of the military administration. The government must consult the lower house of Parliament and obtain its consent before it can order foreign operations not directly relating to the defense of Spain or the national interest. Also, the constitution provides that "Spanish citizens have the right, and duty, to defend Spain."

Spain abolished compulsory military service in 2002. Currently, there are over 126,000 people in the Spanish Armed Forces, of whom 12.2 percent are women. According to the data provided by the Ministry of Defense, by December 2012, the distribution of Spain's armed forces personnel was as follows: Army: 63.5% (80,219); Navy: 17% (21,489); Air Force: 16.9% (21,322); and Common: 2.5% (3,219). By the same year/data, Spain's personnel numbers by category was as follows: Troops: 62.3% (78,696, of whom 16.9% were women); non-commissioned officers: 22.8% (28,777, of whom 3.1% were women); and officers: 14.9% (18,776, of whom 6.7% were women).

Apart from the Spanish Army, Spain has a police force, which is unique due to its complexity. First, they have the national police called *policía nacional*. Second, they have what Spaniards called *guardia civil*, who are similar to the national police. Their main focus is to guard the Spanish civilians, as the name indicates in Spanish (Civil Guard). Third, most towns employ what are called *policía local*, whose salary comes from the local town halls. The duties of the three differ from one another as well as their salaries. Furthermore, two Spanish regions, the Basque and the Catalan, have also created their own regional police called *Ertzanintza* and the *Mossos d'Esquadra* (formed in 1719) respectively. One interesting aspect of the *Mossos d'Esquadra* is that they are considered the oldest police force in all of Europe.

In 1844 the *Guardia Civil* was created as a national police by the Basque aristocrat Francisco Javier Girón y Ezpeleta, Duke of Ahumada. After the Ecclesiastical Confiscations of Mendizábal (*La Desamortización*: 1835–1837) that resulted in the expropriation, and privatization, of monastic properties, the government of Luis González Bravo abolished the national militia in 1844, making an urgent case to create a national institution which is independent from the continuous oscillations of the different governments. Most towns all over Spain now have a *Guardia Civil* station (or house, as Spaniards call it: *Casa cuartel de la Guardia Civil*), which is easy to recognize by its distinctive logo inscribed visibly on the main entrance: "Todo por la patria," meaning, "Everything for the country."

See also: Chapter 2: Overview; Juan Carlos I of Spain. Chapter 3: Constitutions; King Felipe VI.

Further Reading

Hooper, John. *The New Spaniards*. 2nd ed. London: Penguin Books, 2006.

Ross, Christopher J. *Contemporary Spain: A Handbook*. 2nd ed. London: Arnold, 2002.

Constitutions

So far Spain has written nine constitutions:

1808: *Constitution of Bayona*: It can be considered the first written Spanish constitution. Napoleon himself was in charge of this project in which he attempted to link the New French regime to the Spanish tradition. However, it was hardly operative and it was never followed.

1812: *Constitution of La Pepa*: Popularly known as *La Pepa* because it was proclaimed on March 19, which is the day of Saint Joseph; Pepe is the nickname for José. It had great prestige and influence in other countries in Europe and America. However, King Ferdinand VII abolished it in 1814; he refused to swear allegiance to it or to apply it.

1834: *The Royal Statute*: More than a constitution, it was a charter granted by the government and promulgated by the regent Queen María Cristina de Borbón. It was repealed in 1836.

1837: *Constitution*: Inspired by the constitution of 1812, this constitution introduced the constitutional monarchy and set up direct suffrage. It was operative until 1845.

1845: *Constitution*: Promulgated by Queen Isabel II, this text attempted to consolidate the moderate bourgeoisie in power and reinforce the position of the Crown. It was operative until 1868.

1869: Constitution: It is the first democratic Spanish constitution. It established male universal suffrage and declared Spain a secular country. It was operative until 1873.

1876: *Constitution*: It was a new conservative text and a step backward with respect to the previous one. Catholicism was imposed as the main religion in the country as well as a censitary suffrage. It was operative until 1923.

1931: *Constitution*: This constitution was Spain's most idealistic and progressive constitution. For the first time in Spanish history, women were allowed to vote. Also for the first time, divorce was legalized. Freedom of conscience and religion and separation of Church and State were legally recognized. It was operative until 1939.

1978: *Constitution*: It was possible thanks to agreement of the different political parties with a parliamentary presence, which marked a milestone in Spanish history. It has been classified as the Constitution of consensus. This constitution defines Spain as a social and democratic state which adopts parliamentary monarchy as its form of government. The "fathers" of the constitution were: Gabriel Cisneros (UCD, center party), Manuel Fraga (AP, right-wing party), Miguel Herrero de Miñón (UCED), Gregorio Peces-Barba (PSOE, left-wing party), José Pedro Pérez-Llorca (UCD), Miquel Roca Junyent (CDC, liberal conservative political party), and Jordi Solé Tura (PSUC, left-wing Catalan party). On December 6, 1978, there was a referendum in which Spaniards voted 87.87 percent in favor of the constitution; 7.83 percent voted against; and 3.55 percentage registered a protest vote. With a preamble, 169 articles divided into 10 parts and various provisions, the current constitution is, after the 1812 Constitution, the longest in Spain's history. The Magna Carta contains a long list of fundamental rights and public freedoms of all citizens and protects the State of the Autonomous Communities.

As a constitutional monarchy, Spain's head of State is the king, who reigns in accordance with the constitution: the rule of law. Other constitutional monarchies include: Australia, Canada, Denmark, Japan, Jordan, Morocco, New Zealand, Norway, Sweden, Thailand, and The Netherlands.

See also: Chapter 2: Overview; Alcalá Zamora, Niceto; Azaña, Manuel; Franco, Francisco; Juan Carlos I of Spain; Largo Caballero, Francisco; Negrín, Juan; Pasionaria, La; Primo de Rivera, Miguel. Chapter 3: Overview; Electoral Scheme and the "No Molestar" System; Political Challenges of Spain's 21st Century; Regional Government and Regionalism; Scandals and Political Corruption; Serra, Eduardo. Chapter 4: Overview.

Chapter 6: Overview; Nationalism. Chapter 7: Overview; Feminism in Spain. Chapter 8: Overview. Chapter 16: Overview.

Further Reading

Phillips, William D., and Carla Rahn Phillips. *A Concise History of Spain*. Cambridge: Cambridge University Press, 2010.

Ross, Christopher J. *Contemporary Spain: A Handbook*. 2nd ed. London: Arnold, 2002.

Electoral Scheme and the "No Molestar" System

The current law of political parties does not include an annual external independent audit review like, for instance, in Germany. Therefore, even if the political party is accused of wrongdoing, the two major political parties are immune to outside scrutiny. Apart from the issue of corruption, political reform is also needed in order to break the constant duopoly between the two major political parties in Spain. The conservatives and the socialists have been alternating in power for the last 35 years. In doing so, they have had little incentive to make changes to the political system; while these changes could possibly benefit the citizens of the country, they would also decrease their party's influence. According to opinion polls, if the two-party system changes, not only would neither side get an absolute majority, but neither could get enough seats to govern alone. This would mean that a coalition with more than one political party would be necessary. Hence, it would generate more transparency. Within this particular context, it is interesting to observe that new political parties (i.e., Podemos, Ciudadanos) were born during the economic crisis.

As Eduardo Serra mentions in *Transforma España*, the Spanish electoral system needs to be reviewed and adjusted to fulfill the new needs of the country. The CIS conducted a study on democratic quality in 2009 and the results speak for themselves: 39.5 percent believed that the citizens should select the candidates of a political party as opposed to 13.4 percent, who believed it should be done by internal means. The CIS of 2009 also highlights that very few Spaniards (8.3%) feel that their views are taken into account when making policy decisions.

As in the United States, in Spain there is very little ideological difference between the two major political parties: Democrats and Republicans would equate to the PSOE (Socialists) and the PP (Conservatives), as both parties defend the free-enterprise capitalist system. Following the comparison and perhaps political "Americanization" of Spain, it is broadly possible to say that working class society votes for the Democrats (= PSOE: Socialists) while the middle class and wealthy people vote for the Republicans (= PP: Conservatives). One major difference from the U.S., however, is that in Spain the general or federal election happens on one particular day set by the current president while the regional president of each region (17 in total) decides which day to vote.

One of the most lucid and critical studies published on the current political scenario was written by sociologist/professor José Manuel Roca, *La oxidada transición* (2013), which can be translated as "the rusty transition," referring to the old constitution signed during the Spanish transition in 1978. Roca's central thesis is that currently Spain is at an impasse. Therefore, it needs to revise every political structure that was established during what is called in Spanish politics the transition period (1975–1982). Within a short period of time, Spain went from being an emerging country with a powerful economy (in 2007 Spain's GDP was 3.8%, which was higher than the G-8 countries) to a nation plagued with financial shortfalls.

For Roca, Spain has become once again a terribly polarized country, in which two major political parties or a duopoly alternate power. They both rule under a simple mandate: the *no molestar* system, meaning "do not disturb"—a way of governing that has been extended to all Spanish institutions: do not disturb the monarchy; do not disturb the Church; do not disturb Francoism; do not disturb the oligarchy who control the main businesses in Spain. As a solution, Roca advocates a social movement that already exists called *15-M Movimento* that started on May 15, 2011. This civilian movement seems to be still ongoing from time to time in the main squares in Spain. However, the political test for Spain will be during the next general election (held on December 20, 2015), which will determine whether Spaniards can overcome their past and move toward a united future.

See also: Chapter 2: Overview. Chapter 3: Overview; Political Challenges of Spain's 21st Century; Scandals and Political Corruption. Chapter 16: Youth Culture.

Further Reading

Colomer, Josep María. *Handbook of Electoral System Choice*. New York: Palgrave Macmillan, 2006.

Erk, Jan, and Wilfried Swenden, eds. *New Directions in Federalism Studies*. New York: Routledge, 2010.

Roca, José Manuel. *La oxidada transición*. Madrid: La Linterna Sorda, 2013.

ETA

During Franco's dictatorship (1939–1975), any nationalism was heavily repressed in Spain. As a result of the friction between dictatorship and Basque nationalism, the terrorist group ETA was created in 1959. ETA stands for *Euskadi Ta Askatasuna*, which means "Euskadi (Basque homeland) and Freedom." The region of the Basque country has more power than any other territory of Spain. However, ETA supporters still champion full independence and have historically taken violent measures as a means to fight for their independence. More than 800 people have been killed by the ETA, including politicians, public figures, and hundreds of civil guards. Over 700 ETA activists are currently imprisoned in Spain, France, the United Kingdom, and Canada.

In 2011 ETA publicly announced their intent to end violence. However, ETA also announced ceasefires in 1989, 1996, 1998, and 2006. *Herri Batasuna* (HB) (Popular Unity) has been the political wing of ETA since 1978. In 2013 it was banned by the

Policemen search through the wreckage of a bombing that killed Spanish president Luis Carrero Blanco on December 20, 1973. The bomb was planted along the route that Blanco regularly took to church. (AFP/Getty Images)

national government, after having been found guilty of financing ETA with public money. Currently, other active political parties that show sympathy with ETA include Bildu and Askatasuna. On the other hand, some Basque leftist pro-independence political parties, like Aralar, denounce the violence and choose dialogue and negotiation as their main political tool.

In the 1990s PSOE's political party secretly created a "dirty war" against ETA, founding the GAL (*Grupos Antiterroristas de Liberación* / Anti-Terrorist Liberation Groups). Ex-judge Baltasar Garzón found evidence of the Spanish government being involved with the GAL affair. As a result, former PSOE Interior Minister José Barrionuevo was sent to prison in 1995, which became one of the major political scandals in Spain's recent political history.

See also: Chapter 3: Scandals and Political Corruption. Chapter 6: Nationalism.

Further Reading

Clark, Robert P. *Negotiating with ETA: Obstacles to Peace in the Basque Country, 1975–1988*. Reno: University of Nevada Press, 1990.

Whitfield, Teresa. *Endgame for ETA: Elusive Peace in the Basque Country*. New York: Oxford University Press, 2014.

Foreign Policy: Marca España

The *Marca España* strategy was broadcast by royal decree 998/2012 by the current conservative government (PP). According to their website, www.marcaespana.es, "we are all Marca España," meaning, every Spaniard is Marca España. In essence, Marca España is an attempt to create a national brand that is recognized worldwide. Following the dossier *Spain Today 2013* (Corral 2013) written by the People's Party government, Spain's foreign policy must act effectively to foster the country's values and interests. In doing so, during the economic recession, Marca España focuses on four main objectives: stimulating the economic recovery; strengthening Spain's position in the world; reinforcing citizens' security inside the country and abroad; and supporting Spain's companies nationally and internationally. Spain's foreign policy continues to focus on its traditional areas: the Euro-Atlantic, the Ibero-American, and Mediterranean axis, with a growing commitment toward Asia and the Pacific and the consolidation of Spain's relations with Africa.

Initially, the new concept of Marca España makes sense. However, there is a precedent that still resonates in the minds of many. The previous motto "Spain is different" was created by another conservative politician, Manuel Fraga, in the 1960s to promote tourism in Spain. Because of the political ideology associated with its creator, some Spaniards simply refused to recognize the intrinsic value of having a national common slogan. The old slogan "Spain is different" is still widely used not only by Spaniards but also by foreigners to describe Spain. Other Spaniards, however, still ignore (or worse, refuse to credit) the power and positive impact that a worldwide recognizable national brand has nowadays. Time will tell whether Marca España is effective in creating the positive image of a united Spain that is needed nationally and abroad.

The main objective of Marca España is to improve Spain's image nationally and internationally. In doing so, Marca España has created what is called "The Observatory," which basically collects perceptions of Spain abroad. Several institutions study the percentages, barometers, and different analyses in this area:

- The Elcano Royal Institute think-tank is entrusted with collecting this information through the Observatory. A series of indicators help project Spain's image to the world in an objective manner. This also requires opinion surveys, studies, and interviews from which action proposals are derived.
- The Center for Sociological Investigations (CIS) is another think-tank that also handles and provides information through its barometers.
- Asia House has three different observatories:
  - Asia-Pacific Ibero-American Observatory. Its main purpose is to provide knowledge on the Asia-Pacific in Latin American nations, especially in the area of the economy, business, and education.
  - GovernAsia. Its intention is to provide information on socio-economic situations of developing Asiatic countries and to promote the improvement of existing knowledge on emerging economies of the Asia-Pacific region.

- ○ Central Asia Observatory. It was created in 2007 by Asia House, CIDOB, and the Elcano Oil Institute to represent Central Asia in Spain.
- Arab House. The Andalusí Observatory is an institution for observing and monitoring the situation of Muslim citizens and Islamophobia in Spain. Each year it publishes the data of the Muslim population, offers and demands of Islamic religious classes, those attending services and institutions, and special reports.

See also: Chapter 3: Overview; Rajoy Brey, Mariano.

Further Reading

García, David, and Ramón Pacheco Pardo. *Contemporary Spanish Foreign Policy*. London: Routledge, 2014.

Marca España. http://www.marcaespana.es/en

Ulldemolins, J. R., and M. M. Zamorano. "Spain's Nation Branding Project Marca España and Its Cultural Policy: The Economic and Political Instrumentalization of a Homogeneous and Simplified Cultural Image." *International Journal of Cultural Policy* 21 no.1 (2015): 20–40.

King Felipe VI

Initially known as Prince of Asturias, in recognition of the key role that the region of Asturias played during Spain's Christian *Reconquista*, Felipe (born in 1968) became Spain's new king on June 19, 2014, after his father King Juan Carlos abdicated, leaving behind 39 years of *juancarlismo* (followers of the King Juan Carlos). The ceremony of his proclamation as Spain's new king was comparatively low key, since the Spanish economy was still in crisis. He was 46 years old at the time of the ceremony and was accompanied by his wife, who automatically became Queen Letizia Ortiz Rocasolano (41), and their daughters, Princess Leonor and Princess Sofia.

King Felipe VI has an international education including high school studies in Canada (Lakefield College School, Ontario); a law degree from one of Spain's best public universities (Universidad Autónoma de Madrid); and a Master of Science in foreign service from Georgetown University in Washington, D.C. He belongs to the new generation of Spaniards who have access to a better education than their predecessors—hence, the epithet of "the best educated king in Spanish history" being intimately associated with his public persona.

Supporters of the Spanish monarchy have been especially in decline during Spain's economic recession. Also, numerous scandals, including the previous king being photographed hunting elephants in Africa while Spaniards lost their jobs; and Infanta Cristina being summoned for embezzlement, do not help the monarchs with the new image that they want to give the country. Nevertheless, recent polls suggest Spaniards prefer the new king, because he is perceived as being well prepared for the current problems affecting Spain. Furthermore, immediately after Felipe VI became the new king of

Spain, he modified the *casa real* website, which included a new link called "transparency." This link is an attempt to provide Spain with more transparent service, and, more specifically, to broadcast the allocation of Spanish taxes. More recently, in 2015 Felipe VI reduced his salary 20 percent (50,000 euros). Time will tell if the current monarchs become the new symbol for millennial Spain.

See also: Chapter 2: Overview; Juan Carlos I of Spain. Chapter 6: Overview; Aristocracy; Monarchy.

Further Reading

"Spain's King Yields to Next Generation." *Wall Street Journal*, June 3 (2014): A7.

"Three Essential Facts about: Spain's Next King." *Time*, June 16 (2014): 12.

Van der Kiste, John. *A Divided Kingdom: The Spanish Monarchy from Isabel to Juan Carlos.* Charleston: History Press, 2011.

Molinas, César

The mathematician and economist César Molinas is an essential voice that needs to be mentioned due to his lucid book *Qué hacer con España* (*What to Do with Spain*, 2013). Molinas argues that Spain constitutes a political anomaly. He identifies Spain's abnormality as having its root in the following three historical reasons:

1) The decision of Charles V to combat Protestantism instead of embracing it was, perhaps, the most counterproductive decision. It broke Spain away from Europe irreversibly. His son Philip II isolated Spain even more when he moved the capital to Madrid, far from the ebb and flow of European life. Historically Spanish industries began in the periphery, close to navigable waters in regions like Galicia, Catalunya, Valencia, the Basque country, and Andalucía. During the Golden Age, Spain occupied Flanders. However, because the capital of Spain was isolated, in terms of ideas Flanders was far more developed than Spain at the time. As a result, it was the first northern European territory that Spain lost in the 17th century. The next Spanish losses were Napoli, Cuba, Puerto Rico, and the Philippines, for the same reasons—Spain did not have a clear national plan.

2) Spain did not embrace the main ideas of the 18th-century Enlightenment. As a consequence, Spain did not progress with the rest of Europe. Instead, the Inquisition made sure there were no new ideas in the country. This hostility to science and innovation can still be seen being practiced by many current politicians. In fact, there have been very few national debates around important issues in the 18th, 19th, and 20th centuries in comparison to the rest of Europe.

3) Another differential factor was the civil wars. Spain did not participate in the European wars of the 19th and 20th centuries, in which the idea of nationhood flourished and the people of various countries united among themselves. Instead, Spaniards killed each other. Subsequently, national cohesion among Spaniards is extremely weak.

Now here we are in the 21st century, with some politicians like the current president, Mariano Rajoy, who cannot clearly explain the idea of a nation. What is even worse is that there is no clear plan for the country. In order to avoid repeating the same mistakes again, Molinas underlines four political reforms that Spain urgently needs in order to remain in the EU:

1) A change in the electoral system is paramount. It needs to be changed not only to make room for more political parties but also internally, because the way they currently operate is through connections and dubious legality. A prime example is the scandal of Bárcenas in the conservative government (PP); Rajoy appointed Bárcenas to be in charge of the party's treasury, but in 2013 Bárcenas was sent to prison for fraud.

2) The regional map of Spain must be re-thought. Decentralization of the State, which started in the 1980s, is not working properly. The idea of "coffee for everyone" is simply unsustainable. Decentralization created 17 administrations with regional governments; 17 parliaments; and literally thousands of new public territorial entities whose main goal was and still is to create diets and salaries for certain people close to the political party in power. Molinas estimates that there are around 300,000 people whose jobs have been obtained through favor.

3) Areas that should be totally independent in the first place must be de-politicized, particularly in the following three sectors: the banking system; the justice system; and the major energy companies, where it is not uncommon for ex-politicians to end up after retiring from the public sector. In other words, the Spanish political sphere has been busy in the last few decades colonizing areas in which they should not be allowed because these areas require independence.

4) Parliament must authentically debate contemporary issues. Spanish politics has abandoned their main arena; because the parliament is currently an absolute majority, it acts by decree (*por decreto ley*). That means no explanations are given in Parliament, though explanations are a basic rule in any healthy democracy. One of the most recent scandals was the bailout of the bank Bankia in 2012. Despite the international attention it received, it was not discussed in the Spanish parliament and it was treated like a natural catastrophe, with no individuals to blame and no victims in need of assistance.

Since the 1990s, Spain has generated four major scandals known as *burbujas* (bubbles) in which nobody has been held responsible for bad management: 1) the real estate market; 2) the phenomenon of *cajas*, which operate like banks but are heavily controlled by the regional governments; 3) renewable energy companies—Spain pays the most expensive electricity bill in the EU and has a debt of 24,000 million euros that nobody knows how to pay back, but not surprisingly they are ruled by ex-political members; 4) building new toll highways that were not needed (i.e., Madrid built a toll highway that has generated a debt of 3,000 million euros). In fact, according to the *Ministerio de Fomento* (Ministry of Public Works), in 2013 there were seven toll highways in bankruptcy.

See also: Chapter 3: Overview; Electoral Scheme and the "No Molestar" System; Political Challenges of Spain's 21st Century; Scandals and Political Corruption. Chapter 4: Overview.

Further Reading

Molinas, César. *Qué hacer con España. Del capitalismo castizo a la refundación de un país.* Barcelona: Destino, 2013.

Political Challenges of Spain's 21st Century

The year 2015 will be a real test for Spain as the country celebrates its regional and general elections. Based on the summary of the *OECD Economic Surveys SPAIN November 2012* (overview), Spain has four major challenges ahead: 1) Spain needs to recover from a prolonged recession; 2) the financial crisis needs to be addressed quickly; 3) confidence in public finance needs to be restored; and 4) a broad range of reforms is needed to address high unemployment rates.

Spanish politicians have to admit first that Spain's problems are not due to external factors. The global financial crisis has been used *ad nauseam* as the main culprit for Spanish national internal disasters. Some Spaniards even believe this is so. However, that does not explain why by January 2014 there were over six million Spaniards unemployed; a financial system partially broken, and a public sector that could not make ends meet.

As William Chislett has pointed out, Spanish politicians have not done anything significant to restore confidence in the political class such as passing a transparency law, improving internal democracy within parties, or renewing the electoral law, to name a few measures that could have been taken. Instead, Spanish politicians share a disrespect for education, innovation, and business, as well as a certain level of hostility toward research and the sciences.

Spaniards are very discontented over unprecedented unemployment and corruption scandals. Perhaps the good news is that new political voices are coming to the platform. On January 16, 2014, a new party called Vox (voice, in Latin) was created from Spain's ruling People's Party (PP). According to Santiago Abascal, a former PP member on the Vox executive committee, "Millions of Spaniards feel abandoned by the political system, which is infested with corruption scandals" (Press). The new party accused Spain's president Mr. Rajoy of being too lenient on the issue of Catalan and Basque separatism. Vox pledged to be more active than the president in defending Spanish national unity. In its party program, Vox calls for a rewriting of the country's constitution, including a measure that would scrap regional autonomy and regional parliaments. Likewise, the conservative political party AES shares similar goals for the country.

Within this particular context, it is worthwhile to look back at two important voices. Jordi Solé Tura was a politician, jurist, and one of the co-authors and "fathers" of the Spanish Constitution, who admitted that the Senate was the big mistake of the constitution (*La Marea*, October 2013). In a similar vein, Juan José Laborda, who was president of the Senate (1989–1996), stated that if the Senate were to disappear, it would affect nothing (*La Marea*, October 2013).

Explaining the political situation of Spain in the new millennium is not easy. Perhaps the best way to describe Spain's politics is with the recurring words "anomaly" and "unique." One fact, however, remains. Here we have a country that continually battles with internal political problems. For instance, two civil wars occurred in the 20th century alone. On the other hand, Spain managed to be in the top 10 economies in the world during the same period. Is it in the Spaniards' DNA that they are destined to be simultaneously belligerent and self-destructive?

See also: Chapter 3: Overview; Electoral Scheme and the "No Molestar" System; Scandals and Political Corruption. Chapter 4: Overview. Chapter 7: Representation in Government.

Further Reading

Chislett, William. *Spain: What Everyone Needs to Know*. Oxford: Oxford University Press, 2013.

Gunther, Richard, and José Ramón Montero. *The Politics of Spain*. Cambridge: Cambridge University Press, 2009.

Zapata-Barrero, Ricardo. *Diversity Management in Spain: New Dimension, New Challenges*. Manchester: Manchester University Press, 2013.

Political Parties

In Spain's latest election held on November 20, 2011, more than 10.7 million voted for the right-wing party PP, gaining 186 (of 350) seats in the Parliament. Other political parties represented in the Spanish Parliament include PSOE (110 seats); CiU (16); IU (11); AMAIUR (7); PNV (5); UPyD (5); ERC (3); CC (2); BNG (2); FAC (1); Compromis (1); and Geroa Bai (1). In Spain's last general election of 2011, 16 different political parties gained seats out of 350 total seats in the Spanish Congress. With the exception of Albert Rivera's *Ciutadans* (center Catalan political party), which is gaining momentum in the current political scene, Table 3.1 is a list of the political parties with a presence in the Spanish Congress from 2011–2015.

Spain offers a wide range of political parties with different ideologies that vary from radical left to extreme right. Also, some Spanish regions are governed by their own regional parties that may not have representation (seats in parliament) in the national *Cortes* (parliament). Some Spanish cities are even governed by a local party that has no representation elsewhere. In this way, Spain has created a multilevel governance that has served as a model emulated by other countries (Gunther 2009). Some 3,200 parties are officially entered in the Register of Political Parties, although few have a minimum organizational capacity and even fewer have a significant national or regional parliamentary presence. Currently the political groups that make up the Lower House of Parliament are divided into the following parliamentary groups:

Table 3.1 SPAIN'S POLITICAL PARTIES

Party	President / Leader	Ideology
PP: Partido Popular (People's Party)	Mariano Rajoy	Right-wing, conservative
PSOE: Partido Socialista Obrero Español (Spanish Socialist Workers' Party)	Pedro Sánchez	Left-wing, liberal, socialism
CiU: Convergència i Unió (Convergence and Union)	Artur Mas	Right-wing, conservative, Catalan nationalism & separatism
IU: Izquierda Unida (United Left)	Alberto Garzón	Left-wing, communism, republicanism, secularism
Amaiur: (Amaiur)	Xabier Mikel Errekondo	Left-wing, socialism, Basque nationalism & separatism
PNV: Partido Nacionalista Vasco (Basque Nationalist Party)	Andoni Ortuzar	Right-wing, conservative
UPyD: Unión Progreso y Democracia (Union, Progress & Democracy)	Andrés Herzog	Centralism, secularism, European federalism
ERC: Esquerra Republicana de Catalunya (Republican Left of Catalunya)	Oriol Junqueras	Left-wing, Catalan nationalism & separatism, republicanism
BNG: Bloque Nacionalista Galego (Galician Nationalist Bloc)	Xavier Vence	Left-wing, Galician nationalism, socialism
CC: Coalición Canaria (Canarian Coalition)	Paulino Rivero	Right-wing, Canarian nationalism
ICV: Iniciativa per Catalunya Verds (Initiative for Catalunya Greens)	Dolors Camat & Joan Herrera	Left-wing, Green politics, eco-socialism, Catalan nationalism
CC: Coalició Compromís (Commitment Coalition)	Mònica Oltra & Enric Morera	Left-wing, Valencian nationalism, green politics
FAC: Foru Asturies (Asturian Forum)	Cristina Coto	Right-wing, Asturian regionalism, conservatism
GB: Geroa Bai (Yes to the Future)	Uxue Barkos	Left-wing, Basque nationalism
UPN: Unión del Pueblo Navarro (Navarrese People's Union)	Javier Esparza	Right-wing, Navarrese regionalism, conservatism
CHA: Chunta Aragonesista (Aragonese Union)	José Luis Soro	Left-wing, Aragonese nationalism, environmentalism

Grupo Parlamentario Popular (People's Parliamentary Group): 185 members

Grupo Parlamentario Socialista (Socialist Parliamentary Group): 109 members

Grupo Parlamentario Catalán-Convergència i Unió (Catalán Parliamentary Group-Convergence and Union): 16 members

Grupo Parlamentario de la Izquierda Plural: Izquierda Unida, Iniciativa per Catalunya-Verds-Esquerra Unida i Alternativa (Parliamentary Group of the Plural Left: United

Left, Initiative for Catalunya-Greens-United and Alternative Left) (ICV-EUiA) and
Chunta Aragonesista (Aragon Nationalist Party) (CHA): 11 members

Grupo Parlamentario de Unión Progreso y Democracia (Parliamentary Group of
Union, Progress, and Democracy): 5 members

Grupo Parlamentario Vasco–Euzko Alderdi Jeltzalea-Partido Nacionalista Vasco
(Basque Parliamentary Group–Basque Nationalist Party) (EAJ-PNV): 5 members

Grupo Parlamentario Mixto (Mixed Parliamentary Group): 18 members

The last group is formed by Coalición Amaiur (Amaiur coalition): 7 members; Esquerra Republicana de Catalunya (Republican Left of Catalunya): 3 members; Coalición Canaria-Nueva Canarias (Canary Island Coalition-New Canary Islands) (CC-NC-PNC): 2 members; Bloque Nacionalista Galego (Galician Nationalist Bloc)

Table 3.2   ELECTION RESULTS FOR THE PARLIAMENT

Lower House of Parliament or Congreso		
Party	Seats 2011	Seats 2008
PP	186	154
PSOE	110	169
CiU	16	10
IU-LV	11	2
AMAIUR	7	–
UPyD	5	1
EAJ-PNV	5	6
BNG	2	2
ERC	3	3
CC-NC-PNC	2	2
COMPROMIS-Q	1	–
FAC	1	–
GBAI	1	–
NA-BAI	0	1
Upper House of Parliament or Senado		
PP	136	101
PSOE	48	89
PSC-ICV-EUIA	7	12
CiU	9	4
EAJ-PNV	4	2
AMAIUR	3	–
CC-NC-PNC	1	–

(BNG): 2 members; Compromis-Q: 1 member; Foro de Ciudadanos (Citizens' Forum) (FAC): 1 member; Geroa Bai (Yes to the Future) (GBAI): 1 member; Unión del Pueblo Navarro (People's Union of Navarre) (UPN): 1 member.

See also: Chapter 2: Overview. Chapter 3: Overview; Constitutions; Electoral Scheme and the "No Molestar" System; Political Challenges of Spain's 21st Century; Regional Government and Regionalism; Scandals and Political Corruption. Chapter 6: Nationalism; Spanish Youth. Chapter 7: Feminism in Spain. Chapter 16: Youth Culture.

Further Reading

Gunther, Richard, and José Ramón Montero. *The Politics of Spain*. Cambridge: Cambridge University Press, 2009.

Loughlin, John, and David Hanley. *Spanish Political Parties*. Cardiff: University of Wales Press, 2006.

Sánchez-Cuenca, Ignacio, and Elías Dinas. *Voters and Parties in the Spanish Political Space*. New York: Routledge, 2014.

Rajoy Brey, Mariano

Mariano Rajoy Brey earned a degree in law from the Universidad de Santiago de Compostela. Immediately afterwards, he studied the *oposiciones* (competitive exams in order to become a civil servant) to be a registrar, a position he obtained at the age of 23, becoming the youngest registrar of his generation. In the early 1980s, Rajoy joined the right-wing party Alianza Popular (AP), which later became the People's Party (PP). Since then his political career has been on the rise. However, he was not chosen democratically within his own party. His predecessor, José María Aznar, chose Mariano Rajoy personally as his successor. Rajoy gained respect and influence from his party colleagues after occupying different ministerial positions under Aznar's government including Minister of Public Administration (1996–1999), Minister of Education and Culture (1999–2000), and Minister of the Interior (2001–2002).

Three days before Spain's general elections, on March 11, 2004, between 7:30 a.m. and 8:00 a.m., 10 bombs exploded in Madrid's Atocha train station, killing 191 people and injuring 1,857. This event is still to date the biggest terrorist attack that ever happened in Spain's history, and the deadliest on European soil since World War II. It is only comparable to September 11, 2001, in New York. As a result, it generated panic and confusion before the imminent general elections which, instead of being canceled, took place as scheduled with politicians using the terrorist attack as a political weapon. The PP in particular developed multiple conspiracy theories about the attack. After the PSOE's victory, Mariano Rajoy became the PP's opposition leader for the conservatives.

After the resignation of Zapatero, early elections were celebrated in Spain on November 20, 2011, resulting in a clear victory for the conservatives. Rajoy's main goal as the new president was to restore confidence during the biggest economic recession in

Spain's contemporary history. In fact, at the beginning of his term, Spain was on the brink of economic collapse. Rajoy's government received a bailout from the European Union (European Stability Mechanism) of 40 billion euros ($52 billion) in order to refinance the economy. The Spanish banks were subjected to international scrutiny, particularly the *cajas,* the majority of which were nationalized. Under this critical scenario in 2012, Rajoy's government rolled out a series of austerity measures for Spain in order to remain within the European Union. These implementations have already been labeled as the harshest cuts in recent Spanish history. Apart from cutting unemployment payments and increasing taxes (contrary to Rajoy's initial promise of reducing taxes), Rajoy also froze the minimum wage and the salaries of public workers (*funcionarios*).

New general elections will be held in Spain at the end of 2015. Interestingly, Rajoy has already announced a modest increase for the minimum wage and for government funded pensions. Technically Spain came out of its economic recession in 2014. However, time will tell if Spaniards will vote for Mariano Rajoy again, especially considering that Spain's unemployment remains one of the highest in the EU. Similar to previous governments—regardless of their ideology—Rajoy's first term in Spanish government (2011–2015) has experienced a significant number of scandals within his own political party, including the Gürtel affair (bribery, money laundering, and tax evasion by some politicians from the People's Party), and the case of Luis Bárcenas, former treasurer and senator of PP, who was sent to prison for maladministration and embezzlement. Furthermore, a young generation of politicians with refreshing political discourses are

Spanish President Mariano Rajoy waves as he leaves a meeting of the Eurozone heads of state at the EU Council building in Brussels on July 13, 2015. (AP Photo/Francois Walschaerts)

reviving the public's enthusiasm for politics in Spain. Among these newcomers to the political arena are Pablo Iglesias and Albert Rivera.

See also: Chapter 2: Overview. Chapter 3: Overview; Scandals and Political Corruption; Zapatero, José Luis Rodríguez. Chapter 4: Overview. Chapter 8: Testing.

Further Reading

Chislett, William. *Spain: What Everyone Needs to Know*. Oxford: Oxford University Press, 2013.

Encarnación, Omar G. *Spanish Politics*. Cambridge: Polity, 2008.

Regional Government and Regionalism

The Constitution of 1978 divided Spain's territory into 17 regions, and two autonomous cities (Ceuta and Melilla) in the north of Morocco. Each region, or "autonomy," as they are called, has an elected legislature where regional laws are passed. Each region has a president whose role is similar to that of Spain's president in the federal government.

According to the Organization for Economic Co-operation and Development (OECD) and based on data from 2011, Spain is one of the most decentralized countries of the eight federal countries listed. In fact, Spain is not listed by the OECD as a federal country. Instead, it is classified as a regional country, because its political structure is highly decentralized. In 2011, in a list of eight federal countries of the OECD, the central government of Spain keeps 29.9 percent of the public income, which is below Germany (31.7%); France (32.6%); Japan (33.3%); Switzerland (36.3%); U.S. (40.6%); and Canada (41.5%). On the other hand, the regional administrations of Spain received 23.1 percent of the public income, which is more than any other country in the list, with the exception of Canada (39.7%) and Switzerland (24.2%).

See also: Chapter 2: Overview. Chapter 3: Overview; Constitutions. Chapter 4: Overview. Chapter 6: Multiculturalism; Nationalism.

Further Reading

Balfour, Sebastian. *The Politics of Contemporary Spain*. New York: Routledge, 2005.

Centeno, Miguel Ángel, and Agustín Ferraro. *State and Nation Making in Latin America and Spain: Republics of the Possible*. Cambridge: Cambridge University Press, 2013.

Scandals and Political Corruption

Every country has scandals, and Spain is no exception. In fact, the recent history of Spanish politics is inextricably linked to scandals. For instance, during the 1990s the government in power, PSOE, was accused of multiple cases of corruption that ultimately ended the career of well-known politicians such as Felipe González and Alfonso

Guerra. These political scandals involved abuse of public funds (i.e., the Alfonso Guerra affair); political party-funding outrages (i.e., PSOE's own apparatus); and maladministration by the Interior Minister José Barrionuevo (GAL affair) and corruption charges against Director General of the Civil Guard Luis Roldán (Roldán affair), for which both ended up in prison.

Since 2007, Spain has witnessed another round of political scandals. Although dirty political affairs have happened since the beginning of civilization, the magnitude of wrongdoings by the current government officials is staggering. One of the most inexcusable crimes was the labor union UGT scandal in Andalucía (November 2013). Regional government is still investigating whether the labor union illegally received 7.5 million euros of public money. To make matters even worse, Spanish judges are battling against their own apparently corrupted justice system. According to a report written in English by *El País*, "fear makes some judges opt to only go after low-profile criminals" (Andreu 2013). As William Chislett explained in an interview for *El País*, "one likes to think that trade unions are whiter than white; you expect unions to behave more ethically than corporate Spain but it hasn't been the case in Andalucía" (Badcock 2014). Another disturbing incident of misconduct came from a member of the Spanish Crown. On January 7, 2014, Judge José Castro summoned *Infanta* Cristina (48 years old), who is the sister of King Felipe VI. She was accused of fraud and money laundering. On June 12, 2014, King Felipe VI officially dispossessed his sister of her title as Duchess of Palma.

It is easy to see why many Spanish citizens feel at best leery and at worst disgusted about anything related to politics. One of the main causes of public discontent is the fact that Spanish politicians do not resign regardless of how guilty they may be. For instance, Federico Trillo used to be the Minister of Defense in 2003 when a Yak 42 plane crashed in Turkey and killed 75 people of whom 62 were Spanish military returning from their mission in Afghanistan. Instead of assuming any responsibility in the case, Trillo removed the generals who signed the contract for the plane. Currently, he is the Spanish ambassador in London. Another scandal is the case of Bárcenas. The president of Spain, and current president of the Partido Popular, Mariano Rajoy, named Luis Bárcenas as party treasurer in 2008. Although it was proven in 2013 that Bárcenas paid some members of his political party under the table, including several members who are in the current government, Rajoy has not assumed any responsibility.

In this historical context, some recent contemporary Spanish art sends a clear message. Such was the case, for instance, with Pedro L. Trujillo aka Le Frère, a Spanish artist who from February 10 to March 1, 2014, had an exhibition in Madrid under the title "IS PAIN"—a vision of the political class system made in toilet paper. A previous exhibition by the same artist took place in Gijón on September 27, 2013, under the title "SHIT HAPPENS, *papel y ladrillo, el retrato de una crisis*," in which he depicted the current crisis of Spain using toilet paper as his main material to portray in pencil the faces of some of the culprits.

See also: Chapter 2: Overview. Chapter 3: Overview; Electoral Scheme and the "No Molestar" System; Political Challenges of Spain's 21st Century. Chapter 4: Overview. Chapter 16: Overview.

Further Reading

Bull, Martin J., and James Newell, eds. *Corruption in Contemporary Politics*. New York: Palgrave Macmillan, 2003.

Chislett, William. *Spain: What Everyone Needs to Know*. Oxford: Oxford University Press, 2013.

Little, Walter, and Eduardo Posada Carbó. *Political Corruption in Europe and Latin America*. New York: St. Martin's Press, 1996.

Serra, Eduardo

The lawyer and politician Eduardo Serra has spent half of his life working in the public administration, was Minister of Defense from 1996 to 2000 during the government of José María Aznar, and is the only Spanish public servant who has served with all three governing parties in democratic Spain (UCD, PSOE, and PP). In 2012 he co-wrote with Marc Alba and David García *Las claves para transformar España* (*The Keys to Transform Spain*). The written study was initially born in 2010 through the website platform *Transforma España* (www.transformaespaña.es), in which they diagnosed the problems of Spain as well as provided solutions. With a conciliatory voice, they wrote a book and created a website with a simple goal in mind: to help Spain. For Serra, a country that cannot make up its mind on the international stage is a country without credibility. The country, or the civil society, should begin to realize that public decisions also affect them. Marc Alba mentions in a video available on their website that "in the end, the transformations that this country has to go through are so deep that any effort is important." For Serra, "it is very important for society to realize the potential effectiveness of its activity. We need to work together. We need to persevere in the direction that we think is the most correct. I am optimistic. I think we can only have a better future if we reinforce what unites us."

According to Serra, the old motto "Spain is different" should be replaced with "Spain is unique," because it defines an evolution of Spain that is more exclusive, glamorous, and positive as part of its modern identity. To support this particular view, they intentionally compare their solutions with the success of the Spanish national soccer team in an attempt to inspire optimism rather than the pessimism that resonates from the old axiom (Spain is different). In their report *Transforma España*—available free online in English—they provide twelve solutions. For instance, their claims include a new responsible welfare state; new efficient administrations; a new influential country brand; and a new strategy roadmap for Spain.

See also: Chapter 2: Overview. Chapter 3: Overview; Electoral Scheme and the "No Molestar" System; Political Challenges of Spain's 21st Century; Scandals and Political Corruption. Chapter 4: Overview. Chapter 16: Overview.

Further Reading

Fundación Transforma España. http://ftransformaespana.es

Serra, Eduardo, Marc Alba, y David García. *Las claves para transformar España*. Barcelona: Destino, 2012.

Spanish Politicians

After the death of Franco, Spain has had six presidents and several important politicians. This subheading focuses on other Spanish politicians who have played—and some who still play—a significant role in the Spanish political arena. The following is Spain's general elections' timeline since democracy was restored in the 20th century:

1977: First general election (15 June) won by the *Unión de Centro Democrático* (UCD: Center Democractic United) presided by Adolfo Suárez.

1979: New elections again won by Adolfo Suárez (UCD).

1981: Adolfo Suárez resigns as president of the government. H. M. The King asks Leopoldo Calvo Sotelo to be president of Spain; he is appointed immediately after the election on February 25, 1981.

1982: General election (October 28) with an absolute majority for the PSOE. New government presided by Felipe González (December 3).

1986: Spain and Portugal become full members of the European Community (January 1). Prince Felipe swears his allegiance to the constitution at the Spanish Parliament (January 30). Another absolute majority of Felipe González (and his left-wing party PSOE) in the general elections (June 22).

1989: The PSOE is re-elected.

1993: Fourth consecutive victory of Felipe González with an absolute majority.

1996: The Partido Popular (right wing party PP), under José María Aznar, wins the general elections.

2000: José María Aznar and his party (PP) are re-elected.

2004: The PSOE of José Luis Rodríguez Zapatero wins the general elections.

23-F COUP D'ETAT

23-F coup d'état, also known in Spain as *el tejerazo*, takes its name from Antonio Tejero, a colonel who stormed Spain's parliament on February 23, 1981. The right-wing sector of the country thought at the time that democracy was not a good fit for Spain and, in particular, Spain's recent constitution of 1978. The 23-F coup d'état's main goal was to force King Juan Carlos I to terminate the constitution, dissolve the parliament, and rule Spain with a military council including the king as a collaborator. However, Spain's king's appearance on nationwide television on Februrary 23, 1981, made him famous when he, wearing his uniform as commander-in-chief, declared his support for Spain's constitution.

2008: José Luis Rodríguez Zapatero and his party (PSOE) are re-elected. Zapatero resigns on November 20, 2011.

2011: The PP of Mariano Rajoy wins the general elections.

Noteworthy Spanish Politicians of the Current Time

Federico Mayor Zaragoza

Federico Mayor Zaragoza (1934–) is an academic specializing in pharmacology who has also developed a political profile that extends beyond Spain. For instance, he held political positions in Spain during the 1970s and 1980s, including parliamentary member (1977–1978), Minister of Education and Science (1981–1982), and member of the European Parliament (1987). Professor Mayor has also been director-general of UNESCO from 1987 to 1999. Since 1999 he has worked for the *Fundación Cultura de Paz* (Foundation for a Culture of Peace), which he created and of which he is chairman.

Javier Solana

Javier Solana (1942–) received his doctorate in physics from the University of Virginia (U.S.) in 1971 and in 1975 became a professor at the Universidad Complutense de Madrid, where he did his undergraduate studies. Solana started his political career in the PSOE party, where he was appointed as Minister of Foreign Affairs of Spain (1992–1995). From 1995 to 1999 he was secretary-general of the North Atlantic Treaty Organization (NATO). Immediately after, Solana worked for a decade as secretary-general of the Council of the European Union as well as secretary-general of the Western European Union (1999–2009). He is currently president of the ESADEgeo-Center for Global Economy and Geopolitics and is a Distinguished Fellow at the Brookings Institution.

Soledad Becerril

Soledad Becerril (1944–) was the first woman to hold a Spanish cabinet post since the civil war. Becerril served as deputy mayor of Sevilla from 1991 to 1995, and also from 1995 to 1999, becoming the first female mayor of Sevilla. Only once before in Spanish history has a woman become minister in what has traditionally been an exclusive men's club—Federica Montseny, an anarchist, became health minister at the outbreak of civil war in 1936. Becerril entered politics during the last years of the Franco dictatorship. A native of Madrid, she graduated in philology from Madrid University, did graduate work in linguistics in England, and studied political science at Columbia University in New York. As a minister of culture (1981–1983), she emphasized the importance of females having an education in order to move into traditionally male-dominated professional careers, or, in her particular case, a job surrounded by an entire government formed by men with her as the only woman.

Joaquín Almunia

Joaquín Almunia (1948–) graduated in law (1965–1972) and economics (1965–1971) from the Universidad de Deusto (Bilbao), and also studied for a year in both France

(1970–1971) and the U.S. (1991). For three years he worked as an associate lecturer of social law at the Universidad de Alcalá de Henares (1991–1994). Under the PSOE party, Almunia was a member of the Spanish Parliament (1979–2004). He was Minister of Employment and Social Security (1982–1986); Minister of Public Administration (1986–1991); and eventually replaced Felipe González as leader of the PSOE (1997–2000). Later he became the European Commissioner for Economic and Financial Affairs (2004–2010). Since February 2010, Almunia has been vice-president of the European Commission.

María Teresa Fernández de la Vega

María Teresa Fernández de la Vega (1949–) was the first woman to occupy the vice-presidency of Spain (2004–2010). At the beginning of the 1970s she graduated in law studies from the Universidad Complutense de Madrid. Under the PSOE party, she worked in the Ministry of Justice in the 1980s and became a magistrate in 1989. She has had an extensive career campaigning in favor of women's rights in Spain, including the legalization of abortion and the creation of Spain's Womens Institute. Currently she teaches in several universities in Spain.

Rodrigo Rato

Rodrigo Rato (1949–) is a lawyer and also holds an MBA from the University of California at Berkeley (1974) and a Ph.D in economics from the Universidad Complutense de Madrid (2003). He served as vice-president of the conservative government of José María Aznar as well as minister of the economy (1996–2004). From 2004 to 2007 he was managing director and chairman of the International Monetary Fund. According to the *Financial Times*, Rato was "the former head of Bankia and the man who presided over the worst corporate collapse in recent Spanish history" (Buck 2013). Rato was sent to prison on April 15, 2015, over allegations of false accounting, fraud, and embezzlement with regards to the collapse of Bankia.

Rosa Díez

Rosa Díez (1952–), although she does not have a university degree, passed a civil servant exam to work in the administration of the Basque country (*Diputación Foral de Vizcaya*), which is the regional council of Biscay, where she worked from 1973 until 1977, when she joined the PSOE. In 1999 she was elected as a European deputy member and was re-elected in 2004. In 2000, Díez ran against Rodríguez Zapatero, José Bono, and Matilde Fernández to become the secretary general leader of the PSOE. However, she lost the election. After the split between the PNV and the PSOE in the Basque region, Díez became more critical of her own party. In August 2007 she participated in various events organized by Ciutadans de Catalunya, and immediately afterwards resigned from her political position within the PSOE. On March 9, 2008, Díez ran for office under the political party, Unión Progreso y Democracia (UPyD), becoming the first Spanish woman candidate for the position of president. She earned one seat in the Congreso de los Diputados (lower house of Parliament). In 2011, she obtained five seats (four from Madrid and one from Valencia run by the actor Toni Cantó). In 2012 Díez accused Spain's fourth largest bank, Bankia, of carrying out "a massive fraud" on its small investors because, in her opinion, its stock market launch was based on falsification of data. For Díez, there was no doubt that Spain received a bailout from the European Union in the amount of €41.000 million ($56,534 million), although several politicians and even some Spaniards denied that the EU rescued Spain in 2012.

Pablo Iglesias

Pablo Iglesias (1978–) holds a double degree in law (2001) and political sciences (2004), both from the Universidad Complutense de Madrid, where he teaches communications. He also has a Masters in humanities (specializing in cultural studies) from the Universidad Carlos III de Madrid (2010) and a Master of Arts in communication (specializing in philosophy, film, and psychoanalysis) from the European Graduate School (Switzerland / U.S.). Apart from being an eloquent speaker, Iglesias is fluent in English, French, and Italian. He is one of the co-founders of a new Leftist party called Podemos (We Can), which was registered on March 11, 2014, and obtained five seats in the European elections of May 25, 2014. According to several polls in Spain, Podemos could win the next general election of Spain, which will be held on December 20, 2015. On their website, his political party's goals include recovering the economy and conquering inequality. Globally, Podemos can be seen as similar to the Greek *aganaktismenoi* or the international Occupy Movements, including the Spanish *indignados,* as a new political phenomenon.

Albert Rivera

Albert Rivera (1979–) studied law at ESADE Business School (Barcelona). He is the president of the regional party *Ciutadans*, which in 2006 managed to win three seats in the Catalan Parliament. In the 2012 regional elections, his party attracted 7.5 percent of the vote and tripled its number of seats to nine. His popularity is on the rise. He has transformed his initial political Catalan party *Ciutadans* to a national one called *Ciudadanos* for the next Spanish election predicted to be held in 2015. On their website, his political party highlights the critical problems that currently affect Spain: the economy, institutional crises, separatism, and ethical issues. His way to tackle them is through a sweeping reform. In 2010, after Catalunya banned bullfighting in the entire region, Rivera was quoted by the BBC as saying, "They are trying to get independence and they think if they highlight differences it will help" (*BBC*, July 28, 2010). In essence, his political aura resonates with the British concept of the "third way." Rivera does not believe in black and white ideologies. He proclaims himself to be a third option.

See also: Chapter 2: Overview. Chapter 3: Overview; Political Challenges of Spain's 21st Century; Political Parties; Regional Government and Regionalism. Chapter 4: Overview. Chapter 6: Overview.

Further Reading

Casanova, Julián, and Carlos Gil Andrés. *Twentieth-Century Spain: A History*. Cambridge: Cambridge University Press, 2014.

Chislett, William. *Spain: What Everyone Needs to Know*. Oxford: Oxford University Press, 2013.

Dicken, Peter. *Global Shift: Mapping the Changing Contours of the World Economy.* 7th ed. New York: The Guilford Press, 2014.

Phillips, William D., and Carla Rahn Phillips. *A Concise History of Spain.* Cambridge: Cambridge University Press, 2010.

Zapatero, José Luis Rodríguez

José Luis Rodríguez Zapatero earned a degree in law from the Universidad de León. He became leader of the PSOE (Spanish Socialist Workers' Party) in June 2000 when he was 43 years old, but was still relevatively unknown nationwide, despite the fact that he was 26 years old when he became Spain's youngest congressman. Against all the odds that predicted another conservative win, the socialist Zapatero won Spain's general election in 2004. Perhaps two of the main reasons were his intention of withdrawing Spain's troops from the Iraq war, and his support for the idea of converting Spain into a federal state. The latter implied a radical break not only from some of his own political colleagues but also from those Spaniards who in general are more inclined to adopt a centralist approach with regards to regionalism.

During his first term in government (2004–2008), Zapatero introduced one of the most pro-LGTB agendas in the world. His social reform included: legalization of same-sex marriage (only legalized in Canada and the Netherlands at the time); allowing gay couples to adopt children; lifting all restrictions previously set on divorces; and removing religious education as a compulsory subject in public schools. Also, for the first time in Spain's political history, in 2004 Zapatero formed a government with seven women and a female vice-president. Furthermore, in 2005 Zapatero granted Spanish citizenship to 700,000 illegal Africans, giving Spain the most generous inmigrant policy in Europe. Zapatero also generated controversy when the Law of Historical Memory passed in Fall 2007. It repudiated the previous *Pacto del Olvido*. The latter is an unofficial term created by scholars, which essentially consisted of burying the past, so no politician could use the past (Spanish Civil War and Franco's dictatorship) as a political instrument.

Zapatero was re-elected in 2008. However, he was unable to tackle the global financial crisis. Besides, his image further took a hit with his statement in 2008 that "the financial crisis is a fallacy and there is no need to be catastrophic" (*la crisis es una falacia, puro catastrofismo*). To make things worse, a series of scandals came to the public attention, including his justice minister, Mariano Fernández Bermejo, who resigned after allegations of allegedly being involved in bribary.

Mainly due to an unprecedented record high of unemployment in conjunction with other negative factors during his last term, Zapatero was essentially forced to resign before his term ended in November 2011. Zapatero achieved during his first term Spain's lowest rate of unemployment since the Transition (7.95% in 2007), yet, he left the government during what is already known as the Great Recession in Spain. That is to say, he started as a hero of European social democracy, but he ended up as an anti-hero for many Spaniards.

See also: Chapter 2: Overview. Chapter 3: Rajoy, Mariano, Scandals and Political Corruption. Chapter 4: Overview. Chapter 6: Overview. Chapter 7: Overview.

Further Reading

Field, Bonnie N. *Spain's 'Second Transition'?: The Socialist Government of José Luis Rodríguez Zapatero*. New York: Routledge, 2011.

Field, Bonnie N., and Alfonso Botti, eds. *Politics and Society in Contemporary Spain: From Zapatero to Rajoy*. New York: Palgrave Macmillan, 2013.

REFERENCES

Andreu, Jerónimo. "The Lone Rangers of Justice." *El País,* March 10, 2013.

Ayllón, Daniel. "Griñán, el último elefante del Senado." *La Marea*, October 2013: 34–37.

Badcock, James. "I Don't Believe That This Country Has a 26 Percent Unemployment Rate." *El País,* January 13, 2014.

Buck, Tobias. "Former Bankia Head Joins Santander Advisory Board." *Financial Times,* September 17, 2013.

Burgen, Stephen. "Bankia Board Faces Investigation over Corruption Claims." *The Guardian,* July 4, 2012.

Burridge, Tom. "Spanish Princess Infanta Cristina Summoned over Fraud." *BBC News,* January 7, 2014.

"Catalonia's Bullfight Ban Provokes Emotional Response." *The Guardian*, July 28, 2010.

Chislett, William. *Spain: What Everyone Needs to Know*. Oxford: Oxford University Press, 2013.

Corral Cortés, Esther. *Spain Today 2013*. Madrid: Ministry of the Presidency, 2013. http://publicacionesoficiales.boe.es

Gallego-Díaz, Soledad. "La arrogancia de un simple programa." *El País,* September 22, 2013.

Gómez, José Luis. *Cómo salir de esta. España toca fondo. ¿Llega la reactivación?*. A Coruña: Actualia Editorial, 2013.

Kamen, Henry. *Imagining Spain*. New Haven: Yale University Press, 2008.

Markham, James M. "Interview with Soledad Becerril." *The New York Times,* February 21, 1982.

Martorell, Miguel y Santos Juliá. *Manual de historia política y social de España (1808–2011)*. Barcelona: RBA, 2012.

Molinas, César. *Qué hacer con España. Del capitalismo castizo a la refundación de un país*. Barcelona: Destino, 2013.

Moreno Luzón, Javier, and Xosé M. Núñez Seixas, eds. *Ser españoles. Imaginarios nacionalistas en el siglo XX*. Barcelona: RBA, 2013.

Muñoz Machado, Santiago. *Informe sobre España. Repensar el Estado o destruirlo*. Barcelona: Crítica, 2012.

Payne, Stanley G. *Spain: A Unique History*. Madison: University of Wisconsin Press, 2011.

Roca, José Manuel. La oxidada transición. Madrid: La Linterna Sorda, 2013.

Serra, Eduardo. *Transforma España*. Everis, November 16, 2010. Web. January 23, 2014. http://www.transformaespana.es/

Serra, Eduardo, in collaboration with Marc Alba and David García. *Las claves para transformar España*. Barcelona: Destino, 2012.

Tremlett, Giles. *Ghosts of Spain*. London: Faber & Faber, 2006.

Websites

CIS: Centro de Investigaciones Sociológicas. http://datos.cis.es/pdf/Es3008mar_A.pdf

Ertzaintza.net

esadegeo.com. http://www.esadegeo.com/

Fundación Cultura de Paz. Fund-culturadepaz.org

Guardiacivil.es/es. http://www.guardiacivil.es/es/index.html

La Moncloa. http://www.lamoncloa.gob.es/IDIOMAS/9/Espana/ElEstado/index.htm

Marca España. marcaespana.es

Ministerio de Defensa. defensa.gob.es

Mossos.cat. http://mossos.gencat.cat/ca

news-spain.euroresidentes.com. http://news-spain.euroresidentes.com/

OECD: Organization for Economic Co-operation and Development. oecd.org

PressTV. http://www.presstv.ir/detail/2014/01/17/346138/spain-ruling-party-rebels-form-new-party/

Speakerscorner. http://www.speakerscorner.co.uk/speaker/rodrigo-rato

CHAPTER 4

ECONOMY

OVERVIEW

Spain lost the last of its colonies in 1898 (Cuba, Puerto Rico, and the Philippines), and, as a result, began the 20th century in a deep crisis at all levels (economic, political, and, above all, existential). The Spanish crisis of 1898 ended in a civil war (1936–1939), because of unresolved political problems. Current Spanish politicians scarily resemble their counterparts of the early 20th century, who did not create a common national plan for the future of the country. The Spanish economy at present does not show consistency. On the contrary, present-day politicians seem to be unable to create and follow through with a national strategy.

Throughout the 19th century, Spain's economy was mainly based on agriculture because the industrial revolution of the 18th century made no significant impact on the country as a whole. Although the first Spanish industries (set up in Catalunya) were established in 1830 at the same time similar industries were being created in Belgium, France, and Germany, by the end of the century Spain had not progressed economically in comparison with those countries. The main reason for Spain's slow development is that it did not build a railroad system. Furthermore, most Spaniards at that time were poor farmers. In fact, during the Restoration (1875–1916), more than 70 percent of the population was illiterate. The Restoration was characterized by returning power to the monarchy, and the conservative bourgeoisie who benefited did not consider investing in working class industries a priority. The French Revolution had consequences all over Europe, but little impact on the social and economic fabric of Spain. Nevertheless, while Europe was suffering an economic crisis (1873–1896), Spain enjoyed a period of economic splendor—especially in the region of Catalunya from 1876 to 1886. Then, when Europe began a recovery, Spain underwent another economic crisis in the late 19th century, initiated by three factors: inflation, depreciation of the currency, and a decrease of international commerce.

The period between 1914 and 1936 marks a decisive transformation of Spain into an industrial capitalist economy, with the industrial sector growing much faster than in many other European countries. However, this rapid industrialization was impeded by an archaic agricultural sector that was being maintained by impoverished farmers. In 1930, 46 percent of the population was working in agriculture as opposed to 65 percent in 1910; however, the industrialization process was not sufficient to absorb this segment of society. Subsequently, poor, illiterate farmers and outdated agriculture became one of the many causes for the Spanish Civil War (1936–1939), which left Spain economically devastated and in a far worse state than her neighbors after the Second World War.

Because Spain collaborated with Hitler's Nazi Germany and Mussolini's fascist Italy, the country was penalized by a UN economic blockade that lasted until 1950. Spain again attempted to be self-sufficient, but it did not have the capability to do so. As a result, the decade of the 1940s in Spain is known as *los años del hambre* (years of hunger), despite the creation of INI (Institute of National Industry) in September 1941. In fact, due to a lack of basic resources, Spain was forced to ration daily products such as bread, olive oil, soap, and tobacco until 1953. Spain also imported wheat from Argentina, and there were numerous restrictions on energy, especially electricity. Under these conditions, underground businesses emerged, known in Spanish as *estraperlo* or the black market. The figure of the Spanish *maqui* also dates from this period. It refers to a deserter or an insurgent who escaped from Franco's regime and took refuge in the mountains. The *maquis* or *bandoleros* (bandits), apart from having a particular ideology, were also known for dealing on the black market.

In 1955 Spain become a member of the United Nations (UN). During the 1960s, a Stabilization Plan was finally designed and brought some benefits to the country's lagging economy. Spain started to show economic progress between 1961 and 1973, when the country's economy was rising at a rate higher than any other country in the OECD (7% yearly) with the exception of Japan. Also, international companies including Chrysler, John Deere, and Ciba-Geigy became established in Spain. This economic phenomenon known as *milagro español* (Spanish miracle) was also due to an increase of tourism and the money sent home by Spanish emigrants working abroad. In other words, the recovery of the Spanish economy was not due to Spain's economic plan alone but also to the fact that other economies were doing well and that many foreigners chose to spend their money in Spain's expanding tourist industry.

After the death of Franco in 1975, there was a new economic expansion in the cities, which resulted in a movement of the population. The expansion created a disparity in living standards between the urban and the rural areas. For instance, in 1975 five of the seventeen regions generated nearly half of Spain's total GDP. Those regions were Madrid, Catalunya, the Valencia region, the Basque country, and Asturias. Nowadays, although those five regions remain powerful, industrial areas are spread out nationwide. In 1986 Spain joined the European Market, which signified a liberalization of the Spanish economy, transforming Spain into a modern European country. Nevertheless, there are still some uncompetitive industrial sectors such as farming, the northern coal mines, and the political administration system that have become unviable, hampering growth and development. Overall, in economic terms, Spain seems to be unable to create long-term jobs. In the new millennium the economic ground rules have changed and Spain has not yet adjusted to the new order.

The Spanish economy occupies an atypical position within the global economy. In fact, it has been described as an anomaly, different, unique. Although Spain does not belong to the G-8, Spain was the world's eighth largest economy in 2008, surpassing Canada in 2006 (Encarnación 2008). From 2005 to 2007 Spain's economy grew more than any other country in the EU, and even more than some of the G-8 countries. However, Spain does not have much voice within the 28-country European Union, despite the fact that it is the eurozone's fifth largest economy. During the midst of the economic crisis in 2012, Spain's conservative government received 41 billion euros of EU bailout money to refinance its economy; Spain's economy during Europe's economic recession was described as too big to fail.

Ratings agency Moody's raised its outlook for Spain's economy from "negative" to "stable" on December 2013. Technically, Spain ended a two-year recession with 0.1 percent growth in October 2013, ending nine consecutive quarters of losses on GDP. However, very few ordinary citizens are feeling the benefits; over one in four Spaniards remain out of work and many families remain strapped for cash (Burridge 2013). According to the national paper *El País*, during the economic crisis, 80,000 families were bankrupted in Spain in one year alone (Mars 2013). The *Centro de Investigaciones Sociológicas* (CIS: Center for Sociological Research) in February 2015 highlighted that four out of five Spaniards believe that the Spanish economy remains the same or worse.

The term *anomaly* is an apt description of the Spanish economy in the 21st century. Many Spaniards have been forced to abandon their homes and, if possible, they have returned to their parents' houses. In 2008 there were 129,900 families sharing a house with members who were unemployed and/or retired; in 2013 there were over 3,123,000 people living with a retired family member. Without a doubt, the retired population in Spain has played and still plays a key role in the Spanish economy. They have become the only security cushion for the six million plus Spaniards unemployed in 2013.

Spain's economic numbers in 2013 were quite grim: 6.2 million were unemployed, which is 27.16 percent of the total active population in Spain, of which 57.22 percent were the new generation who were less than 25 years old. Once again, Spain seems to be unable to create long-term jobs. In 2012 alone, 850,000 jobs were lost. To make matters worse, Spain's electricity bill is one of the highest in Europe. As reported by *El País* in their special report "The Shocking Price of Spanish Electricity," the high price that Spaniards have to pay for their electricity is mainly due to a lack of authentic competition among the electrical companies. As a result, millions of Spanish homes have had their electricity cut off for nonpayment (over 1.4 million in 2013 alone).

The pillars of the Spanish economy can be divided into four major sectors: service (54% mainly tourism); commerce (24%); construction (15%); and the manufacturing industry (7%, mainly cars). Construction is without a doubt the most problematic one, since it created the Spanish real estate bubble that burst in 2008.

According to the Ministry of Industry in January 2011 (*Spain in Figures 2013*), the most common size for a company in Spain is small and medium, which Spaniards call PYME (stands for Small and Medium Enterprise, in Spanish). In 2011 there were 3,246,986 companies, of which 49 percent were located in three regions: 18.5 percent in Catalunya; 15.4 percent in Madrid; and 15.1 percent in Andalucía. The PYMEs represent 99.9 percent of the total businesses in Spain with a mere 0.1 percent that belongs to the mega companies. In other words, Spain does not have many large companies. On the contrary, 1,793,878 of the companies were businesses with only one person and no workers; 1,297,971 were businesses with less than 10 people employed;

130,448 were small businesses (10–49 employees); 20,888 were medium-sized businesses (50–500 employees); and only 3,801 were big businesses (over 500 employees).

Tax Justice Network (January 13, 2013) ranked Spain as number 10 in the world in regard to financial fraud. According to the Spanish Treasury (Hacienda), 71.7 percent of the fiscal fraud corresponds to large sized companies and multinationals. Spain contributes only 0.13 percent of the GDP to combat economic fraud as opposed to Holland (0.5%). To make matters worse, in 2013 the Spanish Treasury reduced the number of employees and the time dedicated to look for fraud, which makes it challenging to unravel complex fraud schemes.

By January 2014 Spain's economy was still in need of major financial reform. The good news is the many lengthy books recently published by experts in the field, explaining in detail the behavior of Spain's economy since 2008. The bad news is that the two major political party leaders do not seem to be listening to the remedies provided by these many qualified voices. One of the main commonalities shared in these studies is the irrefutable fact that Spain needs to apply drastic financial reforms to become a competitive country again. Spain's economy grew significantly from 1997 until 2007, when it started to show a sharp drop on the global scene.

For economist Gay de Liébana, Spain right now is synonymous with debt, as he explains in his latest book, *España se escribe con E de Endeudamiento* (2012). His main thesis is supported by a basic fact:

Spain's debt in 2011 = €2,863,954,000
Spain's GDP in 2011 = €1,073,383,000 → 266.82%

Spain's debt derives from the sums of: Spanish family debt (€870,987) + nonfinancial corporations (€1,258,006) + public debt (€734,961), which is significantly higher than the national GDP. Without economic growth, there is no progress (Liébana 2012).

The Spanish recession has a dual origin: On the one hand, the international crisis had a huge impact on the Spanish economy. On the other hand, the continuous economic imbalances of the budget created in previous years have generated negative performance in the economy. Currently Spain needs to do what it did not do in the past. Urgent reforms sooner than later have to happen in the financial sector. Similar opinions referring to the need for urgent reform can also be found in other recent studies such as those by Encarnación (2008); Muñoz Machado (2012); Gómez (2013); Chislett (2013); and Llopis (2013).

To conclude with a global picture, the Canadian newspaper *The Globe and Mail* reported on January 10, 2014, referring to the eurozone debt crisis, that "The north (excluding France) is getting stronger while the Mediterranean frontier (including France) is getting weaker. Better northern productivity and efficiency, and lower costs of capital, are pushing the Mediterranean countries into slow-motion suicides" (Reguly, *The Globe and Mail*). For the Spanish economist César Molinas, the solution for Spain is located in Catalunya. For him, Catalunya needs to be more ambitious. First, it needs to abandon the idea of separating from Spain. Then, it needs to make its businesses more global (like the rest of Spain's major businesses are already doing) in order to compete in Europe. For Molinas, the "blue banana" or the business corridor in Western Europe (or European backbone) that goes from the north of Liverpool to the Po River (making Baden-Wüurttember and Rhône-Alpes the four major economic regions in Europe) should be connected to the Mediterranean corridor of Catalunya.

Further Reading

Encarnación, Omar G. *Spanish Politics*. Cambridge: Polity, 2008.

Chislett, William. *Spain: What Everyone Needs to Know*. Oxford: Oxford University Press, 2013.

Agriculture and Fishing Industry

In 1940 half of Spain's population was rural. By 1975, however, less than a quarter was living in the countryside (*éxodo rural*). From backward and unproductive methods of agriculture Spain moved to a more mechanized and free-market system. In doing so, it avoided the relevant issues of large estates (*latifundios*) and in particular the day-laborers (*jornaleros*), who were employed at low wages and in poor conditions. Nowadays, Spain has a large amount of arable land, occupying second place among countries with the greatest utilized agricultural area in the EU in 2010 (*Spain in Figures 2013*).

Table 4.1   ARABLE LAND IN EU

Country	Arable Land (% of Total)
France	16.2%
Spain	**13.8%**
Germany	9.7%
United Kingdom	9.1%
Poland	8.4%
Romania	7.8%
Italy	7.5%

Globally, Spain led in a broad variety of crops, with vineyards, olive groves, and citrus plantations being particularly noteworthy. Spain is also a major producer of meat, in particular, pork, mutton, and goat meat, within the EU. Also, because of Spain's large appetite for seafood, it accounted for 20.1 percent of all aquaculture in 2010 in the EU.

Table 4.2 shows figures for meat production in the EU in 2010.

Table 4.2   MEAT PRODUCTION IN EU (2010)

Swine	Germany 25%	**Spain** **15.5%**	France 8.9%	Poland 8.1%	Denmark 7.7%	Italy 7%	Other 27.8%
Sheep and Goats	U.K. 36.6%	**Spain** **18%**	Greece 13.3%	France 11.7%	Ireland 6.1%	Italy 4.3%	Other 10.1%

Source: Eurostat 2011.

Paradoxically, because of the economic crisis, agriculture has had the highest increase in employment numbers, a place usually occupied by the construction sector—the part of the economy affected the worst during the crisis. Nowadays, there is a tendency, especially among the youth, to cultivate abandoned areas in order to be self-sufficient, and even to live off grid.

Currently, Spain has several multinationals that deal with agricultural products including Ebro Puleva (#1 producer of rice, and #2 of pasta); Grupo SOS (#1 producer of olive oil); and Viscofán (#1 producer of artificial casings for the meat industry). Spain is also the largest producer of lemons, oranges, and strawberries in Europe. However, due to lack of mechanization, soil exhaustion, and lack of water, Spain's agriculture still lags behind other European countries.

The fish industry in Spain is mainly located in the north, between western Galicia and the Basque country. One dish for which the Basques are renowned is *bacalao* (cod). Galicia is the center of the frozen-fish and canning industry in Spain, with more than 100 factories dedicated to sea products. Many countries around the world can now also enjoy a tin of mussels, squid, or tuna manufactured in Galicia and/or Cantabria. Spain is one of the main seafood consumers in the world. The Food and Agriculture Organization of the United Nations, in their report of "Fish and Fishery Products—Apparent Consumption," found that between 2005–2007 Spain had the highest level of fish production among the European Union countries (over one million fish; FAO 2009). According to a research study from 2010, conducted by the University of British Columbia in collaboration with the National Geographic Society and The Pew Charitable Trusts, Spain was in 11th place for fish consumption in the world (Greenberg, "Time for a Sea Change," 2010). Spain's fishing fleet is the largest in Europe with 415,000 gross tons, and is also a major player in aquaculture.

See also: Chapter 1: Overview; Natural Resources and Environment.

Further Reading

FAO.ORG: Food and Agriculture Organization of the United Nations.

Greenberg, Paul. "Time for a Sea Change." *National Geographic,* October 2010.

Phillips, William D., and Carla Rahn Phillips. *A Concise History of Spain.* Cambridge: Cambridge University Press, 2010.

Ross, Christopher J. *Contemporary Spain: A Handbook.* 2nd ed. London: Arnold, 2002.

Automobile Industry

Car production began in Spain in 1950, when SEAT (*Sociedad Española de Automóviles de Turismo*) was founded. In less than 30 years, the country went from no producers to six coexisting ones: Seat, Fasa-Renault, Citroën, Chrysler (now Peugeot), Ford, and

General Motors (with its subsidiary Opel). Spain became one of the world's largest manufacturers of passenger cars. The unique advantages offered by Spain were low labor costs and proximity to the European market. Also, as Peter Dicken explains, the Spanish automobile market was heavily protected in the 1970s. However, after years of negotiations, Ford changed some of its restrictions (like "cars built in Spain had to have 95 percent local content," Dicken 2015).

The story of the automobile industry in Spain is an example of how the Spanish economy is different, unique, and even an anomaly. On the one hand, Spain no longer produces its own national company cars: Elizalde and Hispano-Suiza have disappeared; Pegaso and Seat were taken over by Iveco and Volkswagen, respectively. On the other hand, Spain is a powerhouse in the automobile manufacturing sector: it is the second largest producer in Europe, behind Germany, and in the top 10 worldwide.

However, as explained by Muñiz Alonso (2011), in the last two years Spain's relative position has fallen with the momentum of China, now the leading manufacturer of automobiles, and South Korea, the fifth largest manufacturer, which have advanced their positions internationally. Second place is held by Japan, followed by the U.S. and Germany. The situation has also changed with the emergence of countries like Brazil and India, whose production is already superior, making Spain now the eighth largest producer of vehicles. Nevertheless, Spain remains Europe's leading producer of industrial vehicles.

Currently, there are 18 production centers in Spain; several of these facilities (e.g., Renault in Valladolid, Ford in Valencia, SEAT in Martorell, and General Motors in Zaragoza) are repeatedly well positioned in productivity comparisons made by independent institutions, such as EIU, World Market Research, or Harbour Report, as well as on studies by specialized consultants. Other plants, such as PSA in Vigo, are the internal reference in their groups in terms of productivity and profitability. The automotive industry has been a driving force of industrial development in Spain in the second half of the last century, both due to its marked ability to involve other industries and its high impact on distribution and on a wide variety of activities within the service sector.

While the majority of vehicles produced in Spain are exported, in the case of components, imports are much more important than exports. Electronic chips, catalytic converters, radiators, aluminum welding furnaces, and machines of pipe fabrication are imported. Most components come from Japan, the Philippines, Africa, and Eastern Europe. In Spain, there are 1,000 component manufacturing companies, of which 300 (that is 85 percent of the sector's turnover) are associated with SERNAUTO (Spanish Association of Equipment Manufacturers and Automotive Components), founded in 1967.

Overall growth in industrial vehicle production was 29.5 percent at the end of 2010 with a total volume of 474,387 units. Thus, Spain continues to occupy first place in the European ranking of industrial vehicle manufacturers.

Basic automotive industry data are provided in Table 4.3 (Muñiz Alonso 2011).

Table 4.3 AUTO INDUSTRY DATA (2007–2010)

Vehicle manufacturing industry	2007	2008	2009	2010
No. of vehicle manufacturers in Spain	11	11	10	10
No. of factories in Spain	18	18	18	18
Total motor vehicle production	2,889,703	2,541,644	2,170,078	2,387,900
Passenger car production	2,195,780	1,943,049	1,812,688	1,913,513
Industrial vehicle production	693,923	598,595	357,390	474,387

Table 4.4 contains information on vehicle production in Spain.

Table 4.4 AUTOMOBILE INDUSTRY PRODUCTIVITY IN SPAIN (2007–2010)

Subsectors	2007	2008	2009	2010
Passenger cars	2,195,780	1,943,049	1,812,688	1,913,513
All-terrain vehicles	112,994	70,812	20,311	37,868
Light commercial vehicles	320,989	301,325	239,751	289,255
Vans	165,601	151,191	71,069	110,119
Industrial vehicles	92,793	73,883	25,707	36,891
Buses and coaches	1,546	1,384	552	254
Total	**2,889,703**	**2,541,644**	**2,170,078**	**2,387,900**

Spanish exports according to type of vehicle are listed in Table 4.5.

Table 4.5 SPANISH VEHICLE EXPORTS BY TYPE

Subsectors	2007	2008	2009	2010
Passenger cars	1,803,955	1,655,154	1,555,149	1,658,341
All-terrain vehicles	98,661	64,515	18,336	34,874
Light commercial vehicles	285,294	276,900	223,425	259,227
Vans	137,074	133,919	65,280	100,221
Industrial vehicles	63,144	49,437	20,418	26,771
Buses & Coaches	1,096	927	567	358
Total	**2,389,224**	**2,180,852**	**1,883,175**	**2,079,782**

See also: Chapter 1: Overview; Transportation. Chapter 2: Overview. Chapter 4: Overview; Labor Market; Manufacturing Industry.

Further Reading

Dicken, Peter. *Global Shift: Mapping the Changing Contours of the World Economy.* 7th ed. New York: The Guilford Press, 2015.

Pavlovic, Tatjana. *The Mobile Nation: España cambia de piel (1954–1964).* Bristol: Intellect, 2011.

Thomas, Hugh. *Eduardo Barreiros and the Recovery of Spain.* New Haven: Yale University Press, 2009.

Banks

The major Spanish banks appeared during the 19th century including Banco de Bilbao (1857), Banco Santander (1857); Banco Hispano Colonial (1876), Banco Hispano Americano (1901), Banco de Vizcaya (1901), and Banco Español de Crédito (1902). Nowadays, BBVA is an amalgamation of the Bilbao, Vizcaya, and Americano banks. Banks are omnipresent in every single town and village of Spain. In fact, some studies suggest that Spain has more banks than are needed in a country with less than 50 million inhabitants. They are open from 9:00 a.m. to 2:00 p.m. every day except Sunday, and during summer they start one hour earlier to close at 1:00 p.m. Apart from the ordinary banks, Spain also has what they call cajas. *Cajas* in Spain operate like banks but while the banks are private, the cajas are regulated by the regional government and invest their profits in social improvements such as courses for seniors or employment workshops.

Global Finance, Moody's, Standard & Poor's, and Fitch regularly prepare a list of the 50 safest banks in the world, in which they include four Spanish banks. According to the World Economic Forum, Spanish banks show greater stability and efficiency than other European banks, including those of Germany, Belgium, France, and the U.K. For instance, Banco Santander has become a major bank worldwide and the largest one in the EU with over 100 million customers and 187,000 employees. The financial magazine *Euromoney* ranked Banco Santander as the Best Bank in the World for several years running. Santander currently offers more branches (14,400) worldwide than any other international bank. Santander shares are the most liquid on the main stock markets, including the Madrid, New York, London, Lisbon, Mexico, São Paulo, Buenos Aires, and Milan stock exchanges. They are listed in 63 different stock exchange indexes.

BBVA is Spain's second largest bank with 53 million customers throughout the world. BBVA is the main financial institution in Mexico, and it has a dominant presence in other Latin American countries. BBVA bought American bank Compass in 2007 for $9.6 billion, becoming a leading franchise in the Sunbelt region (it also acquired Valley Bank, Laredo National Bancshares, Texas Regional Bancshares, and State National Bancshares).

La Caixa is the third largest bank in Spain with over 27,000 employees and 13 million customers. However, since the economic crisis, it has been targeted as one of the main culprits of wrongdoing in recent years, mainly due to the debt that political parties have with the bank. According to *La Marea* (October 2013), Spain's main political parties owe La Caixa the following amount of euros: the Catalan Nationalist Party (CiU: 21,490,000; the socialist PSOE: 17,000,000; the Initiative for Catalunya Green (ICV): 12,059,000; the conservative PP: 2,074,000; and the Republican Left of Catalunya (ERC): 480,000. La Caixa has investments in different sectors of the Spanish industry such as communications (Telefónica owing 5.6%), gas (Repsol, owing 12.2%), and has nearly total control of one of the most popular national health insurance companies in Spain (Adeslas, owing 49.9%). La Caixa is also a major player in the Spanish media industry. For example, it controls 20 percent of the media corporation Prisa. The second vice president of La Caixa, Javier Godó, is also the owner of the Spanish media Grupo Godó, and one of the main executive members of La Caixa, Juan Llopart, owns the Spanish media Grupo Zeta.

Bankia is an example of what Spaniards call a *caja* (see "Financial Crisis"). It received 22.4 billion euros to refinance its balance sheet because of mismanagement. Bankia was bailed out by the government, from money that Spain received from the EU. Most cajas in Spain have been nationalized due to poor management.

See also: Chapter 2: Overview. Chapter 3: Overview; Scandals and Political Corruption. Chapter 4: Overview; Financial Crisis.

Further Reading

International Monetary Fund. *Spain: The Reform of Spanish Savings Banks: Technical Note.* Washington, D.C.: International Monetary Fund, 2012.

Kase, Kimio, and Taguy Jacopin. *CEOs as Leaders and Strategy Designers: Explaining the Success of Spanish Banks.* New York: Palgrave Macmillan, 2008.

World Trade Press. *Spain: Money & Banking.* Petaluma: World Trade Press, 2010.

Construction and Transportation

Spain's construction companies are in the top 10 in the world. For instance, ACS continues leading the world ranking as a construction company that generates more international revenue than any other globally. Overall, Spain's infrastructure has gradually developed, including roads, ports, airports, and railways. For example, from 1990 to 2008 Spain extended its highways so much that it has the most miles of highways in Europe. Also, the port of Algeciras (Cádiz) is the busiest in the Mediterranean Sea with over 4.5 million containers processed in 2014, including the *MSC Oscar*—the largest container ship in the world. Apart from ACS, Spain's other major construction companies include

Ferrovial, Abeinsa (Abengoa), OHL, FCC, Técnicas Reunidas, and Isolux Corsán—all among the 50 biggest construction companies in the world. ("Especial España," July 2015).

Spain designated 201,119 million euros in revenues for construction in 2010, remaining on top of the list of construction in Europe (4th). However, Spain led the classification for the past few years due to the construction boom after 2005. For instance, over 700,000 homes were built annually in Spain in comparison to France (400,000) with a much larger population (Pisani-Ferry 2011).

It is no surprise that fewer licenses for building in Spain were issued between 2008 and 2014. The housing market in Spain continued to decrease after 2008. In fact, Spain's average house price index experienced negative fluctuations until 2015 in every single Spanish region. Although early 2015 has seen an increase in the housing market in Spain, it is happening initially in major cities such as Madrid and Barcelona.

The Spanish national rail network, RENFE (*Red Nacional de los Ferrocarriles Españoles*) was one of the first public industries created by the state in 1941. Initially its main goal was to rebuild the rail network damaged during the civil war. Since then, RENFE has been modernizing its network. In general terms, the rail system in Spain can be divided in two groups: the high speed train or AVE, and the standard train or Talgo. Most trains are categorized according to purpose—business, economy, and tourist—and they are priced depending on their speed. A third group is the commercial railway system, which, most studies conclude, benefited least from public industry investments in the sense that Spain invested in it less than in passenger trains.

Currently, Spain has more high-speed rail lines (speed of 200 km/h or over) in service than any other country in the world except China (23,518 km) with a total of 4,900 kilometers of lines built in 2014. However, the decision to build a high-speed system is controversial for some experts. According to professor Germà Bel, Spain's strategy of building high-speed trains known as AVE (stands for Spanish high speed) does not correspond to the necessity of transport but rather corresponds to political reasoning. It denies the need for other required infrastructure such as commercial trains. Nonetheless,

---

AVE

Spaniards are proud of their high-speed trains, which are always on time (if not, AVE will reimburse the full-price ticket as one of their policies), clean, spacious, and affordable, as well as having aesthetically pleasing train stations. Spain has Europe's longest high-speed network with 3,100 kilometers of track and 310 km/h of maximum speed, making it one of the most recent "jewels" of Spain's current achievements and a political selling point used by both socialists and conservatives in the past two decades. However, the cost of AVE has not been without criticism, especially since the economic crisis and considering that Spain has already invested over 45 billion euros, which is far more money dedicated to infrastructure than the country has spent so far to mitigate its high unemployment rate. Not surprisingly, new political party leaders such as Albert Rivera have a different approach to AVE. Instead of following his predecessors, he is proud to stop any more investments in AVE.

Table 4.6   SPANISH TRANSPORT USE BY TYPE (2012)

City Transport	Thousands
Bus	1,663,095
Metropolitan	1,140,946
Total	2,804,040
Inter-city transport	
Road (coach)	658,203
Rail	569,708
Air (domestic)	33,364
Sea (cabotage)	8,320
Total	1,269,595
International transport	
Air	126,440
Sea	5,549

Source: Spain in Figures 2013.

the rationale has been to link Madrid with the capital of each of the 17 regions in a journey that roughly takes three hours (i.e., Sevilla to Madrid). In doing so, Spanish politicians believe they are uniting Spain in a cohesive system. This way of thinking is unique among the EU countries.

Iberia is Spain's largest airline; it was created during the civil war and became state-controlled by the INI. In 2010 Iberia merged with British Airways, becoming the third largest commercial airline by revenue worldwide. Other major Spanish airline companies include Air Europa, Vueling, and Volotea.

In 2011, Spain had the third most passengers transported by airplane in the EU. Passengers transported by airplane in Spain, according to destination, in 2011: European Union: 62.7%; Domestic: 22.9%; and outside the EU: 14.4%.

With regard to local transport, four Spanish cities have a metro: Madrid, Barcelona, Valencia, and Bilbao. They are open from 6:00 a.m. until midnight or 1:00 a.m. the following day. Also, country-wide busses in Spain are very popular, cheap, and reliable to the point that busses are in direct competitions with the train routes.

Table 4.7   BUS USE IN EU (2012)

Country	Thousands	EU Total (%)
United Kingdom	201,535	24.5
Germany	175,316	21.3
Spain	165,153	20.1
France	131,425	16.0
Italy	116,315	14.2

See also: Chapter 1: Overview; Transportation. Chapter 3: Overview; Scandals and Political Corruption. Chapter 4: Overview; Banks; Financial Crisis; Labor Market; Real Estate Market. Chapter 16: Youth Culture.

Further Reading

European Conference of Ministers of Transport. *National System of Transport Infrastructure Planning.* Paris: European Conference of Ministers of Transport, 2005.

Grafe, Regina. *Distant Tyranny: Markets, Power, and Backwardness in Spain, 1650–1800.* Princeton: Princeton University Press, 2012.

Pisani-Ferry, Jean. *The Euro Crisis and Its Aftermath.* Oxford: Oxford University Press, 2011.

Renner, Michael, and G. Gardner. *Global Competitiveness in the Rail and Transit Industry.* Boston: Northeastern University, 2010.

Economic Activity and GDP

Table 4.8 shows the employment per economic activity in 2010, according to Muñiz Alonso (2011).

Table 4.8 EMPLOYMENT PER TYPE IN SPAIN (2010)

Economic activity	Employment Contracts
Agriculture, farming, and fishing	1,860,080
Extractive Industries	8,982
Manufacturing industries	753,956
Supply of electricity, gas, steam, and air conditioning	4,435
Supply of water, management of residues, sanitation	93,766
Construction	1,462,741
Wholesale business and retail trade, and car repair	1,306,906
Transport and storage	494,295
Hospitality	1,628,216
Information and communication	275,619
Financial activities and insurance	59,163
Real estate activities	31,423
Professional, scientific, and technical activities	476,442
Administrative activities and auxiliary services	3,271,471
Public administration, defense, and social care	498,967
Education	489,745
Health activities and social services	922,198
Artistic, recreational, and entertainment activities	469,133
Other services	280,531

Spain's GDP evolution since the new millennium: 2000 (3.2%); 2001 (3.5%); 2002 (3.1%); 2003 (3.3%); 2004 (3.6%); 2005 (3.4%); 2006 (3.9%); 2007 (3.8%); 2008 (0.9%); 2009 (-3.7%); 2010 (-0.3%); 2011 (0.4%); 2012 (−1.2%); 2013 (0.1%). Spain's GDP in 2012 was distributed as follows among five sectors of the economy: services: 65.5%; industry: 15.5%; construction: 8.4%; net taxes on products: 8.1%; and agriculture and fishing: 2.5%. Spain accounts for 11 percent of euro-area GDP, as well as housing major European banks and companies, and it belongs to the G-20.

According to the dossier *Spain in Figures 2013* (prepared by the Spanish Institute of Statistics: INE), the number of active companies in Spain in 2012 was as shown in Table 4.9.

Table 4.9 ACTIVE COMPANIES IN SPAIN (2012)

Type of Company	Number
Industry	14,992
Construction	462,402
Trade	773,657
Rest of Services	1,748,566
TOTAL	**3,199,617**

See also: Chapter 3: Overview; Political Challenges of Spain's 21st Century; Scandals and Political Corruption. Chapter 4: Overview; Financial Crisis.

Further Reading

Camacho, Máximo, and Rafael Doménech. *MICA-BBVA: A Factor Model of Economic and Financial Indicators for Short-Term GDP Forecasting*. London: Springer Heidelberg, 2012.

Gómez Loscos, Ana, et al. *The Impact of Oil Shocks on the Spanish Economy*. Madrid: FUNCAS, 2010.

Financial Crisis

Many experts concur that Spain suffered an unprecedented crisis that played out on at least three fronts: economic, political, and moral. The economic situation in Spain can be summed up in 2013 with the following data: over six million people were unemployed, or 27.2 percent of the total population (in April 2013), which was the highest in Europe. The average within the EU countries was 11.8 percent, which was less than half of Spain, and only two countries in the EU surpassed the EU average: Portugal (16.3%) and Greece (26%). Spain's foreign debt was 167 percent of the GDP, which is one of the highest debts in the world. One of the main problems is Spain's municipal governments, which do not generate as much as they spend. For example, in 2012, municipal governments grew 1.6 percent while they spent 3.7 percent over their given national budget, which is obviously unsustainable.

According to the World Bank, to open a business in Spain takes an average of 47 days as opposed to 13 days on average in OECD countries. One out of five Spaniards is employed in the sector of information and communications. In 2010 they accounted for nearly 20 percent of the total number of people employed in services. Nearly half of the 5.3 million Spaniards employed in services worked in two areas: accommodations and support services, representing 46.5 percent of the total service industry in Spain. In 2013 alone, nearly ten thousand (9,660) businesses and families declared themselves insolvent, that is, in bankruptcy (A.R. *elplural.com,* February 6, 2014).

The Spanish financial sector is also an anomaly in the sense that Spain has not only banks per se but also what they call *cajas,* which is a social type of bank—they cannot make a profit, so they dedicate all proceeds to social improvements. Every single region in Spain used to have at least one caja. There used to be 45 different cajas spread all over the Iberian Peninsula. The main problem with the cajas is that they are heavily politicized. They are run by people with a political agenda, and some of their workers are hired not necessarily due to their qualifications as much as for their political ties. As a result, it is no surprise that very few cajas managed to survive after the crisis. Also, Spain's public deficit has been 9 percent of the GDP every year since 2009. The cuts that have been strongly advised (if not imposed?) from the EU are not a strong enough remedy. Spain did not apply structural reform in the past and the politicians in charge have not acted accordingly since the economic crisis exploded in 2007. Therefore, Spain sooner rather than later will have to reduce expenses in the whole political administration. However, this needed and urgent reform is a delicate matter that no politician in power is willing to do in Spain, because it implies political hara-kiri.

Spain's political situation is at an impasse. Many Spaniards do not believe anymore in any political institution, including the monarchy and the justice system. One of the major problems is the constitution of 1978, which seems to be obsolete in current times. According to César Molinas, about 300,000 Spaniards, including the king, work under some political umbrella. Apart from a fixed salary, they also enjoy certain privileges that come with the job and are paid out of the taxes collected from the rest of the citizenry. In exchange, Spaniards are not allowed to see, for example, how the Spanish Crown spends their budget in a transparent way like the British monarchy. The new king Felipe VI, however, is already making some changes, including a website where one can view the salaries of all members of the Spanish monarchy.

See also: Chapter 3: Overview; Political Challenges of Spain's 21st Century; Scandals and Political Corruption. Chapter 4: Overview; Banks; Economic Activity and GDP.

Further Reading

International Monetary Fund. *Spain: Financial Sector Reform–Final Progress Report.* Washington, D.C.: International Monetary Fund, 2014.

Schuerkens, Ulrike. *Socioeconomic Outcomes of the Global Financial Crisis: Theoretical Discussion and Empirical Case Studies.* New York: Routledge, 2012.

Vetter, Eric. "Is Spain's External Imbalance Sustainable?: An Empirical Study." St. Gallen: University of St. Gallen [Master/Dissertation], 2009.

Yen-Yun Lin, Carol. *National Intellectual Capital and the Financial Crisis in Greece, Italy, Portugal, and Spain*. New York: Springer, 2013.

IBEX 35: Spain's Stock Exchange

Initiated in 1992, Spain's stock exchange is called IBEX 35. It operates in Madrid, Barcelona, Bilbao, and Valencia. The Spanish listings are classified into the following 6 sectors:

1) Petrol and Power
Subsector: 1.1 Petrol
Subsector: 1.2 Electricity and Gas
Subsector: 1.3 Water and Others
Subsector: 1.4 Renewable Energy

2) Basic Materials, Industry, and Construction
Subsector: 2.1 Minerals, Metals, and Transformation
Subsector: 2.2 Manufacturing and Assembly of Capital Goods
Subsector: 2.3 Construction
Subsector: 2.4 Construction Materials
Subsector: 2.5 Chemical
Subsector: 2.6 Engineering and Others
Subsector: 2.7 Aerospace

3) Consumer Goods
Subsector: 3.1 Food and Beverage
Subsector: 3.2 Textiles, Clothing, and Shoes
Subsector: 3.3 Paper and Graphic Arts
Subsector: 3.5 Pharmacy Products and Biotechnology
Subsector: 3.6 Other Consumer Goods

4) Consumer Services
Subsector: 3.1 Food and Beverage
Subsector: 3.2 Textiles, Clothing, and Shoes
Subsector: 3.3 Paper and Graphic Arts
Subsector: 3.5 Pharmacy Products and Biotechnology
Subsector: 3.6 Other Consumer Goods

5) Financial Services and Real Estate
Subsector: 5.1 Banks
Subsector: 5.2 Insurance
Subsector: 5.3 Portfolio and Holding
Subsector: 5.4 SICAV

Subsector: 5.5 Real Estate and Others
Subsector: 5.6 Investment Services

6) Technology and Telecommunications
Subsector: 6.1 Telecommunications and Others
Subsector: 6.2 Electronics and Software

According to the *IBEX 35 Fact Book of 2011*, the financial situation of the Spanish companies listed reflected the weakening in the Spanish economy and in the entire world. They were unable to consolidate the recovery begun in 2010. However, at the end of September 2011, the 21 percent fall in profits (€26,924 million) for all Spanish companies listed on the main market was influenced by the unexpected results in 2010. That year offered some positive points, such as the fact that sales of industrial and service companies rose 7.5 percent, those of the IBEX 35 companies located abroad accounted again for more than 50 percent of their total turnover, and the profits of medium-sized firms increased by almost 4 percent. Looking at the dossier on *Fixed Income Market in 2012* (published also by IBEX), one aspect is worth noting: The number of transactions made in Spain has exponentially increased since 2012. However, around 60 percent of the transactions carried out had a turnover of €15,000 or less, similar to the previous year, despite the rise in the number of transactions.

On January 1, 2012, the number of active companies stood at 3.2 million, 1.6 percent less than the previous year. This was the fourth consecutive year in which the number of active companies decreased. Also, 82.3 percent of the total companies had two wage earners or fewer. Also, as William Chislett points out, "more than 60 percent of the

Table 4.10a   BUYING AND SELLING

Year	No. of Transactions
2008	807,800
2009	917,321
2010	619,781
2011	648,427
2012	1,288,615

Table 4.10b   TRANSACTIONS BY UNIT VOLUME

No. of Transactions	Unit Volume
€6,000	439,952
€6,000–15,000	321,806
€15,000–30,000	204,931
€30,000–60,000	136,757
€60,000	185,169

revenues of the companies that comprise the Ibex-35, [. . .], are generated abroad" (Chislett 2013). In fact, during the first quarter of 2014 alone, 63.6 percent of IBEX 35's total revenue was generated abroad, which hit a record, especially in comparison with the 23.8 percent of 1997. Some Spanish companies that generate revenues from abroad include Grifols (100%), Técnicas Reunidas (98%), Amadeus (94.6%), Gamesa (89.4%), and Abengoa (86.2%), according to the monthly magazine *Ausbanc* ("Especial España," July 2015).

See also: Chapter 4: Overview; Banks.

Further Reading

Chislett, William. *Spain: What Everyone Needs to Know*. Oxford: Oxford University Press, 2013.

Welfens, Paul J., and Cillian Ryan. *Financial Market Integration and Growth: Structural Change and Economic Dynamics in the European Union*. New York: Springer, 2011.

Labor Market

Since 2007 the rate of households where all members were unemployed has been gradually increasing from 2.5 percent in 2007 to 10.1 percent in 2012, which represents

Spanish citizens line up to enter a government unemployment center in Madrid on May 4, 2009. With 4.13 million people out of work in 2009, Spain's unemployment rate hit 17.9 percent. (AP Photo/Daniel Ochoa de Olza)

23 million of Spain's economically active population. Table 4.11 shows the distribution of employed Spaniards by economic sector in 2012.

Table 4.11   SPANIARDS EMPLOYED BY ECONOMIC SECTOR (2012)

Economic Sector	Spaniards Employed
Agriculture	753,200
Industry	2,430,700
Construction	1,147,600
Services	12,950,400
Total	**17,282.000**

Since 2007, self-employed workers increased to 17.5 percent in 2012 while 82.4 percent were salary earners. Also, in 2012 the unemployment rate was 25.0 percent (24.7% male and 25.4% female). Historically, Andalucía has the highest rate of unemployment in the country, reaching 34.6 percent in 2012 as an annual average. Ramón Tamames, one of the most lucid voices on the economy in Spain, points out that Spain has more workers in the public administration sector (3,220,600) than in private business (2,976,900), which partly explains the problems of the Spanish economy (Tamames 2012). The private sector (or *pyme* as Spaniards call it) refers to the small business person who works on his own and/or has a few employees and is actually the heart of the Spanish economy in the new millennium. For the economist Gay de Liébana, a country that kills its *pymes* is a country that commits suicide (Liébana 2012).

There is an inequality in wage distribution both within Spain and within the European Union. For instance, the most common salary in Spain in 2010 was 16,490 euros per year while the median was 19,017 euros/year, and the mean was 22,790 euros/year. According to Tamames, the minimum salary wage in Spain in 2011 was 641.40 euros monthly, paid in 14 salaries a year, which is only superior to Portugal and behind Greece. According to the Eurostat January 2014, a Spaniard earns 14 percent less than a Frenchman. In fact, in 2012 the average salary per hour in France was 36.35 euros; in Germany it was 34.90; in Italy 26.63; while in Spain it was 22.53 euros.

Table 4.12   EMPLOYMENT SECTORS WITH THE GREATEST AVERAGE ANNUAL EARNINGS (2010)

Sector	Euros/Year
Supply of electrical energy, gas, steam & air conditioning	48,803
Financial & insurance activities	41,639
Information & communications	32,426

Table 4.13 EMPLOYMENT SECTORS WITH THE LEAST AVERAGE ANNUAL EARNINGS (2010)

Sector	Euros/year
Administrative & support services activities	15,682
Accomodation	14,630
Other services	16,545

Table 4.14 shows basic data on the Spanish labor market in 2009–2010, according to Muñiz Alonso (2011).

Table 4.14 LABOR MARKET (in thousands)

Active population	23,104.8
Employed (in thousands)	18,408.2
EPA Unemployed (in thousands)	4,696.6
Activity rate	59.99
Estimated unemployment rate	20.33
Social Security members	17,478,095
S.S. general regime members	13,161,364
Autonomous S.S. members	3,100,479
Contracts per year	14,417,150
Foreign contracts	2,912,526
Registered unemployment	4,100,073

Table 4.15 shows data on employment from 2006–2012, according to Martín-Aceña (2013).

Table 4.15 EMPLOYMENT DATA (2006–2012)

2006	2007	2008	2009	2010	2011	2012
3.5	3.0	−0.2%	−6.5%	−2.6%	−2.0	−4.3%

Data of unemployment from 2006–2012, according to Martín-Aceña (2013), are provided in Table 4.16.

Table 4.16 UNEMPLOYMENT IN SPAIN (2006–2012)

2006	2007	2008	2009	2010	2011	2012
8.5%	8.3%	11.3%	18.0%	20.1%	21.6%	25.0%

See also: Chapter 3: Overview. Chapter 4: Overview; Agriculture and Fishing Industry; Automobile Industry; Construction and Transportation; Tourism; Trade.

Further Reading

Bloosfeld, Hans-Peter. *Youth-Workers, Globalization and the Labor Market: Comparing Early Working Life in Eleven Countries.* Northampton: Edward Elgar, 2008.

International Labour Office. *Spain: Quality Jobs for a New Economy.* Geneva: International Institute for Labour Studies, 2011.

Manufacturing Industry

According to the Eurostat, Spain's productivity is 0.91 per kilogram, which is below the European average (1.31). The manufacturing industry revenue, by branch of activity in 2011 was as shown in Table 4.17.

The activities that usually generate the most revenues in Spain are food (18.3%), the automobile industry (11.4%), and the petroleum industry (10.5%). Large companies also tend to create more activity (with a greater percentage of invoicing) and petroleum is traditionally the most dynamic one while the manufacturing of electronics continues to be the least dynamic.

Table 4.17   MANUFACTURING INDUSTRY REVENUE (as percent of total)

Food	18.3
Motor vehicles	11.4
Petroleum industry	10.5
Chemical industry	8.2
Manufacture of metallic products	6.9
Metallurgy	6.9
Electrical, electronic, optical material & equipment	4.4
Paper and graphic arts	4.3
Rubber and plastic products	4.1
Various nonmetallic ore products	4.1
Mechanical machinery and equipment	3.8
Beverages and tobacco	3.6
Textiles, clothing, leather, and footwear industry	3.2
Pharmaceutical industry	3.1
Transport material, excluding motor vehicles	2.4
Various manufacturing industries	2.0
Repair and installation of machinery and equipment	1.4
Wood and cork	1.3

By regions, in 2011 Catalunya led the list for generating revenue. Out of the total revenue of Spain, Catalunya generated 23.6 percent, followed by Andalucía (11.8%), and Comunitat Valenciana plus País Vasco (both with 10.3%). One-third of industrial sales travelled abroad in 2011. The automobile industry had the highest percentage with 62.5 percent in 2011. Also, by size of company, Spain's sales abroad in 2011 by percentage were as shown in Table 4.18.

Table 4.18   SPAIN'S SALES ABROAD (2011)

Size of Company	%
Large	38.9
Medium	33.9
Small	15.7
Total	**32.2**

See also: Chapter 4: Overview; Agriculture and Fishing Industry; Automobile Industry; Banks; Construction and Transportation; Tourism; Trade.

Further Reading

Puig, Francisco, and Helena Marques. *Territory, Specialization and Globalization in European Manufacturing.* London: Routledge, 2011.

Production of Energy

The energy sector in Spain constitutes another interesting anomaly. Although Spain has multinational energy companies like Iberdrola, which is the largest wind farm operator in the world (i.e., it bought Scottish Power in the UK), Spaniards still pay the highest electricity bills in Europe. Acciona, Endesa, Enel, Gas Natural, Red Eléctrica Española, HC Energía, Petronor, and Repsol are the most powerful energy companies in Spain and have a significant presence worldwide. One of the main controversies of these powerful companies in recent years is the fact that they also act as a shelter for previous politicians. This conflict of interests partly explains the reasons why reform in the energy sector has not yet occurred. As a consequence, Spaniards pay a higher electrical bill in comparison with most EU countries while their energy companies earn benefits annually. For instance, in 2007 most of Spain consumed energy (79.5%) that was supplied from abroad. Between 1990 and 2007 energy dependence in the European Union increased from 44.5 percent to 53.1 percent while in Spain alone it rose from 64.3 percent to 79.8 percent. During that period the consumption of energy per EU citizen rose 7.7 percent while the consumption of energy per Spaniard increased 42.3 percent. Major Spanish electrical companies do not compete with each other. On the contrary, they all provide similar billing systems that show that they all protect each other, and do not act separately.

According to INE (National Institute of Statistics), the graph of domestic primary energy consumption and production in 2011 was as follows:

Table 4.19 shows primary energy consumption (in kilo tons of oil equivalent) of 2011.

Table 4.19   SPAIN'S ENERGY CONSUMPTION (2011)

Energy Source	Kilo Tons
Oil (petroleum)	58,317
Natural gas	28,930
Nuclear	15,024
Coal	12,456
Biomass, biofuels, and waste	7,280
Wind, solar, and geothermal	5,226
Hydraulic	2,631
Energy balance (imports-exports)	−524
Total	**129,339**

Table 4.20 shows domestic primary energy production of 2011.

Table 4.20   DOMESTIC PRIMARY ENERGY PRODUCTION (2011)

Energy Source	Percentage
Nuclear	48.6%
Biomass, biofuels, and waste	18.2%
Wind, solar, and geothermal	16.9%
Hydraulic	8.5%
Coal	7.4%
Oil and natural gas	0.5%

Electricity is the main energy consumed in industry. One-fifth of the nation's industrial energy consumption takes place in Catalunya. The main energy products used in industry in 2011 were electricity (51.7%) and gas (28.3%). The two regions that spent the most on energy consumption were Catalunya (19.8%) and Comunitat Valenciana (11.3%). Conversely, Illes Balears (0.3%) and La Rioja (0.8%) carried the least weight out of the total.

The monthly independent newspaper *La Marea* elaborated on a study of the carbon sector in Spain published in November 2013. Two main conclusions can be drawn about the carbon industry: In 1990 the mining industry in Spain generated 45,000 jobs spread out over 200 companies; in 2013 the same sector hardly generated 4,900 jobs via 14 mining companies. Indeed, the carbon sector can be seen as another example of an anomaly in the Spanish economy. While Spain has an abundance of carbon, to produce national carbon in Spain is more expensive than buying it from other countries. Nevertheless, the deficit in the process of extracting carbon also occurs in other countries such as the U.S. In 2012, Spain produced 6.5 million tons of carbon while 22.4 million tons of carbon were bought from other countries such as Columbia (6.2), Indonesia (5.6), Russia (3.2), and South Africa (2.8), among others.

The nuclear energy production in Spain is pretty low in comparison to other major countries. By 2013, Spain had eight nuclear central stations as opposed to 100 in the U.S.; 58 in France; 50 in Japan; 19 in Canada; and 16 in the U.K.

According to reports written by Spain's largest oil company, Repsol, an average Spanish household consumes the following types of energy: electricity (100% of Spain's houses have electricity available); bottle gas (42.1%); gas heating installed (40.5%); liquid fuels (12.5%); others (7.3%); wood (6.7%); and solar panels (0.9%). Solar energy is mainly concentrated in the south of Spain. In fact, 0.3 percent of the total number of solar panels in the country are located in Andalusian homes. Overall, Spain ranks fifth among the world's countries in renewable energy patents. Spain is a country with great potential for exploiting renewable resources, thanks to its privileged climate and location. Following Repsol's studies, the consumption of water in Spain used in 2010 was as follows: 71.1 percent for homes, 19.9 percent for agricultural use, and 9.0 percent for municipal consumption. Spain's water comes from three sources: 67.5 percent surface water (rivers, lakes, reservoirs), 29.2 percent from groundwater, and 3.3 percent from desalinated seawater. The highest users by regions were Cantabria (173 liters), Castilla La Mancha (167 liters), and Extremadura (160 liters), while the lowest users are La Rioja (122 liters) and Balearic Islands (121 liters).

More recently, for the first time in Spain's energy history, wind power contributed most to the annual electricity demand coverage in 2013. According to the British newspaper *The Guardian*, "wind turbines met 21.1 percent of electricity demands on the Spanish peninsula, narrowly beating the region's fleet of nuclear reactors, which provided 21 percent of power" (Murray 2014).

WIND POWER

Apart from Iberdrola being the number one wind energy company worldwide, present in over 20 countries, Spain's involvement in the sector of generating electricity using renewable energy also includes other companies such as EDP Renováveis, Enercon, Electria Wind, Enel Green Power, Enerfín, Gamesa, GasNatural fenosa, and GE Wind, among others. This proliferation of new gigantic windmills in the Spanish scenery is, however, having ecological effects, including aesthetic concerns. In fact, there are already some places in Spain—particularly pronounced on the coasts—where the abundance of these gigantic windmills have become an unpleasant sight as opposed to the iconic image of Spain's Don Quixote fighting the windmills. A similar situation occurs when large areas of fertile land are being covered by massive solar panels.

See also: Chapter 1: Natural Resources and Environment. Chapter 4: Overview; Construction and Transportation; Economic Activity and GDP; IBEX 35.

Further Reading

Jordan, Phillip G. *Solar Energy Markets: An Analysis of the Global Solar Industry*. Amsterdam: Elsevier, 2014.

McMahon, Gary, and Felix Remy. *Large Mines and the Community: Socioeconomic and Environmental Effects in Latin America, Canada, and Spain*. Ottawa: International Development Research Centre, 2009.

Real Estate Market

During the mid-19th century, many Spanish cities experienced a rapid development in the urban landscape. For example, in 1860 Barcelona and Madrid approved the plans for enlargements (*planes de ensanche*), a trend that many other cities followed. The growth of the cities was accompanied by the creation of peripheral districts (*arrabal* or *extrarradio*). In doing so, many cities were extended. For instance, Barcelona expanded the bourgeois area of Sarriá and Pedralbes as well as the zones of Sants and Badalona. Similarly, Madrid absorbed Fuencarral, Hortaleza, and Vallecas. Also, in the 1960s (tourist boom), and during the so called "happy eighties" (after the Spanish transition), the major private real estate companies began to build residences all over the Spanish territory.

For *The Economist*, in 2010 Spain had the most overrated housing market in the world, being +55.1 percent overvalued (*The Economist,* December 30, 2009). To give a brief idea of the magnitude of the real estate market, the following are just a few facts taken from José Manuel Roca's book, *La oxidada transición* (2013): until 2006, there were in Spain about 5,000 real estate companies. In five years, between 2007 and 2012, 3,600 of them applied for suspension of payments. According to Greenpeace, in a period of 18 years, between 1987 and 2005, Spain developed 7.7 hectares every day on the Mediterranean coast. The speculation for construction between the years 2000 and 2006 destroyed 6,500 square meters of forest every hour in Spain, which was converted into condominiums, centers for leisure, massive malls, empty airports, parking spaces, and toll highways that few citizens use.

Economics professor Germà Bel has written extensively on why Spain built so many unnecessary infrastructures. In his recent book, *España, capital París* (2013), he offers an economic answer to a political problem. Essentially, Spain's high-speed system AVE is considered in Spain a symbol of modernity regardless of its cost. Japan was the first country to install high-speed trains (1964). Spain started the high-speed trains in 1992, and in 2000 former President José María Aznar decided to link Madrid through the AVE with every single city in Spain. However, previous studies suggested that Spain did not have enough passengers to self-finance such a major project. In fact, the number of passengers using AVE is still much less than in other countries such as Japan. Nevertheless, Spain is still building high-speed train tracks that are heavily subsidized by European

Union funds, despite the fact that some routes are already generating debts. This debt has been considered illegal by the EU, and it reached 248 million euros in 2007.

The Spanish bank BBVA conducted a survey on the Spanish economy based on the years 1998 and 2007. According to the survey, construction contributed 20 percent of the total growth in Spain, 23 percent of the total employment, and 50 percent of the investment. However, when the housing market crashed, it left 75,000 million euros in what is called a "toxic" state and a total debt of nearly half a billion euros in the construction sector alone.

See also: Chapter 1: Overview; Population and Demography; Chapter 3: Overview; Electoral Scheme and the "No Molestar" System; Chapter 4: Overview; Construction and Transportation; Financial Crisis; Tourism.

Further Reading

Arestis, Phillip. *Housing Market Challenges in Europe and the United States: Any Solutions Available?* Basingstoke: Palgrave Macmillan, 2009.

Gup, Benton E. *The Financial and Economic Crises: An International Perspective*. Cheltenham: Edward Elgar, 2010.

Smith, Susan, and Beverley A. Searle. *The Blackwell Companion to the Economics of Housing: The Housing Wealth of Nations*. Chichester: Blackwell, 2010.

Tourism

Before the tourist boom of the 1960s, Spain's top tourist destinations were Madrid (including nearby areas such as El Escorial), Sevilla, Córdoba, and some beaches like San Sebastián, Costa Brava, and Mallorca. 1992 was also a significant year for tourism in Spain, since the country hosted three major international events: the Olympics in Barcelona, the Universal Exposition in Sevilla, and the European Capital of Culture in Madrid. The three events generated a good amount of international attention and mass tourism.

Since the 1960s, tourism has become one of the major pillars of the Spanish economy. Every year Spain beats a new record of tourists. For example, in 2014 over 65 million tourists visited Spain. Spain is regularly one of the top three most-visited countries

Table 4.21   TOURIST ACCOMMODATIONS (2012)

Accommodation	Overnight Stays (millions)	Average Stay (days)
Hotel establishments	281.3	3.38
Holiday dwellings	63.1	7.13
Tourist campsites	31.3	5.30
Rural tourism accommodation	7.5	2.82

Benidorm Beach in Spain. Tourism is a huge pillar in the Spanish economy. Since the 1960s, Benidorm has been a popular tourist destination. (Bernardo Varela/Dreamstime.com)

in the world. According to the World Economic Forum, Spain ranks first in quality of tourism infrastructure.

In 2012 Spain received 57.7 million tourists, which was an increase of 2.7 percent over the previous year. International tourists spent over 55,594 million euros, making Spain the second most-visited country worldwide, and first in Europe. In fact, Spain became the number one destination in the world in 2014 with over 65 million visitors. Many Europeans spend the summer in Spain. According to the 2015 YouGov survey, out of 7,562 Europeans older than 18 years and including seven countries, the percentage who chose Spain for their next holiday is the following: French: 28%; British: 25%; Italians: 18%; Germans: 17%; Swedish: 16%; and Dutch: 15%. Tourism provides a significant number of jobs in Spain. For example, in 2011 it represented 12.2 percent of employment, and 10.8 percent of Spain's GDP.

Distribution of overnight stays in holiday dwellings in 2012 was as follows: Canarias: 47.3%; Illes Balears: 15.2%; Comunitat Valenciana: 11.9%; Andalucía: 10.0%; Catalunya: 9.6%; and rest of regions: 6.1%. Spain ranked number one in 2011 for overnight stays of nonresidents in tourist accommodation with 239.4 million (second, Italy: 176.5; third, France: 123.0).

Table 4.22 shows the main tourist areas in 2011 in millions of overnight stays.

See also: Chapter 1: Population and Demography. Chapter 3: Overview. Chapter 4: Overview; Economic Activity and GDP.

Table 4.22   MOST POPULAR TOURIST STAYS (2011)

Hotel Establishments	Millions	Holiday Dwellings	Millions
Island of Mallorca	42.5	Island of Gran Canaria	10.1
Island of Tenerife	22.6	Island of Tenerife	9.2
Palma-Calvià	17.3	Island of Lanzarote	7.2
Barcelona	16.9	Island of Mallorca	6.0
Costa del Sol	15.3	Costa Blanca	4.9

Further Reading

Afinoguénova, Eugenia, and Jaume Martí-Olivella. *Spain Is (Still) Different: Tourism and Discourse in Spanish Identity*. Lanham: Lexington Books, 2008.

Pack, Sasha D. *Tourism and Dictatorship: Europe's Peaceful Invasion of Franco's Spain*. New York: Palgrave Macmillan, 2006.

Rosendorf, Neal M. *Franco Sells Spain to America: Hollywood, Tourism, and Public Relations as Postwar Spanish Soft Power*. New York: Palgrave Macmillan, 2014.

Trade: Private, Public, and E-Commerce

Spain's revenues of trade companies generated 654,533 million euros in 2011. Although most of the employment in trade corresponds to retail trade (55.2%), wholesale trade reaped the most benefits (56.8%). Interestingly, in 2012 sales outside the EU increased 13.7 percent, with 62.8 percent of Spain's foreign trade of 2012 going to the EU while 37.2 percent went outside the EU. Also, four Spanish companies were created for every company that was dissolved in 2012. In fact, there were 87,066 new companies registered in 2012, which was an increase of 2.7 percent over the previous year.

Spain still has a significant trade imbalance. The usual trade partners of Spain are France, Germany, Italy, and the United Kingdom. Among Spain's main exports are machinery (i.e., multinational Gamesa is the number four worldwide manufacturer of wind turbines), cars, fruit, wine, and pharmaceuticals (i.e. multinational Grifols is the number three manufacturer worldwide of blood plasma-based products).

According to the dossier *Spain in Figures 2013*, internal expenditure on Research and Development (R&D) in 2011 reached over 14,000 million euros, 2.8 percent less than in 2010. In relative terms, this expenditure represented 1.33 percent of GDP. The Basque country made the greatest effort in these activities, with 2.10 percent of regional GDP. The study further found that 31.1 percent of Spanish companies with 10 or more wage earners were innovative during the 2009–2011 period.

E-commerce is gradually increasing its presence in Spain. For example, in 2011, 22.5 percent of Spanish companies purchased through e-commerce while 14.2 percent did sales via e-commerce. Such online sales and purchases generated 13.7 percent and 19.1 percent, respectively, of total sales.

Furthermore, during the first half of 2013, 2,822 million euros were made via e-commerce in Spain, which represented an increase of 15 percent over the previous year (Frías, *Cinco días* 2014). E-commerce in Spain is synonymous with tourism. The Spanish equivalent of Ebay or Google or Amazon can be seen in platforms such as eDreams, Amadeus, Rumbo, Centraldereservas, Toprural, or Trabber.

Spanish exports have been the main pillar of the economic recovery. However, the figures from the National Accounts for 2013 Q3 show that there has been a substantial deceleration: Exports are still growing but at a slower rate. Specifically, in the first half of 2013, the year-on-year change in goods exported was 8.0 percent in nominal terms, while in Q3 growth it was only 4.4 percent.

See also: Chapter 4: Overview; Agriculture and Fishing Industry; Automobile Industry; Banks; Construction and Transportation; Economic Activity and GDP; Financial Crisis; Tourism.

Further Reading

Lagassé, Paul, ed. *The Columbia Encyclopedia*. 6th ed. New York City: Columbia University Press, 2012.

Sáez, Sebastián. *Let Workers Move: Using Bilateral Labor Agreements to Increase Trade in Services*. Washington, D.C.: World Bank, 2013.

REFERENCES

Álvarez Añibarro, Nuria. "Boletín: Sector financiero: balance de los resultados 2013." *Renta4,* February 10, 2014.

Andreu, Jerónimo. "The Shocking Price of Spanish Electricity." *El País,* January 1, 2014.

Bel, Germà. *España, capital París*. Barcelona: Booket, 2013.

Burridge, Tom. "Spain Ends Two Year Recession According to Central Bank." *BBC News,* October 30, 2013.

Chislett, William. *Spain: What Everyone Needs to Know*. Oxford: Oxford University Press, 2013.

Cocke, Rupert. "Spain's Banks Come Full Circle." *Forbes,* December 11, 2013.

Corral Cortés, Esther. *Spain Today 2013*. Madrid: Ministry of the Presidency, 2013.

"Economic Survey of Spain 2012." *OECD Statistics*. OECD Economic Surveys.

Encarnación, Omar G. *Spanish Politics*. Cambridge: Polity, 2008.

"Especial España" *Ausbanc*, July 2015.

Frías, Óscar. "El turismo, motor del comercio electrónico." *Cinco Días,* January 21, 2014.

Gay de Liébana, José. *España se escribe con E de Endeudamiento. Radiografía de un país abocado al abismo*. Barcelona: Ediciones Deusto, 2012.

Gómez, José Luis. *Cómo salir de esta. España toca fondo. ¿Llega la reactivación?* A Coruña: Actualia Editorial, 2013.

IBEX 35 Fact Book of 2011. Madrid: BMEX, 2011. http://www.ibex35.es/ing/Estadisticas /InformesMercado.aspx

Kulish, Nicholas, and Raphael Minder. "Spain Holds a Trump Card in Bank Bailout Negotiations." *The New York Times,* June 6, 2012. http://www.nytimes.com/2012/06/07/world/europe/spain-holds-a-trump-card-in-bank-bailout-talks.html?_r=2&

La Marea. October 2013.

La Marea. November 2013.

Llopis, Enrique y Jordi Maluquer de Motes, eds. *España en crisis. Las grandes depresiones económicas, 1348–2012.* Barcelona: Pasado y Presente, 2013.

Mars, Amanda. "La crisis borra del mapa 80.000 hogares en España en un año." *El País,* November 3, 2013.

Martín-Aceña, Pablo, Elena Martínez-Ruiz, M.ª, and Ángeles Pons, eds. *Las crisis financieras en la España contemporánea, 1850–2012.* Barcelona: Crítica, 2013.

Molinas, César. *Qué hacer con España. Del capitalismo castizo a la refundación de un país.* Barcelona: Destino, 2013.

Molinas, César. "Lo que no se quiere oír sobre Cataluña." *El País,* January 18, 2014.

Muñiz Alonso, Federico. *Prospective Study: The Automotive Sector in Spain.* Madrid: Public Employment Service, 2011. http://www.sepe.es

Muñoz Machado, Santiago. *Informe sobre España. Repensar el Estado o destruirlo.* Barcelona: Crítica, 2012.

Murray, James. "Wind Power was Spain's Top Source of Electricity in 2013." *The Guardian,* January 6, 2014.

Reguly, Eric. "Euro-zone Debt Crisis Is Over but Serious Issues Persist." *The Globe and Mail,* January 10, 2014.

Roca, José Manuel. *La oxidada transición.* Madrid: La linterna sorda, 2013.

Serra, Eduardo. *Transforma España.* Everis, November 16, 2010. Web. January 23, 2014. http://www.trans formaespana.es/

Serra, Eduard, in collaboration with Marc Alba and David García. *Las claves para transformar España.* Barcelona: Destino, 2012.

Tamames, Ramón. *España, un proyecto de país.* Madrid: Ediciones Turpial, 2012.

Websites

Abengoa. abengoa.com

Acciona. acciona.com

ACS. grupoacs.com

Adecco. adecco.com

A.R. "Nuevo récord de concursos de acreedores tras subir un 6,5% en 2013." *elplural.com* February 6, 2014.

Banco Santander. Bancosantander.es

Bank of Spain. bde.es/bde/en

BBC News. http://www.bbc.com/news/business-25226669

BBVA: Banco Bilbao Vizcaya Argentaria. bbva.com

Center for Global Development. cgdev.org

CIMA: Chartered Institute of Management Accountants. cimaglobal.com

EAPS: Economically Active Population Survey. http://www.ine.es/en/inebaseDYN/epa30308/epa_inicio_en.htm

Euromoney. euromoney.com

Eurostat. http://epp.eurostat.ec.europa.eu

Ferrovial. ferrovial.com

FCC Construcción. fcc.es

Fitch. fitchratings.com

Funcas. http://www.funcas.ceca.es/Indicadores/Indicadores.aspx?Id=1

Global Finance. gfmag.com

Greenpeace. greenpeace.org/canada

IBEX35. ibex35.com

IMF: International Monetary Fund. imf.org

Inditex. inditex.com

INE: Instituto Nacional de Estadística. ine.es

ISO: International Organization for Standardization. iso.org

La Caixa. lacaixa.es

Moody's. moodys.com

Obrascon-Huarte-Lain. ohl.es

OECD: The Organization for Economic Co-operation and Development. oecd.org

Repsol. Repsol.com

Sacyr Vallermoso. sacyr.com

Spain in Figures 2013. Instituto Nacional de Estadística (INE). ine.es

Standard & Poor's. standardandpoors.com

Telefónica. telefonica.com

The Economist. http://www.economist.com/node/15179388

The New York Times. http://www.nytimes.com/interactive/business/global/european-debt-crisis-tracker.html?ref=europe

Trading Economics. http://www.tradingeconomics.com/spain/gdp-growth

Transforma España. transformaespana.es

Transparency International. transparency.org/country

World Bank. worldbank.org

World Economic Forum. weforum.org

World Heritage Foundation. worldheritageproject.com

CHAPTER 5

RELIGION AND THOUGHT

OVERVIEW

The Romans not only left behind a territorial administration on the Iberian Peninsula, they also introduced Hispania to language, religion, and law, as well as important institutions such as the family and municipalities. The first Christian states emerged in Spain in the late fourth century. The integration between the Visigoths and the Hispanic-Romans was marked by the conversion of King Reccared (559–601) to Catholicism, announced at the Third Council of Toledo (589), a city that later became a flourishing cultural center of Jewish learning in Europe. In fact, during the centuries of Reconquista, Jews reemerged as a cultural bridge between Christian and Muslim cultures. Hence, an "'osmosis of manners' was pervasive in all spheres of life, most notably in agricultural techniques and technology, as well as in language and literature" (Gerber 1994).

The impact of Islam on the Iberian Peninsula was huge; Muslims ruled various parts of the peninsula for over 700 years. Today their influence is still visible everywhere, including in architecture, cuisine, agriculture, and language. During Muslim rule, trade, culture, and technological advances flourished while the majority of Europe was fully entrenched in the Middle Ages. In the capital city of Córdoba, the emir's library housed 400,000 books on topics such as higher mathematics, medical advances, and new approaches to philosophy. For centuries, Spain reached an unprecedented level of religious tolerance and peace between Arabs, Jews, and Christians living on the Iberian Peninsula that future generations would find difficult to parallel or surpass.

The merger of the Crowns of Castilla and Aragón with the marriage of the Catholic Monarchs in 1469 had dire consequences for the inhabitants of the Iberian Peninsula. This union was immediately followed by the conquest of the Nasrid Kingdom of Granada in 1492, which marked the expulsion of the Jews and a decline of the Arabic religion practiced in Spain. It subsequently signified that Spaniards were only allowed to practice Catholicism as the one "true religion" or they were forced to leave the kingdom. Cardinal Francisco Jiménez de Cisneros, named Grand Inquisitor by King Ferdinand, began his unrelenting campaign of conversion of the Muslims in 1499. He burned Arabic religious books in public. Muslims were forced to either be baptized or go into exile by a royal decree in 1502. Most Muslims remained in the Iberian Peninsula, becoming known as *moriscos*, or converted Moors. Spain thus became officially a Catholic country, "and gained a reputation for intolerance and cruelty that was to stick with it for many centuries. This gave rise to the *leyenda negra* or Black Legend" (Chislett 2013).

Since the Catholic Monarchs, most Spanish authorities and Constitutions have promulgated laws which include the Catholic religion as part of Spain's political structure. This is the case with the Constitution of 1812, which began with an invocation to "Almighty God, Father, Son, and Holy Spirit." Also, the Constitution of 1869 "recognized the state's obligation to support the Catholic Church without establishing Catholicism as the state religion."

Miguel Primo de Rivera's dictatorship (from 1923 to 1930, which qualified as "moderate despotism") had more in common with a traditional, monarchist, and Catholic philosophy than with the Italian Mussolini's New State (which ruled Italy from 1922 to 1943). Spain became a republic on April 14, 1931, and, after calling for a general election on June 28, the republicans declared freedom of religion in Spain as well as drafting a new Spanish Constitution that passed on December 9. However, one of the major problems of the Constitution of 1931 was precisely its hostility toward Catholicism. As a result, the eruption of liberalism and republicanism (which dated back to the beginning of the 19th century, due to the influence of the French Revolution's anti-monarchal stance) led to the Spanish Civil War in 1936. Religious issues were part of the problem, thus triggering another schism throughout the country.

The two sides of the Spanish Civil War can be divided in general terms into two major groups depending on their beliefs. Most republicans professed to be non-believers while the nationalists tended to be associated with Catholicism. In fact, the Catholic Church openly supported the nationalist party, which constitutes another dark chapter in contemporary Spain's history comparable to the expulsion of the Jews (1492) and the Moors (1502) by the Catholic Monarchs.

If Spanish historiography shows Christianity as a historic pillar of Spain's national identity since the beginning of the country, then varying degrees of intolerance toward other religions has also been a part of Spain's history since the Catholic Monarchs unified the kingdoms in the late 15th century. In other words, religion has been a persistent issue in Spain for centuries (and remains so today), mainly because the leaders—including monarchs and politicians—profusely endorsed one particular faith (usually Catholicism) while simultaneously blatantly disregarding other religious practices.

However, in the last 40 years, since Spain became a democratic country in 1975, religious diversity has been gradually increasing. Having said that, Spain's increased tolerance of pluralism does not mean that religion or religious issues are no longer a source of social or political conflict. Although the Constitution of 1978 explicitly declared that Spain has no official religion (article 16), tensions have sporadically erupted between the Catholic Church and the Spanish government. For instance, this was the case in 2005, when the socialist government of José Luis Rodríguez Zapatero introduced the subject of citizenship instead of religion in the Spanish public school system as a compulsory course. Incidentally, the current conservative government of Mariano Rajoy in 2015 abolished the subject of citizenship and replaced it with religion, making it again compulsory in the program of any public school in Spain.

Religion without a doubt has created numerous debates and tensions throughout the history of Spain. The effective achievement of equal opportunities among citizens regardless of gender, age, ideology, religion, disability, ethnic origin, and sexual orientation was recognized under article 14 of Spain's Constitution of 1978. Since the beginning of the 21st century, religious beliefs have become more complex than a mere religious identity of "Catholic" or "non-Catholic." Nowadays Spaniards are similar to other EU citizens in that they are more comfortable tolerating aspects of the Catholic faith while openly denouncing others. This global religious complexity suggests that religion in Spain does not constitute a Spanish singularity like it did in past centuries.

Apart from Malta, Spain has remained the last Catholic bastion in a highly secularized Europe. However, the current secularization process experienced in Europe has also made its way to Spain (as well as to Ireland, Greece, and France).

The notion of irreligion is relatively new in Spain. The republican Francesc Sunyer i Capdevila (1826–1898), who was a physician and a politician, can be considered one of the pioneers who openly defended atheism in 1869. His epitaph says: "He fought against God, against the Kings, and against tuberculosis." Also, anarchist publications such as *La solidaridad* in 1870 showed a degree of atheism and anti-clericalism in the late 19th century. During the 20th century additional organizations were created such as the association UAL (*Unión de Ateos y Librepensadores*, Union of Atheists and Free-Thinkers), which is the most visible organization, and is located in Barcelona. It promotes atheism nationwide (ateos.org).

One recent case of irreligion in Spain was an incident in Mérida in 2012, where several students carrying flags of the Second Spanish Republic threatened to burn priests alive. Like these students, some Spaniards disagreed with the Spanish model of teaching religion in state schools because this type of schooling is exclusionary against students with non-Catholic beliefs. More importantly, the Spanish Constitution of 1978 does not affirm that most Spaniards are Catholics or that the nation should include teaching Catholicism in the curriculum of the state school system. In fact, it clearly states (article 16c) that "There shall be no state religion. The public authorities shall take the religious beliefs of Spanish society into account and shall in consequence maintain appropriate relationships of cooperation with the Catholic Church and the other religious denominations."

Pope John Paul II (1978–2005) viewed Spain as a bastion of Catholicism to be defended against growing permissiveness and secularism. In 2014, nearly 69 percent of Spaniards self-identified as Catholics, 2 percent described themselves as being of another faith, over 16 percent claimed no religion, and nearly 10 percent were atheists.

Table 5.1   RELIGIOUS IDENTIFICATION IN SPAIN (2014)

Religion	Men	Women	18–24 age	25–34	35–44	45–54	55–64	>65	Total
Catholic	61.3	75.9	49.5	55.0	61.1	71.6	76.3	87.0	68.8
Other religion	1.9	2.0	2.9	2.2	3.3	2.0	0.9	0.7	1.9
No religion	20.5	12.6	23.6	25.7	18.7	15.2	14.2	6.9	16.4
Atheist	13.1	6.5	18.3	14.7	13.0	8.4	5.6	3.2	9.7

Despite the fact that most Spaniards consider themselves Catholics, however, very few participate in a mass regularly. For example, only 16 percent of Spaniards attend church every Sunday, and only 9 percent go to mass monthly. Only 15 percent of Spaniards attend mass frequently throughout the year as opposed to 5–6 percent that go to mass a few times a year. More interestingly, according to the Eurobarometer of 2008, only 3 percent of Spaniards consider religion as a key fundamental value, which is even lower than the 7 percent European average. Furthermore, 59 percent of Spaniards responded that they believe there is a God; 21 percent answered that they believe there is some sort of spirit or life force, and 19 percent answered that they do not believe there is any sort of spirit, God, or life force.

As the sociologist Xavier Costa explains, the tendency toward secularization has existed in Spain since the 1960s, and it is gradually increasing (Costa 2008). Although Catholicism is still very visible in everyday Spanish life, Spaniards are changing their attitudes toward religiosity mainly due to two fundamental factors: the arrival of many northern Europeans since the 1960s, and the impact of new policies implemented by the socialist government. Having said that, the Catholic Church is still very powerful in Spain, owning many cultural heritage buildings, including the Mosque of Córdoba and several universities nationwide (i.e., Comillas, Deusto, Esade) as well as abroad (i.e., Georgetown University).

The 1980 Law of Religious Freedom established that religious organizations in Spain needed to register in order to be recognized and enjoy certain privileges. Also, in 1992, Protestantism, Judaism, and Islam were recognized as deeply rooted faiths. However, those three religious communities still do not receive the same preferential treatment as Catholicism in Spain. For instance, non-Catholic religious groups do not receive as much funding for educational and tax purposes as do Catholics, despite the fact that Spain's constitution separates Church and State. To date, Spaniards do not have the option of donating to charities, which then counts as a tax break, like, for instance, Canadians do.

Like other multicultural countries such as Canada or Australia, history shows that religion has played a huge role in the lives of Spaniards. Like many western nations, Spain is also becoming increasingly secular (rather than more religious), with religion serving as an ongoing topic of debate. For the sociologist Díaz-Salazar, Spain experienced a forced secularization and forced religionization in the 20th century (Díaz-Salazar 1998). On the other hand, for professor José Antonio Souto, the last 20 years of church-state relations can be seen "as highly positive" (Souto 2001). More recently, for the sociologist Javier Noya, Spain currently does not have Islamophobia or anti-Semitism but rather is secularized (Noya 2013).

The way in which the history of ideas has been disseminated historically in Spain, according to the philosopher María Zambrano (1904–1991), "has not been by the path of philosophy, but rather through the novel, which draws from *Quijote* and extends to our modern novelists, from Galdós to Gómez de la Serna, a wide development" (Zambrano *Pensamiento y poesía* 1939, translated by Cyganiak 2011). In other words, the philosophers of Spain tend to be the novelists whose ideas are embedded in literature. One reason for this might be due to Spain's history of intolerance of new ideas or any concept that challenged the status quo and thus the need to camouflage ideas in fiction.

On the other hand, Spain's historical demons still permeate the ideas of Spanish writers. Instead of producing notions of philosophy, they tend to rationalize Spain's identity. Attributed to the most famous Spanish philosopher of the 20th century José Ortega y Gasset (1883–1955) is the dictum, "Spain is the problem, Europe the solution." While chairing the cultural commission at the Congress of Europe (Hague, May 7–10, 1948), the Spanish diplomat and historian Salvador de Madariaga (1886–1978) advocated for a supra-national Europe. As Felix Lessambo explains, "Madariaga claimed that European States would need to surrender part of their sovereignty in the interest of common institutions" (Lessambo 2010). In de Madariaga's famous *Portrait of Europe* (1948), one of his celebrated remarks was: "This Europe must be born. And she will, when Spaniards will say 'our Chartres,' Englishmen 'our Cracow,' Italians 'our Copenhagen,' when Germans say 'our Bruges,' and step back horror-stricken at the idea of laying murderous hands on it. Then will Europe live" (Madariaga 1948). The political theorist and Catholic Ramiro de Maetzu (1875–1936) published *Hacia otra España* (1899, *Towards Another Spain*), in which he envisioned the imperial past of Spain with indignation. The historian José Luis Abellán (1933–) has written extensively (over 30 books) analyzing the history of ideas about Spain. He actually dedicated seven volumes to write *Historia crítica del pensamiento español* (1979–1991, *Critical History of Spanish Thinking*). One of his many observations is, for instance, his approach to philosophy, which he views as not only for academics and experts but also for the "mundane" Spaniard. Another interesting Abellán premise that seems unquestionable is that there is no Spanish thinking if there is no entity called "Spain."

More recently, the influential contemporary Spanish philosopher Fernando Savater (1947–) said: "I want to live in a society where talent is recognized regardless of borders, ethnicity, or religion—now who will lead us there?" (Rosencrantz 2011).

Further Reading

Brunn, Lars K., et al., eds. *European Self-Reflection between Politics and Religion: The Crisis of Europe in the 20th Century*. New York: Palgrave Macmillan, 2013.

Cyganiak, Sarah J. "The Method of María Zambrano: An Analysis and Translated Selection of Essays Centered on the Concepts of the Word, the Person, Compassion, and Love." Michigan: University of Michigan. (Thesis)

Gerber, Jane S. *The Jews of Spain. A History of the Sephardic Experience*. New York: The Free Press, 1994.

Lessambo, Felix. *Fundamentals of European Union Direct Tax*. Pittsburgh: RoseDog Books, 2010.

Martínez-Torrón, Javier. *Religion and Law in Spain*. Amsterdam: Kluwer Law International, 2014.

Perry, Mary Elizabeth. *The Handless Maiden: Moriscos and the Politics of Religion in Early Modern Spain*. Princeton: Princeton University Press, 2005.

Vincent, Mary. *Catholicism in the Second Spanish Republic: Religion and Politics in Salamanca, 1930–1936*. Oxford: Clarendon, 1996.

Averroes, Ibn Rushd (1126–1198)

Ibn Rushd, commonly known by his Latin name Averroes, was one of the last great philosophers of the Islamic kingdom. Additionally, he was a brilliant physician, theologian, political scientist, amateur astronomer, and judge. Born in Córdoba, Spain, both his father and grandfather were recognized scholars and religious figures. He was appointed the Sultan's physician in addition to serving as a religious judge in Sevilla and Córdoba.

Averroes was a visionary, often embracing philosophical ideas centuries before they came into fashion, such as using reason and logical proof to further his understanding of God. According to Averroes, "If the function of philosophy is none other than to study and reflect upon the facts of existence, as they provide evidence of the Maker . . . then the more complete such knowledge is, the more consummate will be our knowledge of the Maker." He went on to declare that if the Quran contradicted the laws of science, then interpretation of the scripture was required. This was a bold assertion as he was writing at a time when philosophy was under attack as a godless discipline. He further provoked the judge-theologians by asserting that philosophers and those versed in using natural reason were better equipped at interpretations of the religious codes.

According to historian and writer Chris Lowney, "Averroes was essentially advocating a degree of academic freedom scandalous in his own time and unusual even today across much of the Islamic world" (Lowney 2005). If questioning the capabilities of religious authorities was not scandalous enough, Averroes championed his own brand of gender equality by arguing that women's talents were far greater than credited by the patriarchal society who expected women to be wives and mothers and little else, stating, "it is not impossible that there may be among them philosophers and rulers" (Lowney 2005).

As is the case with many visionaries who were born into societies governed by the strict laws of religion, Averroes was eventually tried for heresy. He was banished from Córdoba and his works were ordered to be burned; he died shortly after. One could argue that had Averroes been born earlier during the Golden Age of the Islamic empire, his life might have ended differently. As it stands, he was working toward the end of Islamic rule in Spain when suspicion was cast on secular learning. However, his efforts were not in vain. While the great philosopher made little impact in the Arabic world, his writings went on to be studied in European universities shortly after his death.

See also: Chapter 2: Overview; Abderramán III; Don Pelayo; Don Rodrigo; Jaime I "the Conqueror"; Maimónides. Chapter 5: Overview.

Further Reading

Lowney, Chris. *A Vanished World: Medieval Spain's Golden Age of Enlightenment*. New York: Free Press, 2005.

Pasnau, Robert. "The Islamic Scholar Who Gave Us Modern Philosophy." *Humanities* 32:6 (2011): n/p.

Ávila, Saint Teresa de (1515–1582)

Saint Teresa of Ávila, also called Saint Teresa of Jesus, original name Teresa de Cepeda y Ahumada, was a nun at the age of 19, when she entered the Carmelite order. She was the founder of 17 convents as well as the Order of Discalced Carmelites. Teresa de Ávila became well-known for pioneering the Carmelite Reform, which emphasized austerity in one's life. Teresa de Ávila is also famous for her mystical writing, becoming the author of spiritual classics including *The Way of Perfection* (1566) and *The Interior Castle* (1577), both primarily dealing with Christian meditation exercises that make her prose a great example of Catholic mystical literature. Teresa's writing and life has been inspirational for many other writers including French feminist Simone de Beauvoir (1908–1986), who, according to her 1949 treatise *The Second Sex,* considered Teresa perhaps the only woman who lived her life for herself; and American writer R. A. Lafferty (1914–2002) and his novel *Fourth Mansions* (1969), which was inspired by Ávila's *Interior Castle*. Teresa de Ávila was beatified by Pope Paul V on April 24, 1614, and canonized by Pope Gregory XV on March 12, 1622. In 1970 Pope Paul VI named Saint Teresa Doctor of the Church, making her the first woman to receive such an honor.

Detail of the *St Teresa of Avila before the Cross* by Guido Cagnacci, 17th century. Teresa of Avila (1515–1582) was a Spanish mystic and saint who reformed the Carmelite order. (Jupiterimages)

See also: Chapter 5: Overview; Cruz, Saint Juan de la. Chapter 11: Overview.

Further Reading

Kavanaugh, Kieran. *The Collected Letters of St. Teresa of Avila*. Washington, D.C.: ICS Publications, 2001.

Lowney, Chris. *A Vanished World: Medieval Spain's Golden Age of Enlightenment*. New York: Free Press, 2005.

Peers, Allison E., ed. & trans. *The Complete Works of St. Teresa of Avila*. New York: Burns & Oates, 2002.

Starr, Mirabai. *Saint Teresa of Avila: Passionate Mystic*. Boulder: Sounds True, 2013.

Cardinal Cisneros (1436–1517)

Cardinal Cisneros or Francisco Jiménez de Cisneros became a cardinal and grand inquisitor under the Rule of King Ferdinand in 1507. Queen Isabel I of Castilla appointed Cisneros her confessor. Instead of converting the Moors and Jews gradually by education—as his peer the archbishop of Granada, Friar Hernado de Talava, was known for doing—Cisneros instead forced mass conversions. To prove his unwavering determination to convert Muslims, he would burn the Quran in public bonfires. Cisneros in no way honored the surrender treaty pledge to "ever afterwards allow . . . all the common people, great or small, to live in their own religion" (Lowney 2005).

As Granadans suffered the great injustice of a treaty disregarded, one Muslim wrote to the Ottoman sultan in Constantinople for assistance, "Therefore ask their Pope, that is to say, the ruler of Rome, why they permitted treason after having [granted] amnesty, and why they harmed us with their betrayal with no wrong or crime on our part?" (Lowney 2005). Through his open disregard of the Muslim faith, Cisneros is primarily responsible for the Moorish revolts in 1499 and 1568. Subsequently, the decision of Philip III of expelling the *Moriscos en bloc* from Spain in 1609 also can be attributed to him.

In 1508 Cisneros founded the Universidad de Alcalá de Henares, which became a defender of humanistic culture and biblical study. Although it was successful at the beginning, however, due to poor enrollment, it was moved to Madrid, being renamed the Universidad Complutense de Madrid. Nevertheless, the Universidad de Alcalá de Henares reopened in 1977. It was at the Universidad de Alcalá de Henares that Cisneros printed the *Complutensian Polyglot Bible*, which became the first printed polyglot version of the entire Bible; it was completed in 1517 and published in 1522. The influence of Erasmus of Rotterdam (1466?–1536) was particularly influential among professors and students of the Universidad de Alcalá de Henares, thanks to Cisneros's sponsorship on the diffusion of humanism.

See also: Chapter 2: Overview; The Catholic Monarchs; Philip II. Chapter 5: Overview; The Inquisition. Chapter 8: Overview.

Further Reading

Kamen, Henry. *Spain, 1469–1714: A Society of Conflict*. Hoboken: Taylor & Francis, 2014.

Lowney, Chris. *A Vanished World: Medieval Spain's Golden Age of Enlightenment*. New York: Free Press, 2005.

Rummel, Erika. *Jiménez de Cisneros: On the Threshold of Spain's Golden Age*. Tempe: Arizona Center for Medieval and Renaissance Studies, 1999.

Walsh, Michael J. *The Cardinals: Thirteen Centuries of the Men behind the Papal Throne*. Grand Rapids: William B. Eerdmans, 2011.

Churches, Mosques, and Synagogues

Every village has at least one church, usually located in the main plaza or city center. Also, most Spanish cities have magnificent cathedrals (e.g., Santiago de Compostela Cathedral) and/or impressive basilicas; these sites of Catholic pilgrimages include Basilica of Our Lady of the Pillar in Zaragoza. However, one of the current issues in Spain is related to the subsidies that Catholic institutions receive from the state. The Spanish administration forgoes 2,500 million euros every year in taxes to the church. Neither the conservative party (PP) nor the socialist party (PSOE) have made an issue about the fiscal privilege that the Spanish Church enjoys since they have been in power. More surprisingly, a group of citizens has recently documented the lack of religious activity in 82 percent of Catholic buildings, which is a requirement in order to be exempt from taxes (Ayllón 2014).

By the end of 2013, there were 1,703,529 Muslims in Spain (3% of the total Spanish population), of whom 783,137 have a Moroccan passport while 525,842 are native Spaniards. The main four cities with the highest number of Muslims are Barcelona, Ceuta, Madrid, and Melilla (Islam Hoy 2013). In Spain there are 1,177 mosques.

Based on figures provided by the Spanish Federation of Jewish Communities, in 2014 there were about 40,000 Jews living in Spain. The Spanish Jews also maintain educational institutions in all Spanish regions as well as specific schools for childhood, primary, and secondary education in Madrid, Barcelona, and Melilla. There are about 30 synagogues in Spain, some with a capacity of 800 people. More recently, on June 6, 2014, Spain's Cabinet approved a law amending Articles 21 and 23 of the Civil Code. This will allow descendants of Spanish Jews the right to dual citizenship.

Other minorities' religious groups in Spain include Jehovah's Witnesses, who are less than 150,000, Buddhists (approximately 80,000), and Mormons (around 40,000).

See also: Chapter 2: Overview. Chapter 5: Overview.

Further Reading

Beinart, Haim, and Yaacov Jeffrey Green. *The Expulsion of the Jews from Spain*. Oxford: Littman Library of Jewish Civilization, 2005.

Ben-Dov, M. *The Golden Age: Synagogues of Spain in History and Architecture*. Jerusalem: Urim, 2009.

Brassloff, Audrey. *Religion and Politics in Spain: The Spanish Church in Transition, 1962–1996*. New York: St. Martin's Press, 1998.

Callahan, William James. *The Catholic Church in Spain, 1875–1998*. Washington, D.C.: The Catholic University of America Press, 2012.

Ingram, Kevin, ed. *The Conversos and Moriscos in Late Medieval Spain and Beyond, Vol. 2, The Morisco Issue*. Leiden: Brill, 2012.

Martín Muñoz, Gema, et al. *Muslims in Spain: A Reference Guide*. Madrid: Casa Árabe-IEAM, 2010.

Menocal, María Rosa. *The Ornament of the World: How Muslims, Jews, and Christians Created a Culture of Tolerance in Medieval Spain*. New York: Warner Books, 2009.

Cruz, Saint Juan de la (1542–1591)

Saint John of the Cross, original name Juan de Yepes y Álvarez, is considered the greatest Christian mystical poet from Spain. Like Saint Teresa, Saint John also took part in the Carmelite reform in Spain. In fact, they met for the first time in 1567, when they shared their views on the Counter-Reformation. However, due to the numerous problems that occurred, for instance, in the Discalced Carmelites (an order of which he was co-founder in conjunction with Saint Teresa), he removed himself to total solitude by the end of his life. His writing is considered one of the best examples of Spanish mystical poetry of all time. Among his poems are *The Spiritual Canticle* and *Dark Night of the Soul*, both of which were written around 1577, when he was sent to a cell for nine months by the Calced Carmelite brothers, who did not accept his reforms of the Order, and also because he was a close friend of Saint Teresa de Ávila, who was in favor of his reforms.

The Living Flame of Love (1585–1586) is also considered a masterpiece, in which he combines, as in his previous writings, a poetic sensitivity with a religious and philosophical accuracy that resembles Saint Thomas Aquinas. In doing so, Saint John's ultimate virtuosity in his lyricism is to express the spiritual union between the soul and Christ. His lyrical poetry has been inspirational to many other great writers around the world including T. S. Eliot, Edith Stein, and Jacques Maritain. John of the Cross was beatified on January 25, 1675, by Pope Clement X, and canonized on December 27, 1726, by Pope Benedict XIII.

See also: Chapter 2: Overview. Chapter 5: Overview; Ávila, Saint Teresa de. Chapter 11: Overview.

Further Reading

Nicolás, Antonio T. de, ed. and trans. *St. John of the Cross (San Juan de la Cruz), Alchemist of the Soul: His Life, His Poetry (Bilingual), His Prose.* New York: Paragon House, 1989.

Richmond Ellis, Robert. *San Juan de la Cruz: Mysticism and Sartrean Existencialism.* New York: Lang, 1992.

Thompson, Colin P. *St. John of the Cross: Songs in the Night.* London: SPCK, 2008.

The Inquisition: Torquemada

The Inquisition was introduced in 1478 by the Catholic Monarchs, becoming the central instrument of Catholic and monarchical power. Ferdinand and Isabel's crusade against the Jews and the Moors was heavily financed by the Church. Some suspected 2,000 heretics were tortured and burned under the auspices of dominican priest Tomás de Torquemada (1420–1498), confessor and adviser to the Queen. Torquemada thought the Arabs and the Jews were a threat to Spain's religious and social fabric. He became the first grand inquisitor in Spain in August 1483. He expelled over 160,000 Jews from Spain in 1492.

An *auto-da-fé* ("act of faith") in Madrid's Plaza Mayor during the Spanish Inquisition, 17th century. The *auto-da-fé* was the sentencing phase of an Inquisition trial conducted by the Catholic Church against suspected heretics. (Jupiterimages)

The Spanish Inquisition began first in Toledo and then in other towns, with a limited number of personnel but with the cooperation of local authorities. The inquisitorial process used to end with a ceremony called an *auto-da-fé* or act of faith, which took place in a plaza where a group of people including the bishop, inquisitors, and local secular magistrates met, provisionally occupying the public space. As they entered the plaza, a crier would broadcast each person's crime and punishment, including bigamists, freemasons, Protestants, Muslims, and Jews. People who were accused of minor crimes arrived first and the more serious cases were reserved for the end. Feared and detested, the Inquisition was finally abolished in 1831. Over 350 years of history, the Spanish Inquisition is thought to have heard around 150,000 cases, in which they used torture in about 30 percent. Also, it is estimated that 5,000 people were executed, mainly by being burned at the stake.

See also: Chapter 2: Overview. Chapter 5: Overview; Cardinal Cisneros. Chapter 11: Golden Age of Spanish Literature. Chapter 12: Overview.

Further Reading

Edwards, John. *Torquemada and the Inquisitors*. Stroud: Tempus, 2005.

Kamen, Henry. *The Spanish Inquisition: A Historical Revision*. 4th ed. New Haven: Yale University Press 2013.

Sabatini, Rafael. *Torquemada and the Spanish Inquisition: A History*. London: Kessinger, 2004.

Madariaga y Rojo, Salvador de (1886–1978)

Salvador de Madariaga y Rojo was an essayist, diplomat, historian, and journalist who wrote profusely in English, French, German, and Spanish. After graduating in Paris in engineering, he earned a Masters of Arts at Oxford University, where he became professor of Spanish (1928–1931). During his time in Oxford he wrote his first book, *Englishmen, Frenchmen, Spaniards: An Essay in Comparative Psychology* (1929). In 1931 the Spanish republic appointed him ambassador to the United States, and later to France (1932–1934). When the Spanish Civil War erupted in 1936, Madariaga was vehemently opposed to Francisco Franco's regime. He then escaped to England in exile. Among his influential writings are *Anarchy or Hierarchy* (1937), the trilogy *Christopher Columbus* (1939), *Hernán Cortés* (1941), *Simón Bolívar* (1949), and *Spain: A Modern History* (1958). Madariaga's political writings profess the solidarity of mankind. One of his fundamental beliefs is the idea of Europe as a united and cohesive continent.

See also: Chapter 2: Overview; Franco, Francisco. Chapter 5: Overview. Chapter 6: Overview; Diaspora; Multiculturalism; Nationalism.

Further Reading

de Madariaga, Salvador. *Portrait of Europe*. London: Hollis & Carter, 1952.

Preston, Paul. *Salvador de Madariaga and the Quest for Liberty in Spain*. Oxford: Oxford University Press, 1987.

Schopflin, George, and Geoffrey Hosking, eds. *Myths and Nationhood*. New York: Routledge, 2013.

Opus Dei, Compañía de Jesús, and Caritas

The message of Opus Dei is that everyone can become a saint. Opus Dei (The Work of God) was founded in 1928 by the priest Josemaría Escrivá de Balaguer (1902–1975). His philosophy, as expressed in his book *Camino* (1934, *The Way*), constitutes an attempt to find God in daily life. Opus Dei was granted authority to practice in 1947 by Pope Pius XII. Currently, there are about 90,000 members who usually occupy influential positions in the Spanish administration or in the private sector. Opus Dei first gained visibility during the 1960s, when most of Franco's cabinet was formed by the so-called technocrats, a term which refers to those politicians that received an education from the Opus Dei and/or belonged to the religious institution while they tried to regenerate Spain's economy. Currently, Opus Dei is still very much attached to Spain's political and economic arena. That is to say, if Opus Dei was key to the continuation of national-Catholicism in Spain's democracy, nowadays, Opus Dei still represents the survival of Franco.

Compañía de Jesús is known in English as the Society of Jesus. It was founded by Saint Ignatius of Loyola (1491–1556). It is a Christian male religious institution whose members are called Jesuits. Ideologically, Compañía de Jesús can be considered a more progressive society than Opus Dei, whose members tend to be much more conservative. Currently, Compañía de Jesús operates in over 100 nations across the globe, primarily working in the sector of education including founding schools such as the Colegio San Estanislao in Málaga, where the philosopher José Ortega y Gasset studied. Also, some of its major colleges and universities include Wimbledon College (U.K.), the four Loyola Universities, and Georgetown University in the United States. In Spain the Society of Jesus has 68 educational centers, which house more than 75,000 students and about 5,000 teachers. Their main Spanish universities include Deusto (Bilbao), Comillas (Madrid), and Esade (Barcelona).

Caritas still remains the most important non-governmental organization (NGO) set up in Spain since 1947. Its main goal is to help people in need regardless of their religious or political ideology. The first ever Caritas was founded in Germany in 1897. Caritas Spain is attached to the Catholic Church in Spain. Currently, there are over 6,000 parish Caritas and about 70 diocesan offices. Also, Caritas Spain employs around 4,300 people, and has 65,000 volunteers nationwide. In 1999 Caritas Spain received the prestigious Prince of Asturias Award for Concord. Also, in 2013 Caritas Spain invested €36 million; 77,072 people were supported; 12,028 (15.6%) found employment; 2,425 people participated as volunteers; and 670 persons comprised the paid staff. Caritas Spain's motto in 2013 was "Live simply, so that others may simply live."

See also: Chapter 2: Overview. Chapter 5: Overview; Ortega y Gasset, José. Chapter 8: Overview.

Further Reading

Berglar, Peter. *Opus Dei: Life and Work of Its Founder, Josemaría Escrivá*. Princeton: Scepter Publishers, 2000.

Caritas Europe. *The Impact of the European Crisis: A Study of the Impact of the Crisis and Austerity on People, with Special Focus on Greece, Ireland, Italy, Portugal, and Spain*. Brüssels: Caritas Europa, 2013.

Estruch, Juan. *Saints and Schemers: Opus Dei and Its Paradoxes*. Oxford: Oxford University Press, 1996.

Fastiggi, Robert L. *New Catholic Encyclopedia / Supplement 2010*. Detroit: Gale, 2010.

Silf, Margaret. *Just Call Me López: Getting to the Heart of Ignatius Loyola*. Chicago: Loyola Press, 2012.

Ortega y Gasset, José (1883–1955)

José Ortega y Gasset was a philosopher whose essays have been of great influence in Spain since the 20th century. After attending school in the Colegio San Estanislao,

Málaga (1891–1897), he earned a doctorate in philosophy from the Universidad Complutense de Madrid (1898–1904), where he became professor of metaphysics in 1910. He spent the four years from 1904 to 1908 in Germany, where he continued his studies in philosophy. Ortega y Gasset is also known in Spain for being the founder in 1923 of the influential cultural magazine *Revista de Occidente*, which he edited until 1936, when he exiled to Argentina due to the Spanish Civil War. He returned to Madrid in 1948, and founded the Institute of Humanities, where he taught philosophy. One of Ortega y Gasset's main viewpoints is that humans have "no nature, but history." In this context, he argues that before understanding a present situation, we must understand history. Hence, his famous saying *Yo soy yo y mi circunstancia,* meaning, "I am I and my circumstances," which condenses his philosophical thinking. Among his most influential works are *Invertebrate Spain* (1921), *The Dehumanization of Art* (1925), *The Revolt of the Masses* (1930), and *The Origin of Philosophy* (1943).

See also: Chapter 2: Overview. Chapter 5: Overview; Opus Dei, Compañía de Jesús, and Caritas; Zambrano, María.

Further Reading

Dobson, Andrew. *An Introduction to the Politics and Philosophy of José Ortega y Gasset.* Cambridge: Cambridge University Press, 1989.

Graham, John T. *The Social Thought of Ortega y Gasset: A Systematic Synthesis in Postmodernism and Interdisciplinarity.* Columbia: University of Missouri Press, 2001.

Raley, Harold C. *José Ortega y Gasset: Philosopher of European Unity.* Tuscaloosa: University of Alabama Press, 1971.

The Pilgrimage to Santiago de Compostela

The capital of Galicia, Santiago de Compostela, has been drawing pilgrims from all over Europe for more than a millennium. Santiago de Compostela was chosen to be the first European Cultural Route by the Council of Europe in 1987, becoming a UNESCO World Heritage site in 1993. The pilgrimage to Santiago de Compostela started as a way to pay respect to the remains of the Apostle Saint James, who was buried there. Unexpectedly, like many religious festivals in Spain, it has gained a lot of popularity—especially in the last few decades. Nowadays, the pilgrimage is known as the *camino* and it has become Europe's most popular long-distance trail. There are many ways to do the camino. Among the most popular routes are the *Camino Francés* (French route) from Biarritz to Santiago, covering over 700 kilometers; and the *Camino inglés* (English route) also known as the pilgrimage from northern Europe, which usually starts at Ferrol, and is 118 kilometers long. Additionally the Portuguese route from Oporto; the *Vía de la Plata* or silver route from Sevilla; and *Camino Primitivo* from Bilbao are well-known routes.

Countless books have been written explaining the pilgrimage to Santiago de Compostela. More recently, several documentaries and films have been dedicated to the camino. Such is the case of the recent movie *The Way* (directed, produced, written and starring Emilio Estévez, 2010), which explains the spiritual trip from an American perspective. Essentially, the camino consists of a spiritual journey that becomes a multicultural experience, in the sense that a person can meet many international people while doing the trail as well as having the opportunity to experience firsthand the Spanish culture through food and scenery. The pilgrims follow the sign of the shell (*concha*), which is the symbol of Santiago and, therefore, signs bearing the symbol guide hikers in the right direction. Also, the symbol of the shell appears in accommodations known as *refugios* and some restaurants.

Pilgrims can do the camino officially, if they purchase the *credencial*, which is available at tourist offices. With this particular document, which sometimes serves as a pass for free accommodation in refugios along the trail, pilgrims will also receive a *compostela*, if they have successfully completed 100 kilometers of the camino. In order to obtain the compostela, the credencial needs to be stamped in every town where the pilgrim has stopped. The credencial will subsequently show the officer that the pilgrim has walked at least 100 kilometers, which is the minimum distance to get the certificate. In other words, the compostela acts like a passport, in the sense that it validates the pilgrim's daily hiking with the stamps that it contains. Perhaps the popularity of the camino resides in its spirituality regardless of the religious beliefs of the walker.

See also: Chapter 1: Overview; World Heritage. Chapter 2: Overview. Chapter 5: Overview.

Further Reading

Kevin, Tony. *Walking the Camino: A Modern Pilgrimage to Santiago*. Chicago: Scribe Publications, 2009.

Ramis, Sergi. *Camino de Santiago: The Ancient Way of Saint James Pilgrimage Route from the French Pyrenees to Santiago de Compostela*. London: Aurum Press, 2014.

Rudolph, Conrad. *Pilgrimage to the End of the World: The Road to Santiago de Compostela*. Chicago: University of Chicago Press, 2011.

Religious Ceremonies

Freedom of religion is guaranteed by the Spanish constitution of 1978. While in 1975, 80 percent of Spaniards considered themselves practicing Catholics, in 1988 it was less than half of the population (41%) (Díaz-Salazar 2008). It is anticipated that Spain will have more atheists than practicing Catholics in the near future. Several studies (de la Cueva 2005; López Villaverde 2013) suggest that a religious transition is happening in Spain. That is to say, the Catholic majority in Spain is coming to an end. A change of religion will occur over time due mainly to migrants. In 2005, based on the author's own estimates, the religious population of Spain was as follows: Spanish: Catholic=76%; none=20%; Muslim=3%; Buddhist/Hindu=0.1%; Protestant & Others=1%; Migrants: Catholic=44%; Protestant & Other=28%; Muslim=20%; none=6%; Buddhist/Hindu=2% (Skirbekk et al. 2010).

FIRST COMMUNION

Celebrating first Holy Communion in Spain is a very different experience than in North America. While in North America it is usually done around the age of seven or eight, in Spain it is done later, normally at the age of 10. For the event, it is not unusual to hire a professional photographer. In additition, there is often a fully catered meal that tends to be celebrated in a restaurant with numerous courses culminating with a large cake. Family members and guests receive formal invitations well in advance. It normally happens in May. Girls wear elaborate white dresses while boys typically wear a sailor suit. First Communion in Spain is pretty much celebrated like a small wedding.

Although Catholicism is declining in Spain, Spanish families still go to great lengths to celebrate certain religious ceremonies. For example, in 2009 "many Spanish families spent over 2,000 euros on a child's first Holy Communion" (Hampshire 2009). Also, there were over 203,000 marriages in Spain in 2006, with the vast majority (63%) church weddings. However, in 2009 for the first time in Spain there were more civil weddings (94,993) than Catholic weddings (80,174) (INE 2009). The price to celebrate a wedding in the Basilica of Nuestra Señora de Atocha in Madrid is €500, including mass, flowers, and musicians. The service of a photographer is paid separately, and is supplied only by the Church. The average price for similar celebrations in other Spanish churches is no less than €200 (Deiros 2013). The estimated cost for a wedding reception in Spain was about €15,000 for 50 guests in 2012. However, Spaniards are renowned for celebrating big weddings with easily over 100 guests attending.

In 2011 the number of marriages in Spain decreased to 161,724, and in the same year there were also 110,651 divorces (*Espana en cifras* 2013). In 2000 Spain had the lowest rate of divorce within the EU; however, in 2007 Spain had the highest rate. In fact, between 2000 and 2005, Spain's divorce rate rose 277 percent.

See also: Chapter 1: Population and Demography. Chapter 5: Overview. Chapter 7: Overview. Chapter 10: Overview.

Further Reading

Crawford Flitch, J. E., trans. Miguel de Unamuno, and Salvador de Madariaga. *The Tragic Sense of Life in Men and in Peoples*. Mansfield Centre: Martino Pub, 2013.

Hampshire, David. *Living and Working in Spain*. 8th ed. London: Survival Books, 2009.

INE: *Instituto Nacional de Estadística*. ine.es

Savater, Fernando (1947–)

Fernando Savater is a well-known contemporary philosopher. He initially taught ethics at the Universidad del País Vasco, where he is originally from. He then moved to

Madrid, where he currently teaches philosophy at the Universidad Complutense de Madrid. Savater is a very prolific author whose publications deal with such subjects as contemporary ethics, politics, cinema, and literary studies. He is also known for his political activism across various platforms. For example, Savater became a public figure when he engaged with different organizations (i.e., Foro Ermua, ¡Basta ya!) against terrorism and nationalism in the Basque country. He considers himself an agnostic and an anglophile, who also defends the Enlightenment in the tradition of Voltaire.

In an interview with the British newspaper *The Guardian*, Savater said: "I want to live in a society where talent is recognized regardless of borders, ethnicity, or religion—now who will lead us there?" (Rosencrantz 2011). He is the author of nearly twenty books, including novels, essays, and social reflection. He received the National Essay Award in 1982 for *La tarea del héroe* (*The Task of the Hero*). More recently, he received the Premio Primavera de Novela (Spring Novel Prize) for *Los invitados de la princesa* (2012, *The Guests of the Princess*).

See also: Chapter 2: Overview. Chapter 3: Overview; Political Challenges of Spain's 21st Century. Chapter 5: Overview; Madariaga y Rojo, Salvador de. Chapter 6: Multiculturalism. Chapter 15: Bullfighting.

Further Reading

Savater, Fernando. *The Questions of Life: An Invitation to Philosophy*. Cambridge: Polity, 2002.

Savater, Fernando. *Education and Citizenship in the Global Era.* Lecture. IDB Cultural Center. Washington, D.C.: 2003.

Smith, Paul Julian. *The Moderns: Time, Space, and Subjectivity in Contemporary Spanish Culture*. Oxford: Oxford University Press, 2000.

Zambrano, María (1904–1991)

María Zambrano was one of the most important philosophers of the 20th century in Spain. Her life mirrors the turmoil of Spain's contemporary history characterized by the Spanish Civil War (1936–1939) and dictatorship (1939–1975). From her early years, she travelled from one place to another. For example, she was born in Vélez-Málaga (Andalucía) but her parents moved to Jaén, and then to Segovia. She studied philosophy in Madrid and, due to the civil war, she lived in exile (1939–1984) for over half of her life, including working as a University professor in México, Cuba, Puerto Rico, Chile, Italy, Greece, France, and Switzerland.

Based on the notion of exile, and also due to the magnitude of Zambrano's prolific record of publication (over 30 books), her work has been divided into three major periods: 1) Formation (1904–1939) or pre-exile; 2) Expansion (1939–1984) or exile; and 3) Recollection and Conclusion (1984–1991) or post-exile. Zambrano's philosophy engages with the history of Western ideas and, more particularly, the idea of modern European citizenship. Due to her historical context, however, her way of thinking shifted from the universal to the local question of national identity in Spain.

For example, for Zambrano, "it is not fitting for the Spaniard to go raising castles of abstractions, but its anguish for being each one, is immense and runs wherever it wants to be watched. All the literature of '98 and what follows it does not have any other sense" (Zambrano 1977, translated by Cyganiak 2011).

Spain's lack of a philosophical system, according to Zambrano, is due to the Spanish experience of the Counter-Reformation instead of Europe's Reformation. In fact, she states that "the history of Spain is poetic by essence, not because the poets have made it so, but rather because its deep event is a continuous poetic transmutation and perhaps because of all history, that of Spain and that of whichever other place, may be ultimately termed poetry, creation, total realization" (Zambrano 1977). Zambrano won the Premio Príncipe de Asturias in 1981, and the Cervantes Literature Prize in 1988. With the exception of one book (1999), Zambrano's *oeuvre* has not been translated into English, although it has been extensively translated into Italian and French.

See also: Chapter 2: Overview. Chapter 5: Overview; Ortega y Gasset, José.

Further Reading

Cyganiak, Sarah J. "The Method of María Zambrano: An Analysis and Translated Selection of Essays Centered on the Concepts of the Word, the Person, Compassion, and Love." Michigan: University of Michigan, 2011. [Thesis]

Demeuse, Sarah. *Aesthetic Theory in 20th Century Spain: "Style" in José Ortega y Gasset, María Zambrano, and Eugenio d'Ors.* Berkeley: University of California Press, 2004.

Gajic, Tatiana. "In Search of a Lost Nation: Intelleectual Genealogies and Historical Revisions of the Reform of the Spanish Nation in José Ortega y Gasset, María Zambrano, and Rosa Chacel." Durham: Duke University, 2002. [Thesis]

Zambrano, María. *Pensamiento y poesía en la vida española.* México: La casa de España en México, 1939.

Zambrano, María. *Los intelectuales en el drama de España y ensayos y notas, 1936–39.* Madrid: Hispamerca, 1977.

Zambrano, María. *Delirium and Destiny: A Spaniard in Her Twenties.* New York: State University of New York Press, 1999.

REFERENCES

Abellán, José Luis. *Historia crítica del pensamiento español,* 7 vols. Madrid: Espasa-Calpe, 1979–1991.

Ayllón, Daniel. "Mil propiedades de la Iglesia burlan a Hacienda en Valencia." *la Marea,* April (2014): 41–43.

Centro de Investigaciones Sociológicas (Centre for Sociological Research) (April 2014). "Barómetro Abril 2014," p. 153.

Chislett, William. *Spain: What Everyone Needs to Know.* Oxford: Oxford University Press, 2013.

Corral Cortés, Esther. *Spain Today 2013.* Madrid: Ministry of the Presidency, 2013. http://publicacionesoficiales.boe.es.

de la Cueva Merino, Julio, and Ángel Luis López Villaverde. *Clericalismo y asociacionismo católico en España: de la restauración a la transición*. Cuenca: Universidad de Castilla-La Mancha, 2005.

Deiros, Trinidad. "España, paraíso económico de la iglesia." *la Marea,* April (2013): 8–17.

Díaz-Salazar, Rafael. "La transición religiosa de los españoles." In: R. Díaz-Salazar and S. Giner, eds. *Religión y sociedad en España*. Madrid: CIS, 1993.

Díaz-Salazar, Rafael. *La izquierda y el cristianismo*. Madrid: Taurus, 1998.

Díaz-Salazar, Rafael. *España laica*. Madrid: Espasa Calpe, 2008.

Doubleday, Simon R., and David Coleman, eds. *In the Light of Medieval Spain: Islam, the West, and the Relevance of the Past*. New York: Palgrave Macmillan, 2008.

Eaude, Michael. "Obituary—Carlos Castilla del Pino." *The Guardian*, June 29, 2009.

Graff, Marie Louise. *Spain. Cultureshock! A Survival Guide to Customs and Etiquette*. Portland: Marshall Cavendish Editions, 2005.

Hampshire, David. *Living and Working in Spain*. 8th ed. London: Survival Books, 2009.

Hyslop, Stephen G., Bob Somerville, and John Thompson. *Eyewitness History from Ancient Times to the Modern Era*. Washington, D.C.: National Geographic, 2011.

Kamen, Henry. *The Spanish Inquisition: A Historical Revision*. London and New Haven: Yale University Press, 1998.

Lapitan, Giselle. "The Changing Face of the Jesuits." *Province Express,* May 22, 2012.

Lessambo, Felix. *Fundamentals of European Union Direct Tax*. Pittsburgh: RoseDog Books, 2010.

López Villaverde, Ángel Luis. *El poder de la Iglesia en la España contemporánea*. Madrid: Catarata, 2013.

Madariaga, Salvador de. *Spain: A Modern History*. J. Cape: University of Virginia, 1961.

Maestre, Antonio. "Opus Dei, el lobby de Dios." *la Marea,* February (2014): 40–41.

Maetzu, Ramiro de. *Hacia otra España*. Bilbao: Biblioteca Bascongada de Fermín Herrán, 1899.

Margulis, Lynn, and Eduardo Punset, eds. *Mind, Life and Universe: Conversations with Great Scientists of Our Time*. White River Junction, VT: Chelsea Green Publishing, 2007.

Noya, Javier. *Los españoles ante un mundo en cambio. Visiones del exterior. Vol. 2*. 2nd ed. Madrid: Tecnos, 2013.

Phillips, William D., and Carla Rahn Phillips. *A Concise History of Spain*. Cambridge: Unversity of Cambridge Press, 2010.

Souto Paz, José Antonio. "Perspective on Religious Freedom in Spain." *BYU Law Review* 13 no. 2 (2001): 669–710.

Vincent, Mary. *Catholicism in the Second Spanish Republic: Religion and Politics in Salamanca, 1930–1936*. Oxford: Clarendon, 1996.

Vincent, Mary. *Spain, 1833–2002, People and State*. Oxford: Oxford University Press, 2007.

Vincent, Mary. "Religión e identidad nacional." In: Javier Moreno Luzón and Xosé M. Núñez Seixas, eds. *Ser españoles. Imaginarios nacionalistas en el siglo XX*. Barcelona: RBA, 2013: 207–245.

Websites

Ateos. ateos.org

Britannica Encyclopaedia. britannica.com

Cala, Andrés. "As Spain's People Drift from Catholic Church, Government Cozies Up." *The Christian Science Monitor*. http://www.csmonitor.com/World/Europe/2013/0618/As-Spain-s -people-drift-from-Catholic-Church-government-cozies-up

Camino de Santiago. santiago-compostela.net

Catholic News Agency. "Spanish Youths Attack Catholic School, Threaten to Burn Priests Alive." October 19, 2012. http://www.catholicnewsagency.com/news/spanish-youths-attack-catholic -school-threaten-to-burn-priests-alive

"Cardinal Cisneros." Entry in *Britannica Encyclopaedia*. http://www.britannica.com/EBchecked /topic/303923/Francisco-Cardinal-Jimenez-de-Cisneros

Caritas. caritas.org

"Caritas Spain Helped More than 12,000 People to Find a Job in 2013." http://www.caritas.eu /news/caritas-spain-helped-more-than-12000-people-to-find-a-job-in-2013

Costa, Xavier. "Spain between Tradition and the Modern." *Eurotopics*, September 15, 2008. http://www.eurotopics.net/en/home/presseschau/archiv/magazin/gesellschaft-verteilerseite /religion/religion_spanien

Encyclopaedia Britannica. Entry on "Tomás de Torquemada." http://www.britannica.com /EBchecked/topic/600065/Tomas-de-Torquemada

España en cifras 2013. http://www.todofp.es/dctm/todofp/biblioteca/informes/espana-en-cifras .pdf?documentId=0901e72b8175a481

Gagliarducci, Andrea. "Spain, Is It a Kind of Religious War Bulletin?" *Monday Vatican*, April 25, 2011. http://www.mondayvatican.com/religious-freedom/spain-is-it-a-kind-of-religious-war -bulletin

Gagliarducci, Andrea. "Christianity, Is There a Future after Secularization?" *Monday Vatican*, June 20, 2011. http://www.mondayvatican.com/church/christianity-is-there-a-future-after -secularization

Islamhoy.com

Jesuitas. Jesuitas.es

Leahy, Ann, Seán Healy, and Michelle Murphy. "The Impact of the European Crisis: A Study of the Impact of the Crisis and Austerity on People, with a special focus on Greece, Ireland, Italy, Portugal and Spain." http://www.caritas.eu/sites/default/files/caritascrisisreport_web.pdf

Memory on Employment and Social Economy. http://www.caritasespanola.es/memoriaempleo

Opus Dei. http://www.opusdei.org/en-us/article/message

Punset, Eduard. http://www.eduardpunset.es/biography

Rachman, Gideon. "Europe Is No Longer Spain's Solution." *Financial Times*. April 15, 2013. http:// www.ft.com/intl/cms/s/0/f01f5c66-a5b7-11e2-9b77-00144feabdc0.html#axzz375XLyWf6

"Religion Freedom in Spain." In Berkeley Center for Religion, Peace & World Affair (Georgetown University). http://berkleycenter.georgetown.edu/essays/religious-freedom-in-spain

Rosencrantz, Eric. "Interview with Fernando Savater: The EU Needs to Stand Up to the Nationalists." *The Guardian* January 5, 2011. http://www.theguardian.com/commentisfree/2011 /jan/05/eu-nationalists

Scofield, James. "Spain: Religion." *Library of Congress Country Studies*. http://rs6.loc.gov/cgi-bin /query/r?frd/cstdy:@field%28DOCID+es0062%29

Skiberkk, Vegard, Marcin Stonawski, Samir KC, Anne Goujon, Bilal Barakat. "An End to Catholic Majority Spain?" *Vienna Institute of Demography*. Austrian Academy of Sciences. http://www.oeaw.ac.at/vid/empse/download/empse08_06_5.pdf

Spanish Federation of Jewish Communities. http://www.fcje.org

Standford Encyclopedia of Philosophy. plato.stanford.edu

The Jesuit Curia in Rome. http://www.sjweb.info

The Way. The Movie. http://theway-themovie.com/

UCIDE. Unión de Comunidades Islámicas de España. ucide.org

Unión the Ateos y Librepensadores (Union of Atheists and Free-Thinkers). Ateos.org

CHAPTER 6

SOCIAL CLASSES AND ETHNICITY

OVERVIEW

Due to the economic crisis, the social map of Spain has drastically changed. Since 2010 the salary of a Spanish worker has been reduced by 12 percent on average. Currently, Spanish workers earn 25 times less than executives. On the one hand, key Spanish companies made 14 percent more profits by September 2013 than in the previous year. During the same period, an average Spanish worker had to work seven days to receive the equivalent of an executive's hourly wage. On the other hand, an executive at Mondragón, one of Spain's largest companies, cannot make "more in an hour than their workers make in a day" (Inequality.Org, posted on June 2, 2015).

Spanish salaries crashed in 2013. Salaries of 1,000 euros monthly have been reduced to 500–600 euros, which makes it very difficult, if not impossible, to sustain a normal family life. Since the economic crisis began, the average annual wages in Spain have been as follows: 2007 (17,779€); 2008 (18,353€); 2009 (18,796€); 2010 (18,511€); 2011 (18,213€); 2012 (17,392€). The average annual salary of a person living in Switzerland in 2013 was €38,986 ($42,451), which was 287 percent higher than the Spanish average salary in 2013 (€12,880 =$14,025). In contrast, Table 6.1 contains a list of comparative salaries of government positions both in Spain and the EU.

Table 6.1   GOVERNMENT SALARIES IN SPAIN AND EU

Govenrment Office in 2014	Person	Salary
Spain's president	Mariano Rajoy	78,000€
Germany's president	Angela Merkel	266,000€
Italy's president	Enrico Letta	124,000€
Portugal's president	Passos Coelho	58,000€
Greece's president	Antonis Samarás	57,000€
Spanish ministers	Average	68,981€
Spanish secretaries of the state	Average	100,000€
Catalunya's governor	Artur Mas	136,000€
País Vasco's governor	Iñigo Urkullo	97,000€

(continued)

Table 6.1   GOVERNMENT SALARIES IN SPAIN AND EU *(continued)*

Govenrment Office in 2014	Person	Salary
Madrid's governor	Ignacio González	89,000€
Barcelona's mayor	Xavier Trías	110,000€
Madrid's mayor	Ana Botella	101,000€
Zaragoza's mayor	Juan A. Belloch	91,000€
Valencia's mayor	Rita Barberá	60,000€
El Prat de Llobregat's mayor	Lluís Tejedor	77,000€
El Prat de Llobregat's planning consultant	Village planner	78,000€
Spain's president of the Senate	Pío García Escudero	144,000€

The average salary of an executive in Spain in the private sector was 2.2 million euros in 2012. However, the average monthly salaries in Spain for the working class society were as shown in Table 6.2 in 2013 (Pastor 2014).

Table 6.2   WORKING CLASS SALARIES IN SPAIN (2013)

Occupation	Age	Monthly wage
Firefighter	38	1700€
Decorator	41	1200€
Waitress	32	1024€
Nursing assistant	50	1208€
Taxi driver	43	2500€ (13 hrs)
Graphic designer	27	400€ part-time
Nurse (public health)	38	1800€
Technical radiodiagnostic	40	1300€
Driving instructor	30	1200€
Hairdresser	29	1000€+tips
Physiotherapist	28	1200€
Hearing aide	52	1096€
Responsible for cafeteria	41	1400€

The difference between the highest and the lowest pay at the Spanish corporations listed in the IBEX 35 "averages 105 times" (Inequality.Org June 2, 2015).

Spain's main four economic figures were: 0-25-50-100, referring to zero growth; over 25 percent unemployment; over 50 percent decrease in the housing market; and nearly 100 percent public debt (Pérez 2013). With regards to social classes in Spain, one fact remains evident: The Spanish middle class is declining. For example, in 2013, those in executive positions saw an increase in salary by 6.9 percent while those in mid-level positions saw a decrease of 3.8 percent and workers a decrease of 0.4 percent (Blanchar 2014). What is happening is a clear trend toward polarization. On the one hand, there is a small group of people who are getting richer while, on the other hand, there is the majority of ordinary workers who see their salaries frozen or falling.

According to the CIS (Spanish for the Center of Sociological Research), in 2007, 63 percent of Spaniards believed they were middle class. By November 2011, the number dropped to 55 percent, and is still falling. This new phenomenon is so evident that Spanish sociologists have already labeled it "la desmesocratización," referring to the end of the middle class as we know it in Spain. There is a new working class society in Spain. This new working class society has little control over various aspects of life, including the right to decide on factors related to their job. In essence, this new class is formed by some of society's most vulnerable people: the young generation; people over 50 years old; immigrants; people with a low level of education; women; and the *mileuristas* (individuals earning roughly a thousand euros a month).

Another interesting aspect of Spain's social classes is the young professionals. Even if young professionals have the opportunity to gain full time employment, they are paid significantly less than their counterparts in other European countries. Most Spanish professionals in the field of businesses, sciences, social sciences, and the humanities have seen their salaries fall since 2011, and the trend is continuing. According to the Spanish National Institute of Statistics (INE), more than half of the Spaniards employed (62%) earn less than 22,800 euros annually.

Geographically, there are more Spaniards living in medium-sized villages than in the urban spaces. The rural exodus started in the 1960s, when people tended to move to the big cities for better jobs. In general terms, most Spaniards have usually preferred to live in the cities, although they could not afford it. However, a relatively new phenomenon occurred in the 1990s and particularly since 2004, when a number of new town-houses were built near the cities and on the periphery of villages. The new middle class in Spain was able to buy brand new houses close to the city or nearby village. Yet this new way of living on the outskirts has generated problems, such as traffic jams, air pollution, and destruction of fertile land. The extension of cities is also damaging cultural norms like the Spanish tradition of returning home during a workday for lunch with the family (a disruption particularly evident in Madrid and Barcelona). Additionally, this massive construction without real planning has created innumerable ghost towns across the country. About 3.5 million households were estimated to be empty in Spain in 2013, which coincides with the increasing number of social protests across the country and evictions of Spanish families who cannot pay their mortgages or rent (Pereira 2015).

According to the government report *Spain Today 2013*, the Spanish-resident population totaled 46.8 million people as of November 1, 2011. Out of the total population, 5.3 million are foreign nationals (11.2%), of whom 2.1 million are nationals of European Union member states. As of November 1, 2011, 49.4 percent of the total population was male and 50.6 percent was female. Among Spanish nationals, women predominate (51.0%), while among foreign nationals males predominate (52.0%). By age, 16.0 percent of the population is under 16, while 41.0 percent are between the ages of 16 to 44 and 43.0 percent are 44 years old or above.

Spanish-resident foreign nationals who are European Union citizens total 2,084,916. Of these, the leading nationalities are Romanians (798,104), followed by nationals of the United Kingdom (312,098) and Italy (177,520). Among non-EU foreign nationals, the most numerous are nationals of Morocco (773,966), followed by nationals of Ecuador (316,756) and Colombia (250,087) (*Spain Today 2013*).

Immigration has played a significant role on the Spanish economy, particularly in the areas of farming, domestic assistance, and construction. During the economic boom, the availability of jobs began to attract foreign workers. In 1981, there were 198,042 foreign nationals in Spain (0.52% of the total population). By 1996, this figure had increased to 522,314 (1.37%); in 2004 it stood at 3,034,326 (7.02%); and in 2008 it reached a total of 5,220,600 (11.3%). In 2012, foreign nationals came to 5,736,528, or 12.1 percent of the total population. However, the economic recession has hit immigrant workers in Spain especially hard. This is mainly due to their higher exposure to the sectors most affected by the downturn, such as construction (*Spain Today 2013*).

Further Reading

Balfour, Sebastian. *The End of the Spanish Empire, 1898–1923*. Oxford: Clarendon Press, 2010.

Ealham, Chris, and Michael Richards, eds. *The Splintering of Spain: Cultural History of the Spanish Civil War, 1936–1939*. Cambridge: Cambridge University Press, 2010.

Harrison, Lawrence E. *Who Prospers?: How Cultural Values Shape Economic and Political Success*. New York: Basic Books, 1992.

Kamen, Henry. *Spain, 1469–1714: A Society of Conflict*. Hoboken: Taylor & Francis, 2014.

Aristocracy

Aristocracy has existed in Spain since medieval times. One of the oldest Spanish aristocratic titles is the House of Alba, currently hold by Don Carlos Fitz-James Stuart as the new Duke of Alba, after his mother, the Duchess of Alba (1926–2014), recently passed away at the age of 88. She held more nobility titles (more than 40) than any other person in the world (including the British Queen who had to kneel to her). Her immense wealth was inherited. She was one of Europe's richest aristocrats whose fortune was estimated at over $4 billion including palaces, castles, and fine works of art (50,000 paintings and 18,000 rare books). The duchess's full name was María del Rosario Cayetana Alfonsa Victoria Eugenia Francisca Fitz-James Stuart y de Silva, though she was popularly known as Cayetana.

The Spanish aristocracy can be labeled as an anomaly or unique for being particularly wealthy but also acting in a peculiar way. For example, in the case of the Duchess of Alba, she was very well-known through the Spanish media. Her visibility was sensationalized by her way of living. Her image has probably been inspirational to many contemporary women. She became world news on October 5, 2011, for marrying her third husband, Alfonso Diez, a civil servant 24 years younger. Before marrying her, he signed a prenuptial agreement in which he renounced inheritance rights. Instead, her six children each inherited a palace and thousands of acres of land.

Aristocracy in Spain has been synonymous with the rural oligarchy in Spain's 20th century. As Paul Preston recounts, some Spanish aristocrats became paranoiac and lost their minds because of the Spanish Civil War. For example, Preston highlights the case of the Conde de Alba de Yeltes, Gonzalo de Aguilera y Munro, who shot his two sons on Friday, August 28, 1964 (Preston 2013). Nowadays, however, Spanish aristocracy is changing. For instance, apart from being born aristocrats by lineage or inheritance, numerous Spaniards have recently received a nobility title. This has been the case of exemplary Spanish citizens including Spain's national football team manager, Vicente del Bosque, who was named 1st Marquis of Del Bosque in 2011; literary writer Mario Vargas Llosa (1st Marquis of Vargas Llosa), and scientist Margarita Salas (1st Marquis of Canero).

Spain's *Toisón de oro* or Golden Fleece, inherited by current king

The Duchess of Alba arrives for a movie preview in Sevilla, Spain. When she was set to marry again at 85, the Duchess acknowledged that she had to overcome her children's opposition to the wedding, but also insisted that she still controlled her immense wealth. (AP Photo/Paul White)

Felipe VI, is considered one of Europe's oldest and most prestigious orders. However, other citizens around the world have been inducted into the Order including the Emperor of Japan (1985); Javier Solana (2010); Victor García de la Concha (2010); and Enrique Valentín Iglesias (2014). Also, the Spanish monarchy awards a series of annual prizes named Prince of Asturias to distinguished individuals and organizations around the world for their achievements. In 2014 its name was changed to Princess of Asturias. Recent holders include Bob Dylan (Arts, 2007); Umberto Eco (Communications, 2000); Fulbright Program (International Cooperation, 2014); Leonard Cohen (Literature, 2011); Martha Nussbaum (Social Sciences, 2012); New York City Marathon (Sports, 2014); Juan Antonio Cirac (Scientific Research, 2006); and National Organization of Spanish Blind People (Concord, 2013).

The case of contemporary Spanish queen, Letizia Ortiz, constitutes another example of the modernization of the Spanish aristocracy. She was not initially born with a title, nor was she born into upper-class society. However, by her own merits, she has successfully become a current member of the Spanish aristocracy. Letizia Ortiz was a professional worker, a popular news anchor for national television (TVE), and was divorced before marrying Prince Felipe in 2004. With this marriage, as a working member of society, she conquered many stereotypes in regards to the preconceived notion of aristocracy. Currently, she and her husband have two daughters (Leonor and Sofía). If they do not have a male heir, Leonor, already princess of Asturias, will be Spain's next queen.

See also: Chapter 2: Overview. Chapter 3: King Felipe VI. Chapter 6: Overview; Monarchy.

Further Reading

Barton, Simon. *The Aristocracy in Twelfth-Century León and Castile*. Cambridge: Cambridge University Press, 2010.

Zmora, Hillay. *Monarchy, Aristocracy, and the State in Europe, 1300–1800*. New York: Routledge, 2001.

Diaspora

Spain is becoming a country that receives money from citizens who work abroad (emigrant remittances). More often, Spaniards who work abroad send money back to their relatives living in Spain. Conversely, the immigrants who reside in Spain have less money to send to their respective countries. However, the difference between the amount of money that is sent to Spain and the amount that leaves is small. In fact, between April and June 2013, 1,591 million euros came into Spain, which was the highest volume of money ever recorded in the history of Spain, while the output from Spain was 1,563 million euros (Mars 2013). The phenomenon of ex-pats, however, differs greatly from the figure of the emigrant during the 1960s, in the sense that these new ex-pats are usually sent internationally by Spanish multinational companies. In the 1960s, however, the bulk of Spanish emigrants did not go abroad under the Spanish institutional umbrella. Nevertheless, the increasing flow of Spaniards looking for jobs abroad corresponds to the magnitude of a diaspora. The highest selling newspaper in Spain, *El País*, has an entire section dedicated to the *expatriados* (ex-pats).

Looking at the figures of the Spanish Institute of Statistics (INE), the number of Spaniards looking for jobs abroad due to the crisis has increased since 2008. By 2012, nearly 60,000 Spaniards left the country while 135,045 foreign residents in Spain also left the country due to the lack of jobs. Also, by 2013 there were 1.9 million Spaniards living abroad, which was a 6 percent increase over the previous year (INE 2013). During the Spanish Civil War (1936–1939) and Franco's dictatorship (1939–1975) there was an exodus of the Spanish intelligentsia, including Andrés Segovia, Pau Casals, Luis Buñuel, Severo Ochoa, Juan Ramón Jiménez, Pablo Picasso, and Rafael Alberti, among others.

The phenomenon of Spain's diaspora in the 21st century does not correspond to the previous role of the *huídos* (the Republicans who chose to flee the country rather than surrender to Franco) or the *maquis* (insurgents who escaped from Franco's regime and took refuge in the mountains). Nowadays, Spain is witnessing another exodus that

HUÍDOS

Normally the term *huídos* refers to those left-leaning intellectuals who chose to flee the country rather than surrender to Franco's extreme conservatism, which did not allow them to think for themselves. Hence, it provoked the first Spanish diaspora wherein many artists and scientists left Spain and some never came back. This was the case of Antonio Machado, Emilio Prados, Pedro Salinas, and Manuel de Falla. Among other illustrious exiles were Salvador de Madariaga, Pau Casals, Pablo Picasso, Severo Ochoa, Juan Ramón Jiménez, Luis Buñuel, Andrés Segovia, Rosa Chacel, María Zambrano, Rafael Alberti, and Jorge Guillén. More recently, due to the economic crisis, the term *huídos* has become familiar again to many Spaniards, who left the country regardless of their ideology but mainly because of the high unemployment rate as well as the disparity in pay between jobs in Spain and jobs in many Western countries.

constitutes a new Spanish diaspora. This is different from the previous wave, when war and/or repression were the main reasons for leaving. Nevertheless, the new Spanish diaspora produces the same outcome in Spain's 20th century: Spaniards cannot find jobs in their own country, mainly due to political negligence. The 2011–present Spanish protests known as 15-M or the Outrage movement—*los indignados*—partly echoed the political activism of the *huídos, maquis,* and intellectuals.

See also: Chapter 2: Overview. Chapter 6: Overview. Immigration. Chapter 12: Overview.

Further Reading

Avrum Ehrlich, M. *Encyclopedia of the Jewish Diaspora: Origins, Experiences, and Culture.* Santa Barbara: ABC-CLIO, 2009.

Buffery, Helena, ed. *Stages of Exile: Spanish Republican Exile Theatre and Performance.* Oxford: Peter Lang, 2012.

Studnicki-Gizbert, Daviken. *A Nation upon the Ocean Sea: Portugal's Atlantic Diaspora and the Crisis of the Spanish Empire, 1492–1640.* Oxford: Oxford University Press, 2007.

Varela-Lago, Ana María. "Conquerors, Immigrants, Exiles: The Spanish Diaspora in the United States, 1848–1948." San Diego: University of California, 2008 [Thesis].

Disability Services

Public support for people unable to live independently due to illness, disability, or age is provided in Spain's dependent care law. However, due to Spain's recession, it is estimated that over a million elderly Spaniards with severe disabilities could not attend to their basic daily needs in 2011. Other cases of negligence have been reported in the Spanish media in which some families have not received any help from the state, so they have had to rely entirely on their own resources. Spanish journalist Raúl del Pozo wrote an article in 2014 in which he illustrated the disparities among social classes in Spain. His case in point is that even the greatest Spanish writer of all times, Miguel de Cervantes, died in Spain in extreme poverty (in 1616). Just a few hours before dying, Cervantes wrote a letter to the Count of Lemos: "Sobre estar enfermo, estoy muy sin dinero" (*El Mundo*, February 20 2014), meaning, "about being ill, I am very much without any money."

One of Spain's key institutions for providing specialized services to those with disabilities is ONCE (*Organización Nacional de Ciegos Españoles*, National Organization of Blind People). This organization is unique in the world and plays a key role in Spain: They are one of the biggest national and international organizations fully dedicated to supporting not only the blind population but also to helping Spaniards with any kind of disability. As ONCE states on their website, once.es, its three main goals are to provide support for people with disabilities, with specific focus on the blind; promote education; and increase employment. ONCE offers services in education, career assistance, and life skills to Spaniards.

ONCE was founded in 1938. It is funded through voluntary means, specifically though the purchase of the *cupón* (lottery) which first began in May 1939. ONCE gives a percentage of its proceeds to various other groups that aid the disabled. ONCE extends beyond Spain's borders in regards to aid. Currently ONCE is involved in more than 30 international organizations and focuses on high-need international situations such as the natural disaster in the 2010 Haiti earthquake.

Recent studies in the field of disabilities also show interesting facts about the situation in Spain. For example, the Spanish bank la Caixa published an over-200 page report written by the Colectivo Ioé (2012). Among their findings were that the immigrant population in Spain has fewer cases of disability, and that families with an income less than 1,000 euros monthly are four times more inclined to end up with a disability than those earning over 2,500 euros. In other words, poor families tend to experience more cases of disabilities than do the middle and upper classes. This evidence was already highlighted in similar polls taken in 1999 in Spain. Also, the Colectivo Ioé found that most Spanish pensioners do not feel they belong to a particular group with disabilities, nor do they feel discriminated against. In fact, only a very few Spanish pensioners ask for a certificate of disability, which entitles them to extra help, in addition to the package that all pensioners automatically receive, which includes a pension, free health care, and domestic assistance (Colectivo Ioé 2012).

Also, the European Union regularly funds projects such as GINI: Growing Inequalities' Impacts. The country report for Spain concluded that there has been "some periods of large inequality reduction (1985–1993 and 2003–2007) and some important post-recession periods with inequality increases (1993–1996 and 2008–2009)" (Ferrer et al. 2013). Other studies show that deprivation as a notion is understood differently in Spain, Sweden, and the U.K. This is one of the conclusions of Dr. Agnes Nairn. While deprivation in Britain is seen as being closely related to the amount of consumer goods and, by extension, money that the family has, in Spain, the concept of deprivation is more associated with neglect, as a child whose family does not spend time playing with him or her. For a Swedish family, to live in a neighborhood where children have no space to play would be considered "deprivation" (Nairn 2011).

See also: Chapter 4: Overview; Banks. Chapter 11: Golden Age of Spanish Literature.

Further Reading

Anson, Jon, and Marc Luy, eds. *Mortality in an International Perspective*. New York: Springer, 2014.

Chislett, William. *Spain. What Everyone Needs to Know*. Oxford: Oxford University Press, 2013.

Marr, Mathew J. *The Politics of Age and Disability in Contemporary Spanish Film: Plus Ultra Pluralism*. New York: Routledge, 2013.

Nairn, Agnes. *Children's Well-being in UK, Sweden and Spain: The Role of Inequality and Materialism*. London: Ipsos MORI (Social Research Institute), 2011.

Wise, David A. *Social Security Programs and Retirement around the World: Historical Trends in Mortality and Health, Employment, and Disability Insurance Participation and Reforms*. Chicago: University of Chicago Press, 2012.

Immigration

The latter half of the 20th century has brought remarkable changes to Spain's immigrant population. While Spain was a culturally rich country with approximately half a million Roma in addition to the Basques, Catalans, and Gallicians in 1986 when it joined the European community, Spain's immigrant population was minimal, consisting mainly of sub-Saharan Africans working in the agricultural sector. During the latter part of the decade Spain's immigrant population steadily increased. This increase was due to multiple factors: Spain's new found stability, its location on the Mediterranean, and its close proximity to north Africa, as well as its close ties with Latin America, all played a role. During this period many Europeans purchased retirement and vacation homes along Spain's southern coast and in rural areas. Moroccans entered the country through the Strait of Gibraltar, often crossing in *pateras*, dangerously small fishing boats ill prepared to navigate the open seas. A significant number of immigrants from Latin America came to fill jobs that required cheap labor in Spain's larger cities.

The creation of the EU in 1993 made migration both into and out of Spain much easier than previously. At the turn of the century immigrants—most notably from Poland, Russia, and Romania—flocked to Spain for its readily available jobs. While immigration strained Spain's educational and social services, it simultaneously provided workers to fill the void left by Spain's declining birthrate.

The financial crisis has had an impact on immigration. Sectors, such as construction, that traditionally provided jobs to immigrants, have been hit especially hard. Before 2007, Spain used to receive over 700,000 immigrants in one year alone. However, nowadays, Spain hardly receives 100,000. To be precise, 115,557 guest workers obtained Spanish nationality between January 1, 2012 and January 1, 2013 (Sanmartín 2014).

According to INE (January 1, 2013), Spain's total population was 47,129,783 (135,538 less than in 2012). For the second consecutive year, Spain lost foreign population. In 2013, there were 5,546,238 foreigners, which represented 11.70 percent of the total population (down from 2012, when they were 12.14 percent of the population). The highest concentration of foreigners in Spain are in the Illes Balears (20.19%), the Communitat Valenciana, (16.89%) and Murcia (15.69%). Conversely, the lowest percentage of foreign population in Spain are in Extremadura (3.78%), Galicia (3.98%), and Asturias (4.53%). As historians Martorell and Juliá point out, in 2010 there were more foreigners in Spain than in the United Kingdom, Italy, or France, leaving Germany as the only country with more foreign residents than Spain (Martorell 2012).

Obtaining Spanish citizenship is complicated. One of the main problems is the fact that Spain does not provide candidates with a manual, as do countries such as Canada. Because of the lack of a textbook, some candidates have experienced difficulties in grasping the basic cultural knowledge required for the exam. To make matters even worse, the criteria for the general cultural test are totally subjective. In other words, each judge in Spain will decide what questions to ask. Usual questions are the following: Who is the current president of Spain? Who is the current president of your region? Where does the Camino de Santiago end? Who are two famous Spanish sport players? Who was Carrero Blanco? Who is the commander-in-chief of the Spanish Army? Where was Pablo Picasso born? What is the *gaita*? or How do you make a Spanish omelet? The good news is that the Spanish Supreme Court of Justice in 2014 declared that illiteracy is not a sufficient reason to deny Spanish nationality, so long as the candidates can communicate verbally in Spanish.

See also: Chapter 1: Population and Demography; Chapter 6: Overview; Income-Level Groups.

Further Reading

Irastorza, Nahikari. *Born Entrepeneurs?: Immigrant Self-Employment in Spain*. Amsterdam: Amsterdam University Press, 2010.

López Basaguren, Alberto, and Leire Escajedo San Epifiano, eds. *The Ways of Federalism in Western Countries and the Horizons of Territorial Autonomy in Spain*. Vol. 2 New York: Springer, 2013.

Martínez Lirola, María. *Discourses on Immigration in Times of Economic Crisis: A Critical Perspective*. Newcastle: Cambridge Scholars Publishing, 2013.

Income-Level Groups

For sociology professor José Félix Tezanos (UNED), there is no doubt that a deep inequality exists among Spain's social classes. There is a new situation in which we cannot talk about working class society since at the time of his writing, Spain had over six million people unemployed. The evidence is based on the data published by Eurostat, which indicates that since 2007 the inequalities between those who earn more and those who earn less has expanded significantly. In fact, Tezanos applies the concept of "exclusion" to 55 percent of the Spanish population. For him, the excluded group is made up of the unemployed plus the new working poor. This Spanish working class segment of society struggles to make ends meet due to their low income, despite having a university degree and/or other professional titles. His overall conclusion is that there is not a new working class society but a return to the 1970s with uncertain job conditions. Other statistics show that nearly 20 percent of Spaniards over 50 years of age are jobless. Another conclusion is that the population of Spanish youth does not feel that they have a future in Spain. In fact, the youth population of Spain see their future in another country, especially in the Americas and/or Germany (fundacionsistema.com).

The disparities among public salaries in Spain are significant. For instance, the mayor of Pozuelo de Alarcón (a village of 84,000 habitants near Madrid) earns €7,000 more annually than the president of Spain. In fact, one out of five towns with over 50,000 inhabitants has a mayor whose monthly salary is higher than the president of Spain (sueldospublicos.com).

The social map of Spain has changed drastically. During the 1990s Spain was a country primarily receiving immigrants (i.e., in 2007 immigrants sent a record high of nearly 8,500 million euros to their respective countries). From 2008 onward Spain has been a country unable to create jobs. This new scenario can be seen in Spain when a certain number of jobs are advertised, and there is a huge surplus of applicants. A recent case was the opening of a new Ikea shop built in Alfafar (Valencia), which announced 400 jobs and received over 100,000 applications (2014).

In 2013 salaries fell (or *devaluación salarial*) in Spain. Also, there were nearly 20,000 (19,567) eviction notices, which is similar to the previous year 2012 (23,774 evictions). According to the Bank of Spain, 44,745 Spanish homes were reclaimed by the banks in 2012. Also, nearly 600,000 Spaniards were carrying a mortgage that was more than the actual value of their houses in 2014. The average price of a Spanish home fell 38.5 percent, from 245,313 euros in 2007 to 150,787 euros in 2013. However, actual numbers vary depending on the institution publishing the figures.

One of Spain's major problems is the considerable increase in social disparities between the rich and the poor. In particular, the top 20 percent of salaries in Spain have an income that is six times greater than the lowest 20 percent of wages. In Spain, the average number of hours worked annually is 1,690 hours, which is less than the OECD's average of 1,776 hours per year. Interestingly, 6 percent of Spaniards work more than 50 hours weekly, which is far from the 1.9 percent in Denmark. Also, the average Spanish family's income after taxes was €24,000 (approximately $32,888) in 2011.

One positive area across income levels is the field of health services. Spain has been successful in eliminating social inequalities in its *Sistema Nacional de Salud* (SNS / National Health Service). The average unskilled worker uses Spain's primary care and hospital services just as frequently as professionals with university degrees. In 1989, with the Socialist government in power, Spain's health system became universal upon the creation of the National Health Service. The SNS is funded and administered publicly, making the majority of health services free and accessible to Spanish residents (Navarro 1997).

MORTGAGES IN SPAIN

The average length of a mortgage in Spain is 30 years with an interest rate that is called Euribor, which means that it is variable (it varied from a record low of 0.05 to a record high of 5.39 percent in 2008) as opposed to a fixed rate of 3.5 percent, which since 2015 is being heavily advertised by major banks. This is a new situation that breaks Spain's American pattern of 30-year mortgages with hardly any down payment. A 2015 average mortgage was around 118,000 euros with a monthly payment of 581 euros. On the other hand, Spanish banks are now trying to get rid of many holiday houses by offering zero-down mortgages only for those particular homes. For instance, during the last seven years, there were more than half a million foreclosures in Spain. The small town of Fuengirola (a tourist destination) had 13 times the usual number of cases. A traditional Spaniard until very recently did not usually move from one house to another. In other words, as opposed to Canadians, Spaniards tended to live in one house (maximum two) throughout their life span. Eighty-three percent of Spaniards own a property, which is one of the highest ratios in Europe. Spain is low on the list with regards to renting (only around 15% of the population, as opposed to Germany with 55.8% or France with 52.3%). More interestingly, 36.2 percent of Spaniards own a second property, putting Spain second on the list after Cyprus (51.6%), and far ahead of other countries including Italy (24.9%), France (24.7%), and Germany (17.8%).

While the SNS offers access to all, the quality of the services may not be uniform across regions and income level groups. One prime example is civil servants such as teachers and policemen whose jobs grant them access to private general practitioners (their costs are reimbursed with public funds). Such access to private healthcare is not granted to citizens across income level groups.

There are also inequalities in general health based on income and region. Those in high-income groups have better overall health than the middle class. Following the pattern, the middle class has better overall health than the working class. Yet the working class has a higher satisfaction rate with the SNS than the middle class, an indication that the middle class has higher expectations of their healthcare providers. Finally, the worst health was found in regions of Spain with the greatest inequalities between social classes—and not in the overall poorest regions, as one might expect. Therefore, a strong connection exists between class relations and health, indicating that solving inequalities within each region is paramount to improving the health of those in lower income levels.

See also: Chapter 1: Population and Demography. Chapter 6: Overview; Immigration. Chapter 7: Overview.

Further Reading

Caputo, Richard K., ed. *Basic Income Guarantee and Politics: International Experiences and Perspectives on the Viability of Income Guarantee.* New York: Palgrave Macmillan, 2012.

Monarchy

The Spanish monarchy represents an exceptional case, because it is a recently established institution. During Franco's rule, Spain was without a monarchy for 44 years. In 1931 the Bourbon king Alfonso XIII left Spain in exile when it became clear that his presence would result in a civil war between pro and anti-royalists. Alfonso XIII died in Rome in 1941, making the legitimate heir to the throne his third son, Juan. It was Juan's son, Juan Carlos, who was born in Rome and educated briefly in Switzerland, who would eventually restore the monarchy in Spain and establish democracy as well.

While Franco showed no intention of relinquishing his power as head of state to Don Juan (father of King Juan Carlos) under extraordinary circumstances, he did negotiate that he would name Juan Carlos his successor under the provision that he was educated and raised in Spain under the watchful eye of Franco. Thus, at the age of 10, Juan Carlos arrived in Spain for the first time in his life.

King Juan Carlos I has been one of the most important symbols of Spain. However, as Daniel Barredo points out, the restoration and maintenance of the Spanish monarchy are currently under scrutiny. Many world monarchies such as the British (Canada, New Zealand, and Australia), Swedish, and Spanish play a role similar to a trade mark (or corporate brand, *marca corporativa*) (Barredo 2013). For some people, such as John M. T. Balmer, the strongest democracies in the world (U.K., Canada, New Zealand, Australia, and Holland) are monarchies. Similarly, the most socially committed nations (Denmark, Norway, and Sweden), as well as some of the most important economies in the world (most G-8 countries), are also monarchies (Balmer 2013). From another perspective, however, the occupation of monarch is simply obsolete and therefore unnecessary in the 21st century.

The maintenance of a monarchy does not rely solely on the behavior of the monarch. This is particularly proven in the case of the Spanish monarchy. The recent conduct of several members of the Spanish monarchy, including King Juan Carlos I's daughter Cristina (Urdangarín Affair) has been questioned by many Spaniards. Furthermore, even prior to October 2011 (before such scandals as Urdangarín's embezzlement; Froilán's shooting; Corinna zu Sayn Wittgenstein's possible affair with the king; or Botswana's king elephant hunting), the monarchy was already losing the respect of the citizens.

The Spanish monarchy was one of the most valued institutions by the Spanish citizens rating it 6.9 out of 10 total for approval in 1998. However, in October 2011, the same survey produced a lower figure of 4.89 points. The numbers in 2013 were even worse with only 3.68 points. Perhaps the main reason why the Spanish monarchy is still in a deep crisis is simply because it did not adjust before the economic crisis to the current times.

The Spanish monarchy needed to re-invent itself in order to survive in the new global era. The new Spanish monarchs, King Felipe VI and Queen Letizia, have become the more responsible image that many Spaniards desired. Citizens demanded more transparency, and Felipe VI immediately made such changes, publicly updating the Crown website (casareal.es). If the new King and his measures are restoring transparency to Spanish society, questioning and critically examining the Spanish monarchy is becoming no longer taboo in Spain.

See also: Chapter 2: Overview; Franco, Francisco; Juan Carlos I of Spain. Chapter 3: Overview; King Felipe VI; Scandals and Political Corruption.

Further Reading

Carr, Raymond. *Modern Spain, 1875–1980*. Oxford: Oxford University Press, 1980.

Elliott, J. H. *Spain, Europe, and the New World, 1500–1800*. New Haven: Yale University Press, 2009.

Payne, Stanley G. *Spain: A Unique History*. Madison: University of Wisconsin Press, 2011.

Powell, Charles T. *Juan Carlos of Spain: Self-Made Monarch*. New York: St. Martin's Press, 1996.

Multiculturalism

Multiculturalism has long been associated with Spain. However, perhaps it is more accurate to relate Spain to the three religions: Christianity, Islam, and Judaism. Nevertheless, the main issue about considering Spain a multicultural country revolves around two key topics: the quality of the coexistence and the intellectual impact within the European context. The Jewish community was the first known diaspora to occur on the Spanish peninsula. Like the scholar and philosopher Maimónides, Jews had to escape the threat of conversion or death in 1170. This persecution toward non-Catholics was also practiced later under the Catholic Monarchs and even more intensely by Philip II.

One old example of the trilingual cultures still visible in Spain can be seen in the Royal Chapel of the Cathedral in Sevilla. Here there is an inscription on the tomb of Saint Ferdinand III written in four languages: Latin, Spanish, Arabic, and Hebrew, which highlights Spain as a country that practiced tolerance in 1252. His son, Alfonso X, continued his father's multicultural legacy. He actually developed the Toledo School of Translators (*Escuela de Traductores*), where he managed to assemble the best scientists in the world to work together. The medieval city of Toledo is also considered an example of the multiculturalism Spain experienced in the early medieval period. In fact, Toledo became a dynamic city thanks to the input of the three major cultural communities, which made an equal impact into the social fabric of Spain: Jews, Arabs, and Christians.

The old city of Granada represents another modern case of multiculturalism in Spain. The very name "Granada" has dual origins: The Jews named it Garnata, while in the Arabic language it was Garnatah. The inhabitants of al-Andalus built the Alhambra Palace, and the Muslim Nasrid Dynasty expanded the multifunctional complex with gardens (Generalife). The Andalusian troubadours, both Jews and Arabs, "sang of sacred and sensual love and wine more than of war" (Bendiner 1983). Later King Carlos V would add his own mark, building another palace within the same complex (Palace of Charles V). Today, thanks to its rich heritage, Granada has become one of the most visited cities in Spain.

Nowadays, the division of Spain into 17 regions, according to the Constitution of 1978, can be seen as a multicultural mosaic, in the sense that each Spanish region recreates a small but versatile world itself as part of Spain's current diversity. Furthermore, multiculturalism in Spain can be observed not only in the number of people coming from other countries eager to assimilate Spanish culture, but also in the growing number of Spanish cities with a cosmopolitan ambience, multinational companies, and the willingness of many young Spaniards to be transnational citizens.

See also: Chapter 1: Population and Demography. Chapter 2: Overview; The Catholic Monarchs; Maimónides; Philip II. Chapter 9: Overview; Peninsular Languages.

Further Reading

Bendiner, Elmer. *The Rise and Fall of Paradise: When Arabs and Jews Built a Kingdom in Spain*. New York: Barnes & Noble, 1983.

Gerber, Jane S. *The Jews of Spain: A History of the Sephardic Experience*. New York: Free Press, 1994.

Moreno, Luis, et al. *Diversity and Unity in Federal Countries*. Montreal: McGill-Queen's University Press, 2010.

Toguslu, Erkam, et al. *New Multicultural Identities in Europe: Religion and Ethnicity in Secular Societies*. Leuven: Leuven University Press, 2014.

Wright, Susan. *Monolingualism and Bilingualism: Lessons from Canada and Spain*. Clevedon: Multilingual Matters, 1996.

Nationalism

Spain is a mixed country with many different cultures and ideologies. Three regions—Galicia, Catalunya, and the Basque country—have developed their own nationalism and ideology that reflect their unique cultural history.

Historically, the Romans divided Hispania into several major administrative regions. One of them was *Gallaecia*, which refers to the actual Galicia, which became an independent kingdom in the fifth century. During the medieval period Galicia was at the height of its political and cultural splendor. The unification of Spain by the Catholic Monarchs in the 15th century (1492), however, meant a process of gradual isolation for Galicia because of the distance at the time between the capital of the kingdom (Madrid) and the northwest of Spain. Nevertheless, the 19th century saw the beginning of what Gallegos call the *rexurdimento*, meaning the renaissance. Initially, this resurgence of the local roots was primarily cultural as developed by writers such as Rosalía de Castro and Emilia Pardo Bazán. Later, Galicia adopted political ideologies unique to Spain with the ambition of becoming a regional autonomy. In fact, in June 1936 the Spanish parliament voted in favor of the "Estatuto de Autonomía Gallego," which recognized Galicia as its own autonomy/region. But that same summer the Spanish Civil War took place and with the victory of Franco in 1939, nationalism was strictly forbidden in Spain.

When democracy was restored to Spain in 1975, Galician nationalism was very weak in comparison to the Catalan and Basque countries, mainly due to its lack of financial independence. Despite having a distinctive regional language and fulfilling all the requirements of the Spanish constitution (1978) to be recognized as one of the historic nations of Spain, Galicia was not officially recognized as an autonomous region until 1981—two years after Catalunya and the Basque country (1979). Currently, the nationalist vote in Galicia remains comparatively weak. In fact, after the 2009 regional election, the Bloque Nacionalista Gallego (BNG), which is the main nationalist party in Galicia, had an internal crisis and was split into several political parties.

Nationalism in Galicia is synonymous with the Galician cultural movement called "Xeración Nós," which despite being repressed by Franco, has survived abroad. One of its most prominent political and intellectual figures was Alfonso Daniel Rodríguez Castelao (1886–1950), who wrote *Sempre en Galiza* (1944, *Always in Galicia*) during his exile in Argentina. Castelao suggested the idea of a federal Spain in which regional idiosyncrasies and universality could be united. More recently, Galician writers such as Manuel Rivas, Suso de Toro, and Xavier Alcalá are well known throughout Spain. They write in their local language (and their work has been translated into Spanish and other languages) and express their concerns about the globalization of Galicia.

The region of Catalunya used to be called *Tarraconense* by the Romans. During the medieval period, Catalunya was divided into multiple regions that were united by the counts of Barcelona in the 11th century. Between the 12th and 14th centuries, Catalunya (which included the Crown of Aragón, Valencia, Illes Balears, Sicily, and Sardinia) was a political and economic powerhouse in the Mediterranean; however, its power was diminished in the 14th century due to the European Black Death. Also, with the conquest of the New World by the Catholic Monarchs (1492), the center of the European economy changed from the Mediterranean Sea to the Atlantic Ocean. According to César Molinas, who has written about the current problems of Catalan nationalism, Catalunya did not take advantage of the commerce with the Americas simply due to lack of ambition and not because they were not allowed by the rest of Spain ("por falta de ambición y de emprendimiento, no porque tuviese ningún impedimento legal para hacerlo" (Molinas 2014).

Between the 18th and 19th centuries, Catalunya developed prosperous wine and textile industries. During the second half of the 19th century poet Bonaventura Carles Aribau published *Oda a la Pàtria* (1833, *Homage to the Nation*) and started what the Catalans call *Renaixença*, a Catalan cultural movement with a strong nationalist ideology. It represented a cultural boom in many areas (music, poetry, theater, philosophy, and architecture). For instance, the first train line in Spain was built between Barcelona and Mataró in 1848. However, the loss of the last Spanish colonies (1898) created tensions among Spaniards. In fact, it ignited a strong Catalan nationalism that was represented through a new artistic style—modernism. Also, Enric Prat de la Riba wrote *La nacionalitat catalana* (1906, *The Catalan Nationality*), which is considered one of the foundational works of Catalanism. However, Prat, like most Catalan bourgeoisie of the time, did not aspire to be separated from Spain. The reason was simple: They understood that commerce within the interior of Spain was protected. The political Catalan movement achieved regional autonomy (*estatuto de autonomía*) during the second Republic in 1932. However, it was revoked with the victory of Franco. Josep Tarradellas (1899–1988), who was in exile as the president of Catalunya for over 40 years, returned to Spain in 1977. He was a key figure during the Spanish transition toward democracy and pluralism.

Nowadays the nationalist vote in Catalunya is strong. CiU (Convergence and Union) is a conservative and nationalist Catalan party that has played a significant role regionally but also within the general elections in Spain. They have won most regional elections as well as having representation in the national parliament. Due to the economic crisis, the friction between the regional views of the Catalans and the rest of the country has grown. Artur Mas became the current president of CiU and the president of Catalunya on December 27, 2010. However, because he did not obtain a majority, Mas had to form a coalition with another political party. In 2012 CiU and Oriol Junqueras' ERC (Esquerra Republicana de Catalunya)—a left wing Catalan separatist political party—approved a project to create an independent nation from Spain. The current president of Spain, Mariano Rajoy, declared that the region of Catalunya cannot organize a regional referendum in which they can decide unilaterally by vote if they want to be independent from Spain.

Catalan society has been under political pressure in the past decade, and still is. On the one hand, there is a group of Catalans who want to be separate from Spain at all costs, because they do not feel unified with the ideology of Spain. This is the case of the Catalan political party ERC and CUP. On the other hand, there is another group, perhaps the majority of Catalans, who see themselves as historically belonging to Spain's heritage. The latter identify the Catalan culture with what they call *charnega* identity, that is, a combination of different origins. For many experts the authentic essence of Catalunya resides precisely in being a hybrid society. This particular context provided inspiration for Catalan artists such as Albert Plá, Gato Pérez, and La Cubana, who make fun of any nationalism and/or particular essence of any nation. Catalan writer and cinema director Ramón de España describes the current Catalan wave of nationalism as "the Catalan madhouse." He asks himself how in the 21st century there can exist a song written in Spain to instigate hatreds toward the Spaniards: "Con la sangre de los castellanos haremos tinta roja" (with the blood of the Spaniards we will make red ink) (de España 2013). Another recent book that explains the current situation of Catalunya is Anna Grau's *¿Los españoles son de Marte y los catalanes de Venus?* (*Are the Spaniards from Mars and the Catalans from Venus?*, 2015)

The Basque country, or *Euskadi* in the Basque language, has also generated a nationalist movement in Spain. Because of its geographical location, far from the rest of the peninsula surrounded by mountains and the Cantabrian Sea, the Romans did not have a significant impact on the Basque land. During the medieval period, the Basque region was disputed between the kingdoms of Castilla and Navarra, ending up in the hands of Castilla. However, the Basques managed to maintain their local *fueros* or own laws even after the Catholic Monarchs gained power. In fact, it was not until 1876 that they lost their fueros due to the defeat of the Carlist Wars. The Carlist Basque people were traditionalists, ultra catholics, farmers and aristocrats, who felt threatened by the rise of the liberal urban bourgeoisie.

After losing the fueros the *fuerismo* joined the *carlismo*, which subsequently led to Basque nationalism, which was the personal creation of Sabino Arana (1865–1903). It was he alone who built the theory, the myths, and the symbols (i.e., the flag; the name *Euskadi*, and even development of his own version of the Basque language) for the future of Basque nationalism as a country in his *Lecciones de ortografía del euzkera bizkaíno* (Arana, 1896, *Lessons of Orthography from the Basque Country*). For Arana, the identity of the Basques resides in their particular race and their own moral values such as tradition, family, and solidarity among social classes as well as their total adhesion to Catholicism. He was the founder of the Basque nationalist political party PNV (Partido Nacionalista Vasco) in 1895. Gradually Arana managed to acquire popularity to the point that he achieved the recognition of autonomy (*estatuto de autonomía*) for the Basque region by the Spanish government in 1935.

During Franco's dictatorship (1939–1975), any nationalism was heavily repressed in Spain. This was particularly done in the Basque country, which consequently developed a more radical position. As a result of the friction between the dictatorship and Basque nationalism, the terrorist group ETA (*Euskadi'ta Askatasuna* / Euskadi and Freedom) was created in 1959. Initially this Basque organization only held cultural activities such as literary events. However, during the 1960s they became more radical and decided to reject Spain as an invader and colonizer of their lands. ETA did not see the constitution of 1978 as a solution. On the contrary, they thought that the separation of Spain into 17 regions was simply a maneuver on the part of the government to carry out the exploitation of the Basque people. The outrage of ETA members led to violence and terrorist-related deaths both within the region and in the rest of Spain. However, in 2011 ETA announced publicly the end of violence, which marked a historic date in recent Spanish history. Also, many Basque artists have received the most important awards given by the Spanish authorities, including Bernardo Atxaga (National Literature Prize), Eduardo Chillida (Prince of Asturias), and Fernando Savater (National Literature Prize).

For contemporary writer Javier Cercas, the right to choose is manipulated by certain political groups. They intentionally ignore the Spanish constitution, which clearly establishes that the right to choose belongs to every citizen in Spain, and it cannot be decided unilaterally by one single region against the majority of the Spaniards. In other words, the constitution says that sovereignty resides in the Spanish people as a whole, so that under it, the Catalans have no right to decide as a region on whether they want independence. Subsequently, the problem of nationalism in Spain resides in the politicians. Since Spain became a democracy neither left nor right-wing political actors have spent any time in refuting independent ideas. On the contrary, conservative and liberal politicians in Spain have made alliances and even special concessions, which are now the main cause of the problems. For Nobel Prize writer Mario Vargas Llosa, to belong to a specific nation does not mean to have special privileges.

One of the major challenges of Spain resides in educating citizens about Spain's diversity in the 17 regions. Some Spanish regions still tend to accentuate the local differences rather than the collective richness of the entire nation. Therefore, there are some Spaniards who believe they live in one nation with many regional differences. Also there is another group of Spaniards who believe they live in a pluri-national state, and there is a third group who believe in regional independence from Spain.

See also: Chapter 1: Overview; Population and Demography; Regions of Spain. Chapter 2: Overview. Chapter 3: Overview; Constitutions; Political Challenges of Spain's 21st Century. Chapter 4: Overview. Chapter 5: Savater, Fernando. Chapter 6: Overview. Chapter 9: Overview. Chapter 11: Overview; Rexurdimento.

Further Reading

Beswick, Jaine. *Regional Nationalism in Spain: Language Use and Ethnic Identity in Galicia*. Clevendon: Multilingual Matters, 2007.

Goode, Joshua. *Impurity of Blood: Defining Race in Spain, 1870–1930*. Baton Rouge: Louisiana State University Press, 2009.

Sanabria, Enrique A. *Republicanism and Anticlerical Nationalism in Spain*. New York: Palgrave Macmillan, 2009.

Roma Society

Historically, the Roma have been the largest minority group in Spain. Since their arrival on the peninsula in the early 15th century, the Roma have been Spain's largest minority population from outside the region. The first written document that chronicles the presence of the Gypsies in Spain dates back to 1425, when King Alfonso V signed an authorization to don Juan de Egipto Menor (in Medieval Europe, the area of Siria, Cyprus, and nearby lands were known by the name of Egipto Menor, or "Small Egipt") to travel within Spain's territories. The Spanish word *gitano* derives from *egiptano* to refer to a person from Egypt. Much like the Muslim and Jewish communities, the Roma also fell victim to Ferdinand and Isabel's desire for a homogenous kingdom and were subjected to corporal punishment or exile for such minor offenses as not possessing a job or trade. Ultimately, they were the most marginal group since the Renaissance after the expulsion of the Moors and the Jews by the Catholic Monarchs. The social abandonment of the Gypsies did not end with the reign of the Catholic Monarchs. For the next 300 years, gypsies were pressured to conform to social norms of Catholic Spain or leave. Gypsies were legally banned from using their own language, holding public office, and even from marrying within their own culture.

The 19th century brought improvements in legal rights of the Roma, though social stigmatization and discrimination remained widespread. In 1812 the constitution of Cádiz recognized gypsies for the first time as citizens and legislation aimed at targeting the group ceased. Many ceased their nomadic tradition and became a part of local society, particularly in extremadura and Andalucía where they found a place in the rural society and learned trades such as blacksmithing and horse trading. In cities such as Sevilla and Jerez, entire *barrios* of Roma people came into being. The rising population of Flamenco music during the late 1800s and early 1900s further aided in elevating the status of their culture.

The Roma culture is still an integral part of Spanish society today. The American magazine *Time* dedicated an article in 2010 to Spain's tolerance toward the Gypsies (Cala 2010). This editorial points out that Spain has the second largest community of gypsies in Europe. There are an estimated 970,000 gypsies that comprise almost 2 percent of Spain's total population, of which about 45 percent live in Andalucía. In fact, this region celebrates November 22 annually as The Day of the Andalusian Gypsies, because it was on November 22, 1462, that the gypsies settled on the peninsula. Spain invests approximately €36 million annually on social funding for gypsies. In Spain, almost half of Roma are homeowners, and approximately 75 percent are believed to have consistent income. All have access to healthcare, as well as education, an area that Spain is focusing on in regards to funding. Furthermore, the *Time* article interviews a gypsy, who considers himself "first Spanish, then Gypsy, and I'm proud to be both." Although Spanish gypsies recognize that there is still racism, they also think that their quality of life is better in Spain than anywhere else in Europe (Cala 2010).

Nowadays, the majority of Roma in Spain have abandoned their traditional nomadic life; 88 percent live in a house. Nevertheless, the image of this particular group remains stigmatized by Spanish society. On the one hand, there is no doubt that they contribute positively by strengthening the brand of Spain nationally and internationally with their rich cultural heritage in the art of flamenco music, dancing, and singing. On the other hand, their performance in education is still very low. Following Pereira's data, 70 percent of Spanish gypsies have not completed primary education, and 14 percent of Roma families are in extreme poverty (Pereira 2015).

See also: Chapter 1: Population and Demography. Chapter 2: Overview. Chapter 6: Overview. Chapter 13: Flamenco.

Further Reading

Bercovici, Konrad. *Gypsies in Spain*. Whitefish: Kessinger Publishing, 2010.

Borrow, George. *The Zincali: An Account of the Gypsies of Spain*. Teddington: Echo Library, 2010.

Charnon-Deutsch, Lou. *The Spanish Gypsy: The History of a European Obsession*. University Park: Pennsylvania State University Press, 2004.

Hooper, John. *The New Spaniards*. 2nd ed. London: Penguin Books, 2006.

Tremlett, Giles. *Ghosts of Spain*. London: Faber & Faber, 2006.

Spanish Youth

Being a Spanish youth allows for numerous liberties. Legally a Spanish adolescent (12–18 years old) is authorized to do many things. Table 6.3 lists the age to start.

Table 6.3   MINIMUM AGE IN SPAIN FOR VARIOUS ACTIVITIES

Activity	Minimum Age
Vote	18 years old
Health	12 years old, have the right to be heard before accepting medical treatment.
Piercings and tattoos	16 and 18, respectively. However, it does not apply in practice.
Make a will	14

Criminal responsibility	At the age of 14, Spaniards can be sentenced.
Emancipation	16, but with parental consent. However, the real average age is 29.
Hunting license	16; however, they can carry firearms with the consent of their parents.
Sexual intercourse	16.
Work	16, after finishing the compulsory secondary education
Marriage	17
Abortion	At 16 and 17 can interrupt their pregnancy without parental consent.
Alcohol and tobacco	It is forbidden to sell to a minor of 18. However, the average age for beginning to smoke and to drink alcohol in Spain is 13.
Driving license	Scooters can be driven at the age of 15; cars at the age of 18.
Social networks	Tuenti, Facebook, and Twitter establish a minimum age of 14. However, in practice Spaniards do not comply.
Divorce	Children at the age of 12 have the right to be heard in custody disputes.
Disco and gambling	18

Young men carry drinks in a shopping cart during a *macrobotellón* (drinking session) in Granada, southern Spain, on March 17, 2006. Hordes of teenagers and students swarmed into Spanish streets for a mass drinking session, flying in the face of legislation introduced to stop the mass binges, known as "botellones." (STR/Reuters/Corbis)

The conservative government in Spain is preparing new social reforms that will affect the new generation. The disparity between minimum legal age to do certain things is huge. For example, the age for sexual intercourse in Spain is still a controversial issue. The Spanish philosopher Victoria Camps welcomes the increase of the age for sexual consent. For her, people confuse the notion of freedom for minors with the idea of being modern or progressive. Within the context of what is legal among teenagers in Spain, the judge Emilio Calatayud has become famous in Spain for judging exemplary sentences including when he condemned a youngster to finish the ESO (compulsory secondary education). With regards to the age of sexual consent, he thinks that the legal age should be 14, which is the same age for criminal responsibility. However, he also adds that nowadays the youngsters are taller and more handsome, but not necessarily more mature. Therefore, he is also inclined to establish the age of sexual consent at 18, which is the legal age of being an adult in Spain.

See also: Chapter 1: Population and Demography. Chapter 6: Overview. Chapter 8: Overview. Chapter 16: Overview; Social Media; Youth Culture.

Further Reading

Antonucci, Lorenza, et al., eds. *Young People and Social Policy in Europe: Dealing with Risk, Inequality, and Precarity in Times of Crisis*. Basingstoke: Palgrave Macmillan, 2014.

Pérez Vidal, Carmen, et al., eds. *A Portrait of the Young in the New Multilingual Spain*. Clevedon: Mulitlingual Matters, 2008.

REFERENCES

Arana, Sabino. *Lecciones de ortografía del euzkera bizkaíno*. Bilbao: Bizkaya'ren Edestija ta Izkerea Pizkundia, 1896.

Aribau, Bonaventura Carles. *Oda a la pàtria*. Barcelona: El Vapor, 1944.

Ayuso, Miguel. "Todos somos pobres: por qué el 55% de España es ya proletaria." *El Confidencial*, October 19, 2013.

Balmer, John M. T. Prologue to *El tabú Real. La imagen de una monarquía en crisis,* by Daniel Barredo (Córdoba: Berenice, 2013).

Barredo, Daniel. *El tabú Real. La imagen de una monarquía en crisis*. Córdoba: Berenice, 2013.

Blanchar, Clara. "Wage Gap in Spain Widens Hastening the Decline of the Middle Classes." *El País*, January 14, 2014.

Cala, Andrés. "Spain's Tolerance of Gypsies: A Model for Europe?" *Time,* September 16, 2010.

Cercas, Javier. "Democracia y derecho a decidir." *El País*, September 15, 2013.

Cercas, Javier. "Right to Decide." *El País,* September 18, 2013.

Colectivo Ioé (Carlos Pereda, Miguel Ángel de Prada, Walter Actis). *Discapacidades e inclusión social*. Barcelona: la Caixa, 2012.

Domínguez Ortiz, Antonio. *España: Tres milenios de historia*. Madrid: Marcial Pons, 2000.

España, Ramón de. *El manicomio catalán*. Madrid: La Esfera de los Libros, 2013.

Ferrer-i-Carbonell, Ada, Xavier Ramos, Mónica Oviedo. *Growing Inequalities and Its Impacts in Spain*. European Union: GINI, 2013.

García Álvarez, Jacobo. "Los mapas." In: Javier Moreno Luzón y Xosé M. Núñez Sixas, eds.. *Ser españoles. Imaginarios nacionalistas en el siglo XX*. Barcelona: RBA, 2013: (315–363).

"Generaciones desechadas" (no author signed). *El País*, January 11, 2014.

Marco, José María. *Una historia patriótica de España*. Barcelona: Booket, 2013.

Mars, Amanda. "España vuelve a ser un país receptor neto de remesas de emigrantes." *El País*, October 2, 2013.

Martorell, Miguel y Santos Juliá. *Manual de historia política y social de España (1808–2011)*. Barcelona: RBA, 2012.

Molinas, César. "Lo que no se quiere oír sobre Cataluña." *El País*, January 18, 2014.

Nairn, Agnes. *Children's Well-Being in UK, Sweden, and Spain: The Role of Inequality and Materialism*. London: Ipsos MORI (Social Research Institute), 2011.

Navarro, Vicente. "Topics for Our Times: The 'Black Report' of Spain—The Commission on Social Inequalities in Health." *American Journal of Public Health* 87 no. 3 (1997): 334–335.

Pereira-Muro, Carmen. *Culturas de España*. Instructor's Edition. Stamford: Cengage Learning, 2015.

Pérez, Claudi. "Las coordenadas de España: 0-25-50-100." *El País*, October 12, 2013.

Pozo, Raul del. "Miguel, viejo soldado." *El Mundo*, February 20, 2014.

Prat de la Riba, Enric. *La Nationalitat catalana*. Barcelona: Tip. L'Anuari de la Exportació, 1906.

Preston, Paul. *The Spanish Holocaust*. New York: Norton, 2013.

Regàs, Rosa. *España. Una nueva mirada*. Barcelona: Lunwerg, 1997.

Rincón, Reyes. "Qué difícil es ser español." *El País*, December 2, 2013.

Rodríguez Castelao, Alfonso Daniel. *Sempre en Galiza*. Buenos Aires: As Burgas, 1944.

Queralt del Hierro, María Pilar. *Historia de España*. Madrid: Tikal, 2009.

Sánchez-Mellado, Luz. "Niñatos según para qué." *El País*, September 14, 2013.

Sanmartín, Olga R. "España pierde 200.000 extranjeros en sólo un año." *El Mundo*, January 17, 2014.

Tezanos, José Félix. *Los nuevos problemas sociales*. Madrid: Editorial Sistema, 2013.

Vargas Llosa, Mario. "El derecho a decidir." *El País*, September 22, 2013.

Websites

Banco de España. bde.es

CIS: Centro de Investigaciones Sociológicas. cis.es

Consejo General del Notariado. notariado.org

Consejo Superior de Investigaciones Científicas (CSIC). csic.es

Encuesta de Población Activa. http://www.ine.es/inebaseDYN/epa30308/epa_inicio.htm

Fundacionsistema.com

García Ferreras, Antonio. "T1C60/Desigualdad: el que parte y reparte." *La Sexta Columna* lasexta.com (aired on January 24, 2014)

IBEX 35. ibex35.com

INE. Instituto Nacional de Estadística: ine.es

Inequality.org

Kelisto.es

OECD. *How's Life? 2013*: "Country Snapshot Spain." http://www.oecd.org/howslife

OECD. *OECD Health Data 2013*: "How Does Spain Compare?" http://www.oecd.org/spain

ONCE. once.es

Pastor, Ana. "T2/C17/Una bajada de sueldo frenada por las protestas." *El Objetivo*. www.lasexta .com (aired on January 26, 2014)

Spain Today 2013. Madrid: Ministry of the Presidency, 2013. http://publicacionesoficiales.boe .essueldospublicos.com

CHAPTER 7

GENDER, MARRIAGE, AND SEXUALITY

OVERVIEW

Spanish people, including the LGBT community, since June 2005—when same-sex marriage became legal in Spain—have achieved a high level of legal protection in comparison with other countries. The Organization for Economic Cooperation and Development (OECD) finds that, at 78 percent, Spaniards report the seventh highest community tolerance of minority groups—ethnic minorities, migrants, gays, and lesbians (OECD average = 61%), and the third highest tolerance in OECD-Europe after the Netherlands, Ireland, and Iceland. Despite some reliable data like the OECD's reports, however, Spain can still be seen as a "macho" country with regards to sexuality.

Some public manifestations by several members of the Spanish community in the 21st century show a degree of intolerance. For instance, the new Spanish cardinal Fernando Sebastián Aguilar made global news, as reported by the British newspaper *The Telegraph*, when he insisted that "homosexuality can be cured with treatment" and likened it with "other 'bodily deficiencies' such as high blood pressure" (Govan 2014). This kind of opinion is not an isolated case. On the contrary, similar views have been made public and also made the headlines beyond the national Spanish media. For example, Canada's *The Globe and Mail* reported the publication in Spain of "a new book that urges wives to be submissive to their husbands" (Anderssen 2013). The unexpected bestseller *Cásate y sé sumisa* (2013, *Get Married and Be Submissive*) was written by an Italian journalist mother of four, Constanza Miriano, under the auspices of the Catholic Archdiocese of Granada. The archbishop of Granada, Francisco Javier Martinez, said the outrage over the book was ridiculous and hypocritical. The conservative Spanish ex-Health Minister Ana Mato unsuccessfully tried to ban the book. Undoubtedly, it generated a new feminist debate in Spain, where many women disagree with her two main premises—get married and be submissive. Surprisingly, Miriano declared in an interview to the BBC program *Newsnight* that perhaps the reason why women around the world are angry with her book is because "maybe we are not free from the need for recognition from outside ourselves" (BBC aired on December 14, 2013). One thing is clear: Gender issues are very much present in Spain's 21st century.

In 2000 Laura Freixas edited the book *Ser Mujer* (*Be a Woman*), in which she compiled 10 well-known female authors who write about the experience of being a woman in Spain. For Freixas, Spanish women of her generation are very different from their grandmothers. She opens her prologue narrating a personal episode of her grandmother who experienced domestic violence from her husband/grandfather during Franco's time. In the new millennium, key indicators on Spain's gender equality data and statistics from the World Bank Organization (last accessed on February 27, 2014) show that: 48 percent of women are employed in the nonagricultural sector; the maternal mortality ratio (modeled estimate, per 100,000 live births) was 6 in 2010; the number of weeks for maternity leave was 16 (2009); and the ratio of seats held by women in national parliament in 2013 was 36 percent. Furthermore, the age of sexual consent in Spain was 13 until very recently. In 2013 it was raised to 16 years old, after the United Nations admonished Spain and the Vatican for being the two countries in the world with the lowest age for legal sexual consent.

The most common issues that Spaniards have to deal with in terms of gender equality are "measures aimed at balancing working, personal, and family life" (Valdés 2010). Similarly, several studies show that there is still an imbalance with regards to gender equality in Spain. One of the main findings is that in Spain there is less access to high-ranking positions for women. Also, there is less public recognition of women's professional achievements. Other worrying conclusions are that in Spain there is an imbalance in salaries and unequal gender representation in all sectors, including culture (Gautier 2011). More recently, AMIT (Association of Women Researchers and Technologies), CIMA (Women filmmakers), Clásicas y Modernas (association for gender equality in culture), and MAV (Women Visual Artists) signed a *Manifesto for Equality in Culture*. They declared that in the cultural world today in Spain, a deep inequality still reigns between women and men. This manifesto is available in English on any website of the above associations.

Spain's *machismo* is gradually relenting. However, "profoundly sexist attitudes have survived into an era in which women are acquiring much genuine freedom and equality" (Hooper 2006). Since Spain criminalized male violence against women in 2003, 658 women in Spain have been killed by their partners or spouses over the last decade. In 2013 alone, 48 women and 5 children were killed due to male violence (Sahuquillo 2014). According to the latest statistics provided by the National Institute of Women Studies in Spain, nearly a thousand Spanish women have died (984) due to domestic violence in Spain: 1999 (54); 2000 (63); 2001 (50); 2002 (54); 2003 (71); 2004 (72); 2005 (57); 2006 (69); 2007 (71); 2008 (76); 2009 (56); 2010 (73); 2011 (61); 2012 (52); 2013 (54); 2014 (51). By 2015, about 2.5 million Spanish women have experienced a case of domestic violence physically or sexually. The figure of 2.5 million women represents 12.5 percent of Spain's total female population. The figure shows an increase over previous years: 2011 (10.8%) or 2006 (6.3%). If Spanish women are changing, however, men are not. This is one of the main conclusions of the Spanish physician and professor Miguel Lorente Acosta, who in 2001 published *Mi marido me pega lo normal* (*My Husband Beats Me Just Like Normal*), whose provocative title, however, summarizes the fundamental problem.

Ten years after the previous socialist party administration introduced laws aimed at combating gender-specific violence, there has been no reduction in domestic abuse: Judges, police, and NGOs all warn that Spanish society is still failing to grapple with the issue. In fact, over decades male violence against women has been largely ignored in Spain. It has actually been exacerbated due to the economic crisis, which has seen soaring unemployment rates. In other words, because of Spain's recession, those women economically dependent on their partners nowadays receive less help from the state.

Furthermore, around 22 percent of Spanish women say they have experienced gender-specific violence at least once in their lives, yet the number of reports over the last decade has never exceeded more than 130,000 annually. Only 10 of the women killed in 2013 reported being abused to the police. Also, there is no racial profile or pattern related to gender violence in Spain. The majority of the victims were born in Spain (37, which is 76.6%) while 11 were foreigners (23.4%) in 2013.

According to the National Institute of Statistics (INE 2013), in 2012 there were 29,146 women who registered as victims of violence. By age, more than half of this group was between 25 and 39 years old. Also, two out of three victims were born in Spain (65.5% of the total). By areas, the regions with more gender violence in 2012 were Andalucía (7,161), Comunitat Valenciana (4,172), and Comunidad de Madrid (3,427). Conversely, the regions with less gender violence were Navarra (311) and La Rioja (194).

Apart from the national research institute of Women Studies (*Instituto de la Mujer*), the state also offers the 016 free phone helpline services for abused women. Equally important is the help provided by the public platform and website called *Observatorio de la violencia de género* (Observatory against gender violence), which provides useful information, including reports and analysis of the situation of women in Latin America. The *Observatorio* is the only judiciary organ run by the state accounting for male violence against women in Spain. Also, the non-governmental website afavir.org is worth noting because it provides good information and helps families in need.

Further Reading

Ackelsberg, Martha A. *Free Women of Spain: Anarchism and the Struggle for the Emancipation of Women*. Oakland: AK Press, 2005.

Bezhanova, Olga. *Growing Up in an Inhospitable World: Female Bildungsroman in Spain*. Tempe: AILCFH, 2014.

de Ros, Xon, and Geraldine Hazbun, eds. *A Companion to Spanish Women's Studies*. Woodbridge: Tamesis Books, 2014.

Family Roles

While the makeup of a family in contemporary Spain has multiple combinations, there are commonalities that have occurred over the past few decades: Spain's family structure no longer follows the rigid structure of Franco's time; the birthrate has significantly decreased, and the family is becoming multigenerational as children reside longer in family homes and grandparents help raise the younger generation.

There is no prototypical model like there used to be. For instance, during Franco's time, it was a mother and a father with several children and Catholic beliefs. Although the traditional model is still prevalent, new ways of coexistence have developed. The new ideas of diversity, pluralism, and globalization that characterize the 21st century have also made an impact on the Spanish family. Hence, a Spanish family can be: urban or rural; living with multiple relatives vs nuclear (only close family members); extended vs one-parent family; have international or mixed members vs only national members; be same sex; have adopted children; or be a young couple living together (*de facto* partnership or by common-law marriage) vs a registered partnership (*pareja registrada*).

Another distinctive feature of the Spanish family of the 21st century is the low birth rate. In Spain, one or two children in a family are the norm. To see a family with three children or more is a rarity. A family of three children is referred to as a *familia numerosa*, and they are eligible to receive special welfare and education assistance. The large Catholic families of six or seven children that were promoted under Franco's rule are a thing of the past.

Another common feature of the Spanish family is the extended childhood of the younger generation. It is not uncommon for children to remain living with their parents until their late twenties. The average age that a woman leaves home in Spain is between 27 and 28 years, and for the men it is several years older. Another common characteristic of the Spanish family of the 21st century is the huge role that the grandparents play. Due to the economic crisis, the help supplied by the older generation in the Spanish family is not only invaluable, it also denotes one unique common attribute of the Spanish families—they are very resilient. It is predicted that by 2018 Spain will have more multigenerational families, where the income from the different members will be shared. In fact, between 2014 and 2018 there will be a gradual decline of Spain's welfare due to the shared economic nature of Spain's families.

Regardless of changes in the family structure over the past few decades, the role of the women in the family has been very slow to evolve. Within the family unit, Spain leads the EU countries in regards to gender inequalities. Based on INE's statistics of 2009–2010, on average, Spanish women spend four hours and 29 minutes per day on domestic chores while men only spend two hours and 32 minutes. According to Eurostat, on average, women in Spain spend 200 percent more time than men on domestic work (in comparison to 50% more in Sweden). To further illustrate the domestic imbalance, men in Spain spend two hours more per day on leisure activities than women (in contrast to just 26–27 minutes a day in Finland and Sweden). Finally, men in Spain spend on average 99 minutes a day in physical activity including walking, while women spend only 48 minutes a day. In addition to domestic work, women also tend to be primarily responsible for child care. More recently, in 2014, the care of children in Spain was in the following order: mothers (82%); grandmothers (7.5%); fathers (4.8%); daycare (4.3%); and nannies (1.8%). With their responsibilities of maintaining a job, running the family home, and raising the children, many women in Spain are finding the only solution is to opt out of having children or having one at most. Domestic chores as well as taking care of the children are usually family tasks done by women. The role of men in the family still seems to be limited to that of provider. It is uncommon to see Spanish men take paternity leave.

Finally, if the role of the mother is difficult, the role of the child in Spain is golden. In today's culture, children are revered in Spain in a way that would be unfathomable for most North American or English-speaking countries. With the declining birthrate, young children in Spain are treated as rare and delicate novelties to be coddled, admired, and catered to. Yet the Spanish child in turn evolves into a teenager that appreciates the family and avoids the teenage rebellion common to their North American peers. When youth between the ages of 15 and 29 were asked, an overwhelming 96 percent were content with their families.

See also: Chapter 2: Overview. Chapter 4: Overview. Chapter 5: Overview. Chapter 6: Overview. Chapter 7: Overview; Gender Roles. Chapter 10: Overview. Chapter 15: Family Outings and Vacation. Chapter 16: Overview; Youth Culture.

Further Reading

Kraler, Albert, et al. *Gender, Generations, and the Family in International Migration*. Amsterdam: Amsterdam University Press, 2012.

Radcliff, Pamela Beth. *Making Democratic Citizens in Spain: Civil Society and the Popular Origins of the Transition, 1960–78*. New York: Palgrave Macmillan, 2011.

Tremlett, Giles. *Ghosts of Spain*. London: Faber & Faber, 2006.

Feminism in Spain

While women's rights in Spain have increased over time, and particularly since Franco's reign, Spanish women are still battling with the *machismo* attitude that remains prevalent today, particularly in the older generation. Over the past few decades Spain has made strides in gender equality parallel to most EU countries: equal rights, equal salaries, protection from domestic violence, the right to divorce, and the right to abortion, yet often those laws do not translate to reality nor do they change the mindset of traditional Spanish *machismo*. These men are often unapologetic and public about their views on gender equality. One Spanish journalist recently wrote, "I do not share any ideas coming from the feminist pests and I could care less about the so-called gender equality" (Diego 2012). This is not an isolated case of intolerance. Similar views toward feminism appear in recent history books. For example, another writer noted that, "in my opinion, feminism and similar ideas constitute a true plague, whose effects are just starting to come out" (Moa 2013).

Other Spanish historians do not share these misogynistic views. According to historians Martorell and Juliá, there has been a revolution among Spanish woman brought about in part by recent exposure to immigrants, particularly Scandinavians. This change of attitude has subsequently evolved toward changes within the Spanish family. For example, Spanish women with more education tend to postpone marriage and maternity—if they decide to partake in marriage or family at all. Like northern European countries, Spain has also seen a proliferation of couples living together *de facto*. The number of children born out of wedlock has increased in recent years. For instance, in 1976 it was 2.16 percent while in 2010 it exceeded 30 percent. Also, the age for having the first child has been delayed, from being 25 years (1976) to being nearly 30 years in 2011 (Martorell and Juliá 2012). Women in Spain are able to access these choices in career, family, and education due to the long history of Spanish women who fought to obtain these rights (i.e., Clara Campoamor).

There was little effort to promote women's education throughout the 19th century in Spain. In some areas of the country 70 percent of women could not read or write at the turn of the century. Yet the pioneers of the early 1900s set in motion what would be more than a century-long fight for women to gain (or at least move toward) parity with men in Spain. In 1912, the socialist women's group *Agrupación Femenina Socialista* was formed in Madrid and one year later the magazine *El Pensamiento Femenino* (Feminine Thought) was founded by Benita Asas and Pilar Fernández. In 1918 one of the most important feminist organizations to date was created, the *Asociación Nacional de Mujeres Españolas* (ANME: National Association of Spanish Women). They championed causes such as the abolition of legalized prostitution, equal salaries, and the right to work in certain official occupations. They also provided help for working class women.

While in 1924 some women were able to vote in municipal elections, the right was limited to emancipated women who were at least 23 years old or married. In the pivotal year 1931 three women were democratically chosen as members of the Spanish Parliament and Spanish women were able to vote in general elections. Clara Campoamor (Partido Radical / Radical party), Victoria Kent (Izquierda Republicana / Republican Left), and Margarita Nelken (PSOE, Socialist party) were voted into office this year and Clara Campoamor in a historical discourse in Parliament defended suffrage for Spanish women. On October 1, 1931, the bill was passed and included in the constitution (of the Republic). This was truly a historic victory, as it would be over a decade before women's suffrage was allowed in countries such as France, Italy, or Belgium. The momentum of the 1930s continued when in 1932 the Divorce Law was passed with the support of Victoria Kent and feminist writer and politician María Martínez Sierra (or María de la O Lejárraga). This law legalized divorce under mutual consent. This then-revolutionary law would not appear in countries such as Britain and Denmark for another 40 years. This was also one of the first laws that Franco would throw out once he gained power.

In 1934 Pilar Primo de Rivera created the *Sección Femenina,* which was the women's section of the *Falange Española*, a pro-Fascist movement formed by her brother José Antonio Primo de Rivera. She would go on to lead the *Sección Femenina* from 1934–1977, gathering over half a million members while maintaining a public political profile for over 40 years. In 1936 Federica Montseny was appointed Spain's first female minister as the Minister for Health and Social Assistance.

With Franco's rule in 1937, many of the rights women previously achieved were revoked. Women's role was limited to the confines of the family home. When Franco died on November 20, 1975, women's lives in Spain were dictated by laws that resembled the rest of Europe's laws of the 1930s. A significant regression had occurred.

Yet progress since Franco's death has been impressive. Only months after his death a feminist movement emerged that rapidly advanced the right of Spanish women to equal those of other European countries. Certain articles of Spain's Civil Code were abolished such as those designating the male as head of the family and limiting the roles of married women. In 1978 adultery and cohabitation were no longer considered criminal offenses and contraception was legalized.

The Spanish constitution of 1978 also brought additional reforms such as the addition of article 14, which prohibits discrimination based on gender, as well as the

THE 20TH CENTURY

Spain's 20th-century feminism experienced multiple but significantly different ideologies from being socialist and anarchist between 1920 to 1933, when women voted for the first time, to a solid period of conservatism during Franco's time (i.e., abortion was treated as a criminal offense). Yet during a conference in Granada attended by 3,000 women from all over the country in 1979, they chose a "difference feminism" (differences between men and women should not be considered equally), which was becoming a trend in other countries. However, other feminisms, including radical feminism, disagreed with the new adopted positioning within the movement, and immediately after 1979 Spain's women's movement became fragmented. Furthermore, only 70 out of 600 women's organizations considered themselves feminist in 1987, a year when Spanish women became news in Europe for being the largest segment of Spaniards unemployed in comparison to other EU women. On the other hand, Lidia Falcón (1935–) has been considered the mother of Spain's feminism, equivalent in caliber to Simone de Beauvoir and Betty Friedan. Falcón is a lawyer, a journalist, and, above all, a very prolific feminist activist, whose style is versatile, alternating dramas (16 plays), essays (15 essays), narratives (10), chronicles (4), biographies (3), and many articles in different national journals, as well as being the founder of the magazine *Vindicación Feminista* (*Feminist Vindication*) and the theoretical journal *Poder y Libertad* (*Power and Freedom*), both in 1979, and the founder of Spain's first feminist party, the *Partido Feminista*.

legalization of divorce in 1981. The 1982 elections saw the Socialist Party (PSOE) gain power; it would remain in power for another 12 years in which women's rights would continue to gain momentum. In 1985 abortion became legal under the Ley Orgánica 9/1985 (Organic Law 9/1985), but only in cases of rape or if the fetus was deformed. In 1983 the PSOE (Socialist Party) created the *Instituto de la Mujer* (Institute of Women Studies). And in 1988 the PSOE established a quota of 25 percent of women in its voting lists. Later the Izquierda Unida (United left / Communist party) raised the quota to 35 percent. During this decade, women entered the workforce in jobs traditionally reserved for males and entered universities in record numbers. By the late 1980s women made up half of the university student body. However, despite the fact that women were now working out of the home, they still had primary responsibility for housework and childrearing. Many women opted to postpone marriage, if they married at all, and put off or forego altogether having children. The birthrate continued to fall, giving Spain the lowest birthrate in the world by 2000.

In 1993 the PSOE named three women to its government: Ángeles Amador (Minister of Health), Cristina Alberdi (Minister of Social Matters), and Carmen Alborch (Minister of Culture). Women continued to infiltrate the traditionally male-dominated government in the new millennium. In 2004 the PSOE named María Teresa de la Vega as vice president, becoming the first female to hold the position in the history of Spain. Also, there was an equal number of male and female ministers. In 2005 the legalization of marriage by two people of the same sex occurred and in 2007 the Law of Equity was passed mandating a quota of women in the public and private sector in Spain. The year

Spain's feminism won the battle against the Spanish government's plan to implement major restrictions on abortion and women's rights on International Women's Day in Madrid on March 8, 2014. (AP Photo/Andres Kudacki)

2010 brought with it Zapatero's progressive abortion law. Yet with the election of the conservative party (PP) in 2011, women's rights are once again regressing.

Despite decades of reform, the word "feminism" is not universally accepted in Spain. Demographically speaking, by 2014 only 1.5 percent of Spaniards consider themselves feminists while self-definitions of ecologist (5%) or non-political (7%) have a much higher representation. Perhaps the word "feminism" never was accepted in the Iberian Peninsula since Spain has not produced a strong visible and distinctive corpus of theoretical feminism as did, for instance, France (i.e., Simone de Beauvoir), the U.K. (i.e., Mary Wollstonecraft), or the U.S. (i.e., Betty Friedan). Nevertheless, Spain's feminism(s) has steadily developed in the modern era, especially due to the groundwork of Spanish female philosophers such as Celia Amorós's *Hacia una crítica de la razón patriarcal* (1985, *Towards a Critique of Patriarchal Reasoning*); Amelia Valcárcel's *Sexo y filosofía* (1991, *Gender and Philosophy*), Victoria Camps's *El siglo de las mujeres* (1998, *The Women's Century*), Silvia L. Gil's *Nuevos feminismos* (2011, *New Feminisms*), and, more recently, the 2012 anthology edited by Roberta Johnson and Maite Zubiaurre, *Antología del pensamiento feminista español (1726–2011)*. As its title suggests, this anthology has as its primary purpose to highlight the broad range of Spanish feminist thought. For Johnson and Zubiaurre, Spanish feminist thought is different from other Western countries, being generally concerned with more abstract considerations. Due to Spain's tumultuous history, repeatedly swinging between conservative regression and progressive modernization, socio-historical factors have assumed greater weight. Hence, issues such as class and religion have arguably had a more lasting impact on women's rights, bodies, and their relationship with the private, domestic, and public spheres. This anthology reconstructs a feminist genealogy, in all its varied textures, that has been preserved beyond the confines of socio-historical forces.

See also: Chapter 1: Population and Demography. Chapter 2: Overview. Chapter 5: Overview. Chapter 6: Overview. Chapter 7: Overview. Chapter 11: Overview. Chapter 16: Cinema; Cultural Icons; Fashion.

Further Reading

Enders, Victoria L., and Pamela Beth Radcliff, eds. *Constructing Spanish Womanhood: Female Identity in Modern Spain*. Albany: State University of New York Press, 1999.

Femenías, María Luisa, and Amy Oliver, eds. *Feminist Philosophy in Latin America and Spain*. New York: Rodopi, 2007.

Labanyi, Jo, ed. *Constructing Identity in Contemporary Spain: Theoretical Debates and Cultural Practice*. Oxford: Oxford University Press, 2003.

Twomey, Lesley K., ed. *Women in Contemporary Culture: Roles and Identities in France and Spain*. Portland: Intellect, 2000.

Vollendorf, Lisa, ed. *Recovering Spain's Feminist Tradition*. New York: Modern Language Association of America, 2001.

Gender Roles

Over the centuries, Spanish women have been dominated by their husbands. In fact, only in the 20th century have women started to take a more assertive role in society. Gender roles as viewed in society are without doubt changing in Spain's 21st century. Today most Spanish women aspire to have a professional career as well as to maintain control of their bodies, including the right to decide the terms of conceiving children. A recent Spanish film *Planes para mañana* (*Plans for Tomorrow*, directed by Juana Macías, 2010) portrays, however, the current difficulties experienced by most contemporary Spanish women in achieving total autonomy—including economic independence. Furthermore, a magazine's recent cover photo of two *falleras* (local women from Valencia) kissing each other generated controversy in the Spanish media (*EGF and the City,* March 2014). For the president of the Basque country LGBT, Ascensión Parron, "Spanish society already understands what it means to be homosexual. They do not see us as sick people. However, there is still a long way to go" ("La sociedad ya entiende lo que es ser homosexual. Ya no nos ven como enfermos pero queda mucho camino por hacer," Sánchez 2014).

The patriarchal system in Spain cannot be abolished with one or two laws, nor with eight years of the same government. The reason is simple. Conservative views claim that equality already exists; thus feminism is no longer necessary and, therefore, obsolete (Pérez Garzón 2012). For instance, the socialist Zapatero's abortion law of 2010 allowed females age 16 to have an abortion without parental consent and without the need to provide a reason for the abortion. On December 2013, the conservative Rajoy government passed a bill in which abortion is legal only in cases of rape or in cases where an extreme health risk is present. In response to the bill, countrywide protests erupted in Spain. In fact, on February 1, 2014, there was a protest against this new abortion reform, which became the biggest feminist action ever to take place in Spain (Varela 2014). The controversy of Spain's new abortion law was also news in other countries such as Britain. In a 2012 poll, 81 percent of Spaniards were opposed to changes to Spain's abortion laws. Within this particular new scenario, Spain made a step backward, that is, "women's organizations predict the re-emergence of 'abortion tourism,' with many travelling to Britain for operations" (Fotheringham 2013).

According to article 14 in the Spanish constitution of 1978, in terms of the law, all Spaniards are equal in regards to race, gender, religion, or any other personal or social condition and/or circumstance. However, the reality is different. Spain still has one of Europe's highest rates of discrimination between the sexes. Spanish women have more difficulties in finding a job than men, and their wages are usually 13 percent lower than men's salaries.

The European Commision Eurostat published a document entitled *The Life of Women and Men in Europe: A Statistical Portrait* (2008), which analyzes gender roles in the European Union. One interesting finding is that while it varies from country to country, women on average leave the parental home two years earlier than men. In the EU, 66 percent of women aged 18–24 lived at home while 78 percent of men aged 18–24 lived at home. The average age that a woman leaves home in Spain is between 27–28 years. Not only do men tend to leave the home later, they also on average marry later. The average age for a man in the EU to marry is 29.8 years old. This is 2.5 years older than the average woman (27.4). The age that women are having their first child has increased in the majority of EU countries over the past 10–15 years while fertility rates have decreased. Statistically speaking, only 6 percent of women live alone in Spain (as opposed to 20–21% in the U.K., Finland, and Germany), and 7–8 percent of males live alone in Spain (as opposed to 10–15% in most EU countries).

Spain—along with Portugal and the Netherlands—has one of the largest prison populations in the EU with 7–9 percent of the total population imprisoned. Females tend to have a lower rate of conviction in EU countries, rarely exceeding 6 percent. On the other hand, as of January 31, 2014, there were 5,461 men in jail for crimes of gender violence (Sahuquillo 2014).

See also: Chapter 1: Population and Demography. Chapter 2: Overview. Chapter 4: Overview. Chapter 5: Overview. Chapter 6: Overview. Chapter 7: Overview; Family Roles; Feminism in Spain; LGTB Community; Representation in Government; Representation in the Workforce. Chapter 8: Overview. Chapter 10: Overview. Chapter 11: Overview. Chapter 13: Overview. Chapter 16: Cinema.

Further Reading

Johnson, Roberta. *Gender and Nation in the Spanish Modernist Novel.* Nashville: Vanderbilt University Press, 2003.

Krook, Mona Lena, and Sarah Childs, eds. *Women, Gender, and Politics: A Reader*. Oxford: Oxford University Press, 2010.

Threlfall, Mónica, et al. *Gendering Spanish Democracy*. London: Routledge, 2004.

LGBT Community

There are approximately four million lesbian, gay, bisexual, or transgendered (LGBT) Spaniards, who represent about 10 percent of Spain's total population. In 1998 Catalunya was the first region to pass laws on civil union. On July 1, 2005, Spain passed Law 13/2005, which legalized marriage between two people of the same sex. Two years later, the Spanish government on March 15, 2007, approved Law 3/2007, which allows citizens to change their gender in the Spanish Registry without proof of gender-reassignment surgery. Spain also provides "access for same-sex married couples to rights of inheritance, residence, adoption of the other spouse's children, tax benefits, and to divorce rights" (Platero Méndez 2007). More recently, in 2013 Spain topped world gay-friendly rankings. According to the Washington-based think tank Pew Research Group, 88 percent of people in Spain believe that "homosexuality should be socially accepted" (Mills 2013).

However, as professor Gema Pérez-Sánchez points out in her article, "Transnational Conversations" (2010), despite the spectacular legal gains achieved by the Spanish LGBT community in the last decade in Spain, nevertheless, it is "a form of belated and overdue compensation, on the part of the progressive political class, for the

Socialist deputy and gay rights activist Pedro Zerolo, right, poses with his partner Jesús Santos while holding the Spanish Constitution, after getting married in a civil ceremony in Madrid, on October 1, 2005. In June 2005, the Spanish parliament legalized gay marriage, defying conservatives and clergy who opposed making traditionally Roman Catholic Spain the third nation to allow same-sex unions. (AP Photo/Bernat Armangue)

suffering that LGBTQ individuals experienced under repressive laws such as the 1970 *Ley de Peligrosidad y rehabilitación social*—a law that was in effect until 1978 and subjected gays, lesbians, transvestites, and transsexuals to security measures and internment in rehabilitation camps" (Pérez 2010). For Professor Silvia Bermúdez, "the important social and political achievements for the LGBTQ communities cannot be trivialized, neither can the brutal immigration policies [Rodríguez Zapatero's] government began enforcing more forcefully since the onset of the economic recession in 2008. The draconian measures include the implementation of weekly quotas for the police in Madrid and Barcelona to arrest illegal immigrants" (quoted in Pérez 2010).

The picture of Spain's LGBTQ community has significantly changed. This was thanks to the contributions of many experts who incidentally are often foreigners or Spaniards who work in English-speaking universities and have been able to do research in the field of queer studies in the last decades. In fact, it was British professor Paul Julian Smith with the publication of *Laws of Desire: Questions of Homosexuality in Spanish Writing and Film, 1960–1990* (1992), who inaugurated the field of queer peninsular studies, combining analysis of novels and films. Since then, the existing corpus on Spain's LGBTQ studies has been gradually increasing through the work of specialists, some of whom live in Spain but particularly by experts from around the world.

Chris Perriam's *Spanish Queer Cinema* (2013) deserves special mention, as in it, the author covers much more than the title suggests. Equally important is the volume edited by Nancy Vosburg and Jacky Collins, *Lesbian Realities/Lesbian Fictions in Contemporary Spain* (2011). Additionally, Lourdes Torres and Immaculada Pertusa's edition of *Tortilleras* (2003) and Gema Pérez's monograph *Queer Transitions* (2007) constitute milestones in the field of queer peninsular studies. As Pérez points out, Spain in the 1980s was no longer the Spain designed or desired by Franco. Her monograph can be interpreted as homage to those artists living at the so-called margins, who have been central to the consolidation of contemporary Spanish democracy with regard to gender and sexuality. Pérez's conclusion still holds true: "they and their works have enabled multiple queer transitions" (Pérez 2007).

See also: Chapter 1: Population and Demography. Chapter 6: Overview; Spanish Youth. Chapter 7: Overview; Feminism in Spain; Gender Roles. Chapter 16: Cinema; TV Outlets; Youth Culture.

Further Reading

Bergmann, Emile L., and Paul Julian Smith, eds. *¿Entiendes?: Queer Readings, Hispanic Writings*. Durham: Duke University Press, 1995.

Calvo Borobia, Kerman. *Post-Marriage LGBT Politics in Spain*. Salamanca: Gredos/Universidad de Salamanca, 2014.

Calvo Borobia, Kerman, and Gracia Trujillo. *Fighting for Love Rights: Claims and Strategies of the LGBT Movement in Spain*. Salamanca: Gredos/Universidad de Salamanca, 2011.

Guasch, Gustavo. "Social Stereotypes and Masculine Homosexualities: The Spanish Case." *Sexualities* 14.5 (2011): 526–543.

Maternity (and Paternity) Care

The regulations on maternity and paternity leave in Spain date back to Law 3/1989, when Spain passed the bill. Since the new millennium, a significant number of Spanish women have been deciding whether or not to become a mother based on their working conditions and, more particularly, on their salary. A higher salary implies more options. Without a doubt, salary conditions are a factor that separates Spanish women from women in most northern European countries.

According to a report produced by the NGO *Save the Children 2012*, being a mother in Spain differs to a great extent from, for example, being a mom in Norway, where mothers can choose a maternity leave permit between 392 days (56 weeks), earning 80 percent of their salary or 322 days (46 weeks), earning 100 percent. In addition, by law, Norwegian mothers have 21 days' leave before the delivery day and another 42 after. Furthermore, the mother can share the leave with the father, who also has the right of 70 days (10 weeks) for paternity leave while receiving his full salary (Lobo 2013). These conditions are among the best in the world and differ greatly from the case of Spain, where maternity leave as of 2013 was for 112 days (16 weeks) at full salary. This time period can be extended if she delivers more than one baby or the child has some disability. Paternity leave, however, is reduced to 15 days (20 if the family already has 2 children or more), and the mother can share it with the dad during the last 10 weeks.

Among the population who decide to be unemployed in order to take care of their children, 82.2 percent are women, 38.2 percent of women choose maternity leave for a year which contrasts with 7.4 percent of men. Also, 97.3 percent of women prefer to be employed part-time, so they can help with their children younger than 14 years old.

One public case of the difficulties of being a mother in modern Spain is Gemma Sesar, an art historian and editor of El Patito Editorial—a small publishing house that mainly publishes Galician classic comics and art books. Apart from being the mother of two children and a business woman in Spain's tumultuous economy, she became popular among artists for being the scriptwriter of her blog *Vida de madre* (*Life of a Mother*). This is a comic that illustrates the current economic crisis from the distinctive point of view of a mother, whose small business company is tremendously complicated to run due to the particular labor market of Spain. Interestingly, Sesar describes herself first as a mother, then, as an entrepreneur, and, only if there is any time left, as a woman.

See also: Chapter 1: Population and Demography. Chapter 2: Overview. Chapter 4: Overview. Chapter 6: Overview. Chapter 7: Overview; Family Roles; Gender Roles. Chapter 8: Overview.

Further Reading

Hass, Linda, ed. *Families and Social Policy: National and International Perspectives*. Binghamton: Taylor and Francis, 2012.

Kamerman, Sheila B., and Peter Moss, eds. *The Politics of Parental Leave Policies: Children, Parenting, Gender, and the Labour Market*. Bristol: Policy Press, 2011.

Robila, Mihaela, ed. *Handbook of Family Policies across the Globe*. New York: Springer, 2014.

Representation in Government

Spain pursued a distinctly egalitarian agenda under the socialist government of José Luis Rodríguez Zapatero (2007–2011). For the first time in Spain's history, a cabinet was composed of nine women ministers and eight men. Never before had the country achieved such a sexually balanced government. On March 22, 2007, the Zapatero socialist government passed the Law of Equity (LOI is its Spanish acronym). The LOI aimed to eliminate the social obstacles and stereotypes standing in the way of achieving real, effective equality between men and women. In essence, it established the presence in public institutions as well as in political parties of no more than 60 percent and no less than 40 percent for each sex. However, Spain's High Tribunal, which is divided into five sections (Criminal, Contentious, Civil, Social, and Military), did not have a woman in their 200 years of history in the branch of Criminal Law until February 27, 2014, when Ana María Ferrer García became the first woman to occupy a seat.

Spain is not an isolated case in the EU for having a strong female representation nor is it alone in implementing policy focused on achieving balanced gender representation. For example, in 2006 over half of Austria's senior cabinet members were women. Sweden and Norway both implemented a similar policy, resulting in half of their senior ministers being female, a statistic that Spain matched. In Finland just under half of the positions were held by women. Historically, Spain's most visible periods to observe women in power were during the Catholic Monarchs and the 16th century. Particularly interesting are the cases of power exercised by Isabel I of Castilla, followed by Joanna of Austria and Isabel Clara Eugenia.

See also: Chapter 2: Overview; The Catholic Monarchs; Eugenia, Isabel Clara. Chapter 3: Overview; Zapatero, José Luis Rodríguez. Chapter 6: Overview. Chapter 7: Overview; Feminism in Spain; Representation in the Workforce.

Further Reading

Cuevas Gutiérrez, Tomás, and Mary E. Giles. *Prison of Women: Testimonies of War and Resistance in Spain, 1939–1975*. Albany: State University of New York Press, 1998.

Jansen, Sharon L. *The Monstrous Regiment of Women: Female Rulers in Early Modern Europe*. New York: Palgrave Macmillan, 2010.

Radcliff, Pamela Beth. *Making Democratic Citizens in Spain: Civil Society and the Popular Origins of the Transition, 1960–78*. New York: Palgrave Macmillan, 2011.

Representation in the Workforce

The main employer of women in Spain used to be the state until 2012. Due to budget cuts in the public sector, the main victims of the collapse of Spain's economy were women. However, in a historical period hit by an unprecedented economic crisis, the number of self-employed women reached a peak. In 2008, 20 percent of companies were owned by women; in 2011 this percentage was up to 31 percent.

On the other hand, in Spain as of August 2010, "companies within IBEX 35 (the Spanish stock market) have as a whole 54 women on their boards out of a total of 500 members, which means a rate of 10.8 percent, far away from a balanced composition" (Valdés 2010). Also, the reality of female workers in Spain is that women earn less than their male peers. The economic crisis has further exacerbated the wage gap between men and women in Spain, which recently was a 23 percent difference. To put this figure in perspective, a woman would have to work an additional 84 days each year to earn the same as a man. The average salary of a man was approximately €25,667 ($27,690), while the average salary of a woman was €19,767 ($21,326). So on average, a woman earns approximately €5,900 ($6,365) less than a man in Spain.

While Spain is making progress in regards to female representation in government, that progress is not shared in private industry. In fact, there are no countries in the EU where women make up even a quarter of the board of managers in the largest 50 companies. Only Bulgaria and Sweden have female representation of over 20 percent. In Spain, the female representation was under 5 percent, along with Italy, Luxembourg, and Malta.

By 2015, 6 out of 10 holders of a university degree within the EU countries are women. However, 80 percent of board members of large companies are men. In Spain, the number of women in executive positions in companies that are registered in the IBEX 35 is low. In fact, there are only three cases: Ana Botín (who become the most important female bank director in the world after replacing her father, Emilio Botín of Banco Santander); Ana María Llopis (president of Spain's supermarkets *Día*); and María Dolores Dancausa (managing director of the Spanish bank Bankinter).

The workforce in Spain is also characterized by a higher number of people employed part-time because they cannot find a full-time job. For instance, in 2012 Spain had 2.7 million Spanish workers (63%) in contrast to Holland (9.1%), Germany (16.6%), and France (31.5%). Also, the workforce in Spain is composed of a large number employed on very short-term contracts. In fact, 64 percent of Spanish women and 62 percent of men had contracts of less than six months. Finally, according to the OECD 2014, Spain was the country with the highest level of disparity between rich and poor people. In fact, 10 percent of the poor population in Spain lost one-third (14%) of their income while the 10 percent of the rich community only lost 1 percent.

See also: Chapter 2: Overview. Chapter 3: Overview. Chapter 4: Overview; Banks; IBEX 35. Chapter 6: Overview. Chapter 7: Overview; Feminism in Spain; Representation in Government.

Further Reading

Lombardo, Emanuela, et al., eds. *The Discursive Politics of Gender Equality: Stretching, Bending, and Policy-Making.* London: Routledge, 2012.

Mora Sanguinetti, Juan, and Andrés Fuentes. *An Analysis of Productivity Performance in Spain before and during the Crisis.* Paris: OECD, 2012.

Rialp Criado, Àlex. *Internationalization and International Marketing: Export Behavior, International Marketing Strategy and Export Performance in Spanish Small and Medium-Sized Enterprises.* Bellaterra: Universitat Autònoma de Barcelona, 2010.

REFERENCES

Almeida, Cristina. *En defensa de la mujer.* Barcelona: Martínez Roca, 1999.

Amorós, Celia. *Hacia una crítica de la razón patriarcal.* Barcelona: Anthropos, 1985.

Anderssen, Erin. "The Message to Women in This Best-Selling Book: Be Submissive." *The Globe and Mail,* December 16, 2013.

Arkinstall, Christine. "Book review of *Antología del pensamiento feminista español (1726–2011).* Edited by Roberta Johnson and Maite Zubiaurre. Madrid: Cátedra, 2012." In: *Revista Canadiense de estudios hispánicos* 37 no. 3 (2013): 565–567.

Bergmann, Emilie L., and Paul Julian Smith, eds. *¿Entiendes?: Queer Readings, Hispanic Writings.* Durham, NC: Duke University Press, 1995.

Caballé, Anna. *El feminismo en España. La lenta conquista de un derecho.* Madrid: Cátedra, 2013.

Camps, Victoria. *El siglo de las mujeres.* Madrid: Cátedra, 1998.

De Diego, Enrique. *Carta a los jóvenes españoles.* Madrid: Rambla, 2012.

De Vega, Eulalia. *La mujer en la historia.* 3rd edition. Madrid: Anaya, 1996.

Fotheringham, Alasdair. "New Hard-Line Abortion Law Prompts Protests across Spain." *The Independent,* December 22, 2013.

Freixas, Laura, ed. *Ser mujer.* Madrid: Temas de hoy, 2000.

Fusi, Juan Pablo. *Historia mínima de España.* Madrid: Turner Publicaciones, 2012.

Gautier, Andrea. *Mujeres y cultura: políticas de igualdad.* Madrid: Ministerio de Cultura, 2011.

Gil, Silvia L. *Nuevos feminismos. Sentidos comunes en la dispersión. Una historia de trayectorias y rupturas en el Estado español.* Madrid: Traficantes de sueños, 2011.

Govan, Fiona. "New Spanish Cardinal Insists, 'Gays Can Be Cured' ahead of His New Appointment to Rome." *The Telegraph,* January 20, 2014.

Granados, Óscar. "Busco trabajo de lo que sea." *El País,* March 9, 2014.

Hernández, María. "Empleo, en femenino." *El Mundo,* March 3, 2014.

Hooper, John. *The New Spaniards.* 2nd ed. London: Penguin, 2006.

Johnson, Roberta, and Maite Zubiaurre, eds. *Antología del pensamiento feminista español (1726–2011).* Madrid: Cátedra, 2012.

The Life of Women and Men in Europe: A Statistical Portrait. Luxemburg: Eurostat, 2008.

Lobo, A. "Ser madre en España: peor que en Noruega y mucho mejor que en Níger." *Qué!* November 21, 2013.

Macías, Juana. Dir. *Planes para mañana*. España: Teoponte P.C., 2010.

Martorell, Miguel, and Santos Juliá. *Manual de historia política y social de España (1808–2011)*. Barcelona: RBA, 2012.

Miriano, Constanza. *Cásate y sé sumisa*. Granada: Nuevo Inicio, 2013.

Moa, Pío. *Ensayos polémicos. España en la encrucijada*. Lorca: editorial Fajardo el bravo, 2013.

Mujeres y hombres en España. Madrid: Instituto de la Mujer, 2013.

Pérez-Sánchez, Gema. *Queer Transtions in Contemporary Spanish Culture. From Franco to la Movida*. New York: State University of New York Press, 2007.

Pérez-Sánchez, Gema. "Transnational Conversations in Migration, Queer, and Transgender Studies: Multimedia Storyspaces." *Revista Canadiense de Estudios Hispánicos* 35 no.1 (2010): 163–184.

Pérez Garzón, Juan Sisinio. *Historia del feminismo*. 2nd ed. Madrid: Catarata, 2012.

Perriam, Chris. *Spanish Queer Cinema*. Edinburgh: Edinburgh University Press, 2013.

Platero Méndez, Raquel/Lucas. "Love and the State: Gay Marriage in Spain: Spanish Law no. 13/2005, 1 July 2005, Concerning, through a Change in the Civil Code, the Access of Lesbians and Gay Men to the Institution of Marriage." *Feminist Legal Studies* 15 (2007): 329–340.

Sahuquillo, María R. "A Decade of Male-on-Female Violence Leaves a Tragic Total of 658 Deaths." *El País,* March 21, 2014.

Sánchez, Ainhoa. "Entrevista a Ascensión Parron, presidenta de GEHITU." *EGF and the City*. Number 8. March 2014. 30–35.

Sánchez Robles, Carmen. *Retratos de familia*. Madrid: Ministerio de Trabajo y Asuntos Sociales, 2007.

Segarra, Marta y Àngels Carabí, eds. *Feminismo y crítica literaria*. Barcelona: Icaria Editorial, 2000.

Smith, Mikey. "Submissive Wives Book Is Controvesial Bestseller in Spain Angering Feminists." *Mirror,* December 15, 2013.

Smith, Paul Julian. *Laws of Desire: Questions of Homosexuality in Spanish Writing and Film, 1960–1990*. Oxford: Oxford University Press, 1992.

Torres, Lourdes, and Immaculada Pertusa, eds. *Tortilleras: Hispanic and U.S. Latina Lesbian Expression*. Philadelphia: Temple University Press, 2003.

Valcárcel, Amelia. *Sexo y filosofía*. Barcelona: Anthropos, 1991.

Valdés de la Vega, Berta. "Gender Equality in Private Enterprises in Spain: The New Equality Plans." *European Gender Equality Law Review* 2 (2010): 17–25.

Varela, Nuria. "Feminismo. Guía práctica." *La Marea,* March 2014: 31–34.

Vosburg, Nancy, and Jacky Collins, eds. *Lesbian Realities/Lesbian Fictions in Contemporary Spain*. Lewisburg, PA: Bucknell University Press, 2011.

VV.AA. *Retratos de familia*. Madrid: Egraf, 2007.

Websites

22 de febrero, día de la igualdad salarial. Madrid: UGT, 2014. http://www.ugt.es/actualidad/2014/febrero/2014-02-22-%20Dia%20de%20la%20igualdad%20salarial_web.pdf

Abbadessa, Ivano. "Spain's Gender Wage Gap Widens." *WEST* / WElfare Society Territory. http://www.west-info.eu/spains-gender-wage-gap-widens/

AFAVIR. afavir.org

AMIT. Asociación de Mujeres Investigadoras y Tecnológicas. amit-es.org

CIMA. Asociación de mujeres CIneastas y de Medios Audiovisuales. cimamujerescineastas.es

CIS: Centro de Investigaciones Sociológicas. cis.es

Clásicas y Modernas. clasicasymodernas.org

Constitución 1978. http://www.boe.es/buscar/act.php?id=BOE-A-1978-31229

Estatuto de los trabajadores. http://www.empleo.gob.es/es/sec_leyes/trabajo/estatuto06/

Eurostat. http://epp.eurostat.ec.europa.eu/portal/page/portal/eurostat/home/

INE. Instituto Nacional de Estadística. ine.es

Instituto de la Mujer. inmujer.gob.es

Juan Carlos I. "Mensaje de Navidad de su Majestad el Rey." December 24, 2013. http://www.casareal.es/ES/Actividades/Paginas/actividades_actividades_detalle.aspx?data=11760

Manifesto for Equality in Culture. March 1, 2013. http://www.mav.org.es/documentos/manifiesto%20igualdad%20cultura%201%20marzo.pdf

MAV. Mujeres en las Artes Visuales. mav.org.es

Mills, George. "Spain Tops World Gay-Friendly Rankings." *The Local. Spain's News in English.* http://www.thelocal.es/20130605/spain-tops-world-gay-friendly-rankings

Mujeres en Red. nodo50.org/mujeresred

"Newsnight." *BBC*: 'Interview with Constanza Miriano.' December14, 2013. http://www.bbc.com/news/uk-25374805

No fueron solos. Madrid: Museo Naval, 2012. http://www.armada.mde.es/archivo/dirorcun/No_fueron_solos_dossier.pdf

Observatorio de la violencia de género. observatorioviolencia.org

OECD. oecd.org/spain

Save the Children (2012 report). http://www.savethechildren.net/about-us/our-finances

Sesar, Gemma. *Vida de Madre.* http://blog.elpatitoeditorial.com/wp-content/uploads/2015/04/VdM-I.pdf

Soteres González, Alberto. *2.826.549 razones. La protección de la infancia frente a la pobreza: un derecho, una obligación y una inversión.* Madrid: Save the Children, 2014. http://www.savethechildren.es/docs/Ficheros/644/INFORME.pdf

"Spanish Women's History in the 20th Century" (last accessed on March 7, 2014) http://www.estelacantabra.com/comenius/SPANISHCENTURY.pdf

Teléfono 016. http://www.msssi.gob.es/ssi/violenciaGenero/Recursos/telefono016/home.htm

Trotta, Tiziana. "Same Crisis, Different Consequences." *WEST* / Welfare Society Territory. http://www.west-info.eu/spains-gender-wage-gap-widens/

World Bank Organization. *Spain's Gender Equality Data and Statistics.* http://datatopics.worldbank.org/gender/country/spain

CHAPTER 8

EDUCATION

OVERVIEW

Spain has a long history of education, as Europe's first universities were founded on the Iberian Peninsula. One of the oldest was the University of Córdoba (968), where Christians and Jews studied with Muslims. Other historic Spanish universities include *Universidad de Salamanca* founded in 1218, *Universidad de Alcalá de Henares* founded in 1508, and the *Residencia de Estudiantes* established in 1910 in Madrid—which became the first cultural center of Spain in the 20th century. Despite being affordable for only a few of Spain's elite families at the time, the *Residencia de Estudiantes* was an intellectual hub for artists such as Federico García Lorca, Salvador Dalí, and Luis Buñuel. There they developed their avant-garde ideas, which earned Spain the reputation of being a hub of modernity during the first half of the century.

Spain's history of education was, for centuries, intertwined with the Catholic Church and until relatively recently was reserved for the elite. Before the 1900s many children, especially rural children, went without any formal education. For example, in 1840 less than 10 percent of Spaniards knew how to read and write. However, a century later, by 1940, two-thirds of Spaniards were literate. Historically, Spain's tumultuous political situation has interfered with education; it has resulted in changes to the curriculum and textbooks and in pressure being put on teachers to support the ideology of those in power.

The 19th century was a time of multiple school reforms under the mandate of María Cristina, who was the mother of the *infanta* Queen Isabel II. Some reforms included allowing the State to run the universities (1835) and to regulate primary schools in Spain (*La Ley de Instrucción Pública*, 1838). In 1846, the Queen established the General Directorship of Public Instruction, which monitored both primary and secondary schools, including instruction. This led to a formal group whose job was to oversee primary teaching. However, in 1851, many of these reforms, which ultimately gave the state power over the schools and decreased the stronghold of the Catholic Church on education, were reversed when the partnership between the church and monarch was reestablished. Some Spaniards viewed this as a regression from the liberal ideals whose way was paved with the occupation of the French in Spain during the early 1800s.

One of the most important reforms in Spain's education was the creation of the *Institución Libre de Enseñanza* (Free Institute of Education), founded by the philosopher Francisco Giner de los Ríos (1839–1915) in late 19th-century Spain. From its beginnings in 1876, it evolved into an Institute, offering both primary and secondary education separate from both the state educational systems and the religious educational system which had dominated Spain's education since the eighth century. Courses included anthropology, social sciences, technology, economics, art, drawing, singing, and physical education, most of which were not taught in schools run by the state or Church. The Institute was influenced by French and English educational philosophies as well as the writings of Rousseau and Frobel. In keeping with liberal ideas that were sweeping through Europe, the Institute emphasized the importance of inquiry, learning through observation, and development of the whole person. Traditional methods of learning such as the use of the textbook and assessment through formal examinations were discouraged. Instead, student progress was reflected in personal notebooks that offered a synthesis of learned material. The Institute was closed due to the civil war of 1936; however, traces of its philosophy permeate Spanish society today.

Under the rule of Franco's government, the state allowed the Church to maintain primary responsibility for educating students through a private educational system. Upon Franco's rise to power, he had the Church rewrite all school curricula; hence, both state- and Church-run schools used curricula based on religious and Fascist convictions. Autonomy was taken away from regional education as Franco pushed his Catholic Nationalistic agenda into the schoolrooms. The year that Franco came to power, over half of Spain's teachers were released from their positions and many of those were persecuted for having ideologies other than that of Franco's State.

While the Church provided schools in prosperous city centers or their affluent suburbs, they often neglected the rural areas, leaving many Spaniards with minimal schooling at best. During the 1960s in order to meet both demands of employers and demands of the upwardly mobile workers living in industrial areas formerly ignored by the Church, the state played a more active role in Spain's education. Consequently, state schools experienced a dramatic increase in students with female students increasing in numbers as well. Between 1960 and 1980, the student population rose by 60 percent, while the student population in secondary schools increased a staggering 753 percent, with the vast majority of the students attending state schools.

The 1970s brought additional reform to Spanish schools with the *Ley General de Educación* (LGE), which was successful in introducing free mandatory education for students ages 6 to 14 as well as removing discrepancies in school policy toward children of the elite and those from less affluent families. This legislation began what would be over two decades of school reform that would transform education at every level. During the 1990s Spain began to examine the role of non-compulsory early education as a means to negate classism. Money was allocated for providing free textbooks to families that could not afford them, and courses were offered to young students who had dropped out of their compulsory education. Legislation of the 1990s put early education under state regulation and guaranteed to have the facilities to meet the demands of the people. Reforms continued into the 21st century such as the *Ley Orgánica de Calidad de Educación* (Education Quality Act) of December 2002 that altered the university entrance examination, introduced new subjects in secondary education, and provided free pre-school education.

In the 21st century, debate over the role of religion in Spain's schools remains. On May 17, 2013, the Spanish government approved a draft educational reform supported by many bishops that placed Catholic religious education in the core curriculum and made assessment in the subject count toward whether a pupil progresses to the class above or wins a scholarship. Although pupils will be able to choose between religious education or taking "social and cultural values" classes in primary school and "ethical values" classes at the secondary level, the reform has met with widespread criticism, especially from state schools and PSOE, the opposition party. A recent survey shows that 70 percent of Spaniards disagree with an item in the bill that will elevate religion to the same status as other core subjects, with the goal of attracting more students and halting a decades-long drain in attendance. According to the proposed bill, grades in religion class would be weighted equally with core subjects such as math or language arts in an attempt to raise the enrollment in religion classes. The recent Metroscopia survey shows that Spaniards almost unanimously (86%) feel the education system will only improve when parties come together to produce a long-lasting pact, rather than making partisan reforms each time one of them attains power, as has been the case since 1975. The bill proposed by former Education Minister José Ignacio Wert appears to fall squarely into the second category (Toharia and Planelles, *El País*, May 27, 2013).

In April 2007 under the socialist government, a new bill was signed (*Ley Orgánica de Educación* or LOE) in the Parliament, in which the subject "Education for Citizenship and Human Rights" had to be taught in the last two years of primary education as well as during the first three years of ESO. However, in November 2013, when the conservatives were in power, a new LOE was approved. Officially known as LOMCE, it is popularly identified as *Ley Wert* (taken from the last name of the minister of education, José Ignacio Wert, who incidentally was removed from office in June 2015). With the bill's approval, the previous subject of education for citizenship was abolished from the curriculum along with "philosophy." Instead, the subject of religion was reintroduced, with the student's grade in the course counting equally to any other subject.

Spain's schools today are experiencing numerous challenges. Currently, most national newspapers have carried extremely negative reviews about the new education system in Spain. For instance, *El País* published an article written in English entitled "Dangers to Education" (December 10, 2013), which warns that current budget cuts should not impede action to solve the problem of Spain's school system. While some indicators seem to suggest that the economic cycle is changing, education ministry and regional government budgets for 2014 show new cutbacks. While the austerity measures may prove to be less severe than those seen in the recent past, the country's administrations that have control of the education system will have cut their spending by 7.298 billion euros between 2010 and 2014. Coming hot on the heels of the latest PISA report—which exposed a stagnation in the test scores of Spanish students—a labor-union report has revealed that the shrinkage of education budgets in the course of the crisis so far has been as much as 16.7 percent on average. The chief losers by percentage are Castilla-La Mancha (–31.1%), Catalunya (–24.1%), and Castilla y León (–20.4%) (*El País*, December 10, 2013).

MARGARITA SALAS FALGUERAS (1938–)

Margarita Salas Falgueras is a prestigious Spanish scientist who received her Ph.D. in Science from the Universidad Complutense de Madrid (*Cum Laude*) in 1963 and continued her postdoctoral studies at New York University (1964–1967) under the direction of Severo Ochoa, who won the Nobel prize in 1959. Following her return to Spain, she has worked at the CSIC (Consejo Superior de Investigaciones Científicas / Spanish National Research Council). She is also the current president of Severo Ochoa Foundation in Madrid and a member of the Academy of Sciences not only in Spain but in Europe and the United States. Salas has published over 300 articles in international journals and books. In 2008 Spain's King Juan Carlos I honored Dr. Salas with the hereditary noble title of *Marquesado de Carnero* (Marquise of Carnero) for her outstanding contributions in the field of biochemistry and molecular biology.

On the other hand, according to information provided by the state website *Marca España*, the percentage of young Spaniards aged 25–34 with a university degree is 37 percent, while the European average is 26 percent, according to 2003–2012 data (*Marca España,* March 21, 2014). The publication of 113 academic essays in the book *La Uni en la calle. Libro de textos* (2013, *The University in the Street: A Textbook*) constitutes another recent example of the current crisis in Spanish education. The book defends the public universities and advocates for free education at all levels and increased funding to support academic research.

Looking at the last time that a Spaniard received a Nobel Prize for science we have to go back to 1959 with Severo Ochoa (who was also an American citizen at the time), and before him to Santiago Ramón y Cajal in 1906. Spain's contribution to the world of innovation is significantly low in comparison to other EU countries as evidenced by the modest number of Spanish patents registered with the European Office of Patents. Furthermore, many of the current scientists born in Spain are developing their research abroad. One of the main reasons is the fact that Spain does not invest as much in research and development as do other countries, Spain's R+D spending being slightly below the European average in 2014.

Further Reading

Boyd-Barrett, Oliver, and Pamela O'Malley, eds. *Education Reform in Democratic Spain*. London: Taylor & Francis, 2003.

Breiner, B. F., and C. W. Troll. "Christianity and Islam," in J. L. Esposito, ed. *The Oxford Encyclopedia of the Modern Islamic World*. Vol. 4. Oxford: Oxford University Press, 1995: 277–284.

Domke, Joan. "Education, Fascism, and the Catholic Church in Franco's Spain." Chicago: Loyola University Chicago, 2011. [Thesis].

Groves, Tamar. *Teachers and the Struggle for Democracy in Spain, 1970–1985*. New York: Palgrave Macmillan, 2013.

CSIC: Consejo Superior de Investigaciones Científicas

The CSIC dates back to 1907, when it was initially named JAE, an acronym that refers to the *Junta para Amplicación de Estudios* or Board for Advanced Studies. Its main goal was to connect with other European researchers. The JAE's first president was Santiago Ramón y Cajal (1852–1934), who was supported by José Castillejo (1877–1945) as the Bursar, and the organization had various goals, including a study extension service, studying abroad, sending academics to conferences, and promoting research. To achieve these aims, the JAE was an active grant-awarding body, and its funding benefited many students, researchers, and professors through scholarships to work on different continents. These grants became an essential feature of cultural and scientific development in Spain at the time.

On May 19, 1938, in the midst of the Spanish Civil War, Franco's government declared a cessation of the activities of the JAE, although the board kept open an office in Valencia (later relocated to Barcelona), which was supported by the legitimate government of the republic. In October of that year, Tomás Navarro Tomás (1884–1979) appointed Luis Calandre (1890–1961), director of the Hospital de Carabineros which was installed in the *Residencia de Estudiantes*, subdelegate of the JAE in Madrid, in order to maintain its activities and inventory its laboratories, one of which—Microscopic Anatomy—had been under his management. The end of the war condemned Luis Calandre to internal exile, twice facing trial and finally being sent to prison.

Over the course of the war many of the JAE's scientists found themselves obliged to leave the country. One example of the intellectual Spanish diaspora was a group of scientists in Mexico, who founded the journal *Ciencia, Revista hispano-americana de ciencias puras y aplicadas* (*Science: Hispano-American Journal of Pure and Applied Science*), which served as a focus for Spanish scientists in exile.

In 1939, Franco's newly installed regime created the Spanish National Research Council (CSIC: *Consejo Superior de Investigaciones Científicas*) out of the JAE's laboratories, offices, and centers. The law passed on November 24, 1939, creating the CSIC and mandating that all the centers belonging to the dissolved Board for Advanced Studies and Scientific Research (JAE) would become part of the CSIC. The CSIC is Spain's largest public institution devoted to research, and the third largest in Europe. It is run by the government through the Ministry of Economy and Competitiveness. One of its main goals is to produce and disseminate research nationwide as well as to collaborate with foreign institutions.

The CSIC currently employs around 15,000 people including over 3,000 staff researchers and about 3,000 research students. Approximately 20 percent of all Spanish scientific production comes from the CSIC.

See also: Chapter 2: Overview; Franco, Francisco. Chapter 8: Overview; Elcano Royal Institute.

Further Reading

CSIC: http://www.csic.es

Martínez-Alonso, Carlos. "Re-founding the Spanish National Research Council: New Methods, New Culture" in *Max-Planck-Forum 7: Perspective of Research,* Ringberg-Symposium May (2006): 59–70.

Elcano Royal Institute

Apart from the CSIC, which is run by the state, the Elcano Royal Institute is the second largest privately run think-tank in the country. The Institute was established in 2001 as a private foundation under the honorary presidency of HRH The Prince of Asturias. Its Board of Trustees comprises prominent figures linked to Spanish foreign policy and representatives of both the companies that fund the Institute and of the Spanish Ministries of Foreign Affairs and Cooperation; Defense; Education, Culture, and Sports; and Economy and Trade.

The Elcano Royal Institute focuses on both specific topics and geographical areas. Among the former are energy and climate change, security and defense, international terrorism, Spain's image abroad, and demography and migrations. The latter includes Europe, the Atlantic world, Latin America, North Africa, and the Middle East. The Institute has a stable team of highly qualified analysts along with a wide-ranging network of contributors and associate experts. The Institute's work is made available in a wide range of publications, all of which are also freely accessible on its website (realinstitutoelcano.org). In 2013–2014 Elcano Royal Institute was rated 32nd worldwide and 29th in Western Europe among the top think tanks. Furthermore, the Institute organizes frequent working groups, seminars, and conferences on topics of current interest. Participation in leading international networks and projects enhances its external projection and outreach. The *Red Iberoamericana de Estudios Internacionales* (RIBEI: ribei.org) was also founded by Elcano Royal Institute in 2010, and has already become one of the 20 best think-tank networks in the world.

See also: Chapter 2: Overview. Chapter 8: Overview; CSIC.

Further Reading

Elcano Royal Institute: http://www.realinstitutoelcano.org

Fabry, Elvire. *Think Global—Act European IV. Thinking Strategically about the EU's External Action: The Recommendations of 16 European Think Tanks.* Paris: Notre Europe, 2013.

Preschool, Primary, and Secondary Education

In regards to Spain's current system, the Ministry of Education, Culture, and Sports (*Ministerio de Educación, Cultura y Deporte*) oversees the educational system in Spain while each of the 17 regions maintains partial responsibility for schooling. The new Organic Law on the Quality of Education (LOMCE, *Ley Orgánica de Calidad de la Educación*) established some commonalities for all Spanish schools such as: school is mandatory and free for all children aged 6–16; accommodations will be made for children with special needs; and vocational training is available for all students in secondary education.

The Spanish schools consist of nursery school (*Guardería*) for children aged 0–3; preschool (*Educación infantil*) for children aged 3–6; primary education (*Educación primaria*) for children aged 6–12; and compulsory secondary education (ESO) for students aged 12–16. Once students successfully complete their four years of compulsory secondary education, they receive their *graduado en educación secundaria* certificate. At the age of 16, students can continue their education by either attending post-secondary education for students aged 16–18 (*Bachillerato*), which allows them to go on to a university; or they can go on to a two-year vocational school (*formación profesional*).

There are three main types of schools in Spain: public schools, which are funded entirely by the state, though parents are responsible for purchasing textbooks and school supplies; semi-private schools, which are partially subsidized by the state; and private schools, which are independently funded via tuition costs. During the 2008/2009 academic year, 67.7 percent of Spain's students attended state schools, 26.0 percent attended semi-private schools, and 6.6 percent attended fully private schools. Also, Spain has a strong presence of international educational institutions which operate mainly on the Mediterranean coast including American, British, German, and French schools, which are all highly regarded.

Spain's preschool system is divided into two parts: (1) school for children aged 0–3; and (2) school for children 3–5 years old. School for children aged three to five is free in Spain. Since the mid-1970s Spain's goal has been to increase the number of students attending preschool, thus having a more prepared populace entering the compulsory primary school. Over the past few decades, the enrollment rate has increased significantly from just under 350,000 children under the age of 6 attending from 1975–1976 to over a million children under the age of 6 attending during the 2007–2008 school year. While two-thirds of preschools are publicly funded, private or Church-run preschools still play a significant role in early education, with over 570,000 children enrolled during the 2007–2008 school year. In the 21st century, Spain consistently has had one of the highest enrollment rates in the EU for preschool. For example, in 2010, Spain was second only to France, for percentage of children aged 3–5 attending educational programs.

Spaniards use the term *colegio* or *escuela* (school) to refer to public or private primary school which consists of first through sixth grade and may include preschool for aged 3–5. Another particular Spanish name is *instituto*, which refers to public secondary school that includes both *ESO* and *bachillerato*.

Primary education (*educación primaria*) for students aged 6–12 is both required and free of charge for students attending state schools. Secondary education (*educación secundaria*) is provided for students aged 12–16 years and is also required and free of charge. During the fourth year of secondary education, students receive guidance on both university-bound continuing education options as well as employment possibilities or vocational studies. At the end of the fourth year students will receive the certificate *Título de Graduado de Educación Secundaria* or, as it is now called, *Título de Graduado de Educación Secundaria Obligatoria* (ESO).

There are some significant differences between secondary education in Spain and that of the United States, one difference being that in Spain education is only required up until the age of 16, which is the completion of ESO. Once the ESO is earned, students have four main routes they can take in education. The first is the *Bachillerato* which prepares students for university training and is equivalent to the American high school diploma. The second option is to receive vocational training (*formación profesional de grado medio)*. A third option is for students to receive education geared toward artistic training (*las enseñanzas de artes plásticas y diseño de grado medio)*, and the final option is vocation sports education (*las enseñanzas deportivas de grado medio)*.

See also: Chapter 1: Population and Demography. Chapter 6: Overview; Spanish Youth. Chapter 8: Overview; Testing: Selectividad and Oposiciones; University and Vocational Education. Chapter 16: Overview; Social Media; Youth Culture.

Further Reading

Hagemann, Karen, et al. *Children, Families, and States*. New York: Berghahn Books, 2014.

OECD: *Family Database* (01/05/2014): www.oecd.org/social/family/database: http://www .oecd.org/els/soc/PF3_2_Enrolment_in_childcare_and_preschools.pdf

Testing: Selectividad and Oposiciones

Selectividad or *Prueba de Acceso a la Universidad* (PAU) is the national exam taken by students in the last year of post-secondary education (*bachillerato)*. The grade received on the exam is combined with the overall average grade from both years of bachillerato and is used for the university admissions process. When calculating this number, known as the *Nota de acceso*, the bachillerato grade counts for 60 percent of the total number, and the selectividad number accounts for the remaining 40 percent. If a student has taken the voluntary subject specific portion of the exam, this may also be factored into the Nota de acceso depending on how well the student did.

The general portion of the exam covers subjects taught in the second year of bachillerato, including Spanish language and literature, foreign language, history or philosophy (student's choice) and one other school subject (student's choice). The subject portion of the exam is optional. A student may take up to four subject exams, but only the two highest grades will be counted. Typically, a student will take subjects related to the desired university program. Students may take the PAU as many times as they wish; the best grade received will be the one counted toward the Nota de acceso. The general portion grade does not expire, while the subject portion is only valid for two years. The PAU is given twice a year (June and September). Although there is no official ranking for universities in Spain, different schools and courses of study typically have a minimum required grade (Nota de acceso) for entrance into a particular program. The minimum required grade may vary slightly from year to year, depending on the

Students take a university entrance examination at a lecture hall in the Andalusian capital of Sevilla, southern Spain, on June 16, 2015. Students in Spain must pass the exam after completing secondary school in order to gain access to university. (Marcelo del Pozo/Corbis)

demand for that program or university and the number of available spaces for new students.

In April 2015 the conservative government announced that the selectividad will be abolished by 2017. Instead, the current administration proposes to replace it with a test of 350 multiple choice questions (200 questions will be based on the specialization of the students; 100 on the optional subject chosen, and the remaining 50 will be a personal choice by the student). While there may be pedagogical reasons for the change, the economic incentives are clear: Once the selectividad is abolished, professors will no longer be paid to assess them. The two new political parties in Spain, Podemos and Ciudadanos, have both already stated that they will not support the proposed bill in Parliament.

Being a civil servant in Spain means having a job for life, but applicants for public-sector jobs must pass competitive exams called *oposiciones*. The candidates (*opositores*) must sit for a written exam, a practical test and, if you pass these first two exams (theo-retical and practical), then you sit for the final oral interview in front of a panel of experts. Some applicants spend years studying for and re-sitting exams, so preparing candidates for oposiciones is a major source of work for many *academias* (private insti-tutions specialized in many subjects including the different exams for the oposiciones). All public-sector appointments that are open to competition are published in the BOE (*Boletín Oficial del Estado*), an official government publication. In essence, oposiciones are public examinations held to fill vacancies in the public sector on a national, regional, or local basis. The positions attained through these State exams imply a job for life (with a working day from 8:00 a.m. to 3:00 p.m.), and they are much sought after in a country with a tradition of high unemployment.

There are usually far too many candidates for every job advertised, so the requirements listed can be extremely rigorous: If you apply to be a street cleaner (*barrendero*) or a clerk at the post office you may have to show an in-depth knowledge of the constitution. This is why many people spend years preparing for these examinations, especially for occupations with more responsibility. In 1962 the American professor Lawrence B. Kiddle published an article entitled "*Las Oposiciones*: An Old Spanish Custom," whose insights are surprisingly still applicable in today's Spain. For instance, he cited the Spanish poet Pedro Salinas (1891–1951), who on several occasions used to refer to the oposiciones as "the quintessence of Spanish culture since in them one could see all that was typical of Spanish life: a bit of the bullfight, a bit of the Inquisition, and a bit of the national lottery" (quoted in Kiddle 1962).

See also: Chapter 8: Overview.

Further Reading

Newton, Michael, and Graham Shields. *Studying and Working in Spain: Student Guide*. New York: Palgrave, 2001.

Ross, Christopher J. *Contemporary Spain. A Handbook*. 2nd ed. London: Arnold, 2002.

University and Vocational Education

Two major differences from North American universities are that Spanish university students do not receive sports grants to study and student residences are not as common as in the English-speaking countries. In fact, Spaniards usually go to the university that is near home in order to reduce costs. The typical Spanish university student tends to rent a room in an apartment with other students, if not living at home. Also, the idea of having a university student loan was until very recently unheard of for a Spaniard. However, this situation is rapidly changing, and Spain is shifting closer to the North American method of financing a university education through a student loan rather than via scholarships. Scholarships have been common in some European countries such as France and Germany, while in others, university education is altogether free (as in Norway and Finland). In 2015 only eight EU-countries paid higher tuition fees than Spain (between 713 to 2,011 euros per academic year).

The Universidad Nacional de Educación a Distancia (UNED), founded in 1972, is the only Spanish university run by the government and the second largest in Europe with roughly over 250,000 students per academic year. However, a typical university in Spain usually has around 60,000 students registered annually. Most Spanish universities in Spain are public although a new boom by the private sector has occurred in the

A panorama of Magdalena Palace in Santander. This former Summer Royal Palace is now the home of the International University Menéndez Pelayo. Recently, the popular Spanish TV series "Grand Hotel" was filmed at the palace. (Manuel Alvarez Alonso/Dreamstime.com)

last two decades. However, on average, the typical Spaniard attends a public university. According to the 2015 *Financial Times* business school rankings, the MBAs from IESE Business School (7), the IE Business School (12), and Esade Business School (19) are among the best 20 MBAs in the world ("Global MBA Ranking 2015" *Financial Times*).

Vocational training (*formación profesional*) has always had a stigma in Spain. Popularly known as FP students, this vocational training is traditionally for those adolescents who have not performed well enough to be on the bachillerato track. On the other hand, FP students tend to pursue a professional career early in their lives. In other words, instead of following the traditional academic path of studying usually for four years to get a university degree, FP students can complete a *grado medio* program, obtaining a "technical specialist" (*técnico especilista*) certificate, and complete a *grado superior*, receiving a "superior technical" (*técnico superior*) certificate. The latter title will allow FP graduates to enroll, if they wish, to the university without the need to do the entry exams for the university (*selectividad*).

Spain does not limit higher education to university studies or vocational studies. Spain offers more options than the traditional binary system of higher education that some of its European neighbors provide. In Spain higher education may consist of a university education, advanced art studies, advanced vocational training, or advanced sports education. For those students seeking university entrance, they must take a national university entrance exam called *Prueba de Acceso a la Universidad* (PAU), which is also known as selectividad, and then apply to the university program of their choice where they will be accepted based on their exam results along with their GPA from their bachillerato. Since most students in Spain will apply for the public university in their town or region, the application process is much less complex than application for universities in the United States.

See also: Chapter 8: Education; Testing: Selectividad and Oposiciones.

Further Reading

Boakari, Francis Musa, et al., eds. *Power, Voice, and the Public Good: Schooling and Education in Global Societies*. Bingley: Emerald JAI, 2008.

Otero Hidalgo, Carlos et al. *Vocational Education and Training in Spain: Short Description*. Luxembourg: Office for Official Publications of the European Communities, 2002.

REFERENCES

Fernández Liria, Carlos; Pedro Fernández Liria y Luis Alegre Zahonero. *Educación para la Ciudadanía. Democracia, Capitalismo y Estado de Derecho*. Madrid: Akal, 2007.

Gentile, Alessandro, Anna Sanmartín Ortí, Ana Lucía Hernández Cordero. *La sombra de la crisis. La sociedad española en el horizonte de 2018*. Madrid: Centro Reina Sofía Sobre Adolescencia y Juventud. Fundación de Ayuda contra la Drogadicción (FAD), 2014.

Hampshire, David. *Living and Working in Spain*. 8th ed. Bath: Survival Books, 2009.

Kiddle, Lawrence B. "Las *Oposiciones*: An Old Spanish Custom." *The Modern Language Journal* 46 no.6 (1962): 255–258.

Lassibille, Gérard, and María Lucía Navarro Gómez. "How Long Does It Take to Earn a Higher Education Degree in Spain?" *Research in Higher Education* 52 no.1 (2011): 63–80.

Nadeau, Jean-Benoît, and Julie Barlow. *The Story of Spanish*. New York: St. Martin's Press, 2013.

Noya, Javier. *La imagen de España en el mundo. Visiones del exterior. Volumen 1*. 2nd ed. Madrid: Tecnos, 2013.

VV.AA. *La Uni en la calle. Libro de textos*. Madrid: Cooperativa MásPúblico, 2013.

Websites

Chislett, William. "The Way Forward for the Spanish Economy: More Internationalisation." In http://www.realinstitutoelcano.org/wps/portal/web/rielcano_en/contenido?WCM_GLOBAL_CONTEXT=/elcano/elcano_in/zonas_in/image+of+spain/dt1-2010#.U4y2OXJdXsZ

CSIC: Consejo Superior de Investigaciones Científicas. csis.es

"Dangers to Education." *El País,* December 10, 2013. http://elpais.com/elpais/2013/12/10/inenglish/1386699834_218308.html

Elcano Royal Institute. realinstitutoelcano.org

FRIDE. fride.org

Fullbright España. http://eca.state.gov/fulbright/country/spain

"Global MBA Ranking 2015," *Financial Times.* http://rankings.ft.com/businessschoolrankings/global-mba-ranking-2015

Hernández Revuelta, Ana. *Enseñanzas artísticas. Situación actual en España y Europa: oferta académica*. Madrid: Universidad Complutense de Madrid, 2012. https://bellasartes.ucm.es/data/cont/media/www/pag-11069/ense%C3%B1anzas%20artisticas.pdf

InterNations. http://www.internations.org/spain-expats/guide/living-in-spain-15487/education-and-healthcare-in-spain-3

Marca España. http://marcaespana.es/en/espana-al-dia/378/spain-above-the-european-average-for-the-number-of-young-university-students

Ministerio de Economía y Competitividad. http://www.mineco.gob.es/portal/site/mineco

Nuffic. *Contry module: Spain. Information about the Structure of the Education System of Spain and the Evaluation of Degrees Obtained in Spain.* http://www.nuffic.nl/en/library/country-module-spain.pdf

OECD Skills Outlook 2013 report. http://www.oecd.org/site/piaac/Country%20note%20-%20Spain.pdf

Physical Education and Sport at School in Europe. Eurydice Report. Luxembourg: Publication Office of the European Union, 2013. http://eacea.ec.europa.eu/education/eurydice/documents/thematic_reports/150en.pdf

Real Instituto Elcano. realinstitutoelcano.org

Residencia de estudiantes. http://www.residencia.csic.es/

Span¡shD!ct. spanishdict.com

Toharia, José Juan y Manuel Planelles. "70 Percent of Spaniards Reject New Plans for Religion Classes in School." *El País,* May 27, 2013. http://elpais.com/elpais/2013/05/27/inenglish/1369657255_146639.html

UNED. http://portal.uned.es/portal/page?_pageid=93,1&_dad=portal&_schema=PORTAL

Universia. universia.es

Valis, Noel M. "Reform in Spanish Education: The *Institución Libre de Enseñanza.*" In http://www.american-buddha.com/lit.reformspaneducvalis.toc.htm

Villar, Antonio. "Education and Cognitive Skills in the Spanish Adult Population. Intergenerational Comparison of Mathematical Knowledge form PIAAC Data." In *Fedeablogs.net.* http://www.fedeablogs.net/economia/?p=33217, pages 1–24.

"Youth on the Move." *Eurobarometer.* May 2011. http://ec.europa.eu/public_opinion/flash/fl_319b_en.pdf

CHAPTER 9

LANGUAGE

OVERVIEW

Over 500 million people all over the world speak Spanish. In fact, Spanish is the second most-spoken language in the world after Mandarin. After English, Spanish is the most used language for business. Also, Spanish is the most used language on the Internet, and in 2015 there were over 20 million people who wanted to learn Spanish. For instance, in 1995 Spanish became and still is the most studied language in the United States, including at the university level.

A sign of this trend is the network of centers all over the world established by the *Instituto Cervantes*. Spanish is spoken as an official language in 21 countries, and is the unofficial second language in the United States. Spanish is the only international language that has two distinctive names: Spanish and Castilian. Apart from Castilian Spanish, there are another four official languages spoken in Spain: Catalan (in Catalunya and the Balearic Islands); Valencian (in the region of Valencia); Galician (in Galicia); and Euskera (in the Basque country). San Millán de la Cogolla (Logroño), in the north of Spain, is considered the birthplace of the Spanish language. In the monasteries of Yuso and Suso the first words of what we now know as Spanish were written. Spanish is a romance language, and these early written expressions are called *Glosas emilanenses*. One of the first poets who wrote in Spanish was Gonzalo de Berceo (1197–1264). During the medieval period, monasteries were the focal point of culture. As Jean-Benoît Nadeau and Julie Barlow (2013) explain,

> The origins of Spanish are similar to those of French. Both languages grew out of the Roman occupation of Western Europe and the "barbarian" invasions of Germanic tribes that followed Rome's decline. But before the Dark Ages ended, the two languages headed in radically different directions. [. . .]. In Spain, the Germanic Visigoths ceded power to the Arabs, who, in turn, were unseated by Christian kings, punctuating the evolution of Spain's history with radical new influences. (Nadeau and Barlowo 2013)

Like the origin of the country, the Spanish language is a fusion of different communities, including the Visigoths, whose influence on the Spanish language can be seen in the Spanish suffixes –engo (i.e., *realengo, abadengo*) and -ez and –oz (i.e., Rodrígu-ez,

The monastery of Yuso, San Millán de la Cogolla in La Rioja, Spain. The Spanish language originated in San Millán de la Cogolla. (Carlos Soler Martinez/Dreamstime.com)

Muñ-oz). Other linguistic influences came from the Greeks (i.e., demo-cracia, erot-ico, gineco-logía), the Romans (Latin), the Arabs (i.e., *alambique, alfombra, baladí*), the Hebrews (i.e,. names such as *José, María, Gabriel*, or *alfabeto, sábado, eden, mesías*), and more recently, the French (i.e., *chalet, bulevar*) and the English (i.e., *club, chat, premiere*). Conversely, many English words have a Spanish origin, such as tomato, vanilla, ranch, as do numerous North American places, including Florida, California, San Francisco, and Los Angeles.

Today, twice as many people speak Spanish as French. Yet *what is the world role of Spanish?* This seems to be the fundamental question, as expressed in the headline of an article written in English in Spain's best selling national newspaper *El País*, in which it was stated that "English is spoken by 1.5 billion people around the world, a quarter of the global population, and is without doubt the *lingua franca* of diplomacy and economics. But even *The Economist* admits that Spanish deserves to be used more, particularly in the United Nations" (Galarraga 2013). Despite the fact that the Spanish language is growing every year in countries such as the United States (roughly 55 million), Philippines (nearly 3 million), Canada (over 500,000), and Israel (over 50,000), nevertheless, Spanish-speaking nations do not challenge the status quo.

Perhaps one of the reasons why Spanish-speaking people do not complain about being linguistically underrepresented in international institutions is because they think Spanish will spread naturally. For the award-winning writer Antonio Muñoz Molina (1956–), however, there is a profound economic reason. In 2007, during his speech to the IV International Congress of the Spanish Language, he said that the enemy of the Spanish language is not English but poverty (Muñoz Molina 2007).

Internationally, among the first institutions to support the Spanish language was the Queen Sofía Spanish Institute, which was founded in 1954 in New York City to promote the Spanish language and the culture of Spain. Apart from organizing numerous cultural events, in 1978, the Queen Sofia Spanish Institute also established the annual Gold Medal Gala, in which they recognize individuals who have contributed to the appreciation of Spain and Ibero-America globally through any discipline including the arts, science, and business. Furthermore, in 2010 an award was created, consisting of a $10,000 prize for the best translation of any Spanish literary work translated by an American. The first recipient was Dr. Edith Grossman for her translation of Antonio Muñoz Molina's *A Manuscript of Ashes* (originally entitled *Beatus Ille*, 1986).

The orthographic, grammatical, and lexical rules of Spanish are decided by the Spanish Royal Academy (*Real Academia Española*), founded in 1713, and by the Association for Academies of the Spanish Language. Its motto in Spanish is *Limpia, fija y da splendor*, which literally means "it cleans, sets, and casts splendor." In the United States the first endowed chair in modern languages, the Smith Chair established at Harvard in 1815, was, not by chance, first held by Hispanists. As Joan Ramón Resina points out, they "realized the importance of South American independence for their commercial interests and encouraged the teaching of Spanish by funding the new academic discipline" (Resina 2013).

If initially early Hispanists turned to the study of Spain for reasons of prestige, nowadays, the role of Hispanism in English academia is changing drastically. One of the problems has to do with the fact that most languages departments have a degree of rivalry between different languages in English-speaking universities. Also, those departments typically represent Spanish under the old term "Hispanic Studies," which usually refers to Castilian only, ignoring Basque, Catalan, Galician, and Valencian. Furthermore, another disturbing change happening in the United States and Canada is the gradual dissolution of the programs of individual foreign literatures and cultures, which end up being replaced under the new term "World Languages."

The teaching of the Spanish language in Spain was not an issue until 1900. However, since the dictatorship of Miguel Primo de Rivera (1923–1930) and Franco's persecution of Iberian diversity (1936–1975), both dictators converted the Spanish language and teaching into symbolic battles around the concept of nationhood. Spanish nationalism did not disappear in 1975. Despite Franco's death, Spain's nationalism persisted and even managed to re-adapt itself under new political agents after 1978.

Further Reading

Nadeau, Jean-Benoît, and Julie Barlow. *The Story of Spanish*. New York: St. Martin's Press, 2013.

Penny, Ralph J. *A History of the Spanish Language*. Cambridge: Cambridge University Press, 1991.

Pharies, David A. *A Brief History of the Spanish Language*. Chicago: Chicago University Press, 2007.

Resina, Joan Ramón, ed. *Iberian Modalities: A Relational Approach to the Study of Culture in the Iberian Peninsula*. Liverpool: Liverpool University Press, 2013.

Instituto Cervantes

The Instituto Cervantes is a language institution run by the state to promote the Spanish language abroad. It was created in 1991 (Article 3 of Law 7) to promote and teach Spanish. Its headquarters are in Madrid and in Alcalá de Henares, where Miguel de Cervantes (1547–1616) was born. It takes its name from the most universal Spanish writer of all times. Currently there are over 55 centers across five continents.

One of the most important educational titles that is offered at the Instituto Cervantes is the DELE diploma. The acronym in Spanish stands for *Diploma de Español como Lengua Extranjera* (Diploma of Spanish as a Foreign Language). DELE are official certificates recognized worldwide in the field of Spanish. There are six different DELE diplomas, depending on the level of the candidate and in accordance with the common European reference framework.

See also: Chapter 8: Overview. Chapter 9: Overview. Chapter 11: Golden Age of Spanish Literature.

Further Reading
Instituto Cervantes: http://www.cervantes.es

Linguistic Landscape of Spain

The Spanish Reconquista would last almost eight centuries (711–1492). One of the main reasons why the Christian kingdoms were at each other's throats is because "one of the biggest stakes of the Reconquista was deciding which of Spain's northern kingdoms would dominate the Iberian Peninsula" (Nadeau and Barlow 2013). Like *El Poema del Mio Cid* (*The Poem of the Cid*, composed between 1195–1207), the earliest texts in the history of Castilla were not actually written in Spanish. The first written examples of vernacular Ibero-Romance were the *Gloss of San Millán de la Cogolla* and the *Gloss of Silos*.

In Spain the former is called *Glosas emilianenses* for San Millán (St. Emiliane), who retired to the mountains of La Rioja to become a hermit and died at the age of 101. After his death, his fame grew, spurred by the legend recounting his miraculous appearance mounted on a stallion assisting the Christians against the Moors in the battle of Simancas. Another story from the period recounts how King García, son of Sancho, arranged to have the saint's mortal remains transferred to the Monastery of Santa María in Nájera, but the oxen pulling the cart refused to move, which was interpreted as the refusal of San Millán to be moved from the place he so dearly loved in life.

EARLY TEXTS

Juglaría and *Clerecía* were the earliest texts written on the Iberian Peninsula, dating back to the eighth century "when Arab sources began to use *al-Quila* (the castles, Latin *castella*) to refer to a small mountainous area" (Elliott 1991). Similarly, *El Poema del Mio Cid*, like all literature of *juglaría* (characterized by being anonymous) belongs to an oral tradition where other Iberian languages including Aragonese, not Castilian, were added to the text. This was also the case with the popular *jarchas*, which were not written in Spanish but transliterations of Mozarabic, in the sense that *jarchas* (in Arabic *kharjas*) belonged to a type of Arabic poetry known as *muwashshahs* (in Spanish *moaxahas*) that were made of five stanzas where the *jarcha* was the last verse sung by the local jugglers. On the other hand, the *Mester de Clerecía* was cultivated by clerics in the 13th century. They distanced themselves from the *Mester of Juglaría* by following a regular meter (*cuaderna vía*). One of their best examples is the Castilian deacon Gonzalo de Berceo (1190–1264), who initially borrowed vocabulary from the oral traditions (i.e., jugglers) to write poems to the Virgin such as *The Miracles of Our Lady* (written around 1260) and became the "father" of poetry written in Spanish.

It was then that the monarch decided to build the Lower Monastery called the Monastery of Yuso in the year 1053 (Tomé 2003). Both monasteries—de Suso (6th century) and de Yuso (11th century)—were declared World Heritage Sites by UNESCO in 1997. They are considered the birthplace of the Castilian language on account of the *Glosas emilianenses*, annotations written in Castilian in the margins of a work. Since parchment was expensive and rare, monks scribbled in the margins of already written parchment. These glosses date from around 980, each coming from neighboring monasteries near Burgos.

Several centuries later, the figure of Gonzalo de Berceo (1197–1264), a priest from the monastery, would emerge from this same focal point of religious and cultural illumination. He is considered the first poet in the Castilian language and precursor of the mystic writers of later times. His style of verse belongs to the *Mester de Clerecía*. Another historical date for the Spanish language was during the kingdom of Alfonso X of Castilla y León (1252–1284), who was the first monarch who promoted the Castilian language. In fact, he replaced Latin with Castilian for use in official court and church documents, as well as in books. Also, Alfonso X codified the *Siete Partidas* (Seven Parts), which remained the basis of the Spanish legal system until the 19th century, and "became a foundational law of the United States" (Nadeau and Barlow 2013). Furthermore, Alfonso made Castilian a language of higher learning despite the fact that he was a prolific writer of Galician poetry including *Cántigas de Santa María* (*Songs of Saint Mary*). The reason why Alfonso chose the Galician language for his poetry was that "during his reign the prestige of Galician was still unmatched—in fact it was bolstered by the powerful Crown of Portugal" (Nadeau and Barlow 2013).

Another great promoter of the Spanish language was the Andalusian scholar at the Universidad de Salamanca, Antonio de Nebrija (1441–1522), who understood that vernacular tongues had a grammatical structure. "With his *Gramática de la lengua Castellana* (1492, *Grammar of the Spanish Language*), he became the first European to record and thoroughly systematize the grammar of a vernacular tongue" (Nadeau and Barlow 2013). His publication coincided with the discovery of the new world—a time of conquests and discoveries in which Castilian spread to other lands as the ambassador of Spain's vision of the world. At the end of the 19th century, Miguel de Unamuno (1864–1936), a Spanish philosopher and writer, said that no people could become truly cultured except through trade with others, through free intellectual exchange.

In the early 16th century, Castilian could be heard throughout the Iberian Peninsula and was becoming an international language. Its prestige swept across the rest of Europe, particularly the Italian and Flemish states, but also France, Great Britain, and Germany. In the dissemination of the Spanish language, its arrival in America in 1492 was to be crucial. Castilian was to be the language that travelled to the new overseas territories. For over five centuries, Castilian took hold and reached from Tierra del Fuego to the Río Grande and across the Pacific Ocean to the Philippines. Spanish is a language that has been expanding globally since the 16th century.

Other major influential books written in Spanish include Juan Luis Vives (1493–1540)'s *De ratione studii puerilis* (*On the Right Method of Instruction for Children*) in 1523, and *De disciplinis libri XX* (*Twenty Books on Discipline*), in 1531. In the latter he advocated the use of the vernacular in schools, argued for the building of academies, and supported the education of women. It constitutes the first systematic study to address, explicitly and exclusively, the universal education of women.

Sebastián de Covarrubias (1539–1613)'s *Tesoro de la lengua castellana o española* (*Treasury of Castilian or Spanish Language*) published in 1611 also deserves special attention, since it was the first monolingual dictionary in Europe, and likewise the first dictionary to describe Castilian entirely *in* Castilian. With regards to prominent dictionaries written in the Spanish language, two without any doubt are among the most important ones: María Moliner (1900–1981)'s *Diccionario de uso del español* (*Dictionary of Spanish Usage*) published in 1966, and an immediate success, selling nearly two hundred thousand copies by 1967; and the *Diccionario de americanismos* (*Dictionary of Americanisms*) in 2010. Contrary to what the title may suggest to English readers, this is not a book on Spanglish or U.S. Anglicisms but a celebration of the dialectal Spanish of Latin America. The goal was to create unity in diversity, not uniformity.

Another important linguistic achievement was the *Enciclopedia universal ilustrada europeo-americana* (*Universal Illustrated European-American Encyclopedia*) published by Espasa-Calpe (1908–1930), which contained 82 volumes. "Today's version, which has 110 volumes, 175,000 pages, and 200 million words, is even bigger than the *Britannica* and rivals it in the quality of its articles" (Nadeau and Barlow 2013).

Nowadays, the U.S. with its 55 million Hispanics, is the second country in the world in terms of the number of Spanish speakers, after Mexico, and ahead of Spain, Colombia, and Argentina. Spanish speakers are—if only countries where it is an official language are taken into account—around 6 percent of the world's population, compared to 8.9 percent of English speakers and 1.8 percent of French speakers. Another significant fact is that Spanish is spoken by 94.6 percent of the population living in countries where it is the official language, a far higher percentage than the 34.6 percent of the population of French-speaking countries and 27.6 percent of the population of the English-speaking countries (*Spain Today 2013*).

See also: Chapter 1: Overview; Population and Demography; Regions of Spain. Chapter 2: Overview. Chapter 3: Overview. Chapter 5: Overview. Chapter 6: Multiculturalism; Nationalism. Chapter 8: Overview. Chapter 9: Overview. Chapter 11: Overview.

Further Reading

Gorter, D. *Linguistic Landscape: A New Approach to Multilingualism*. Buffalo: Multilingual Matters, 2006.

Turell, María Teresa. *Multilingualism in Spain: Sociolinguistic and Psycholinguistic Aspects of Linguistic Minority Groups*. Buffalo: Multilingual Matters, 2001.

Peninsular Languages

The Romans converted the Iberian Peninsula (*Hispania*) into a province in 206 BCE. The common language of the Roman Empire in Hispania was Latin, except in the north, in the area that corresponds to the Basque country and part of Navarra. Isolated by the mountains, the Roman influence hardly penetrated into these two northern regions, preserving the Basque language, whose origin is still uncertain. In fact, the Basque, or Euskera, language has no associations with any European tongue. In the rest of Spain, Latin evolved naturally into other languages. Like the other Romance languages, Spanish was formed over the long period ranging from the fourth to the 10th centuries as a result of the fragmentation of Latin. In the 13th century Spanish was already a language of culture. The popular epic gave rise to *The Poem of the Cid*, an anonymous 12th century poem that suggests the existence of an old literary tradition prior to it.

The official language of Spain, Castilian, is the language of the former kingdom of Castilla. When it spread across the world in the 16th and 17th centuries, it became increasingly referred to as "Spanish." Since then both names have coexisted. Internationally, the most widely accepted name is "Spanish," while "Castilian" tends to be used in the north of Spain and in its bilingual areas, as well as across the countries of South America. Most Spanish citizens will speak and understand Spanish even if some Spaniards (mainly from the Basque or Catalan regions) do not want to. Although the Spanish language can be easy to learn, especially after understanding the complexity of the verbs and the orthography of the accentuations, the pronunciation still remains a major obstacle. This is perhaps due to the huge variety of accents not only in Spain but in all Latin American countries. For instance, the region of Andalucía is well known for its complicated accent, which varies significantly from one city to another.

Basque is one of the oldest languages in Europe. Its origins are subject to a wide range of hypotheses; some linguists argue that it could be related to Caucasian languages, due to certain similarities with Georgian. Today it is spoken in the Spanish Basque country, in the north of Navarra, and French Basque territory. The first texts written in Basque are dated from the 16th century when Bernat Dechepare or Beñat Etsepare published *Linguae Vasconum Primitiae*. Later, in 1571, Joanes Leizarraga translated the *New Testament* (*Testamentu Berria*) into Basque. In 1979 the Statute of Regional Autonomy declared Basque the official language of the Basque country. Since then many rules have been developed and various bodies and institutions have been created. The rules of this language have been established by the Royal Academy of the Basque Language (*Euskaltzaindia*), founded in 1918. Currently, there are about 600,000 Basque people who speak Euskera (Basque language), of whom half a million live in the Basque country.

Together with Castilian, Catalan is the official language of the region of Catalunya and the Balearic Islands. Outside Catalunya it is spoken in the Principality of Andorra, on the border of Aragón with Catalunya, in the French territories of Rosellón, and in the Italian city of Alguer (Sardinia). Catalan first appears in written documents in the second half of the 12th century. Legal, economic, religious, and historical texts written in Catalan have been preserved since that time. The first great universal literary talent in this language appeared in the 13th century: Ramón Llull (1232–1315). He was the first writer to use Catalan in literary prose as a normal instrument of communication and as a tool for cultural expression. The creation of the Catalan Studies Institute (*Institut d'Estudis Catalans*) (1907) enabled the language to be systematized through the publication of *Normes ortogràfiques* (1913), *Dicionari ortográfico* (1917) and *Gramática catalana*, produced by Pompeu Fabra (1918). In 2000 Institut Ramón Llull was created to promote the Catalan language outside Spain. Nowadays the Catalans (over seven million) represent 15.9 percent of Spain's total population. After Andalucía, Catalunya is the region with the second highest number of Catalan inhabitants. Thirteen percent of Catalunya's residents are foreigners.

Galician is spoken across practically the whole of Galicia and on its borders with Asturias, León, and Zamora. Its literature thrived in the Middle Ages. The *Cántigas de Santa María* of King Alfonso X the Wise exemplifies its use and prestige as a literary language at the close of the 13th century. In 1905 the Galician Royal Academy was established. This represented the institutionalization of the Galician language and rules regarding its idiomatic usage. The 1978 constitution and subsequent linguistic and educational regulation of Galician have enabled Galician to be used in schools and as a respected language in social communication.

Article 7 of the Statute of Regional Autonomy of the Community of Valencia establishes that the two official languages of the region of Valencia are Valencian and Castilian and later states that the Generalitat Valenciana (regional government of Valencia) shall guarantee the normal and official use of both languages, adopting the necessary measures to ensure that it not become obsolete. In addition, it states that special protection and respect for the recovery of Valencian shall be afforded. The Valencian language reached the peak of its literary splendor in the 15th century and part of the 17th century. The dukes of Calabria commenced a gradual process of writing more documents in Castilian, but its presence continued in daily use. In 1932 the rules on the orthography called "de Castellón" were agreed upon. In 1998 the *Cortes Valencianas* (Legislative Assembly of Valencia) approved an act creating the Academy of the Valencian

Language (*Ley 7/1998*). Article 3 of the above act states that the purpose of the academy is to determine and compile, if applicable, the linguistic rules of the Valencian language.

One of the latest reports produced by the Instituto Cervantes entitled *El uso de las lenguas en la red* (2011, *The Use of Languages on the Internet*), which covers the linguistic map of Spain, shows some interesting recent figures: Catalan, which is spoken in three regions represents 29 percent of Spain's total population (47,021,031 in 2010); Euskera represents 6 percent of the Spanish population, and Galician also represents nearly 6 percent (5.95% of the Spanish population). More interestingly, the article also provides the current number of Spaniards who are able to read in their respective regional languages (page 5), as shown in Table 9.1.

Table 9.1   SPANIARDS ABLE TO READ THEIR LOCAL LANGUAGE

Region	Population 2001	Population able to read in their local language 2001	Population 2010	Population able to read in their local language 2010
Catalunya	6,343,110	4,808,077	7,512,381	5,694,385
Comunidad Valenciana	4,162,776	1,948,179	5,111,706	2,392,278
Balears Islands	841,669	508,368	1,106,049	668,054
Basque Country	2,082,587	503,986	2,178,339	527,158
Navarra	555,829	257,349	636,924	294,896
Galicia	2,695,880	1,860,157	2,797,653	1,930,381
Total of Spain	40,847,371		47,021,031	

See also: Chapter 1: Overview; Population and Demography; Regions of Spain. Chapter 2: Overview. Chapter 3: Overview. Chapter 5: Overview. Chapter 6: Multiculturalism; Nationalism. Chapter 8: Overview. Chapter 9: Overview; Linguistic Landscape of Spain. Chapter 11: Overview.

Further Reading

Grenfell, Michael, ed. *Modern Languages across the Curriculum*. London: Routledge, 2002.

Pérez Vidal, Carmen, et al. *A Portrait of the Young in the New Multilingual Spain*. Buffalo: Multilingual Matters, 2008.

Spanish Language Mixed

A major weakness of the current population of Spain is their lack of knowledge of a second language. Spaniards remain resistant to some elements of globalization.

Although most Spaniards study English since the country joined the European Union in 1986—which increased the linguistic homogenization brought about by MTV, CNN, and the Internet—it is primarily in tourist areas that English is spoken fluently. Nevertheless, since Spain colonized the New World, the Spanish language has been in contact with many native languages such as Guaraní, Quechua, and Nahuatl, producing their own "fusion" languages. A contemporary example of the linguistic interaction between Spanish and other languages is the so-called *Spanglish*. As Nadeau and Barlow explain, "Spanglish is actually a blanket term for a variety of different Spanish slangs, including *Cubonics* (from Miami Cubans); *Nuyorican* (from New York Puerto Ricans); and *Dominicanish* (from New York Dominicans). The Spanglish of Mexicans is roughly divided among *Pocho, Pachuco, Chicano,* and *Tex-Mex*" (Nadeau and Barlow 2013). In Gibraltar, the local Spanglish is called *Llanito*. In the Panama Canal Zone, it is *Zonian*. Brazil has *Portuñol,* and France has *Fragnol*, while Peru has *Quechuañol* and *Japoñol* (Spanish slang among second-generation Japanese immigrants). The term *Spanglish* was coined in 1948 by Salvador Tió, a Puerto Rican columnist. In 1971, he recoined it *El Inglañol*, but the Spanglish label stuck.

Two features distinguish Iberian Spanish (the type of Spanish spoken in Spain) from Latin American Spanish. One is the lisp-heavy pronunciation of the letters c and z. Thus, in Spain, *cerveza* (beer) is pronounced thehr-be*h*-thah. And the second is that the native population uses the third-person *vosotros* (you) form, rather than the *ustedes* form common throughout Latin America. Furthermore, the Spanish spoken in Spain is very diverse. For instance, apart from the official recognized languages of some regions (i.e., Basque, Catalan, Valencian, Galician), other regional accents are also particularly distinctive. For example, each Canary island has its own accent. A similar situation occurs in the eight cities in the region of Andalucía, which differ significantly from the tone of *Madrileños*, the people of Madrid.

The percentage of Spaniards who speak and understand their own regional language is as follows: Galician (88% of their regional population); Catalan-Valenciano (65%); and Basque (20%). On the other hand, the five most-spoken languages in Europe are English (38%), French (12%), German (11%), Spanish (7%), and Russian (5%).

See also: Chapter 1: Overview. Chapter 9: Overview; Linguistic Landscape of Spain; Peninsular Languages.

Further Reading

Nadeau, Jean-Benoît and Julie Barlow. *The Story of Spanish*. New York: St. Martin's Press, 2013.

Ostler, Nicholas. *Empires of the Word: A Language History of the World*. London: Folio Society, 2010.

Stewart, Miranda. *The Spanish Language Today*. London: Routledge, 2003.

REFERENCES

Galarraga, Naiara. "What Is the World Role of Spanish?" *El País,* April 30, 2013.

López-Davalillo Larrea, Julio. *Geografía regional de España*. Madrid: UNED, 2014.

Nadeau, Jean-Benoît and Julie Barlow. *The Story of Spanish*. New York: St. Martin's Press, 2013.

Noya, Javier. *La imagen de España en el mundo. Visiones del exterior*. Vol. 1. 2nd ed. Madrid: Tecnos, 2013.

Núñez Seixas, Xosé Manuel. "La(s) lengua(s) de la nación" in *Ser españoles. Imaginarios nacionalistas en el siglo XX*. Edited by Javier Moreno Luzón and Xosé M. Núñez Seixas. Barcelona: RBA, 2013.

Resina, Joan Ramón. *Iberian Modalities. A Relational Approach to the Study of Culture in the Iberian Peninsula*. Liverpool: Liverpool University Press, 2013.

Tomé, Javier. *The Route of the Castilian Language*. 2nd ed. Madrid: Turespaña, 2003.

VV.AA. *El español en España*. Barcelona: EGEDSA, 2007.

Websites

El uso de las lenguas en la red. http://www.cervantes.es/imagenes/File/cidic/El%20uso%20de%20las%20lenguas%20en%20Internet_El%20caso%20de%20Espaa.pdf

España. Spain.info/en

Europeans and Their Languages. Special Eurobarometer 386. European Commission. http://ec.europa.eu/public_opinion/archives/ebs/ebs_386_en.pdf

Instituto Cervantes. cervantes.es

Muñoz Molina, Antonio. *Ciudadanía hispánica de la literatura* 2007.

OECD 2014. oecd.org

Oxford Bibliographies. Entry on "Juan Luis Vives." http://www.oxfordbibliographies.com/view/document/obo-9780195399301/obo-9780195399301-0113.xml

Queen Sofía Spanish Institute. spanishinstitute.org

Real Academia Española. rae.es

Spain is Culture. http://www.spainisculture.com/

Spain Today 2013. Madrid: Ministry of the Presidency, 2013. http://publicacionesoficiales.boe.es

CHAPTER 10

ETIQUETTE

OVERVIEW

Spaniards are generally warm and passionate people yet they can be complex and their mannerisms sometimes may appear contradictory. Mannerisms and social behavior are both influenced by the Spanish temperament and Catholic religion. For example, Spaniards do not wear a hat at church and generally speaking they sometimes behave with bravado, which echoes the passion experienced during a bullfight. That being said, it is very difficult to accurately generalize about the social norms of Spanish citizens as they embrace at least three different cultural heritages: from the Celtic and Basque peoples of the north to the more typically Mediterranean culture that stretches across the peninsula from Catalunya to Andalucía. As with its formation, 21st-century Spain is a melting pot.

To further complicate matters, in addition to differences in lifestyle and cultural traditions that still exist, Spain's socials norms are globally changing. The English writer Chris Stewart (1950–), who moved to Spain to become a farmer and an author, noted that in the 1990s, Spain was markedly different from 1970, at which time he decided to live in the mountains of the Alpujarras in Granada. For him, Spain had until very recently a very strong culture, a certain way of dressing and a way of being. However, like most Western nations, these distinctive national features of the past have been eroded by globalization. For instance, cultural concepts such as the *siesta* and two hour lunch breaks, formal clothing worn to mass, culinary customs, and ways of greeting each other are all evolving.

The Catholic religion still permeates the language and daily life of Spaniards, though less so than in previous times. For instance, Spanish people say "Jesus" after a person sneezes but this is only the Spanish equivalent of "Bless you." One of the rituals in which Spanish decorum and etiquette can be observed is the traditional mass on Sundays. The ceremony lasts about 25 minutes, involves the whole family, and provides an occasion to dress elegantly. Attending a Sunday mass usually becomes an all-day event. It also involves a walk (*paseo*) before or after having a family lunch or dinner at home or in a restaurant.

Another tradition entrenched in Catholic ideology is that Spaniards celebrate their saint name day in addition to their birthdays. Many Spaniards have a given name that is based on the name of a Catholic saint. Their saint name day falls on the feast day of their patron saint. In fact, for some their saint name day is more special than birthdays.

The custom is a special lunch or dinner, which is accompanied by sweets or cake. This day is relatively low key in comparison to North American birthdays. Usually it is a small family celebration.

Spanish surnames can be confusing due to the fact that Hispanic people carry double surnames. The first surname of a Spaniard is his/her father's father's surname and the last one is his/her mother's father's name. For example, based on the name Enrique Ávila López, foreigners should assume that Ávila is his paternal grandfather's surname while López is his maternal grandfather's surname. If he has any children, their first last name would be Ávila followed by his partner's father's surname. Compared to the English tradition, the Spanish custom can be considered more inclusive of the family lineage.

Spaniards' relaxed attitude can also be detected through their language use. Spaniards tend to swear more freely than the average person in North America and have many expressions that exemplify their culture. *Hombre*, which literally translates to "man," is frequently exclaimed and has numerous applications ranging from joy at seeing an old friend to surprise upon hearing unexpected news to appreciation upon tasting an excellent paella. *Mañana por la mañana* is a Spanish saying that literally means "tomorrow morning," although another meaning is the polite way for Spanish people to tell you that something is not going to happen. *Mañana, mañana* is perhaps the most well-known phrase used by foreigners to describe the Spanish attitude toward work. Especially abroad, Spaniards still have the reputation of being unpunctual, often showing up late for a meeting or appointment. However, this is changing, particularly in the more urbanized towns and cities.

Socializing is an integral aspect of being Spanish. In contrast to North Americans, Spaniards embrace the street culture. That is to say that homes are generally private spaces, not reserved for socializing. Parties and gatherings of friends are more likely to happen at restaurants, bars, or cafes than in the home. One distinctive Spanish way of socializing, especially in rural villages, is to see a group of people, including children, standing or sitting around the front of their house visiting and exchanging the latest news of the village. It is rare for Spaniards to formally entertain in their homes with the exception of a birthday party for children. When invited to a Spaniard's home for a meal or a party, a small gift is acceptable. As opposed to children's birthday parties, in which parents arrange lavishly, inviting a lot of little friends and organizing games, the birthday of a Spanish young adult consists of inviting his/her friends, coworkers, or classmates out for a cup of coffee, a drink, or meal to celebrate his/her birthday.

Another aspect of Spanish behavior that distinctly differs from many other cultures is the Spanish preferential treatment toward children. Children are considered "kings" (*los reyes de la casa*) in Spain. Spaniards indulge their children and like to spend as much time with them as possible. Children are welcome almost anywhere, including restaurants and bars, when accompanied with their parents. It is not uncommon to see children—particularly in the warmer summer months—playing in the plazas, or at outdoor concerts or in sidewalk cafes late into the evening.

On the other hand, if foreigners are pleasantly surprised about the polite respect that children receive in public spaces, the same positive conduct cannot be applied when

People enjoy food and drink at a busy tapas bar in Sevilla, Spain. Tapas consist of a small portion of food. In some cities, tapas are free and most bars are proud of serving a few specialties. (Arenaphotouk/Dreamstime.com)

Spaniards queue in front of a bus or at the butcher. Certainly, queuing in Spain can be a unique social experience that can lead to misunderstanding. As Jonathan Packer explains, the Spanish version of queuing is "an anarchic mass of humanity of which the queue-jumper is king. In Spain, it is not a question of lining up politely, but of being first" (Packer 1998).

In 1985 the Italian prime minister Giulio Andreotti (1919–2013), who firmly supported Spain's intention to join the EU despite the strong opposition of France at the time, defined the Spaniards as *Gli spagnoli, brava gente, ma tagliata con l'accetta* ("los españoles, buena gente, pero cortada con hacha"), meaning that Spaniards are good people, but cut with an ax. In other words, as the Italian journalist Josto Maffeo explains, Andreotti meant that Spanish people are not very polished or refined, and usually have some "rough edges." They tend to be more black and white thinkers rather than allowing the necessary grey areas that a position of moderation entails (quoted in Íñigo and Zurdo 2013).

Further Reading

Packer, Jonathan. *Live and Work in Spain and Portugal.* 2nd ed. Oxford: Vacation Work, 1998.

Stewart, Chris. *Driving over Lemons: An Optimist in Andalucía.* New York: Pantheon Books, 1999.

Clothing and Fashion

Spaniards take their clothing very seriously, and will go to great lengths about their appearance before stepping out of their homes to complete even the simplest of errands. They adhere to the changing trends of the season and it is not uncommon when walking through the streets of a city to see the women wearing this season's footwear or the men dressed smartly in slacks and a shirt with a designer label prominently displayed. According to Graff, "women are very clothes-conscious and fashion is of supreme importance. They will spend huge amounts of money buying dresses and accessories just to keep up with the latest fashion trends" (Graff 2008). For the Spanish middle class, following the fads of the season takes priority over even the more practical aspect of "need." However, due to the recent financial crisis, Spaniards are turning more toward *rebajas* or sales, and companies have been willing to comply by drastically reducing the initial price through large scale sale campaigns and temporary discounts. The semiannual rebajas are becoming even more popular as discretionary spending becomes tighter for the average Spanish household.

For the Spaniard fashion is not so much about self-expression as it is about having a proper or respectable appearance. Therefore, Spaniards' look is more visually coherent and conformist than those in other metropolitan cities such as London or New York, where the look may be more eclectic. Additionally, the fashion industry is not monopolized by only the youth or the trend setters; fashion brands are worn by both men and women, married and unmarried, as well as professional and career people.

With regards to dressing for occasions, Spaniards tend to be formal. For example, even in the heat of the southern regions of Spain, it will be rare to see men wearing T-shirts or women in strapless tops. Flips flops would be considered acceptable only at the beach or poolside and men tend to prefer jeans or trousers to shorts. Similarly, gym wear is just that—clothing reserved for the gym. Women will rarely be seen walking through the streets in workout gear and men are held to the same standards. Gym shoes or running shoes are not commonly worn out in the streets of Spain, though, again, this is changing with the younger generation. When working or going to a government office or place of business, more formal dress is advised. Similarly in church, conservative, formal dress is

---

SALES

Rebajas means "sales" and they now happen twice a year throughout Spain after having been regulated by the government. These annual sell-offs used to occur during the second week of January and the last week of July. However, because of the economic crisis, at the beginning of 2013, the government allowed shops to display the notice of rebajas at any time, although most shops respect the tradition of doing it just twice a year. The only difference has been that they have extended the period of time, with the first period of rebajas being from January to March and, in most parts of Spain, the second period being from July to the end of August.

common. Shorts or revealing tops are not considered socially acceptable, and neither are baseball caps or casual hats, especially at church or when eating in a restaurant.

Fashion is not limited to adults; even the youngest of children are quickly indoctrinated into the habit of wearing the proper clothes. From the moment a baby is taken out of the house for the first time, his/her appearance is of great importance. Even today, it is not uncommon for baby girls to have their ears pierced shortly after birth and before they leave the hospital. At the earliest age, appearance surpasses convenience as many of the baby clothes in Spain still contain buttons as opposed to the North American snaps. Seeing toddlers walking in shorts sets or trousers complete with knee socks and leather shoes is again common particularly in cosmopolitan areas.

Spain has a variety of contemporary designers and fashion labels ranging from the more affordable Sfera, Stradivarius, Bershka, Hoss Intropia; to the middle of the road Massimo Dutti, Armand Basi, Desigual, MANGO, and Zara; to the more exclusive Adolfo Dominguez, Manolo Blahnik, Roberto Verino, and Ágatha Ruíz de la Prada.

See also: Chapter 12: Overview. Chapter 16: Overview; Fashion.

Further Reading

Euromonitor International. *Passport: Apparel in Spain*. July 2013.

Smith, Paul Julian. *Contemporary Spanish Culture: TV, Fashion, Art, and Film*. Cambridge: Polity, 2003.

Food and Dining Out

Food is an integral part of the Spanish culture. On average, Spaniards spend almost double (20%) what their North Americans counterparts spend (13%) on food and dining out according to 2010 data. Spanish meals are usually eaten much later than North American meals, with lunch beginning around 2:00 p.m. and dinner starting between 9:00–10:00 p.m. or even later in the summer months. In Spain lunch is the main meal of the day and can often last several hours. Immediately after lunch, Spanish has the word, *sobremesa*, which refers to the very distinctive custom in Spain of enjoying a conversation after lunch. *Sobremesa* typically happens on weekends or during a party, and frequently it takes place during the serving of coffee or tea, and sweets. If the *sobremesa* tends to be more of a drink and the relevance is in the conversation, however, Spaniards also have the word *merienda*, which is a snack in the afternoon that can be a sandwich (*bocadillo*), a nibble on sweets, or even the famous sugared, fried dough dipped in thick hot chocolate (*churros con chocolate*).

Traditionally lunch was followed by a nap or *siesta* though it is not as common as it used to be. Many individuals such as business executives, shift workers, and working mothers no longer have time for this one fundamental nap. In the more globalized companies the long lunch break is being replaced by the one-hour lunch break. However, most Spaniards now work eight hours from 8:00 a.m.–6:00 p.m. or 7:00 p.m. with one or two hours for lunch. In the summer (July and August), this schedule usually changes, with work beginning one or two hours earlier in order to leave earlier. During summer, it is considered ill-mannered to drop in after the post-lunch period, since many Spaniards still enjoy a *siesta*.

Fresh bread is always present at meals and many Spanish families prefer to break it with their own hands rather than cut it with a knife. Since Spaniards have deep respect for food, wasting food would be considered bad manners. Therefore, Spaniards tend to refuse an additional serving as opposed to leaving food on their plate. However, if in a restaurant, it is very rare to see a Spaniard asking for a "to go" container to take home the leftover meal. Spaniards tend to eat meals sitting down at a table, and even in the most cosmopolitan cities, a drive-through restaurant is a rarity. Likewise, ordering coffee or tea "to go" is not the social norm. However, dining traditions are changing due in part to globalization, in part to the economic crisis as Spaniards are looking for cheaper dining alternatives, and in part due to the busy lifestyle of the younger generation with both partners working full-time jobs. The result is that Spaniards are eating more ready-made meals and processed foods, with direct consequences: In 2011 Spain ranked among the top of the list in the world for overweight and obesity rates and almost 30 percent of Spanish children are overweight.

Despite the economic downturn, Spaniards still consider eating out to be a priority. In 2010 Spain maintained one of the highest rates of spending dedicated to eating out and catering (8.4% compared to the European average of 4%). Tapas bars are a favorite of Spaniards for combining food with socializing. *Tapas* is a traditional meal in Spain consisting of ordering drinks accompanied by small plates of food to share. Spaniards often dine out in groups and when that happens, the bill is not split as is common in North America. Rather, one person pays for a round of drinks and tapas and then another person pays for the next round. When eating out, a meal can take several hours and, therefore, the waiter will not present the bill until it is asked for. To do so would not be considered efficient but rather offensive as the restaurant patrons would assume they were being rushed. Tipping when eating out is optional as it is added into your bill. A few coins at a tapas bar is considered fine; in more formal eating establishments a 10 percent tip would be considered generous.

See also: Chapter 14: Overview. Chapter 15: Overview.

Further Reading

Agriculture and Agri-Food Canada. *Foodservice Profile Spain: Market Analysis Report,* June 2011.

Graff, Marie Louise. *Spain. Cultureshock! A Survival Guide to Customs and Etiquette.* New York: Marshall Cavendish Editions, 2008

Greetings and Language

A common way in which Spaniards greet each other is by saying *buenos días* (good morning), *buenas tardes* (good afternoon), or *buenas noches* (good evening). The expression *¿qué tal?* (what's up? or what is new?) exemplifies Spain's relaxed etiquette, and frequently follows the greeting.

When Spaniards are talking to a stranger or to a superior, they use a different pronoun and verb tense than when speaking to a friend or equal; the formal pronoun *usted* accompanies the formal third person verb tense and the casual pronoun *tú* accompanies the informal second person verb tense. When speaking to a Spaniard, *Señor* (Mr), *Señora* (Mrs), or *Señorita* (Miss) should come before the surname of the person. In a more polite way, *Don* (male) or *Doña* (female) are used with the Christian name. Teenagers or adolescents are simply called by their given names.

Due to globalization, greetings in Spain are changing from a kiss on both cheeks if you are a woman to a more international standard handshake. However, a kiss on both cheeks is still normal in Spain after leaving a party or social gathering. Women tend to kiss the men and the other women, but men will opt to give another man a hug—or in more formal situations a handshake—as a form of greeting. Traditionally, Spanish men only kiss their family members. Also, most Spanish men will always open doors for women or stand aside to let them pass. In general terms, Spaniards can be seen as far more tactile than northern Europeans in the way they embrace each other.

Spaniards are expressive people. Choral conversations, or conversation where multiple people are speaking simultaneously, are fairly common and verbal expressions are illustrated with frequent hand gestures. Swearing, which is often considered taboo in other cultures, is more widely accepted in casual conversation in Spain. A newcomer to Spain can be scandalized by the colorful language used, for instance, between two friends or a mother toward her child. Nevertheless, the use of bad language (*palabrotas*) is common nationwide among Spaniards regardless of their position in society. Cursing is an integral part of the Spanish language, and definitely has become less taboo than in English.

A constantly changing slang language is embraced particularly by the younger generation of Spaniards. Spain's slang has a tendency to contain subtle sexual connotations which again is less offensive than it would be in the English language. *Piropos* are the Spanish equivalent of the English pick-up lines. They are admiring statements that some Spanish men still say in public in front of others to beautiful women. However, as *machismo* is disappearing, so is the street custom of the *piropo*. These supposedly innocuous compliments still occur from time to time. Nevertheless, not every man in Spain uses it as a mechanism of social control, just like not every Spanish woman reacts to a *piropo* in the same manner (modestly as culturally expected).

While Spanish—or Castilian—is spoken in most of Spain, Catalunya, Valencia, the Basque region, and Galicia each have their own language, which are Catalan, *velenciano* Euskera, and Galego, respectively. While on the Iberian Peninsula it is relatively easy to recognize certain regional accents (i.e., Basque, Catalan, *Madrileño*, *Andaluz*), another matter would be to detect the social status of a native Spaniard by the way he/she speaks, as is normally done in Britain. In other words, if in England it is quite easy to socially label a person according to his/her use of the language, in Spain, this linguistic social scan is much less accurate, simply because a person from the Spanish aristocracy can talk as well or as bad as a Spanish fisherman.

See also: Chapter 9: Overview. Chapter 10: Overview.

Further Reading

Schlecht, Neil E. *Spain for Dummies*. Hoboken: Wiley, 2007.

Zollo, Mike, and Phil Turk. *World Cultures: Spain*. Chicago: Contemporary Books, 2000.

Shopping

Prices have risen with inflation, while salaries have not (i.e., the situation of millions of *mileuristas*—individuals earning roughly a thousand euros a month in Spain). However, Spaniards love going shopping or *de compras* as they say, as part of the street culture which truly characterizes them. The cost of living in Spain is relatively cheaper than in northern European countries, and the price of food, public transport, tobacco, and alcohol still tend to be less in Spain.

In regards to supermarkets, most towns and cities have modern supermarkets where a variety of products can be found (i.e., *Mercadona, Día, SuperSol*). Most stores and supermarkets will close from 2:00 p.m.–5:00 p.m. for the *siesta* in summer and re-open again until 8:00 p.m. During Sundays and holidays it is not uncommon for many of the local shops to be closed altogether. Food shopping can be a positive experience as the selection and quality of fruits and vegetables that are in season is excellent. In small towns particularly, a Spaniard may make separate trips to the baker, the fruit and vegetable vendors, and the indoor market for fresh meat, fish, or eggs. Shopping is in some places still a daily affair that is combined with socializing among other locals in the village.

Apart from the large supermarkets and department store chains, smaller markets are common in towns and villages and may be set up on certain days outdoors or have a more structured indoor location. *Rastros* or flea markets are set up in various locations usually once a week or on specific dates that are advertised locally. An eclectic variety of items can be found at rastros ranging from inexpensive household items to art, antiques, and jewelry. Stamp and coin collectors may also be present, attracting those looking for a rare piece or an odd bargain.

The larger stores are becoming dominated by the department store chains such as *El Corte Inglés* or *Eroski*. Unlike the smaller shops, these chains stay open continuously from 10:00 a.m.–10:00 p.m. Spanish stores have their sales or rebajas twice a year—once in January and again in July.

See also: Chapter 4: Overview; Manufacturing Industry; Tourism; Trade. Chapter 12: Overview. Chapter 14: Overview. Chapter 15: Family Outings and Vacations.

Further Reading

Euromonitor International. *Passport: Apparel in Spain*. July 2013.

Holton, Harvey. *Working and Living: Spain*. London: Cadogan Guides, 2007.

Shoppers walk in front of El Corte Inglés in Barcelona. The view from the restaurant at El Corte Inglés offers a panoramic view of the whole city. (Viorel Dudau/Dreamstime.com)

Standards of Public Decency

Topless tanning is quite common all over the Mediterranean coast and acceptable by most Spaniards with perhaps the exception of the rural areas, where some people may feel upset. Nude bathing, on the other hand, is strictly forbidden except on the authorized nude beaches. Otherwise, there is a warning to cover up or a direct fine will be given by the authorities. Furthermore, Spaniards tend to be very clean in their private domestic space. However, while in the public domain, littering in the street as well as throwing napkins and olive pits on the floor in restaurants is still usually the custom, especially in the countryside of Spain.

Nonetheless, Spaniards consider it very rude to wear swim clothes while walking in the street or in a beach restaurant (called *chiringuito*). Likewise, it is very rare to see a Spaniard completely drunk while in the company of people, especially in front of a woman.

Smoking is still prevalent in Spain. Although it was banned in the workplace, on public transportation, and in other public areas such as cultural centers in 2006, however, around 50,000 Spaniards die yearly due to smoking related illnesses. In 2011 Spain also banned smoking in bars and restaurants as well as anywhere near hospitals and school playgrounds. Moreover, Spain prohibited the showing of smoking on television broadcasts.

Tipping is not mandatory in Spain except for taxi drivers, barbers, and hairdressers. Although service is included in restaurant bills, the waiter will expect a tip (compulsory in Catalunya). A generous tip, if the service was good, would be 10 percent.

Public toilets in Spain can be an experience. Normally they are clean but often they have no paper and/or no soap. In this case, what most Spaniards do is to stop in a bar for a quick drink after using the washroom. The name of the restroom in Spanish can be confusing, since there are different names to say toilet (i.e., *servicios*, *baños*, *aseos*, *lavabos*, *retretes*, *sanitarios*).

See also: Chapter 10: Overview.

Further Reading

Hickey, Leo, and Miranda Stewart. *Politeness in Europe*. Buffalo: Multilingual Matters, 2005.

Novas, Himilce, and Rosemary Silva. *Passport Spain: Your Pocket Guide to Spanish Business, Customs, and Etiquette*. Petaluma: World Trade Press, 2008.

Weddings, Funerals, and Etiquette in Religious Places

The idea of a small wedding in Spain is very rare. This is definitely a huge contrast with the average English nuptials, which usually involves around 50 guests while the standard expected in any Spanish village is no less than 100. Apart from the number of guests, there are other major differences between the typical English wedding and the Spanish one. For instance, there are no bridesmaids or groomsmen, nor best man or maid of honor in a Spanish wedding. Unlike the custom in North America where traditionally the bride's family pays for the wedding, the Spanish tradition requires the wedding expenses to be paid equally by both families. Another distinctive feature in a Spanish wedding has to do with the attire of the bride, who will decide if she will wear the *mantilla* (a form of headdress) instead of a *velo nupcial* (wedding veil). The mother walks with the groom down the aisle while the father walks with the bride. The entire wedding party—guests and family—wait outside the church for the bride to arrive. Once she arrives, she is the first to walk into the church with the wedding party following her.

During the wedding celebration, speeches are not usually given. Instead, the tradition is for the groom to give the bride 13 coins, which is symbolic of his commitment to provide for her. However, as many couples have collective responsibility for finances today, the custom is changing so that both the bride and groom exchange coins as a symbolic gesture of future wealth and shared fiscal duties. In Spain the wedding ring or *alianza* is a simple band traditionally of gold and is worn on the right hand. The North American diamond engagement rings are not traditionally given in Spain. While the prospective groom may present his bride to be with a necklace or a ring, the ring is not worn with the wedding band as is the custom elsewhere. Another tradition during the wedding party is to cut the groom's tie into three parts and auction it off as a token of good luck. During the wedding feast the bride and groom walk from table to table carrying a basket with small wedding gifts (*detalles*) that they personally give to each of their guests. *Detalles* may consist of a cigar or small bottle of wine for the men. The women will receive a small present of some sort such as a pendant or hand-painted fans. During this time the guest is expected to give the bride and groom the wedding gift of choice: money. It is not uncommon for couples to include their bank account numbers on wedding invitations. The wedding gift is expected to be worth more than the meal the guests will be offered.

With regards to nontraditional weddings, it is important to note that in 2009 for the first time in Spain there were more civil weddings (94,993) than Catholic church weddings (80,174), based on the statistics of the Spanish National Institute (INE). This new phenomenon in Spain, according to some Spanish sociologists, is due mainly to the economic crisis but also because of the fact that there is a secularization process currently underway in Spain. The average cost of a civil wedding in Spain was 20,353 euros and for a Catholic celebration 25,050 euros in 2012. In the same year (2012), only 74,021 people got married in Spain: 1,981 couples were of same-sex (2.7%): 1,132 weddings between men (57.1%), and 849 between women (42.9%).

Cemeteries are usually located on the outskirts of the town or the village, and are surrounded by walls bordered by cypress trees. Most Spaniards place the deceased into above-ground graves. Some families own a family vault (*panteón familiar*), which traditionally they visit on "the Day of the Dead" on November 1st (All Saints' Day). This day is a time for the entire family to congregate at the grave and pay homage to the deceased member of their family. However, this is not necessarily a sad occasion, but rather a time for family members to visit and exchange the latest news of the family.

Spain has numerous shrines dedicated to Catholic Saints or the Virgin Mary and great attention is paid to maintaining these holy places. For example, statues of the Virgin Mary usually have their outfits (dresses, cloaks, jewelry, and ornaments) changed on a regular basis. These are considered sacred areas and are treated with the utmost respect. Statues and shrines are taken out of the church and paraded through the town on the feast day of the saint, and more especially during Easter (*Semana Santa*).

Churches in Spain are usually open to visitors, the basic protocol being that if the building is unlocked, all are welcome to enter. However, respect must be shown by wearing proper clothes (no hats, no flip-flops, conservative dress) and if there is a mass in session, visitors are expected to act accordingly.

See also: Chapter 5: Overview. Chapter 10: Overview.

Further Reading

Graff, Marie Louise. *Culture Shock! Spain: A Survival Guide to Customs and Etiquette*. New York: Marshall Cavendish Editions, 2008.

Macfarlane, Michael. *The Little Giant Encyclopedia of Etiquette*. New York: Sterling, 2001.

REFERENCES

Graff, Marie Louise. *Spain. Cultureshock! A Survival Guide to Customs and Etiquette*. New York: Marshall Cavendish Editions, 2008.

Hampshire, David. *Living and Working in Spain*. 8th ed. London: Survival Books, 2009.

Hooper, John. *The New Spaniards*. 2nd ed. London: Penguin Books, 2006.

Íñigo, José María, and David Zurdo. *Chupa la gamba*. Madrid: la esfera de los libros, 2013.

Packer, Jonathan. *Live and Work in Spain and Portugal*. 2nd ed. Oxford: Vacation Work, 1998.

Marías, Julián. "Prólogo: Carta abierta al estudiante americano" in *Modos de vivir. Un observador español en los Estados Unidos. Selections from the writings of Julián Marías*. Edited by Edward R. Mulvihill and Roberto G. Sánchez. New York: Oxford University Press, 1971: 1–8.

Mulvihill, Edward R., and Roberto G. Sánchez, eds. *Modos de vivir. Un observador español en los Estados Unidos. Selections from the writings of Julián Marías*. New York: Oxford University Press, 1971.

Websites

Asociación Empresarial del Comercio Textil y Complementos: ACOTEX: http://www.acotex.org/

"Spanish Weddings" in *Don Quijote Spanish Language Learning*. http://www.donquijote.org/culture/spain/society/customs/spanish-weddings.asp

Urquhart, Conal. "Graduates Who Come to the UK Will Do Anything to Pay the Rent." *The Guardian*, June 3, 2012. http://www.theguardian.com/world/2012/jun/03/spanish-graduates-come-to-uk

CHAPTER 11

LITERATURE AND DRAMA

OVERVIEW

The beginning of Spanish literature dates back to the 9th–12th centuries, when Spain was a multilingual country of Muslims, Jews, and Christians. During the medieval period, literature was a privilege accessible primarily to scholars who were able to read and write. Some cultivated Muslims and Jews started writing erudite poems called *muwashaha*, in which at the end they added popular songs in romance language called *jarchas*. The jarchas were brief compositions usually written by a male writer who often employed a female character as the main protagonist of a love story. The tradition of the jarchas would develop into the birth of medieval literature. The discovery of the jarchas reveals at least one significant aspect about Spanish literature: the fact that, like any other art, the jarchas highlighted the reality of people living in Spain—a country that was seen as the locus or particular setting in which multiple cultures coexisted.

During the Renaissance period, the most important Spanish writers probed deeply into religion, like Santa Teresa de Jesús (1515–1582), Fray Luis de León (1528–1591), and San Juan de la Cruz (1542–1591). They attempted to connect with God through their mystical poetry.

The Baroque period (1600–1750) is known in Spanish as the Golden Age due to the fact that a significant number of writers and painters would create what is considered the most important Spanish art of all time.

The 18th century, known as the Enlightenment or the Age of Reason, would generate modern writers who attempted to bring education to the populace. This was the case of Benito Jerónimo Feijoo (1676–1764), José Cadalso (1741–1782), and Gaspar Melchor de Jovellanos (1744–1811).

Spain's 19th-century literature was partly romantic with poets such as José de Espronceda (1808–1842), who sadly died at the age of 34, leaving behind an important legacy. Also, the playwright José Zorrilla (1817–1893) renewed the Spanish drama with *Don Juan Tenorio* (1844)—a new version of Tirso de Molina's (1579–1648) *El burlador de Sevilla* (1616, *The Seducer of Seville*).

Spanish literature of the 20th century can be divided into three major groups, each of which was affected by the Spanish Civil War and its consequences. The first literary group was the "Generation of '27," comprised of poets such as Pedro Salinas (1892–1951), who died in Boston (U.S.); Luis Cernuda (1902–1963), who died in Mexico City; and Federico García Lorca (1898–1936), who did not escape the dictatorship like many of his peers and was assassinated by Franco's regime. A second important literary movement was the Spanish Civil War novel (1940–1970), which produced a type of realistic novel characterized by the *tremendismo* (recreates a sordid world where the reader is tremendously impacted) created by Camilo José Cela in the 1940s. The third major literary movement coincided with the universal generation of writers known as "Generation X," a term coined by the Canadian writer Douglas Coupland (1961–)'s *Generation X: Tales from an Accelerated Culture* (1991). Gen X is the generation born after the Western Post–World War II baby boom, of which Spain had their own distinctive writers such as Gabriela Bustelo (1962–), Lucía Etxebarría (1966–), Ray Loriga (1967–), and Ángel Mañas (1971–). The boom of the subsequent writers who appeared in the 1990s has been, however, rejected by some critics for being, as Christine Henseler points out in her book *Spanish Fiction in the Digital Age: Generation X Remixed*, "trendy, unrefined, and selling out to commercial culture" (Henseler 2011).

The division between different groups of Spaniards can also be noticed in literature. On one hand, some Spanish authors are considered to be fairly commercialized and influenced by the English-speaking world (i.e., Agustín Fernández Mallo). Other Spanish authors, however, create a more committed literature that deals with social realism and does not make concessions to the capitalist world (i.e., Belén Gopegui). And in between there is a vast plethora of writers who practice different types of literature. For instance, Najat El Hachmi (1979–) is a recent example of a transnational writer in Spain whose literature deals with immigration and has already been translated into multiple languages including English. Her case is diametrically opposed to Luis Goytisolo (1935–), who has received prestigious Spanish literary awards, including the National Literary Award in 2013, but is hardly known outside Spain.

Like many other countries in the Western world, it is more common for Spaniards to buy books in the superstores and over the internet than in a bookstore. The list of Spanish writers of the 20th and 21st centuries is extensive. In fact, with the abundance of high quality writers, one could conclude that Spanish literature is already experiencing another Golden period. Spain is the fourth leading editorial powerhouse in the world after the United States, Great Britain, and Germany. Currently less than 24 authors from

---

TREMENDISMO

Tremendismo refers to a type of writing initiated by Cela with his first novel, *The Family of Pascual Duarte* (1942), where he describes the situation of his time during the post-civil war and more specifically known as the "years of hunger." The tremendismo technique essentially consisted of a very objective and brutal but realistic description of the 1940s and even the 1950s in Spain. Cela's writing emphasizes violence, and the ugly and repulsive. Hence the term *tremendismo* from the Spanish word *tremendo* (tremendous). Others refers to this kind of writing as neorealism. Cela's technique is also characterized by employing "gallows humor" and being intentionally distorted, which resembles Valle-Inclán's *esperpentos*.

Spain are translated annually into English; more translations would make them more well-known in the global market. *Hispabooks Publishing* (www.hispabooks.com) is one of the few Spanish independent publishers located in Madrid that translates into English the most current Spanish literature. For some Spanish authors like Laura Freixas (1958–), the universe of a writer is not limited to writing within the borders of a country in her national language, but rather is formed by a whole array of cultural experiences, including reading more foreign than national literature.

Further Reading

Corbalán, Ana, and Ellen C. Mayock, eds. *Toward a Multicultural Configuration of Spain: Local Cities, Global Spaces*. Lanham: Fairleigh Dickinson University Press, 2015.

Labanyi, Jo. *Spanish Literature: A Very Short Introduction*. Oxford: Oxford University Press, 2010.

Martin-Estudillo, Luis, and Nicolás Spadaccini, eds. *New Spain, New Literatures*. Nashville: Vanderbilt University Press, 2010.

21st-Century Literature

Jon Juaristi (Bilbao 1951–) is a prolific poet, novelist, and essayist, as well as a professor of Spanish literature at the Universidad de Alcalá de Henares since 2005. He was the director of the National Library in Spain (1999–2001) and of the Cervantes Institute (2001–2004).

Juaristi's essay on Basque nationalism, *El bucle melancólico* (1997, *The Melancholy Ringlet*) received three important awards (Essay Award by the publisher Espasa in 1997; the National Award in 1998; and the Fastenrath Award given by the Spanish Academia in 2000). *El bucle* is a controversial but riveting essay that disentangles the legends of Basque nationalism. Juaristi, a former member of ETA, committed sacrilege by exposing the construction of Basque nationalism. In doing so, he has lived under a death threat issued by ETA, requiring a police escort to his classes when he taught at the Universidad del País Vasco.

Espaciosa y triste. Ensayos sobre España (2013, *Spacious and Sad: Essays on Spain*) is another eloquent essay about the construction of Spanish identity. Starting from the Cervantes tradition to the Generation of '98, Juaristi illustrates that Spain became a nation before any other village in Europe. For Juaristi, Spain was formed before any other regional culture in the Iberian Peninsula.

Rosa Montero (1951–) is an award-winning journalist (National Award in 1981) and acclaimed writer who is also the recipient of many literary awards such as the Primavera prize in 1997 for her novel *La hija del caníbal* (*The Cannibal's Daughter*) and the Grinzane Cavour Prize 2004 for best foreign book for her essay, autobiography, and/or novel *La loca de la casa* (2003, *The Crazy Woman Inside Me*, or, *The Lunatic of the House*). Since the end of 1976, she has worked exclusively for the daily newspaper *El País* and has published over 26 novels, many short stories, and two autobiographical essays. Although Montero's extensive literary work has been translated into more than

20 languages, most of her novels are not yet available in English. *Instrucciones para salvar el mundo* (2008) can be translated as "Instructions on how to save the world." From the very title Montero signals to the reader the ironic tone of her novel, which deals with major world issues from unorthodox points of view. A widowed taxi driver, a jaded doctor, an African prostitute, and an old scientist star in this urban novel set in a background rife with serial killers and sadomasochistic housewives. *Lágrimas en la lluvia* (2011) has been translated into English as *Tears in the Rain* (2012), and it will be the first introduction for many readers to Montero's hypnotic way of writing.

See also: Chapter 2: Overview. Chapter 3: Overview; ETA. Chapter 6: Overview; Multiculturalism; Nationalism. Chapter 7: Feminism in Spain. Chapter 8: Overview.

Further Reading

Epps, Bradley S., and Luis Fernández Cifuentes, eds. *Spain beyond Spain: Modernity, Literary History, and National Identity*. Lewisburg: Bucknell University Press, 2005.

Knights, Vanessa. *The Search for Identity in the Narrative of Rosa Montero*. Lewiston: The Edwin Mellen Press, 1999.

Mueller, Stephanie Ann. "Conflicting Identities in Spain's Peripheries: Centralist Spanish Nationalism in Contemporary Cultural Production of Catalonia and the Basque Country." Iowa: University of Iowa, 2013. [Thesis].

Smith Balena, Ashlee. *Loss, Death, Procreation, and Writing in the Metafictive Narrative of Rosa Montero*. Chapel Hill: University of North Carolina, 2007.

Award-Winning Writers

José Echegaray y Eizaguirre (1832–1916) was the first Spanish writer to win the Nobel Prize, in 1904, and not without controversy, since that year the Nobel was shared with the French writer Frédéric Mistral. In fact, during the period between 1890 and 1910 there were several disputes between the old and new generation of writers. One such episode occurred when Echegaray received national homage and some Spaniards attempted to boycott his literary achievement. Echegaray's main background was science; specifically, he was a civil engineer, a mathematician, and a statesman, despite the fact that he became the most important playwright of the last quarter of the 19th century. One of his most famous plays is *El gran Galeoto* (1881, *The Great Galeoto—Out of the Wings*), which deals with the toxic consequences that unfounded gossip can have on a middle-aged man's happiness. Paramount Pictures made a silent drama adaptation with the title *The World and His Wife* (1920). The novelist Leopoldo Alas Clarín considered Echegaray the best playwright of Spain's 19th century.

Jacinto Benavente (1866–1954) received the Nobel Prize in 1922. Benavente achieved tremendous success in Spain and managed to renew the theatre during the first quarter of Spain's 20th century. He was very prolific and wrote 172 literary pieces. *Los intereses creados* (1907, *The Bonds of Interest*) remains his most famous comedy. Here he draws upon the heritage of the old Spanish theatre, the play within the play. This work is a cynical reflection on how vanity and egoism are the main engines of human actions.

Juan Ramón Jiménez (1881–1958) received the Nobel Prize in 1956 for his poetry. He travelled often around Spain, France, and the U.S., and exiled to Puerto Rico during the Spanish Civil War. The language building of the University of Puerto Rico was named after him. He also became a professor at the University of Miami. Apart from creating several literary journals and writing many erotic poems, Jiménez's most famous pieces were actually written in lyrical prose, such as "Platero y yo" (1914, "Platero and I"), which is an elegy to a donkey. Here the poet dialogues with his donkey friend about the life and landscape of the Andalusian village Moguer (Huelva), where he was born. *Españoles de tres mundos* (1942, *Spaniards from Three Worlds*) was his last book written in prose. Here he chronicles his memoirs during his stay in Madrid's *Residencia de Estudiantes*.

Vicente Aleixandre (1898–1984) received the Nobel Prize in 1977. Although he studied law, he dedicated his life to literature. His first poems appeared in the journal *Revista de Occidente* in 1926. His poetic style evolved from a pessimistic tone (i.e., *Sombras del paraíso,* 1939–1943, *Shadows of Paradise*) to a more positive voice (i.e., *Historias del corazón,* 1954, *Stories from the Heart*). Although there is no specific message, his poetry emphasizes freedom of expression and, as in Lorca's *Poeta en Nueva York*, he adds dreams and surrealistic elements in order to reflect on the interaction between the human being and the world. In essence, his poetry seeks harmony with the universe.

Camilo José Cela (1916–2002) received the Nobel Prize in 1989. Although he studied medicine and law, Cela never completed a university degree. He came from a middle-class, conservative family who favored Franco's dictatorship. He published his first novel *La familia de Pascual Duarte* (1942, *The Family of Pascual Duarte*) at the age of 26. It became a huge success and since then Cela dedicated his life to literature. In fact, he cultivated most of the literary genres from poetry, travel writing, and journalistic articles to plays and novels. Cela was the creator of the so-called tremendismo novel, despite the fact that he always denied this label. Because it focuses on illnesses, violence, and repulsive characters, creating a sordid world, the reader is tremendously impacted as a result of his writing. His short stories *El gallego y su cuadrilla y otros apuntes carpetovetónicos* (1949, *The Galician and His Group and Other Spanish Notes*) and his well-known novel *La colmena* (1951, *The Hive*) also depict a harsh Spain during the post-civil war.

Ana María Matute (1925–2014) has received the most important literary awards that Spain grants to artists. Her monumental *oeuvre* constitutes perhaps the best example of literature ever written on the causes of the Spanish Civil War. Her writing is characterized by its violence and deprivation. Due to the civil war, Matute lost her childhood and her confidence as a person. This loss became a constant theme in her literature. Matute mainly wrote short stories and novels in which the main characters appear alienated and have to deal with solitude. Despite belonging to the literature of protest, Matute managed to escape the censorship of the time thanks to the lyrical tone of her writing. Her first short story, "el chico de al lado" ("The Boy Next Door"), was published in 1942 and her first novel *Los Abel* (1948) was a finalist for the Nadal award. *Los hijos muertos* (1958, *The Dead Children*), *Fiesta del noroeste* (1959, *Party from the North East*), and *Primera memoria* (1960, *First Memory*) are three novels that strongly criticize Franco's regime and his attempt to generate a stable and idealized image of Spain.

See also: Chapter 2: Overview; Franco, Francisco. Chapter 3: Overview. Chapter 8: Overview. Chapter 9: Overview.

Further Reading

Boruszko, Gabriela Susana. *A Literary Map of Spain in the 21st Century*. New York: Peter Lang, 2013.

Luebering, J. E. *The Literature of Spain and Latin America*. New York: Britannica, 2011.

Best-Selling Writers

Vicente Blasco Ibáñez (1867–1928) was a writer, politician, and journalist. His novels, written with distinct social tones, follow the naturalist style. He was a prolific author with a republican (left wing) ideology. He settled in Madrid and suffered two brief periods of exile, during which he came into contact with the French naturalist movement. In 1894 he founded the newspaper *El Pueblo*, which would become his political platform. He was elected six times as a member of the Spanish parliament.

The publication of *Los cuatro jinetes del Apocalipsis* (1916, trans. into English 1918: *The Four Horsemen of the Apocalypse*) brought him international renown. In 1921, with the arrival of Primo de Rivera's dictatorship, he decided to retreat to his house in Nice (France), where he wrote his last novels. *La barraca* (1898, *The Holding*) recreates the world of the Valencian farming communities and the bitter social conflicts that erupted between farm laborers and landowners. His later books were more commercial than those written during his years of political fight. Most of his novels were adapted into Hollywood blockbuster films during the 1920s.

María del Socorro Tellado López (1927–2009) has published 4,000 novels and sold more than 400 million books, becoming the best-selling Spanish author of all time after Miguel de Cervantes. When she was little, Tellado López was known as Socorrín, which she adapted to her nickname Corín. She published her first novel, *Atrevida apuesta* (1946, *Daring Gamble*) when she was 19 to earn money due to the financial problems of her family after the death of her father. In 1951 she signed a contract with *Vanidades*, a popular magazine in Latin America. Her two short novels published monthly for this journal instantly increased sales from 16,000 to 68,000 copies. *Corín Ilustrada* (1966, *Corín Illustrated*) is a collection of photo novels whose first edition, *Eres una aventurera* (*You Are an Adventurer*), sold 750,000 copies in one week. Her novels *Tengo que abandonarte* (1969, *I Have to Leave You*) and *Mi boda contigo* (1984, *My Wedding with You*) were her first adaptations to the cinema screen in 1970 and 1984, respectively. Many of her works were adapted to cinema, television, and also aired on popular radio shows like *Lorena* in 1977. Tellado considered *Lucha oculta* (1991, *Hidden Fight*) to be her best novel.

José Mallorquí Figuerola (1913–1972) was the best selling writer of Spain's 20th century. Although relatively unknown among Spanish academia, Mallorquí was the pioneer of Spanish pulp fiction. He started as a translator of Agatha Christie and Earl Derr Biggers' works for Molino Publisher. Mallorquí also created a series of novels inspired by the Wild West, including *Tres Hombres Buenos, Jíbaro,* and *Miss Moniker.* He brought to Spain the American pulp magazine *Weird Tales* and was a pioneer on radio shows with series such as *Los Bustamante, Dos Hombres Buenos,* and *El Coyote.* The latter derived from his short novel *El Coyote* (1943) written under the pseudonym Carter Mulford. The figure of El Coyote would become the main character of more than 190 novels and comics, and several movie adaptations. Mallorquí was a great aficionado of North American history as well as the role of Spain in the conquest of America. Like many great storytellers of his caliber, Mallorquí put emphasis on the adventure, making his writing educational while also entertaining.

Arturo Pérez-Reverte (1951–) became a novelist after 21 years as a war correspondent for national Spanish television *RTVE. El húsar* (1986, *The Hungarian Soldier*) was his first novel set during the Napoleonic Wars. However, his fame started with his *Alatriste* series of novels of which his daughter Carlota co-authored the first book, *El capitán Alatriste* (1996, *Captain Alatriste*). This series was created when her father realized that Carlota was not taught Spanish history properly. The director Agustín Díaz Yañez adapted it to the screen and *Alatriste* (2006) became the second most expensive Spanish language film ever made in Spain (about €24 million or $30 million). Javier Marías, a well-known Spanish writer and one of Reverte's close friends, coined the term *totalización del gusto* to refer to Reverte's literature as a captivating product that is able to appeal to both intellectuals and mass consumers. Most of Reverte's novels have been adapted into blockbuster films.

Julia Navarro (1953–) has already spent over 30 years as a journalist specializing in political affairs. She regularly publishes a column in the online magazine *Escaño Cero,* where she highlights the current political situation of Spain. Aside from writing several essays on Spanish politics, her first novel was *La Hermandad de la Sábana Santa* (2004, *The Brotherhood of the Shroud of Turin*). Since then, her career as a novelist has been very successful. *Dime quien soy* (2010, *Tell Me Who I Am*) was another popular novel where Navarro depicts the history of the 20th century, incorporating several aspects such as history, love, intrigue, betrayal, and espionage. Navarro's novels have been translated into multiple languages and sold in 30 countries. Her latest best seller is *Dispara, yo ya estoy muerto* (2013, *Shoot, I Am Already Dead*) in which Navarro tells the story of two families, one Jewish and the other Palestinian.

Ildefonso Falcones de Sierra (1958–) works as both a lawyer and a writer and became famous with his first historical thriller *La catedral del mar* (2006, *Cathedral of the Sea*). This historic novel is set in 14th-century Barcelona, when the Catalonian empire was at its greatest. It was published in 40 countries and won many literary awards such as the Fundación José Manuel Lara literary prize for the top-selling novel of 2006, the prestigious Italian Giovanni Boccaccio award 2007 for best foreign author, and the

French Fulbert de Chartres 2009 award. Falcones's second novel, *La mano de Fátima* (2009, *The Hand of Fatima*) received the Roma award in 2010 and sold over 50,000 copies the very first day of its release. More than seven million copies of his novels have been sold.

Matilde Asensi (1962–) is a journalist and contemporary writer specializing in historical novels. From her first publication, *El Salón de Ámbar* (1999, *The Amber Room*), her success was instant and she has become known as the "queen of adventure novels." The quality of her novels resides in the amount of documentation provided as well as in her particular technique of generating suspense. Her books meticulously recreate a given time in history. In 2007 she was honored twice by the International Latino Book Awards for the best mystery novel (*El último Catón*, 2001, *The Last Cato: A Novel*) and for the best fiction novel written in Spanish (*Todo bajo el Cielo*, 2006, *Everything under the Sky: A Novel*). Her most recent success is the trilogy of *Martín Ojo de Plata* (2011, *Martin's Silver Eye*) which has already sold over a million copies. It centers on the Spanish Golden Age. Asensi is considered the best female writer of her generation. Her novels have been translated into 15 languages and have sold over 20 million copies.

Carlos Ruiz Zafón (1964–) is a recent famous writer, who has become one of the most recognized authors outside Spain. His first novel, *The Prince of Mist* (1993) met with huge success abroad. It was followed by *The Midnight Palace* (1994) and *September Lights* (1995) as a trilogy, and *Marina* (1999). Zafón's writing is heavily influenced by the classics, English mysteries, and American noir authors such as Dashiell Hammett and Raymond Chandler. The *Shadow of the Wind* (2001) sold over 15 million copies worldwide, becoming an instant literary phenomenon. Other novels include *The Angel's Game* (2008) and *The Prisoner of Heaven* (2011). His style is very appealing, successfully combining fictional narratives and historical settings. Zafón has already received multiple awards nationally and internationally since his novels have been translated into over 50 languages.

Jordi Galcerán (1964–) is a playwright, script writer, and translator, who writes in Catalan. His fame started with his play *El mètode Gröholm* (2003, *The Gröholm Method*), which has been performed in 60 countries and continues to be successful. It was adapted into a 2005 thriller film (*El método*, *The Method*). Galcerán's other plays have also been adapted into popular Spanish psychological thrillers like *Palabras encadenadas* (2003, *Killing Words*) or the Spanish/U.K. horror film *Frágiles* (2005, *Fragile*). His play *Dakota* (1995) received the Ignasi Iglesias award. One of his most recent plays is *El credit* (2013), which became an instant success in Barcelona and Madrid. Galcerán also adapted the movie *Conversaciones con mamá* (2004, *Conversations with Mother*, by Santiago Carlos Oves) into a play which was performed with great success in 2013.

Dolores Redondo (1969–) studied law and gastronomy, and owned a restaurant before she began to write children's stories. In 2009 she published her first novel, *The Privileges of the Angel* (Eunate Editorial), and in January 2013 she published *The Invisible Guardian*, the first volume of the *Baztán Trilogy*. The latter was published simultaneously in Spain's four official languages (*valenciano*, Catalan, Basque, and Galician), as well as being translated into other languages and published in 22 countries. Redondo's

Baztán Trilogy has been bought by NadCon Films, a joint venture of Peter Nadermann, the German producer who acquired the film rights for Stieg Larsson's *Millenium* (2005–2007). Redondo's main character, inspector Amaia Salazar, belongs to a matriarchal family. Her novels depict strong women who display good but also sinister sides.

Javier Sierra (1971–) is a journalist, essayist, and best-selling novelist who became famous with his fourth novel, *La cena secreta* (2004, *The Secret Supper*), which made the top 10 on *The New York Times* Best Seller list of 2006. Like most writers of his generation, Sierra writes thrillers based on historical facts. He is well known in Spain thanks to his frequent participation as a guest speaker on radio and television programs in which he talks about mysteries in history and science. Sierra is also the host of the weekly TV program *The Other Side of Reality* for *Telemadrid*, the television channel for the region of Madrid. His novels have been translated into 25 languages.

Juan Gómez-Jurado (1977–) is another award-winning writer who is also a journalist. In fact, he still works as a columnist for the Spanish national newspapers *ABC* and *La Voz de Galicia* as well as participating in television and radio programs in Spain. While some critics define him as "an impossibly young master of the thriller," his way of writing has been described as "energetic and cinematographic." In 2010, he celebrated the three-million-reader mark worldwide. His first novel, *Espía de Dios* (2006, *God's Spy*), became an immediate success in Spain. It also sold over 1.5 million copies worldwide. Located in the Vatican, immediately after the death of Pope John Paul II, there is a hunt for a serial killer who knows the details of a disturbing conspiracy. His second novel, *Contrato de Dios* (2007, *The Moses Expedition*), recently published by Atria Books as *Contract with God*, became an international best seller too. On September 27, 2008, Gómez-Jurado won the prestigious Premio de Novela Ciudad de Torrevieja ($500,000 prize) for his latest novel *El emblema del traidor* (2008, *The Traitor's Emblem*). The storyline takes place after the First World War in Germany. This novel has been translated into 40 languages including English.

See also: Chapter 2: Overview. Chapter 11: Overview.

Further Reading

Arturo Pérez-Reverte. perezreverte.com

Carlos Ruiz Zafón. carlosruizzafon.com

Corín Tellado. corintellado.com

Fundación Centro de Estudios Vicente Blasco Ibáñez. blascoibanez.es

Hispabooks Publishing. Hispabooks.com

Ildefonso Falcones. ildefonsofalcones.com

Javier Sierra. javiersierra.com

José Mallorquí, el Coyote. novelascoyote.com

Juan Gómez-Jurado. juangomezjurado.com

Julia Navarro. julianavarro.es

Matilde Asensi. matildeasensi.net

Costumbrismo

Costumbrismo is a literary and artistic movement that depicts specific Spanish customs (preocupied with minute details) usually from a comical perspective in an attempt to reflect and criticize such traditions. This way of writing was practiced in the late 18th century and more particularly during the 19th century.

Mariano José de Larra (1809–1837) is considered one of the best Spanish journalists of all time and one of the early Costumbrismo writers. During the 19th century, journalism became the main medium to connect with the public and the intelligentsia. His article "Vuelva usted mañana" ("Come Back Tomorrow") became famous. With a heavy dose of irony, Larra compared the commercial dynamism of the French neighbors with the lack of ambition and laziness of the Spaniards. This idleness begins with the very title "Vuelva usted mañana" ("Come Back Tomorrow"), which epitomizes the plot. It tells the story of a Frenchman (Mr. Sans-délai) who attempts to do business with the Spaniards. Despite his efforts, he receives the same old phrase everywhere he goes.

Larra's writing goes beyond satire or a simple description of the society of his time. His literature reflects his political, social, and moral commitment. To read Larra is to understand the psyche of many Spaniards. His narrative unravels the reasons for the national decay and at the same time illustrates to the reader the backwardness of Spain in comparison to the rest of the world. Larra strongly criticizes the indolence of the Spaniards, the false patriotism, the false appearances of the bourgeoisie, and the lack of good manners. In fact, there are very few aspects of the culture that he does not criticize. His criticism and intrinsic pessimism, however, should not be interpreted as disloyalty to Spain. On the contrary, Larra's life as well as the modernity expressed in his writing, exemplifies his twofold love for Spain and France.

See also: Chapter 2: Overview. Chapter 11: Overview. Chapter 12: Overview.

Further Reading

Schurlknight, Donald E. *Power and Dissent: Larra and Democracy in Nineteenth-Century Spain.* Lewisburg: Bucknell University Press, 2009.

Sherman, Alvin F. *Mariano José de Larra: A Directory of Historical Personages.* New York: Peter Lang, 1992.

Generation of '27

Generation of '27 refers to a group of poets who championed "pure poetry" and whose main inspiration was Luis de Góngora (1561–1627). They believed in the universality of the arts.

Federico García Lorca (1898–1936) is the most universally recognized poet and playwright of Spain's 20th century. His literature integrates tradition with modernity. In 1919 he moved to Madrid to study at the university and lived in the Residencia de

Estudiantes, a university residence whose main goal was to train the young generation to become the future leaders who would transform Spain into a modern country. In this particular environment García Lorca met most members of the Generation of '27, a group of poets who championed "pure poetry" and whose main inspiration was Luis de Góngora. Hence, the year 1927 was a reference to the three-hundred-year anniversary of Góngora's death. The Generation of '27 believed in the universality of the arts while introducing innovative language based on local folklore such as the flamenco culture. Like the European avant-gardes, the Generation of '27 expressed a desire for change.

The publication of *Romancero gitano* (1928, *Gypsy Ballads*) catapulted García Lorca to the top of his field and he became one of the most important voices in contemporary Spanish poetry. *Poema del cante jondo* (1931, *Poem of the Deep Song*) and *Llanto por Ignacio Sánchez Mejías* (1935, *Lament for Ignacio Sánchez Mejías*) are considered masterpieces of modern Spanish poetry. Perhaps the most fascinating feature of his poetry is the abundance of images that he associates with Andalusian culture as a starting point; later he transforms these local representations into universal imagery.

A sculpture of Federico García Lorca at the Plaza de Santa Ana in Madrid. Lorca renewed Spanish poetry, becoming Spain's most universal poet of the 20th century. (Sasaperic/Dreamstime.com)

After a trip to New York he wrote *Poeta en Nueva York* in 1930, although it was not published until 1940. In this book of poems García Lorca expresses a more committed voice in the sense that his writing becomes a reflection of reality instead of focusing on "pure poetry." Here the poet is a modern person who feels alienated and has anxieties.

His first play released for the public was *Mariana Pineda* (1927). García Lorca's reputation as a playwright began with his trilogy of rural tragedies: *Bodas de sangre* (1933, *Blood Wedding*), *Yerma* (1934), and *La casa de Bernarda Alba* (1936, *The House of Bernarda Alba*). These three plays are set in rural Andalucía and their main characters are women who are oppressed by the traditional norms imposed by the patriarchal society. Although women dominate throughout the three plays, they end up defeated in the end by the archaic tradition characteristic of the era.

See also: Chapter 2: Overview. Chapter 11: Overview. Chapter 13: Overview; Flamenco.

Further Reading

Bonaddio, Federico, ed. *A Companion to Federico García Lorca.* Woodbridge: Tamesis, 2007.

Delgado, Maria M. *Federico García Lorca.* New York: Routledge, 2008.

Generation of '98

Called *Generación del '98* in reference to the year, 1898, when Spain lost their last three colonies (Cuba, the Philippines, and Puerto Rico), this group of intellectuals attempted to break with the past with the goal of rediscovering and rejuvenating the nation. Consequently, these artists criticized Spain for being an apathetic nation.

Ramón María del Valle-Inclán (1866–1936) was a writer whose work is essential to understanding Spain's 20th-century literature. His work connects symbolism, modernism, and Generation '98. His first publication *Féminas* (1895, *Women*) and his collection of sonatas (*Sonata de otoño* 1902; *Sonata de estío* 1903; *Sonata de primavera* 1904; and *Sonata de invierno* 1905) are good examples of the influence of symbolism and modernism on his writing. Like Rubén Darío, in these sonatas, Valle-Inclán detested the vulgar, the ordinary, and the mundane, showing nostalgia for the life of the aristocracy as opposed to the middle class.

Valle-Inclán's modernist aesthetics would evolve into a new way of writing that he called *esperpentos*. Valle-Inclán defined *esperpento* as a distortion of reality. In 1920 he published two plays that would become instant classics, *Divinas palabras* (1918–1920, *Divine Words*) and *Luces de Bohemia* (*Lights of Boehmia*). *Los cuernos de don Friolera* (1921, *The Horns of Don Friolera*), however, is considered his best example of esperpento, in which the author contemplates the characters from above, looking down upon them as inferior people. The writer assumes the position of God, who acts indifferently toward the miseries of the characters. Hence, the playwright makes a vicious critique against the Spanish society of his time, which coincided with the critical views of the intellectuals of the Generation of '98 group. His invention of the concept of esperpento essentially became a biting satire of Spain which, in the eyes of Valle-Inclán, was synonymous with the grotesque distortion of European society.

Miguel de Unamuno (1864–1936) was a versatile and prolific writer of Spain's 20th century. He cultivated most genres, including the novel, the essay, poetry, and drama. His name is usually attached to the Generation of '98 group. Unamuno was particularly critical of the Spanish society of his time. The bulk of his literary work has traditionally been divided into two periods: before and after his existential religious crisis in 1897. Before that year, Unamuno used to criticize the economic and social backwardness of Spain. In doing so, he favored *europeización*, that is, Spain becoming more like other European countries. In his collection of essays entitled *En torno al casticismo* (1895, *On the Essence of Spain*), he strongly criticized the false idea of *casta* (race) of Spaniards, which subsequently promoted laziness and vulgarity from the low classes associated with the pimp (*chulo*) and the flamenco-gipsy. He also detested the literary figure of *Don Juan*, which generated a popular *donjuanismo*, which still persists in the 21st century: a man who spends his time conquering women and partaking in sexual exploits, while avoiding making a positive contribution to society.

Because Spanish society was in decline, Unamuno proposed to find the real soul of Spain in what he called the *intrahistoria*, referring to the interior landscape of the community. He argued that, instead of promoting the myth of *Don Juan*, Spaniards should look into the authentic legends such as the spirit of Sancho Panza of *Don Quixote*, and the willingness of Saint Teresa in searching for ideals. Unamuno developed a literary model based on individualism featuring two fundamental themes—freedom of spirit and austerity—as the only alternative in order to prosper as a nation.

San Manuel Bueno, mártir (*Saint Manuel the Good, Martyr*) is one of Unamuno's most well-known but provocative novels. The latter presents a strong maternal figure in opposition to a male counterpart, who still needs to find himself. The presence of a woman-mother figure is a constant feature in his writing.

Antonio Machado (1875–1939) was one of the main writers of Generation of '98. The poems of *Campos de Castilla* (*Fields of Castile*), which are considered a masterpiece in modern Spanish poetry, embody the philosophy of Generation of '98. Although it contains the pessimism of this generation, it also encapsulates the beauty and admiration for this region of Spain. In these poems Castilla is depicted as a place where time has stopped and the space is characterized by old cities and arid land. The image of Castilla can be extended as a symbol of Spain.

His first book of poetry, *Soledades* (1902, *Time Alone*) contains two key aspects that characterize his writing: time and landscape. *Soledades* was strongly influenced by French symbolism (Paul Verlaine) and modernism from Latin America (Rubén Darío). Miguel de Unamuno, however, became his primary literary influence. After reading *Soledades*, Unamuno advised Machado to abandon his *arte por el arte*, that is, to shift his art into a cause more committed to social injustices, which he did. Machado abandoned his bohemian life and became a teacher in Soria, a town whose landscape typifies what he describes in *Campos de Castilla*. Like Unamuno, Machado advocated a recovery based on the old virtues, that is, austerity and spirituality, in order for the country to prosper.

See also: Chapter 2: Overview. Chapter 11: Overview. Chapter 5: Overview; Madariaga y Rojo, Salvador de. Chapter 6: Diaspora; Multiculturalism; Nationalism.

Further Reading

Anderman, Gunilla M. *Europe on Stage: Translation and Theatre*. London: Oberon books, 2005.

Edwards, Gwynne. *Dramatists in Perspective: Spanish Theatre in the Twentieth Century*. New York: St. Martin's Press, 1985.

Fernández-Medina, Nicolás. *The Poetics of Otherness in Antonio Machado's 'Proverbios y cantares.'* Cardiff: University of Wales Press, 2011.

Krogh, Kevin. *The Landscape Poetry of Antonio Machado: A Dialogical Study of Campos de Castilla*. Lewiston: The Edwin Mellen Press, 2001.

Olson, Paul Richard. *The Great Chiasmus: Word and the Flesh in the Novels of Unamuno*. West Lafayette: Purdue University Press, 2003.

Round, Nicholas G., ed. *Re-reading Unamuno*. Glasgow: University of Glasgow Press, 1989.

Golden Age of Spanish Literature

Also known as the Baroque period, during this time a significant number of writers and painters would create what is considered the most important Spanish art of all time.

El ingenioso hidalgo Don Quijote de la Mancha (Part 1, 1605; Part 2, 1614) combines the mentality of both centuries, that is, the Renaissance optimism and celebration of life in the 16th century with the pessimism and bitterness of the 17th century. In the time of Miguel de Cervantes (1547–1616) there was no place for a noble knight who wanted to remedy social injustices; hence, the continuous illusions that Don Quixote experiences and the hard disappointment that reality presents to him. A good example is the famous episode of Don Quixote fighting against the windmills that he believes are giants.

Cervantes had firsthand knowledge of the Muslim world since he was captured by pirates of North Africa when he participated in the famous Lepanto battle against the Turks. He also lost his left hand and was in prison for several years as a result. During Cervantes's time, *Don Quijote* was considered a hilarious work. However, the adventures of Don Quixote behaving candidly in the company of his squire Sancho Panza, who represents practicality, have been interpreted as a sign of the human condition, which constantly oscillates between realism and hopeless idealism.

According to the experts, *Don Quixote* represents a key novel in the Western world's shift toward modernity. The novel initially depicts an old society that still clings to medieval values like honor and knighthood. However, the reader gradually observes a more modern society based on Sancho Panza's materialistic self-interests. For many Spaniards, like Miguel de Unamuno, for example, Don Quixote represents a national hero who fights in vain for the values of a nobler past.

Francisco de Quevedo (1580–1645) was very proud of his aristocratic origins and despised people who used money to climb the social ladder. He was a witness to the dismantling of the Spanish empire. He saw Portugal and Holland achieve their independence from Spain at a time when Catalunya and Andalucía also experienced separatist revolts. For Quevedo, the new social and economic system was destroying traditional Spanish values. Hence, he wrote a famous poem entitled "Poderoso caballero es don Dinero" ("A Powerful Lord Is Money"), in which he made a stinging criticism of money— the favorite theme of the Baroque. According to him, money can masquerade as reality and one can buy anything to maintain the appearance of social status. With money, anyone can buy social origin, religion, or even love. Money transforms people into someone else. Even ugliness can be seen as beauty if the ugly person is rich.

Quevedo cultivated different literary genres, such as the novels *La vida del Buscón* (1603, *The Life of Buscón*), *Los sueños* (1627, *The Dreams*), moral essays, and philosophical and historical literature. However, above all, he is well-known for his poetry. *Miré los muros de la patria mía* (*I Looked upon my Native Country's Walls*) deals with many themes such as religion, nationality, culture, and love. Overall, his poetry is a satire on society.

Quevedo also developed the idea of *conceptismo*, a new way of writing poetry, although this style was inherited from medieval times. In essence, conceptismo means to seek to create complex poetry through the exchange of themes that appear explicitly as well as implicitly in the poem. This particular technique was in direct opposition to his counterpart Luis de Góngora's *culteranismo*, whose poetry is characterized by the different registers in the language, introducing Latin words, and the use of hyperbaton.

Félix Lope de Vega y Carpio (1562–1635) was the most popular playwright of the Golden Age. He became a perfect fit for the masses' *cultura del espectáculo de masas* (popular culture). During the 17th century, the lower class and marginalized society was rapidly growing. In order to contain the spreading social disillusionment, one of the main vehicles of the government was to foster popular culture. Theatre, in particular, became extremely popular as an escape from the rather dismal daily reality.

Lope de Vega wrote an essay, *Arte nuevo de hacer comedias en este tiempo* (1609, *New Rules for Writing Plays at This Time*) in which he clearly states that he was not interested in creating "art" but in achieving success. He was extremely prolific and wrote more than 1,000 comedies, which made him an iconic figure. Lope de Vega was not only liked by the populace; he also managed to obtain the protection of the monarchy.

His plays were usually represented in the *corrales de comedias* (old theatres such as the one in Almagro). These venues were interior patios of a house with a rudimentary decor and the seats were divided according to social status and gender. In other words, the physical space was a mirror of the actual society of the time in which the hierarchy could be seen in the theater physically as well as metaphorically through the comedies. This was the case of *Fuenteovejuna*, which has been recently translated again into English by G. J. Racz (2010).

Pedro Calderón de la Barca (1600–1681) was another great playwright of the Golden Age. He became the official playwright for the court of King Philip IV, who was an *aficionado* of the theatre. Needless to say that the plays represented at the court were far more serious, complex, and luxurious than the ones presented in the old theatres (comedies).

The personality and plays of Calderón differ enormously from his peer Lope de Vega. Calderón's plays are more philosophical and intellectual. Later on in his life Calderón became a priest. One of his most famous plays is *La vida es sueño* (*Life Is a Dream*). The plot enacts one of the most important themes of his time: life on earth can be seen as theatre, artifice, or dream. During a period characterized by skepticism, disillusionment, and escape from mundane reality, Calderón concludes in this play that

---

AUTOS SACRAMENTALES

These were short plays presented outdoors (in the main plazas), intentionally written to be intelligible by everyone, in which the Catholic dogma was transmitted allegorically—in particular, the Eucharist. They were usually presented during the day of Corpus Christi (or Holy Thursday). This dramatic genre was very popular during the 16th and 17th centuries, and the playwright Calderón de la Barca was the first to apply it to non-sacramental subjects. During the 18th century the *autos* were accused of being irreverent toward the sacramentals and, subsequently, were banned by royal decree in 1765. Do not confuse *auto sacramental* with *auto-da-fé* (trial of faith). The latter started earlier with the Spanish Inquisition, dating back to 1481 in Sevilla, where the first auto-da-fé took place, when six *conversos* were burnt publicly at the stake. The painters Pedro Berruguete and Francisco Rizi both depicted the *autos-da-fé* (or the act of public penance) held publicly in Spain. Later, Goya's *The Tribunal of the Inquisition* (c. 1816) was largely a personal interpretation.

God is the only reality in which we can trust. He is also the author of a great number of *autos sacramentales* (sacramental acts).

See also: Chapter 2: Overview. Chapter 5: Overview. Chapter 11: Overview. Chapter 12: Overview.

Further Reading

Cascardi, Anthony J., ed. *The Cambridge Companion to Cervantes.* Cambridge: Cambridge University Press, 2002.

Close, A. J. *Miguel de Cervantes: Don Quixote.* Cambridge: Cambridge University Press, 1990.

Davis, Rick. *Calderón de la Barca: Four Great Plays of the Golden Age.* Hanover: Smith & Kraus, 2008.

Honig, Edwin. *Calderón and the Seizures of Honor.* Cambridge: Harvard University Press, 1972.

McKendrick, Melveena. *Playing the King: Lope de Vega and the Limits of Conformity.* London: Tamesis, 2002.

Olivares, Julián. *The Love Poetry of Francisco de Quevedo.* Cambridge: Cambridge University Press, 2009.

Schmidt, Rachel. *Critical Images: The Canonization of Don Quixote through Illustrated Editions of the Eighteenth Century.* Quebec: McGill-Queen's University Press, 1999.

Selig, Karl-Ludwig. *Studies on Cervantes.* Kassel: Reichenberger, 1993.

Walters, D Gareth. *The Cambridge Introduction to Spanish Poetry.* Cambridge: Cambridge University Press, 2002.

Wright, Elizabeth. *Pilgrimage to Patronage: Lope de Vega and the Court of Phillip III, 1598–1621.* Lewisburg: Bucknell University Press, 2001.

Medieval Period

The *Cantar de Mío Cid* (1207) constitutes the first national myth. As a large poem, it tells the epic acts of a hero during the Reconquest of Spain. His name is Rodrigo (Ruy) Díaz de Vivar (1043–1099), but he is known by the nickname given to him by the Arabs, *El Cid* (the Lord / the Chief, in Arabic) *Campeador* (fighter). El Cid was a great warrior and mercenary who indistinguishably served either Christian or Arabic people.

At the end of the 11th century, El Cid conquered the kingdom of Valencia to keep it for himself as his own kingdom. Contrary to the Spanish legend, his conquest did not enlarge the power of the Christian region of Castilla. On the contrary, Valencia remained mainly Muslim. However, the oral tradition and political interests magnified his persona, converting him into a Christian national hero. The first manuscript of the poem dates back to 1207 and it can be found in the National Library of Spain, located in Madrid. The anonymous author depicts El Cid as a perfect Christian, perfect warrior, and perfect noble who fights for his king (Alfonso VI). He was also a perfect husband and a perfect father.

The epic poem is characterized by a plot that contains action, historical references, and realism. Its style was closer to narration than lyrical rhyme due to the number of irregular verses. With these blockbuster ingredients, perhaps it is no surprise that Hollywood made a colossal adaptation directed by Anthony Mann, *El Cid* (1961), with Charlton Heston and Sophia Loren as the main protagonists.

Don Juan Manuel (1282–1348) was a noble and the nephew of Alfonso X, who continued the tradition of his uncle of writing books. His most famous manuscript is

In this 19th-century engraving, El Cid orders the chief magistrate, or *qadi,* of Valencia burned alive along with his supporters. El Cid was an accomplished mercenary who controlled much of Spain. When the capital of his personal principate revolted in 1094, he laid siege to the city and dealt harshly with the rebels. (Ridpath, John Clark, *Ridpath's History of the World,* 1901)

El Conde Lucanor (*Tales of Count Lucanor*), which is a collection of 51 short stories (*exempla*) written at the beginning of the 14th century (1335). His goal was educational as well as moralistic. He was inspired by oriental short stories like *Calila e Dimna* (1251) as well as other classical fables.

Don Juan Manuel represents the ideology of the new aristocracy, who strove to be not merely combatants like the hero of *El Cantar de Mío Cid*, but also intelligent and well educated. *El conde Lucanor* starts with a prologue in which the author states his goal of educating his readers. Juan Manuel presents the dialogue between a noble, el conde Lucanor, and his adviser, Patrocinio. While Count Lucanor asks him for advice on politics and ethical issues, as well as personal matters, Patrocinio narrates a history incorporating an example for each question. Every *exemplum* contains a moral ending that the author indicates was written thanks to the wise communicative interchange between el conde Lucanor and Patrocinio. The full text contains 50 different examples. From a literary point of view, *El conde Lucanor* introduces the novel in Europe, before Bocaccio's *Decamerone* (1353) and Chaucer's *Canterbury Tales* (1387–1400).

Juan Ruiz, known as Arcipreste de Hita (1283–1350) wrote *El libro de buen amor* (1330–1343, *The Book of Good Love*) in verse, and it mainly constitutes a parody of the shifting mentality of the bourgeoisie. The book is full of vitality as well as irony and a sense of humor. It is dedicated to the pleasures of life, since the success of the Reconquest brought peace and prosperity to the cities.

Based on Aristotle, the realist philosopher and poet Juan Ruiz depicts love as a sexual instinct that human beings share with every animal. In his poetry he gives practical and immoral advice to his readers. His use of irony and parody can also be seen in the technique of his writing. He uses the *cuaderna vía*, which is a type of verse mainly associated with the scholarly poetry practiced by the *mester de clerecía*, that is to say, for religious matters and having nothing to do with sexuality. However, Juan Ruiz utilizes poetry (particularly the uses of antithesis and epithet) in a profane theme with a burlesque tone to highlight the use of parody as his main message.

Jorge Manrique (1440–1479) was the ideal Renaissance knight. A noble warrior and an artist at the same time, Manrique wrote poetry that was characterized as scholarly and similar to a ballad. He died very young during the civil war of Castilla, which brought Catholic queen Isabel I to power. His most famous work is *Coplas por la muerte de su padre*—a long poem dedicated to the life and death of his father, Don Rodrigo Manrique who died in 1476.

His *coplas* are written in *pie quebrado,* a combination of verses of eight and four syllables, which creates a fluid and rhythmic pace. His poem has a solemn and melancholic tone, combining Christian reflections about the transience of life with the new Renaissance mentality, which consisted of a mixture between medieval supernaturalism and critical scientific attitude. He also incorporates the theme of death as a character. In doing so, death is seen as less grotesque and more pleasantly personified as the figure of his father. The structure of the poem is divided into three major parts with the topic of death as the main aspect: the first part deals with death in general terms; the second part examines the life and death of different historical characters; and the third part is about the life and death of his father. The style of the coplas is uncomplicated and perhaps the most original attribute is the emphasis given to the immediate political history of the 15th century in an attempt to elevate the heroic acts of the Spaniards to a universal level. Hence, the coplas contain comparisons of Rodrigo with classic historical characters.

See also: Chapter 1: Overview. Chapter 2: Overview. Chapter 5: Overview. Chapter 6: Overview. Chapter 9: Overview. Chapter 11: Overview. Chapter 13: Coplas.

Further Reading

Domínguez, Frank. *Love and Remembrance: The Poetry of Jorge Manrique.* Lexington: University Press of Kentucky, 2015.

Hart, Thomas R. *Allegory and Other Matters in the Libro de buen amor.* London: University of London, 2007.

Hart, Thomas R. *Studies on the Cantar de Mio Cid.* London: University of London, 2006.

Haywood, Louise M. et al., eds. *Companion to the Libro de buen amor.* Rochester: Tamesis, 2004.

Himelblau, Jack J. *Morphology of the Cantar de mio Cid.* Potomac: Scripta Humanistica, 2010.

Keller, John E., and L. Clark Keating. *The Book of Count Lucanor and Patrimonio: A Translation of Don Juan Manuel's El Conde Lucanor.* Lexington: The University Press of Kentucky, 2015.

Marino, Nancy F. *Jorge Manrique's Coplas por la muerte de su padre: A History of the Poem and Its Reception.* Woodbridge: Tamesis, 2011.

York, James. *Count Lucanor: or, The Fifty Pleasant Stories of Patrimonio.* Honolulu: University Press of the Pacific, 2003.

Naturalism

If Espronceda (1808–1842) depicted the women of his time as passive and beautiful objects created to bring happiness to men, Emilia Pardo Bazán (1851–1921) portrayed the women of her time under a very different light in her novel *La Tribuna* (*The Tribune*). This novel reflects the social anxieties among the urban working-class society of Spain's 19th century. In particular, Bazán illustrates the situation of women workers in the tobacco factory in La Coruña. In doing so, Bazán is one of the pioneers of Spain's feminism. *La Tribuna* can be read as a document that shows the growing number of women in the workforce and in politics.

Bazán came from an aristocratic family, which she later criticized in her famous novel *Los pazos de Ulloa* (1886, *The Manors/House of Ulloa*). Due to her popularity, Bazán was one of the very few Spanish women who enjoyed prestige and respect from her male counterparts in the 19th century.

Bazán wrote 19 novels, 21 short novels, and more than 500 short stories. She was also a literary critic and the founder of the literary magazine *Revista Ibérica*, in which she published her first short story "El indulto" (1883, *The Pardon*). Pardo Bazán is mainly known for being one of the pioneer Spanish feminists. She believed that education was the only vehicle for women to excel in society. Bazán was a strong advocate of equality between men and women, especially in education. Despite the considerable influence of Emile Zola's naturalism on Bazán, she did not accept the concept completely since she was Catholic. However, her husband abandoned her when she published *La cuestión palpitante* (1883, *The Burning Question*), an essay in which Bazán explained Zola's theory of naturalism.

See also: Chapter 2: Overview. Chapter 4: Overview. Chapter 6: Overview. Income-Level Groups. Chapter 11: Overview.

Further Reading

Hemingway, Maurice. *Emilia Pardo Bazán: The Making of a Novelist*. Cambridge: Cambridge University Press, 2009.

Tolliver, Joyce. *Cigar Smoke and Violet Water: Gendered Discourse in the Stories of Emilia Pardo Bazán*. Lewisburg: Bucknell University Press, 1998.

Realism

Benito Pérez Galdós (1843–1920) is considered, after Cervantes, Spain's greatest novelist. During a visit to Paris, Galdós met Balzac. The novels of this famous French writer influenced him enormously in his career as a young writer. Galdós was a very prolific writer. He wrote 68 novels, 26 plays, and several short stories, essays, and journal articles.

Galdós chronicled the Spanish society of his time in 46 novels under the title *Episodios Nacionales* (*National Episodes*). Reading these novels is reading the history of Spain's 19th century. They begin with the defeat of the Spaniards in the battle of Trafalgar in 1805. The main characters of the novels participate in the historical events. For Galdós, in order to progress into a modern nation, Spaniards need to know first the history of their century to comprehend the times in which they live. Hence, he brought the genre of literary realism to Spain. In doing so, Galdós developed *novelas de tesis*, that is, novels that deal with social injustices (i.e., *Doña Perfecta*, 1876). He is also well-known for his *Novelas contemporáneas* where he depicts the daily routine of the middle class in Madrid. He thought that the future of the nation was in the bourgeoisie. In writing these novels, Galdós's main goal was to provide the middle class with harmful examples of living such as adultery and the desire to climb the social ladder. For instance, Galdós's *La desheradada* (1881, *The Disinherited*) illustrates the repercussions for those who do not obey the social duties of citizenship.

See also: Chapter 2: Overview. Chapter 3: Overview. Chapter 11: Overview.

Further Reading

Labanyi, Jo. *Galdós*. Hoboken: Taylor & Francis, 2014.

Varey, J. E., and Nicholas Grenville Round, eds. *New Galdós Studies*. Woodbridge: Tamesis, 2003.

Renaissance Literature

The year 1492 is considered the beginning of the Renaissance in Spain. The period is characterized by multiple stylistic features of writing within the same genre. For instance, there were two major schools that developed Renaissance poetry in Spain along different lines: the Salmantine used concise language, realistic themes, and simple ideas, whereas the Sevillian school employed grandiloquent language with long and complex verses and was particularly refined.

La vida de Lazarillo de Tormes (1554, *The Life of Lazarillo de Tormes*) is considered the first example of a picaresque novel: a narration written in the first person by a poor child (an anti-hero), who often has to survive through tricks and lies. The innovative realism of the picaresque novel portrays with critical humor the crisis that Spain experienced in the mid-16th century. If the novel of chivalry and the pastoral novel used to represent an ideal and artificial world, the picaresque novel depicted very crude and realistic scenery in which an anti-hero (*pícaro*), a crafty adolescent, has to fight against a world characterized by cruelty, hunger, misery, hypocrisy, and superfluous ambitions. Despite these negative aspects, the *Lazarillo* is written with a comic tone in which the important message is the satire and criticism of society.

Although ignored, it is believed that the actual author of the *Lazarillo* was a converted Jewish writer. This is due to his strong sarcastic views toward materialism, the ignorance of the clergy, and the suicidal pride of the *hidalgos* (noblemen), who prefer to die of hunger before having a job which they considered a humiliation.

The *Lazarillo* represents the first picaresque novel in Europe. As the protagonist works as a servant for a blind man, a monk, a knight, and an archpriest, the whole spectrum of society is displayed. All of his bosses abuse him physically or with starvation. Through these injustices, the pícaro unravels the fabric of his society, which is characterized by corruption where appearances deceive. The reader observes that the moral and economic corruption constitutes a common feature at every level of society. The novel provides concrete historical contexts of Spain's 16th century, mentioning specific cities like Toledo and Salamanca. The conclusion is full of irony. While the pícaro has managed to find a more stable job and get married to the servant of the archpriest, the rumor (or *malas lenguas*) of the village is that the archpriest is fornicating with the pícaro's wife.

The *Tragicomedia de Calisto y Melibea*, better known as *La Celestina*, was written by Fernando de Rojas in 1499. This is a crucial novel that acts as a bridge between the Renaissance and the Baroque periods. It tells the dramatic story of Calisto who falls in love with Melibea. The different registers of language vary from erudite and sophisticated used by the lovers to the more popular and marginal employed by La Celestina. The latter is an old street-wise procurer that Calisto hires to satisfy his love for Melibea. The diversity of language and the psychological refinement of the characters make *La Celestina* a universal masterpiece. Contrary to the sentimental novels of the time, the lovers of *La Celestina* do not follow the rules of *amor cortés*, that is, courtly love. Their love is essentially of a sexual nature. Also, the protagonists do not deal with the ideal and artificial world of the nobility. *La Celestina*, on the other hand, portrays the urban upper classes as well as the lower classes with assistants, prostitutes, and roughnecks. The final message, if any, is quite pessimistic. Not a single character can be redeemed. No one is loyal to anyone and everybody perpetrates sins such as lust, greed, and revenge. This pessimism, in conjunction with the parody of the Christian beliefs as well as the Inquisition, caused critics to argue that *La Celestina* was written by a converted person, because these people were jaded. His bitterness and skepticism were due to the injustices that the converted people (i.e., *conversos* and *moriscos*) used to experience at the time in Spain.

See also: Chapter 2: Overview. Chapter 3: Overview. Chapter 6: Overview. Chapter 11: Overview.

Further Reading

Cruz, Anne J., ed. *Approaches to Teaching Lazarillo de Tormes and the Picaresque Tradition.* New York: Modern Language Association of America, 2008.

Deyermond, Alan. *Lazarillo de Tormes: A Critical Guide.* 2nd ed. London: Grant & Cutler in association with Tamesis, 1993.

Kallendorf, Hilaire. *A Companion to Early Modern Hispanic Theater.* Leiden: Brill, 2014.

Sánchez, Francisco J. *An Early Bourgeois Literature in Golden Age Spain: Lazarillo de Tormes, Guzmán de Alfarache, and Baltasar Gracián.* Chapel Hill: University of North Carolina Press, 2003.

Severin, Dorothy Sherman. *Tragicomedy and Novelistic Discourse in Celestina.* Cambridge: Cambridge University Press, 2009.

Rexurdimento

Rexurdimento refers to a Galician literary and art movement during the 19th century that coincided with the Catalan *Renaixença*. Both were influenced by romanticism and both paid central attention to regional traditions with particular emphasis on regional languages.

Rosalía de Castro (1837–1885) was one of the first influential writers of the 19th century known for writing in her regional language—Galician. During her time, there were a series of initiatives to centralize power under a single Spanish nation. As a consequence, several regions protested against a unified political system and embraced their unique cultural identity to counter the nationalist movement.

Although Castro wrote novels, her fame is due to her poetry. *La Flor* (1857, *The Flower*) was her first book of poems, which was highly influenced by the romantics. *Cantares Gallegos* (1863, *Galician Songs*) was one of her most important books written in Galician. The local habits and folklore are the two main themes of this collection of poems, which again echoed the ideals of romanticism. In essence, Castro emphasizes the love for her local land and her heritage. *Follas novas* (*New Leaves*) was her last poetry book written in Galician. As Kathleen March observed, "after decades of being relegated to the periphery, Castro has emerged as a nationalist and feminist writer, with a clear vision of her regional conditions, of women's difficulties in being taken seriously as writers, and of her role as an advocate for the language of the people" (March 2011).

See also: Chapter 2: Overview. Chapter 6: Nationalism. Chapter 7: Feminism in Spain. Chapter 9: Overview. Chapter 11: Overview.

Further Reading

Dever, John P., and Aileen Dever. *The Poetry and Prose of Rosalía de Castro: A Bilingual Facing Page Edition*. Lewiston: The Edwin Mellen Press, 2010.

March, Kathleen. "Rosalía de Castro," in *World Literature in Spanish*. Edited by Maureen Ihrie and Salvador A. Oropesa. Santa Barbara: ABC-CLIO, 2011. 161–163.

Stevens, Shelley. *Rosalía de Castro and the Galician Revival*. London: Tamesis, 1986.

Romanticism

Ángel de Saavedra, Duke of Rivas (1791–1865), is the best example of a playwright of the new romantic theatre, which abandoned the 18th-century technique of the French neoclassic school (or Enlightenment). In essence, he combines verse with prose and mixes the tragic with the comic, creating a complexity in dramatization and producing visual effects as well as an intense emotional impression.

Don Álvaro o la fuerza del sino (1835, *Don Álvaro, or, The Force of Fate*) signified a huge triumph for romanticism in Spain. The plot is full of inaccuracies and eccentric elements, which were typical of the epoch. *Don Álvaro* appears to be an improvised play: the scenes are without continuity, giving the impression of a broken rhythm. The action is enthusiastic with a sudden and unexpected ending. The characters are mainly cliché: he is impulsive while she is feminine and sweet. Overall, due to the combination of dynamism, tragic force, lyrical intensity, and the use of color during the representation, *Don Álvaro* is the most romantic Spanish play of all time. Ultimately, *don Álvaro* can be considered as evidence of the author's *españolismo*. If *Don Álvaro* was a mere product of Saavedra's time, however, his *Romances* (1841) reflect a more authentic enthusiasm for the customs of Spain.

Gustavo Adolfo Bécquer (1836–1870) was the most important poet of the 19th century. His father died when he was five years old and he became an orphan at the age of 13. His interest in literature began when he read the romantic literature of Chateaubriand, Byron, Hugo, and Espronceda. Gustavo Adolfo Bécquer wrote his first piece of literature, *Los conjurados*, when he was 10 years old. One year after his death, in 1871, Bécquer's friends compiled his poems and published them under the title of *Rimas*. The experts tend to put his poems in the category of "post-romantic" due to the subjectivity and the feeling of solitude found in them. Bécquer's poetry is highly emotional. The poet expresses his feelings about bygone times, poetry, feminine beauty, and love.

In addition to his poetry, Bécquer also developed the literary genre of *Leyendas*. These are lyrical pieces in which he poetically narrates medieval stories, deliberately incorporating elements of fantasy and romanticism. These legends deal with several themes, the most common being love and the search for utopia.

See also: Chapter 2: Overview. Chapter 11: Overview. Chapter 12: Overview.

Further Reading

Bynum, B. Brant. *The Romantic Imagination in the Works of Gustavo Adolfo Bécquer*. Chapel Hill: University of North Carolina Press, 1993.

Fedorchek, Robert M. *Don Álvaro, or, The Force of Fate (1835): A Play by Ángel de Saavedra, Duke of Rivas*. Washington, D.C.: Catholic University of America Press, 2005.

Sullivan, Henry W. *The Poems of Gustavo Adolfo Bécquer: A Metrical, Linear Translation*. Rock Hill: Spanish Literature Pub, 2002.

Trimble, Robert G. *A Translation of Don Álvaro, o la fuerza del sino*. Lewiston: The Edwin Mellen Press, 2002.

Social Realism

Carmen Martín Gaite (1925–2000) belongs to the generation of the 1950s, also known as the children of the post-civil war, who practiced social realism due to the dictatorship that she experienced. Her compilation of short stories *Balneario* (1955, *The Spa*) won the Café Gijón literary award. It mainly deals with aspects of feminism and key issues the country faced under Franco's regime. Her novel *Entre visillos* (1958, *Behind the Curtains*) received the Nadal award, Spain's oldest literary prize. One of her most famous novels is *El cuarto de atrás* (*The Back Room*), which won the national literary award, making Martín Gaite the first woman to receive the award. Martín Gaite depicts the daily routine of women during the post-civil war. She started a new way of writing called *Memoria Histórica*, which has become very popular in the new Spain's millennial literature. The main character of *El cuarto de atrás*, C., in company with a mysterious conversational partner, remembers several episodes of the childhood of a young girl that have marked the lives of many women of her generation. C's review of the past history is also a reflection on Franco's dictatorship and the vestiges of it that remain.

See also: Chapter 2: Overview; Franco, Francisco. Chapter 3: Overview. Chapter 11: Overview.

Further Reading

O'Leary, Catherine, and Allison Ribeiro de Menezes. *A Companion to Carmen Martín Gaite*. Woodbridge: Tamesis, 2008.

Womack, Marian, and Jennifer Wood, eds. *Beyond the Backroom: New Perspectives on Carmen Martín Gaite*. New York: Peter Lang, 2010.

Spanish Enlightenment Literature

Leandro Fernández de Moratín (1760–1828) is considered a pioneer in the modern comedy of Spain. His plays are a bridge between the 18th and 19th centuries. He was the son of a famous literary figure of the time, Nicolás, who started the process of regenerating the Spanish theatre. His father was heavily influenced by the new French drama. Moratín continued his efforts, while enjoying the favor of the king José Bonaparte. However, with the expulsion of the French and the return of King Fernando VII, Moratín exiled to France.

After the death of Pedro Calderón de la Barca in 1681, Spanish theatre began a period characterized by decadence. Nevertheless, new modern plays from France helped to regenerate the traditional Spanish drama that was stuck in the glorious past of the Golden Age. This friction between tradition and modernity ended initially with a victory for the moderns, when in 1765 Spain forbid the *autos sacramentales*. However, despite the attempts of the new government to revive the drama, the majority of Spaniards still demanded to see representations of the traditional Golden Age theatre. Being fully aware of this context, Moratín managed to succeed with two plays. *La comedia nueva, o el café* (1792, *The New Comedy*) was actually an ironic critique of the contemporary plays. It was well received in spite of the opposition of the popular playwrights. Another huge success was his drama *El sí de las niñas* (1806, *The Maiden's Consent*, or, *A Daughter's Consent*), in which Moratín advocates educating the female youth. This play criticizes the exploitation of some parents with respect to the marriage of their daughters. Moratín's major literary contribution was not a critique of the masterpieces of the Golden Age period, but a satire of the heroic comedy written by most of his peers. For him, the new theatre and art in general should be educational and a reflection of contemporary society based on ordinary lives.

See also: Chapter 2: Overview. Chapter 6: Overview. Chapter 11: Overview; Golden Age of Spanish Literature.

Further Reading

Komocki, Kirt Edward. "The Representation of Domestic Servants in Eighteenth-Century Spanish Theatre." Columbus: Ohio State University, 2011. [Thesis].

Mackenzie, Ann L., and Jeremy Robbins. *Hesitancy and Experimentation in Enlightenment Spain and Latin America*. Hoboken: Taylor & Francis, 2013.

REFERENCES

Aldaz, Anna-Marie, Barbara N. Gantt, and Anne C Bromley. *Poems by Rosalía de Castro*. Albany: State University of New York Press, 1991.

Applebaum, Stanley. *Rhymes and Legends by Gustavo Adolfo Bécquer*. Mineola, NY: Dover Publications, 2006.

Cervantes Saavedra, Miguel de. *The History and Adventures of the Renowned Don Quixote de la Mancha*. New York: Modern Library, 2001.

Coupland, Douglas. *Generation X: Tales for an Accelerated Culture*. New York: St. Martin's Press, 1991.

Delage, Fernando. "El bucle melancólico. Historias de nacionalistas vascos." *Foreign Policy* 113 (Winter, 1998–1999): 104–107.

Fernández de Moratín, Leandro. *La comedia nueva*. Madrid: Castalia. 1970.

García Lorca, Federico. *The House of Bernarda Alba / La casa de Bernarda Alba*. London: Methuen Drama, 2009.

Henseler, Christine. *Spanish Fiction in the Digital Age: Generation X Remixed*. New York: Palgrave, 2011.

Juan Manuel. *El conde Lucanor*. Madrid: Cátedra, 2012.

Juaristi, Jon. *El bucle melancólico. Historias de nacionalistas vascos*. Madrid: Espasa Calpe, 1997.

Larra, Mariano José de. *Vuelva usted mañana y otros artículos*. Madrid: El País, 2005.

Lewis-Smith, Paul, ed. *Calderón de la Barca: La vida es sueño*. London: Grant & Cutler, 1998.

Machado, Antonio. *Campos de Castilla / The Landscape of Castile*. Translated by Mary G. Berg. Dennis Maloney. Buffalo, N.Y.: White Pine Press, 2005.

March, Kathleen. "Rosalía de Castro." In: Maureen Ihrie and Salvador A. Oropesa, eds. *World Literature in Spanish*. Santa Barbara: ABC–CLIO, 2011. 161–163.

Marino, Nancy F. *Jorge Manrique's Coplas por la muerte de su padre. A History of the Poem and its Reception*. New York: Tamesis, 2011.

Martín Gaite, Carmen. *The Back Room*. San Francisco: City Lights Books, 2000.

Montero, Rosa. *Instrucciones para salvar el mundo*. Madrid: Santillana ediciones, 2009.

Pardo Bazán, Emilia. *La Tribuna*. Edited by Benito Varela Jácome. Madrid: Cátedra, 2009.

Pérez Galdós, Benito. *Episodios Nacionales*. Edited by Francisco Caudet. Madrid: Cátedra, 2007.

Racz, G. J. *Fuenteovejuna*. New Haven: Yale University Press, 2010.

Rojas, Fernando de. *La Celestina: Tragicomedia de Calixto y Melibea*. Edited by Dorothy Sherman Severin. Madrid: Alianza Editorial, 2013.

Rowland, David, and Keith Whitlock. *The Life of Lazarillo de Tormes*. Warminster: Aris & Phillips, 2000.

Ruiz, Juan. *El libro del buen amor*. Barcelona: Linkgua, 2004.

Smith, Colin. *Poema de mío Cid*. Madrid: Cátedra, 2011.

Trimble, Robert G. *A Translation of Don Álvaro, o la fuerza del sino*. Lewiston: Edwin Mellen Press, 2002.

Unamuno, Miguel de. *Miguel de Unamuno. San Manuel Bueno, mártir*. Edited by John Butt. London: Grant & Cutler, 1981.

Valle-Inclán, Ramón del. *Luces de Bohemia*. Warminster: Aris & Phillips, 1993.

Walters, Gareth. "Five Modes of Translation: About Quevedo's 'Miré los muros de la patria mía.'" *Bulletin of Hispanic Studies* 75 no.1 (1998): 55–67.

CHAPTER 12

ART AND ARCHITECTURE

OVERVIEW

Spain is one of the most visited countries in the world, and part of its natural beauty is due to the vast number of monuments that glorify its long history. Spanish art derives from the old civilizations that have influenced Spain's history since ancient times. The first examples of Iberian art can be found in caves such as Altamira (Santillana del Mar) and in rock shelters, such as Albarracín (Teruel). Later examples of Spanish art are the Neolithic pottery and astounding megalithic constructions (huge stone monuments) such as the dolmens (stone tombs) of La Menga and El Romeral in Antequera (Málaga), and funeral chambers. It is unknown how these were built. Apart from the dolmens of Antequera (circa 2500 BCE), Spain's oldest constructions are the megaliths of the Balearic Islands. Megalithic constructions indicate the dawn of civilization in Spain. The Balearic island of Menorca contains examples of *talayots* (defensive towers), *taulas* (a kind of altar), and *navetas* (funeral chambers) such as *Es Tudons*, making the entire island an open air museum of prehistoric architecture.

Spanish art was influenced by people who came by sea—in particular, by the Phoenicians, Greeks, Carthaginians, and Moors. For example, the *Dama de Elche* and the *Dama de Baza* (both believed to have been created between the fourth and sixth centuries BCE) are two distinctive examples of beautiful and ancient types of sculptures from Spain. Both are busts representing priestesses or goddesses.

All the previous civilizations including Phoenician merchants, Greek colonists, and Carthaginians left an artistic heritage on the Iberian Peninsula. In the north, the

---

LADY OF ELCHE

Dama de Elche or Lady of Elche is for most Spaniards one of the most iconic symbols of timeless Iberia, dating from 500 BCE through 150 CE. However, for the American art historian John Moffitt, who wrote extensively on Hispanic art, the Lady of Elche constitutes an art forgery made around 1896–1897. To demonstrate his theory, he wrote a book entitled *Art Forgery: The Case of Lady of Elche* published by the University Press of Florida in 1995. Since then, art historians from Spain have ignored him despite the fact that he was probably right, because Spaniards have not yet proven him wrong.

influence of the first great European civilization, the Celts, can be seen in the fortresses and settlements of Galicia's *castros* (fortified villages). The Celtic culture also left stone reliefs and exquisitely fashioned jewelry, which are on display in the Museum of Pontevedra, near where they were discovered. In the central regions of Spain, early artists created sculptures of totemic animals, including the Bulls of Guisando (Ávila). In the south of Spain, figures of deities and priestesses show the influence of peoples who arrived by sea.

The church of San Juan de Baños, located in the town of Baños de Cerrato in Palencia, is considered the oldest church in Spain, having been built in the seventh century. The Roman legacy is still visible in many places of Spain. For instance, the aqueduct of Segovia and the amphitheater of Mérida are the two most impressive Roman legacies usually visited among the ruins of Itálica in Santiponce, Sevilla. Also museums such as the Museum of Roman Art in Mérida and the National Archaeological Museum of Tarragona are Spain's Roman legacy.

The Moors developed their own style, and in doing so, they influenced the Christians with whom they shared the peninsula. As a consequence, two separate styles were developed by the *Mozarabs* (Christians who lived under Muslim rule) and later the *Mudejars* (Moors who remained in territory conquered by Christians). Spain's Jewish community was also influenced by Islamic art, creating a distinctive Sephardic style. The Moors' greatest period of cultural splendor is the so-called Córdoba period. Al-Andalus, also known as the Islamic Iberia, referred to the land occupied by the Muslims in Spain, which at one time covered most of the peninsula. Examples of art of the Córdoba period are the *Giralda* of Sevilla, the *Aljafería* of Zaragoza, and the Córdoba mosque, which was built on the site of an old Visigothic basilica. The Alhambra Palace in Granada with its intricately patterned interior, flowing fountains, and adjoining Generalife gardens is the crowning achievement of Nasrid art, which corresponds to the last years of Moorish rule in Spain.

The Jewish community also played an important role in Spanish history, especially serving as an important safeguard between Muslim–Christian rivalry. Rather than develop a separate art, Spanish Jews adapted Moorish—and Mudejar—forms of art. Evidence of their presence is also scattered all over Spain. Known as the "routes of Sepharad," there are many places with a strong Jewish influence such as the city of Ávila, which is considered the Jerusalem of Castilla. The architecture of Toledo is also distinctive with its very narrow streets. It used to be the great center of Jewry for the West that, for centuries, was a reference for all the Jews of Europe.

Spain preserves many medieval *juderías* or *calls*—Jewish quarters—some as evocative as the *judería* in Córdoba (birthplace of Maimonides), the call in Girona, and the Besalú call with its ritual baths, which are three of Europe's oldest and most beautiful synagogues. Remains of other synagogues are spread out in several Spanish towns such as Tudela, Agreda, and Segovia.

During the Medieval Age (8th to 15th centuries), Christian kings were engaged in war with the Moorish rulers. As a result of that long period of time and fighting, Spanish paintings were dispersed in different kingdoms and lack the refinement of their neighboring countries such as France or Italy. The first painter labelled as "painter of the king" (*pintor del rey*) was Rodrigo Esteban, who was employed by King Sancho IV of Castilla (1258–1295). Another early Spanish painter was Juan Cesilles, who in 1382 signed a contract for 320 florins of Aragón to paint the altar for the church of San Pedro in Reus (Catalunya). These two cases exemplify the fact that the arts in Spain during that time were in the hands of the monarchy or at the mercy of religious institutions.

Catholic churches, basilicas, and cathedrals are without a doubt the most distinctive architectonic feature that characterizes the scenery of Spain. In fact, every town on the Iberian Peninsula has at least one church, which is usually located in the main square or *plaza de España*, as Spaniards call it. The *plaza* is another typical mark of Spanish architecture. Nowadays the term *plaza* can be found in most western societies. For Spaniards, a plaza is a gathering place where they usually go for a stroll to socialize, have a drink, or to attend mass. Interestingly enough, if we pay attention to the layout of a main square in Spain, we see that there is often a church on one side and a town hall in front of it. This particular distribution of power between religion and government sharing the same geographical space is a distinctive architectural feature of the landscape in Spain. No wonder, then, that this physical connection between religion and politics in the plaza becomes inseparable in the minds, perhaps unconsciously, of many Spaniards.

Other forms of Christian art include illustrations for manuscripts in the early ages such as the *Comes* manuscript, which can be found in the Academy of History in Madrid. This manuscript was created in 744 (eighth century) by the abbot in the monastery of San Emiliano. There are several manuscripts that contain illustrations and most of them are held in the National Library of Spain in Madrid. Furthermore, cathedrals such as the one in Toledo or Sevilla also hold manuscripts and paintings that date back to the 12th and 13th centuries. The main conclusion that can be drawn from these early art forms, however, is that all of them were strongly influenced by foreign artists from Italy, Holland, France, and Germany. In other words, the history of Spanish painting, like the country itself, is a mix of cultures.

Sculpture assumed a decorative and didactic function during the 12th century, mainly due to illiteracy. Hence, the figures on the facade of the Ripoll monastery constituted an illustrated Bible for the people with little understanding of the world around them. Another old Spanish sculpture is "El Doncel" of Sigüenza (Guadalajara), which is considered a jewel of funerary sculpture because of its quality. It represents a young noble of the Order of Santiago who died fighting against the Muslims. The sculptor is not known, although it is associated with Sebastián de Almonacid (1460–1526). Cathedrals, especially with their frescoes, also fulfilled an educational purpose.

In the 14th century and, even more so, since the 15th century, due to Spain's colonization of the Americas, Spain flourished as a great civilization. Initially Spanish artists travelled abroad to gain additional knowledge, and their paintings were more or less a continuation of the Italian and Flemish style. During the Renaissance, however, more foreign artists came to Spain on salary, such as to the court of Juan I and Juan II who brought various artists from Italy. In fact, the first names of painters registered in the history of art in Castilla were Italian names. This mixture of multicultural influences can be seen as an essential step that enabled Spanish painting to flourish and, subsequently, to acquire the authentic and distinctive style that distinguished it through the following centuries. The cathedrals and universities built during this period all over Spain contain many examples of the development of this distinctive style of painting.

The history of Spanish painting is complex and cannot be understood in a vacuum without the influence of other countries. As art historian Janis Tomlinson points out, "the story of painting in Spain cannot be reduced to the history of Spanish painting, since some of the painting, and many critical influences, were the work of artists with no claim to the title of 'Spanish'" (Tomlinson, 1997). This is the case, for instance, of the foreign painter El Greco (the Greek), who exemplifies the fact that the Spanish monarchs always searched for the best artists regardless of their nationality. The Flemish Antonis Mor and the Italian Sophonisba Anguissola are also two cases in point. As Tomlinson notes, "the traditions of portraiture established by Mor and Sánchez Coello, like the Italian traditions imported to the Escorial, remain crucial influences in the development of painting in Spain during the later sixteenth and seventeenth centuries" (Tomlinson, 1997).

Since the Spanish Renaissance—represented by El Greco in the 16th/early 17th century until the 18th century with Goya as the first modern painter—most artists had to choose between the Court or the Church as their main patron, which could provide stability for their careers. The Golden Age of Spanish art includes such artists as Zurbarán and Velázquez, both of whom at one time benefited from the patronage of King Philip IV, in addition to Ribera and Murillo.

The 18th century began with the Spanish throne in the hands of the French house of Bourbon followed by the War of Spanish Succession, which would last until 1913. While the rest of Europe was embracing an Age of Enlightenment, Spain was experiencing political instability, decreasing military power, and a decline in the arts. Although two schools—*La Escuela Nacional* (for architects) and *La Real Academia de Bellas Artes de San Fernando*—were founded, artistic control reigned over the land and royal oversight prevented much artistic experimentation. As in the 14th and 15th centuries, again, foreign artists were brought to Spain—this time under the rule of the Bourbon court. Spanish artists such as Francisco de Goya were forced to cater to the demands of the Court or look elsewhere for patronage.

The function of 19th century academic painting in Spain was mainly to teach and its subject matter was predominately historical with attention to realism and accuracy. The 20th century is marked with European influences as seen in the impressionistic paintings of Joaquín Sorolla y Bastida, whose bright and airy works were a welcomed reprieve from the deathbed and battle scenes of the previous century and were embraced by Spain's growing middle class. However, this is contrasted by Ignacio Zuloaga, whose art is reflective of the ideals of the Generation of '98, defining the nature of Spanishness. This philosophic mindset would be studied by rising art stars such as Pablo Picasso, Juan Gris, Salvador Dalí, and Joan Miró.

The *Gauche Divine* refers to a group of Catalan intellectuals from the bourgeoisie, who secretly (hence the sarcastic nickname of "divine") managed to bring from overseas other cultures to Spain during the 1960s, that is, during the Spanish dictatorship. It was a cultural movement that can be considered one of the first multicultural milestones that occurred in 20th-century Spain. Their main premise was to look abroad in a purposeful transgression of the social norms imposed by Franco. It was formed by architects such as Ricardo Bofill and Óscar Tusquets, photographers such as Colita and Xavier Miserachs, singers, filmmakers, editors, poets, writers, and models.

On June 15, 1977, the majority of Spaniards were extremely happy to vote for the first time after 40 years of dictatorship. *La movida madrileña* represented a boom in the cultural scene of Spain. It was an influential movement whose main protagonists came from all cultural sectors. Here we have cinema directors (Pedro Almodóvar, Fernando Trueba), singers (Alaska, Nacha Pop), fashion designers (Ágatha Ruiz de la Prada, Manuel Piña), painters (Ceesepe, Costus), photographers (Ouka Leele, Alberto García-Alix), writers (Umbral, Luis Antonio de Villena), and cultural publications known as *fanzines* (such as *Premamá*, which stands for *Prensa Marginal Madrileña* [Madrid Marginal Press], and *La Luna*).

21st-century art in Spain today manifests itself in various forms—from traditional painting, sculpture, and architecture to contemporary expressions, including graphic design, street art, and comics.

Further Reading

Moffitt, John F. *The Arts in Spain*. London: Thames & Hudson, 1999.

Tomlinson, Janis. *From El Greco to Goya: Painting in Spain, 1561–1828*. New York: H. N. Abrams, 1997.

Alhambra Palace

The Alhambra Palace is an architectural structure that deserves recognition based on aesthetics alone. However, it is also a cultural rarity: It is one of the few medieval Islamic structures to survive near to true form.

The palace contains a rich historic past. Granada's geographical location, protected by the mountains of the Sierra Nevada yet with access to the Mediterranean, made it an ideal location for a fortress. With the kingdoms of Castilla, Aragón, and Portugal gaining in power, Muhammad ibn Nasr (Muhammad I: 1237–1273), founder of the Nasrid dynasty, was in need of a geographical stronghold. The southern kingdom of Granada offered Nasrid rulers independence from their Catholic neighbors to the north. The Nasrid rule of Granada lasted another 250 years until the union of Ferdinand and Isabel sealed its demise (they conquered Granada in 1492). Its art and architecture is reflective of the region's earlier styles as well as of Moroccan and Egyptian influences.

Muhammad ibn Nasr chose Granada as the capital of his dynasty and began the expansion of the existing structure on the hillside. This expansion grew into an ornate city known as Qal'at al-Hamra' (the red fortress) due to the red color of its clay bricks, which eventually became Alhambra in Spanish. The structure consists of multiple fortified towers along an outer wall with six royal palaces on the interior of the edifice (though only two are in existence today) and a summer palace—the Palacio de Generalife—which is

The Gardens of the Generalife, part of the Alhambra. The original fortress in Granada was built in 889. The Alhambra was added in 1333 by Yusuf I, who converted the space into a royal palace. (Shchipkova Elena/Dreamstime.com)

surrounded by lush garden grounds. The formidable exterior is deceptive, for inside the fortress awaits a world of softly flowing fountains, cool wading pools, and intricate patterns on every possible surface constructed in wood, plaster, and clay. Marble is used for flooring, columns, and in the fountains, many of which were ornately painted.

During medieval times, glossy, brightly colored ceramics were rare and only affordable by the wealthy and the nobility, yet they decorated the expansive Alhambra walls, making a final display of wealth for an empire in decline. The ceilings were created by thousands of carved wooden elements that connect to the pattern in the tile. Plaster was utilized between the tile mosaic and the wooden ceilings, though some ceilings were entirely adorned with plaster, such as in the Palace of the Lions and the Hall of the Two Sisters. A main feature of the plaster decor is the prisms, which formed eight- and 16-pointed stars; the dome of the Two Sisters has more than 5,000 individual prisms cast onto its surface.

See also: Chapter 2: Overview. Chapter 12: Overview.

Further Reading

Dodds, Jerrilynn Denise. *Al-Andalus: The Art of Islamic Spain*. New York: Metropolitan Museum of Art—H. N. Abrams, 1992.

Rosser-Owen, Mariam. *Islamic Arts from Spain*. New York: Harry N. Abrams, 2010.

Architects

José Rafael Moneo (Tudela, 1937–) contributed, not without controversy, to the modern look of Spain. Examples of his work are the modern town halls of Logroño (1980) and Murcia (1998), the Kursaal Auditorium and Congress Center in San Sebastián (1999), and the controversial renovation of Mercado Grande in Ávila (2002). Moneo also taught architecture at the Harvard Graduate School of Design and has built several buildings in the United States such as the Davis Art Museum at Wellesley College (1993), the Houston Museum of Fine Arts (2000), and the Cathedral of Our Lady of the Angels in Los Angeles (2002).

Ricardo Bofill (Barcelona, 1939–) is another talented national architect whose impact inside and outside Spain has been remarkable. One of his most recent buildings is the Cultural Center Miguel Delibes in Valladolid (2007). He completed the new terminal at Barcelona airport (2008) and designed the Picasso terminal at Málaga airport (1991), among many other landmarks in Spain. Bofill's architecture is characterized by a distinctive fusion between technology and classical elements. This particular mixture is especially visible in his work abroad such as the Donnelly Building in Chicago (1992), Old Port of Montréal (1989), and the Antigone District in Montpellier (2000).

Santiago Calatrava (Valencia, 1951–) epitomizes the state of excellence in contemporary Spanish architecture. His extraordinary achievements are still to be measured, since he is currently one of the busiest architects in the world. His buildings become icons immediately. For instance, the Monjuic Communication Tower (1991) for the Barcelona Olympics in 1992, the bridge of Alamillo in Sevilla (1992), and the Auditorium of Tenerife (2003), which was his first performing arts facility, are clear examples of postmodern architecture in Spain. The City of Arts and Science (2004) in Valencia, his birth place, deserves special attention since it has become one of the most visited places in Spain due to the eye-catching effect of its white, seemingly weightless, futuristic buildings. Perhaps one of the reasons for his enormous success is his ability to incorporate nature into his organic designs, as can be seen at the BCE Place Galleria in Toronto (1992); the Milwaukee Art Museum (2001); Turning Torso in Malmö, Sweden (2005); or the Peace Bridge in Calgary, Canada (2012).

Enric Miralles (Barcelona, 1955–2000), who died in 2000 from a brain tumor, also left his mark abroad. Perhaps his main—although controversial—building is the new Scottish Parliament finished in 2004 in Edinburgh. Its structure includes abstract panels of glass and wood which, according to Miralles, evoke Henry Raeburn's painting *The Skating Minister*. Bill Price includes Miralles in his book about great modern architecture (2009), though he is aware of the effect that the abstract elements of the new Parliament have on some locals, who, he claims, "have suggested they give the building the appearance of a herd of cows, a comparison which might not be welcomed by MSPs" (132).

The urban landscape of Spain is becoming increasingly more homogeneous compared to the richest countries in the world. The abundance of skyscrapers in Madrid, Barcelona, and other cities such as Bilbao, and even in tourist destinations such as Benidorm highlight the fact that Spain has built too much in a short period of time. It epitomizes the Mediterranean explosion of buildings resulting from the lack of planning and fueled by the tourist boom.

See also: Chapter 2: Overview. Chapter 12: Overview.

Further Reading

Kleihues, Jan, et al. *Spanish Architects Abroad / Arquitectos españoles en el extranjero*. Berlin: Jovis, 2011.

Price, Bill. *Great Modern Architecture. The World's Most Spectacular Buildings*. London: Canary Press, 2009.

Comics and Cartoons

The history of comics in Spain is long and successful. It stretches back three centuries. According to a recent report in the daily newspaper *El País* (Intxausti 2013), the *Tebeosfera* project has recently catalogued 17,000 titles of Spanish comics dating from the 19th century through to the present day. Works by thousands of authors and tens of thousands of collections have been identified. The project started as an unfinished doctoral thesis. The objective of *Tebeosfera* is to compile these publications and study and popularize Spanish comics and cartoons. Many aficionados of this art form have already joined the project, and *Tebeosfera* now has 93 partners. Currently, 180 researchers of different nationalities are studying different aspects of these publications from the semiotics used through to their narrative form, history, and sociology. Some 182,369 technical sheets have already been completed, with almost 16,000 authors and over 17,000 collections identified.

The first political satire magazine known in Spain was *En Caricatura* (1865) and the first illustrator, who was also a poet and a writer, was Apeles Mestres, who published his vignettes in the magazine *Granizada* (1880). Both of these magazines have since disappeared. Before the Spanish Civil War, the first comic collection was born. It was called *Dominguín* (1915) and was published in Barcelona. Since then the Catalan city has become the main center for comics and graphic design.

Joaquín Buigas Garriga (1886–1963) bought the magazine *TBO* in 1917 and converted it into a national phenomenon, where a group of talented illustrators created different series. After the success of *TBO*, other comic magazines began to appear, such as *Pulgarcito* (1921), *Pocholo* (1931), and *La Revista de Mickey* (1935), the three of them imitating the realist style of North American cartoonists. However, this initial development of the comic industry was dismantled by the Spanish Civil War (1936–1939).

In 1940 the comic *Roberto Alcázar y Pedrín* came into being which, against all odds, due to its poor quality and use of populist language, maintains the record for being the longest comic collection of a hero ever published in Spain. *El Guerrero del antifaz* (1944) was another phenomenon that still remains in the memory of many Spaniards. *Diego Valor* (1954) was the first science-fiction comic in Spain, ironically, for a country where science at the time was practically nonexistent.

Francisco Ibáñez (1936–) is considered the master of Spanish comics. In fact, *Mortadelo y Filemón* (1958) is arguably the most well-known Spanish comic character ever produced. Ibáñez has been awarded prestigious comic prizes like the Grand Prize of the Saló del Còmic de Barcelona in 1994, and the Golden Medal for Contributions to the Fine Arts in 2001. In essence, *Mortadelo y Filemón* can be seen as the Spanish version as well as a parody of the famous English detective Sherlock Holmes and his assistant Watson.

Peridis (José María Pérez González) (1941–) is an architect and a comic illustrator. His vignettes are mainly published in *El País*, where he humorously analyzes the political context of the time. His work can be seen in the following books: *Los animalillos políticos de la transición de Peridis* (1977), *De la Constitución al golpe* (1981), and *Seis años para el cambio* (1977–1982). He has also published his memoirs under the title *Memorias con Arte. Peridis* (2006). Apart from being recognized as an architect with many awards to his name, he received the Golden Medal for his professional career, an honor bestowed by the Spanish government in 2006.

Forges (Antonio Fraguas) (1942–) is a draughtsman and a comic illustrator. He has also directed two movies and four television comedy series. The Spanish government honored him with the Golden Medal for his professional career in 2007; he received the Leyenda Award from the *Asociación de Libreros* (The Association of Bookshops). In 2011 he was awarded the Golden Medal for his contribution to the Fine Arts in Spain.

El Roto (Andrés Rábago García) (1947–) is a comic illustrator who has worked with many newspapers and magazines in Spain. Currently he publishes his work in the newspaper *El País*. In 2011 *Círculo de Lectores* and Random House re-published *La edad del silencio*, which is a compilation of his early work under the pseudonym OPS. He was awarded the 35th Award Diario de Avisos for the best script in his vignettes in 2011 and was the recipient of the National Award for Illustration in 2012.

Francesc Capdevila (1956–) is known solely as Max, and has collaborated with most Spanish newspapers and magazines as an illustrator, designer, and cartoonist. His work has been recognized nationally and internationally. He has received numerous honors for his work, such as: *Licantropunk* (Best Award given by the International Saló del Còmic de Barcelona, 1988); *Como perros!* (Best Work, 1996), *El prolongado sueño del Sr. T* (Best Script, 1998); and the Grand Award by the Saló de Còmic in 2000 for his professional career, among a long list of other important awards.

Manel Fontdevila (1965–) is a comic illustrator. He began with the now defunct newspaper *Público* and now works for *ElDiario.es*. He has also collaborated since 1993 for one of the most well-known Spanish comic magazines, *El Jueves*, and more recently has worked for *Orsai*. Fontdevila has already published three books: *Mantecatos* (2004), *Súper Puta* (2007), and *La crisis está siendo un éxito* (2012).

Paco Roca (1969–) is a draughtsman and illustrator. Roca bases his work on references to real characters, places, and events, and particularly to the history and culture of Spain. For example, in *El juego lúgubre* he finds similarities between Dalí and Dracula. In *El invierno del dibujante,* Roca recounts the real-life experience of five draughtsmen in 1950s Spain. In 2007 he published *Arrugas* (*Wrinkles*), a comic novel where two male characters deal with current problems while one of them is a patient with

Alzheimer's. For the latter Roca received the National Comic Award in 2008. In 2011 he was the screenwriter and designer for the film adaptation of *Wrinkles*, winner of two Goya awards in 2012. Roca's works are published in France and Italy, where he has received numerous accolades. Since March 2010 he has published a weekly page in the newspaper *Las Provincias* in Valencia.

Other contemporary Spanish cartoonists include Mauro Entrialgo (1965–); Miguel Brieva (1974–), well-known illustrator for the educational book *Educación para la ciudadanía* (2007, *Education for the Citizens*) as well as for the movie *Sobre ruedas* (Oscar Clemente, 2011); and Mamen Moreu Bibián (1985–), who works semi-regularly with the magazine *El Jueves*, where she created the character "Marcela." However, due to the economic crisis, this series was cancelled in October 2012. A new satirical magazine called *Orgullo y Satisfacción* (*Pride and Satisfaction*) was created in 2014.

See also: Chapter 2: Overview. Chapter 12: Overview. Chapter 16: Overview.

Further Reading

Beaty, Bart. *Unpopular Culture: Transforming the European Comic Book in the 1990s*. Toronto: University of Toronto Press, 2007.

Rodgers, Eamonn, ed. *Encyclopedia of Contemporary Spanish Culture*. New York: Routledge, 1999.

Dalí, Salvador

The Surrealist painter Salvador Dalí (1904–1989) once said that the only difference between a mad man and himself was that he was not mad. However, much about Dalí—his life, his appearance, and his work—contained a provocative element of madness about it.

Born in 1904 in the town of Figueres, Dalí studied at San Fernando Academy of Fine Arts in Madrid, where he was eventually expelled. If Pablo Picasso was a genius with many revolutionary artistic accomplishments, Dalí's paintings represent the Surrealist movement par excellence. According to the Surrealist founder, André Breton, Dalí "incarnated the Surrealist spirit" (Hunter and Jacobus, 1985). Dalí joined the Surrealist movement in 1929 and, unlike his fellow Catalan Joan Miró's style of automatism, Dalí's branch of Surrealism explored illusionistic images. His painting, *The Persistence of Memory* (1931), with melting watches, and eerily barren landscape, is indicative of his knowledge of abnormal psychology; it is still one of the best-known Surrealist works today.

Despite the fact that his artwork exemplified the Surrealist style, the 1930s brought conflict between the Surrealist founder Breton and Dalí, resulting in Dalí's eventual disbarment from the group. He achieved fame early in his life not only in Spain but in Europe and later on in the United States where he and his wife fled during WWII, and he lived for a period of time. During this time, Dalí collaborated with Alfred Hitchcock to create a series of dream-like shorts.

The 1950s marked Dalí's classical period, where geometry, science, and religion were key factors in his large, detailed paintings. Dali declared himself both a devoted Catholic and Monarchist and thus was accepted in Spain under Franco's rule. Later in his life he returned to his hometown of Figueres to construct the Teatro-Museo Dalí (The Dali Theatre-Museum). One of Spain's highest distinctions, the Grand Cross of the Order of Isabel the Catholic, was awarded to Dalí in 1964.

See also: Chapter 1: Cities: Barcelona, Madrid, Sevilla, Valencia. Chapter 2: Overview. Chapter 12: Overview.

Further Reading

Grenier, Catherine et al. *Salvador Dalí: The Making of an Artist.* London: Thames & Hudson, 2012.

Shanes, Eric. *Salvador Dalí.* New York: Parkstone International, 2014.

Spanish painter Salvador Dalí at work in 1945. Dalí was one of the most famous figures in the surrealist movement. (The Illustrated London News Picture Library)

El Greco

El Greco (1541–1614), originally Doménikos Theotokópoulos, is the only Spanish painter of the 1500s to receive international recognition today. Yet his work was not wildly popular at his time, often underwhelming his patrons, including King Philip II. Originally born in Crete, he lived in Italy for the 10 years preceding his move to Toledo in 1577. While his early work can be classified as post-Byzantine style, El Greco was influenced by Titian's work, which can be seen in El Greco's use of rich colors and twisting figures. Venetian artists such as Tintoretto and Veronese also played a role in shaping El Greco's style. He distinguished himself from the more conservative Spanish painters by remaining true to his artistic vision, being well read, and having a knowledge of Mannerist theory.

Upon El Greco's arrival in Toledo, he was commissioned to paint the *Disrobing of Christ* (1577–1579) for the Cathedral of Toledo. However, when payment was to be settled for the finished piece, the patrons offered far less than El Greco's asking price (350 ducats to El Greco's 900 ducats) and cited reasons such as the head of Christ was not placed high enough on the composition, and the work was historically inaccurate by including the Three Marys in the painting.

El Greco's desire to be true to his artistic vision again did not align with the strict and narrow expectations of Counter-Reformation art, this time with the commission of King Philip II, who often hired Italian artists to complete the large altarpieces of his residence in El Escorial. The commissioned piece was *The Martyrdom of St. Maurice and the Theban Legion* (1580–1582), which Philip II eventually had replaced with a second painting done by Romulo Cincinato. One can infer that Philip II found El Greco's focus on the graceful figures of the soldiers distasteful. Additionally, the subject of the painting itself, the martyred St. Maurice, is cast to the side of the painting, shown in the distant mid-ground. El Greco paints the portraits of contemporary military officers into the painting, once again turning his back on historical accuracy, a pattern that continues throughout his work. This contrasts with Cincinato's version, which has the decapitated bodies front and center. After this commission, El Greco returned to Toledo where he would spend the remainder of his life working surrounded by a close circle of intellectuals, artists, and patrons. Here he enjoyed a successful career. It was also the site of his painting, *View of Toledo* (1598–1599).

In the following years, El Greco's work would undergo significant change, evolving from the Italian Mannerist style to that which could be classified as conceptualized; he included elements of the unreal in his work. One of his best paintings is *The Burial of Count Orgaz* (1586–1588), which is based on a legend that dates back to 1323. However, El Greco reinterpreted the myth in his own time, dressing the count and his mourners in 16th-century fashions.

See also: Chapter 1: Overview. Chapter 2: Overview. Chapter 12: Overview.

Further Reading

Moffitt, John F. *The Arts in Spain*. London: Thames & Hudson, 1999.

Tomlinson, Janis. *From El Greco to Goya: Painting in Spain, 1561–1828*. New York: H. N. Abrams, 1997.

Gaudí, Antoni

The Barcelona architect Antoni Gaudí (1852–1926), though still controversial, has only recently—in the latter part of the 20th century—been recognized for his brilliance as an architect, specifically in countries abroad such as Germany. To date, Gaudí remains one of the most cited individuals in contemporary Spanish architecture because of the immensity of his works, which essentially reshaped Barcelona into an avant-garde city.

His architecture is an extension of his religious piety and his Catalan patriotism, as well as his infatuation with the natural world, resulting in structures that astonish the viewer with their defiance of convention. Naturally, his work was not without controversy. His designs for the Barcelona garden suburb of Park Güell resulted in only two of his proposed 60 houses being built. The designs of his Casa Milà apartment block, with their undulating rooftops and bizarre wrought iron balconies, resulted in disputes regarding his spiritual voice along with court battles between Gaudí and his client over unpaid fees—fees which when collected, Gaudí immediately gave away to charity. Thus, it is surprising that a young Gaudí was selected as the architect for the greatest work of his lifetime: the building of the *Temple Expiatori de la Sagrada Familia* (Expiatory Church of the Holy Family). This is a project that would consume 43 of Gaudí's 48 years as an architect, leading to fanaticism the last decade of his life so intense that he eventually moved into the unfinished building to be on site all hours of the day.

The building was commissioned by the Spiritual Association of the Devotees to Saint Joseph, or the Josephines, a group of citizens who desired to provide a church for Barcelona's growing working class. It is not surprising that Gaudí was not their first choice, but rather the reputable architect Francisco de Paula del Villar was selected to create a modest design for the church, which was then located on a plot surrounded by a field on the outskirts of Barcelona. Villar resigned from the project as he was unwilling to make the artistic concessions to fit the limited budget offered by the Josephines, so they turned to the young Gaudí instead, having no idea that this small church would result in a massive architectural project. It began in 1883. Over 130 years later it is still under construction today.

Seven of his buildings have been declared World Heritage Sites by UNESCO. The seven buildings are: Parque Güell; Palacio Güell; Casa Milà; Casa Vicens; Gaudí's work on the Nativity façade and crypt of La Sagrada Familia; Casa Batlló; and the crypt in Colonia Güell.

See also: Chapter 1: Cities: Barcelona, Madrid, Sevilla, Valencia. Chapter 2: Overview. Chapter 12: Overview.

Further Reading

Burry, Mark, ed. *Gaudí Unseen: Completing the Sagrada Familia*. Berlin: Jovis, 2007.
Constantino, Maria. *Gaudi*. Secaucus: Chartwell Books, 1993.

Goya, Francisco de

Francisco de Goya's (1746–1828) *oeuvre* comprises almost 2,000 paintings, drawings, lithographs, and engravings from the late Baroque to the modern period. Though born in a small country town in the south of Aragón, near Zaragoza, Goya spent most of his life in Madrid where he worked to elevate his status during the 60 years of his life as an artist.

He began working in Madrid at the royal tapestry factory of Santa Barbara, a job secured through the connections of his brother-in-law, the painter Francisco Bayeu. Traditionally, artists commissioned to illustrate a series of tapestries chose common themes such as the seasons or pastoral images from a story, whereas Goya chose scenes of contemporary life, often contrasting members of various social classes and ethnicities as seen in such tapestry paintings as *The Blind Guitarist, The Fair of Madrid,* or *The Crockery Vendor*, all completed in 1778.

At the age of 40, he was appointed court painter to Carlos III and subsequently to Carlos IV. While his collection of royal portraiture is significant, including works such as *The Family of Carlos IV* (1800–1801), he is better known for his drawings that critique both the social inequalities of the time and the violence of the Napoleonic wars. The 18th century was tumultuous in Spain in general and the painting of the time reflected the chaos. If the Enlightenment led many European artists to criticize the monarchy, Goya was perhaps the first painter in Spain who made a social critique of his times through his series of *Los caprichos* (1797–1799) and in several of his paintings such as *The Family of Carlos IV* (1800) or his extremely famous work, *The Third of May 1808* (1814), despite the fact that he was working for the court.

In 1792, Goya became seriously ill, and though he recovered, he permanently lost his hearing and was in a weakened state. This change in physique had a psychological impact on him that is reflected in his work. While he continued to paint Madrid's elite, he began smaller works of drawings and etchings. These noncommissioned pieces offered Goya the artistic freedom not possible in the large-scale tapestry paintings.

Los Caprichos (1797–1799) was a series of 80 aquatint etchings first published in 1799 featuring animals, monsters, beasts, and elements of witchcraft in often melancholic and disturbing arrangements. Imagery is prevalent throughout these works with the donkey or ass portraying the foolishness of mankind, or the bat symbolizing humanity's fears. Generally these works speak of the flawed human condition while exploring concepts such as love, morality and ignorance. Specifically, Goya was showcasing the follies of 18th-century Spanish society as seen in etchings such as *What a Sacrifice!* (1779), *One Hunting for Teeth* (1799), and *The Sleep of Reason Produces Monsters* (1799).

The latter part of Goya's life was marked with political unrest, including the invasions of Napoleon's armies in 1808, which resulted in the fall from power of Charles IV, the restoration of the monarchy with an intolerant Ferdinand VII, and the reinstating of the Inquisition followed by a reign of terror. Works of this time include *The Second of May 1808* (1814), *The Third of May 1808* (1814), and a series of 85 prints entitled *The Disasters of War* (1810–1823). Ill at ease with the political stance of Spain at the time, Goya moved to Bordeaux in 1824, where he spent his final years.

See also: Chapter 2: Overview; de Farnesio, Isabel; de Godoy, Manuel. Chapter 12: Overview; Painters. Chapter 15: Bullfighting. Chapter 16: Cinema.

Further Reading

Hughes, Robert. *Goya*. New York: Alfred A. Knopf, 2003.

Loeb Stepanek, Stephanie, et al. *Goya: Order and Disorder*. Boston: Museum of Fine Arts, 2014.

Tomlinson, Janis A. *From El Greco to Goya: Paintings in Spain 1561–1828*. New York: H. N. Abrams, 1997.

Graphic Design

Graphic design is another modern form of artistic expression that has a significant number of well-known artists in Spain.

Alberto Corazón (1942–) is one of the most well-known graphic designers in the world. In fact, he is the only European designer who has been awarded the Golden Medal by the American Institute of Graphic Arts, which is the most important international award in Visual Communication. His designs become instant iconic logos for the Spanish people, who can easily identify institutions by their logos created by Corazón such as ONCE, Paradores, RENFE (Cercanías), MAPFRE, Junta de Andalucía, Biblioteca Nacional, and Casa de América. His long career has also been recognized internationally. The Spanish authorities have bestowed upon him the Spanish National Award in Design in 1989; in the United States he is a member of the Arts Director Club of New York; and in the United Kingdom he won the Gold Medal given by the Designers Association of London.

Javier Mariscal (1959–) is another well-known designer who acquired international attention with the design of the Barcelona Olympics logo, *cobi*. Since then, Mariscal's work has been very prolific. One of his recent works is the movie *Chico y Rita* (2010) by Fernando Trueba and himself. Among other achievements is the creation of the first multidisciplinary studio in Spain.

Mikel Casal (1965–) works for different newspapers, magazines, and book publishers in Spain and abroad. He has also illustrated children's books such as *El Señor Navidad* (editorial SM 2003) and *Industrias Gon* (Macmillan Iberia 2009). In 2011 he received the Silver Medal from the Society for News Design (SND-E).

Luis Grañena (1968–), after receiving several international awards by the Society of New Design, established his permanent residence in 2009 in Valderrobres, Teruel (Aragón). From his village he regularly collaborates with newspapers and magazines from all over the world. Among his clients are the *New Yorker*, *Vanity Fair*, *Financial Times Weekend*, *La Tercera* (Chile), *Libération* (France), *La Vanguardia*, *Tiempo*, and other European magazines.

Luciano Lozano (1969–), after studying for an MA in illustration at EINA in Barcelona in 2007, currently resides in the Catalan city as a professional *illustrista*, working for different newspapers and magazines such as *Público*, *la Marea*, *The Guardian*, *Le Monde,* and *House and Garden*. In 2011 he won the Junceda award given by the Catalonian Association of Illustrators (APIC) for the best book published abroad, which was his *Operation Alphabet* (Thames & Hudson 2011), published in the U.K., U.S., and Germany first and available also in France since 2012.

See also: Chapter 1: Cities: Barcelona, Madrid, Sevilla, Valencia. Chapter 2: Overview. Chapter 12: Overview.

Further Reading

Gil, Emilio. *Pioneers of Spanish Graphic Design*. New York: Mark Batty, 2009.

Mariscal, Javier. *Mariscal Drawing Life*. New York: Phaidon Press, 2009.

Nichols, William J., and H. Rosi Song, eds. *Toward a Cultural Archive of La Movida: Back to the Future*. Madison: Fairleigh Dickinson University Press, 2014.

Miró, Joan

Joan Miró (Barcelona, 1893–1983) is another world-renowned Spanish painter whose work reflects the ideologies of the Surrealist movement. Born in Barcelona, Miró abandoned his plan of studying business to become an artist instead. In 1920, he made his first trip to Paris where he met the native *malagueño*, Pablo Picasso, and he would continue to divide his time between Paris and Spain. In Paris he became involved in the nonsensical Dada movement, eventually joining the Surrealist movement in 1942. The Surrealist movement was influenced by Freudian psychology's exploration of the subconscious, repressed desire, and the dream world, and it manifested itself in two different directions artistically: automatism and dream imagery.

The founder of the Surrealist movement, André Breton, described Miró as, "the most Surrealist of us all" (Hunter and Jacobus 1992), and the artist himself wrote, "I began gradually to work away from the realism I had practiced . . . until in 1925, I was drawing almost entirely from hallucinations. At the time I was living on a few dried figs a day" (Hunter and Jacobus 1992). Yet Miró formally declined to classify himself with any one movement and remained stubbornly independent in regards to his style. As a prolific artist, he worked in a variety of mediums including painting, collage, lithography, etchings, and sculpture.

Miró's Fauve-like brightly colored work has a playful, dreamlike quality that can be seen in his pivotal painting, *The Harlequins' Carnival* (1924–1925), where amorphous shapes, curving figures, and bright blues, yellows, and reds are used throughout the composition. This painting marks a shift from his earlier more realistic pieces (such as *The Farm*, 1922) to those dealing with the subconscious. It is not surprising that he was asked by the Spanish government to design a national logo. Spain was the first country having a promotional emblem to promote tourism. His *España logo* designed in black, red, and yellow, with a tiny bit of green is still considered one of the best logos in the world.

See also: Chapter 1: Cities: Barcelona, Madrid, Sevilla, Valencia. Chapter 2: Overview. Chapter 12: Overview.

Further Reading

Erben, Walter et al., *Joan Miró, 1893–1983: The Man and His Work*. New York: Taschen, 1998.

Hunter, Sam, and John M. Jacobus. *Modern Art: Painting, Sculpture, Architecture*. New York: H. N. Abrams, 1985.

Mink, Janis. *Joan Miró, 1893–1983: The Poet among the Surrealists*. Los Angeles: Taschen, 2012.

Museums

Located in the heart of Madrid, just west of the vast Retiro Park, stretches a wide, historic, tree lined street called El Paseo del Prado. Near this street reside three of Spain's most prominent art museums, collectively known as "the golden triangle": *Museo del Prado* (the Prado), *Museo Reina Sofía* (the Reina Sofia), and *El Museo de arte Thyssen-Bornemisza* (the Thyssen-Bornemisza). Within a mere fifteen minute walk lie some of the greatest artistic treasures of all time.

The Prado Museum is without a doubt the most prestigious museum in Spain. It opened for the first time to the public in 1819. It hosts a variety of European art from the 12th to the 19th century. Multiple schools are displayed in its rooms from the early Flemish and Italian schools to the German, French, and Dutch schools, as well as the works of the Spanish school, which covers a long list of iconic artists such as El Greco, Tintoretto, Diego Velázquez, and Goya. In fact, the museum has one of the largest collections in the world, consisting of approximately 19,000 artifacts. It is estimated that only one-seventh of the museum's pieces are on display at any given time.

Located a few blocks southwest of the Prado is the Museo Nacional Centro de Arte Reina Sofía or the Reina Sofia. Formerly a hospital constructed in the 18th century, the structure now houses Spain's greatest collection of contemporary art. Opened in 1992 by then Spanish King Juan Carlos and Queen Sofia, the museum is named after Doña Sofía as a tribute to her commitment to culture on all levels. Here the collection is divided between two floors. The first floor displays painting from the years 1900–1939 (the latter being the year the Spanish Civil War ended). Among some of its most famous pieces are Pablo Picasso's *Guernica* (1937), a piece that is over 26 feet long and 11 feet tall, and Salvador Dalí's *Invisible Man* (1929–1932).

The Thyssen-Bornemisza opened its doors in 1992, showcasing over 1,000 works of art; it is considered one of the most impressive private art collections in the world. The collection began with Dutch-born Baron Heinrich Thyssen-Bornemisza and was completed by his son Baron Hans Heinrich. The two complemented each other—while the first collected Old Masters, the second acquired works from the 19th and 20th centuries. The top floor of the museum displays the older works, while the first floor houses the more modern, including artists such as Renoir, Monet, Degas, Picasso, and Hopper.

However, art in Spain is not located only in the capital. On the contrary, it is spread out all over the country with, for example, another three museums in Barcelona: the Museum of Contemporary Art (MACBA), the Fundación Joan Miró, and the Fundación Antoni Tàpies. Furthermore, the Valencia Institute of Modern Art (IVAM), the Guggenheim Museum in Bilbao, the Museo Picasso in Málaga, and the National Museum of Roman Art in Mérida, aside from housing many important paintings, are also among the most visited museums in Spain.

See also: Chapter 1: Cities: Barcelona, Madrid, Sevilla, Valencia. Chapter 2: Overview. Chapter 12: Overview.

Further Reading

Garín Llombart, Felipe Vicente. *Treasures of the Prado*. New York: Abbeville Press, 1993.

Museyon Guides. *Art + Travel Europe: Step into the Lives of Five Famous Painters*. New York: Museyon Guides, 2010.

Painters

Bartolomé Esteban Murillo (1617–1682) was one of the most important representatives of Spanish Baroque. The popular subjects of his religious paintings brought the Counter-Reformation to the common people. Murillo founded a prestigious art school in 1660 and he became an artist of great popularity. Murillo's influence on Spanish painting lasted over the centuries. Murillo is currently considered one of the great masters and his paintings are distributed in all the great museums of the world. Unusual for an artist, Murillo found fame in his own lifetime. In his twenties, Murillo created a series of paintings depicting Franciscan saints, which brought him to the attention of the art establishment and led to many commissions. *Grape and Melon Eaters* (c.1650) exemplify Murillo's interest in depicting the street life of Spain, often using children and women as his models. *St Francis of Assisi at Prayer* (1645–1650), *The Flight into Egypt* (1647–1650), and *Madonna and Child* (1650) are a few examples of his religious works.

Joaquín Sorolla y Bastida (1863–1923) represents a bridge between the most ethnically authentic (*castizo*) type of painting known as *Costumbrismo* (developed in the second half of the 19th century) and the current European influences—particularly from French Impressionism. For instance, Sorolla's *Children on the Beach* (1910) can be seen as a masterpiece of "*plein-air* effects of light sparkling off water and rosy flesh; his art remains very popular today" (Moffitt, 1999). Sorolla resided in Madrid, where there is a museum named after him, the Museo Sorolla, which opened in 1932.

Juan Gris (1887–1927), born as José Victoriano González Pérez, was a Spanish painter and sculptor who was born in Madrid, where he studied engineering before moving to Paris in 1906, where he worked most of his life. His heavily analytical, mainly still-life Cubist works are notable for their purity and lucidity. He followed Georges Braque and Picasso by progressing into a more accessible "synthetic" phase. In his last period Gris became obsessed with color, as seen in *Guitar and Newspaper*, which was painted just two years before his tragically early death from asthma.

Maruja Mallo (1902–1995) was the first widely recognized female Spanish painter of the 20th century. Her paintings belong to the literary movement known as Generation of '27 in Spain. Her first exhibit was for the salons of the *Revista de Occidente* directed by the philosopher José Ortega y Gasset in 1928. Later Mallo exhibited in Paris in 1932 for the Gallery Pierre Loeb, and met other artists such as André Breton, who bought her *Espantapájaros* (1929, *The Scarecrow*). There she also met Jean Cassou, Picasso, Miró, Aragón, Arp, Magritte, and Torrés-García. During the Spanish Civil War, Mallo moved from her native Galicia to Lisbon, thanks to her friendship with the Nobel prize-winning poet Gabriela Mistral, who invited her to her house while she was at the time the ambassador for Chile in Portugal. Later, Mallo developed her paintings in Uruguay and Argentina and returned to Spain in 1964. She received the Golden Medal of Fine Arts in 1967.

Apart from the Surrealist movement, another prominent collective of Spanish painters in the 20th century was *El Paso*, comprised of Antonio Saura (1930–1998), Antoni Tàpies (1923–2012), Manuel Millares (1926–1972), Martín Chirino (1925–), Manuel

Rivera (1927–1995), Luis Feito (1929–), and Rafael Canogar (1935–), among a long list of other artists. The El Paso group was, as the name indicates, a collective of artists at the end of the 1950s whose work was instrumental in reviving Spanish art after the post-war era. The group began in Madrid in 1957, and their last joint exhibition was in 1960, in the L'Attico gallery in Rome. One example of the paintings of this group is *Cuadro 122* by Manuel Millares, in which he depicted—exclusively in black and white—human barbarity and irrationality. Between May and June 2004, the Marlborough gallery in Madrid held a retrospective of the group with an exhibition titled "El Paso, 1957–1960."

Juana Mordó (1899–1984) opened a gallery in Madrid on March 14, 1964, during the post-civil war. The role of the Juana Mordó Gallery (closed in 1985) in contemporary Spanish art is immense. She managed to display in Spain a whole array of national and international artists as well as to act as an extraordinary cultural agent for many contemporary Spanish painters who are well-known nowadays, such as Carmen Laffón (1934–) and Antonio López (1936–). Her artistic legacy, donated to the Círculo de Bellas Artes in Madrid, constitutes more than 250 paintings, sculptures, and drawings, plus 3,000 books, which sum up her contribution of 20 years as an artistic patron who provided a platform for more than 200 artists in her gallery. For her outstanding contribution to the Spanish arts during a grey period of Spain, Mordó received the Golden Medal of Fine Arts in 1979.

Carmen Laffón (1934–) is an honorary "Daughter of Andalucía," who, like Gordillo, has achieved official recognition by the Spanish authorities. Laffón won the National Prize in Arts in 1982 and the Golden Medal in 1999. Her paintings deal with death, nature, daily objects, and, particularly, native landscapes of the Coto de Doñana, where she established herself as a painter. Along with Antonio López, she is one of the pillars of Spanish contemporary art in the style known as lyrical realism. Magdalena Illán Martín, a history professor at the Universidad de Sevilla, has written a book entirely dedicated to the paintings of Laffón entitled *Carmen Laffón. La poética de la realidad en el arte español contemporáneo* (Illán Martín, 2012).

Antonio López (1936–) is without doubt one of the most well-known painters alive in Spain. Robert Hughes has defined him as a master realist, although for others he has been criticized for neo-academism and, interestingly enough, for being a slow painter. For instance, in 1997 he was given a contract by the Spanish monarchy to paint the Royal family, and it took him 17 years until he finished it in 2014. López said that "una obra nunca se acaba, sino que se llega al límite de las propias posibilidades" ("a painting never is finished; you just reach the limits of your own attempts," arteespaña.com). Despite the fact that he is not a prolific artist, López's paintings have already acquired not only a national but also an international reputation. His work has been exhibited three times in New York as well as in several major U.S. museum collections, in addition to appearing in several exhibits in Madrid. In 2004, López was inducted as an honorary member of the Academy of Arts and Letters in New York, and in 2006 he was awarded the Velázquez Prize for Fine Arts. For more information, López is featured in an award-winning 1992 film, *El sol del Membrillo*, directed by the Spanish cult film director Victor Erice, and written by both. The film portrays López's struggles to paint.

Eduardo Arroyo Rodríguez (1937–) is another prestigious Spanish painter who was recognized by the Spanish academy in 1982, when he won the National Prize of Fine Arts. His style can be described as a reinterpretation of the Spanish stereotypes with a Surrealist touch. Examples of his particular style of painting are *Caballero español*, painted in 1970 in Paris, where he emigrated because he was expelled by the Franco regime. Another interesting sample of his painting is *Carmen Amaya asa sardinas en el Waldorf Astoria* (1988), where his figurative style is connected to the influences of pop art. Arroyo's work is currently displayed in many important worldwide art centers.

Miquel Barceló (1957–) is probably one of the most well-known Spanish artists of the 21st century. His artistic production has acquired a huge reputation mainly due to two fundamental works—the gothic decoration for the cathedral in Palma de Mallorca, locally known as *La Seu*, which Barceló invested seven years to complete; and the ceiling painting called *Chamber XX of Human Rights and Alliance of Civilizations* at the European headquarters of the United Nations in Geneva, Switzerland, which constitutes his most ambitious project to date. Barceló used 77,000 pounds (35,000 kilos) of paint to decorate the hall, of which Spain paid 40 percent of the €14.5 million ($23 million) redecoration budget. It took him one year to finish. It was inaugurated by the king and queen of Spain on November 18, 2008.

Recalling the importance of the Altamira caves as one of the early examples of Spanish painting, Barceló's monumental 1,500 square meters of multicolored stalactite forms echoed the first primitive paintings ever found in Spain. Barceló's idea of the world as a planet cave brings together men who think into the future. According to the artist, the hall reflects infinity and the multiplicity of viewpoints. Interestingly enough, all Barcelo's works (paintings, drawings, sculptures, and ceramics) are exclusively represented not in Spain but abroad by Galerie Bruno Bischofberger in Zürich. In 2010 Spain paid tribute to his legacy with an exhibition of his work both in Madrid and Barcelona.

See also: Chapter 2: Overview. Chapter 12: Overview.

Further Reading

Mangini González, Shirley. *Maruja Mallo and the Spanish Avant-Garde*. Burlington: Ashgate, 2010.

Saavedra, Santiago. *Spanish Painters, 1850–1950: In Search of Light*. Madrid: P.E.A.C.E., 1984.

VV.AA. *The 20th Century Art Book*. London: Phaidon Press, 2007.

Photographers

The history of Spanish photography is often overlooked within the subject of visual arts in Spain. However, in 1994, the Ministry of Culture created the National Award for Photography with an annual prize of 30,000 euros. The blog fotoruta.com is a good source for more information about current Spanish publications on photography. However, as noted in the entry on "Photography" written by Mihail Moldoveanu, "the new generation of photographers, despite their different approaches, shared a rejection of 'photogenic' reality" (Rodgers, 1999). Currently, most professional Spanish photographers work and live abroad.

José Ortíz-Echagüe (1886–1980) is considered the "father of photography" in Spain. He was a versatile man, becoming an entrepreneur, a military pilot, and an industrial engineer. Due to his extensive career, he was nominated *Gentil hombre de cámara con ejercicio* (Gentleman of the Bedchamber). For 60 years, Ortiz depicted the changes of Spain's landscapes and people. He also published a number of books, which have been translated into different languages including English, such as his first series *Tipos y Trajes* (1930, *Characters and Outfits*), and *España, Pueblos y Paisajes* (1939, *Spain: Peoples and Landscapes*). More recently, his works have been exhibited around the world as well as being included in English anthologies, including the one by Francis Ribemont (2006).

Darío Villalba (1939–) is a painter and photographer. He was a pioneer in Europe in the use of photography as painting. He is considered one of the most prestigious Spanish visual artists on the international art scene. He abandoned painting in 1972 and turned to black-and-white photography, experimenting with processes of decomposition and recomposition and exploring themes such as dementia, cruelty, and violence. In 2001 the Galician Contemporary Art Centre (CGAC) hosted an exhibition entitled *Documentos básicos 1957–2001* (*Basic Documents 1957–2001*), a diary in images that describes the general aims of his work. He has received international awards such as the Sao Paulo International Painting Prize (1973); the International Jury Prize, 13th Graphic Arts Biennial, Ljubljana (1979); the Grand Prize in the 8th International Sports Biennial in Fine Arts (1982); the National Painting Award (1983); and the Golden Medal for Merit in Fine Arts (2002). Surprisingly, he has no website as of the writing of this volume.

Isabel Steva Hernández (1940–) is known as "Colita," a name she was given after her parents told her she had been found under a "col"—the Catalan name for a cabbage—just like in the folktale of Catalan origin, *Patufet*. She studied French Civilization at University of Paris–Sorbonne. When Colita returned to Barcelona she discovered the world of photography, thanks to Oriol Maspons, Julio Ubiña, and Xavier Miserachs, renowned photographers of the post-civil war period. Colita was linked to cultural anti-Francoist and feminist movements. She alternated her tasks as a photojournalist with work in the cinematographic movement of the School of Barcelona and in the visual chronicle of the artist group of the 1960s known as the *gauche divine*. Colita also worked for the record label Edigsa, the company in charge of promoting the Catalan music *Nova Cançó*, in which she photographed singers such as Joan Manuel Serrat and Guillermina Motta. Since the death of Franco and the reinstatement of democracy, her work has focused on the urban landscapes of Barcelona. Colita is currently working on a study of women photographers. In 2012 Colita was awarded an honorary doctorate by the Universitat Autónoma de Barcelona for her contributions to the field of photography. In 2014 she received the National Award of Photography, but she rejected it.

Cristina García Rodero (1949–) is a Spanish photographer and member of *Magnum* and *Vu* (photo agency). She used to work as a teacher. García Rodero has received many prizes, including the National Award of Photography in 1996. Her work has been exhibited worldwide. Rodero has also published several books, including *Festivals and Rituals of Spain* (1994) and more recently *Transtempo* (2011). García Rodero is the first Spanish female photographer who works for the agency *Magnum*.

Ouka Leele (1957–) was born Bárbara Allende Gil de Biedma and is a contemporary Spanish photographer. She started in the early 1980s during the counterculture movement following Franco's death known as *La movida madrileña*. Since then, she has published several poetry books as well as being an illustrator and a renowned Spanish photographer whose work has appeared in recent prestigious exhibitions of contemporary Spanish arts, such as that held by the curator Blanca Berlín entitled *Women & Women* (2010). More recently, she has been included in the 2013 anthology by the prestigious art critic Francisco Calvo Serraller.

Other contemporary Spanish photographers include Francesc Català-Roca (1922–1998); Miguel Reveriego (?), who is a world fashion photographer; and Cristina Otero (1995–), who became a well-known artist for her self-portraits. Despite her young age, her portraits have already been showcased in exhibits across Spain. More recently, she has an ad campaign with the Spanish train company Renfe.

See also: Chapter 2: Overview. Chapter 12: Overview. Chapter 16: Overview.

Further Reading

Calvo Serraller, Francisco. *The Museo del Prado and the Contemporary Artists*. Barcelona: Fundación Amigos del Museo del Prado, 2013.

Fontcuberta, Joan, and Betty Hahn. *Contemporary Spanish Photography*. Alburquerque: University of New Mexico Press, 1987.

Morino, Beatriz, et al. *Women & Women: Exhibition*. Washington, D.C.: Embajada de España, 2010.

Ribemont, Francis. *Impressionist Camera: Pictorial Photography in Europe, 1888–1918*. New York: Merrell, 2006.

Picasso, Pablo Ruiz

The prolific artist Pablo Ruiz Picasso (1881–1973) had a career that spanned decades, often shaping the direction of the art world. As one of the most pivotal artists of the 20th century, his work launched or encompassed numerous movements including Cubism, Neo-Classicism, Dada, and Surrealism and included the mediums of painting, drawings, collage, etchings, printmaking, sculpture, metalworking, ceramics, and tapestry. He traveled extensively, working in Spain, France, England, The Netherlands, and Poland.

Born in Málaga, he was a prodigy completing his first oil painting, *The Picador* (1889), at the age of eight. When Picasso was 10 his family moved to A Coruña in northern Spain, and then later to Barcelona where his father took a position as an instructor at the School of Fine Arts. Between 1900–1904 Picasso moved back and forth between Paris and Barcelona before settling in Paris permanently. It was during this time that Picasso began his Blue Period and later his Rose Period. His Blue Period paintings are associated with melancholic images of longing. His subject matter includes the homeless, the impoverished, and the outcasts of Paris as seen in *Two Women in a Bar* (1902). The work of this period might have been influenced by his personal financial troubles.

Picasso had strong political ideologies. As a Loyalist, from the safety of France, he voiced his dissent from Franco in various forms including The *Dream and Lie of Franco* (1937), a series of etchings depicting Franco as a hairy, vegetable-like figure wearing a paper crown. Picasso wrote a poem to accompany the series, describing Franco as "an evil-omened polyp . . . his mouth full of the chinch-bug jelly of his words." One of his most monumental works, *Guernica* (1937) was painted the same year in response to the Basque town of Guernica being bombed by German planes under the consent of Franco. Painted in black, white, and greys, this work of art stretches over 25 feet long and 11 feet high. It depicts the horror of the day, creating a nightmarish effect through brutal distortion of the figures, including a woman holding her dead child in her arms and a soldier lying mutilated on the ground, still clutching his broken sword. In 1939, with the beginning of WWII, Picasso exiled himself to the United States.

There are two Picasso Museums in Spain; one in his native Málaga and the other in Barcelona, and his works are celebrated throughout the world. Any of his works now cost millions and represents a piece of contemporary art history. How many paintings did Picasso make in his lifetime—a career that lasted until his death at the age of 92? There is debate and answers vary from nearly 2,000 to over 20,000. Picasso wrote, "I paint the way some people write their autobiographies. The paintings, finished or not, are the pages of my journal, and as such they are valid. The future will choose the pages it prefers. It's not up to me to make the choice." (http://www.picasso.fr/us/picasso_page_index.php)

See also: Chapter 2: Overview. Chapter 12: Overview.

Further Reading

Daix, Pierre. *Picasso: Life and Art*. New York: Icon Editions, 1994.

Richardson, John, and Marilyn McCully. *A Life of Picasso*. New York: Alfred A. Knopf, 2010.

Sculptors

Alonso Berruguete (1488–1561), considered the most important sculptor of the Spanish Renaissance, is known for his religious figures sculpted in ecstasy or torment. Berruguete travelled to Italy to study the latest artistic trends. Examples of his skills are Granada's decorations of the Royal Chapel and Zaragoza's tomb of Cardinal Sevagio. Other works include: Toledo's Cathedral left choir stall, Valladolid's altarpiece of San Benito, and Salamanca's high altar of the College of Los Irlandeses.

Alonso Cano (1601–1667) was a painter, sketcher, maker of altarpieces, sculptor, and architect. Cano was a many-sided artist and a central figure in Spain's Golden Age. He was influenced by Italian Mannerism and the Baroque. His drawings are outstanding for their perfection, making him perhaps the greatest sketcher of his age. His *Bust of Saint Paul* and the carved *Immaculate Virgins* formed the basis of another school of art in Spain at the time, which published works from artists such as Pedro de Mena and José de Mora.

Francisco Salzillo (1707–1783) was a prolific sculptor of religious figures. His legacy, however, is disputed, being regarded by some as Spain's greatest sculptor of the 18th century while others consider him an outstanding folk artist. While most European sculptors chose secular subjects, Salzillo focused on religion as his main theme. He was the son of a Neapolitan sculptor and his Italian parentage can be seen in his Holy Week images and nativity figures, so dear to the tradition of Naples. The Salzillo Museum in Murcia contains much of his work.

Mariano Benlliure (1862–1947) created numerous monuments for prominent figures in Spain and Latin America. Benlliure is considered the last master of 19th-century realism. Everyday life constituted the main focus of his art, which he fully dedicated to sculpture after travelling to Rome in 1879, when he saw Michelangelo's works. Examples of Benlliure's sculptures are the statue of Alfonso XII or the monument to Emilio Castelar, both located in Madrid.

Jorge Oteiza Enbil (1908–2003) was a versatile artist who abandoned his studies in order to devote himself to sculpture. Apart from being a well-known sculptor, he was also a painter, designer, and writer. In fact, the Center for Basque Studies (Nevada University) published a volume dedicated to *Oteiza's Selected Writings* (2003). Oteiza announced in 1959 that he gave up on sculpture and, instead, would spend his time developing aesthetic and anthropologic studies. Hence, his essay entitled "Quosque tandem!" (1963), in which he envisioned a particular Basque aesthetics based on the ancient roots of the Basque.

Eduardo Chillida (1924–2002) is probably the most well-known Spanish sculptor of the 20th century for his monumental abstract works. However, one of the most controversial cases of contemporary Spanish art was his Tindaya project in the Canary Island of Fuerteventura. Chillida planned to hollow out a mountain, and "offer it up to men of all races and colors, a gigantic sculpture to tolerance," as he said to interviewers. The project immediately drew the attention of many Spaniards, who were against his idea of colonizing a sacred mountain. Following Simon Schama's *Landscape and Memory* (1996), Chillida's case represents the colonization of nature by culture. In Schama's own words, "landscapes are culture before they are nature" (Schama, 1996). Apart from the controversial project in the mountain of Tindaya, his sculptures have become iconic places to visit in Spain. Examples of his work are *El Peine del Viento* (San Sebastián 1976), *Elogio del Agua* (Barcelona 1987), and *Elogio del Horizonte* (Gijón 1990). In 1985 Chillida was recipient of the Wolf Prize in Sculpture, and in 1998 he received the Lifetime Achievement in Contemporary Sculpture Award, among other national honors and awards. There is now a Museum Chillida-Leku in Hernani.

Susana Solano (1946–) belongs to a generation of Spanish sculptors working in the country's ironwork tradition who gained prominence after the death of dictator

Francisco Franco in 1975. Solano constructs her abstract metal sculptures as autonomous, enclosed receptacles, often reminiscent of cages, in which inaccessible interior space plays an essential role. Solano's work has been exhibited in many galleries and exhibitions around the world.

Jaume Plensa (1955–) trained at the School of Fine Arts in Barcelona. After his first exhibition in 1980, his fame began to spread. Since then Plensa has lived and worked in countries such as Germany, Belgium, England, and France. He has worked as a teacher at the National School of Fine Arts in Paris. Plensa is one of the leading figures in the current plastic arts scene. A significant part of his career has been dedicated to creating sculpture for public spaces, and his work can be seen in cities throughout the world. Some of his most brilliant creations include *The Crown Fountain* in Chicago's Millennium Park, and the project *Breathing* for the BBC in London. Among other distinctions, in 2012 he won the National Plastic Arts Award. He is also the recipient of the Chevalier de l'Ordre des Arts et des Lettres of France in 1993 and the Atelier Calder Foundation Award in 1996.

Cristina Iglesias (1956–) was described by *Time* Magazine as a promising young artist for her part in the Venice Biennale 1986. The Guggenheim in New York gave her an exhibition in 1997, and she received the National Plastic Arts Award in 1999, which she shared with the painter Pablo Palazuelo. In 2007, Iglesias made the door-sculpture for the extension to the Prado Museum designed by Spanish architect Rafael Moneo.

Jordi Colomer (1962–) is a sculptor and video artist whose residency and place of work oscillates between Barcelona and Paris. Colomer's sculptural work is mixed with other elements including, for instance, theatre staging (he in fact is also a theatre set designer) and architectural references like the walkable building *L'avenir* (2011). Colomer's works have been exhibited in several museums around the world such as the Reina Sofia (Madrid), Center George Pompidou (Paris), Mumok (Vienna), and Macba (Barcelona).

Dau al Set was one of the first post-Civil War movements that aimed to renew Spanish art. It was founded in Barcelona in 1948. Following the example of Joan Miró, a group of young painters and critics who were open to French artistic currents met to take up pre-civil war Spanish surrealism and combine it with Cubism and new contemporary trends. The founders included the poet Joan Brossa and the painter Joan Ponç, who were soon joined by Antoni Tàpies, Arnau Puig, Modest Cuixart, and the critic Juan Eduardo Cirlot, among others. The group's main instrument for spreading its message was its magazine, also called *Dau al set*. The group played a key role in opening up Spanish art to outside influences. Its works tended toward material informalism and were the precursors of this movement in Spain. It broke up in 1954 after six years of activity.

See also: Chapter 2: Overview. Chapter 12: Overview.

Further Reading

Helmstufler Di Dio, Kelley, and Rosario Coppel. *Sculpture Collections in Early Modern Spain*. Burlington: Ashgate, 2013.

Whittaker, Andrew. *Speak the Culture: Spain*. London: Thorogood, 2008.

Street Art

In Spain, street art is very much alive. Apart from the two major cities of Spain (Madrid and Barcelona), Valencia, Zaragoza, and Ibiza also have a vibrant street art scene.

Sergio Hidalgo (1975–) is a multidimensional graffiti artist known as Sixeart, who started painting in the 1980s in Barcelona. Currently he has also exhibited his paintings in the N2 Gallery of Barcelona and the Alice Gallery of Brussels. He considers himself a self-taught artist. *Portrait of a Family while the Father Has Gone Hunting* is an example of his painting, in which he mixes the animal world with technological circuits that add the three dimensions to his distinctive style.

Gómez Bueno (1964–) is a Spanish artist living in Los Angeles since 1988. He has a Bachelor of Fine Arts from Universidad de La Laguna (Tenerife) and Universidad Complutense de Madrid. His situationist self-promotion tactics have included doctoring billboards so that they read "Gómez Bueno for President."

Boris Hoppek (1970–) is a German artist who lives in Barcelona. He has been making art on the streets since 1990. His work usually deals with political issues such as immigration, racism, and sexuality.

Ripo (Max Rippon aka Ripo) (1983–) was born and raised in New York, where he graduated from art school in 2005. He left his country to live in Barcelona, where he produces text-based work, influenced by calligraphy, sign painting, and graffiti.

Kenor (1976–) is the son of a Sevillian photographer and a painter. His art is usually characterized by swirling, abstract, and geometric forms with plenty of color and movement. He already has an impressive amount of work all over Europe.

Eltono (1975–) started writing graffiti and "decorating" the trains that connect Paris with his native suburb of Cergy-Pontoise in 1989, under the name Otone. When he arrived in Madrid a decade later he renamed himself Eltono (*el tono* is Spanish for "the tone") and began experimenting with the image of a tuning fork instead of a tag. Although he began his studies of plastic arts in Saint Denis, Paris, he moved to Madrid in 1999, when he was part of an international exchange program at the Universidad Complutense. Since then, he resides in Spain.

Nuria Mora (? -) is an artist based in Madrid. She started painting on the street with Eltono in an attempt to reach as many people as possible, whether they were sensitive or not to art in general. She still collaborates with Eltono, although her solo output has a calmer, more organic feel and often appears to merge into its surroundings.

Aryz (1988–), although born in the United States to Spanish parents, was raised since he was three years old in Spain. Aryz established his residence in Cardedeu, near Barcelona. His colorful artwork is usually huge.

Zosen (1978–), originally from Argentina, came to Barcelona in 1989 at the age of 12. He became an active member of the Barcelona graffiti scene during the 1990s and still paints frequently, sometimes collaborating with Pez and Aryz.

Pez (1976–) is a well-known graffiti artist who started in 1999 in his native Barcelona. Since then, his art has been exhibited all over the world, and his name appears as a constant reference in the world of graffiti. Pez now lives in Bogotá, Colombia, where he works.

According to www.fatcap.com, which has a list of graffiti artists around the world, Spain counts 45 artists and 182 pictures (researched on October 3, 2015), occupying the third position in street art in Europe after France and the United Kingdom.

See also: Chapter 2: Overview. Chapter 12: Overview. Chapter 16: Overview.

Further Reading

Bou, Louis. *NYC-BCN Street Art Revolution*. New York: Collins Design, 2006.

Chaffee, Lyman G. *Political Protest and Street Art: Popular Tools for Democratization in Hispanic Countries*. Westport: Greenwood, 1993.

Jake. *Mammoth Book of Street Art*. Philadelphia: Running Press Pub., 2012.

Martín, Luz A. *Textura: Valencia Street Art*. New York: Mark Batty, 2009.

Schacter, Rafael, and John Fekner. *The World Atlas of Street Art and Graffiti*. New Haven: Yale University Press, 2013.

Velázquez, Diego Rodríguez de Silva y

Diego Rodríguez de Silva y Velázquez (1599–1660) was born in Sevilla and at the age of 23 moved to Barcelona where he was promptly appointed court painter by Philip IV. Though he traveled to Italy twice, where he was greatly influenced by the art of Titian, Tintoretto, and Veronese, he always returned to his native country, where he worked as a portraitist to the court of King Philip IV of whom he was a favorite. Eventually he was named knight of the Order of Santiago, the highest order of Spain and his popularity allowed him to be free of the artistic limitations and financial burdens that most artists of his time faced. He had the luxury of leading a truly artistic life, one that included reading, traveling, and self-cultivation. Although he is one of the most important painters of the Spanish Golden Age, he was not prolific. The number of his paintings is estimated as between 110 and 120, many of which are housed at the Prado Museum in Madrid.

Although Velázquez painted numerous portraits of the king, and also of the royal family, he remained interested in painting those struggling in everyday life. Early works of this genre include *The Water Carrier of Seville* (1618) and *An Old Woman Cooking Eggs* (1618).

His court paintings include such works as *The Equestrian Portrait of the Count-Duke of Olivares* (1633) and *Philip IV in Brown and Silver* (1635). He also painted subjects of a mythical nature including his *Feast of Bacchus* (1692), *Toilet of Venus* (1647), *Mars* (1647), and his rather epic *The Fable of Arachne* (1655–1660)—one of Velázquez's most innovative canvases in conjunction with *Las Meninas* (1656). The fundamental question to be asked is what is the subject of these two paintings? Looking at the arrangements of the background and the use of different light and even illegibility of the face of one of the characters in the middle of the frame makes the viewer think about the influential genre of theatre at that time. Velázquez astutely manipulates our eyes in a manner that to a 21st-century viewer could be interpreted as visionary because of his use of light, which seems to anticipate the technique of cinematic action. Alfonso E. Pérez Sánchez, art historian and former head of the Museo del Prado, wrote, "Velázquez may be, forever, the most perfect example of the pure painter, that is, one who besides being gifted with a phenomenal eye also possesses the unerring hand that can freeze reality, suspending it within an instant of radiant life" (Domínguez et al., 1989).

See also: Chapter 1: Cities: Barcelona, Madrid, Sevilla, Valencia. Chapter 2: Overview. Chapter 12: Overview. Chapter 16: Overview.

Further Reading

Domínguez Ortiz, Antonio, et al. *Velázquez*. New York: Metropolitan Museum of Art: H.N. Abrams, 1989.

Moffitt, John F. *The Arts in Spain*. New York: Thames & Hudson, 1999.

Payne, Laura, et al. *Essential History of Art*. Bath: Parragon Publishing, 2003.

Tomlinson, Janis A. *From El Greco to Goya: Painting in Spain, 1561–1828*. New York: H. N. Abrams, 1997.

REFERENCES

Anderson, James M. *Guía arqueológica de España*. Madrid: Alianza, 1997.

Burry, Mark. *Gaudí Unseen: Completing the Sagrada Familia*. Berlin: Jovis Verlag, 2007.

Hunter, Sam, and John M. Jacobus. *Modern Art: Painting, Sculpture, Architecture*. New York: H. N. Abrams, 1985.

Hunter, Sam, and John M. Jacobus. *Modern Art*. 3rd ed. New York: Prentice Hall, 1992.

Hunter, Garry. *Street Art from Around the World*. London: Arcturus, 2012.

Illán Martín, Magdalena. *Carmen Laffón. La poética de la realidad en el arte español contemporáneo*. Sevilla: Universidad de Sevilla, 2012.

Íñigo, José María y David Zurdo. *Chupa la gamba. España es diferente...* Madrid: la esfera de los libros, 2013.

Intxausti, Aurora. "Tres siglos de tebeos españoles." *El País,* July 23, 2013.

Jake. *The Mammoth Book of Street Art*. London: Robinson, 2012.

Jodidio, Philip. *Architecture in Spain*. Los Angeles: Taschen, 2007.

Lechado, José Manuel. *La movida: una crónica de los 80*. Madrid: Algaba, 2005.

Lefort, Paul. "Historia de la pintura española." *deyave.com*. N.p.. Web. Oct 4, 2013. Deyave.com /Arte/Pintura/historia-de-la-pintura-espanola/Portada.html.

Martín, Luz A. *Textura: Valencia's Street Art*. Brooklyn, NY: Mark Batty Publisher, 2009.

Pascual, Carlos. *Art in Spain*. Madrid: Egesa, 2005.

Price, Bill. *Great Modern Architecture: The World's Most Spectacular Buildings*. Eastbourne: Canary Press, 2009.

Prout, Ryan, and Tilmann Altenberg. *Seeing in Spanish: From Don Quixote to Daddy Yankee. 22 Essays on Hispanic Visual Cultures*. Newcastle: Cambridge Scholars Publishing, 2011.

Regàs, Rosa, and Oliva María Rubio. *"Gauche divine."* Barcelona: Lunwerg, 2000.

Riambau, Esteve, and Casimiro Torreiro. *La Escuela de Barcelona: el cine de la 'gauche divine'*. Barcelona: Anagrama, 1999.

Riera, Carme. *La Escuela de Barcelona*. Barcelona: Anagrama, 1988.

Robinson, William H., et al. *Barcelona and Modernity: Picasso, Gaudí, Miró, Dalí*. Cleveland: Cleveland Museum of Art in association with Yale University Press, 2006.

Rosser-Owen, Mariam. *Islamic Arts from Spain*. New York: N. H. Abrams, 2010.

Ruiz Mantilla, Jesús. "La interminable espera por la Ley de Mecenazgo." *El País,* November 20, 2012.

Schama, Simon. *Landscape and Memory*. New York: Knopf, 1996.

Schroth, Sarah, ed. *Art in Spain and the Hispanic World: Essays in Honor of Jonathan Brown*. London: Paul Holberton Publishing, 2010.

Sureda, Joan. *The Golden Age of Spain: Painting, Sculpture, Architecture*. New York: Vendome Press, 2006.

Tomlinson, Janis. *From El Greco to Goya: Painting in Spain 1561–1828*. New York: Abrams, 1997.

VV.AA. *Essential History of ART*. Bath: Parragon Publishing, 2003.

VV.AA. *Museo Nacional Centro de Arte Reina Sofía*. Madrid: Visual Egap, 1992.

Zollo, Mike, and Phil Turk. *World Cultures: Spain*. London: Hodder Headline, 2004.

Websites

artespain.com

arteespana.com

fatcap.com

fotoruta.com

franciscodegoya.net

fundacionfuendetodosgoya.org

guiadelcomic.es

madrid-uno.com/society/movida.htm

marcaespana.es

mav.org.es

mcu.es/patrimonio

miquelbarcelo.org

museodelprado.es

spainisculture.com

tebeosfera.com

The Metropolitan Museum of Art: "The Art of the Nasrid Period" (1232–1492). http://www.metmuseum.org/toah/hd/nasr/hd_nasr.htm

CHAPTER 13

MUSIC AND DANCE

OVERVIEW

The first evidence of music from Spain can be found in the *jarchas* and *cantigas*, which date back to medieval times. One of the first Spaniards who wrote about music was San Isidoro de Sevilla in the sixth century. Religious music still has a considerable influence on contemporary music. The organist and organ maker Ramón González de Amezúa Noriega (1921–) and José López Calo (1922–), a Jesuit priest who has written over 60 books on musicology, are two contemporary examples of the presence of religion in Spanish music. Before them, Cristóbal de Morales (1500–1553), together with Tomás Luis de Victoria (1548–1611), Francisco de Salinas (1513–1590), and Francisco Guerrero (1528–1599), are considered golden examples of Spanish Renaissance music.

Mateo Albéniz (1755–1831) was a Spanish composer in the 18th century who dedicated his musical talent mainly to writing sonatas, including "Larrañaga," "Gallés," and "Misón." However, the most important Spanish figure during the Classicism period in Spain was without a doubt Crisóstomo Arriaga (1806–1826). Like Wolfgang Amadeus Mozart, Arriaga was a child prodigy who composed his first opera *Los esclavos felices* (*The Happy Slaves*) in 1820 at the age of 13, and music for string quartets when he was 16. Arriaga also wrote church music including *cantatas* (i.e., Agar, All'Aurora, Patria) and *Salve Regina* (Et vitam venture saeculi), among many other compositions. He died at the age of 20, due to exhaustion and tuberculosis. The Teatro Arriaga in Bilbao was named after him.

In the 20th century, two Spanish composers enlightened the global music scene with their compositions and theories. One was Joaquín Rodrigo (Sagunto 1901–1999), who is one of the greatest Spanish composers. He was named First Marqués de los Jardines de Aranjuez—Spain's highest civilian honor—in 1996. Among his long musical repertoire, *Concierto de Aranjuez* (1939) is his best-known work, which has been incorporated into several film soundtracks. The second is Ramón Barce Benito (1928–2008), who is considered the originator of European vanguard music. Barce created a harmonic system of his own, which he called "harmony of levels." He is one of the representatives of the Generation of '51, and founder of *Grupo Nueva Música* (1958). More recently, the works of Jesús Torres (1965–), who won the National Music Award in 2012, and Elena Mendoza (1973–), who was the first woman to win the National Music Award (2010), both exemplify the current situation of many musicians in Spain.

GENERATION OF '51

Because of the Spanish Civil War, Spain did not evolve musically like other European countries until the 1950s with musicians such as Luis de Pablo (i.e., Módulos We, who also introduced Spain's first electronic music studio), Cristóbal Halffter (i.e., Microforms), Ramón Barce (i.e., Canadá Trío), and Carmelo Bernaola (i.e., Heterofonías). Another prominent Generation of '51 member was Juan Hidalgo, who explored experimental forms influenced by the American composer John Cage. The latter also influenced Spanish musicians in the 1980s and 1990s, when there was a boom of different trends of music.

Mendoza lives in Berlin, which can be seen as another example of Spaniards who go abroad in order to pursue their professional career.

Like Spanish cuisine, every region has its own distinctive heritage with its own regional music and dance. In Catalunya the dance is the *sardana*; in the Basque country it is the *zortzicos*, and in Aragón it is the *jota*. In Galicia and Asturias they play the *muñeiras, alboradas, saudades*, and *pandeiradas* while in the two regions of Castilla they dance the *jota segoviana* (of Segovia), apart from originating the *seguidillas, las canciones de Ronda, los pasacalles*, and *la rueda*. Other popular dances are: *el fandango, el chotis, el pasodoble, el paloteo* or *ball de bastons, las pardicas, la charrada, el contrapás, las habas verdes, la isa canaria, la revolada, los verdiales*, and *la rumba*. Although the last is originally from Cuba, different Spanish groups have been able to adapt it into distinctive Spanish songs. Musicians such as Peret, El Pescaílla, and bands like The Gipsy Kings, Los Manolos, Estopa, and more recently Melendi have achieved a huge success with this particular fusion sound, in which they manage to mix rumba, flamenco, and pop successfully.

As Eva Moreda explains in her article, there was a monolithic Spanish identity imposed upon the whole population during Franco's dictatorship (1939–1975). *La copla* and *la zarzuela* became the two most popular styles of music during Franco's time. Nowadays, contemporary Spanish music does not refer only to rural music (*copla*) or to Spain's version of opera (*zarzuela*). However, this used to be the case under Franco, who attempted to construct "Spanish folklore as a monolithic, essentialist entity of preeminently rural roots for national conscience-building" (Moreda 2012). In fact, it is not a coincidence that the late 1970s and early 1980s witnessed the Golden Age of Spanish popular music, partly due to Spain's process of internationalization.

Spain has embraced multiculturalism in the new millennium. Nowadays Spanish music has become more international and it offers a huge variety of styles. Perhaps the most apparent one is the strong influence from English-speaking countries, mainly from the U.K and the U.S. As the popular singer Ruth Lorenzo points out, "the English language is a reality in Spain" (Piña 2014). This explains the abundance of groups with names such as Dover, Deluxe, Arizona Baby, Russian Red, Love of Lesbian, and Sweet California, who also sing in English.

The Spanish pop tune "Así Me Gusta A Mí (X-Ta Sí, X-Ta No)" by Chimo Bayo (1961–) reached number one in Spain, Greece, Israel, Japan, and some Latin American countries in 1991. The single "Macarena" by Los del Río became another international hit in 1995 and 1996, and it was ranked number one greatest one-hit wonder of all time by *VH1* in 2002. Las Ketchup manufactured a huge global hit with the song "Aserejé" in 2002, which became number one in 27 countries. It has sold over seven million copies worldwide, which places it in the category of one of the best-selling singles of all time. More recently, the song "Loca People" by Sak Noel became another one hit wonder in Spain, Austria, Belgium, Denmark, Holland, the U.K., Canada, and Sweden in 2011.

One current aspect of the Spanish music scene is the disparity between the super famous singers/bands and the underground groups/singers. In other words, there are massive record-sales by a few groups, on the one hand, while, on the other hand, there is a proliferation of alternative bands. The latter remain widely ignored by the big corporations. In fact, the only television channel that fully supports independent music in Spain is Sol Música. Their website and their free iTunes application is loaded with a large number of current videos and information on music festivals across the country. Another key platform on independent Spanish music is the *Unión Fonográfica Independiente* (*UFI*, which stands for Independent Phonographic Union)—the Spanish association of independent music publishers and record producers. Their website ufimusica .com also offers plenty of relevant information.

Spain is very diverse in music regionally, nationally, and more recently, internationally. For instance, you can hear global music like Electronic; Hip Hop; Indie; funk; and poet-singers known in Spain as *cantautores*, who differ from the *canción protesta* in the sense that they do not usually include a political message in their lyrics. However, due to the long economic crisis in Spain (2008–), many contemporary singers add a social meaning to their lyrics. This is the case of Enrique Bunbury's popular songs "Despierta" ("Wake Up") and Amaral's "Ratonera" ("Mousetrap").

Electronic music in Spain started in the 1990s with groups like OBK's first album *Llámalo sueño* (Call It a Dream, 1991), Locomía (i.e., Locovox 1991), and Fundación Tony Manero (1996–). The influence of the Balearic island of Ibiza as a factory of chill-out music also played a significant role in the techno dance music industry around the world with well-known disco venues like Pacha, Privilege, and Amnesia. Additionally, Café del mar and well-known DJs like José Padilla (1955–) have made a big impact on techno music. Cristian Varela, DJ Panko, Ismael Rivas, Los Suruba, Julio Navas, and Álex Under are also recognized DJs. Perhaps the most important DJ event organized in Spain is the Sónar Festival in Barcelona.

Joaquín Cortés (Córdoba 1969–), Tamara Rojo (Montreal 1974–), and Farruquito (Sevilla 1982–) are renowned international dancers. Spain also has a National Ballet located in Madrid. It was founded by the Ministry of Culture in 1978 and its first director was the famous dancer Antonio Gades (1936–2004). Throughout the years, it has received numerous international awards. However, the lack of official support plus the 21 percent tax increase on any cultural event in Spain has had two major consequences. First, many artists—in particular, classical musicians and dancers—have had to leave Spain in order to excel in their professional fields. Second, because of the lack of audience, several cultural theatres, cinemas, and musical arenas have been forced to close down in Spain since 2008, with that trend continuing to date.

New cultural forums like La Casa Encendida (2002) and the transformation of a former slaughterhouse Matadero (2007) into an Arts Center, both located in Madrid, are two modern spaces to help young artists reflect on the contemporary sociocultural environment. Madrid is also home to the Nave de Música, which is a multifunctional building for music, small concerts, and radio studios.

One of Matadero's main goals is to engage in the process of hybridization, which is currently happening among different genres of music. On the other hand, there is a problem with regards to music space in Spain due to the lack of large buildings entirely dedicated to music concerts. In other words, apart from numerous medium-sized auditoriums across the country such as the Auditorio de Tenerife (2003) with 1,616 available seats, the multifunctional Palau Sant Jordi in Barcelona—which was built for the Olympic Games 1992 and has over 24,000 seats—still remains the largest covered building to hold major music concerts.

According to the Spanish association of music producers in Spain, PROMUSICAE (Asociación de Productores de Música de España), the 10 top-selling albums in Spain in 2012 consisted of six national, two British, and two American artists. In other words, 66 percent of the best-selling albums in 2012 were national Spanish music. But what is national music in Spain's 21st century? Looking closely at the type of music that many of the well-known groups are creating, the quintessential Spanish formula appears clear. Successful Spanish national music is synonymous with fusion. This consumption of fusion (or hybrid music) exemplifies Spain as a multicultural country in terms of taste but, more interestingly, in the sense that Spanish musicians are able to produce a distinctive hybridism or *mestizaje* in their music. By extension this particular taste and creation based on fusion defines the authentic essence of Spain.

Flamenco fusion is perhaps the most popular music played nowadays in Spain. Among the favorite flamenco fusion artists is Kiko Veneno (1952–), who is a multidisciplinary musician moving between flamenco, rumba, and modern pop. Santiago Auserón (Zaragoza 1954–) is another versatile artist who successfully integrates pop, rock, and flamenco. He got his start as the singer-songwriter for Radio Futura, which was a famous rock band in the 1980s. In 1992, when the band disintegrated, he began his solo career under the name Juan Perro. Auserón has also published books on philosophy and music. Diego el cigala (1968–) is another good example of fusion music; he has won three Latin Grammy awards (2004, 2006, and 2011). He is constantly integrating other genres into flamenco like *jazzmenco*. His well-known album *Lágrimas negras* (2003) successfully combined Latin music like the bolero and Cuban *son* with flamenco. More recently, *Romance de la luna Tucumana* (2013) was nominated for a Latin Grammy of the same year, and once again combines flamenco with popular Latin music such as tango. Chambao (2002–) is a flamenco-electronic band that effectively mixes flamenco with "chill out" music. Their first album *Flamenco Chill* (2002)—and, in particular, *Pokito a Poko* (2005)—helped establish them in the current musical scene of Spain.

Jazz is still relatively new in Spain. In fact, the Universitat Politècnica de Valencia organized—for the first time in Spain—an international conference dedicated to jazz music on November 28–30, 2013. Among the most important Spanish jazz musicians was Pedro Iturralde (1929–), who combined jazz and flamenco in a radical fusion. In 1967 he recorded the legendary *Jazz Flamenco*, with the participation of Paco de Lucía.

Tete Montoliu (1933–1997), who was born blind, is another important jazz musician from Spain. During the 1960s he played in numerous concerts in New York. He consolidated his reputation as the leader of the hard bop movement in the 1970s. His album *Tete!* (1974) is a good example of his jazz abilities with the piano. La Locomotora Negra is the oldest Spanish jazz band originally from Catalunya, which started in the 1970s. Their first record was *La Locomotora Negra Number 1* (1982). They have recorded over a dozen albums. Carles Benavent (1954–) is a well-known bassist of jazz and flamenco. He has collaborated with a long list of artists not only from Spain but abroad, like Miles Davis in *Live in Montreaux* (1993), Gil Goldstein in *Zebra Coast* (1991), and several times with the Spanish jazz guitarist Max Sunyer. Chano Domínguez (1960–) is another recognized jazz musician from Spain. His early records already show a strong influence of flamenco, which was first introduced by his father. He has released more than a dozen records, from *Chano* (1992) to his latest *Flamenco Sketches* (2012). Chano was the only Spanish jazz musician included in Fernando Trueba's film *Calle 54* (2000), which is dedicated to Latin jazz.

The list of records sold over the Internet is very similar to the list of records sold in stores. However, Spanish music industry sales dropped 12 percent in 2013, registering a historic low, while the digital market, in particular selling on streaming, increased 18 percent in the same year. Due to the economic crisis, some musicians are financing their own albums through crowdfunding before they are even made. Based on the Latin Grammy Award created in the United States in 2000 and, arguably, a good indicator of the global music industry in Latin countries, Spain occupied the third position in 2012 with a total of 57 awards, behind Mexico (131) and Brazil (125).

A study on "Consumer Attitudes towards Music Piracy: A Spanish Case Study" written by three academics from the University of Valencia pointed out that regional music, ethnic music, and world rock were the least preferred as opposed to pop rock from Spain and international and Latino pop rock. Also, in terms of owning a record collection, "23 percent said they had more than 100 CDs" (Cuadrado et al. 2009).

Among Spain's best guitarists of all time are Francisco Tárrega (1852–1909), Andrés Segovia (1893–1987), and Paco de Lucía (1947–2014). Spain has also produced great pianists such as Isaac Albéniz (1860–1909), Manuel de Falla (1876–1946), and Alicia de Larrocha (1923–2009).

Apart from guitarists and pianists, Spain has been the birthplace of only five internationally renowned instrumentalists. Pablo Sarasate (1844–1908) was one of the world's best concert violinists. He was a precocious child who gave his first violin recital at the age of seven. Pau Casals (1876–1973) is considered one of the greatest cello soloists of all time. One of his most famous compositions is "Hymn to the United Nations," or "Hymn to Peace," composed in Puerto Rico during his exile. Casals was an anti-Francoist and he refused to perform in countries unless they denounced Spain's dictatorial regime. His mother was originally from Puerto Rico, where he resided since the 1950s and where he died at the age of 96. Nicanor Zabaleta Zala (1907–1993) is considered one of the most important harpists of the 20th century. He invented the eight-pedal harp. Several contemporary musicians composed for him, including Joaquín Rodrigo and Alberto Ginastera. Carmelo Alonso Bernaola (1929–2002) was mainly a composer of marches and other types of music for bands as well as a clarinetist. Jordi Savall Bernardett (1941–) is currently considered by critics to be one of the world's greatest viola da gamba players as well as a musicologist.

Spain has also produced a significant number of experts who write about music (musicologists). Musicology became a degree in Spanish universities in the late 1980s. In 1986 the Goya Film Awards included, for the first time, the category of Best Original Film Score. As Lluís i Falcó points out, "the most important thing about the Goya awards is their media impact" (Falcó 2010). Felipe Pedrell (1841–1922) was the creator of Spanish musicology. He also created what is known as Spain's musical nationalism. His opera *Los Pirineos* constitutes an example of the *Renaixença* cultural movement, which originated in Catalunya in the 19th century. Jesús Guridi (1886–1961) is considered one of the founding fathers of Basque opera. Josep Soler Sardá (1935–) is one of Spain's foremost musicologists. He has also composed 16 operas and many symphonies and concerts. Juan José Falcón Sanabria (1936–) is a conductor and composer. Among his works are *Canarias canta* (1982), *Ergo* (1986), the soundtrack for the film *Guarapo* (1987), and, more recently, the opera *La hija del cielo* (2007).

Other contemporary composers include Mauricio Sotelo (1961–), César Camarero (1962–), and Alberto Posadas (1967–), who won the National Music Award in 2011.

Further Reading

Boyd, Malcom, and Juan José Carreras, eds. *Music in Spain during the Eighteenth Century*. Cambridge: Cambridge University Press, 1998.

Klugherz, Laura. *A Bibliographical Guide to Spanish Music for the Violin and Viola, 1900–1997*. Westport: Greenwood Press, 1998.

Kreitner, Kenneth. *The Church Music of Fifteenth-Century Spain*. Woodbridge: The Boydell Press, 2004.

Llano, Samuel. *Whose Spain? Negotiating 'Spanish Music' in Paris, 1908–1929*. New York: Oxford University Press, 2013.

Ribera, Julian. *Music in Ancient Arabia and Spain*. Peterborough: Vincentpress, 2014.

Canción Protesta—Protest Songs

During the last part of the Franco regime, 1960–1975, Spain begun to receive external cultural influences from abroad. For instance, Bob Dylan's *Blowing in the Wind* (1961) became an anthem for a generation around the world. His impact on the Spanish scene generated a type of music associated with social injustices popularly known as *canción protesta* (protest songs), which in the Catalunya region is known as *Nova Cançó* with artists like Pau Riva, Oriol Tranvía, Ovidi Montllor, María del Mar Bonet, and Joan Manuel Serrat. While the Nova Cançó was gaining popularity, a similar phenomenon was occurring in Madrid with figures such as Moncho Alpuente, Rosa León, Hilario Camacho, and Luis Eduardo Aute. More recently, the music of Rosana (i.e., *Lunas rotas* 1996), Ismael Serrano (i.e., *Principio de incertidumbre* 2003), and Pedro Guerra (i.e., songs like "Contamíname" and "Mararía") have influenced the canción protesta. Paco Ibáñez (1934–) has set to music some of the best-known Hispanic poetry ever written. In 1964 he released his first album *Lorca y Góngora*, with a sleeve design by Salvador Dalí. His songs were soon adopted as anthems against the dictatorship of Franco.

Other important canción protesta singers include José Antonio Labordeta (1935–2010), who had one of the most unique voices of the cultural scene in recent decades. His song "Canto a la libertad" ("I Sing to Freedom") became a hymn to freedom. He was also one of the most popular faces of television in the 1990s thanks to the program "Un país en la mochila" ("A Country in a Backpack"). Labordeta was also a political member of the Aragonese Union party.

Joan Manuel Serrat (1943–) is one of the most prominent singer-songwriters of Spain's 20th century. His first album *Una guitarra* was recorded when he was 22. In 1967 he achieved a number one hit with two songs composed in Catalan. In 2006 he received the Gold Medal for Merit in Work. His song "Mediterráneo" became one of Spain's popular anthems.

Luis Eduardo Aute (1943–) had as his first vocation painting, but he is better known for his outstanding contribution to Spanish music. He was a member of the group Los Tigres, and composed songs with a distinct air of protest for the singer Massiel. His first book of poetry was *La matemática del espejo* (1975, *The Mathematics of the Mirror*). He has worked with many artists and composed music for numerous films and plays. One of his famous songs is "Al Alba" (1975), which is a condemnation of the Franco regime.

Mari Trini (1947–2009) composed her first song at the age of 14 entitled "Mi pájaro." She travelled to London to act for the BBC. In Paris, she studied singing for over six years. Given her songs' tone of protest, during the 1960s she became the muse for intellectual movements of the time. Over the course of her career, she acquired 18 platinum records. Her song "Una estrella en mi jardín" was one of the most emblematic and best-selling popular songs of its day.

María del Mar Bonet (1947–) became internationally known as "the voice of the Mediterranean." In 1965, she was invited by the Youth Music Association of Palma to sing in what would be her first public recital. Two years later she moved to Barcelona to become part of "Els Setze Jutges," a pioneer New Song movement. In 1968, the censorship of the Franco regime forbid her to sing "Què volen aquesta gent?" During the early 1970s, she traveled through Europe and recorded a live record at the Olympia in Paris. Her interest in music of ethnic origins led her to record "Anells d'Aigua" (1985) in collaboration with the Tunisian Traditional Music Ensemble.

Lluis Llach (1948–) is a crucial figure in the Catalans' Nova Cançó. Llach was a member of the group "Els Setze Jutges" in 1967, which later would change to Nova Cançó. His first album *Les seves primers cançós* was recorded in 1969, and in 1970 he made his debut at the Teatro Español in Madrid. Llach was the first non-opera singer to perform at the Gran Teatre del Liceu of Barcelona in 1979. Llach's song "L'estaca" (1968) constitutes a hymn against Franco's dictatorship.

Joaquín Sabina (1949–) is another key figure with regards to the genre of protest songs in Spain. Sabina wrote his first lyrics when he was 14, and he exiled to London in 1970 for political reasons. After three years in England, he returned to Spain where he recorded his first album, *Inventario* (Inventory, 1978). Since then, Sabina has established himself as a very successful musician with over 20 records. Also, he has written a dozen books dealing mainly with poetry and essays.

See also: Chapter 2: Overview; Franco, Francisco. Chapter 13: Overview.

Further Reading

Marco, Tomas. *Spanish Music in the Twentieth Century*. Cambridge: Harvard University Press, 1993.

Martínez, Silvia, and Héctor Fouce, eds. *Made in Spain: Studies in Popular Music*. New York: Routledge, 2013.

Copla

Spanish music is inextricably identified with *flamenco, zarzuela, cuplé,* and *copla.* The latter is actually a mix of the first three and it appeared at the beginning of the 20th century. The *copla* consists of a fusion of cuplé, flamenco without a guitar, and sometimes with an orchestra—an element derived from the zarzuela. A typical copla is an emotional song that deals with love, jealousy, and betrayal. Nevertheless, at the beginning of the 20th century, the lyrics of a copla referred directly to social injustices experienced by marginalized people like prostitutes and the poor. Sincere and sentimental, the copla touched the emotions of many Spaniards. It was extremely popular between 1940–1960 during the regime of Franco, who was an admirer of the copla. One example of a well known copla is for instance "¡Ay, pena, penita, pena!," which was written by the Quintero brothers in 1932, and recently has been adapted into a short film *Ay pena* by Elisa Cepedal (2012, coproduced by U.K. and Spain). Antonio Quintero, Rafael de León, and Manuel Quiroga wrote more than five thousand coplas.

The prodigal voice of Joselito in the film *El pequeño Ruiseñor* (1956) and Juan Valderrama's *El Emigrante* (1958) deserve attention as they combine copla and movie, which became a virtual hymn for thousands of Spaniards who abandoned the country after the civil war. Valderrama is one of the greatest male copla singers of all time. He appeared as an actor in seven highly successful films. With more than 1,500 recordings, he remained actively performing until his death. Also, the composer Juan Solano not only cultivated the copla, but also ventured into symphonic, pop, and film soundtrack genres such as *Bienvenido Mister Marshall, El último cuplé,* and *Carmen la de Ronda.* His last composition was the theme music for the television program *La Copla* on the regional channel Canal Sur in Andalucía.

Other great copla singers include Concha Piquer ("Romance de la Reina Mercedes," "Eugenia de Montijo," "La parrala,," "Tatuaje," "Ojos Verdes"), Imperio Argentina

("Antonio Vargas Heredia "Falsa monea"), Juanita Reina ("Capote de grana y oro," "Lola la piconera," "Yo soy esa," "Callejuela sin salía," "Francisco alegre"), Lola Flores ("La Guapa de Cádiz," "Copla y Bandera," "La Zarzamora," "La niña de Fuego"), Rocío Jurado ("Como una ola," "Señora," "Como yo te amo," "Se nos rompió el amor"), Rafael Farina ("Mi Salamanca," "Vino amargo," "A Barcelona llegan los oles," "Twist del faraón"), Manolo Escobar ("El Porompompero," "Suspiros de España," "España cañi," "Por los caminos de España"), Antonio Molina ("Soy minero," "Toros y coplas," "Adiós a España," "Mujer extranjera," "Como en España ni hablar"), el Fary ("Toro guapo," "Apatrullando la ciudad," "el cuponazo," "el bichito de amor"), and Carlos Cano ("Verde, blanca y verde," "María la Portuguesa," "La murga de los currelantes").

More recently, other copla singers who are revitilizing the traditional Spanish genre include Pasión Vega (*Banderas de nadie* 2003), Isabel Pantoja (*Sinfonía de la Copla* 2006), Estrella Morente (*Mujeres* 2006), Pastora Soler (*Toda mi verdad* 2007), Soledad Giménez (*La Felicidad* 2008), Miguel Poveda (*Coplas del querer* 2009), Pablo Alborán (*Pablo Alborán* 2011), and Enrique Vargas, known as "el príncipe gitano" (*el Principe Gitano* 2012).

See also: Chapter 2: Overview. Chapter 6: Overview; Immigration; Income-Level Groups; Roma Society.

Further Reading

Biddle, Ian, and Vanessa Knights,.eds. *Music, National Identity, and the Politics of Location: Between the Global and the Local.* Burlington: Ashgate, 2008.

Pring-Mill, Robert. *The Uses of Spanish-American So-Called "Protest" Song.* Liverpool: Institute of Popular Music, 1993.

Cuplé

Popular music was a huge phenomenon all over the world at the beginning of the 20th century, with the foxtrot, Charleston, and jazz in the United States and the birth of the bolero, tango, and mambo in Latin America. Spain also created a distinctive music genre which Spaniards call *cuplé*. As Fernando Operé and Carrie B. Douglass point out, the word appears for the first time in the librettos of *zarzuelas* around 1880. Its etymology comes for the French word *couplet*, which refers to a type of melody sung with a monologue. The first singers or *cupletistas* were women, although in the 1920s some transsexuals appeared on the scene. The origin of the cuplé can be traced back to 1893, with the German singer Augusta Bergés, who revolutionized the apathetic society of the time with her cuplé "La pulga" ("The Flea"). Here she deliberately performed a type of erotic dance without ever being naked while she was trying to find the flea on her body.

From this erotic ambience the *salones* came into being, where the *cupletistas* would dance provocatively for men. In 1912 there were around 6,000 salones in Spain, especially in Madrid and Barcelona. They were shows "only for men." The term *vedette* appeared at that time. The most popular timeframe of the cuplé was between 1900–1950. Among the most famous singers were Pastora Imperio, Bella Dorita, Julita Fons, and Raquel Meller. The latter became legendary also in Paris and New York. Some of the most famous cuplés are *Clavelitos, Ven y ven, El Polichinela, La violetera,* and *El relicario.* During the 1960s, Carmen Sevilla and Sara Montiel achieved popularity. The latter gained success as a cinema star not only in Spain but also in Hollywood, becoming the first Spanish woman who succeed in both the music and cinema industries. More recently, the female singer Martirio mixes cuplé and flamenco.

The cuplé was very successful during the first part of the 20th century, when Spain was in crisis due to the civil war and dictatorship. Ironically the cuplé is back in the new Millenium, when Spain is once again in crisis. This is the case of new cabaret-concerts as an updated version of the cuplé. For instance, in Madrid alone in December 2012, the public has enjoyed three successful performances: *Showtime Burlesque* (in the theater Arlequín), *La Mirilla* (in Garage Lumière), and *Vuelve el Cabaret* (in Joy Eslava). Other cities like Barcelona (in El Molino) and Alcalá de Henares (in Corral de Comedias) are also currently enjoying the return of the cuplé converted into a cabaret.

See also: Chapter 12: Overview. Chapter 13: Overview; Copla.

Further Reading

Torres Hortelano, Lorenzo J. *Spain: Directory of World Cinema*. Bristol: Intellect, 2011.

Woods Peiró, Eva. *White Gypsies: Race and Stardom in Spanish Musicals*. Minneapolis: University of Minnesota Press, 2012.

Flamenco

Originating in the region of Andalucía, *flamenco* is without a doubt Spain's most distinctive music. Flamenco has become a universal dance and music. In fact, 2013 was named the official International Year of Flamenco. Flamenco music includes *cante* (singing), *toque* (guitar playing), *baile* (dance), and *palmas* (handclapping). There are many types of flamenco, but the most genuine one is the *cante jondo*.

In 2010 UNESCO declared flamenco one of the masterpieces of the Oral and Intangible Heritage of Humanity. One example of its popularity around the world is the fact that currently there are more flamenco academies in Japan than in Spain. The Cátedra de Flamencology de Jérez (1958) was the first to grant flamenco an academic status. The Universidad de Granada in 1987, and more recently the universities of Córdoba (2004) and Sevilla (2012), also offer a Ph.D. in flamenco studies. Nowadays, there are many flamenco dancers and singers not only in Spain but across the globe, for instance, the Canadian flamenco guitarists Jesse Cook and Harry Grimwood-Knight.

Flamenco dancers in Costa Dorada, Spain. Flamenco is not only popular in the south, where it was born, but all over the country. It has become the symbolic dance of Spain. (Corel)

La Niña de los Peines (1890–1969) was considered by Federico García Lorca to be the prototype of the charismatic singer. The Cultural Department of the Regional Government of Andalucía declared her voice to be "Property of Cultural Interest" in 1996. La Niña de la Puebla (1908–1999) was one of the greatest flamenco and Andalusian copla singers of all times. Her voice was particularly outstanding in *tonadillas, fandangos,* and *malagueñas.* Blinded shortly after birth, she began her special education and musical training when she was eight years old. Antonio Mairena (1909–1983) is another central reference in the history of flamenco because of his technique in singing as well as his own research into the subject of flamenco. Lola Flores (1923–1995) was known artistically as "La Faraona" and is considered the "Queen of Flamenco." Apart from recording albums, she also appeared in many films such as *Los tres amores de Lola, Maricruz, La Faraona,* and *María de la O.* She married Antonio González "el Pescaílla" and they had three children, who also became famous musicians (Antonio, Lolita, and Rosario Flores). Bernarda de Utrera (1927–2009) was a specialist in singing *bulerías.* In 1952 she participated in the film *Duende y misterio del flamenco* (*The Spirit and the Mystery of Flamenco*) by Edgar Neville. That same year she recorded her first album with her sister Fernanda, under the direction of Antonio Mairena. Antonio Fernández Díaz (1932–), known as Fosforito, has made over 20 recordings in which he sings all styles and variants of flamenco. La Paquera de Jerez (1934–2004) owned one of the most passionate flamenco voices of all time, and was especially renowned for singing *fandangos* and *bulerías.* Her heartfelt performance was captured by Carlos Saura in his film *Flamenco* (1995).

CANTE JONDO

Cante hondo or *cante jondo* (literally, deep song) derives from the Hebrew *jontoh*, which refers to songs sung on holidays. Flamenco began to be popular at the beginning of the 18th century, particularly in the region of Andalucía among the gypsy communities. The *saeta* is an example of the Jewish and Christian religious music performed on the Iberian Peninsula related to *cante jondo*; it is a type of flamenco characterized by expressing the sorrows and joys of daily life. Normally the cante jondo is sung in religious processions which happen at night, and the first word of the lyrics is usually *¡Ay!*, echoing the nocturnal sorrow of previous nomads traveling in unkonwn lands. There are several cante jondo festivals in Andalucía. This type of music subsequently influenced other ethnic music such as regional folk music developed by groups like Jarcha (Andalucía), Los Sabandeños (Canary Islands), Voces Ceibes (Galicia), Ez Dok Amairu (Euskadi), Al Tall (Valencia), and Grup de Folk (Catalunya). The latter is associated with the *Nova Cançó*.

Other contemporary flamenco artists include El Lebrijano (1941–), who is well-known for his cante jondo style as well as introducing the symphony orchestra into his flamenco creations. Enrique Morente (1942–2010) was a leading figure of the renewal of modern flamenco. He worked in all types of cante jondo. Camarón de la Isla (1950–1992) is considered to be one of the greatest flamenco singers ever, who revolutionized the art of flamenco singing. His success spread across international borders. *Soy gitano* (1989) is still the best-selling album in the history of flamenco. Carmen Linares (1951–) cultivated all of the varied traditions within flamenco. She combined traditional *cante* with the search for new forms of expression. She collaborated on the film *Flamenco* (1995) by Carlos Saura. Miguel Poveda (1973–) is currently one of the most successful flamenco voices; he won the 1993 Lámpara Minera Award at Las Minas Festival in La Unión (Murcia), which is the most prestigious award in the world of flamenco. Apart from singing all over the world, Poveda has also participated in several films directed by Bigas Luna, Carlos Saura, Nicolas Klotz, and Pedro Almodóvar. La Niña Pastori (1978–) is also a current famous female flamenco singer. Her album *Esperando verte* (2009) received a Latin Grammy Award, as did *La orilla de mi pelo* in 2011.

See also: Chapter 1: Overview. Chapter 6: Overview; Income-Level Groups, Roma Society. Chapter 11: Overview; Generation of '27. Chapter 13: Overview.

Further Reading

Hass, Ken, and Gwynne Edwards. *Flamenco!* New York: Thames & Hudson, 2000.

Thiel-Cramér, Barbro, and Sheila Smith. *Flamenco: The Art of Flamenco, Its History and Development until our Days.* Lidingö: Remark, 1991.

Washabaugh, William. *Flamenco Music and National Identity in Spain.* Burlington: Ashgate, 2012.

Iconic Musicians

María Malibrán (1808–1836) became an opera legend despite having lived a very short life. The public, critics, and composers, such as Bellini, Rossini, or Donizetti, were all captivated by her. At the age of 17 she debuted at London's Royal Theatre. Soon after, the García-Sitches family travelled to New York, where María married the banker Eugene Malibrán, and was thereafter referred to as "La Malibrán." She could change from pure soprano in *Desdemona* to contralto as Angelina in *La Cenerentola*. She also appeared as a character in a poem by William McGonagall.

Xavier Cugat (1900–1990) was a very versatile artist who successfully combined his talents as a singer, songwriter, actor, director, and screenwriter. However, he is well remembered for his Spanish American orchestra, which played in major Hollywood movies. For instance, in 1940, his recording of "Perfidia" became a big hit. Cugat followed trends closely, making records for the conga, the mambo, the cha-cha-cha, and the twist when each was in fashion during his time. In 1943, "Brazil" was another big hit, reaching No. 17 on the Billboard Top 100.

Montserrat Caballé (1933–), a soprano *tessitura* opera singer. is known for her vocal technique and her performances of the *bel canto* repertoire. She is considered one of the best sopranos of all time. Her repertoire includes over 90 operas. She achieved international fame when she replaced Marilyn Horne in *Lucrezia Borgia* at Carnegie Hall in 1965. Through her interpretation of "Barcelona," the official song of the Barcelona Olympic Games (1992), with Freddie Mercury, her voice became familiar to people of all ages.

Teresa Berganza (1935–) has acted on stages all over the world, performing a wide ranging repertoire of Spanish and European music. One of the highlights of her career was her performance during the Universal Exhibition in Sevilla at the La Maestranza theatre, where she sang *Carmen*, by Bizet. In 2002 together with her daughter, the soprano Cecilia Lavilla, Berganza gave one of her last stage performances at the Liceo theatre in Barcelona.

Plácido Domingo (1941–) is renowned as one of the greatest tenors of all time. His career is filled with successes and awards. His debut was as a baritone at the Degollado Theatre in Guadalajara (Mexico) in 1959. He recorded the official song for the World Cup held in Spain in 1982. He has performed at the most important opera houses around the world with a repertoire of nearly one hundred different roles. Domingo has been directed by the most prestigious directors. Together with José Carreras and Luciano Pavorotti, Domingo formed "The Three Tenors," the trio that made opera more accessible to a wider audience.

Daniel Barenboim (1942–) is a well-known pianist and conductor who debuted in Buenos Aires in 1949. His family moved to Israel in 1952. He began working as a conductor from an early age. In addition to symphonic music, he has worked in genres such as opera and ballet. He has gained recognition for his work to promote music. He founded West-Eastern Divan Workshop and Orchestra in 1999, which has been based in Sevilla since 2002. He is the first musician to give annual BBC Reith Lectures.

José Nieto (1942–) specializes in cinema soundtracks. He has six Goya awards to date for best soundtrack. He started out by playing drums and working on musical arrangements for a record company, before he made his film debut with Jaime de Armiñán. Without renouncing his jazz origins, he composed works with a flamenco influence. He composed the music for the Universal Exhibition in Sevilla in 1992. He has also created music for BBC documentaries and over 30 soundtracks for Spanish films.

Julio Iglesias (Madrid 1943–) is considered the Frank Sinatra of Spain. Iglesias is a well-known singer of ballads around the world. Due to a car accident in 1963, he started to write songs such as "La vida sigue igual" ("Life Goes On"), which became a major hit, winning the first prize at the Benidorn International Song Festival in 1968. Since then, he has achieved tremendous success nationally and internationally. He has sold more records than any other Spanish singer to date (over 260 million). His son, Enrique Iglesias, appears to be following his father's success in the music industry, having already sold over 100 million albums worldwide.

Alberto Iglesias (San Sebastián 1955–) is a composer of numerous film sound tracks. His career in films began with his brother, José Luis, and the director, Montxo Armendáriz. After creating the sound tracks for various feature films, he worked with Julio Médem and Pedro Almodóvar, with whom he won national and international awards. He has been nominated on various occasions for the Oscars in Hollywood in the category of Best Original Soundtrack (in 2005 for *The Constant Gardener* by Fernando Meirelles; in 2007 for *The Kite Runner*; and in 2012 for *The Mole*). He has also composed various pieces for the National Dance Company.

Ainhoa Arteta (1964–) is one of the most renowned Spanish opera singers of the present day. She is also an outstanding performer of *zarzuela*. Her success in important competitions in Paris and New York launched her on her current international artistic career. The acclaim she received at the New York Metropolitan Opera House was continued in Covent Garden in London. She works frequently with Plácido Domingo in concerts in different countries around the world. She is one of the few Spanish artists to have performed at the White House.

Carlos Álvarez Rodríguez (1966–) is a baritone, who has become one of the best interpreters of the Verdi canon of the early 21st century. In 1990 he made his debut in the Teatro de la Zarzuela with *La del manojo de rosas* by Pablo Sorozábal. He turned down an offer from Riccardo Muti to sing *Rigoletto* at La Scala in Milan, as he considered himself too young and inexperienced at the time. In 1998 he first performed at the Salzburg Festival in *Don Carlo*. Mentored by Plácido Domingo, his career has gone from great to greater. He has already sung in all the world's top theatres.

Alejandro Sanz (1968–) is one of Spain's outstanding international pop stars, although his style and voice have traces of flamenco. He has sold more than 25 million copies throughout his career and won many prizes, among them 20 Grammys, as well as working with numerous artists of great international prestige such as Shakira, Alicia Keys, and The Corrs. His first album *Viviendo deprisa* (1991) was the year's biggest seller in Spain. His international fame came with his album *Más* (1997), which sold more than five million copies.

Ainhoa Arteta as "Musetta," second from left, Angela Gheorghiu as "Mimi," far right, and Ramón Vargas as "Rodolfo," second from right, in their starring roles during the dress rehearsal of the Franco Zeffirelli opera *La bohème* at the Metropolitan Opera in New York, on March 27, 2008. (AP Photo/Bebeto Matthews)

See also: Chapter 13: Overview. Chapter 16: Overview.

Further Reading

Gray, Anne. *The World of Women in Classical Music*. La Jolla: WordWorld, 2007.

Russell, Peter E. *Spain: A Companion to Spanish Studies*. New York: Routledge, 1989.

Pop

The influence of the Beatles was huge in Spain. Spanish pop music started in the 1960s with the group Duo Dinámico (1958–present), which is considered the pioneer of pop music in Spain. Their popularity was so influential that they are considered "the Beatles of Spain." Duo Dinámico (i.e., popular song "Quisiera ser" 1962) are still active and perform their hits yearly in live tours around Spain. Other important pop figures of the 1960s and 1970s were Concha Velasco ("La chica yeye" 1965), Raphael ("Yo soy aquel" 1966), Marisol ("Corazón contento" 1968), Nino Bravo ("Un beso y una flor" 1972), José Luis Perales ("Primer amor" 1973), Camilo Sesto ("¿Quieres ser mi amante?" 1974), and Jeanette ("Porque te vas" 1974).

The second most popular Spanish pop band of all time is Mecano (1981–1992). Some of their biggest number one singles include "Me colé en una fiesta," "Me cuesta tanto olvidarte," "La fuerza del destino," "Hijo de la Luna," "Cruz de navajas," and "El 7 de Septiembre." Other successful Spanish pop artists/bands are: Alaska y Dinarama (*Canciones profanas* 1983), La Unión (*Mil siluetas* 1984), Gabinete Caligari (*Cuatro rosas* 1984), Hombres G (*Hombres G* 1985), El último de la fila (*Enemigos de lo ajeno* 1986), Duncan Dhu (*El grito del tiempo* 1987), Ella baila sola (*Ella baila sola* 1996), Jarabe de palo (*La Flaca* 1996), Los Planetas (*Pop* 1996), Mónica Naranjo (*Palabra de Mujer* 1997), La oreja de Van Goth (*Dile al Sol* 1998), Café Quijano (*La Extraordinaria Paradoja del Sonido Quijano* 1999), La Casa Azul (*Tan simple como el amor* 2003), El Canto del Loco (*Zapatillas* 2005), Despistaos (*Lo que hemos vivido* 2009), and Sergio Dalma (*Via Dalma* 2010).

Marta Sánchez (1966–) is considered the "Queen of Spanish Pop" and one of the biggest sex symbols of the 1980s. She became famous with the pop group Olé Olé (i.e., "Lilí Marlen" 1985, "Supernatural" 1988). Her solo album *Miss Sánchez* (2007) remains her top selling album, achieving number one in digital sales. Her song "Colgando en tus manos" was number one on *Billboard* Latin Pop Songs for two weeks in a row in 2007. David Bisbal (1979–) has also achieved great success since he was the runner up in the first *Operación Triunfo* (equivalent of *American Idol* in Spain) in 2001. As of 2012, David Bisbal has sold more than 5 million records in Spain and America. *Corazón latino* (2002) was his first album, which catapulted him to fame as the winner of many national and international awards like the Grammy Latino in 2003.

Other Spanish pop singers include Raphael (1943–), who is considered one of the most representative voices of the 20th century. Raphael has earned 300 gold records, 50 platinum records, and even one uranium record, awarded both in Spain and in a multitude of Latin American countries. His songs "Como yo te amo" (1980) and "Escándalo" (1991) are part of the collective memory of many Spaniards. He remains the third top-selling singer from Spain (72 million), after Julio and Enrique Iglesias. Miguel Bosé (1956–) became famous with his album *Bandido* (1984). His compilation album *Papito* (2007) has sold over eight million copies. He also works in film and television. Luz Casal (1958–) is one of the most highly regarded ballad singers and the undisputed "Queen of Galician Pop-Rock." After her success in the happy 1980s during *la movida* in Spain (i.e., "Quiéreme aunque te duela" 1987), she achieved international fame, particularly in France, due to Pedro Almodóvar's film *Tacones Lejanos* (1991, *High Heels*), which includes two of her songs. Amaral (1992–) is a pop duo from Aragón with singer Eva Amaral and guitarist Juan Aguirre. They have been successful since the outset and sold millions of records. Their first album *Amaral* (1998) won gold and platinum discs for their millions of records sold. *Estrella de mar* (2002), however, remains their biggest album, including the MTV Europe Music Award of 2002.

See also: Chapter 13: Overview. Chapter 16: Overview.

Further Reading

Regev, Motti. *Pop-Rock Music*. Malden: Polity, 2013.

Rodgers, Eamonn, ed. *Encyclopedia of Contemporary Spanish Culture*. New York: Routledge, 1999.

Rock

The influence of rock music with influential groups such as the Rolling Stones left an impact on the Spanish music scene. Sabino Méndez (1961–) is considered one of the best composers in the history of Spanish rock. His song "Cadillac solitario" (1983) and the entire album *¿Dónde estabas tú en el 77?* (1984) by Loquillo y los Trogloditas are good examples of his musical talent. Other important Spanish rock bands are: Triana (*El Patio* 1975), Barón Rojo (*Larga vida al rock and roll* 1981), Loquillo (*Morir en primavera* 1988), La Guardia (*Vámonos* 1988), Los Rebeldes (*Básicamente . . . Rebeldes* 1995), Barricada (*Hombre mate hombre* 2004), Héroes del silencio (*Senderos de traición* 1990), and Dover (*The Devil Came To Me* 1997). The latter mainly sings in English.

Miguel Ríos (1944–) is one of the pioneers of rock music in Spain. He recorded his first album in 1962, and in 1969 achieved probably the most important hit of his career with the song "Himno de la alegría" ("Ode to Joy"). Based on Beethoven's Ninth Symphony, it brought him international fame and reached number one in numerous countries. In the 1970s and 1980s his reputation grew with songs that became classics in his repertoire, such as "Bienvenidos" and "Santa Lucía." He has also presented music programs on television including *Qué noche la de aquel año* and *Buenas noches, bienvenidos*.

Other rock singers include Rosendo (1954–), who has been a member of several rock bands such as Leño and Barricada. He currently works as a solo artist and tours with other bands. In 2008, he began the "Otra Noche sin Dormir" tour in Spain together with Barricada. Ramoncín (1955–) became very popular during the 1980s with punk songs like "El Rey del Pollo Frito," "Marica de terciopelo," and "Cómete una paraguaya." *Arañando la ciudad* (1981) remains his best album. More recently, he has been a regular commentator for several Spanish television programs. Antón Reixa (1957–) is mainly known for being the leader of the rock band Os Resentidos (1982–1994). When he was 19 he founded the group Poética Rompente. He has written poetry, plays, and prose. "As ladillas do travesty," "Historia del Rock and Roll," and "El silencio de las Xigulas" are some of his literary productions. He also works as a newspaper columnist and in radio and television. He was one of the creators of the TV series *Mareas vivas*. He directed the film *El lápiz del carpintero* (2003), based on the novel with the same title by Manuel Rivas.

Other contemporary rock bands include Medina Azahara (1979–), which echoes the fusion between flamenco and symphonic rock sound initially created by the rock band Triana. Their song "Paseando por la Mezquita" from their first album *Medina Azahara* (1979) was successful nationwide, and became the group's hymn. After 30 years of activity, they have recorded over 20 albums. More recently, Pony Bravo (2006–) is another Andalusian rock group that has already produced three albums. Their most recent album, *De Palmas y Cacería* (2013), incorporates satire and Surrealism in a manner reminiscent of *No me pises que llevo chanclas* (1986–), a well-known Andalusian band that created the distinctive sound known in Spain as "agropop."

See also: Chapter 13: Overview. Chapter 16: Overview.

Further Reading

Lechner, Ernesto. *Rock en español: The Latin Alternative Rock Explosion.* Chicago: Chicago Review Press, 2006.

Zarzuela

La *zarzuela* is Spain's version of the opera. The term *zarzuela* comes from the word *zarzas* (blackberries), which were planted in the Palacio de la Zarzuela—a royal hunting lodge near Madrid. Allegedly, this Spanish operetta was first presented in this particular palace. However, the origin of its etymology is still unknown. There are two types: the *género chico*, which contains only one act; and the *zarzuela grande*, which has three. Zarzuela began in the 17th century, became extremely popular between the 19th and 20th centuries, and continued during Franco's regime. In fact, Franco's regime added the zarzuela as part of their television programming. The Teatro de la Zarzuela in Madrid used to be exclusively dedicated to playing zarzuela. A zarzuela is normally structured with spoken and sung scenes, including popular songs as well as dances.

If Emilio Arrieta's greatest contribution (with over 50 works) to the history of Spanish music was his decisive role in consolidating the zarzuela, Francisco Asenjo Barbieri is considered the creator of the zarzuela. His first important zarzuela was *Gloria y peluca* (1859), where he successfully combined Italian opera with Spanish popular music. Barbieri also played an important role in the building of the Teatro de la Zarzuela in 1856. He also published the *Cancionero musical de los siglo XV y SVI* (1890), which contains 459 transcriptions of music manuscripts from the 15th and 16th centuries.

Other zarzuela figures were Ruperto Chapí, Manuel Penella, and Anselm Clavé. The latter was a composer, poet, and a Barcelona politician. Clavé was also the founder of the choral movement in Spain and promoter of the associative movement. The works of Manuel López-Quiroga (i.e., "La Niña de los Perros," 1921, "The Girl with Dogs"), Jancinto Guerrero (i.e., "Los gavilanes," 1924, "Hawks"), maestro Francisco Alonso (i.e., "La Calesera," 1925, "The Rickshaw Puller"), and Federico Moreno Torroba with over 50 zarzuelas (i.e., "La chulapona," 1934, "Madrid Jacket") renewed the zarzuela in the 20th century.

Spain has not produced a new zarzuela since 1981. However, the main goal of the new director of the Teatro de la Zarzuela (2011–), the Italian Paolo Pinamonti, is to revitalize this genuine Spanish operetta as well as to make the zarzuela more international.

See also: Chapter 13: Overview. Chapter 16: Overview.

Further Reading

Chase, Gilbert. *The Music of Spain.* New York: 2nd ed. Dover Publications, 1976.

Webber, Christopher. *The Zarzuela Companion.* Lanham: Scarecrow Press, 2002.

REFERENCES

Baker, Trevor. "Spanish Music Now: From Alicante to Zaragoza." *The Guardian*, June 19, 2012.

Bermúdez, Silvia, and Jorge Pérez. "Introduction: Spanish Popular Music Studies." *Journal of Spanish Cultural Studies* 10 no.2 (2009): 127–133.

Cuadrado, Manuel, María José Miquel, and Juan D. Montoro. "Consumer Attitudes towards Music Piracy: A Spanish Case Study." *International Journal of Arts Management* 11 no.3 (Spring 2009): 4–15.

Fairley, Jan. "Spain: Flamenco, A Wild, Savage Feeling." In *The Rough Guide to World Music: Europe, Asia, and Pacific*. Edited by Simon Broughton, Mark Ellingham, and Jon Lusk. London: Rough Guides Ltd. (2009): 388–412.

Falcó, Josep Lluís i. "The Film Composer in Spain: The Generation of '89." *Music, Sound, and the Moving Image* 4 no.2 (Autumn 2010): 225–235.

Fraile, Teresa, and Eduardo Viñuela. "Recent Approaches to Sound and Music in Spanish Audiovisual Media." *Music, Sound, and the Moving Image* 4 no.2 (Autumn 2010): 135–138.

Holguín, Sandie. "Música y nacionalismo." In *Ser españoles*. Edited by Javier Moreno Luzón y Xosé M. Núñez Seixas. Barcelona: RBA, 2013 (497–529).

Khan, Andrew. "Sounds of Spain—Day One: A History of Spanish Pop in 10 Songs." *The Guardian,* June 18, 2012.

López González, Joaquín. "Los estudios sobre música y audiovisual en España: hacia un estado de la cuestión." *Trípodos* 26 (2010): 53–66.

Manuel, Peter. "Composition, Authorship, and Ownership in Flamenco, Past and Present." *Ethnomusicology* 54 no.1 (Winter 2010): 106–135.

Martínez, Silvia, and Héctor Fouce, eds. *Made in Spain: Studies in Popular Music*. New York: Routledge, 2013.

Moreda, Eva. "La mujer que no canta no es . . . ¡ni mujer española!: Folklore and Gender in the Earlier Franco Regime." *Bulletin of Hispanic Studies* 89 no.6 (2012): 627–644.

Operé, Fernando, and Carrie B. Douglass. *España y los españoles de hoy. Historia, sociedad y cultura*. New Jersey: Pearson, 2008.

Piña, Raúl. "Ruth Lorenzo: 'El inglés es una realidad en España, por eso he incorporado más a la canción.'" *El Mundo,* March 15, 2014.

Rutherford-Johnson, Tim, ed. *The Oxford Dictionary of Music*. 6th ed. Oxford: Oxford University Press, 2012.

Websites

Cadena100.es

Cadenadial.com

dvdgo.com

Flamenco-world.com

https://www.youtube.com/user/FlamencoworldTV/about

Los40.com

Promusicae.es

Revistaflamenca.com http://www.revistalaflamenca.com/

Ritmic.com

Solmusica.com

Spainisculture.com

ufimusica.com

CHAPTER 14

FOOD

OVERVIEW

Spanish cuisine has become a global phenomenon thanks to the achievements of local and well-renowned international chefs. Part of the success of Spanish gastronomy is due to the tradition of using fresh local products. The thirst for sustainable agriculture quite often plays an invisible role in Spanish cuisine. For instance, in the book *Culinaria Spain,* a countryman from Majorca clearly states that "we have all we need here" (Trutter 2004), referring to the small island of Majorca in the Balearic Islands. Having all they need is especially important to the islanders. It epitomizes the Spanish mentality towards food. Spaniards appreciate their local vegetables, fruits, cheeses, wines, olive oil, ham, meat, and seafood, which they proudly cultivate, raise, or catch.

Spaniards usually buy their fresh food in what is called a *mercado*—a traditional market that sells mainly fresh fish, meat, fruits, and vegetables. Every village and city in Spain has a mercado that is open certain days of the week. A few of the most famous and historical mercados are the *Boquería* in Barcelona, *Mercado de San Miguel* in Madrid, and the *Mercado Central* in Valencia, which is one of the oldest European markets still running. To go to any of these mercados is a great cultural experience. Here, one is able to see and smell some of the varieties of meat and fish available in Spain. Furthermore, one can enjoy many different kinds of fresh fruits for which Spain is justifiably famous, as Spain is considered the land of fruits and vegetables of Europe.

Part of the secret of Spanish cuisine is that it is based on the Mediterranean diet, which has been proven to have health benefits (i.e., it prevents certain cancers, inhibits coronary diseases, lowers weight, and generally helps one to live longer). The Mediterranean diet was recognized in 2013 as part of the World's Intangible Cultural Heritage by UNESCO. However, the Mediterranean diet is more than just food; it is an attitude toward food. For example, eating together is part of the cultural identity of the Mediterranean basin, which includes the countries of Spain, France, Italy, Greece, and Turkey. Typical ingredients of the Mediterranean diet are fresh seasonal vegetables, fish, legumes, eggs, fruit, rice, pasta, olive oil, and a bit of meat. A 2013 survey showed that Spaniards follow a Mediterranean diet, although not 100 percent, due to the arrival of fast food chains and processed food. Also, due to the recent economic crisis in Spain (since 2008), in the last few years the number of Spaniards with obesity is on the rise. For instance, in 2014 one out of six adults was obese, and half of Spain's adult population was overweight.

Some American celebrities or television reporters have also contributed to the popularity of Spanish cuisine in the world. This is the case of the actress Gwyneth Paltrow and her participation in the American television program *Spain . . . On the Road Again* (Pinsky 2008, 13 episodes) with Chef Mario Batali, among others. More recently, Anthony Bourdain, CNN broadcaster (and chef-at-large for Brasserie Les Halles in New York) included Spain in his broadcast as one of the best cuisines in the world.

The Spanish Mediterranean diet differs from the North American or English diet in that it tends to emphasize dishes that use the spoon as opposed to the fork. Although Spanish cuisine is rich and diverse depending on regional variations, it has the common feature of being eaten with the spoon. This is the case of the humble shepherd's dish *migas* (literally translates as "bread crumbs"), many types of soups (i.e., *consomé*), and, above all, the distinctive Spanish stews such as the *potaje* (lentil stew), *puchero* (chickpea stew), the *cazuela de fideos* (noodle stew with clams), and the *estofado* (beef stew).

Spanish cuisine derives from Mediterranean gastronomy, which is mainly based on cereals, legumes, fish, vegetables, fruits and, in particular, extra virgin olive oil. In fact, Spain is the number one producer of olive oil in the world. "Some 300 million olive trees—200 million of those in Andalucía—produce nearly 1.5 million tons of olive oil annually" (Koehler 2013). According to the International Olive Council, Spain's production now totals three times more than Italy and well over four times more than Greece. The cultivation of olive trees dates back 3,000 years, initiated by the Phoenicians, the Greeks, and the Romans (who expanded the cultivation), and followed by the Arabs (who improved the techniques of irrigation and pressing oil). Nowadays, Spain cultivates over 250 varieties of olives, still following a traditional method of pressing oil at the *almazara* (mill where the olives are pressed within 24 hours of harvesting). Spaniards consume olive oil on a daily basis. For instance, Spanish people love olive oil with their popular breakfast *pan con tomate* (toasted slices of fresh bread with tomato juice and olive oil on top).

Olive trees in the mountains of Granada on October 19, 2014. (Grantotufo/Dreamstime.com)

Perhaps the best way to understand a culture is to immerse yourself in its food. Spanish cuisine is an amalgamation of different cultures. For example, the Romans left the text *De re Coquinaria* written in the first century, which can be considered one of the first cookery books. Apart from describing the culinary habits of the Iberian Peninsula, the manuscript contains culturally relevant information. For instance, the author noted that the Carthaginians from the north of Africa named the peninsula *Ispania*, which translated into their language to "land of rabbits." The latter is still a very populous animal in Spain that Spaniards like to cook in different ways.

Wheat has been cultivated on Earth since the beginning of civilization and in Spain for centuries. Similarly, the origin of wine is difficult to track down, although in the Spanish context, we know that it was brought by the Phoenicians in the eighth century. The Arab influence on Spanish gastronomy is huge. Apart from improving the techniques of irrigation, they also introduced many dry fruits (quince, grenade, figs, dates, almonds); legumes (lima beans, chickpeas, lentils); citrus (oranges, lemons, grapefruit); and cereals (oats, barley, rye, rice). Although rice probably originated in Asia, the first European cultivation of rice was in Valencia in the eighth century by the Arabs. The Arabs also left a written legacy, including *Libro de la agricultura* by Abu Zacaría in the 12th century, and *Cocina hispano-magrebí o el tratado de Ibn Rain al Tuybi, el Andalusí*, written between 1243 and 1328.

Cacao came to Spain from Mexico via the conquistadors. During this time a plethora of ingredients came to Spain, which subsequently revolutionized European cuisine, including potato, tomato, corn, pepper, paprika, vanilla, mango, and many more.

During the 18th century French cuisine also influenced Spanish gastronomy. However, Spain did not produce a cuisine based on social status like France did. Looking at the menu served to the Spanish monarchy, one can observe that the difference between a noble and an average citizen in Madrid had to do more with the number of dishes served than the quality of the cooking. That is to say, historically nobles and common folk ate similar food with the exception of some sweets, cold cuts, and chocolate that the aristocrat would eat on a more regular basis.

Furthermore, Spanish gastronomy cannot be understood without recognizing the contributions of nuns and monks, who could be considered the first anonymous Spanish chefs. The nuns created divine sweets such as the popular *tocino de cielo* (Spanish heavenly custard) while the monks appear on the label of wines such as Kina San Clemente—a popular non-alcoholic wine that was usually given until very recently to Spanish children to increase their appetite.

Eating is a cultural experience in Spain due to the different habits to which Spaniards are accustomed. If every country has its own particular customs to start a day and eat their meals, Spain is notorious for its unique and unorthodox meal times. For example, most Spanish people tend to have a light breakfast around 8:00 a.m. Then, they do not have lunch until 2:00 p.m., which is their main meal of the day. Many public institutions such as banks, schools, and shops close from 2:00 to 4:00 p.m. to have lunch—a meal that is often eaten with the family. A light dinner is usually eaten at 9:00 p.m., although in summer it can be as late as 11:00 p.m.

Breakfast in Spain

Spaniards tend to have a light continental breakfast, which basically consists of a fresh glass of orange juice, a cup of coffee, and toast with butter and marmalade. Spain actually produces many types of wonderful marmalades and jams including pomegranate (Granatum), Autum fruit jam (Can Bech); blueberry jam (Los arándanos), peach marmalade (La Jalacina), and Spain's oldest and famous quince paste or jelly from the company El Quijote, which started in 1840 in Puente Genil (Córdoba). It would be worthwhile to go to any Spanish supermarket to see and/or buy their variety of jams and marmalades.

Cola Cao is also another typical Spanish product that many Spaniards enjoy for breakfast. This is cocoa powder mixed with warm milk, and it is usually combined with biscuits (i.e., cuétara, Gullón, Siro). Any child in Spain is a master chef of making a great cola cao with biscuits. Depending on summer or winter season, it is used with hot or cold milk to mix it up in a mug in varying strengths from mild to bold.

If there is a uniquely distinctive Spanish breakfast, it is *churros con chocolate*, a dish consisting of warm thick chocolate with tasty *churros* (pastry made of fried flour). As the Spaniards like to say, *las cosas claras y el chocolate espeso*, which essentially means that "things [ideas] should be clear and the chocolate should be thick" (in order to dip the churro). Spaniards enjoy their *chocolate con churros* throughout the whole year, although it is most popular in winter because it is hot food. This is typically eaten on weekends in the morning but also in the afternoon between 5:00 to 7:00 p.m. in winter, particularly before going to the cinema. Also, this is common comfort food eaten around 6:00 a.m. in the morning in many parts of Spain. *Tejeringos* is another version of *churros*. The difference is that they are more crispy and circular.

Quedar para tomar un café is another popular Spanish expression which refers to the typical Spanish custom of meeting for coffee. However, Spaniards are not as heavy coffee drinkers as other European countries (i.e., Holland, Finland, Sweden), although within Europe, Spain remains the fourth largest coffee market. Most Spaniards take two cups of coffee daily, one at home for breakfast, and another one in a bar. Spain offers a variety of coffee drinks. When ordering coffee at a diner, it is served quickly and consumed quickly, oftentimes with the customer standing at the bar. By North American standards the coffee is served in comparatively small portions. Coffee can be served in Spain in many ways, with or without milk. If it is served with milk, the milk can be served in a variety of temperatures: *templada* (mild), *caliente* (very hot), or *fría* (cold). The nine most common types of coffee include:

Café solo—a small cup of black coffee or basically an expresso
Café suizo—café solo topped with whipped cream
Café con leche—coffee with milk. This type of drink is the most common one. However, it can be unusually strong for a North-American drinker.
Leche manchada—hot milk "stained" with a very small amount of coffee
Café cortado—the opposite of *leche manchada*; that is to say, black coffee with a dash of milk

Carajillo—black coffee served with brandy

Café con hielo—black coffee served with a glass full of ice

Café canario—*café solo* with sweet condensed milk, a specialty from the Canary Islands

Café del tiempo—a remedy for a hangover; coffee served with ice, plus a slice of lemon

The date when coffee arrived in Spain is still unknown, although the most common belief is that it was brought by the first Bourbon king, Phillip V, whose reign began in 1700. Coffee drinking became customary in the 18th century. Initially, Spain's main source of coffee was Colombia as one of Spain's former colonies. Currently, most Spanish coffee comes from Brazil and Vietnam. The Swiss company Nestlé owns most of Spain's popular coffee brands including Nescafé, Nespresso, and Bonka. Spain's national coffee brands include Café Bahía, Café Fortaleza, Café Dromedario, and Cafè Cornellà to name a few.

Lunch—The Feast at 2:00 P.M.

Lunch in Spain normally starts at 2:00 p.m. and often lasts over an hour. Without a doubt, this is the main meal of the day for Spaniards. Restaurants have what it is called *Menú del día* meaning "Menu of the day," which is the best option economically speaking. This choice provides a full meal including starter, main dish, and *pan, bebida, y postre*—bread, a drink, and desert. The price varies between 7.50 and 15 euros. Sunday is more expensive.

The pleasure of eating in Spain not only consists of a wonderful meal. In addition, it is associated with family time which is considered almost "holy." Therefore, it is normal to see Spaniards going back home for their lunch to be eaten with the family. The globalization of the new millennium, however, is pushing some Spanish industries into a mainstream eating style. The idea of a 30-minute lunch or grabbing a quick sandwich on the go is still relatively rare, especially in small/medium-sized cities and rural areas.

Following a special lunch is the custom of what Spaniards call *sobremesa*. Essentially, it consists of chatting while enjoying a cup of coffee followed by liquor after a good meal that usually happens on a Sunday lunch in the company of family members and/or friends. The term *tertulia* also refers to the discussion group that takes place in a *cafetería* (coffee shop) as opposed to the *sobremesa*, which normally is at home with family and/or friends. Café Gijón and Café Barbieri, both in Madrid, have probably the longest history of what in other European countries is known as coffee houses, understood as a group of intellectuals or friends who get together around coffee.

Dinner—The Light Snack

The amount of food eaten during dinner time is much smaller in comparison to lunch. The most important aspect of a Spanish dinner is perhaps the fact that it is the last meal of the day, so all family members eat together at a table usually at 9:00 p.m. in winter (much later in summer time). It would be very unusual to see a Spanish family eating, seated on a couch while watching the television.

Although it is small in quantity, Spaniards usually eat three dishes as well for their dinner: starter, main, and dessert. The last is normally at least one piece of fruit. Spain produces all kind of fruits, so it is common to see Spaniards eating seasonal fruits—such as, oranges, melons, mangos, and grapes—for breakfast, lunch, and dinner. In fact, Spaniards eat at least three pieces of fruit every day, which constitutes an essential part of their Mediterranean diet. They also eat all their meals around a table where it is common to see a *frutero*, a bowl containing fruits of the season.

Generally speaking, Spaniards tend to have the famous *paella* on weekends, perhaps because it is the most popular dish of Spain. Originally from the Valencia region, the ingredients of a standard *paella* exemplify the diet of the average Spaniard: rice, olive oil, saffron, chicken, peas, tomatoes, red pepper, (optional seafood) and garlic. Garlic is a featured addition to the Spanish diet; it is very common to see in bars garlic inside the bottle of olive oil, which is often used to spread on toast for breakfast. Apart from the *paella*, other popular dishes contain garlic as an ingredient including *gambas al ajillo* (shrimp garlic) or *conejo al ajillo* (rabbit with garlic). Spain is among the top 10 garlic producers in the world. On average, every Spaniard eats over three pounds (1.5 kilograms) of garlic annually.

The impact of Spanish cuisine on the world market is visible by the growing number of Spanish delicatessens that are now noticeable in foreign supermarkets. In

Although Spain has no national dish, paella is the most popular. There are different types of paella including rabbit, seafood, fideua, and vegetable. (iStockPhoto.com)

metropolitan cities in North America, it is possible nowadays to buy a whole array of Spanish goods such as the typical *manzanilla* olives, a jar of red peppers or artichokes, a can of anchovies or mussels or the real Spanish *chorizo* (sausage), cheeses like Manchego, and even the authentic Spanish *jamón* (cured ham). There are also the omnipresent bottles of olive oil, different types of vinegars and fruit juices, some Spanish biscuits, and the popular Christmas sweet of *turrón* (almond candy or nougat) and other brands of sweets such as the Spanish chocolate brand *Valor*.

Around 15 percent of the total exports of Spain are food items, which are mainly delivered to the EU market (71%), and it is projected to increase to 40 percent by 2020. For instance, in 2013 Spain exported food and drinks for a revenue of 22,594 euros while in the same year they imported other food and drinks for a total cost of 19,128 euros (Muñoz Cidad et al 2013). Having said that, finding Spanish products abroad is not as easy as buying other countries' food items in the world. Spanish food companies still need to improve in their international distribution, if they are to compete with the more prominent Italian and French products.

Spanish cuisine has received international attention not only from their visitors but also for their cooks such as Juan Mari Arzak, who was the first to be awarded three Michelin stars in Spain in 1989. Soon after, Ferrán Adriá, the Roca brothers, Quique Dacosta, and Martín Berasategui also received international acclaim. In fact, the number one restaurant in the world in 2013 and 2015, according to the prestigious culinary magazine *Restaurant*, was El Celler de Can Roca in Catalunya. According to the *2014 Michelin Guide to Spain and Portugal* eight Spanish restaurants were rated among the best in the world. DiverXO (chef David Muñoz) was the latest Spanish restaurant to join the list of the three Michelin star restaurants in Spain, which include Arzak (San Sebastián); Berasategui (Lasarte, Guipúzcoa); Sant Pau de Carme Ruscalleda (San Pol de Mar, Barcelona); Akelarre de Pedro Subijana (San Sebastián); El Celler de Can Roca (Girona); Quique Dacosta Restaurant (Dénia, Alicante); and Azurmendi de Enejo Atxa (Larrabetzu, Vizcaya).

Further Reading

Batali, Mario. *Spain: A Culinary Road Trip*. New York: HarperCollins, 2008.

Koehler, Jeff. *Spain*. San Francisco: Chronicle Books, 2013.

Radford, John, and Mario Sandoval. *Cook España, Drink España: A Culinary Journey around the Food and Drink of Spain*. New York: Hachette Book Group, 2009.

Trutter, Marion. *Culinaria Spain: Cuisine. Country. Culture*. Potsdam: h.f.ullmann, 2010.

Alcohol: Beer, Brandy, Cava, Sherry, Wine

When it comes to alcohol, Spaniards are changing their Mediterranean habits. Nowadays they prefer to drink beer over the traditional local wine. This global trend happens not only among youngsters but at all age levels. However, the new generation of Spaniards tend to drink as much beer as their English counterparts (Argandoña et al. 2009).

The weekend is by far their favorite time to drink to excess. Therefore, *botellón* or binge drinking appears as a global phenomenon changing cultural traditions. Among students between 15 and 16 years old from all over the world, nearly 90 percent have drunk alcohol at least once. In Spain, the number is 82 percent, according to EDADES 2004 (Argandoña et al. 2009). The legal age to drink any alcohol in Spain is 18, which contrasts with Germany or France, where the legal drinking age for beer or wine is 16. The price of alcohol in Spain is one of the cheapest in the European Union.

According to the survey by the American news channel *CNBC*, Spain occupies the 12th position among the top 20 beer-drinking countries in the world, with 83.8 liters per person. Eighty percent of the beer industry in Spain is controlled by three major companies: Heineken, Mahou-San Miguel (Madrid/Málaga), and Damm (Barcelona), of which the last two are Spanish-owned. The typical beer from Spain is lager. Like food, everywhere you go, depending on the region, you will taste and enjoy a local beer/drink. Some of the most famous Spanish beers are Damm inedit (created by Ferran Adrià), Alhambra 1925, Mahou Cinco estrellas, San Miguel 1516, and Ámbar especial.

Brandy de Jerez is a protected trademark exported throughout the world. Like sherry, Brandy de Jerez ages depending on the solera process. The origin of brandy is actually quite accidental. First, the Moors brought *alquitaras* (distilling machines) to Andalucía in the eighth century, converting wine of the Jerez region into high-proof alcohol, which they used for perfumes and medicinal purposes. Once the Moors left Spain, the alcohol was used for the production of sherry, which then became popular around Europe. However, one day a Dutch customer cancelled his order, and the barrels of this invoice were almost forgotten in the cellar for years until the owner sampled it and realized that the sherry had matured into a quite different alcoholic beverage. *Brandy de Jerez* was born. There are three different types of Spanish brandy according to the length of time spent in the barrel: *Solera* (matured at least for six months), *Solera Reserva* (at least 12 months), and *Solera Gran Reserva* (at least 36 months, although it normally matures for 10 to 15 years).

If the French invented champagne, Spaniards produced its equivalent called *cava*, which in Catalan means cave or cellar. It is mainly produced in Catalunya with approximately 95 percent of the production, followed by Valencia, Extremadura, Navarra, Rioja, Aragón, and the Basque country. It is illegal to call it "Spanish champagne" under the European Union law, because champagne has protected geographical status. However, cava is gaining momentum against French champagne competition all over the world when it comes to sales figures. The Brits, who constitute an important market for the Spanish wine industry, have already changed their palate to cava, and this is not necessarily due to the fact that it is cheaper. As Neil Martin mentions in his article "Give a Little Respect: Cava," there are cavas out there that "deserve as much respect as the fêted champagnes and should not be bracketed in with cheaper, commercial brands, but with some of the greatest sparkling wines in the world" (Martin 2013). Catalunya, Valencia, Aragón, Extremadura, and La Rioja are all regions that produce cava.

Sherry was invented in the south of Spain, where wine was cultivated in western Andalucía for 3,000 years. However, sherry was not discovered until the 13th or 14th century. The town of Jerez used to be called *Xeris*, a word that the English could not pronounce well when Sir Francis Drake attacked Cádiz in 1587 and British sailors began to transport sherry from the south of Spain to their homeland, where it became very popular. The town of Jerez de la Frontera borrows its name from the Spanish *jerez*, which is of Arabic origin (*scherisch*), but the English call it "sherry." The production of sherry in Spain covers what is known as the Sherry Triangle which refers to the towns of Jerez de la Frontera, Sanlúcar de Barrameda, and El Puerto de Santa María, all of which are in the city of Cádiz. Most traditional sherries go through an aging process that lasts for years and is called the *solera* system. Sherry usually has an alcohol content of 15 to 20 percent.

There are six types of sherries including *finos* (a pale golden dry sherry, which literally means "refined" and is a classic aperitif—although fino is also drunk together with the meal in Andalucía); *manzanilla* (a pale, very dry fino, which is also the name of chamomile tea in Spanish and resembles a bit of its flavor); *amontillado* (with an orangey color and hazelnut aroma, it can be dry or medium dry but always with a nutty bouquet as it is considered the most elegant of sherrys); *oloroso* (meaning "aromatic," it is a dark, full-bodied sherry); *palo cortado* (dark and can be described as a fusion between amontillado and oloroso); and finally what Spaniards call *Pedro Ximénez* (to refer to the East India type of sherry, which is a pale cream or cream sherry containing sweet Pedro Ximénez or Moscatel grapes). The latter tastes very sweet, so it is usually drunk for dessert.

The wine industry in Spain is huge. In fact, Spain has more vineyards than any other country in the world (1,080,000 million hectares). Spain dedicates 28 percent of its land to wine production, which is more than any other European country including France (25%) and Italy (23%). Currently, Spain is number three in production (after France and Italy) with 29.7 million hL (11.8% worldwide and 21% of the European Union). Geographically, Castilla-La Mancha is the biggest wine region with more than half of the Spanish production; Extremadura is the second; and Catalunya the third. Among the main wineries, with more than 100 million euros in sales annually, are the following: Freixenet, J. García Carrión, Codorníu, Arco Wine Invest Group, Grupo Domenecq Bodegas, Grupo Miguel Torres, S.A., Félix Solis Avantis, and Grupo Faustino. The letters DO in Spanish stand for *Denominación de Origen* (guarantee of region of origin) status. Overall, there are approximately 70 wine regions with DO. The DO Rioja has the

---

THE *SOLERA* SYSTEM

In the solera system, "at least three rows of barrels are stacked on top of each other; the barrels containing the oldest wines, the soleras (derived from *suelo*, floor) are at the bottom. The vintner takes a certain amount of wine out of this solera at regular intervals. This is replaced by the same amount from the *criadera* above it, and this in turn is topped up from the next row. So all the rows are gradually transferred and the top one is made up with young wine. Over the years, the sherry from the top row of barrels moves down to the bottom one. . . . The minimum aging time permitted for sherry is three years, but this is far exceeded by most of the bodegas" (Trutter 2004).

most registered number of wineries (826), followed by DO Cava (419), DO Ribera del Duero (286), DO La Mancha (256), DO Catalunya (203), DO Penedés (187), and DO Rías Baixas (181). However, three distinctive regions have a more revered and stricter status known as *Denominación de Origen Calificada* (Qualified Denomination of Origin), which corresponds to La Rioja, Ribera del Duero, and Priorat. For instance, in the region of La Rioja alone, which only covers 1 percent of Spain's total area and less than 350,000 people, there are over 800 registered winenries.

Among the most spectacular Spanish wineries, due to its modern avant-garde architecture, is the Ysios winery in Alava which was founded in 2001 and designed by the famous Spanish architect Santiago Calatrava. It is a very long futuristic type of cellar that can be seen from different distances creating different effects. For instance, at close range it gives the impression of a pixilated landmark but from far away it resembles giant wine barrels. Also, the CVNE winery, which stands in Spanish for *Compañía Vinícola del Norte de España* (Winery Company of the North of Spain), was founded in 1879 by two brothers originally from the Basque country who moved to La Rioja for better weather. The current owners are Victor Urrutia and his sister María. Currently, CVNE has three wineries and each of them run independently. The Viña Real winery was designed by the French architect Philippe Mazières in 2004. The shape of the building evokes a wine barrel. Divided into two floors, the basement contains the barrels of wine while the main floor is dedicated to the process of wine making.

The Marqués de Riscal vineyard is a spectacular Spanish bodega that started in 1850, and since 2006 shares the grounds with a hotel and a wine center designed by the Canadian architect Frank Gehry. Similar to the Guggenheim museum near the city of Bilbao, the Marqués de Riscal winery is located about an hour from Bilbao in the small rural village of Elciego in the Rioja region. The new complex also includes a spectacular spa which offers wine therapy and other vinous treatments. Additionally, the shop of R. López Heredia designed by Zaha Hadi is very modern. Although the winery itself continues to use the traditional craft initiated by the legendary great-grandfather of Mercedes López de Heredia-Viña Tondonia in Haro, the new shop is a delight to the eyes.

In 2012 Spain sold 2,062 million liters of wine and brought in 2,499 million euros. The wine without DO (sold in the cask) is still the best-selling product abroad with 934 million liters sold in 2012, which comprised 45.3 percent of the total production (Foodswinesfromspain.com).

In terms of markets, in 2012 only Russia reduced its investments in Spanish wines. Germany, U.K., U.S., and France are the main clients, although the Asian markets are also purchasing a large amount of Spanish wine recently, with Japan and China as the main buyers. However, Mexico, Switzerland, and Ireland are the three main countries that buy the most expensive wine, paying over three euros per liter.

See also: Chapter 4: Overview.

Further Reading

Koehler, Jeff. *Spain*. San Francisco: Chronicle Books, 2013.

Raezer, David, et al. *Spanish Wine Guide*. Kindle Edition 2014.

Read, Jan. *Wines of Spain*. London: Mitchell Beazley, 2005.

Trutter, Marion. *Culinaria Spain. Cuisine. Country. Culture*. Potsdam: h.f.ullmann, 2010.

Cheeses and Jamón

The pig has been the symbol of Spain since Roman times. When the Muslims conquered most parts of the Iberian Peninsula in the eighth century, they removed pigs from the menu. However, in the Reconquista period, the consumption of pig served as proof of being a good Christian. People who refused pork were suspected of being nonbelievers in Christ and, subsequently, the pig become a symbol of division between religions. A Castilian *cochinillo* (roast suckling pig) at the *asadores* (local restaurants) of Segovia is a popular image at most restaurants in the city. The word *matanza* refers to the Spanish tradition of the winter pork butchering season, which is still practiced in some small villages. It basically consists of a two-day affair in which one or two pigs are cooked and prepared in different ways so one or two families can have pork for the entire year. Spain has two main types of ham: *jamón ibérico* and *jamón serrano*. *Jamón ibérico* is more expensive because it comes from the specific breed of black Iberian pigs. The *cerdo ibérico* or *Jamón de Pata Negra* (black foot ham), as it is sometimes called, resides in the Dehesa, a large area in southwest Spain comprised of grasslands and oak trees. These pigs are free-range and their main food is acorns, which gives the pork its characteristic taste to the palate. The ham is salt cured, then dried for anywhere between two to four years and sometimes even longer.

Joselito's hams from Salamanca are currently considered the best *jamones ibéricos* in the world. More recently, Spain has developed new regulations for ibérico products to facilitate the different types of Spanish ham. Since 2014 Spanish hams have been labeled for easy identification. Hence, four different labels have been established:

- Red label. A free-range swine fed exclusively with acorns.
- Green label. A free-range animal fed with grains and legumes.
- White label. Farm-dwelling swine fed with grains and legumes.
- Black label. This label refers to the highest quality ham, exclusive for swine which are 100 percent genetically ibérico and have been afforded the freedom of roaming the Dehesa, eating as many acorns as they wish.

CHORIZO

"In every respectable household in Spain, they make as many *chorizos* as there are days in the year: 365 sausages for their own consumption, and 50 more for days when they have guests" (French writer Alexandre Dumas who toured Spain in 1846–1847, and wrote extensively on world cuisine including *From Paris to Cádiz*, 1847).

The second type of ham is called *jamón serrano* or mountain ham, which is made from pigs fed a grain diet and takes 6–18 months to be cured (hanging in dry mountains). Though the ham is not as prized as the *jamón ibérico,* it has a unique, rich taste of its own.

The pork industry in Spain is the second largest in Europe. Only Germans manufacture more pork than the Spaniards. The variety of merchandise related to pork is quite significant. Among the most popular pork products consumed by the Spanish are the following: *chorizo* (sausage)*, salchichas* (small sausages), *longaniza* (mixed type of sausage), *chistorra* (a thin soft paprika-red sausage lightly cured), *salchichón* (a firm sausage similar to salami)*, queso cerdo* (pork cheese), *lomo embuchado* or *caña de lomo* (long think tenderloin matured for at least two months), *sobrassada* (typically Mallorcan soft spreadable minced pork sausage), *fuet* (Catalan thin cured dry sausage), and *botifarra* (Catalan version of longaniza). The last two are specialties of Catalunya, where the main factories of pork are located in Spain.

There are over a hundred distinct types of cheeses in Spain, whose origins date back to medieval times in monasteries near the pilgrim route to Santiago de Compostela. Over 30 cheeses of Spain have been awarded *Denominación de Origen* (DO) or *Indicación Geográfica Protegida* (IGP) status. Because goats live in most areas of Spain, goat cheese is popular (i.e., *Cabrales, queso de cabra*). Other Spanish cheeses are made from the milk of cows, sheep, and in some places they blend two or even three types of milk. *Picón* is a three-milk blue cheese from the Cantabrian Mountains of the Picos de Europa. Well-known sheep cheeses are *zamorano* (made from esparto grass in the city of Zamora), *burgos* (a very soft moist cheese made from Castilian sheep milk), *manchego* (made from the sheep of La Mancha region), *Roncal* (a hard cheese from Navarra), *Idiazábal* (a Basque hard cheese), and cow cheeses such as *Mahón-Menorca* (from the Balearic Islands), *San Simón, Arzúa-Ulloa*, and *tetilla* (the last three originally from Galicia).

See also: Chapter 14: Overview.

Further Reading

Escorial, José Manuel. *España y sus quesos: Spain and its Cheeses.* Spain: Akasa, 2006.

Koehler, Jeff. *Spain.* San Francisco: Chronicle Books, 2013.

Trutter, Marion. *Culinaria Spain: Cuisine. Country. Culture.* Potsdam: h.f.ullmann, 2010.

Weinstein, Bruce, and Mark Scarbrough. *Ham: An Obsession with the Hindquarter.* New York: Stewart, Tabori & Chang, 2010.

Chefs and Restaurants

The Arzak family has been in the forefront of the culinary tradition for more than 100 years. In fact, the building that houses the restaurant was built in 1897and started as a tavern and wine cellar for the local village of Alza. Elena Arzak was named the best female chef in the world in 2012. Perhaps the main contribution of Arzak is that its success is due to a great family team effort rather than an individual inspiration.

Arzak is the name of a famous Spanish restaurant located in the Basque country. It is currently run by father and daughter—Juan Mari and Elena Arzak, who also own the *Ametsa* in London (U.K.), which in 2013 received the first Michelin star given to a Spanish restaurant abroad. This family is a living legend of Basque cuisine, although they are not afraid to look further afield for flavors.

Ferran Adrià is without a doubt one of the best chefs in the world. His cuisine has been defined as "molecular gastronomy," although he identifies his cooking as deconstructivist. His goal is to provoke with the flavors. As he likes to say, "the ideal customer doesn't come to *elBulli* to eat but to have an experience." *elBulli* is another Michelin 3-star restaurant near the town of Roses, which is situated in Catalunya. Although temporally closed until it reopened as a creativity center in 2014, its chef Ferrán Adrià successfully managed to associate haute cuisine with molecular gastronomy. *Restaurant Magazine* judged *elBulli* to be number one on its Top 50 list of the world's best restaurants for a record five times—in 2002, 2006, 2007, 2008 and 2009, and number two in 2010.

The Roca brothers from Girona—Joan, Josep and Jordi—are also prominent chefs from Spain. If Ferran Adrià transformed haute cuisine, Jordi Roca has managed to create desserts that taste like many well-known fragrances smell. Due to his success, he now has a fragrance available to purchase in the market called *Núvol de Llimona*, which smells as good as it tastes. Also, their restaurant *El Celler de Can Roca* was named the best restaurant in the world in 2013 and 2015. Located in the northeastern Spanish city of Girona, as they mention on their website, *El Celler* is a free-style restaurant, committed to cuisine and to the avant-garde.

David Muñoz belongs to the youngest generation of successful chefs in the world. He received his first Michelin award in 2010, and a second in 2012 for his creativity with the restaurant *StreetXO*. However, in 2013 David Muñoz became famous worldwide when he won the prestigious three-star Michelin award for his restaurant *DiverXO* (Madrid), becoming Spain's eighth restaurant with three Michelin stars. DiverXO moved in 2014 to Madrid's hotel Eurobuilding, which belongs to the Spanish hotel chain called NH Hotel Group.

Mugaritz in Rentería (Guipúzcoa) has been in the top-five best restaurants in the world for the past eight years. Chef-patron Andoni Luis Aduriz's style of cooking has been labelled as "techno-emotional Spanish" by *The World's 50 Best Restaurants*.

Quique Dacosta has become another stylish name in haute cuisine. One of his innovations is that he does not have only one restaurant, *Dacosta* in Dénia (Alicante). On the contrary, he has expanded his reputation and has created Daco&Co, which is a chain of trendy bars and restaurants like *El Poblet* in Valencia, which offers a varied menu for a good price. *Quique Dacosta* filled the number 26 position on the list of the top 50 restaurants in the world in 2013. Located in Dénia (Alicante), Dacosta is part avant-garde chef, part ecological researcher. His style of food is modern Spanish and he only uses locally sourced ingredients from within 75 kilometers of his restaurant.

Asador Etxebarri, in the Basque country, occupied the 44th place on the list of the world's best restaurants of 2013. Its most distinctive feature is that the chef, Victor Arguinzoniz, cooks everything over a grill, including dessert. The downside is its location, which is about an hour from San Sebastián. Restaurante *Akelarre* (chef Pedro Subijana), *Martín Berasategui* (chef Martín Berasategui with seven Michelin stars), and *Zuberoa* (chef Hilario Arbelaitz) are three other prestigious Spanish restaurants located in the Basque region.

The next following five chefs have been awarded "3 Soles" by Repsol, which is the Spanish equivalent of the Michelin guide:

Angel León is the chef of the *Restaurante Aponiente* located in Puerto de Santa María (Cádiz). He mainly works with seafood. León, in the video available in the Repsol website, also recommends *Casa Sacha* (chef Sacha Ormaechea), a historical restaurant in Madrid; Carles Gaig (another important chef from Barcelona); and Bernardo Etxea in San Sebastián.

Pedro Morán is the chef of *Casa Gerardo* (Gijón). He mainly works with the local cuisine from Asturias, so the *fabada* is a must. The region of Asturias is also the home of *Casa Marcial* by Nacho Manzano in Arriondas (Oviedo).

Paco Roncero is the chef of *la Terraza del Casino* in Madrid, and is renowned for creating an avant-garde cuisine, following the steps of his master, Ferrán Adrià. Also in Madrid you can find famous restaurants such as *Ramón Freixa*, by Ramón Freixa; *Santceloni*, by Óscar Velasco; and *El Club Allard*, by Diego Guerrero.

Jordi Cruz is the chef of Restaurante *ÀBaC* in Barcelona. Perhaps his main peculiarity is that he mixes an almost scientific technique with the rock & roll music which he and his partners listen to as they work. The creative mood that inspires his cuisine can be characterized as innovative and always looking for something new. Also in Catalunya you can find other famous restaurants such as *Enoteca* and *Miramar*, both by Paco Pérez; *Lasarte*, by Martín Berasategui; *Can Fabes*, by the family of Santi Santamaría and Xavier Pellicer; *Les Cols*, by Fina Puigdevall; and *Moments*, by Raúl Balam, the son of Carme Ruscadella.

Dani García is also another prestigious chef who works in the *Restaurante Calima*, located in the hotel Gran Melía Don Pepe in Marbella (Málaga). He is well known for what he describes as "contradición" cuisine, which is mainly based on local products from Andalucía.

Other important restaurants in Spain are: *Atrio* (Toño Pérez) in Cáceres; *Las Rejas* (Manolo de la Osa) in Cuenca; *La Sirena* (Mari Carmen Vélez) in Alicante; and *Sant Pau* (Carme Ruscalleda) in Barcelona. Finally, in 2013 a group of Spanish chefs in conjunction with the tourist office of Spain launched the website tastingspain.es in order to promote the diversity of Spanish cuisine.

See also: Chapter 14: Overview.

Further Reading

Andrews, Colman. *Ferran: The Inside Story of El Bulli and the Man who Reinvented Food*. New York: Gotham Books, 2010.

Michelin, Pneu (Firm). *España & Portugal 2013*. France: Michelin, 2013.

Richardson, Paul. *A Late Dinner: Discovering the Food of Spain*. New York: Scribner, 2009.

Regional Dishes and Drinks

Table 14.1 highlights typical dishes and drinks from each region of Spain.

Table 14.1   REGIONAL FOOD AND DRINKS OF SPAIN

Region	Distinctive Food	Distinctive Drinks
Andalucía	Pescaíto frito [fried fish] Gazpacho, salmorejo & ajo blanco [cold soups]	Jerez /Montilla-Moriles Brandy & Ponche Caballero Ron Montero & Whisky Embrujo de Granada
Aragón	Migas al ajoarriero [Shepherd's breadcrumbs] Frutas de Aragón [sugar-candied fruits]	Somontano / Cariñena
Asturias	Fabada [Asturian bean stew] Queso azul [Blue cheese]	Sidra [cider]
Islas Baleares	Ensaïmada [Majorcans' favorite cake] Sobrassada [Sausage of the Balearic Islands]	Ginebra menorquina, Hierbas de Mallorca, palo de Mallorca
Islas Canarias	Plátano al caramel con ron [Banana with rum and syrup] Papas arrugadas [Wrinkled potatoes]	Vino de tea, ron
Cantabria	Cocido montañés [Cantabrian style stew] Arroz santanderino [Santander style rice]	Leche fresco
Castilla La Mancha	Pisto [Braised mixed vegetables] Queso manchego [Manchego cheese]	Valdepeñas
Castilla y León	Cochinillo asado [Roast suckling pig] Yemas de Ávila [Saint Teresa's egg yolk confection]	Ribera del Duero, Rueda
Cataluña	Escalivada [smoky grilled vegetables] Crema catalana [crème brûlée]	Ratafía catalana, Cava, Penedés
Comunidad Valenciana	Paella Turrón [nougat]	Horchata Agua de cebada Bebidas espirituosas de Alicante, vino de Utiel-Requena

(continued)

Table 14.1 REGIONAL FOOD AND DRINKS OF SPAIN *(continued)*

Region	Distinctive Food	Distinctive Drinks
Extremadura	Caldereta extremeña [Extremadura style meat stew] Jamón ibérico [Iberian ham]	Ribera del Guadiana
Galicia	Marisco [Sea food] Empanada gallega [Galician turnover]	Queimada Orujo de Galicia, Albariño, Ribeiro
La Rioja	Bacalao a la riojana [Cod La Rioja style] Queso camerano [Camerano cheese]	Rioja
Madrid	Cocido madrileño [Chickpeas stew Madrid style] Callos a la madrileña [Madrid style tripe]	Chinchón Vinos de Madrid
Murcia	Caldero murciano [Murcian fish stew] Olla gitana [Gipsy stew]	Licor 43 Jumilla-Yecla Bullas
Navarra	Pimientos de piquillo rellenos [Stuffed peppers] Trucha a la navarra [Trout Navarra style]	Clarete o Rosado de Navarra, Pacharán
País Vasco	Merluza a la vasca [Hake Basque style] Marmitako [Tuna stew]	BitterKas, Kalimotxo, Txacolí, Rioja-Alavesa

See also: Chapter 1: Overview; Regions of Spain. Chapter 3: Overview; Regional Government and Regionalism. Chapter 4: Overview. Chapter 6: Overview; Nationalism. Chapter 9: Overview. Chapter 11: Overview. Chapter 14: Overview.

Further Reading

Koehler, Jeff. *Spain*. San Francisco: Chronicle Books, 2013.

Trutter, Marion. *Culinaria Spain: Cuisine. Country. Culture*. Potsdam: h.f.ullmann, 2010.

Seafood Dishes

Considering that the population of Spain is ridiculously small in comparison to the top countries in seafood consumption, we can better understand the importance of seafood in Spanish gastronomy. In other words, fish in Spain is a staple food that is eaten at least once a week as part of the diet for many Spaniards. As a result, each Spaniard consumes, on average, around 100 pounds (45 kg) a year of fish, which is nearly twice the EU average (about 25 kg per person). By way of comparison, the average consumption in the United States is under 16 pounds (7 kg) a year.

The abundance of fish in any *mercado* (market) shows the importance that Spaniards pay to fish. The fish in Spain comes mainly from the Atlantic Ocean and the Mediterranean Sea, as well as from the fresh water of the Ebro River, the Albufera lagoon in Valencia, the streams of northern Spain (Navarra and Cantabria) and Granada, and the rivers of Asturias (salmon).

Spaniards prepare fish in many ways. For instance, *boquerones fritos* are typical in the south (Andalucía) where they are devoured like popcorn. Grilled sardines are known in Málaga as *espetos,* while in the Basque country they cook fish in stew like the popular *marmitako* (tuna stew). *Bacalao* (cod) and *merluza* (hake) are also two classic dishes in the Spanish cuisine, similar to calamari, which is one of the most traditional *tapas* of Spain.

Among Spain's most popular seafood dishes are *Bacalao al pil pil* (cod with pil pil sauce), *fritura de pescado* (Andalucía-style deep fried fish), *rape con azafrán* (monkfish steaks with saffron), *merluza a la gallega* (Galician-style hake), and *truchas a la navarra* (Navarra-style trout with dry cured *jamón*).

See also: Chapter 4: Overview. Chapter 14: Overview.

Further Reading

Campbell Caruso, James, and Douglas Merriam. *España: Exploring the Flavors of Spain.* Layton: Gibbs Smith, 2012.

Koehler, Jeff. *Spain.* San Francisco: Chronicle Books, 2013.

Trutter, Marion. *Culinaria Spain: Cuisine. Country. Culture.* Potsdam: h.f.ullmann, 2010.

Sweets

In Spain, no matter if it is a city or a small village, one is bound to encounter several *panaderías* (bakery shops) and *pastelerías* (cake shops) as well as some *heladerías* (ice cream shops) and stopping is a must. If the bars are mainly for *tapas* (between 12:00–2:00 p.m. and evenings), the *pastelerías* are common places to go for breakfast, a *merienda* (between 5:00–6:00 p.m.), or dessert. The *pastelería* is often substituted for the *heladería* in summer. These particular shops usually portray their different products in an eye-catching, well-presented showcase. The variety is endless and it is better to ask for the local sweets. Every town has their own specialty and often in plural, specialties. For example, the most common sweets from the city of Granada alone include the small delicate cakes called *piononos* and *felipes,* as well as the famous *roscos de Loja* (ring-shaped cakes), *torta Maritoñi* (a delicate round spongy cake with cream), *pestiños* (fritters of Lent, because they are prepared during the 40-day period before Easter known as *Cuaresma*—Lent), and the sweets made in the convent of Santa Catalina de Zafra. In fact, convent sweets are very popular among the locals, especially in Andalucía.

Normally Spaniards eat fruit at the end of every meal. However, for their *merienda* (5:00–6:00 p.m.), it is common to see them having a sweet. For instance, they might indulge in *magdalenas* (Spanish muffins, which are much smaller than the North American size), *palmeras* (pastries covered in chocolate), or simply some sort of *galletas* (biscuits) like the *torta de aceite tradicional* (aniseed biscuits).

When Spaniards eat out, they tend to order homemade dessert. The most popular Spanish desserts are the following: *flan* (cream caramel), *natillas* (custard), *arroz con leche* (rice pudding), *macedonia de frutas* (fruit salad), or *tarta de helado de whiskey* (whiskey ice cream cake). Other popular sweets are *crema catalana* (Catalan custard), Andalusian *polvorones* (crumbly Spanish shortbread), *tarta de Santiago* (St James's Cake), *ensaimada* (Mallorcan Snails), *torrijas* (Easter Week fritters), or *leche frita* (fried milk). The last two are homemade and hard to find in restaurants but available in certain *pastelerías*.

See also: Chapter 14: Overview; Regional Dishes and Drinks.

Further Reading

Balaguer, Oriol, et al. *Dessert Cuisine*. 2nd ed. Barcelona: Montagud Editors, 2006.

Camorra, Frank, and Richard Cornish. *MoVida Desserts and Pastries: Spanish Culinary Adventures*. Sydney: Murdoch Books, 2011.

Tapas

The culture of tapas is popular in Spain and internationally. Its origins are not fully known. One story states that tapas were created by an ancient king who wanted to curtail the drunkenness of his subjects. Another story claims that in the 18th century, innkeepers would offer refreshments for the customers as they changed horses. The innkeepers put a small piece of bread or cheese over the glass of wine to prevent the flies from getting in the glass. The world *tapas* translated literally means "a cover" or "a lid."

Tapa is a small portion of food that varies depending on where you are. For instance, *pescaíto frito* (fried small fish), *tortilla española* (Spanish omelette), or *croquetas* (ham croquettes) are popular samples of what in North America are called appetizers or starters and in Spain are christened as tapas. In fact, in the Spanish language there is a verb "tapear," which means to go for tapas. Tapas is another strong tradition deeply rooted in the Iberian culture, which reflects the country's rich gastronomical heritage. In essence, Spaniards know how to enjoy life, and tapas inextricably constitute an integral part of its charm. Hence, it is very common to see many quaint Spanish *bares* with clients talking enthusiastically about soccer and politics while they are having a drink and enjoying a tapa, which usually is eaten standing up before lunch or as a substitute for dinner. This kind of a ritual is practiced all over Spain, which highlights the cordiality of the Spanish people.

There are many tapas bars in Spain. Each bar usually specializes in certain tapas. Some of them are served in a small bowl (*gambas al ajillo* [prawn garlic] / *albóndigas* [meat balls], etc.) or on a small plate (*jamón* [cured ham] / *chorizo* [Spanish sausage] / *queso* [cheese]). The waiter serves as many forks as clients at the table and everyone eats from the central plate, which constitutes another cultural experience. The price of a tapa is quite reasonable and can be very practical if you are not yet fully immersed in the highly diversified Spanish cuisine. Each region has its own gastronomical specialties, so the options for different items of food and drink are immense. Some places in Spain even offer a free tapa with a drink, which emphasizes the tradition that wine and food go together in Spain. In other words, Spaniards do not drink wine alone but with food. Free tapas are very popular in Granada and Jaén (both cities located in Andalucía), although there are great tapas bars at an unbeatable price all over Spain.

See also: Chapter 14: Overview.

Further Reading

Evans, Polly. *It's Not about the Tapas*. New York: Bantam Dell, 2003.

Lawson, Jane, ed. *Cooking Spanish*. Vancouver: Whitecap, 2005.

Lewis, Emma. *200 Tapas and Spanish Dishes*. London: Hamlyn, 2013.

Traditional Dishes

Traditional Spanish dishes were created "not in palace kitchens, but as country fare" (Koehler 2013). The following is a general list of food items that any tourist should try at least once when visiting Spain, because they define the richness of Spanish gastronomy:

Traditional tapas: *tortilla española* (Spanish omelette), *calamares a la romana* (calamari), *gambas al ajillo* (garlic prawns), *mejillones al vapor* (steamed mussels), *una tabla de embutidos* (a tray of cold cuts), *una tabla de quesos* (a tray of cheeses), *ensaladilla rusa* (Russian salad), *croquetas* (croquettes), and *albóndingas* (meat balls).

Traditional lunches: *paella* (Spain's most iconic dish), *migas* (fried breadcrumbs), *carne en salsa con patatas* (meat in a sauce with fried potatoes), *chistorra con patatas a lo pobre* (fast-cured sausage with potatoes cooked Spanish-style).

Traditional dinners: *sopa de merluza* (soup of hake), *bacalao al pil pil* (cod cooked in a tasty sauce), *ensalada mixta* (mixed salad).

Traditional fruits: cherimoyas and persimmons (only available from November to January), oranges, quinces, figs, prickly pears (*higos chumbos* only in summer), melons, watermelons, plums, peaches, pears, apricots, and bananas from the Canary Islands.

Traditional home-made desserts: *arroz con leche* (rice pudding), *natillas* (custard), *flan* (caramel cream), *cuajada* (curd), *crema catalana* (Catalan cream).

Traditional sweet drinks: *chocolate a la taza* (chocolate in the cup), *horchata* (tiger-nuts or almond juice), *leche rizada* (curly milk), *leche merengada* (meringue milk), *granizada de limón* (slushy lemon slurp), *mosto* (non-alcoholic wine), Licor 43 (alcoholic liquor).

Traditional after-dinner drinks: Apart from producing the best sherries in the world, Spaniards are expert in creating superb brandies. *Fundador* is a popular brand of cognac from the Pedro Domecq family. Also, *103* white label is a very smooth brandy sold at a good price in Spain. In addition, the following are quintessential drinks from Spain: *agua de Valencia* (orange juice and cava), cava, sangria (summer red wine mixed with fruits), *aguardiente de orujo* (burning water), *ponche caballero*, *pacharán* and any Rives liquor, as well as any Anís liquor.

See also: Chapter 14: Overview.

Further Reading

Aris, Pepita. *The Real Taste of Spain in 150 Traditional Dishes*. Wigston: Lorenz Books, 2013.

Torres, Marimar. *Traditional Dishes from Spain*. Sausalito: Torres Wines North America, 1981.

Vegetarian Dishes

Spain used to be a difficult country for vegetarians. In fact, until very recently, it was hard to find just one vegetarian restaurant in a medium-sized town. Due to the new multiculturalism in Spain, this has changed. Nowadays it is relatively easy to find vegetarian restaurants in most Spanish cities. The traditional Spanish cuisine, however, has always had a few staple vegetarian dishes. The following is a list of 10 popular veggie starters. But remember to ask for the local vegetarian food. Most Spanish restaurants include a section of food for vegetarians. Here are, probably, the ten most common vegetarian dishes:

Pisto is a mélange of fresh fried vegetables that originated in the La Mancha region, where vegetables grow abundantly. Basically pisto consists of sautéed onions, zucchini, tomatoes, and peppers, and it is normally served with a poached egg as a starter. It also goes well with grilled lamb or beef as a main course. Pisto can also be accompanied with Manchego cheese and it is very popular in the summer season.

After the *paella*, the *tortilla española* is without a doubt another of Spain's iconic foods. It translates as Spanish potato omelette, although most Spaniards also add a white onion to make it more spongy. It goes well with many other food items, including cheeses, olives, grilled peppers, salad, and even as a food for breakfast.

Garbanzo con espinacas is a stew of chickpeas with spinach that is also called *olla gitana* (Gipsy stew). It is usually served in a small terra-cotta *cazuelita* (casserole dish), which is typical of Andalusian style. Hence, *olla gitana* is also popular as a tapa in a bar in Andalucía. Do not confuse with *ensalada gitana* or *remojón*, also from Andalucía, which consists of a combination of ingredients such as cod, boiled eggs, boiled pota-toes, oranges, a tin of tuna, black olives, and a lot of extra-virgin olive oil left to soak for a few hours before serving. People in Granada call it *remojón*, which translates to "soak," meaning that the best part of the dish is dipping fresh bread into the sauce mixed with all the ingredients.

Pimientos del Padrón are fried small green peppers from Padrón, which is a village in A Coruña (Galicia). They are served very hot as a tapa. These particular green pep-pers are small but very tasty and fresh. Currently they can be found in the United States in places such as Whole Foods, and abroad they can be found under the Japanese name "shishito peppers."

Salmorejo is essentially a cold purée of fresh tomatoes and garlic. In Andalucía it is usually served with slices of boiled egg and breadcrumbs as a topping. Warning: Some-times it also contains a slice of *jamón* on top! *Salmorejo* is very refreshing on a hot sum-mer day. The difference from the other popular Andalusian cold soup, *gazpacho*, is that the latter is much thinner in texture and served typically in a glass with ice as opposed to *salmorejo*, which is served in a small bowl. Both, however, are starters and popular as a tapa.

Revuelto de espárragos trigueros are scrambled eggs with wild green asparagus, which can be as long as 8 inches (20 centimeters) when pulled out of the ground. They are very common in late winter and spring, especially in the Dehesa region in the south of Extremadura. In fact, the region of Extremadura has become a huge exporter of wild vegetables, including mushrooms, to France.

Berengenas fritas (fried eggplant) and *croquetas vegetarianas* (vegetarian croquettes) are another two popular vegetarian dishes in Spain. The first is simple, while the latter requires a bit more preparation. Instead of the traditional chicken and ham croquettes, the veggie version usually constains leeks and mushrooms.

Escalivada is a Catalan word that means "to cook on hot embers." It consists of smoky grilled vegetables which usually are red peppers, eggplant, and onions. Traditionally this dish is prepared in the oven, although the authentic way is to cook it on hot charcoal or over a gas flame. It goes very well accompanined with a Spanish omelette and cheese.

Ensaladilla rusa means "little Russian salad" and the origin perhaps has to do with Russia. In particular, Spain's dictator Francisco Franco sent the *División Azul* (the Blue Division) as volunteer soldiers (around 20,000) to fight with Germany during World War II on the eastern front, confronting Boshevism, and some Spanish soldiers ad[o/a] pted the name. It contains mashed potatoes, a big tin of tuna, green olives for pickles, sweet peas, and two hard-boiled, chopped eggs. After all the ingredients have been mixed in a big bowl, it is served covered in mayonnaise with some tinned grilled red peppers or anchovy fillets on top as the final frill.

See also: Chapter 14: Overview.

Further Reading

Barlow, John. *Everything but the Squeal: Eating the Whole Hog in Northern Spain*. New York: Farrar, Straus & Giroux, 2008.

Christian, Rebecca. *Cooking the Spanish Way: Revised and Expanded to Include New Low-Fat and Vegetarian Recipes*. Minneapolis: Lerner Publications, 2002.

REFERENCES

Argandoña, Antonio; Joan Fontrodona, and Pilar García Lombardía. *Libro Blanco del Consumo Responsable de Alcohol en España*. Madrid: IESE, CBS & Diageo, 2009.

Greenberg, Paul. "Time for a Sea Change." *National Geographic* October (2010). http://ngm.nationalgeographic.com/2010/10/seafood-crisis/greenberg-text

Harráiz, Alberto. *Spain: Mediterranean Cuisine*. Cambridge: KÖNEMANN, 2006.

Martin, Neil. "Give a Little Respect: Cava." In *catalanwinesusa.com* May 6, 2013: http://catalanwinesusa.com/2013/05/give-a-little-respect-cava-by-neil-martin

Muñoz Cidad, Cándido et al. *Informe Económico 2013*. Madrid: Fiab.es, 2013.

Operé, Fernando, and Carrie B. Douglass. *España y los españoles de hoy. Historia, sociedad y cultura*. New Jersey: Pearson, 2008.

Paratore, Monika. *Cooking Spanish*. Vancouver: Murdoch Books Pty Limited, 2005.

Pinsky, Charles dir. *Spain . . . On the Road Again*. PBS, 2008 (13 episodes).

Thring, Oliver. "Champagne Sales Lose Their Sparkle." *The Guardian,* July 23, 2012.

Trutter, Marion. *Culinaria Spain*. Cambridge: KÖNEMANN, 2004.

Websites

Arzak.es

http://asadoretxebarri.com/en

Cellercanroca.com

cnbc.com/id/26789471

elbulli.com

http://europa.eu/index_en.htm

Foodswinesfromspain.com

guiarepsol.com

iberianature.com/material/spain_food/galician_food.html

Iberico.com

Joselito.com

Quiquedacosta.es

spainisdelicious.com/en/iberico-ham-label

spainontheroadagain.com

travelchannel.com/tv-shows/anthony-bourdain/episodes/spain

worldsofflavorspain.com

CHAPTER 15

LEISURE AND SPORTS

OVERVIEW

Spain likes to play. It is a nation where one can participate in sports from all over the world, including skiing, snowboarding, and extreme sports such as kite surfing. Most Spaniards grow up playing soccer and basketball, the two most popular sports in the country with the exception of cycling. Other typical sports include tennis, golf, field hockey, and water (aquatic) sports.

The swimmer Mireia Belmonte, the sprint canoer David Cal, and the taekwondo specialists Joel González, Nicolás García, and Brigitte Yagüe, are all Olympic medalists, and examples of Spain's recent success in sporting events. Gisela Pulido, who was the youngest European Junior Champion in 2003 in kite surfing was also the youngest sportswoman ever nominated to the Laureus World Sport Awards. Carolina Marín became two times number one in the world in badminton (2014, 2015), and was the 2014 European Champion. The Spanish men's national team of roller hockey is the most successful team in the world with 16 titles, and counting. The Paralympics swimming champion Teresa Perales has won 22 Olympic medals (6 gold) in the Olympic Games, the same number as American swimmer Michael Phelps. The celebration of the Summer Olympics in Barcelona 1992 marked a milestone in the Spanish history of sport. During these Summer Olympics, Spain won 22 medals in total (13 gold) and ranked sixth in the world. In essence, this put Spain among the best countries of athletes on the globe.

Sport is more than an area of honor for Spain; it is also an important factor that attracts many tourists to the region. Spain is the second most mountainous country in Europe, and thus lends itself well to climbing, mountain biking, skiing, and hiking. Although the Iberian Peninsula is full of mountains, there are two unique places that experts enjoy rock climbing in Spain: the Costa Blanca (Alicante) in the Mediterranean Sea, perhaps Europe's best winter climbing venue; and El Chorro in Málaga, which also offers excellent climbing adventures. Mountain biking is also a sport that is growing rapidly. Spain has the highest average altitude in Europe, offering the best selection of terrain and trail conditions for enthusiasts. One of the best venues in Spain is the Almanzora Valley in the Sierra de los Filabres, located on the Costa de Almería, Andalucía. The Valley de Castril, Pico del Buitre, and Cazorla routes are also excellent locations to enjoy mountain biking. Hiking is becoming popular as well, especially among the younger generation. Furthermore, equestrian tourism is another trendy way to see the countryside.

There are more than 30 established ski resorts in the mountains of Spain. Valdelinares is a small town and ski resort located in Teruel, in the region of Aragón. The altitude of the village is 1,690 meters above sea level, making it one of the highest ski resorts on the Iberian Peninsula. Baqueira-Beret in the Catalan Pyrenees is the biggest, and also most exclusive, ski resort in Spain with more than 80 kilometers of marked runs. Sierra Nevada in Granada, Andalucía, is the southern-most ski resort in all of Europe. It is very modern with 70 kilometers of marked runs. Here you can easily spend half of your day skiing and the other half swimming in the Mediterranean Sea, which is only 45 minutes away. Sierra Nevada contains the highest point of continental Spain called Mulhacén at 3,478 meters (11,411 feet). Among many ski events, Sierra Nevada held the FSI Alpine World Ski Championships in 1996. Other major ski resorts in Spain are La Molina, Astún, Candanchú, Cerler, Formigal, Panticosa, and Navacerrada. The latter is located in the mountains of Madrid. The most famous skiers from Spain are the Fernández Ochoa family and María José Rienda Contreras, who has six World Cup victories, all in giant slalom.

Spain has more than 100 leisure ports for boats to dock, good winds, and 300 days of sun, plus three different seas. Apart from the warm Mediterranean Sea, the cold Cantabrian Sea, and the Atlantic Ocean, Spain also offers a variety of navigable rivers, lakes, and reservoirs. More than one hundred sailing clubs and many other sporting ports are located around the coast—mostly on the Mediterranean, where conditions are better for sailing. One of the popular water sports in Spain is windsurfing, and one of the most visited destinations, if not the best in Europe, is Tarifa, a name synonymous with windsurfing in Spain. The Mediterranean Sea is also a magnet for divers who want to explore submarine life. Alejandro Abascal was the first Spanish sailor to win the gold Olympic medal in 1980. Luis Doreste remains Spain's sailing Olympic champion, winning the gold medal in the Summer Olympics in Los Angeles (1984) and in Barcelona (1992) as well as being three times European Champion (1976, 1985, and 1988). Marina Alabau is a sailor and windsurfer, has won five gold medals at the European championships, was the winner of the World Championships in 2009, and was gold medalist of the Olympic games of 2012 in the category of windsurfing. The International Descent of the River Sella is a kayaking race on the famous river Sella that winds through the rolling green landscape of Asturias. This race attracts over a thousand participants from around the globe and ends in the historic northern coastal town of Ribadesella, where in keeping true to Spain's love of mixing all things with pleasure, a four-day festival is planned around the race featuring live musicians and street vendors. This race, which originally began in 1929, was recognized by UNESCO as a World Heritage tourism event.

Spain's 422 golf clubs make it Europe's leading golfing country. The Valderrama course in San Roque (Cádiz) is considered the best on the entire continent. Spain has four major golf courses that rank among the top 10 golf courses in Europe, according to *Golf Monthly* senior staff, contributors, and some well-travelled members: Valderrama (1), PGA Catalunya (3), Sotogrande (5), and El Saler (8). The region of Andalucía is a major attraction—especially during the winter season, which offers golf courses in a warmer climate while the rest of Europe is frozen. Visitors are guaranteed 300 days of sun and golf per year.

Spain celebrates annual international sporting events such as the Linares chess tournament, which is usually described as the Wimbledon of chess, and the Teresa Herrera Trophy, which is one of Spain's most prestigious preseason soccer tournaments organized by the town hall of A Coruña. Spain also has achieved international recognition for holding major international sports celebrations such as the Olympic Games in Barcelona 1992, the World Biking Championships in Sierra Nevada 2000; and the 1997 Ryder Cup in Sotogrande, marking the first time this golf event was hosted in Europe. Spain also hosted the America's Cup 2007 international yachting competition in Valencia, which was the first America's Cup ever to be held in Europe; and in 2010 Valencia held the 33rd annual America's Cup competition. America's Cup is the oldest sports trophy in the world. Hosting these major sports events has also contributed to the economic development of Spain as a powerhouse in tourism.

Tourism aside, a much simpler sport is gaining popularity among the locals in Spain. As reported by the journalist Pablo R. Suanzes, jogging has become without a doubt the most popular sport practiced in Spain since 2005. Because many Spanish families cannot pay a gym fee, they are turning to a more economical solution. In 2013, 2.2 million sports shoes were sold in Spain, which was double the amount of 2009. In other words, the economic crisis in Spain has been very beneficial for the jogging industry. For instance, carreraspopulares.com in 2013 listed over 3,000 popular races in Spain, without including decathlons and triathlons.

Possibly surpassing Spain's enthusiasm for sport is its love of leisure, and this includes its festivals. Spain is considered the land of fiestas, because literally there is a fiesta every day somewhere in Spain. Despite the fact that Spain is a secular country according to the constitution of 1978, Spaniards observe the Christian calendar. Following this almanac, every day results in a celebration somewhere in the Iberian Peninsula in honor of the patron saint of a particular city, town, or village. That also means that Spaniards celebrate their name days by throwing a fiesta similar to a birthday party. For some, their saint day celebration is more important than their birthday.

Spaniards commemorate religious festivities such as Easter, Christmas, and the Feast of St. James the Apostle on July 25 ("Santiago Apostol"). Also, Spain has festivals in recognition of their history like the "Capitulaciones" of Santa Fe (Granada) on April 16–18, "Día de la Hispanidad" or Columbus Day on October 12, and the mock battles of Moors and Christians, to name a few. There are also strange festivities such as the snail festival in Lleida, the garlic event in Zamora, or the seafood gala in O'Grove, for instance, all of which have a common element—the celebration of harvest. Furthermore, Spain reinvents itself and creates new festivals such as La Tomatina in Bunyol (Valencia) and the festival of Water in Lanjarón (Granada). Therefore, there are more fiestas in Spain than days in a year.

Further Reading

Campbell, Polly et al. *Focus on Spain*. Millwaukee: World Almanac Library, 2007.

Powell Kennedy, Brittany. *Between Distant Modernities: Performing Exceptionality in Francoist Spain and the Jim Crow South*. Jackson: University Press of Mississippi, 2015.

Vaczi, Mariann. *Soccer, Culture, and Society in Spain*. New York: Routledge, 2015.

Basketball

Basketball is the second most popular sport in Spain. Like soccer, there is also a very competitive league called "Liga ACB" or *Asociación de Clubs de Baloncesto* (Basketball Clubs' Association), which according to some experts is the best basketball league in Europe. The Spanish national team has won the Euro league title in 2009, 2011, and 2015. Spain also has won the Olympic silver medal in 1984, 2008, and 2012. In 2006, they became World Champions, and currently are listed second in the FIBA world rankings for men. Fernando Martín was the first Spanish player to play in the NBA in 1986 for the Portland Trail Blazers. Several Spaniards now play in the NBA such as José Calderón, Ricky Rubio, Marc Gasol, and Víctor Claver.

Pau Gasol is the greatest Spanish basketball player of all time. In 2010 he was considered the best pivot in the world. He played for the Memphis Grizzlies (2001–2008), Los Angeles Lakers (2008–2014), and currently plays for the Chicago Bulls (2014–). While he played for the Lakers, he won the NBA Champion in 2009 and in 2010, and the gold medal in the Eurobasket 2011 and 2015 with his national team, among many other important awards. The female basketball team won the title of European Champions in 1993 and in 2013. The lower categories of "Under 16," "Under 18," and "Under 20" female basketball teams also became the European Champion in the year 2013. In other words, the national women's basketball team won the European championship in every single category from "Under 16" onwards.

See also: Chapter15: Overview. Chapter 16: Overview.

Further Reading

Gasol Sáez, Pau, and Lori Shepler. *Pau Gasol. Life = Vida*. Huntington Beach: CTK Productions LLC, 2013.

Nauright, John, and Charles Parrish, eds. *Sports around the World: History, Culture, and Practice*. Santa Barbara: ABC-CLIO, 2012.

Shubert, Adrian. *A Social History of Modern Spain*. New York: Routledge, 1996.

Bullfighting

The "art" of bullfighting can be traced back to the early 18th century. And although Spain has modernized itself since the death of the dictator Francisco Franco in 1975, the bull industry remained unchanged. For some, it is the last bastion of genuine national identity. For this group, the map of Spain itself resembles the skin of a bull and, therefore, it is an essential cultural component inextricably linked to the Spanishness of Spain. The Spanish philosopher Fernando Savater published *Tauroética* in 2010, in which he argues that the *fiesta nacional* is very much linked to Spanish art, Spanish music, Spanish poetry, and even to the Spanish language. For Savater, the bull constitutes the symbol of Spain. And yet for others, it is the last vestige of Franco's shadow. And for others still, the bullfight is a barbaric anachronism which is an embarrassment to Spain's reputation as a progressive country.

According to famed matador Joselito Ortega: "You are born to be a bullfighter" (http://www.andalucia.com/history/people/joselito-ortega.htm). Like an artist, it seems that you cannot become a bullfighter, if you do not have it "in your blood," so to speak. Perhaps that is the reason why many bullfighters come from previous generations of prestigious bullfighters and/or famous bull breeders. The weekly income of a well-known bullfighter reaches the level of British soccer stars. For instance, Madrid-born José Tomás is considered the world's most sought-after bullfighter in contemporary Spain, earning a minimum of 300,000 euros per fight. On July 23, 2011, in the popular *plaza de toros* of Valencia, it is estimated that Tomás made an estimated 400,000 euros for bravely fighting two bulls.

Training to be a matador starts early. There are 42 schools of bullfighting in Spain where teenagers are taught how to kill a bull. The law in Spain does not allow children younger than 16 years old to kill a bull. Some Spanish families send their youngsters to schools in Mexico, where there is no age restriction. In contemporary Spain, among the most legendary bullfighters were Juan Belmonte (1892–1962), Antonio Ordoñez (1932–1998), Manuel Rodríguez "Manolete" (1917–1947), Francisco Rivera Paquirri (1948–1984), Manuel Benítez "El cordobés" (1936–), and Curro Romero (1933–), all of them born in Andalucía.

The oldest bullring in the world is La Maestranza (built in 1761) in Sevilla and one of the most beautiful ones is the plaza de toros in the Andalusian town of Ronda (built

A bullfighter faces off with a bull in Sevilla, Spain. Bullfighting is popular in Spain, though some Spaniards consider it an art while others view it as barbaric. (Corel)

in 1784), Málaga. However, the most important plaza de toros in Spain is without a doubt Las Ventas (built in 1931) in Madrid. Maximum glory will be recognized to any bullfighter who triumphs in this particular bullring.

The price of a ticket varies from €10 to €100, depending on where you want to be seated: *sol* (under the sun) or *sombra* (under the shadow). The bullfighting industry employs about 200,000 people—from bull breeders to bullfighters' assistants—and turns over about €1.5 billion a year. The European Union subsidizes bull breeders with €220 per bull annually. About 12,000 bulls were killed in the year 2000 in annual *corridas* (bullfights) in the country, where top matadors are celebrities comparable to movie stars. In 2006, 11,458 bulls were killed in official plazas de toros in Spain. The taxpayers in Spain dedicate €550 million to the bullfighting industry every year. However, the financing of bullfighting is now disputed by the anti-bullfighting association www .stopourshame.com, whose study reflects that 72 percent of Spanish taxpayers are against this tax.

There are three countries in the European Union that have bullfighting: Spain, France, and Portugal. This Spanish tradition also expanded to eight former Spanish colonies in the New World countries of Colombia, Costa Rica, Ecuador, Mexico, Panama, Peru, Venezuela, and Uruguay. By the new millennium, however, Spain experienced a multicultural force with the arrival of many immigrants from all over the world, who are making a significant impact into the new Spanish culture. In other words, if bullfighting used to be considered a respectable tradition until a few decades ago, nowadays, many Spaniards feel at best indifferent about it.

Historically the artistic dance between matador and bull has inspired numerous artists and writers. Francisco de Goya, for instance, dedicated a series of 33 etchings to the subject entitled, *La Tauromaquia*. Many others, like the Spanish painters Sorolla and Picasso and the French artist Manet, were inspired to create art on the subject, while writers and philosophers such as Lorca, Machado, Vargas Llosa, Hemingway, and Ortega y Gasset wrote about the experience. The Spanish philosopher Ortega y Gasset was an advocate, writing "not only is the bullfight an important reality in the history of Spain since 1740 . . . but—and I say this in the most express and formal manner—one cannot write the history of Spain from 1650 to our own time without keeping the bullfight clearly in mind" (Shubert 1999). On the other hand, there are also a significant number of artists who were against this Spanish tradition such as Hans Christian Andersen, Victor Hugo, Franz Kafka, George Bernard Shaw, Mark Twain, and H. G. Wells.

There is no doubt that the popularity of bullfighting in Spain is declining every year. Perhaps the most illustrative survey is the Gallup 2006, which shows that 72.1 percent of Spaniards are not interested at all in bullfighting and just 7.4 percent are very interested. Other independent statistics reiterate similar results like a survey run by the national television news *Telecinco* in March 2010 (available at http://www.animanaturalis .org/n/10637/), where 68 percent are in favor of banning bullfighting in Spain in contrast with 32 percent opposed. Furthermore, visitors to Spain are not interested in attending a bullfight either. For example, 89 percent of the British public (the number one tourist nationality in Spain) would not visit a bullfight when on holiday; 76 percent said that it is wrong for the tourist industry to promote bullfighting in any way; and a survey done by the Franz Weber Foundation in 2003 found that 93 percent of German visitors, 81 percent of visitors from Belgium, and 82 percent of visitors from Switzerland expressed opposition to the *corridas de toros* (bullfightingfreeeurope.org).

With these numbers, it can be argued that the tourist industry in Spain may even attract more tourists once bullfighting has been banned in the whole country. The fact that in August 2007 the Spanish national television channel *RTVE* banned live coverage of any corrida de toros demonstrates that there is a shift of mentality in the Spanish culture. This change of mentality can also be observed in the Spanish news. Until very recently the Spanish media used to cover the news on bullfighting in the culture section as part of the artistic shows or cultural spectacles available in Spain. However, as it is controversial to associate bullfighting with art, news on bullfighting is now placed in the sports section.

The Canary Islands was the first region of Spain banning bullfighting in 1991. In 2010 the region of Catalunya decided to do the same. The ban on bullfighting became official in Catalunya in 2012, not without political implications. As Catalan separatists desire autonomy from Spain, they view bullfighting as a representation of the very country that they are trying to distance themselves from. On the other side of the spectrum, the regions of Madrid, Murcia, and Valencia measured bullfighting as a national heritage of cultural interest.

In 2012 the conservative government of Mariano Rajoy (2011–) reintroduced the corridas de toros on national public television. On December 2013, the Spanish government passed the bill called "Pentauro," which in Spanish stands for *Plan Estratégico Nacional de la TAUROmaquia*. It essentially protects bullfighting nationally as part of Spain's cultural heritage.

See also: Chapter 1: Overview. Chapter 5: Ortega y Gasset, José; Savater, Fernando. Chapter 15: Overview. Chapter 16: Overview.

Further Reading

Kennedy, Alison Louise. *On Bullfighting*. New York: Anchor Books, 2001.

Shubert, Adrian. *Death and Money in the Afternoon: A History of the Spanish Bullfight*. New York: Oxford University Press, 1999.

Cycling

Cycling was always a popular sport in Spain, especially thanks to the victories of Federico Bahamontes in 1959 and Luis Ocaña in 1973 in the Tour de France, who were the first Spaniards to win the most prestigious cycling event in the world. Pedro Delgado won it in 1988, and also twice won the Vuelta a España in 1985 and 1989, becoming an idol for the new generations of cyclists in Spain.

The early 1990s are indisputably marked by Miguel Induráin, one of the most talented cyclists in the world. This athlete grew up in a small town on the outskirts of

Pamplona in the mountainous region of northern Spain. He made cycling history in 1995 when he became the first person to win the Tour de France five times for consecutive years (1991–1995), an event which over six million Spaniards watched on TV. In addition to that honor, he won two Giro d'Italia races (1992, 1993), was an Olympic champion in 1996, and world champion in 1995, an array of impressive achievements that made him a legend in the world of sport. He retired at the age of 32, but has greatly increased the popularity of cycling in Spain.

Spanish cyclists are often in the top positions in any major international cycling event. For instance, Óscar Pereiro (2006) and Carlos Sastre (2008) won the Tour de France once while Alberto Contador won twice (2007 and 2009) plus two Giro d'Italia (2008, 2015), and one Vuelta a España (2008), and counting.

The Spanish national cycling team has won a total of 19 medals throughout its history in the world of road racing. It has held three world championships in the road race and two in the timed trials. The stars in this field are Abraham Olano, Óscar Freire, and Igor Astarloa. In women's cycling the star is Joane Somarriba, the winner of the Tour de France in 2000, 2001, and 2003, and of the Giro d'Italia in 1999 and 2000. With the women's national cycling team she won the gold medal at the world timed trials in 2003, the silver medal in 2005, and the bronze medal in the world championship road race in 2002.

Another cycling discipline practiced in Spain is track racing. Its top exponent is Joan Llaneras, a seven-time world champion, a gold medal winner in the 2000 Sydney Olympics, a silver medal winner in Athens in 2004, and a double medalist (gold in overall score and silver in Madison along with Antonio Tauler) in Beijing in 2008. Llaneras even surpassed another track cycling legend, Guillermo Timoner, who was a six-time world champion.

In cross-country mountain biking, Spain's winners include Marga Fullana, three-time world champion and bronze medal winner at the 2000 Sydney Olympics, and José Antonio Hermida, a three-time world champion in relay and silver medal winner at the 2004 Athens Olympics.

See also: Chapter 15: Overview. Chapter 16: Overview.

Further Reading

Fallon, Lucy, and Adrian Bell. *Viva la Vuelta!* Norwich: Mousehold Press, 2005.

Lowe, Felix. *Climbs and Punishment.* London: Bantam Press, 2014.

Tsaneva, Petya. *Mediterranean Spain by Bicycle.* www.meetlovevisit.com

Family Outings and Vacations

Spaniards tend to go out to a restaurant for a big lunch as a family group traditionally on the weekend. Also, it is quite common among families with small children to visit their grandparents and enjoy a family lunchtime gathering. Another popular family outing is to go to the mountains for a hike, or to spend the day at the beach, which is usually done on Sundays. This type of family outing is distinctively called *domingueros*, which comes from the word *domingo* (Sunday) to refer to the people who come to the beach on Sunday. Therefore, it is not unusual to see more people at the beach on the weekends, when it is typical for an entire family with an arsenal of food and their dog to occupy a portion of the beach.

Spaniards usually receive their salaries monthly but it is also a custom to have two extra payments for the vacations: one extra payment at Christmas and another at the beginning of summer. This may lead you to believe that Spaniards make more money but the reality is otherwise. Most Spanish salaries are below the average of their counterparts in the European Union. In fact, due to the recession in Spain (2008–2014), the government cut one extra salary to all civil servants in 2013. As a result, the average Spanish family does not go abroad. This particularly happens during the Christmas period, when Spaniards traditionally prefer to stay with family. Christmas vacation usually means a visit and stay with the grandparents. The summer holidays, on the contrary, is the period when Spaniards tend to go abroad, although the average Spanish family still prefers to go for a few days to the nearest beach and/or travel domestically.

See also: Chapter 10: Overview; Food and Dining Out. Chapter15: Overview. Chapter 16: Overview.

Further Reading

Dickin Schinas, Jill. *A Family Outing in the Atlantic*. London: Imperator Publishing, 2008.

Medina, F. Xavier. *Food Culture in Spain*. Westport: Greenwood Prescs, 2005.

La Tomatina

La Tomatina is the most popular food festival in Spain due to the fact that this annual event is gaining more international attention every year. On the last Wednesday of every August, thousands of people gather in the *Plaza del pueblo* of Bunol, a small village near Valencia. This normally unassuming town tucked in the countryside of Valencia normally consists of about 9,000 habitants, yet swells in size receiving over 40,000 visitors during La Tomatina.

The first Tomatina dates back to 1945. There are several theories about the origin of this celebration. According to Hispanist professors Muñoz and Marcos, it started due to a fight between several youngsters who could not participate in the procession. Because they were upset, they picked up tomatoes from a nearby stand and threw them at the authorities. The following year, the "victims," looking for revenge, brought their own tomatoes and started another tomato fight. The number of participants increased every year but it was banned in 1950 and 1956. However, the locals enjoyed "la tomatina" so much that the authorities recognized it officially. Certain rules have been established, however, such as: to respect the signals between the beginning and

People throw tomatoes at each other during the La Tomatina festival in Buñol, Spain, on August 28, 2013. (Iakov Filimonov/Dreamstime.com)

the end of the battle; to open the tomatoes before throwing them to avoid injuring anyone; not to rip off the clothes of your adversary; and not to bring any type of glass or bottles to the main plaza where it takes place for exactly one hour. Although this festival is in honor of the town's patron saints, St. Louis Bertrand and the Mare de Déu del Desemparats, it was banned for a few years during Franco's regime for having no religious significance.

The night before La Tomatina, participants of the festival compete in a paella cooking contest. Also, following the tradition, women usually wear a white t-shirt and/or swimming clothes while men wear no shirts. Over 125 tons of tomatoes are provided by the local town hall for this annual event. In 2008 the total cost of La Tomatina was €120,000 euros, much of which is subsidized by the local government, revenues from tourism, and television rights. In 2013 the town hall also added a €10 entry fee in order to access the "tomato area." Also, they limit attendance to a maximum of 15,000 partcipants. Thanks to this festival, Bunol is now known around the globe at zero cost in publicity.

See also: Chapter 15: Overview. Chapter 16: Overview.

Further Reading

Galván, Javier A., ed. *They Do What? A Cultural Encyclopedia of Extraordinary and Exotic Customs from around the World*. Santa Barbara: ABC-CLIO, 2014.

Hannan, Nicolette, and Michelle Williams. *Spanish Festivals and Traditions*. Bedfordshire: Brilliant Publications, 2011.

Las Fallas

The origin of Las Fallas dates from the 1400s in medieval Spain, when local carpenters used to burn candles on large scraps of wood in order to see, especially during the winter. Every March they lit the whole structure on fire, since they no longer needed it, as the longer daylight of spring was sufficient. Hence, Las Fallas honors the arrival of spring and the memory of Saint Joseph, the patron saint of carpenters.

The word *falla* in Valencian means bonfire. The festival is comprised of two main events: the papier mâché figures (*ninots*) and the fireworks. The fireworks of Las Fallas takes place every March 15–19 in Valencia to celebrate the feast of San José. The Valencia region has one of the most advanced industries on pyrotechnics. In fact, *la Nit del Foc* (the Night of Fire) on March 18 and the loud daytime fireworks of the *Mascletà* (every day until March 19) are recognized as one of the best fireworks shows in the world. Valencia's town hall has an annual budget dedicated entirely to this particular celebration.

During the festival of Las Fallas there are hundreds of painted cardboard, papier mâché, and wooden figures (*ninots*). These playful, fantastical structural feats can tower up to 100 feet. They are burned during the last day of Las Fallas, on March 19, known as *Mascletà*. Usually these figures are a caricature of people who have been in the news for different reasons such as politicians, artists, celebrities, cartoon characters, and even religious icons. This satirical representation of society will be exhibited to the public for a few days and the community will judge the best one to be exempted from burning on March 19. Every year the winning one is kept in the *Museo del Ninot*.

Las Fallas can be seen as a religious experience in the sense that creating huge lifelike figures only later to have them destroyed could be considered as a representation of Life and Death. Everything on Earth is ephemeral like a firework. In an amalgamation of religious, social, and superstitious nuances, on March 19th Valencia is converted into an *inferno* to exorcise social problems and bring luck to farmers in the coming summer.

See also: Chapter 1: Overview; Cities: Barcelona, Madrid, Sevilla, Valencia. Chapter 15: Overview. Chapter 16: Overview.

Further Reading

Mendelson, Jordana. *Documenting Spain*. University Park: Pennsylvania State University Press, 2005.

Zollo, Mike, with Phil Turk. *World Cultures: Spain*. London: Hodder Headline, 2000.

Los Reyes Magos

The festival of "The Three Wise Men" occurs every January 5 at 5:00 p.m. in the main streets of any town in Spain. There are processions all over Spain, where sweets and some small presents are thrown from the floats to spectators below. Every city has its own variation such as the one celebrated in the mountains of Sierra Nevada in Granada, where the Three Kings can be seen skiing down to the village. This festival is a prelude to January 6, a bank holiday in Spain when Spaniards traditionally open their Christmas gifts. However, due to globalization, many Spanish families nowadays have to budget for two Christmas presents: one for December 25 in order to follow Santa Claus, who is relatively new in the Spanish culture; and another Christmas gift for the traditional Three Wise Men on January 6, when the whole family usually gets together to eat the typical *Roscón de Reyes*, a big creamy cake with presents inside.

See also: Chapter 15: Overview. Chapter 16: Overview.

Further Reading

Forbes, Bruce David. *Christmas: A Candid History*. Los Angeles: University of California Press, 2008.
McLenighan, Valjean. *Christmas in Spain*. Lincolnwood: Passport Books, 1995.

Lottery Games

The first Spanish lottery in Spain took place on December 10, 1763, under the monarchy of Carlos III, who imported the game from a tradition in Naples. Later the National Lottery was created and run by the State. Its main goals were to increase the public treasury without burdening the taxpayers and to give the general populace hope of gaining instant wealth.

For the past two centuries, Spaniards have been running a lottery. Even during the Spanish Civil War (1936–1939) the lottery continued, with both sides creating their separate National Lottery. The National Lottery has become a tradition especially during the Christmas season, when two particular games, *el Gordo* and *el Niño*, are inextricably associated with this festivity; it is a custom among Spanish families to include lottery numbers when they send their Christmas cards. *El Gordo* affectionately means "the Fat One" and it is played on December 22. This special event is aired on national television and it usually takes the whole morning due to the large number of prizes. The winning numbers on this particular occasion are announced by the children of the School of San Ildefonso in Madrid. The price of one Christmas lottery ticket is currently €20, which will result in €400,000 if it is the winning number. However, you can still win your money back if the last number of your ticket coincides with the last number of one of the winning tickets. In only one year, Christmas of 1931, was there no winner. More recently, in 2013, the region of Catalunya created its own Christmas version of *el Gordo*. *El Niño* (The Kid) is the second most popular raffle in Spain, giving away half the amount of prizes as *el Gordo*. As of January 1, 2013, individuals who have won 2,500 euros or more in any lottery are required to pay back 20 percent to the treasury. This applies to any prize won by a Spaniard nationally or internationally.

In addition to the National Lottery, the *Quiniela* is another common lottery game in Spain. The Quiniela is the name for the football pool sponsored by the *Loterías y Apuestas del Estado* (State Lotteries and Gambling), an institution that is run by the government. The first official game of the Quiniela was on September 22, 1946, and Spaniards have been playing ever since, with a few changes in the format. Nowadays one has to predict the winner of 15 soccer matches to win the Quiniela. It normally consists of 10 soccer teams from the First Division and 5 from the Second Division. So far the Quiniela has given away over 10,500 billion euros. For instance, the Quiniela of August 18, 2013, which was the first of the soccer season 2013–2014, managed to pool the amount of 4,857,762 euros, which was distributed among the winners.

ONCE stands for the National Organization of the Blind in Spain (*Organización Nacional de Ciegos en España*). ONCE is also a very popular raffle with distinctive yellow and green stands that can be seen on streets throughout the cities of Spain. It was created in 1938 with the goal of providing aid to the disabled. The price of one ticket from Monday to Thursday is 1.5 euros on which you can win 300,000 euros. They also have a big ticket called *cuponazo*, which happens on Fridays. It costs 2.5 euros with the winner earning up to 6,000,000 euros. According to this private organization, it is the lottery that makes the existence of the charitable organization possible.

See also: Chapter 4: Overview. Chapter 15: Overview. Chapter 16: Overview.

Further Reading

Andreff, Wladimir, ed. *Contemporary Issues in Sports Economics*. Northampton: Edward Elgar Publishing, 2011.

Labanyi, Jo, ed. *Constructing Identity in Contemporary Spain*. Oxford: Oxford University Press, 2002.

Moros y Cristianos

The mock battle of Moors and Christians is an example of how beautifully Spain integrates history, religion, and social mores into a civilized fiesta, which ends with a traditional drink between the Catholic king and the Arab chief. This festival takes place in many towns, especially close to the Mediterranean Sea in Spain. It enacts the battles between the Christians and the Moors, who subsequently left by the sea after more than seven centuries in power (during the period known as *Reconquista* from the eighth to the 15th century). The best places to enjoy this historic festival are Alcoy (Alicante) on April 21–24, and Guardamar del Segura (Alicante) on the second fortnight of July. Almansa (Albacete) is also famous for its *Moros y Cristianos* festival from May 1–6, which adds a distinctive cuisine during the celebration.

See also: Chapter 1: Overview. Chapter 2: Overview. Chapter 15: Overview. Chapter 16: Overview.

Further Reading

Guia, Aitana. *The Muslim Struggle for Civil Rights in Spain, 1985–2010*. Sussex: Sussex Academic Press, 2014.

Harris, Max. *Aztecs, Moors, and Christians: Festivals of Reconquest in Mexico and Spain*. Austin: University of Texas Press, 2000.

Motor Sports

No matter where you go in Spain, you will almost always find motorbikes. Perhaps it is due to the good weather that Spain has a fascination with motor bikers. In 2010, Spain was the only country that held four major international racing events out of eighteen: the Gran Premio de España in Jerez; the Gran Premi de Catalunya; Gran Premio de Aragón; and the Gran Premio Generali de la Comunitat Valenciana. Ángel Nieto was the first to achieve great success in motor biking during the 1970s and 1980s. Nieto (1969–1984) has won 13 Grand Prix World Championships, making him one of the sports legends of all time worldwide.

The Grand Prix in the three disciplines of MotoGP, Moto2, and Moto3 have been usually dominated by Spaniards, and special attention should go to the names of Ricardo Tormo (1978–1981: 2 titles), Jorge Martínez (1986–1988: 4 titles), Sito Pons (1988–1989: 2 titles), Àlex Crivillé (1989–1999: 2 titles), Manuel Herreros (1989: 1 title), Emilio Alzamora (1999: 1 title), Dani Pedrosa (2001–2005: 3 titles), Jorge Lorenzo (2002–2012: 4 titles), Toni Elías (2010: 1 title), Marc Márquez (2008–2015: 4 titles), Álvaro Bautista (2006: 1 title), Julián Simón (2009: 1 title), and Nicolás Terol (2011: 1 title). By nationality, in 2010 Spain was number three in the ranking of Riders' World Championship in road racing. In the last decade Spain continues to enjoy a golden age in the three disciplines of motorcycling, where it is not surprising to see three Spaniards on top of the world ranking. The females Ana Carrasco and María Herrera are also well-known in the professional circuits of Moto3.

The names of Toni Bou and Jordi Tarrés in motorcycle trials and Carlos Sainz in world rally should also be mentioned since the three of them have achieved record history in their respective sports.

FORMULA 1 used to be a minor sport in Spain. Juan Jover (1951), Alfonso de Portago (1956–1957), Paco Godia (1951, 1954, 1956–1958), Antonio Creus (1960), Alex Soler-Roig (1970–1972), Emilio Zapico (1976), Adrián Campos (1987–1988), Luis Pérez-Sala (1988–1989), Marc Gené (1999–2000; 2003–2004), and Pedro de la Rosa (1999–2002; 2005–2006; 2010–2012) were the first drivers in Spain. However, Fernando Alonso was the first Spanish F-1 champion. He became a two-time world champion in 2005 and 2006, bringing Formula 1 an unprecedented audience record in Spain. More recently, two other Spanish drivers joined this sport: Jaime Alguersuari (2009–2011) and Carlos Sainz Jr. (2013–). Maria de Villota (1980–2013) was the first female Spanish racing driver. Her successful career as a F-1 test driver was abruptly cut off after a car accident in 2012, when she lost one eye, which subsequently led to her sudden death.

See also: Chapter 15: Overview. Chapter 16: Overview.

Further Reading

Pérez de las Rozas, Emilio. *Marc Márquez: Dreams Come True: My Story*. London: Ebury Press, 2014.

Other Sports

Robert Trent Jones, Jack Kicklaus, Severiano Ballesteros (1957–2011), Miguel Ángel Jiménez (1964–), José María Olazábal (1966–),and Sergio García (1980–) have all put their signature on some of the country's most prestigious courses. In women's golf, Carlota Ciganda (1990–) was the Rookie of the Year and winner of the LET Order of Merit in the same season 2012. Beatriz Recari (1987–) already has four professional wins and Azahara Muñoz (1987–) three, and counting.

Field hockey is a minor sport around the world and Spain is no exception. Generally speaking, this game is mainly practiced in the Mediterranean regions of Catalunya, Valencia, and Murcia. The national team has usually done a very good job in competition and proof of their success is the fact that Spain has remained in the top five best countries in the world since the 1970s, winning the Olympic silver medal in 1980, 1996, and 2008, and second place in the World Cup in 1971 and 1998. In the EuroHockey Nations Championship, Spain has been the champion twice—in 1974 and 2005—as well as winning the Champion Challenge in 2003 and the Champion Trophy in 2004. The Spanish women's national field hockey team also deserves a mention, since they won the gold medal for the Olympic Games in Barcelona 1992.

Water polo is also a minor sport in Spain, although there is a national Spanish water polo league. There are 12 teams in the División de Honor and another 12 in the Primera División, plus a Copa del Rey and Super Cup tournaments. Spain's men's national water polo team became world champions in 1998 and 2001. They also won a gold medal in the Olympic Games of 1996. Spain's women's national water polo team became world champions in 2014, having won the 2013 World Championships.

Gymnastics is an important sport in Spain, and a number of Spanish gymnasts have won prestigious titles. Joaquín Blume, the pioneer of this sport, won eight medals in the 1955 Mediterranean Games and the European Championship in 1957. The women's team won the gold medal in 1996. Elena Artamendi, Nerea Esbrit, Laura Muñoz, Eva Rueda, Almudena Cid, Sara Moro, Elena Gómez, and Ana María Izurieta have also received international attention. Among men, Miguel Soler in the 1980s and Jesús Carballo in the 1990s were also well-known by their international victories.

Other sports achievements include figure skating, with Javier Fernández as world champion in 2015, and Sergio Muñoz and Rafael Martínez, among others, also achieving a lot of success. In synchronized swimming, the women won the silver medal twice in the category of duet, in 2008 (Andrea Fuentes and Gemma Mengual) and 2012 (Ona Carbonell and Andrea Fuentes); further, the female national team won the silver medal in the Olympics in 2008 and the bronze medal in 2012.

See also: Chapter 15: Overview. Chapter 16: Overview.

Further Reading

Evens, Tom, and Paul Smith. *The Political Economy of Television Sports Rights*. New York: Palgrave Macmillan, 2013.

Quiroga, Alejandro. *Football and National Identities in Spain*. New York: Palgrave Macmillan, 2013.

San Fermín

The running of the bulls of Pamplona is the most international festival of Spain, whose coverage is reported by several foreign news broadcasts. Pamplona's famous running of the bulls takes place in the historic streets of Pamplona city at 8:00 a.m. beginning on July 7, which is the day of Saint Fermín—the patron of the city. The *pamplonica*s pay respect to their benefactor celebrating their local history. It is a party with a religious origin. This festival starts at midday on July 6 with the famous *txupinazo*, which is one big firework thrown from the local town hall. However, just a few minutes before, a traditional speech is given by a distinguished personality, who officially starts the celebration. During the nine days that follow, the city of Pamplona never sleeps, and there is a special ambience everywhere. The fiestas end on July 14 with the popular song "Pobre de mí" (Poor Me).

One special component of this local celebration is the traditional *encierro* that runs for a few minutes every morning, which consists of the actual bull running accompanied by hundreds of runners, although the majority of people are watching the encierro from their balconies, windows, and, of course, through live television. These encierros are common in other places of Spain, but not at the magnitude of Pamplona, which has acquired an international reputation.

SAN FERMÍN

Perhaps the massive popularity of San Fermín is due to the odes and praises of Nobel Prize-winning writer Ernest Hemingway, in his novel *The Sun Also Rises*, when he elevated the festival into a cultural phenomenon. Hemingway wrote about San Fermín, "The fiesta was really started. It kept up day and night for seven days. The dancing kept up, the drinking kept up, the noise went on. The things that happened could only have happened during a fiesta. Everything became quite unreal finally and it seemed as though nothing could have any consequences" (Hemingway, 1926). Hemingway also idealized the art of bullfighting, writing, "Nobody ever lives their life all the way up except bullfighters" (Hemingway 1926).

See also: Chapter 15: Overview. Chapter 16: Overview.

Further Reading

Hollander, Jim. *Run to the Sun: Pamplona's Fiesta de San Fermín*. Wilmington: Master Arts Press LLC, 2002.

Mouton, Ray. *Pamplona: Running the Bulls, Bars, and Barrios in Fiesta de San Fermín*. New Orleans: Quinn Pub., 2002.

Semana Santa

Semana Santa is Holy Week, which is the full week leading up to Easter Sunday. It takes place all over Spain. In essence, Semana Santa consists of processions in which enormous *pasos* or floats of a religious icon, who normally is a Virgin or the figure of Jesus, are carried around the streets by teams of *costaleros* (bearers) followed by hundreds of *nazarenos* (penitents).

The Semana Santa in Spain is also an opportunity to experience firsthand a multicultural expression of religious artifacts, the aesthetic beauty of floats in the processions, the singing or *saeta* of a flamenco singer, and the enjoyment of the specific gastronomy of Semana Santa, which is only cooked during this Holy Week. Seafood dishes like cod and hake, and sweets such as *torrijas* and *pestiños* are staples for the duration of the Semana Santa in many Spanish homes.

Related to Semana Santa is La Feria de Abril, which is the most important festival in Sevilla. It consists of attending an outdoor party held on a massive grounds called *recinto ferial* where thousands of people wear their traditional Andalusian clothes. Some even bring their own horses and carriages in order to enjoy the festivities from a booth, which are more private. Plenty of food and drinks are available throughout the night. Every night usually ends at 3:00 or 4:00 a.m., and the Feria lasts for a whole week. The origin of La Feria de Abril dates back to medieval times, when farmers used to get together for a week in order to exchange products.

See also: Chapter 5: Overview. Chapter 15: Overview. Chapter 16: Overview.

Further Reading

Mitchell, Timothy. *Passional Culture: Emotion, Religion, and Society in Southern Spain*. Philadelphia: University of Pennsylvania Press, 1990.

Zollo, Mike, with Phil Turk. *World Cultures: Spain*. London: Hodder Headline, 2000.

Soccer

Soccer is indisputably the king of sports in Spain, and you will see children playing the sport anywhere you go. Soccer has a long history in Spain and historically has been intertwined with both regionalism and politics. FC Barcelona was established in 1899 just one year after Spain lost their last colony in South America. Catalans wanted to distance themselves from Spain's shortcomings. FC Barcelona's management historically supported autonomy, which led to trouble when Franco came to power as the regime supposedly preferred Real Madrid. Though there is no longer overt political implications surrounding the two teams, one thing that Spaniards have kept is their fanatical support towards one and hatred of the other.

History aside, Real Madrid Club de Fútbol and Fútbol Club Barcelona are among the best football teams in the world. Real Madrid was voted by FIFA as the most successful club of the 20th century and it is one of the most successful teams in Europe—both in the national league and in the UEFA Champion league with a record 10. According to the 2010 Deloitte "Football Money League" report, Real Madrid and FC Barcelona are the world's richest soccer teams. In 2009, FC Barcelona managed to win six out of six competitions such as La Liga, Copa del Rey, and the Champion League, among others, becoming the first team in Spain ever to win every single title in one season.

The passion for soccer—or, as it is called outside of North America, football—is heightened by pride in "La Liga," the national soccer league of Spain. La Liga is considered the most glamorous league in the world, due to the number of soccer stars who play in the so called *la liga de las estrellas* (League of Stars).

The Spanish national soccer team popularly known as *La Furia Roja* (the Red Fury) also drew international attention as a tough team to beat. From 2006–2009 Spain held the world record of most consecutive games undefeated with 35 (it shared the honor with Brazil between 1993–1996) and the most consecutive wins with 15 in the years 2008–2009. They were world champions (2010) and also the first team to retain the European championships winning in a row in 2008 and 2012 (the championship is held every 4 years); a title that they won for the first time in 1964. They also won the Olympic gold medal in 1992. Nationwide, the international legend David Villa maintains the record of more international goals with 59, and the goal keeper Iker Casillas possesses the most international captains with 162, and counting.

See also: Chapter 1: Cities: Barcelona, Madrid, Sevilla, Valencia. Chapter 15: Overview. Chapter 16: Overview.

Further Reading

Evans, Polly. *It's Not about the Tapas*. New York: Bantam Dell, 2006.

Kuper, Simon, and Stephan Szymanski. *Soccernomics: Why England Loses, Why Spain, Germany, and Brazil Win, and Why the US, Japan, Australia—and Even Iraq—Are Destined to Become the Kings of the World's Most Popular Sport*. New York: Nation Books, 2014.

Lowe, Sid. *Fear and Loathing in La Liga: Barcelona vs. Real Madrid*. New York: Nation Books, 2013.

Tennis

Tennis was not popular in the beginning of the 20th century in Spain. However, a female player should be remembered in the Spanish history of this sport, since Lilí

Álvarez managed to play in the finals for three times in a row in Wimbledon in 1926, 1927, and 1928, and was number two in world ranking from 1927–1928. Also worthy of remembrance are the names Andrés Gimeno, winner of Roland Garros in 1972, and, in particular, Manuel Santana. He won the French Open twice (1961, 1964) as well as the U.S. Open (1965) and Wimbledon (1966), becoming the first Spaniard achieving number one ranking in 1966.

Since the 1990s, Spain has produced many talented tennis players who have won the Roland Garros—the most prestigious tournament on clay. The victories of Arantxa Sánchez Vicario (1989, 1994, 1998), Conchita Martínez (in Wimbledon 1994), Sergi Bruguera (in a row 1993 and 1994), Carlos Moyà (1998), Albert Costa (2002), and Juan Carlos Ferrero (2003) confirmed Spain as a major contender in the history of tennis. Special attention is due to Rafael Nadal, who could be considered the best athlete of all time from Spain. So far Nadal has a world record of Masters 1000 Series (27 to date), 1 gold medal (2008), and 14 Grand Slams to date. He has been number one in the ATP three times—2008, 2010, and 2013.

Nowadays there are hundreds of tennis clubs scattered throughout Spain. Madrid has become one of the tennis capitals of the world since they hold one of the Masters Series. This international tennis tournament takes place in Madrid's "Magic Box," known in Spanish as La Caja Mágica, the most modern and avant-garde scenario for the best world tennis with three main courts and retractable roofs, all in the same arena.

See also: Chapter 15: Overview. Chapter 16: Overview.

Further Reading

Nadal, Rafael, and John Carlin. *Rafa*. New York: Hyperion, 2011.

Wertheim, L. Jon. *Strokes of Genius: Federer, Nadal, and the Greatest Match Ever Played.* Boston: Houghton Mifflin Harcourt, 2009.

REFERENCES

Green, Stewart M. *Rock Climbing Europe*. Guilford: Morris Book Publishing, 2006.

Lowe, Sid. *Fear and Loathing in La Liga: Barcelona, Madrid, and the World's Greatest Sports Rivalry*. London: Nation Books, 2014.

Muñoz, Pedro M., and Marcelino C. Marcos. *España. Ayer y hoy*. 2nd ed. London: Prentice Hall, 2010.

Núñez Florencio, Rafael. "Los toros, fiesta nacional." In *Ser españoles*. Edited by Javier Moreno Luzón and Xosé M. Núñez Seixas. Barcelona: RBA, 2013 (433–463).

Quiroga Fernández, Alejandro. "El deporte." In *Ser españoles*. Edited by Javier Moreno Luzón and Xosé M. Núñez Seixas. Barcelona: RBA, 2013 (464–496).

Savater, Fernando. *Tauroética*. Madrid: Turpial, 2010.

Suanzes, Pablo R. "El negocio del 'running,' en cifras." *El Mundo,* January 19, 2014.

Suárez, Laureano. *Sports . . . in Spain*. Madrid: Turespaña, 1995.

Websites

andalucia.com/history/people/joselito-ortega.htm

animanaturalis.org/n/10637/

bullfightingfreeeurope.org/index_esp.html

carreraspopulares.com

gente5.telecinco.es/sondeos/prohibir_toros/prohibir_toros.html

losmillones.com/quiniela/premios

marbellagolf.com/latest-news/the-number-of-federated-golf-courses-in-spain-rises-to-422

once.es

stopourshame.com

CHAPTER 16

MEDIA AND POPULAR CULTURE

OVERVIEW

During Franco's dictatorship the media was controlled by the authoritarian regime, which imposed censorship on everything that was published. In fact, the censors appointed by Franco had prior access before any book was published or information aired on radio or television to the Spanish citizens. This filter, however, was not 100 percent effective, so some clandestine publications began to appear, especially in the 1970s. This is the case, for instance, with *Demócrito* (1945–1947), which was distributed with precautions among "a new Vanguard, in which an *intelligentsia* composed of students would unite with peasants, workers, and guerrillas in the struggle" (Wright 1986).

In the seventies *Cambio 16* (1971–), whose name already reflected the change (*cambio*) in the Spanish media establishment, played a significant role among Spaniards' consumption of broadcasting. *Cambio 16* is Spain's equivalent of *Time* and *Newsweek*. Soon afterwards another important magazine, *Interviú* (1976–), would also be devoured by millions of Spaniards during the Spanish transition (1975–1982), probably because of its exotic but intentional approach of combining current political affairs and naked women in the same journal. Then, in the 1980s, Spain would develop the so called *prensa rosa* or *prensa del corazón* (romantic press), which refers to popular magazines such as *Semana, Lecturas, Diez Minutos,* and, of course, the pioneer and superfamous *¡Hola!*. The latter started in 1944 and it is still a Spanish emporium, publishing two different versions: *¡Hola!* for the Spanish-speaking countries, and *Hello!* for the English-speaking world. The huge success of these weekly magazines, which are still consumed in large quantities by the Spaniards, is also due to the fact that Spanish newspapers, unlike those in the U.S. and in Britain, do not have gossip columns.

Radio and television were part of Franco's apparatus and, as the only media having the exclusive right to broadcast news, became the two most effective tools of propaganda. Nowadays, Spanish radio remains quite influential among Spaniards, who enjoy listening to radio programs, especially the early morning news, the *tertulias* (intellectual gatherings), and the evening sports programs, all of them reaching several million listeners every day. A similar scenario occurs with Spain's television. However, since the 1980s, its content has been gradually adapted not necessarily to please the average Spanish viewer, who usually demands more Spanish content, but to maximize its profits since some Spanish media networks (i.e., Telecinco) belong to global corporations that demand consumerism.

Carlos Saura's film *La caza* (1965, *The Hunt*) as well as Antonio Buero Vallejo's historical plays both constitute good examples of avoiding Franco's censorship while still promulgating criticism of the endemic violence that seems ingrained within Spanish society and that subsequently ended up in the bloodbath of the civil war. This historic period (1936–1939), plus the whole dictatorship that came afterwards (1939–1975), has been recreated in multiple artistic forms (i.e., theatre, novels, poetry, painting) not only during the post-civil war, when Spain was considered a cultural desert (mainly due to the isolation of the country from the rest of the world), but also recently as reinvented within the popular media. This is the case, for instance, with the movies *Pan's Labyrinth* (2006, Guillermo del Toro) and *Pa Negre* (2010, Agustí Villaronga). Both films achieved great international success but, with regards to popular consumption, they both interestingly exemplify the hunger of the Spanish audience for products that deal with Spain's history. This was precisely the key element for the tremendous success of Jordi Évole's documentary *Operación Palace* (la Sexta) of 2014, which recreated the 23-F coup d'état of 1981 and provoked remarkable repercussions in Spain. In fact, it became the most watched program (with over 5 million viewers and 23.9 percent of screen quota) on Spain's channel *la sexta*. The latter, by the way, is not a porn channel as its name may sound to English ears.

Pornography was strictly censored during Franco's time, a period when some Spaniards used to go to France to watch, for instance, *Last Tango in París* (1972). The last years of Franco, nonetheless, coincided with Spain's sexual revolution. A series of movies depicted this new social attitude becoming a cinematographic phenomenon characterized by *el destape* (uncovering), which essentially meant a sexually explicit sequence(s) was included during the film (i.e., *Españolas en Paris, Asignatura pendiente*). Nowadays, Spain's volume of pornography is similar to the majority of the western European countries. However, unlike other European countries, Spain, with the exception of cinema, has no policies to protect children and adolescents from exposure to pornographic material (which nowadays is an issue that equals in controversy bullfighting being aired on public live television at 5:00 p.m.). Hence, it is not uncommon to see on any of Spain's television channels at any time of the day warnings about "adult" material, including some Spanish commercials.

Other contemporary cinema directors from Spain include: Isabel Coixet (i.e., *The Secret Life of Words* 2005), Icíar Bollaín (i.e., *Even the Rain* 2010); CIMA—the Spanish acronym for the Association of Women Directors in the Spanish Media (cimamujerescineastas.es); Juan Cruz and José Corbacho (i.e., *Tapas* 2005); David Planell (i.e., *La vergüenza* 2009); Javier Rebollo (i.e., *La mujer sin piano* 2009); Isaki Lacuesta (i.e., *Los pasos dobles* 2011); Pablo Berger (i.e., *Snow White* 2012); Paco León (i.e., *Carmina o revienta* 2012); Gracia Querejeta (i.e., *15 años y un día* 2013); Neus Ballús (i.e., *La plaga* 2013); Carlos Marqués-Mercet (i.e., *10,000 km* 2014), and Adán Aliaga's *La casa de mi abuela* (*The House of my Grandmother* 2005), which remains the only Spanish documentary that has won the International Documentary Film Festival Amsterdam (IDFA) award, as well as being the recipient of numerous international awards. With regards to movie magazines, Spanish publications include: *Fotogramas, Cinemanía, Nickel Odeon, ACCIÓN, Cartelera Turia, Los olvidados, Revista de cine Encadenados;*

Revista de la Academia de Cine, and online platforms such as: labutaca.net; cinerama .es; caimanediciones.es; scifiworld.es; 400films.com.

Considering that Spain's population is less than 50 million, which is far below the U.K., Germany, France, or Italy, it is impressive to see the number of different newspapers available not only nationally but also locally. Every Spanish city has at least one local newspaper, apart from the daily national broadsheets. The power of the media in Spain, perhaps like in the U.S., has become so influential that in effect they are the political process, shaping public opinion. Because of the recent economic crisis, as Pere Rusiñol points out in 2013, most of the Spanish major newspapers have been absorbed by the bank. As a result, Spaniards are aware of the political tone of the majority of the Spanish newspapers and media in general. According to the 2014 *Libro blanco de la prensa diaria* (*White Book of the Daily News 2014*, by AEDE), Spaniards dedicated on average 55 minutes a day to reading newspapers in 2013 as opposed to 40 minutes in 2012. Thanks to the Internet, Spanish people are reading more news from a variety of sources. To be precise, in 2001, 96.8 percent of Spanish readers used to read the newspaper while in 2012 that number dropped to 59.8 percent. Nowadays, the tendency to read the news is clearly toward the digital format: 2001 (1.1%) and 2012 (22.3%). Agencies of news in Spain include: *Agencia EFE* (which is the largest news agency in the Spanish-speaking world); *Agencia Atlas; Europa Press;* and *Colpisa*.

After *Telecinco* (13.9%), *Antena 3* (12.5%) and *TVE* (12.2%) are Spain's most watched television channels in recent years. According to CIS of March 2013, Table 16.1 shows Spaniards' favorite mediums of information.

The youth social map of Spain's culture does not differ much from the global picture. In other words, since the 1960s Spain also had *hippies* (i.e., Ibiza); *punks* (i.e., Basque bands such as *La Polla Records, Eskorbuto,* and *Kortatu*); *yuppies* (i.e., Mario Conde); *Generation X* (i.e., see studies by Christine Henseler); and currently the so-called *Millennial Generation*. Since Spain's economic crisis (2008–), the majority of young Spaniards

Table 16.1   MOST USED MEDIUM OF COMMUNICATION (2013)

Medium	Total of All Ages	Age 18–24	Age 25–34
Television	56.8	52.7	54.3
Newspapers	9.0	5.9	6.2
Digital newspapers	11.9	20.9	18.3
Magazines	0.2	0	0.4
Radio	13.7	2.7	9.1
Blogs	0.6	1.4	1.5
Social media	3.6	10.5	5.7
Others	0.4	0.9	1.1
All of them	1.7	1.8	1.5
Neither	1.9	2.7	1.9

are willing to leave the country for jobs abroad. According to Spain's National Statistics Institute (INE), for the first time since 1990, in 2011 more people left Spain than moved in. Time will tell if these young Spanish skilled workers will return to Spain once the situation improves. Since the 1960s, Spanish youth has been an essential component of social movements such as feminism, gay rights, environmental protection, and support of local economies.

Within a strictly national context, as Amparo Novo and Fernando Sánchez point out, there is not a single model of Spanish youth (Novo and Sánchez 2003). Perhaps one distinctive Spanish youth group that is different from the English etymology already mentioned (hippies, punks, yuppies, Gen X, Millennial) is the so-called *Generación Ni-Ni*. The latter refers to the group of Spaniards who are not in school and are not employed (in Spanish *NI estudia NI trabaja*)—the Neither-Nor generation. Looking at the statistics of the EU, Spain has more youngsters who neither study nor work (over 14%) than the EU average (10.8%). However, this is not a new phenomenon in Spain (Areces 2010).

One of the most transformative changes in Spain's history was the generational change of the people in power in the general election of 1982. The young socialists took over from the center-right wing. This political change regenerated the cultural scene with what is known as *la movida* (the cultural boom that started in Madrid during the Spanish transition, especially due to the end of Spain's dictatorship in 1975) in the 1980s. However, before the 1980s, 1957 was another decisive year in Spain's cultural history. As Mercedes Pasalodos explains, it was a definitive moment for art, with *El Paso*, *Equipo 57,* and *Grupo Parpalló* representing new experiences. Nationally, the Spanish textile industry was growing rapidly: Catalonian mills were producing high-quality cotton for export to Morocco, England, Finland, Greece, Lebanon, Australia, Egypt, and South Africa. Although not unaffected by the trends set in Paris, Spanish fashion was characterized by its very "Spanishness," the weight of its tradition, its regional characteristics, and its indigenousness and folkloric aspects. But, above all, it was the work of the Golden Age painters like Zurbarán, Velázquez, and Goya that inspired the creations of Spanish fashion and even cinema (i.e., Goya's *The Third of May 1808* (1814) can be seen as an example of how the painter "manipulates" like a film camera the eyes of his audience). In recognition of his contributions, Spain's major national cinema awards equivalent to the Oscars are named after him, the Goya Awards.

Further Reading

Rodgers, Eamonn, ed. *Encyclopedia of Contemporary Spanish Culture*. New York: Routledge, 1999.

Wright, Eleanor. *The Poetry of Protest under Franco*. London: Tamesis, 1986.

Cinema

The first movie shot in Spain was *Plaza del Puerto en Barcelona* (1896), directed by the Frenchman Alexandre Promio (1868–1926) and produced by a French cinema company (Société Antoine Lumière et ses Fils). Eduardo Jimeno Correas (1869–1947) became the first Spanish cinema director when, in October 1896, he filmed *Salida de la misa de doce en la iglesia del Pilar de Zaragoza* (*Leaving the Midday Mass at the Church of Pilar in Zaragoza*). As its title suggests, it is a documentary showing people leaving the main church of Zaragoza. *Llegada de un tren de Teruel a Segorbe* (*The Arrival of a Train from Teruel to Segorbe*), however, is considered the first Spanish movie directed by a Spaniard, although anonymous. It was released on September 11, 1896, in Valencia. Fructuós Gelabert's *Riña en un café* (1897, *Brawl in a Café*), on the other hand, is considered the first Spanish fiction film. Also, Segundo de Chomón (1871–1929) has been called the Spanish version of Georges Méliès, because of his innovative drive. With more than 500 movies, he pioneered different forms of art cinema (i.e., documentary, literary adaptation, fantasy) as well as introducing the first known Spanish cinema production, *Macaya y Marro*.

The first Spanish co-productions were *Lucha por la herencia* (1911, *Struggle for Inheritance*) and *Ana Kadowa* (1914), both codirected by the Catalan Fructuós Gelabert (1874–1955) and the German Otto Mulhauser with a Spanish cast and financing from an American firm based in Barcelona. As Gerard Dapena et al. (2013) point out, this coproduction exemplified a transnational outlook. Another major influence in Spanish cinema at the time was the Italian director Giovanni Doria. In his *Sangre gitana* (1913, *Gypsy Blood*) he portrayed an archetypical image of the folklore of Spain.

During the early stages of cinema in Spain, Barcelona was—and probably still is to some degree—the main center of the Spanish film industry (i.e., *Escuela de Barcelona* in the 1960s), despite the fact that most Spanish regions have now developed a regional film industry. *Nobleza baturra* (1925) by Juan Vilá Vilamala, shot in the region of Aragón, is interesting in terms of success within the Spanish cinema industry. With a budget of 55,000 pesetas ($458), it generated over 1.5 million pesetas in proceeds at the time, becoming one of the most popular Spanish films ever (Seguin 17).

During the early stages of the Spanish cinema, two movies also need to be mentioned due to their success in spite of their pedestrian origins. The two early important movies for their transitional impact on the Spanish cinema are *Un chien andalou* (1929, *An Andalusian Dog*) and *La aldea maldita* (1930, *The Cursed Village*). The first one was the first movie directed by Luis Buñuel, who can be considered the "father" of the avant-garde Spanish cinema. Buñuel directed this 25-minute feature that was produced by his mother (25,000 pesetas = $202), reviving Surrealism as well as redefining global cinema. Six of Buñuel's films are included in *Sight & Sound*'s 2012 critic's poll of the top 250 films of all time. He was the first Spaniard to receive an Oscar for Best Foreign Language Film (*The Discreet Charm of the Bourgeoisie*; French: *Le Charme discret de la bourgeoisie*) in 1972.

On the other hand, Florián Rey's *La aldea maldita* consists of a rural drama which, despite some influences from the Soviet Union's cinema, deeply revolves around the most traditional roots of Spain. On reflection, both films to some extent epitomize the current situation of the Spanish cinema, in the sense that it is capable of brilliance but at the same time its industry remains rustic and somehow underdeveloped. Some even say that the Spanish cinema industry is cursed, and it does not exist. That is the opinion of new Spanish cinema directors such as Álex de la Iglesia, Freddy Mas, and Fernando Baños.

Rob Stone opens his book *Spanish Cinema* (2002) stating that if there is a common thread through Spanish cinema, its name is Elías Querejeta (1934–2013), who produced the New Spanish Cinema of the 1960s and 1970s, practicing the cinema of resistance under Franco. *Esa pareja feliz* (1951, *That Happy Couple*) was cowritten and codirected by two of the most prominent names in Spanish cinema history: Juan Antonio Bardem (1922–2002) and Luis García Berlanga (1921–2010). Bardem is the uncle of the well-known actor Javier Bardem (1969–), who in 2007 received the Oscar (Best Supporting Actor) for his role in *No Country for Old Men* (directed by Joel and Ethan Cohen).

Spanish movies can be divided into two radically different groups based on their treatment of the Spanish Civil War. This is the premise of *100 Years of Spanish Cinema* by Tatjana Pavlović et al. (2009). Hence, on one hand, there are the Nationalists seeking legitimacy in the glory days of Spanish history (i.e., the Christian Reconquista) and, on the other hand, there are the Republicans, whose position is to defend democracy against Franco's fascism. Two clear examples of this cinematic division are Benito Perojo's *Suspiros de España* (*Sighs of Spain* 1938) and Pedro Puche's *Barrios bajos* (*Slums* 1937).

After the victory of the Nationalists, the Franco regime established censorship on the cinema industry on November 18, 1937, by a decree, in which the state made sure that every movie obeyed the regulations of the Franco authorities. In doing so, Franco's autarky created the NO-DO (*NOticiarios y DOcumentales Cinematográficos*, News and Cinematographic Documentaries) in December 1942, which lasted until 1976. The monopoly of NO-DO particularly forbade the projection of any foreign documentary in Spain. However, despite the attempt to control every movie that was shown in the country, nevertheless, some films managed to escape Franco's censorship. The most notorious examples were Lorenzo Llobet-Gràcia's *Vida en sombras* (1949, *Life in the Shadows*); Luis Buñuel's *Viridiana* (1961); and Luis María Delgado's *Diferente* (1961, *Different*), which paradoxically was the first Spanish movie that dealt with the theme of homosexuality. Two other Spanish movies during the period of dictatorship deserve special attention for their huge influence on Spanish cinematography: Luis García Berlanga's *El verdugo* (1963, *Not on Your Life*) and Carlos Saura's *El jardín de las delicias* (1970, *The Garden of Delights*). The first is widely considered one of the masterpieces of Spanish cinema while the latter was censored by Franco's authorities because of its Franco bourgeois satire and Spanish Civil War references.

When Franco died in 1975, there was a brief period of transition (1975–1981) in the Spanish cinema, which was characterized by disenchantment as expressed by *Jaime Chávarri's El desencanto* (1976, *The Disenchantment*) and Pilar Miró's *El crimen de Cuenca* (1980, *The Crime of Cuenca*). Pilar Miró (1940–1997) also played an important role in the structure of the Spanish cinema industry, since she became the director of Spain's cinematography from 1982 to 1985. During her period, there was a boom of Basque cinema with directors such as Imanol Uribe's *La muerte de Mikel* (1983), Pedro Olea's *Akelarre* (1983), Eloy de la Iglesia's *El pico 1* (1983), and Montxo Armendáriz's *Tasio* (1984). Also, during Miró's time the cinema of Spain became recognized abroad. For instance, after Buñel (1972), another Spanish director received an Oscar for Best Foreign Film thanks to

José Luis Garci's *Volver* (1982); *La colmena* (1982, *The Hive*, directed by Mario Camus) won the Golden Bear in the Berlinale in Germany; and *Los santos inocentes* (1984, *The Holy Innocents*, directed by Mario Camus) starring Alfredo Landa and Francisco Rabal won Best Actor Awards for both stars at the 1984 Cannes Film Festival in France. However, the most internationally recognized name in post-Franco Spain is without a doubt Pedro Almodóvar (1949–). His cinematic contributions have been recognized worldwide, as he has received on multiple occasions the most prestigious cinema awards.

Another Basque generation of young rebel cinema directors regenerated Spain's national cinema in the 1990s, solidifying the idea that there existed a strong cinema tradition in the Basque country with Enrique Urbizo's *Todo por la pasta* (1991, *Everything for the Cash*); Julio Medem's *Vacas* (1992); Alex de la Iglesia's *Acción mutante* (1993, *Mutant Action*) and Juanma Bajo Ulloa's *Airbag* (1996). This new generation of directors are characterized by coming from a very disturbing socio-political context. They grew up in the 1980s in the Basque country, where many people suffered casualties due to the terrorism of ETA. However, their main cinema revolutionary message consists precisely of making a comedy out of their convulsive situation. In other words, Spain's particular scenario of the 1980s and 1990s was so bad that their immediate reaction was to create comedy to laugh about it. Chema de la Peña's documentary *Un cine como tú en un país como este* (2010, *A Cinema Like You in a Country Like This*) provides useful insights into the beginnings of this recognized generation of Spanish cinema directors—among whom might be mentioned Fernando Trueba (i.e., 1992, *Belle Epoque*); Imanol Uribe (i.e., *Días contados*, 1994, *Running Out of Time*); and Fernando Colomo (i.e., 1998, *Los años bárbaros*).

Nowadays, most successful Spanish films made after 2010 are comedies, due not only to the economic crisis but also because of the idea of separatism fracturing Spain, which some people—mainly in the regions of Catalunya and the Basque country—are promoting. This is the case of Borja Cobeaga's *No controles* (2010, *Love Storming*), Pedro Almodóvar's *Los amantes pasajeros* (2013, *I'm so Excited!*), and Emilio Martínez Lázaro's *Ocho apellidos vascos* (2014, *Eight Basque*

Pedro Almodóvar at a press conference in Beverly Hills, California, on November 9, 2011. Almodóvar is Spain's most awarded cinema director, and has received prestigious international awards around the globe. (AP Foto/Katy Winn, Archivo)

Surnames). The latter has become the most successful film ever made in Spain. In fact, it broke more Spanish box office records than any film since Juan Antonio Bayona's *The Impossible* (2012). Paradoxically, according to the report of FAPAE 2012, the Spanish cinema makes 25.5 percent more revenue abroad than nationally (Fapae *Memoria* 2012). Within a global context, Spain still occupies ninth place for number of films produced (182) and fourth place within Europe in 2012, after France (279); Germany (241) and the U.K. (222) (Fapae *Memoria* 2012).

Table 16.2 includes the movies that reached over a million viewers in Spain (2006–2012), with the name of the national director highlighted when appropriate.

Table 16.2 MOVIES WITH OVER ONE MILLION VIEWERS IN SPAIN 2006–2012

Year	Movie	National Director	Spectators
2012	*The Impossible*	Juan Antonio Bayona	5,914,601
	Las aventuras de Tadeo Jones	Enrique Gato Borregán	2,720,152
	Tengo ganas de ti	Fernando González Molina	1,980,358
2011	*Torrente 4*	Santiago Segura	2,630,263
	Midnight in Paris		1,239,355
2010	*Tres metros sobre el cielo*	Fernando González Molina	1,331,895
	Que se mueran los feos	Nacho García Velilla	1,127,131
	Julia's Eyes	Guillem Morales	1,088,368
2009	*Agora*	Alejandro Amenábar	3,318,399
	Planet 51	J.Blanco; J.Abad & M. Martínez	1,643,634
	Cell 211	Daniel Monzón	1,400,422
	Fuga de cerebros	Fernando González Molina	1,176,069
	Spanish movie	Javier Ruiz Caldera	1,072,280
2008	*The Oxford Murders*	Álex de la Iglesia	1,421,063
	Mortadelo y Filemón Misión: salvar la tierra	Miguel Bardem	1,363,275
	Vicky Cristina Barcelona		1,240,343
	Che: The Argentine		1,161,635
	Astérix aux jeux olympiques		1,051,286
2007	*The Orphanage*	Juan Antonio Bayona	4,274,355
	REC	Jaume Balagueró & Paco Plaza	1,341,951
2006	*Alatriste*	Agustín Díaz Yañez	3,130,710
	Volver	Pedro Almodóvar	1,903,583
	Los dos lados de la cama	Emilio Martínez Lázaro	1,537,266
	Pan's Labyrinth		1,346,853
	Los Borgia	Antonio Hernández	1,244,590
	Perfume: The Story of a Murderer		1,184,849

See also: Chapter 2: Overview. Chapter 7: Overview. Chapter 11: Overview. Chapter 12: Overview. Chapter 13: Overview.

Further Reading

Labanji, Jo, and Tatjana Pavlovic, eds. *A Companion to Spanish Cinema*. Malden: Wiley-Blackwell, 2012.

Mira Nouselles, Alberto. *The A to Z of Spanish Cinema*. Lanham: Scarecrow Press, 2010.

Cultural Icons

Concepción Velasco (1939–) popularly known as Concha or Conchita Velasco, is a Spanish film actress, theatre actress, singer, and TV presenter. Velasco became very successful in the comedy films of the 1950s and 1960s, becoming the Spanish *yé-yé* girl in conjunction with Massiel (Eurovision song contest with the song "La, la, la" in 1968) and Karina (i.e., "En un mundo nuevo y feliz" and "El baúl de los recuerdos"). Her recent films include: *Más allá del jardín* (Pedro Olea 1996); *París-Tombuctú* (Luis García Berlanga 1999); *Chuecatown* (Juan Flahn 2007); and *Enloquecidas* (Juan Luis Iborra 2008). She has also appeared in many national television series (i.e., *Motivos personales*, 2005; *Grand Hotel*, 2011) as well as being the TV presenter of popular TV shows such as *Viva el espectáculo* (1990), *Querida Concha* (1992), *Sorpresa, sorpresa* (1999), and *Cine de barrio* (2011–).

Belén Esteban (1973–) is a TV phenomenon thanks to her marriage with the also super famous Spanish bullfighter Jesulín de Ubrique (1973–) in 1998. After three years of marriage, Esteban sold her divorce story to *¡Hola!*, and soon after that was offered a job alongside veteran daytime television presenter María Teresa Campos at the Antena 3 television channel. Esteban says she does not feel that she is anybody's creation, and much less that her life is being manipulated by the Spanish media. However, those who work with Esteban say that she has paid a high price for fame and fortune. As Jesús Rodríguez explains in his article, Esteban is already known by millions of Spaniards as *la princesa del pueblo*—the people's princess, although for her critics she represents a new low for popular culture.

See also: Chapter 2: Overview. Chapter 7: Overview. Chapter 11: Overview. Chapter 12: Overview. Chapter 13: Overview. Chapter 16: Overview.

Further Reading

Agawu-Kakraba, Yaw. *Postmodernity in Spanish Fiction and Culture*. Cardiff: University of Wales Press, 2010.

Hooper, John. *The New Spaniards*. 2nd edition. New York: Penguin, 2006.

Fashion

Professor Luis Casablanca Migueles, from the Universidad de Granada, wrote in 2007 the first Spanish thesis that analyzed in depth Spanish fashion as an artistic discipline in relation to painting, cinema, sculpture, and architecture. That is to say, Casablanca studies fashion as a plural phenomenon. For instance, he mentions Mariano Fortuny y Madrazo (1871–1949) as one of the emblematic artists of Spain in the 19th century, because of his synthesis of art as a way of life. Spanish fashion became well known in the 15th and 16th centuries, especially by the court of Philip II, since Spain was a global reference due to its world empire. *The Portrait of the Infanta María Teresa of Spain* (1659–1660) by Velázquez represents a good example of the new fashion of the time.

The influence of Spain in fashion ceased in the 17th century when France became a global powerhouse in style. Nevertheless, Spain managed to continue independently a more traditional style of fashion (i.e., *capa española, mantilla*) and one of the most international Spanish products was *Casa Loewe* (1846), which is still a world leader in leather. Although *Casa Loewe* was taken over by LVMH, owned by the Frenchman Bernard Arnault, in 1995, *Casa Loewe*'s products are still inspired by Spanish tradition, such as a handbag influenced by Gaudí's architecture or a perfume jar that resembles a Velázquez *menina* (girl).

Spain's 20th-century haute couture began in the 1940s, when the *Cooperativa de Alta Costura* was created in 1940 in Barcelona by five important Spanish designers: Pedro Rodríguez (1895–1990); Asunción Bastida (1902–1995); *Santa Eulalia* (fashion house founded in 1843 by Domingo Tabernera Prims); *el Dique Flotante* (1889 Joaquím Beleta Mir); and Manuel Pertegaz (1917–). According to Casablanca, the golden age of high fashion in Spain corresponds to the period between 1940 and the end of 1970s, when the *prêt-a-porter* appeared.

Cristóbal Balenciaga (1895–1972) in the 1950s and Paco Rabanne (1934–) in the 1970s created new ways of understanding how a woman dresses. During the 1960s a new social and economic phenomenon occurred in Spain, which was the opening of the *Grandes Almacenes* or department stores (i.e., *El Corte Inglés* and the already extinct *Galerías Preciados*). In the mid-1970s a generation of new designers appeared, transforming Spanish fashion to what it is today: Jesús del Pozo, Manuel Piña, Francis Montesinos, Juanjo Rocarfort, Antonio Alvarado, Adolfo Domínguez, Toni Miró; and more recently Sybilla, bimba & lola, Uterqüe, Ágatha Ruiz de la Prada, Devota y Lomba, Purificación García, Jordi Cuesta, Teresa Ramallal, Manolo Blahnik, Felipe Varela, Lorenzo Caprile, and Alexandra Plata, among others. Amancio Ortega's *Grupo Inditex* started in 1980 with its main label *Zara*, which has also revolutionized Spanish fashion beyond its borders.

The 1970s were convulsive years in Spain, which also had an impact on Spanish fashion. On the one hand, as Casablanca points out, on May 28, 1970, a public swimming pool of the city of Zaragoza banned the bikini for being such a daring swimming outfit (Casablanca 2007). On the other hand, some Spaniards were forging ahead with embracing more revealing fashion statements. The actress Susana Estrada, known as one of the "Muses of the Transition" (1949–) generated a lot of controversy in 1978 when she received an award by the now defunct newspaper *Pueblo* for being Spain's most popular person of the year. When accepting the award, she wore an unbuttoned tunic, fully revealing her breasts to all in attendance at the formal event. However, despite the controversial attempts of a few, the general image of Spain in the 1970s can be compared to the customs portrayed in a typical Spanish *pueblo* (village) in the sense that Spain was still very traditional in comparison to most European cities. The Spanish magazines as well as foreign publications like *Life, Elle, Vogue, GQ,* and *Harper's Bazaar* were indispensable in promoting Spanish fashion.

Since the 1990s the Spanish fashion industry has been increasing its number of employees. For instance, in 1995 it had over 180,000 workers, "putting Spain in fifth place in Europe" (Rodgers, 1999) while in 2011 the number reached over 250,000 personnel, with clothing being the largest category (183,267), followed by shoes and leather (40,998), and fabric stores (26,899) (The International Industry Network, 2011). Spain's best customers of Spanish fashion in 2012 were France, which spent over 2.54 billion euros on Spanish fashion, followed by Italy and Portugal (both over 1.6 billion), among other countries around the world including the U.S. (545 million), Mexico (409 million), and China (368 million).

There are 118 Spanish fashion companies (not stores) established abroad, making fashion third within Spain's ranking of industries, which in 2012 generated € 15,365,600,000 in textiles alone (Ramírez Nicolás 2013). This put Spain in fourth place as a producer of textiles (behind Italy, France, and Germany). Spain's Inditex is the world's largest fashion distribution group with Zara as Spain's most iconic fashion shop, and the company Pronovias remains number one worldwide in the bridal sector, among others (Mango, Cortefiel, Jeanología, Camper, Desigual, Massimo Dutti, Munich).

See also: Chapter 2: Overview. Chapter 12: Overview. Chapter 13: Overview. Chapter 16: Overview.

Further Reading

Lomba, Modesto, ed. *Geography of Spanish Fashion*. Madrid: Artes Gráficas, 2009.

Ramírez Nicolás, Inés. *Fashion: The Sweetheart of Electronic Commerce in Spain*. Madrid: eMarket Services Spain, 2013.

News Sources

El País and *El Mundo* are Spain's two largest daily newspapers. Overall, Spain's newspapers are characterized by strong partisan identities. As Laura Chaqués and Frank Baumgartner have recently demonstrated, the two leading newspapers show powerful similarities in the topics of their coverage over time. *El País* was born in 1976 with the beginning of democracy in Spain, and it always opens with an international headline.

El Mundo was created in 1989, and immediately became the "relentless inquisitor" of the socialist PSOE governments and a point of media support for conservative elites, especially the conservative PP. *El País* and *El Mundo* belong to two of the largest Spanish media groups, *Prisa* and *Unidad Editorial*, respectively. The *Prisa* group is the largest media group in the country, and it also controls the main national and Latin American radio stations (*la SER*; *ADN Radio Chile*); publishers such as Grupo Santillana, Alfaguara, Richmond, and Moderna (in the Portuguese language); different magazines (*CincoDías*; *Rolling Stone*; *Cinemanía*; *El Viajero*); audiovisual production companies (*Plural Entertainment*); and television channels such as *Canal+* (the main pay-per-view TV in Spain), *Cuatro, TVI,* and *TVI24*. In June 2012 Prisa created *El Huffington Post*, the Spanish language version of the U.S. *Huffington Post.* However, as Emily Glazer works for *The Wall Street Journal*, Prisa has filed for Chapter 11 bankruptcy protection in the U.S. in order to refinance about $3 billion of debt (Glazer and Bjork 2013).

Vocento is another leading multimedia group in Spain. Its portfolio includes the national conservative daily paper *ABC*—which is the oldest newspaper in Spain, and the free daily *Qué!,* along with a collection of regional papers (grupo Correo). The company also has a stake in Taller de Editores, a publisher of newspaper supplements (*XLSemanal*; *Mujer Hoy*; *Hoy Corazón*) and niche interest magazines (*Inversión & Finanzas*). In addition to publishing, *Vocento* has operations in television broadcasting (*Paramount Channel*; *Disney Channel*), radio (*COPE*; *Cadena 100*; *Radio María España*; *Punto Radio*; *Onda Rambla*; *Rock FM*), and popular websites (finanzas.com; mujerhoy.com; hoymotor.com; hoycinema.com; veralia.com). The company's media reaches an audience of more than 30 million people.

Unidad Editorial (controlled by the Italian RCS) is one of the rival media groups that emerged in 2007 after the merger of Grupo Recoletos3 (owner of the newspapers *Expansión* and *Marca*—Spain's most widely read newspaper, which specializes in sports) and Unedisa (owner of *El Mundo* and several magazines like *Telva*, and a TV network *Veo7* that stopped broadcasting in 2012).

Table 16.3 SPAIN'S MAJOR NEWSPAPERS

National	Digital	Business	Sports
El País	*El Plural*	*Expansión*	*Marca*
El Mundo	*El Confidencial*	*Cinco Días*	*Sport*
La Vanguardia	*Estrella digital*	*El Economista*	*As*
ABC	*Gente digital*	*Capital*	*Mundo deportivo*
La Razón	*Libertad digital*	*La Gaceta*	
El periódico	*Periodista digital*	*Negocios*	
	Público		
	20 minutos		

See also: Chapter 2: Overview. Chapter 12: Overview. Chapter 13: Overview. Chapter 16: Overview.

Further Reading

López de Zuazo Algar, Antonio. *The History of Spanish Newspapers*. Thornton Cleveleys: Ibertext, 2010.

Paffey, Darren. *Language Ideologies and the Globalization of 'Standard' Spanish*. London: Bloomsbury Publishing, 2012.

Social Media

Spanish social media is a new way for Spaniards, especially the younger generations, to be informed and to gain access to educational outlets. Professor Juan López Sierras emphasizes the fact that there is no correlation between the use of social media and problems with social relations (López Sierras 2010). In other words, it is not a good or a bad thing, but simply a different medium altogether. However, the journalist Juan Luis Cebrián (1944–) describes in *La red* (2000, *The Web*) the new generation as "Generación Red" (Generation Web), focusing more on the negative aspects that the new technologies have brought to society,

Although television is still the prime medium chosen by the majority of Spaniards for entertainment, the habit of watching it has changed for two main reasons. One is due to the arrival of the digital television, which resulted in the fragmentation of the audience. Second, like other western countries, Spaniards are also watching more television content online. In Spain, the website of the main national television RTVE was the most visited site in 2011 with over 14 million users. In May 2009 Antena 3 launched a multimedia project series called *El internado*; it was the first Spanish television channel to offer news services on the website. Every episode was simultaneously reproduced online as well as on the traditional television channels of *Antena 3*, *Neox,* and *Nova*.

In a 277-page study on the youth population of Madrid, the preferred content of television includes: films (18%); Spanish comedy series (9.9%); Spanish fictional youth series (8.7%); sports programs (8.4%); sitcoms (8.1%); comedy programs (5.7%); and the rest (40.8%) (Rodríguez *2012*). Also, according to *Informe Juventud en España 2012* (*Dossier on Youth in Spain 2012*), in which different experts collaborate, one of the main highlights is that Spanish youth have been nicknamed in English "the Reset Generation" (*Informe* 2012), referring to the latest generation who allegedly will become the engine to change Spain's social map. Among the changing habits of the Spanish population, 93 percent of Spaniards between 20 and 35 years old prefer to buy over the Internet because of flexibility, offers available online, and variety of products. In 2004 most Spanish homes had a television; they also had a landline phone in 90 percent of homes, a mobile phone (77%), and Internet (31%). However, in 2012 having access to the Internet (67%) and a mobile phone (96%) increased while owning a landline phone dropped (*Informe* 2012).

The main social media in Spain includes: Facebook (55.1%); Tuenti (37.3%); Twitter (2.2%); Google buzz (1.0%); Windows Live Spaces (0.8%); Badoo (0.8%); My Space (0.3%); Hi5 (0.3%); Flickr (0.3%); Bebo (0.3%), and Orkut (0.1%). In a survey in 2011, the population between 15–29 years old used the social media several times a day (55%), once a day (31%), and weekly (14%). The activities on the Internet in 2012 for the population between 15–29 years old include: email (80.4%); social media (77.1%); search for information (73.9%); download music, videos, films (62.6%); Chats and Messengers (55.1%); surfing on the web without a specific goal (48.6%); buying online trips, books, tickets (43%); online banking (36%); looking for a job (33.6%); dealing with administrative paperwork (20.6%); maintenance of a personal blog or website (18.3%); phone calling over the Internet (13.4%); and other (3.7%). Surprisingly, in a survey about the use of Internet to obtain political information in 2011, of a population between 15–29 years old, 56 percent declared they had never used it to obtain political information while 16 percent said they did so more than once a week.

See also: Chapter 2: Overview. Chapter 6: Overview; Spanish Youth. Chapter 12: Overview. Chapter 13: Overview. Chapter 16: Overview; Youth Culture.

Further Reading

Albarrán, Alan B., ed. *The Handbook of Spanish Language Media*. New York: Routledge, 2009.

Kinder, Marsha, ed. *Refiguring Spain: Cinema, Media, Representation*. Durham: Duke University Press, 1997.

TV Outlets

Televisión Española (TVE) is Spain's national television channel, which began on October 28, 1956. Until 1982, Spain had only two television channels, La 1 and La 2, which were rigidly controlled and censored during Franco's time. The monopoly of TVE did not last forever and in the 1980s two regions launched their regional television channels, the Basque television (ETB) and the Catalan television (TV3) in 1982 and 1983, respectively.

During the 1990s *Antena 3*, *Telecinco*, and *Canal+* were launched, becoming the first private commercial channels. On November 30, 2005, Digital Terrestrial Television (Spanish acronym TDT) provided Spaniards with multiple channels and radio stations. By groups and percentage of viewing, according to *Barlovento Comunicación* data published on July 2013, Table 16.4 shows the most popular Spanish television channels.

Table 16.4   MOST POPULAR TV CHANNELS IN SPAIN (per 2013)

GROUPS	PERCENTAGE %
ATRESMEDIA	**28.7**
Antena3	13.0
La Sexta	5.8
Neox	2.4
Nova	2.2
Xplora	1.9
Nitro	1.8
La Sexta 3	1.6
MEDIASET	**28.7**
Telecinco	12.5
Cuatro	6.0
FDF-T5	3.0
Bong	2.2
Divinity	1.7
Energy	1.3
La Siete	1.1
Nueve	0.8
TVE	**17.4**
La1	9.6
Clan	2.6
La2	2.6
Teledeporte	1.7
24h	0.9
Vocento	**4.6**
Disney Channel	1.7
Paramount Channel	1.4
Intereconomía	0.8
MTV	0.7
Unidad Editorial	**3.6**
Discovery	1.7
13 TV	1.3
Marca TV	0.6

Following *Barlovento Comunicación* data, the five most viewed channels by July 2013 were in the following order by share of total viewing in percentage: *Antena 3* (Atresmedia Televisión) with 13.0 percent; *Telecinco* (Mediaset España Comunicación) with 12.5 percent; *La 1* (TVE) with 9.6 percent; *Cuatro* (Mediaset) with 6.0 percent; and *La Sexta* (Atresmedia) with 5.8 percent. On March 2014, Spain's most watched television channel was *Telecinco* (14.8%), and the five most watched programs were: Friendly Soccer Match Spain vs Italy (*Telecinco*: 6,994,000–34.4%); La Voz Kids (*T5*: 5,559,000—34.1%); *El Príncipe* (*T5*: 5,555,000—28.6%); Soccer Champions League Atlético de Madrid vs Milan (*La1*: 5,333,000—27.5%); and *El Príncipe* (*T5*: 5,244,000—27.8%).

Spaniards prefer to watch national productions at all times. In fact, national Spanish series are more popular than any other foreign series. Some have already been exported to many countries and are available also on Netflix and Amazon Prime in North America (i.e., *Grand Hotel* and *Velvet* in Canada and the U.S.). For instance, in 2012 among the most popular television series were: *Águila roja* (TVE1); *Cuéntame cómo pasó* (TVE1); *Isabel* (TVE1); *Amar en tiempos revueltos* (TVE1); *Gran Reserva* (TVE1); *Grand Hotel* (Antena 3); *Luna, el misterio de Calenda* (Antena 3); *Con el culo al aire* (Antena 3); *Pulseras rojas—Polseres Vermelles* (Antena 3); *Bandolera* (Antena 3); *Amar es para siempre* (Antena 3); *El secreto de Puente Viejo* (Antena 3); *BuenAgente* (Antena 3); *Frágiles* (Telecinco); *Familia* (Telecinco); *La que se avecina* (Telecinco); and *Aída* (Telecinco).

Also in 2012, Telecinco was the most watched channel (13.9%), particularly thanks to its news and its national program *La Voz* (Spanish version of the American show *The Voice*). National Spanish TVE has an iPad application so that most of its content can be watched for free. Another popular Spanish app is the one developed by Atresmedia player (mitele.es), which also includes many free programs and successful series such as *Sin tetas no hay paraíso* (2008), *El tiempo entre costuras* (2013–2014), *Sin identidad* (2014–). On May 8, 2014, the U.S. network NBC announced an American adaptation of Spain's series *Los misterios de Laura* (TVE: 2009), entitled *The Mysteries of Laura* (NBC 2014). Similarly, *Red Band Society* (Fox 2014–2015) was adapted from *Polseres vermelles* (TV3 2011–2013).

Apart from films, sport events and music programs, the national content of Spanish television channels include:

Sitcoms *(situation comedy)*: *Aída, Camera Café, 7 Vidas.*

Comedy programs: *El hormiguero, Tonterías las justas, Sé lo que hicisteis, El Intermedio.*

National Fictional Series: *Azul, Farmacia de guardia, Los Serrano, Médico de familia, Los hombres de Paco, Física o Química, Hay alguien ahí, Aída, Hospital Central, Cuéntame.*

Telenovelas *(soap operas): Amar en tiempos revueltos.*

Miniseries or telefilms: *23-F, Una bala para el rey, Felipe y Letizia.*

Travel programs: *Españoles por el mundo, Callejeros viajeros.*

Talk shows & Late night shows: The first one was *Esta noche cruzamos el Mississipi* (Pepe Navarro, 1995). Others include *Buenafuente, En el aire.*

Reality shows: *Gran Hermano, Supervivientes, Princesas de barrio, Operación Triunfo, Factor X, Fama.*

Gossip shows: *Sálvame, DEC.*

Game shows: The first and most successful one in the history of Spanish television was *Un, dos, tres . . . responda otra vez* (Narciso Ibáñez Serrador, running from 1972–2004), *Quién quiere ser millonario, Pasapalabra, La ruleta de la suerte*.

A new global phenomenon that also occurs in Spain is the increase in the number of people who watch television series on the Internet (i.e., *Malviviendo, Con pelos en la lengua, Princesa Rota, Freaklances, Asqueadas, Are you APP?, Muñecas, La Revolución de los Ángeles*). This is partly due to the low cost of production. These new series have already been seen on the Internet by millions, especially among the Spanish younger generations. Spaniards also follow major British and American TV series since the global phenomenon of *Twin Peaks* in 1990–1991. For the academic Paul Julian Smith, what is striking with the Spanish shows in comparison to the U.S. teen series is what is left out, referring in particular to the theme of popularity (fashion and sports in, for example, *Gossip Girl* and *Glee*) and the motif of class conflict, which is greatly reduced in Spain. Perhaps the main reason why Spaniards prefer the national television series is because in Spain producers usually think of a big audience (the whole family watching the television show together) rather than narrowing to a particular group of people (which is generally the case with the U.S. series).

According to the governmental online platform http://www.mesientodecine.com, Spain is one of the countries with more copy-piracy in the world. This platform was actually created to provide Spanish viewers with a list of the legal Internet sites where it is possible to watch movies and/or television series in Spain: 400films; ADNstream; cineclick.com; filmin; filmotech.com; googleplay; margenes.org; mubi; nubeox; totalchannel .com; plat.tv; voddler; wuaki.tv; plus.es; iTunes; movistar; ono; Orange TV; mundo-r.com.

See also: Chapter 16: Overview; Cinema; Youth Culture.

Further Reading

Goddard, Peter, ed. *Popular Television in Authoritarian Europe*. Manchester: Manchester University Press, 2013.

Smith, Paul Julian. *Contemporary Spanish Culture: TV, Fashion, Art, and Film*. Cambridge: Polity Press, 2003.

Youth Culture

Young people have been hit particularly hard by the recent social and economic crisis in Europe. According to the report *Indicadores Básicos de la Juventud* (*Basic Indicators of Youth*) prepared by Anna Sanmartín (2013), the Spanish youth population between 15–24 years old was 10.6 percent of Spain's total population. By the second trimester of 2013, the unemployment rate in Spain was 26.26 percent, and 56.14 percent for youth, which is much higher than the OECD average of 16.3 percent, and is one of the highest rates in the OECD. The rate for dropping out of school is also quite high in Spain in comparison with the average in the EU (see Table 16.5).

Table 16.5 HIGH SCHOOL DROPOUT RATE: EU / SPAIN

Region	2000	2005	2008	2009	2010	2011
EU 27	17.6	15.8	14.9	14.4	14.1	13.5
Spain	29.1	30.8	31.9	31.2	28.4	26.5

Table 16.6 CAUSES FOR UNEMPLOYMENT IN SPAIN / OTHER EU COUNTRIES

Country	Lack of necessary skills	There are no good jobs based on their skills	There are no jobs where they live	There are jobs but badly paid	They ignore the jobs available
EU 27	13.2	20.9	30.2	20.5	11.2
Spain	9.5	28.8	28.8	21.9	9.6
Germany	12.9	11.5	35.7	21.5	12.5
Belgium	17.9	18.6	21.4	16	18.8
France	21.8	18.5	26.9	17.5	12.7
Portugal	7.5	30.3	30.5	17.4	10.7

The most important values for Spanish youth (15–29 years old) in 2012 included: friendship (96.8%); family (93.9%); health (92.8%); job (89.5%); hobbies (89.3%); studies (88.6%); money (86.3%); sexuality (82.7%); travelling abroad (76.1%); physical appearance (76.1%); getting involved in the local community (64.0%). The most popular activities among Spanish youth in their spare time included: using the computer (93.1%); going out with friends (85.7%); listening to music (83.9%); and watching television (81%). Their main topics of interest included: technological development (88.4%); gender equality (84.0%); environment (82.4%); culture (80.3%); cooperation for development (66.6%); international conflicts (63.8%); sports (56.2%); immigration (53.6%); politics (40.7%); and religion (22.3%).

According to the survey *Indicadores* (Sanmartín 2013), by December 2013, Spain had 4,559,964 young people between 15 and 24 years old, who considered themselves: studious (42%); hard workers (23%); fun-loving (17%); consumers (12%); and home-loving (6%). For Spanish youth the most important concerns included unemployment (72.1%); the economy (16.1%); the educational system (13.8%); the housing market (10.3%), and drugs (7.9%).

Perhaps the most distinctive feature of Spanish youth under 30 was and still is the so-called 15-M movement, which started in Plaza del Sol in Madrid 2011, when a mass demonstration of young people protested the lack of future/jobs for the youngsters in Spain. This initial social protest became organized into various young political parties. Apart from Albert Rivera's *Ciudadanos* (Citizens), which obtained two seats in the European Parliament, the young party of Pablo Iglesias's *Podemos* (We Can) won five seats (over 1.2 million Spaniards voted *Podemos*), becoming the main surprise of Spain's European elections on May 25, 2014, considering his political party was formed just

THE 15-M MOVEMENT

The 15-M movement, also known as the movement of *los indignados* (the indignant movement) took place by surprise at the square of Madrid's Puerta del Sol on May 15, 2011, and was quickly reproduced at other major plazas around Spain thanks to the use of media (i.e., smartphones and the Internet). Spain's 15-M inspired the Occupy Wall Street movement in the United States. Spain's 15-M movement had no specific ideology. In fact, most Spaniards (over 80%) felt sympathetic with the indignants. The protesters simply expressed out loud what most Spanish people were already saying at home and in conversations in bars, which was a feeling of disgust with Spain's unemployment rate, the austerity measures imposed by the government (of Spain—although the feeling was that Spain was governed by Angela Merkel), and, more importantly, repulsion toward senior executives who alledgedly received millionaire salaries and severance packages before and after the collapse of several regional banks, particularly the infamous so-called *cajas*. As as example, Caja Madrid was converted into Bankia, and executives such as Miguel Blesa and Rodrigo Rato were subsequently sent to prison in 2014 and 2015 respectively, although they both were released shortly thereafter.

four months before the European elections. Both Rivera (1979–) and Iglesias (1978–) were 34 and 35 years old, respectively, during the elections. If the far-right parties swept the European Parliament elections in 2014 in several EU countries (France, U.K., Denmark, Greece, Austria, Germany), Spain, however, did not have an extreme right-wing party. On the contrary, Spain's new political generations seem to be ideologically more inclined toward the other side of the political spectrum.

In a political context, Spanish youth show a center-left ideological positioning, although they have also been labeled with *pasotismo*, meaning they do not really care or are not interested in politics. In Spanish, a *pasota* person means he/she is indifferent, which is the most numerous group among the Spanish youth (29%). Others classify as: skeptical (21%); involved in politics (21%); pro-active (18%); and apolitical (11%).

Another aspect related to Spain's youth is the presence of *bandas latinas* (Latin gangs). Although the numbers differ from one source to another, according to Juan Pablo Soriano, in Spain there are roughly less than 3,000 Latin gangs, which represent 4/100 of a percent of the total Spanish youth between 15 and 24 years old. The existence of these groups should be seen as a symptom of the problems of a country, not as an illness (Soriano 2008). In another study by Alejandro Portes, they conclude that "there is nothing in [their] results that points to the emergence of an alienated or adversarial stance among foreign-origin youths and nothing that appears to arrest the integrative influence of the passage of time on self-identities and plans toward the future" (Portes et al. 2011).

According to the report *Indicadores Básicos de la Juventud* (*Basic Indicators of Youth*), prepared by Anna Sanmartín (2013), the consumption of drugs among Spanish youth between 15–34 years old from 2005–2011 has decreased in most items with the exception of tranquilizers and sleeping pills (see Table 16.7).

Table 16.7 SUBSTANCE USE IN SPAIN 2005–2011

Substance	2005	2007	2009	2011
Tobacco	42.3	42.2	40.9	40.4
Alcohol	66.3	61.7	63.1	63.7
Cannabis	15.4	13.5	14.1	12.5
Ecstasies	1.1	0.8	0.8	0.6
Hallucinogens	0.5	0.2	0.4	0.3
Speed	0.8	0.5	0.7	0.5
Cocaine	2.8	2.9	2.0	1.7
Heroine	0.1	0.1	0.0	0.1
Inhalable	0.1	0.0	0.0	0.0
Tranquilizers	1.6	2.5	1.8	2.8
Sleeping pills	0.8	1.0	1.2	1.3

The *European Drug Report 2014* shows that Spanish youth (15–34 years old) consumed more cocaine (3.6%) in 2013 than any other country in the EU, followed by the U.K. (3.3%), Ireland (2.8%), and Denmark (2.4%). With regards to cannabis, Spain is fourth (11.2%), the biggest users being the Czech Republic (18.5%), Denmark (17.6%), and France (17.5%). Also, another interesting figure related to drugs among Spanish youth is that Spain is below the EU-average (17.1%) in number of deaths due to drugs, being 11.4 cases per million inhabitants. Estonia (191 cases per million habitants), Norway (76), Ireland (70), Sweden (63), and Finland (58) are the EU countries with the most young casualties due to drugs.

The lack of jobs is one of the main reasons why nearly 30 percent of women and 40 percent of men between 24 and 35 years old still live with their parents. According to the report *Observatorio de Emancipación 2013*, 26.6 percent of Spanish youth between 16 and 29 years old live in poverty. Also, nearly half of the young population of Spain (47.5%) do not have any type of income such as a salary or grant of some sort. By 2013, barely 20.9 percent of the youth population between 16 and 29 had managed emancipation, which constitutes a specific pattern of Spain's youth culture. On the other hand, the website *Home Sapiens* (homesapiens.es) was created in 2014 by a young Spanish couple with the main goal of helping and giving advice to those young Spaniards who might be clueless about the process of emancipation.

Els nens salvatges (*The Wild Children*, directed by Patricia Ferreira 2012), *Hermosa juventud* (*Beautiful Youth*, directed by Jaime Rosales 2014), and *Todos están muertos* (*Everyone Is Dead*, directed by Beatriz Sanchís 2014) are three contemporary Spanish films that examine the current problematic situation of being young in Spain's 21st century.

GENERATION Z

Generation Z refers to the group of people born between 1994 and 2010, which represent 25.9 percent of the world's population, which in Spain translates to 8 million so-called Millennials. One of the main differences with their previous peers is that they go one step further with regards to merchandise, in the sense that Gen. Z'ers want to produce their own design and content. This is the case, for instance, with the latest celebrities who became famous through their own exposure on YouTube, and more particularly in webs such as Playbuzz and Buzzfeed, where the content is uploaded by the users (over 80 million monthly according to Google Analytics). Because of this new way of thinking, major brand names such as Nike are allowing their customers to design their own sports shoes. In other words, consumers are not only personalizing the product but, more importantly for the Gen. Z'ers they are participating in the process. Because of the financial crisis and austerity measures, among the Millennials (also coined Generation K after Katniss Everdeen, the heroine of *The Hunger Games*), 77 percent are concerned about their financial situation and do not want to get into debt. The use of drugs among this group is expected to be minimal in comparison with previous generations. In fact, in Spain since 2005 drug users have gradually been on the decline. Another difference with previous groups is that Gen. Z prefers to use Snapchat, where photos and videos can be sent but are simultaneously destroyed a few seconds afterwards as opposed to the narcisisstic selfies, which characterized the previous generation with uploaded images reproduced ad nauseam in many public platforms.

See also: Chapter 6: Spanish Youth. Chapter 8: Overview. Chapter 16: Overview; Social Media.

Further Reading

Henseler, Christine, ed. *Generation X Goes Global: Mapping a Youth Culture in Motion*. New York: Routledge, 2013.

Leaman, Jeremy, and Martha Wörshching, eds. *Youth in Contemporary Europe*. New York: Routledge, 2010.

REFERENCES

Amago, Samuel. *Spanish Cinema in the Global Context*. New York: Routledge, 2013.

Areces, Miguel Ángel. "Introducción: Generación NI-NI." *Ábaco 2ª Época* 4 no.66 (Generación NI NI 2010): 6–8.

Benet, Vicente J. *El cine español. Una historia cultural*. Barcelona: Paidós, 2012.

Caparrós Lera, J. M. *Historia del cine español*. Madrid: T&B editores, 2007.

Carrión, Jorge. *Teleshakespeare*. Madrid: Errata Naturae, 2011.

Casablanca Migueles, Luis. *La moda como disciplina artística en España. Jesús del Pozo y la generación de los nuevos creadores*. Granada: Universidad de Granada, 2007.

Castaño Collado, Cecilia, Juan Martín Fernández, and José Luis Martínez Cantos. "La brecha digital de género en España y Europa: medición con indicadores compuestos." *Centro de Investigaciones Sociológicas* (Octubre–Diciembre 2011): 127–140.

Castells, Manuel. *The Rise of the Network Society, The Information Age: Economy, Society and Culture Vol. I.* Cambridge: Blackwell, 1996.

Castiella, Antxon Salvador. *Spanish Cinema: A Selection of 250 of the Best Spanish and Latin American Films from Sound Cinema to Today.* Rome: Gremese, 2013.

Cebrián, Juan Luis. *La red.* Madrid: Taurus, 2000.

Centeno, Patrycia. *Política y moda. La imagen del poder.* Barcelona: Península, 2012.

Chaqués Bonafont, Laura, and Frank R. Baumgartner. "Newspaper Attention and Policy Activities in Spain." *Journal of Public Policy* 33 no.1 (April 2013): 65–88.

Dapena, Gerard, Marvin D'Lugo, and Alberto Elena. "Transnational Frameworks." In *A Companion to Spanish Cinema.* Edited by Jo Labanyi and Tatjana Pavlović. Chichester: Wiley-Blackwell, 2013: 15–49.

D'Lugo, Marvin, and Kathleen M. Vernon, eds. *A Companion to Pedro Almodóvar.* Chichester: Wiley-Blackwell, 2013.

Fouce, Héctor. "De la agitación a la Movida: Políticas culturales y música popular en la Transición española."*Arizona Journal of Hispanic Cultural Studies* 13 (2009): 143–153.

Gavarrón, Lola. *La gran dama de la moda. La apasionante biografía de María Rosa Salvador.* Madrid: La esfera de los libros, 2010.

Gentile, Alessandro, Anna Sanmartín Ortí, and Ana Lucía Hernández Cordero. *La sombra de la crisis. La sociedad española en el horizonte de 2018.* Madrid: Centro Reina Sofía Sobre Adolescencia y Juventud. Fundación de Ayuda contra la Drogadicción (FAD), 2014.

Glazer, Emily, and Christopher Bjork. "Spanish Media Firm Has Weighted U.S. Bankruptcy Filing." *The Wall Street Journal,* July 11, 2013.

Gubern, Román, José Enrique Monterde, Julio Pérez Perucha, Esteve Riambau, and Casimiro Torreiro. *Historia del cine español.* 7th ed. Madrid: Cátedra, 2010.

Horcajo, Carlos, ed. *España de moda.* Segovia: Artec Impresiones, 2003.

Hyslop, Stephen G., Bob Somerville, and John Thompson. *Eyewitness History from Ancient Times to the Modern Era.* Washington, D.C.: National Geographic, 2011.

Labanyi, Jo, and Tatjana Pavlović, eds. *A Companion to Spanish Cinema.* Chichester: Wiley-Blackwell, 2013.

López Sierras, Juan. "Evolución del uso de internet y móvil entre niños y jóvenes en España (1996–2010)." *Cicees-Ábaco* 2ª *Época* 4 no. 66 (Generación Ni Ni 2010): 98–105.

Manzanera López, Laura. *Del corsé al tanga. 100 años de moda en España.* Barcelona: Ediciones Península, 2011.

Megías Quirós, Ignacio, and Elena Rodríguez San Julián. *Jóvenes y comunicación. La impronta de lo virtual.* Madrid: Centro Reina Sofía Sobre Adolescencia y Juventud. Fundación de Ayuda contra la Drogadicción (FAD), 2014.

Megías Quirós, Ignacio, and Juan Carlos Ballesteros Guerra. *Mismas drogas, distintos riesgos. Un ensayo de tipología de jóvenes consumidores.* Madrid: Centro Reina Sofía Sobre Adolescencia y Juventud. Fundación de Ayuda contra la Drogadicción (FAD), 2013.

Novo Vázquez, Amparo, and Fernando Sánchez Bravo-Villasante. "Estilos de vida e identidades juveniles".*Cicees-Ábaco*, 2ª *Época* 37/38 (2003): 65–72.

Olmo Arriaga, José Luis. *Marketing de la moda.* 2nd ed. Madrid: Eiunsa, Ediciones Internacionales Universitarias, 2008.

Outumuro, Manuel. Genio y Figura. *La influencia de la cultura española en la moda.* Barcelona: Disparo editorial, 2006.

Pavlović, Tatjana, Inmaculada Álvarez, Rosana Blanco-Cano, Anitra Grisales, Alejandra Osorio, and Alejandra Sánchez. *100 Years of Spanish Cinema.* Chichester: Wiley-Blackwell, 2009.

Plaza Orellana, Rocio. *Historia de la moda en España: el vestido femenino entre 1750 y 1850.* Córdoba: Almuzara, 2009.

Pohl, Burkhard, and Jörg Türschmann, eds. *Miradas glocales. Cine español en el cambio de milenio.* Madrid: Iberoamericana, 2007.

Portes, Alejandro, Erik Vikstrom, Rosa Aparicio. "Coming of Age in Spain: The Self-Identification, Beliefs and Self-Esteem of the Second Generation." *The British Journal of Sociology* 62 no.3 (September 2011): 387–417.

Richardson, Nathan E. "Youth Culture, Visual Spain, and the Limits of History in Alejandro Amenábar's *Abre los ojos.*" *Revista Canadiense de Estudios Hispánicos* 27 no.2 (Invierno 2003): 327–346.

Richardson, Nathan E. "New Media and Democracy in Spain: Culture and the Mediated Politics of March 11–14, 2004." *Revista Canadiense de Estudios Hispánicos* 31 no.1 (Otoño 2006): 147–160.

Richardson, Nathan E. *Constructing Spain: The Re-Imagination of Space and Place in Fiction and Film, 1953–2003.* Lanham: Bucknell University Press, 2012.

Rodríguez San Julián, Elena y Juan Carlos Ballesteros Guerra. *Crisis y contrato social. Los jóvenes en la sociedad del futuro.* Madrid: Centro Reina Sofía Sobre Adolescencia y Juventud. Fundación de Ayuda contra la Drogadicción (FAD), 2013.

Rodríguez San Julián, I. Megías Quirós y T. Menéndez Hevia. *Consumo televisivo, series e Internet.* Madrid: Centro Reina Sofía Sobre Adolescencia y Juventud. Fundación de Ayuda contra la Drogadicción (FAD), 2012.

Rusiñol, Pere. "Introducción." In *Papel Mojado. Reality News/Mongolia.* Barcelona: Debate, 2013.

Sanmartín Ortí, Anna. *Indicadores básicos de la juventud.* Madrid: Centro Reina Sofía Sobre Adolescencia y Juventud. Fundación de Ayuda contra la Drogadicción (FAD), 2013.

Seguin, Jean-Claude. *Historia del cine español.* Madrid: Acento editorial, 1995.

Shary, Timothy, and Alexandra Seibel, eds. *Youth Culture in Global Cinema.* Austin: University of Texas Press, 2007.

Smith, Paul Julian. *Contemporary Spanish Culture: TV, Fashion, Art, and Film.* Cambridge: Polity Press, 2003.

Soriano Gatica, Juan Pablo. "Adaptación social de las pandillas juveniles latinoamericanas en España: Pandillas y organizaciones juveniles de la calle." *Revista CIDOB d'Afers Internacionals,* 81 (Marzo/Abril 2008): 109–137.

Sousa Congosto, Francisco de. *Introducción a la Historia de la Indumentaria en España.* Madrid: ISTMO, 2007.

Stone, Rob. *Spanish Cinema*. London: Pearson, 2002.

Triana Toribio, Núria. *Spanish National Cinema*. London: Routledge, 2003.

Websites

AEDE. Asociación de Editores de Diarios Españoles. *LIBRO BLANCO de la prensa diaria 2014* http://www.aede.es/publica/libro_blanco.asp

Barlovento Comunicación. Julio 2013 http://www.barloventocomunicacion.es/images/pub licaciones/NOTA%20JULIO%202013%20BARLOVENTO%20COMUNICACION%20%20 AUDIENCIAS.pdf

Barlovento Comunicación. *Análisis Televisivo 2013*. http://www.barloventocomunicacion.es /blog/82-analisis-televisivo-2013-actualizado.html

Barlovento Comunicación. *Audiencia TV Marzo 2014* http://www.barloventocomunicacion.es /blog/86-informe-audiencias-tv-marzo-2014.html

Centro Reina Sofía sobre Adolescencia y Juventud. Adolescenciayjuventud.org

Consejo de la Juventud de España. cje.org/es

Encyclopaedia Britannica. britannica.com

European Drug Report 2014. European Monitoring Centre for Drugs and Drug Addiction. em cdda.europa.eu

FAPAE. Federaciones y Asociaciones de Productores Audiovisuales Españoles. *Memoria 2012*. Fapae.es

Home Sapiens. homesapiens.es

INE: Instituto Nacional de Estadística. ine.es

Informe Juventud en España 2012. Injuve.injuve.es/observatorio

Me siento de cine. mesientodecine.com

Ministerio de Educación, cultura y deporte. mecd.gob.es http://www.mecd.gob.es/portada -mecd/

Museo del Traje. Museodeltraje.mcu.es

Observatorio de Emancipación 2013. Consejo de la juventud de España. cje.org

OECD Skills Outlook 2013 report. http://www.oecd.org/site/piaac/Country%20note%20-%20 Spain.pdf

Pasalodos Salgado, Mercedes. "Haute Couture, High Fashion in the 50s." *Indumenta 1* (2009): 1–47. http://museodeltraje.mcu.es/index.jsp?id=462&ruta=6,25,368

Radio TeleVisión Española. RTVE.es

Rodríguez, Jesús. "The Very Public Life of Belén Esteban." *El País* 10 January 2011. http://elpais. com/elpais/2011/01/10/inenglish/1294640443_850210.html

Smith, Paul Julian. "Youth Culture in Spain: Between Cinema and Television." *IV Congreso Internacional de la Sociedad Española de Estudios Literarios de Cultura Popular*. Palma de Mallorca: 20–22 Octubre 2010. http://www.uibcongres.org/congresos/ponencia.en.html?cc=175 &mes=22&ordpon=4

"Youth on the Move." *Eurobarometer*. May 2011. http://ec.europa.eu/public_opinion/flash/fl _319b_en.pdf

A DAY IN THE LIFE

A DAY IN THE LIFE OF A UNIVERSITY STUDENT

I get up at 8:00 in the morning. I brush my teeth, comb my hair, and begin to get ready for class. At 8:45 I go to the garage and grab my bike to go to the university. I arrive at 9:05. I lock up the bike in special parking for bikes and I attend my classes. Then I sit on the benches (which are like in the churches but inclined) and prepare my books and notes.

At 9:15 my first class begins, which is Human Rights. In this course, the teacher talks without following a specific script, although we have a book and we listen. The exam will be on July 12 and will be multiple choice. This class ends at 10:30. Then we have a break until 11:00 and on that break I eat a sandwich and talk to my classmates.

At 11:00 another class begins, which is Civil Law. In this class the teacher starts talking but she is following a script and we listen while taking notes to study later. The exam will be on July 5 and will be essay questions.

At 13:00 (1:00 p.m.) this class ends. Then I take the bike to go home. I usually arrive at 13:15 (1:15 p.m.) and leave the bike tied to a pole. When I get home, I make a meal and change my clothes before going to the gym. At 13:30 (1:30 p.m.) I pick up my bike to go to the gym.

When I get to the gym, I leave my backpack in the locker. Then I start to do the exercise of the week. Each day I do different exercises. I'm in the gym until approximately 15:00 (3:00 p.m.). After completing all the exercises, I gather my things from the locker, and bike home.

I get home at 15:15 (3:15 p.m.). I leave the bike in the garage, and I get more comfortable clothes before eating. At 15:45 (3:45 p.m.) I finish my food and lie down for a short nap until 16:30 (4:30 p.m.)

At 16:30 (4:30 p.m.) I get up and brush my teeth. Then at 16:45 (4:45 p.m.) I start studying until 19:00 (7:00 p.m.), when I eat a snack. I finish studying at 20:00 (8:00 p.m.), and then I take my dog out for about an hour. Then, at approximately 21:30 (9:30 p.m.) I take a shower and I put on my pajamas.

I relax a bit watching some television or going online. At 22:15 (10:15 p.m.) I have dinner with my family and we usually watch a movie or series. When the series or film ends, usually at 00:00 (midnight) or 00:15 (12:45 a.m.), I brush my teeth before going to bed until 08:00 a.m., when I get up to start a new day.

A DAY IN THE LIFE OF A SCHOOL TEACHER

The deafening noise of the alarm clock rings at 7:45 announcing the beginning of my day.

After stretching for a few seconds in the overstuffed and comfortable mattress of my bed, I stand up and I start the marathon-morning. I let the water run from the faucet while I prepare myself mentally to deal with the mess that I will inevitably have to confront before I get to work. I go in the kitchen.

The teddy bear in the drawing that appears in the children's menu of my small son Miguel (3 years old) looks at me suspiciously like it is telling me what I have to put in his backpack for breakfast at school. I prepare backpacks for Miguel and Álvaro, who is my eldest son (6 years old).

I come into the room of my kids softly, singing and in a very good mood, as I remember my mother used to do when I was myself a child. I awake them in the sweetest way I know—with a kiss Good Morning!

After passing through the bathroom, they drink their glasses of milk on the couch in the living room while watching *Doraemon*. My coffee is in the cup waiting for the milk that is heating up in the microwave and the bread in the toaster. Now is the time when I take a few minutes to get cute applying some mascara until I hear the toast pop up. I dress Miguel and I help Álvaro, who already knows how to dress himself.

I say goodbye to my children at the door of the school and I walk toward my work. I get ready for my students of only 4 months old, who are unwillingly left at the kindergarten by their moms after exhausting their official maternity leave. They can stay there up to 3 years. Fate, love, and reconciling work and family life led me to change my regular English classes for adults to teaching in a bilingual children's center. Twelve years ago when I looked into this adventure to teach very young children, I had a confused feeling, somewhere between tenderness and fear. Today, however, I really enjoy guiding their first steps in the knowledge of a second language, singing, playing, and laughing a lot.

At 14:00 (2:00 p.m.) I pick up my children and go home. Due to the global economic crisis—and, in particular, to my country, Spain—my workday has been cut. I wait for my partner and when he comes, we eat while we talk about daily work happenings. After resting for a moment we then face the extracurricular music lessons and soccer for my children.

When we return home, the routine begins of bathrooms and children's dinners. Since today is Monday, I get to burn some calories in the gym in the class Body-Pump. My partner and I take turns with sports activities, so he goes to the gym on Tuesdays and Thursdays for spinning classes and I go on Mondays and Wednesdays. In doing so, I can consider myself a woman who, despite being a mother, has not given up her body so she still looks and feels good about herself.

I go home and pick up something for dinner. Once the children are in bed, which is an awaited moment of quietness and tranquility, it is also the only time I have for my partner. We laugh for a while watching TV. Then we make our way to bed for a decent night's sleep, as it will all start over very early the next day . . .

A DAY IN THE LIFE OF A HOUSEWIFE

At 7:30 the alarm clock sounds: *Arriba, arriba*! I say to myself to start the day with motivation. Then, I go to the children's bedroom to awake them: "Come on, come on . . . or else we will arrive late to school."

After struggling with the little boy to put him into the uniform and prepare the hair for the oldest girl, finally we can go downstairs for breakfast. While they eat something, I prepare some snacks to put in their backpacks for school. Then, we leave home to walk quickly to the school.

I return home to organize and clean the house . . . . making beds, cleaning the bathrooms, putting clothes in the washing machine, and deciding on what I'm going to cook today.

Then I usually go shopping for the food for the day. I come back home with the trunk full. I go upstairs to put the food away. The washing machine has finished. Therefore, I have to hang up the clothes.

At 13:45 (1:45 p.m.) I go to school to pick up the children. We walk home to eat. While I clean up the kitchen, the oldest starts doing some of her homework.

When I manage to get them upstairs in the bathroom, the little boy fights fiercely and screams at me: "Mommy, I do not want to bathe!" Then, I start losing my patience.

Once they both have been bathed, I take the oldest to English, dance, or catechism classes, depending on the day of the week. About seven o'clock we arrive back home. We eat some snacks, and I help the oldest to finish with her homework.

While they put on their pajamas, I get dinner ready.

21:30 (9:30 p.m.) is the time to put them to bed. Kisses, stories, and a hug for goodnight is a must.

Then I step out outside to take out the garbage immediately after cleaning up the kitchen. Also, I pick up the clothes from the rack to iron the next day.

At 22:30 (10:30 p.m.) I go to bed. Finally I try to disconnect a bit by reading a book until it falls on my face. I sleep, if no child incident occurs at night (i.e., vomiting, wetting the bed, monsters, etc.).

Thus ends one of my days. All are equal and repetitive. No matter if it is a holiday or a weekend break. They are all the same. However, I always, always enjoy these days with the joy of my children garnished with kisses, hugs, and games. Although sometimes I wish I had endless patience, nevertheless, I always have to have a good sense of humor.

A DAY IN THE LIFE OF A FOREIGNER

The sound of my flat mate rustling up his breakfast wakes me, but no longer does the much earlier nightly noise of the waste and recycling trucks emptying the collection bins on the streets my window faces. I'm out of bed to either prepare my breakfast or off to stop in to eat at any of the early opening cafés between my flat and the bus station near the center of town. One can read the newspapers or football papers at a café.

I catch my bus and chat about the weather and discuss current events with the passengers. What life is like where I'm from also comes up, along with how Canada is depicted on a show about antique hunters airing here on Xplora, one of a handful of networks that are soon to be pulled. The bus is intercity sized, with seating for sixty, but it is running a local route connecting Logroño, La Rioja to some small towns to the south. We're only ever five at most riding, and everyone sits right up front to be able to talk with the driver.

At the cinema I had found out that they run assigned seating. I was early for the show and my ticket had me in the middle of a twelve seat row halfway up the aisle. Next a young couple arrived. They sat right in front of me. Eventually we were joined by three more couples, each strangers to the others, of which one sat behind me, with the other two making it six people in a line in front of me. Not one had opted to make a buffer seat. I chuckled at this demonstration of the Spanish concept of personal space.

When strolling home from the bus station, the same cafés are open, the schoolchildren are out in droves, but all the shops are closed. However, siesta time is an opportunity to grocery shop at the supermarket. Lines to the cashier are longest later, around six or seven p.m. It's best to have your fridge stocked before holiday weekends. Some ethnic grocery shops and halal butchers are open on Sundays, though, and a traditional bakery may be open the first half of a festival day.

People here are very friendly and very eager to help. You can get to know your neighborhood greengrocer, butcher, hairstylist . . . Folks in small towns who see you frequently will pull up to the bus stop you're waiting at and offer you a lift into the city. You will hear the cries and shouts of national pride echo out into the street and your upstairs neighbors stomping their feet any time Athletic Madrid scores against Chelsea. You may catch F1 or Moto GP fever. You'll find after hours at the bar or disco last until dawn, and that a Spanish day isn't over until the sun is rising on the next.

GLOSSARY OF KEY TERMS

al-Andalus: term referring to Muslim Spain.

Altamira caves: caves near Santillana del Mar, Cantabria, which contain mysterious and beautiful paintings of animals and hands created by prehistoric man. (Upper Paleolithic period)

autos sacramentales: small liturgical plays presented outdoors that were prohibited in 1765, after some authors began to use them in an irreverent manner.

AVE: acronym of Spanish High Speed that also means bird, *ave*, as appears on the logo.

Bachillerato: a route of post-secondary education that prepares students for university training and is equivalent to the American high school diploma.

Bourbons: Originally French, this European royal lineage ruled Spain for centuries. The current monarchy of Spain is Bourbon.

café con leche: coffee with milk—the most common way to serve coffee in Spain.

cajas: a Spanish institution which operates like banks but are heavily controlled by each regional government. The mismanagement of these institutions was partially responsible for Spain's current economic crisis.

cancíon protesta: Known in the Catalunya region as *Nova Cançó,* these songs of protest were associated with social injustice and were initially popular during Franco's rule.

cántigas: Medieval narrative songs on religious topics such as miracles or praise of the Holy Virgin.

Castilian: the language spoken by the majority of the Iberian Peninsula (Spanish).

Catalán: a language spoken in Catalunya.

cava: a Spanish sparkling wine made in the same manner as champagne.

churros con chocolate: a dish consisting of warm thick chocolate with pastry made of fried flour.

City of Arts and Sciences: a large complex in Valencia devoted to scientific and cultural dissemination. It was designed by internationally renowned architect Santiago Calatrava.

conceptismo: a form of poetry that began in the 17th century, although this style is inherited from the medieval time. In essence, *conceptismo* means to seek for a complex poetry through the exchange of themes that appear explicitly as well as implicitly in the poem.

Constitution of 1978: Spain's most recent constitution which among other things states in article 14, in terms of the law, all Spaniards are equal in regards to race, gender, religion, or any other personal or social condition and/or circumstance.

Conversos: a Jew or Muslim who converted to Catholicism, particularly during the 14th and 15th centuries.

Copla: 20th-century genre of music that is a blend of *flamenco, zarzuela*, and *cuplé*. Extremely popular in Spain between 1940–1960, the lyrics of a *copla* referred directly to social injustices experienced by marginalized people.

Costumbrismo: a literary and artistic movement that took place in Spain in the 19th century. Its focus was artistic realism and Romanticism, often showing pictorial images of everyday life.

CSIC: *Consejo Superior de Investigaciones Científicas* or Board for Research Studies. Spain's largest public institution devoted to research. It is run by the government through the Ministry of Economy and Competitiveness. One of its main goals is to produce and disseminate research nationwide as well as to collaborate with foreign institutions.

cuaderna vía: a type of poetry mainly associated with the scholarly poetry practiced by the *mester de clerecía*, that is to say, for religious matters and having nothing to do with sexuality.

culteranismo: a form of poetry that began in the 17th century. The poetry is characterized by the different registers in the language, introducing Latin words and the use of hyperbaton.

cuplé: a distinctive type of popular music created in Spain in the late 19th century.

Dau al Set: one of the first post-civil war art movements that aimed to renew Spanish art. It was founded in Barcelona in 1948.

Descent of the River Sella: a kayaking race on the famous river Sella that attracts over a thousand participants from around the globe.

desmesocratización: Spanish term referring to the end of the middle class as we know it in Spain.

domingueros: slang term used to classify a Spanish family going on an outing to the beach or the mountains during the weekend, specifically Sunday (*Domingo*).

donjuanismo: the concept of a man who spends his time conquering women and partaking in sexual exploits, while avoiding making a positive contribution to society. Based on the literary figure of *Don Juan.*

Educación Secundaria Obligatoria (ESO): the certificate a student receives at the end of the fourth year of secondary education.

Elcano Royal Institute: second largest privately run think-tank in the country. It focuses on both specific topics and geographical areas. Among the former are energy and climate change, security and defense, international terrorism, Spain's image abroad, demography, and migrations.

El Cid: "The Lord or Master" in Arabic. The first national myth of Spain. As a large poem, it describes the epic acts of a great warrior and mercenary who indistinguishably serves either Christian or Arab people.

El Paso: a group of artists at the end of the 1950s whose work was instrumental in reviving Spanish art after the post-war era.

Enlightenment: also known as the Age of Reason, a period of scientific and cultural exploration during the 18th century.

esperpento: a new way of writing created in the 20th century. It refers to a distortion of reality used in order to critique society.

ETA: Basque terrorist group created in 1959 that champions full independence from Spain. ETA stands for *Euskadi Ta Askatasuna*, which means Euskadi (Basque homeland) and Freedom.

Euskadi: the name of the Basque country in the Basque language.

Euskera: the language of the Basque people, spoken in the Basque country.

familia numerosa: the title given to a family with three or more children. These families are eligible to receive special welfare and education assistance.

(Fifteen) 15-M movement: started in Plaza del Sol in Madrid 2011 when a mass demonstration of young people protested the lack of future/jobs for the youngsters in Spain. This initial social protest became organized into different young political parties.

Flamenco: type of music originating from the Gypsy people of Andalucía. It can be traced back to the late 18th century.

Flamenco **fusion:** popular type of contemporary Spanish music. It mixes Flamenco music with other genres such as rock, pop, or jazz.

Formación Profesional de grado medio: a route of post-secondary education that prepares students for vocational training.

Free Institute of Education: one of the most important reforms in Spain's education. It was founded in 1876 and evolved into an institute. It offered primary and secondary education separate from both the state educational systems and the religious educational system.

fusion languages: mixture of Spanish with another language. A contemporary example of the linguistic phenomenon between Spanish and other languages is so-called *Spanglish*.

Galician: language spoken in Galicia (*gallego*).

Gauche Divine: cultural movement of the 1960s created by a group of Catalan intellectuals from the bourgeoisie, who secretly managed to bring other cultures to Spain during the Spanish dictatorship. It could be considered one of the first multicultural milestones that occurred in 20th-century Spain.

Generación Ni-Ni: contemporary term referring to the younger group of Spaniards who are not in school and are not employed (Neither-Nor generation).

Generation of '27: a group of poets who championed "pure poetry" and whose main inspiration was Luis de Góngora. They believed in the universality of the arts.

Generation of '98: a group of intellectuals who attempted to break with the past and their main goal was to rediscover as well as rejuvenate the nation. The name refers to 1898, the year that Spain lost its last three colonies.

Generation X: the generation born after the western post-World War II baby boom, of which Spain had their own distinctive writers.

Golden Age: 1492–1659. Also known as the Baroque period. During this time a significant number of writers and painters would create what is considered the most important Spanish art of all time.

Goya Film Awards: Spain's national film awards. Named after the iconic Spanish painter, Francisco José de Goya y Lucientes.

Guernica: Basque town that was bombed by German planes on April 26, 1937, under the consent of Franco. Also refers to the monumental painting by Picasso that depicted the horrific event.

Hispania: The Romans converted the Iberian Peninsula (*Hispania*) into a province in 206 BCE. The common language of the Roman Empire in Hispania was Latin.

huídos: the Republicans who chose to flee the country rather than surrender to Franco.

IBEX 35: Spain's stock exchange. It opened in 1992 and operates in Madrid, Barcelona, Bilbao, and Valencia.

Invincible Armada: Philip II attempted to invade Protestant England by sea with this infamous group of ships. He was defeated. This loss in 1588 marked the beginning of the decline of Spain's empire.

jamón ibérico: a type of salt-cured ham that comes from the specific breed of black Iberian pigs. It usually takes two to four years to be cured, but sometimes will take longer.

jamón serrano: a type of mountain ham made from pigs fed a grain diet; it takes 6–18 months to cure.

jarchas: brief compositions usually written by a male writer who often employs a female character as the main protagonist of a love story. The tradition of the *jarchas* would develop into the birth of medieval literature.

juderías: Jewish quarters.

Law of Equity: a law Zapatero's socialist government established in regards to gender representation. The law requires the presence of no more than 60 percent and no less than 40 percent for each sex in public institutions as well as in political parties.

Loyalists: also known as Republicans. During the Spanish Civil War (1936–1939), this group supported the established Spanish Republic and opposed the Nationalist Party led by Franco.

machismo: the concept of aggressive masculine pride. It is often associated with male chauvinism.

Mañana por la mañana: Spanish saying that literally means "tomorrow morning," although it is also the polite way of Spanish people to tell you that something is not going to happen.

Manchego: sheep's cheese from the region of Castilla-La Mancha.

maquis: deserters or insurgents who escaped from Franco's regime and took refuge in the mountains. They played a prominent role in the French Resistance to fascism.

Marca España: attempt to create a national brand that is recognized worldwide and that fosters the country's values and interests.

Mediterranean diet: a type of eating popular in the Mediterranean basin. It includes using mainly fresh seasonal vegetables, fish, legumes, eggs, fruit, rice, pasta, olive oil, and a bit of meat.

Memoria Histórica: a new way of writing that has become very popular in the New Spain's millennial literature. It also refers to the Law of Historical Memory, which passed during Zapatero's government in 2007.

mileuristas: individuals earning roughly a thousand euros a month.

Moriscos: Muslims who were forced to convert to Christianity.

Mozárabes: Christians who lived under Muslim rule (Mozarabs).

mudéjares: Muslims who remained in territory conquered by Christians. The term Mudejar also refers to the architecture practiced between the 12th and 17th centuries that combined Moorish and Gothic styles.

Nadal award: oldest literary prize of Spain.

Nasrid: final period of Muslim rule in Spain. It began with the rule of Muhammad ibn Nasr (Muhammad I: 1237–1273), who chose Granada as his capital, and ended with the loss of Granada to the Christians in 1492.

Nationalists: Led by Franco during the Spanish Civil War (1926–1939), this group opposed the Loyalists or Republicans who fought to maintain the Spanish Republic and supported the Franco Regime.

NHS: NHS is in Britain. In Spain we call it *Seguridad Social*: Spain's universal health system. It is funded and administered publicly, making the majority of health services free and accessible to Spanish residents.

no molestar **system:** Literally meaning "do not disturb," this term refers to a way of governing that has been extended to all Spanish institutions: do not disturb the Monarchy; do not disturb the Church; do not disturb Francoism; do not disturb the oligarchy who control the main businesses in Spain. Coined by sociologist José Manuel Roca Vidal in his book (*La oxidada transición,* 2013).

ONCE: *Organización Nacional de Ciegos Españoles* / National Organization of Blind People. One of Spain's key institutions in providing a system of specialized services to those with disabilities.

oposiciones: competitive exams that one must pass in order to become a civil servant in Spain.

paella: iconic dish of Spain consisting of rice, olive oil, saffron, chicken, peas, tomatoes, red pepper, (optional seafood) and garlic.

paseo: a popular custom in Spain where residents informally stroll the streets of their town. May occur after mass on Sunday or in the evenings in summer.

picaresque novel: a narration written in the first person by a poor child (an anti-hero), who has to survive often through tricks and lies. This type of writing originated in mid-16th-century Spain.

pícaro: the anti-hero of a picaresque novel.

piropos: the Spanish equivalent of the English pick-up lines.

PP: Popular party, also known as the People's Party. This is a right-wing political party in Spain.

PSOE: Partido socialista obrero Español / Spanish Socialist Workers Party. Founded in 1872, it is the second oldest political party in Spain. PSOE was in power between 1982 and 1996, and between 2004 and 2011.

pyme: refers to the small- and medium-sized businesses in the private sector or the small business man who works on his own and/or has a few employees. These types of business are the heart of the Spanish economy in the new millennium.

Queen Sofía Spanish Institute: founded in 1954 in New York City to promote the Spanish language and the culture of Spain.

Quiniela: popular lottery in Spain based on the football pool and regulated by the *Loterías y Apuestas del Estado*: Lotteries and Gambling of the State. One has to predict the winner of 15 soccer matches to win.

RENFE: *Red Nacional de los Ferrocarriles Españoles*, the Spanish national rail network.

Rioja: region in Spain famous for its wine.

Roma: Historically, the gypsies (or Roma) have been the biggest minority group in Spain.

Saint's name day: the day that Spaniards celebrate the feast day of their patron saint (*santo*).

Selectividad: national exam taken by students in the last year of post-secondary education (*Bachillerato*).

siesta: an afternoon nap. Usually taken after lunch, particularly during the summer. Due to globalization, the tradition of the *siesta* is not as strong as previously.

Sima de los Huesos: the largest collection of hominid bones in the world found near the Gran Dolina cave in Burgos. Over 30 human remains were found that date to 400,000 years ago.

sobremesa: The Spanish custom of having coffee followed by an alcoholic drink at the end of a Sunday lunch.

Surrealist movement: movement founded in 1924 by French writer André Breton, it sought to explore the subconscious through literary works and writing. Spanish artists Joan Miró and Salvador Dalí were greatly influenced by this movement.

tapas: small Spanish dishes often served at a bar with wine or beer.

Teide: an enormous volcano formed from a crater, *Las Cañadas*, located in the center of the Tenerife. At 16 km (52,493 ft) of diameter, it is one of the largest craters in the world.

Valencian: language spoken in the region of Valencia (*valenciano*).

zarzuela: Spanish musical production consisting of opera, theater, and dance.

FACTS AND FIGURES

Table 1:   GEOGRAPHY

Location	Spain occupies 80% of the Iberian Peninsula in southwestern Europe. It is bordered by France to the north and Portugal to the west, and has coastlines on the Bay of Biscay to the north, the Atlantic Ocean to the west and southwest, and the Mediterranean Sea to the southeast. The nation also encompasses the Canary Isles, situated in the Atlantic Ocean; the Balearic Islands, located in the Mediterranean Sea; and some enclaves within Morocco.
Time Zone	6 hours ahead of U.S. Eastern Standard
Land Borders	1,183 miles
Coastline	3,084 miles
Capital	Madrid
Area	194,834 sq. miles
Climate	Less temperate than most areas of western Europe, Spain has hot summers in most regions, with temperatures averaging about 95°F. The mountainous areas of the interior have cold winters.
Land Use	25.5% arable land; 9.7% permanent crops; 22.2% permanent meadows and pastures; 37.1% forest land; 5.5% other.
Arable Land	26% (2007)
Arable Land Per Capita	1 acre per person (2007)

Sources: ABC-CLIO World Geography database; CIA World Factbook. http://www.cia.gov; FAO (FAOSTAT database). http://www.fao.org; World Bank. http://www.worldbank.org.

Table 2: POPULATION

Population	48,146,134 (estimate) (2015)
World Population Rank	32nd (2009)
Population Density	240.0 people per square mile (estimate) (2011)
Population Distribution	77% urban (2011)
Age Distribution	
0–14:	14.00%
15–64:	67.10%
65+:	18.40%
Median Age	41.6 years (estimate) (2014)
Population Growth Rate	0.9% per year (estimate) (2015)
Net Migration Rate	8.3 (estimate) (2015)

Sources: ABC-CLIO World Geography database; CIA World Factbook. http://www.cia.gov; U.S. Census Bureau (International Data Base). http://www.census.gov.

Table 3: HEALTH

Average Life Expectancy	81.5 years (2014)
Average Life Expectancy, Male	78.5 years (2014)
Average Life Expectancy, Female	84.7 years (2014)
Crude Birth Rate	9.6 (estimate) (2015)
Crude Death Rate	9.0 (estimate) (2015)
Maternal Mortality	92 per 100,000 live births (2005–2012 projection)
Infant Mortality	4 per 1,000 live births (2012)
Doctors	3.7 per 1,000 people (2012)

Sources: ABC-CLIO World Geography Database; U.S. Census Bureau (International Data Base). http://www.census.gov; World Bank. http://www.worldbank.org; World Health Organization. http://www.who.int.

Table 4: ENVIRONMENT

CO_2 Emissions	6.3 metric tons per capita (2009)
Alternative and Nuclear Energy	17.7% of total energy use (2011)
Threatened Species	240 (2010)
Protected Areas	47,661 (estimate) (2010)

Sources: ABC-CLIO World Geography database; UN Statistical Database. http://unstats.un.org/unsd /databases.htm; United Nations Statistical Yearbook http://unstats.un.org/unsd/syb/; World Bank. http:// www.worldbank.org

Table 5: ENERGY AND NATURAL RESOURCES

Electric Power Generation	276,800,000,000 kilowatt hours per year (estimate) (2011)
Electric Power Consumption	249,700,000,000 kilowatt hours per year (estimate) (2011)
Nuclear Power Plants	7 (2014)
Crude Oil Production	33,600 barrels per day (2013)
Crude Oil Consumption	1,204,100 barrels per day (2013)
Natural Gas Production	61,000,000 cubic meters per year (estimate) (2012)
Natural Gas Consumption	35,820,000,000 cubic meters per year (estimate) (2010)
Natural Resources	Coal, lignite, iron ore, copper, lead, zinc, uranium, tungsten, mercury, pyrites, magnesite, fluorspar, gypsum, sepiolite, kaolin, potash, hydropower, arable land

Sources: ABC-CLIO World Geography database; CIA World Factbook. http://www.cia.gov; U.S. Energy Information Administration. http://www.eia.gov.

Table 6: NATIONAL FINANCES

Currency	Euro
Total Government Revenues	$505,100,000,000 (estimate) (2013)
Total Government Expenditures	$597,300,000,000 (estimate) (2013)
Budget Deficit	−6.8 (estimate) (2013)
GDP Contribution by Sector	Agriculture: 3.3% industry: 26.4% services: 70.3% (2012 est.)
External Debt	$2,278,000,000,000 (estimate) (2012)
Economic Aid Extended	$2,281,710,000 (2011)
Economic Aid Received	$0 (2011)

Sources: ABC-CLIO World Geography database; CIA World Factbook. http://www.cia.gov; IMF (World Economic Outlook). http://www.imf.org; OECD (Organization for Economic Cooperation and Development). http://www.oecd.org/dac/stats/idsonline.htm.

Table 7: INDUSTRY AND LABOR

Gross Domestic Product (GDP)—official exchange rate	$1,466,357,000,000 (estimate) (2015)
GDP per Capita	$31,601 (estimate) (2015)
GDP—Purchasing Power Parity (PPP)	$1,411,493,000,000 (estimate) (2013)
GDP (PPP) per Capita	$30,620 (estimate) (2013)
Industry Products	Wine, cement, iron, steel, sulfuric and nitric acids, automobiles, metals, chemicals, machine tools, textiles, clothing and footwear, food and beverages. Shipbuilding and tourism are also major industries.
Agriculture Products	Wine grapes, olives, vegetables, sugar beets, citrus fruit, potatoes, barley, wheat, poultry, sheep, pigs, cows' milk and other dairy products, fish.
Unemployment	25.2% (2012)
Labor Profile	agriculture: 4.2% industry: 24% services: 71.7% (estimate) (2009)

Sources: ABC-CLIO World Geography database; CIA World Factbook. http://www.cia.gov; ILO (LABORSTA database). http://www.ilo.org; IMF (World Economic Outlook). http://www.imf.org; World Bank. http://www.worldbank.org.

Table 8: TRADE

Imported Goods	Machinery and transportation equipment, electrical equipment, textiles, plastics, chemicals, rubber, wood and wood products, base metals, fish, mineral fuels and products, cinematographic equipment.
Total Value of Imports	$287,775,000,000 (2009)
Exported Goods	Machinery, motor vehicles, base metals, chemicals, vegetable products, alcoholic beverages, textiles, footwear and accessories.
Total Value of Exports	$303,800,000,000 (estimate) (2012)
Import Partners	Germany—15.0%; France—12.8%; Italy—7.2%; China—5.9%; Netherlands—5.2% (2009)
Export Partners	France—19.3%; Germany—11.1%; Portugal—9.2%; Italy—8.2%; United Kingdom—6.2% (2009).
Current Account Balance	$2,100,000,000 (estimate) (2013)
Weights and Measures	The metric system is in use.

Sources: ABC-CLIO World Geography database; CIA World Factbook. http://www.cia.gov; Europa World Year Book; IMF Direction of Trade Statistics.

Table 9: EDUCATION

School System	Spanish students begin their primary education at the age of six. After six years, they continue to four years of early secondary education, followed by two years of academic or technical upper secondary school.
Mandatory Education	10 years, from ages 6 to 16.
Average Years Spent in School for Current Students	17 (estimate) (2012)
Average Years Spent in School for Current Students, Male	17 (estimate) (2012)
Average Years Spent in School for Current Students, Female	18 (2012)
Primary School–age Children Enrolled in Primary School	2,816,584 (2012)
Primary School–age Males Enrolled in Primary School	1,452,603 (2012)
Primary School–age Females Enrolled in Primary School	1,363,981 (2012)
Secondary School–age Children Enrolled in Secondary School	3,296,129 (2012)
Secondary School–age Males Enrolled in Secondary School	1,686,545 (2012)
Secondary School–age Females Enrolled in Secondary School	1,609,584 (2012)
Students Per Teacher, Primary School	12.6 (2012)
Students Per Teacher, Secondary School	11.4 (2012)
Enrollment in Tertiary Education	1,965,829 (estimate) (2012)
Enrollment in Tertiary Education, Male	911,887 (estimate) (2012)
Enrollment in Tertiary Education, Female	1,053,942 (estimate) (2012)
Literacy	98% (2012)

Source: ABC-CLIO World Geography database; Country government; UNESCO. http://www.unesco.org; World Bank. http://www.worldbank.org.

Table 10: MILITARY

Total Active Armed Forces	128,013 (2010)
Active Armed Forces	0% (2010)
Annual Military Expenditures	$11,700,000,000 (2009)
Military Service	Service in the Spanish military is voluntary.

Sources: ABC-CLIO World Geography database; Military Balance.

Table 11: TRANSPORTATION

Airports	152 (2012)
Paved Roads	99.0% (2003)
Roads, Unpaved	0 (2006)
Passenger Cars per 1,000 People	481 (2010)
Number of Trucks, Buses, and Commercial Vehicles	4,908,000 (2005)
Railroads	9,500 (2008)
Ports	Major: 19, including Algeciras, Valencia, Barcelona, Bilbao, Santa Cruz de Tenerife, Cartegena, Las Palmas, Cádiz.

Sources: ABC-CLIO World Geography database; CIA World Factbook. http://www.cia.gov; World Bank. http://www.worldbank.org.

Table 12: COMMUNICATIONS

Facebook Users	17,000,000 (estimate) (2013)
Internet Users	28,119,000 (2009)
Internet Users (% of Population)	71.6% (2013)
Television	55 sets per 100 population (2004)
Land-based Telephones in Use	19,220,000 (2012)
Mobile Telephone Subscribers	50,663,000 (2012)
Major Daily Newspapers	151 (2004)
Average Circulation of Daily Newspapers	6,183,000 (2004)

Sources: ABC-CLIO World Geography database; CIA World Factbook. http://www.cia.gov; Facebook. https://www.facebook.com/.

Table 13: **LIST OF SPAIN'S PRESIDENTS IN THE 20th CENTURY**

1900 (Oct. 23): Marcelo de Azcárraga

Kingdom of Alfonso XIII:
1901 (Mar. 6): Práxedes Mateo Sagasta

1902 (Dec. 6): Francisco Silvela

1903 (July 20): Raimundo Fernández Villaverde

1903 (Dec. 5): Antonio Maura Montaner

1904 (Dec. 14): Marcelo de Azcárraga

1905 (Jan. 27): Raimundo Fernández Villaverde

1905 (June 23): Eugenio Montero Ríos

1905 (Dec. 1): Segismundo Moret y Preendergast

1906 (July 6): José López Domínguez

1906 (Nov. 30): Segismundo Moret y Prendergast

1906 (Dec. 4): Antonio Aguilar y Correa, Marquis de la Vega de Armijo

1907 (Jan. 25): Antonio Maura Montaner

1909 (Oct. 21): Segismundo Moret y Prendergast

1910 (Feb. 9): José Canalejas y Méndez

1912 (Nov. 12): Manuel García Prieto, provisional government

1912 (Nov. 14): Álvaro de Figueroa y Torres, Count de Romanones, provisional government

1912 (Dec. 31): Álvaro de Figueroa y Torres, Count de Romanones

1913 (Oct. 27): Eduardo Dato Iradier

1915 (Dec. 9): Álvaro de Figueroa y Torres, Count de Romanones

1917 (Apr. 19): Manuel García Prieto

1917 (June 11): Eduardo Dato Iradier

1917 (Nov. 1): Manuel García Prieto

1918 (Mar. 22): Antonio Maura y Montaner

1918 (Nov. 9): Manuel García Prieto

1918 (Dec. 5): Álvaro de Figueroa y Torres, Count de Romanones

1919 (Apr. 15): Antonio Maura Montaner

1919 (July 19): Manuel Allendesalazar (resigned without forming a government)

1919 (July 20): Joaquín Sánchez de Toca

1919 (Dec. 12): Manuel Allendesalazar

1920 (May 5): Eduardo Dato Iradier

1921 (March 12): Manuel Alledensalazar

1921 (Aug. 13): Antonio Maura Montaner

1922 (March 8): José Sánchez Guerra

1922 (Dec. 7): Manuel García Prieto

1923 (Sept. 15): Miguel Primo de Rivera y Orbaneja

1925 (Dec. 3): Miguel Primo de Rivera y Orbaneja

1930 (Jan. 30): Dámaso Berenguer Fusté

1931 (Feb. 18): Juan Bautista Aznar y Cabañas

Second Republic

1931 (Apr. 14): Niceto Alcalá Zamora, provisional government

1931 (Oct. 14): Manuel Azaña Díaz, provisional government

1931 (Dec. 16): Manuel Azaña Díaz

1933 (Sept. 12): Alejandro Lerroux García

1933 (Oct. 8): Diego Martínez Barrio

1933 (Dec. 16): Alejandro Lerroux García

1934 (Apr. 28): Ricardo Samper Ibáñez

1934 (Oct. 4): Alejandro Lerroux García

1935 (Sept. 25): Joaquín Chapaprieta Torregrosa

1935 (Dec. 14): Manuel Portela Valladares

1936 (Feb. 19): Manuel Azaña Díaz

1936 (May 13): Santiago Casares Quiroga

1936 (July 19): Diego Martínez Barrios (didn't manage to take possesion)

1936 (July 19): José Giral Pereira

1936 (Sept. 3): Francisco Largo Caballero

1937 (May 8) to 1939 (Apr. 1): Juan Negrín López (Republican Spain)

1936 (July 24): Miguel Cabanellas Ferrer (Council of National Defense)

1936 (Oct. 3): Fidel Dávila Arrondo (Technical Council of State)

1937 (June 3): Francisco Gómez Jordana (Technical Council of State)

Franco's dictatorship

1938 (Jan. 30) to 1969 (Oct. 29): Francisco Franco Bahamonde

1973 (June 8): Luis Carrero Blanco

1974 (Jan. 3): Carlos Arias Navarro

Kingdom of Juan Carlos I

1975 (Dec. 12): Carlos Arias Navarro

1976 (July 7) to 1980 (Sept. 8): Adolfo Suárez González

1981 (Feb. 25) to 1981 (Dec. 1): Leopoldo Calvo-Sotelo Bustelo

1982 (Dec. 3) to 1995 (June 30): Felipe González Márquez

1996 (May 5) to 2003 (Sept. 4): José María Aznar López

2004 (Apr. 18) to 2011 (Nov. 20): José Luis Rodríguez Zapatero

2011 (Dec. 21) to present: Mariano Rajoy Brey

Kingdom of Felipe VI

2011 (Dec. 21) to present: Mariano Rajoy Brey

Table 14: SPAIN'S TOP TEN MULTINATIONALS

Company	Industry	Global Market Position
Inditex	Clothing	#1 fashion retailer by sales
Tavex	Textiles	#1 producer of denim
Pronovias	Clothing	#1 maker of bridal wear
Acerinox	Steel	#1 producer of stainless steel
Repsol	Energy	#3 privately owned shipper of liquefied gas
Roca	Sanitary equipment	#1 maker of sanitary equipment
Grupo Antolín	Car components	#1 producer of interior linings
Zanini	Car components	#1 producer of wheel trims
Iberdrola	Electricity	#1 wind farm operator
ACS/Hochtief	Infrastructure	#1 developer & manager of transportation infrastructure

Chislett, William. *Spain. What Everyone Needs to Know.* Oxford: Oxford University Press, 2013.

Guillén, Mauro F. *The Rise of Spanish Multinationals: European Business in the Global Economy.* Cambridge: Cambridge University Press, 2005.

HOLIDAYS

Date/Day	Holiday
January 1	New Year's Day (*Día de Año Nuevo*). First day of the Gregorian or Western calendar.
January 5	The Three Wise Men Procession (*Cabalgata de los Reyes Magos*). It happens all over Spain, no matter how small the village. Normally starts at 5:00 p.m. with a parade through popular streets and ends up in a major square (*plaza*). The festival usually ends with a free concert. Children then go to bed with many candies in their pockets from the festival, waiting to open their Christmas presents next morning.
January 6	Feast of the Epiphany (*Día de los Reyes Magos*), when traditionally Spaniards exchange gifts—hence, the importance of January 5 (no bank holidays) for the children in particular. Nowadays, Santa Claus or Papá Noel has also been incorporated into the Spanish culture.
February	Carnivals in Spain (*Carnavales*): Days change every year. Best places are Cádiz and Tenerife, both holding Europe's biggest festivals during February. It involves a heavy dose of sarcasm known as *comparsas* in Cádiz and *murgas* in Tenerife. These satirical songs are accompanied by bands (*chirigotas*) that continuously play on words.
March	Easter, the date of which varies every year. Easter in Spain is known as *Semana Santa*, which literally means Holy Week. Religiously it covers the week from Palm Sunday to Easter Sunday. However, holidays normally take two days off—Good Friday and Easter Monday.
March 15–19	*Las Fallas* of Valencia. Without a doubt, one of the most cultural festivals of Spain. Massive cardboard statues (*fallas*) are burned in Valencia's downtown.

April 22–24	The Battle of the Moors and Christians (*Moros y Cristianos*). It takes place in several towns across the Mediterranean corridor. The best place, however, is Alcoy (Alicante). It recreates Spain's *Reconquista*.
April 23	Saint Jordi Festival in Catalunya (*Fiesta de San Jordi*). It takes place in the whole region of Catalunya but is especially celebrated in Barcelona. Catalans pay tribute to their Patron Saint Jordi. Traditionally women received a rose and men a book, coinciding with World Book Day. Catalans also call it the Day of the Rose, which is similar to Valentine's Day. The Catalans' human towers (*castellers*) are also part of this tradition in Catalunya, which also happens during the national Day of Catalunya (September 11), and for *La Mercè* (Barcelona's main festival on September 24).
May 1	Labor Day (*Día del Trabajador*). Spain celebrates the accomplishments of workers.
May 2	Provincial Holiday (*Fiesta de la Comunidad de Madrid*). Each province in Spain has its own provincial holiday day. Every province in Spain honors their local saint. For instance, San Isidro is Madrid's patron saint. Then, people from Madrid (*madrileños*) enjoy food fairs, parades, parties, concerts, and bullfights at Las Ventas.
May 15	Rocío Pilgrimage (*La romería del Rocío*). It takes place in El Rocío, which despite being a very isolated and small village in Huelva (Andalucía) most of the year, holds arguably Spain's biggest festival during El Rocío.
June 3	Corpus Christi (*Día del Corpus*). Spain celebrates the body of Christ. Big processions take place in many cities across Spain. Barefoot *penitentes* (penitents) dressed in pointed hoods and robes are usually accompanied by local authorities including politicians seeking forgiveness. During the procession, women usually dress in a specific pious attire consisting of a black *mantilla* (silk veil worn over the shoulders) and *peineta* (a high comb worn over the head). This particular attire is used for religious events only.
June 18–20	Barcelona International Sonar Festival. Spain's most progressive and multimedia arts festival.
June 23–24	Bonfires of St John (*Hogueras de San Juan*). Although it happens all along Spain's coasts, Alicante, Menorca, and Almuñecar (Granada) prepare a particularly magnificent display of fireworks at the beach, which, for the occasion, allows campers to spend the night.

June 28	Gay Pride Day (*Día del Orgullo Gay*). It is celebrated all over Spain, although Madrid celebrates it for a week, especially in the district of Chueca.
July 7–14	San Fermín Running of the Bulls (*Los San Fermínes*). It takes place in Pamplona (Navarra). Arguably Spain's most famous festival.
Mid-July	Benicàssim Festival (*Festival de Benicàssim*). It takes place in Benicàssim (Castellón) and it is Spain's biggest international outdoor music event—currently known as FIB (*Festival Internacional de Benicàssim*).
July 22–26	San Sebastián International Jazz Festival. Spain's most important venue for jazz music.
July 25	Feast of Saint James (*Fiesta de Santiago*). It takes place at Santiago de Compostela (Galicia). St. James—Spain's patron saint—is buried in Santiago de Compostela.
July 29	Festival of Near Death Experiences (*La Fiesta de Santa Marta de Ribartem*). It takes place in the small village of As Nieves (Galicia), where a statue of Saint Martha is celebrated as the saint of resurrections.
August 15	Assumption (*Asunción de la Virgen* or *Virgen de la Paloma*). Spain celebrates the ascension of the Virgin Mary to Heaven. Like other events, Spaniards celebrate this day with family and friends.
Last Wednesday of August	*La Tomatina* (The Tomato Festival). It only occurs in Bunol (Valencia), where the biggest tomato festival in the world is held. Due to the number of people now, there is a fee of €10 to participate.
Days vary	Sanlúcar Horse Races on the Beach. They take place in Sanlúcar de Barrameda (Cádiz), where riders do not compete but run for the sport. Some prizes are involved and it is free.
September 16–26 (days vary)	San Sebastián Film Festival (*Festival Internacional de San Sebastián*) is the oldest and largest cinema festival in Spain. It is held in the Basque city of San Sebastián (in euskera *Donostiako Zinemaldia*), and has become one of the most prestigious film festivals worldwide.
October 12	Spain's National Day (*Fiesta Nacional de España o Día de la Hispanidad*). Spain celebrates Christopher Columbus's first day in the Americas. The *Instituto Cervantes* has become the great ambassador of the Spanish, organizing special events for this particular day not only in Spain but across the five continents where the *Instituto Cervantes* is present. This festival is also known as *Fiestas del Pilar* (The Pilar Festival), which is hugely celebrated in Zaragoza.

November 1	All Saints Day (*Día de todos los santos*). On this day Spaniards usually go to the cemetery to honor family members who are dead. They decorate the graves and tombs with flowers, and they also reunite with other family members.
December 6	Constitution Day (*Día de la Constitución*). Spaniards commemorate this day to honor Spain's constitution.
December 8	Immaculate Conception Day (*Día de la Immaculada Concepción*). Spain honors the belief of the Virgin Mary's Immaculate Conception.
December 22	Spanish Lottery (*El Gordo*). It takes places all over Spain and the party is celebrated with *gusto* by the winners of the Christmas lottery.
December 24	Christmas Eve (*Nochebuena*). It is not a bank holiday but is celebrated nationwide at dinner time with a good meal (hence, *Nochebuena*, meaning good night) followed by midnight mass (*Misa del Gallo*).
December 25	Christmas Day (*Natividad del Señor*). Spain celebrates the birth of Jesus Christ. Nativity scenes are exhibited and are very popular in many churches nationwide.
December 31	New Year's Eve (*Nochevieja*). It is not a bank holiday but it is celebrated at midnight in every main square (plaza) of Spain.

SELECTED BIBLIOGRAPHY

GEOGRAPHY

Anderson, James M. *Guía arqueológica de España*. Madrid: Alianza Editorial, 1997.

Atlas Climático Ibérico / Iberian Climate Atlas. Agencia Estatal de Meteorología (España); Ministerio de Medio Ambiente y Medio Rural y Marino (España). Instituto de Meteorología de Portugal. 2011.

Atlas cronológico de la historia de España. Madrid: Real Academia de la Historia, 2008.

Carandell, Luis. *Celtiberia Show*. Madrid: Guadiana de Publicaciones, 1971.

Carandell, Luis. *Spain*. Madrid: Incafo, 1980.

Castles, Stephen, Hein de Hass, and Mark J. Miller. *The Age of Migration. International Population Movements in the Modern World*. 5th ed. New York: The Guildford Press, 2014.

Champion, Neil. *Countries of the World: Spain*. New York: Facts on File, 2006.

Copons, Elisenda. *Montañas de España. Rutas, paseos y aventuras*. Barcelona: ElCobre Ediciones, 2006.

Dunlop, Fiona. *National Geographic Traveler: Spain*. Washington, D.C.: National Geographic, 2012.

Farino, Teresa, and Mike Lockwood. *Travellers' Nature Guides: Spain*. Oxford: Oxford University Press, 2003.

Harris, Patricia, and David Lyon. *Frommer's Spain*. Frommer Media LLC, 2015.

Lucia, Paul. *Through the Spanish Pyrenees. GR11: A Long Distance Footpath*. 2nd ed. Milnthorpe: Cicerone Press, 2000.

Morris, Jan. *Spain*. London: Faber & Faber, 2008.

Nadeau, Jean-Benoît, and Julie Barlow. *The Story of Spanish*. New York: St. Martin's Press, 2013.

Ollé Martín, Albert. *Pueblos de España*. Barcelona: Lunwerg, 2009.

Ostergren, Robert C., and Mathias Le Bossé. *The Europeans: A Geography of People, Culture, and Environment*. 2nd ed. New York: The Guilford Press, 2011.

Pla, Josep. *Viaje en Autobús*. Barcelona: Destino, 1942.

Regàs, Rosa. *España. Una nueva mirada*. Barcelona: Lunwerg, 1997.

Tukker, Arnold, et al. *The Global Resource Footprint of Nations. Carbon, Water, Land, and Materials Embodied in Trade and Final Consumption*. Delft: Leiden University, 2014.

HISTORY

Barton, Simon. *A History of Spain*. New York: Palgrave, 2004.

Bendiner, Elmer. *The Rise and Fall of Paradise: When Arabs and Jews Built a Kingdom in Spain*. New York: Barnes & Noble, 1983.

Carr, Raymond, ed. *Spain: A History*. Oxford: Oxford University Press, 2000.

Casanova, Julián, and Carlos Gil Andrés. *Twentieth-Century Spain: A History*. Cambridge: Cambridge University Press, 2014.

Cassanyes García, Xavier. *La España que SÍ puede ser*. Madrid: Editorial Síntesis, 2015.

Castro, Américo. *The Meaning of Spanish Civilization: The Inaugural Lecture of Américo Castro*. New Jersey: Princeton University, 1941.

Chislett, William. *Spain: What Everyone Needs to Know*. Oxford: Oxford University Press, 2013.

Domínguez Ortiz, Antonio. *España, tres milenios de historia*. Madrid: Marcial Pons, 2000.

Elliot, J. H., ed. *The Hispanic World: Civilization and Empire. Europe and the Americas. Past and Present*. London: Thames & Hudson, 1991.

Eslava Galán, Juan. *Historia de España contada para escépticos*. Barcelona: Booket, 2013.

Fusi, Juan Pablo. *Historia mínima de España*. Madrid: Turner, 2012.

García de Cortázar, Fernando, and José Manuel González Vega. *Breve historia de España*. Madrid: Alianza Editorial, 2011.

Gioseffi, Daniela. *Women on War: Essential Voices for the Nuclear Age*. New York: Simon & Schuster, 1988.

Grau, Anna. *¿Los españoles son de Marte y los catalanes de Venus?* Barcelona: Península, 2015.

Hill, Fred James. *Spain. An Illustrated History*. New York: Hippocrene Books, 2001.

Hooper, John. *The New Spaniards*. 2nd ed. London: Penguin, 2006.

Hyslop, Stephen G., Bob Somerville, and John Thompson. *Eyewitness History from Ancient Times to the Modern Era*. Washington, D.C.: National Geographic, 2011.

Marco, José María. *Una historia patriótica de España*. Barcelona: Booket, 2013.

Phillips, William D., and Carla Rahn Phillips. *A Concise History of Spain*. Cambridge: Cambridge University Press, 2010.

Pierson, Peter. *The History of Spain*. Westport: Greenwood Press, 1999.

Powell, Charles. *España en democracia, 1975–2000*. Barcelona: Plaza y Janés, 2001.

Preston, Paul. *Franco: A Biography*. New York: BasicBooks, 1994.

Preston, Paul. *Juan Carlos: Steering Spain from Dictatorship to Democracy*. New York: W. W. Norton, 2004.

Preston, Paul. *The Spanish Holocaust*. New York: W. W. Norton, 2012.

Queralt del Hierro, María Pilar. *Historia de España*. Madrid: Tikal, 2009.

Quiroga, Alejandro. *Making Spaniards: Primo de Rivera and the Nationalization of the Masses, 1923–30*. New York: Palgrave Macmillan, 2007.

Sánchez-Albornoz, Claudio. *España: un enigma histórico*. Buenos Aires: Ed. Latinoamericana, 1956.

Treglown, Jeremy. *Franco's Crypt. Spanish Culture and Memory since 1936*. New York: Farrar, 2013.

Tremlett, Giles. *Ghosts of Spain*. London: Faber & Faber, 2006.

GOVERNMENT AND POLITICS

Balfour, Sebastian. *The Politics of Contemporary Spain*. New York: Routledge, 2005.

Centeno, Miguel Ángel, and Agustín Ferraro. *State and Nation Making in Latin America and Spain: Republics of the Possible*. Cambridge: Cambridge University Press, 2013.

Colomer, Josep María. *Handbook of Electoral System Choice*. New York: Palgrave Macmillan, 2006.

Corral Cortés, Esther. *Spain Today 2013*. Madrid: Ministry of the Presidency, 2013.

Encarnación, Omar G. *Spanish Politics*. Cambridge: Polity, 2008.

Field, Bonnie N., and Alfonso Botti, eds. *Politics and Society in Contemporary Spain: From Zapatero to Rajoy*. New York: Palgrave Macmillan, 2013.

García, David, and Ramón Pacheco Pardo. *Contemporary Spanish Foreign Policy*. London: Routledge, 2014.

Gómez, José Luis. *Cómo salir de esta. España toca fondo. ¿Llega la reactivación?*. A Coruña: Actualia Editorial, 2013.

Gunther, Richard, and José Ramón Montero. *The Politics of Spain*. Cambridge: Cambridge University Press, 2009.

Kamen, Henry. *Imagining Spain*. New Haven: Yale University Press, 2008.

Kern, Robert W. *The Regions of Spain: A Reference Guide to History and Culture*. Westport: Greenwood Press, 1995.

Loughlin, John, and David Hanley. *Spanish Political Parties*. Cardiff: University of Wales Press, 2006.

Martorell, Miguel y Santos Juliá. *Manual de historia política y social de España (1808–2011)*. Barcelona: RBA, 2012.

Molinas, César. *Qué hacer con España. Del capitalismo castizo a la refundación de un país*. Barcelona: Destino, 2013.

Moreno Luzón, Javier y Xosé M. Núñez Seixas, eds. *Ser españoles. Imaginarios nacionalistas en el siglo XX*. Barcelona: RBA, 2013.

Muñoz Machado, Santiago. *Informe sobre España. Repensar el estado o destruirlo*. Barcelona: Crítica, 2012.

Payne, Stanley G. *Spain: A Unique History*. Madison: University of Wisconsin Press, 2011.

Phillips, William D., and Carla Rahn Phillips. *A Concise History of Spain*. Cambridge: Cambridge University Press, 2010.

Roca, José Manuel. *La oxidada transición*. Madrid: La Linterna Sorda, 2013.

Sánchez-Cuenca, Ignacio, and Elías Dinas. *Voters and Parties in the Spanish Political Space*. New York: Routledge, 2014.

Serra, Eduardo, Marc Alba y David García. *Las claves para transformar España*. Barcelona: Destino, 2012.

Smith, Angel. *Historical Dictionary of Spain*. Lanham: Scarecrow Press, 2009.

Van der Kiste, John. *A Divided Kingdom: The Spanish Monarchy from Isabel to Juan Carlos*. Charleston: History Press, 2011.

Whitfield, Teresa. *Endgame for ETA: Elusive Peace in the Basque Country*. New York: Oxford University Press, 2014.

Zapata-Barrero, Ricard. *Diversity Management in Spain: New Dimension, New Challenges.* Manchester: Manchester University Press, 2013.

ECONOMY

Afinoguénova, Eugenia, and Jaume Martí-Olivella. *Spain Is (Still) Different: Tourism and Discourse in Spanish Identity.* Lanham: Lexington Books, 2008.

Bel, Germà. *España, capital París.* Barcelona: Booket, 2013.

Dicken, Peter. *Global Shift: Mapping the Changing Contours of the World Economy.* 7th ed. New York: The Guilford Press, 2015.

Gay de Liébana, José. *España se escribe con E de Endeudamiento. Radiografía de un país abocado al abismo.* Barcelona: Ediciones Deusto, 2012.

Gómez, José Luis. *Cómo salir de esta. España toca fondo. ¿Llega la reactivación?* A Coruña: Actualia Editorial, 2013.

Gómez Loscos, Ana, et al. *The Impact of Oil Shocks on the Spanish Economy.* Madrid: FUNCAS, 2010.

Grafe, Regina. *Distant Tyranny: Markets, Power, and Backwardness in Spain, 1650–1800.* Princeton: Princeton University Press, 2012.

International Monetary Fund. *Spain: Financial Sector Reform—Final Progress Report.* Washington D.C.: International Monetary Fund, 2014.

Jordan, Philip G. *Solar Energy Markets: An Analysis of the Global Solar Industry.* Amsterdam: Elsevier, 2014.

Kase, Kimio, and Taguy Jacopin. *CEOs as Leaders and Strategy Designers: Explaining the Success of Spanish Banks.* New York: Palgrave Macmillan, 2008.

Llopis, Enrique y Jordi Maluquer de Motes, eds. *España en crisis. Las grandes depresiones económicas, 1348–2012.* Barcelona: Pasado y Presente, 2013.

Martín-Aceña, Pablo; Elena Martínez-Ruiz, M.ª Ángeles Pons, eds. *Las crisis financieras en la España contemporánea, 1850–2012.* Barcelona: Crítica, 2013.

Molinas, César. *Qué hacer con España. Del capitalismo castizo a la refundación de un país.* Barcelona: Destino, 2013.

Muñiz Alonso, Federico. *Prospective Study: The Automotive Sector in Spain.* Madrid: Public Employment Service, 2011.

Muñoz Machado, Santiago. *Informe sobre España. Repensar el Estado o destruirlo.* Barcelona: Crítica, 2012.

Roca, José Manuel. *La oxidada transición.* Madrid: La linterna sorda, 2013.

Rosendorf, Neal M. *Franco Sells Spain to America: Hollywood, Tourism and Public Relations as Postwar Spanish Soft Power.* New York: Palgrave Macmillan, 2014.

Ross, Christopher J. *Contemporary Spain. A Handbook.* 2nd ed. London: Arnold, 2002.

Serra, Eduardo, in collaboration with Marc Alba y David García. *Las claves para transformar España.* Barcelona: Destino, 2012.

Tamames, Ramón. *España, un proyecto de país.* Madrid: Ediciones Turpial, 2012.

Vetter, Eric. "Is Spain's External Imbalance Sustainable?: An Empirical Study." St. Gallen: University of St. Gallen [Master/Dissertation], 2009.

RELIGION AND THOUGHT

Abellán, José Luis. *Historia crítica del pensamiento español*, 7 vols. Madrid: Espasa-Calpe, 1979–1991.

Beinart, Haim, and Yaacov Jeffrey Green. *The Expulsion of the Jews from Spain*. Oxford: Littman Library of Jewish Civilization, 2005.

Callahan, William James. *The Catholic Church in Spain, 1875–1998*. Washington, D.C.: The Catholic University of America Press, 2012.

Caritas Europe. *The Impact of the European Crisis: A Study of the Impact of the Crisis and Austerity on People, with Special Focus on Greece, Ireland, Italy, Portugal, and Spain*. Brüssel: Caritas Europa, 2013.

de Madariaga, Salvador. *Portrait of Europe*. London: Hollis & Carter, 1952.

Díaz-Salazar, Rafael. *España laica*. Madrid: Espasa Calpe, 2008.

Ingram, Kevin, ed. *The Conversos and Moriscos in Late Medieval Spain and Beyond, Vol. 2, The Morisco Issue*. Leiden: Brill, 2012.

Kamen, Henry. *Spain, 1469–1714: A Society of Conflict*. Hoboken: Taylor & Francis, 2014.

Kamen, Henry. *The Spanish Inquisition: A Historical Revision*. New Haven: Yale University Press, 2014.

Krauel, Javier. *Imperial Emoticons: Cultural Responses to Myths of Empire in fin-de-siècle Spain*. Liverpool: Liverpool University Press, 2013.

López Villaverde, Ángel Luis. *El poder de la Iglesia en la España contemporánea*. Madrid: Catarata, 2013.

Lowney, Chris. *A Vanished World. Medieval Spain's Golden Age of Enlightenment*. New York: Free Press, 2005.

Maetzu, Ramiro de. *Hacia otra España*. Bilbao: Biblioteca Bascongada de Fermín Herrán, 1899.

Margulis, Lynn, and Eduardo Punset, eds. *Mind, Life and Universe: Conversations with Great Scientists of Our Time*. White River Junction: Chelsea Green Publishing, 2007.

Martín Muñoz, Gema, et al. *Muslims in Spain: A Reference Guide*. Madrid: Casa Árabe-IEAM, 2010.

Martínez-Torrón, Javier. *Religion and Law in Spain*. Amsterdam: Kluwer Law International, 2014.

Menocal, María Rosa. *The Ornament of the World: How Muslims, Jews, and Christians Created a Culture of Tolerance in Medieval Spain*. New York: Warner Books, 2009.

Ramis, Sergi. *Camino de Santiago: The Ancient Way of Saint James Pilgrimage Route from the French Pyrenees to Santiago de Compostela*. London: Aurum Press, 2014.

Savater, Fernando. *Education and Citizenship in the Global Era: Lecture*. Washington, D.C.: IDB Cultural Center, 2003.

Savater, Fernando. *The Questions of Life: An Invitation to Philosophy*. Cambridge: Polity, 2002.

Smith, Paul Julian. *The Moderns: Time, Space, and Subjectivity in Contemporary Spanish Culture*. Oxford: Oxford University Press, 2000.

Vincent, Mary. *Spain, 1833–2002: People and State*. Oxford: Oxford University Press, 2007.

Zambrano, María. *Delirium and Destiny: A Spaniard in Her Twenties*. Albany: SUNY University Press, 1999.

SOCIAL CLASSES AND ETHNICITY

Antonucci, Lorenza et al., eds. *Young People and Social Policy in Europe: Dealing with Risk, Inequality and Precarity in Times of Crisis*. Basingtoke: Palgrave Macmillan, 2014.

Balfour, Sebastian. *The End of the Spanish Empire, 1898–1923*. Oxford: Clarendon Press, 2010.

Barredo, Daniel. *El tabú Real. La imagen de una monarquía en crisis*. Córdoba: Berenice, 2013.

Bendiner, Elmer. *The Rise and Fall of Paradise: When Arabs and Jews Built a Kingdom in Spain*. New York: Barnes & Noble, 1983.

Bercovici, Konrad. *Gypsies in Spain*. Whitefish: Kessinger Publishing, 2010.

Borrow, George. *The Zincali: An Account of the Gypsies of Spain*. Teddington: Echo Library, 2010.

Buffery, Helena, ed. *Stages of Exile: Spanish Republican Exile Theatre and Performance*. Oxford: Peter Lang, 2012.

Caputo, Richard K., ed. *Basic Income Guarantee and Politics: International Experiences and Perspectives on the Viability of Income Guarantee*. New York: Palgrave Macmillan, 2012.

Carr, Raymond. *Modern Spain, 1875–1980*. Oxford: Oxford University Press, 1980.

Charnon-Deutsch, Lou. *The Spanish Gypsy: The History of a European Obsession*. University Park: Pennsylvania State University Press, 2004.

Colectivo Ioé (Carlos Pereda, Miguel Ángel de Prada, Walter Actis). *Discapacidades e inclusión social*. Barcelona: la Caixa, 2012.

Domínguez Ortiz, Antonio. *España. Tres milenios de historia*. Madrid: Marcial Pons, 2000.

Ealham, Chris, and Michael Richards, eds. *The Splintering of Spain: Cultural History of the Spanish Civil War, 1936–1939*. Cambridge: Cambridge University Press, 2010.

España, Ramón de. *El manicomio catalán*. Madrid: La Esfera de los Libros, 2013.

Ferrer-i-Carbonell, Ada, Xavier Ramos, and Mónica Oviedo. *Growing Inequalities and its Impacts in Spain*. European Union: GINI, 2013.

Irastorza, Nahikari. *Born Entrepeneurs?: Immigrants Self-Employment in Spain*. Amsterdam: Amsterdam University Press, 2010.

López Basaguren, Alberto, and Leire Escajedo San Epifiano, eds. *The Ways of Federalism in Western Countries and the Horizons of Territorial Autonomy in Spain*. Vol. 2 New York: Springer, 2013.

Marco, José María. *Una historia patriótica de España*. Barcelona: Booket, 2013.

Martínez Lirola, María. *Discourses on Immigration in Times of Economic Crisis: A Critical Perspective*. Newcastle: Cambridge Scholars Publishing, 2013.

Martorell, Miguel y Santos Juliá. *Manual de historia política y social de España (1808–2011)*. Barcelona: RBA, 2012.

Moreno, Luis, et al. *Diversity and Unity in Federal Countries*. Montreal: McGill-Queen's University Press, 2010.

Nairn, Agnes. *Children's Well-being in UK, Sweden and Spain: The Role of Inequality and Materialism*. London: Ipsos MORI (Social Research Institute), 2011.

Pérez Vidal, Carmen, et al., eds. *A Portrait of the Young in the New Multilingual Spain*. Clevedon: Mulitlingual Matters, 2008.

Powell, Charles T. *Juan Carlos of Spain: Self-Made Monarch*. New York: St. Martin's Press, 1996.

Preston, Paul. *The Spanish Holocaust*. New York: Norton, 2013.

Sanabria, Enrique A. *Republicanism and Anticlerical Nationalism in Spain*. New York: Palgrave Macmillan, 2009.

Tezanos, José Félix. *Los nuevos problemas sociales*. Madrid: Editorial Sistema, 2013.

Toguslu, Erkam, et al. *New Multicultural Identities in Europe: Religion and Ethnicity in Secular Societies*. Leuven: Leuven University Press, 2014.

Varela-Lago, Ana María. "Conquerors, Immigrants, Exiles: The Spanish Diaspora in the United States, 1848–1948." San Diego: University of California, 2008 [Thesis].

GENDER, MARRIAGE, AND SEXUALITY

Ackelsberg, Martha A. *Free Women of Spain: Anarchism and the Struggle for the Emancipation of Women*. Oakland: AK Press, 2005.

Almeida, Cristina. *En defensa de la mujer*. Barcelona: Martínez Roca, 1999.

Amorós, Celia. *Hacia una crítica de la razón patriarcal*. Barcelona: Anthropos, 1985.

Bergmann, Emile L., and Paul Julian Smith, eds. *¿Entiendes?: Queer Readings, Hispanic Writings*. Durham: Duke University Press, 1995.

Caballé, Anna. *El feminismo en España. La lenta conquista de un derecho*. Madrid: Cátedra, 2013.

Calvo Borobia, Kerman. *Post-Marriage LGBT Politics in Spain*. Salamanca: Gredos/Universidad de Salamanca, 2014.

Camps, Victoria. *El siglo de las mujeres*. Madrid: Cátedra, 1998.

de Ros, Xon, and Geraldine Hazbun, eds. *A Companion to Spanish Women's Studies*. Woodbridge: Tamesis Books, 2014.

Enders, Victoria L., and Pamela Beth Radcliff, eds. *Constructing Spanish Womanhood: Female Identity in Modern Spain*. Albany: State University of New York Press, 1999.

Femenías, María Luisa, and Amy Oliver, eds. *Feminist Philosophy in Latin America and Spain*. New York: Rodopi, 2007.

Freixas, Laura, ed. *Ser mujer*. Madrid: Temas de hoy, 2000.

Gautier, Andrea. *Mujeres y cultura: políticas de igualdad*. Madrid: Ministerio de Cultura, 2011.

Gil, Silvia L. *Nuevos feminismos. Sentidos comunes en la dispersión. Una historia de trayectorias y rupturas en el estado español*. Madrid: Traficantes de sueños, 2011.

Johnson, Roberta, and Maite Zubiaurre, eds. *Antología del pensamiento feminista español (1726–2011)*. Madrid: Cátedra, 2012.

Kraler, Albert, et al. *Gender, Generations and the Family in International Migration*. Amsterdam: Amsterdam University Press, 2012.

Labanyi, Jo, ed. *Constructing Identity in Contemporary Spain: Theoretical Debates and Cultural Practice*. Oxford: Oxford University Press, 2003.

The Life of Women and Men in Europe: A Statistical Portrait. Luxembourg: Eurostat, 2008.

Lombardo, Emanuela et al., eds. *The Discursive Politics of Gender Equality: Stretching, Bending, and Policy-Making*. London: Routledge, 2012.

Lorente Acosta, Miguel. *Mi marido me pega lo normal*. Barcelona: Ares y Mares, 2001.

Miriano, Constanza. *Cásate y sé sumisa*. Granada: Nuevo Inicio, 2013.

Moa, Pío. *Ensayos polémicos. España en la encrucijada.* Lorca: editorial Fajardo el bravo, 2013.

Mujeres y hombres en España. Madrid: Instituto de la Mujer, 2013.

Pérez Garzón, Juan Sisinio. *Historia del feminismo.* 2nd ed. Madrid: Catarata, 2012.

Pérez-Sánchez, Gema. *Queer Transitions in Contemporary Spanish Culture: From Franco to la Movida.* New York: State University of New York Press, 2007.

Segarra, Marta y Àngels Carabí, eds. *Feminismo y crítica literaria.* Barcelona: Icaria Editorial, 2000.

Smith, Paul Julian. *Laws of Desire: Questions of Homosexuality in Spanish Writing and Film, 1960–1990.* Oxford: Oxford University Press, 1992.

Threlfall, Mónica, et al. *Gendering Spanish Democracy.* London: Routledge, 2004.

Torres, Lourdes, and Immaculada Pertusa, eds. *Tortilleras: Hispanic and U.S.–Latina Lesbian Expression.* Philadelphia: Temple University Press, 2003.

Twomey, Lesley K., ed. *Women in Contemporary Culture: Roles and Identities in France and Spain.* Portland: Intellect, 2000.

Valcárcel, Amelia. *Sexo y filosofía.* Barcelona: Anthropos, 1991.

Vollendorf, Lisa, ed. *Recovering Spain's Feminist Tradition.* New York: Modern Language Association of America, 2001.

Vosburg, Nancy, and Jacky Collins, eds. *Lesbian Realities/Lesbian Fictions in Contemporary Spain.* Lewisburg, PA: Bucknell University Press, 2011.

EDUCATION

Boyd-Barrett, Oliver, and Pamela O'Malley, eds. *Education Reform in Democratic Spain.* London: Taylor & Francis, 2003.

Domke, Joan. "Education, Fascism, and the Catholic Church in Franco's Spain." Chicago: Loyola University Chicago, 2011. [Thesis].

Fabry, Elvire. *Think Global—Act European IV. Thinking Strategically about the EU's External Action: The recommendations of 16 European Think Tanks.* Paris: Notre Europe, 2013.

Fernández Liria, Carlos, Pedro Fernández Liria y Luis Alegre Zahonero. *Educación para la ciudadanía. democracia, capitalismo y estado de derecho.* Madrid: Akal, 2007.

Gentile, Alessandro, Anna Sanmartín Ortí, and Ana Lucía Hernández Cordero. *La sombra de la crisis. La sociedad española en el horizonte de 2018.* Madrid: Centro Reina Sofía Sobre Adolescencia y Juventud. Fundación de Ayuda contra la Drogadicción (FAD), 2014.

Groves, Tamar. *Teachers and the Struggle for Democracy in Spain, 1970–1985.* New York: Palgrave Macmillan, 2013.

Hagemann, Karen, et al. *Children, Families, and States.* New York: Berghahn Books, 2014.

Hampshire, David. *Living and Working in Spain.* 8th ed. Bath: Survival Books, 2009.

Newton, Michael, and Graham Shields. *Studying and Working in Spain: Student Guide.* New York: Palgrave, 2001.

Noya, Javier. *La imagen de España en el mundo. Visiones del exterior. Volumen 1.* 2nd ed. Madrid: Tecnos, 2013.

Otero Hidalgo, Carlos, et al. *Vocational Education and Training in Spain: Short Description.* Luxembourg: Office for Official Publications of the European Communities, 2002.

Ross, Christopher J. *Contemporary Spain: A Handbook*. 2nd ed. London: Arnold, 2002.

VV.AA. *La Uni en la calle. Libro de textos*. Madrid: Cooperativa MásPúblico, 2013.

LANGUAGE

Gorter, D. *Linguistic Landscape: A New Approach to Multilingualism*. Buffalo: Multilingual Matters, 2006.

Grenfell, Michael, ed. *Modern Languages across the Curriculum*. London: Routledge, 2002.

López-Davalillo Larrea, Julio. *Geografía regional de España*. Madrid: UNED, 2014.

Nadeau, Jean-Benoît, and Julie Barlow. *The Story of Spanish*. New York: St. Martin's Press, 2013.

Noya, Javier. *La imagen de España en el mundo. Visiones del exterior. Volumen 1*. 2nd ed. Madrid: Tecnos, 2013.

Núñez Seixas, Xosé Manuel. "La(s) lengua(s) de la nación," in *Ser españoles. Imaginarios nacionalistas en el siglo XX*. Edited by Javier Moreno Luzón, and Xosé M. Núñez Seixas. Barcelona: RBA, 2013 (246–286).

Ostler, Nicholas. *Empires of the Word: A Language History of the World*. London: Folio Society, 2010.

Penny, Ralph J. *A History of the Spanish Language*. Cambridge: Cambridge University Press, 1991.

Pérez Vidal, Carmen, et al. *A Portrait of the Young in the New Multilingual Spain*. Buffalo: Multilingual Matters, 2008.

Pharies, David A. *A Brief History of the Spanish Language*. Chicago: Chicago University Press, 2007.

Resina, Joan Ramón. *Iberian Modalities. A Relational Approach to the Study of Culture in the Iberian Peninsula*. Liverpool: Liverpool University Press, 2013.

Stewart, Miranda. *The Spanish Language Today*. London: Routledge, 2003.

Tomé, Javier. *The Route of the Castilian Language*. 2nd ed. Madrid: Turespaña, 2003.

Turell, María Teresa. *Multilingualism in Spain: Sociolinguistic and Psycholinguistic, Aspects of Linguistic Minority Groups*. Buffalo: Multilingual Matters, 2001.

VV.AA. *El español en España*. Barcelona: EGEDSA, 2007.

ETIQUETTE

Agriculture and Agri-Food Canada. *Foodservice Profile Spain. Market Analysis Report* June 2011.

Euromonitor International. *Passport: Apparel in Spain*. July 2013.

Graff, Marie Louise. *Culture Shock! Spain: A Survival Guide to Customs and Etiquette*. New York: Marshall Cavendish Editions, 2008.

Hampshire, David. *Living and Working in Spain*. 8th ed. London: Survival Books, 2009.

Hickey, Leo, and Miranda Stewart. *Politeness in Europe*. Buffalo: Multilingual Matters, 2005.

Holton, Harvey. *Working and Living Spain*. London: Cadogan Guides, 2007.

Hooper, John. *The New Spaniards*. 2nd ed. London: Penguin Books, 2006.

Íñigo, José María y David Zurdo. *Chupa la gamba*. Madrid: la esfera de los libros, 2013.

Macfarlane, Michael. *The Little Giant Encyclopedia of Etiquette*. New York: Sterling, 2001.

Mulvihill, Edward R., and Roberto G. Sánchez, eds. *Modos de vivir. Un observador español en los Estados Unidos. Selections from the writings of Julián Marías*. New York: Oxford University Press, 1971.

Novas, Himilce, and Rosemary Silva. *Passport Spain: Your Pocket Guide to Spanish Business, Customs & Etiquette*. Petaluma: World Trade Press, 2008.

Packer, Jonathan. *Live & Work in Spain and Portugal*. 2nd ed. Oxford: Vacation Work, 1998.

Richardson, Bill. *Spanish Studies. An Introduction*. New York: Oxford University Press, 2001.

Schlecht, Neil E. *Spain for Dummies*. Hoboken: Wiley, 2007.

Stewart, Chris. *Driving over Lemons: An Optimist in Andalucía*. New York: Pantheon Books, 1999.

Zollo, Mike, and Phil Turk. *World Cultures: Spain*. Chicago: Contemporary Books, 2000.

LITERATURE AND DRAMA

Álvarez-Blanco, Palmar, and Toni Dorca, eds. *Contornos de la narrativa española actual (2000–2010)*. Madrid: Iberoamericana, 2011.

Boruszko, Gabriela Susana. *A Literary Map of Spain in the 21st Century*. New York: Peter Lang, 2013.

Cascardi, Anthony J., ed. *The Cambridge Companion to Cervantes*. Cambridge: Cambridge University Press, 2002.

Corbalán, Ana, and Ellen C. Mayock, eds. *Toward a Multicultural Configuration of Spain: Local Cities, Global Spaces*. Lanham: Fairleigh Dickinson University Press, 2015.

Epps, Bradley S., and Luis Fernández Cifuentes, eds. *Spain beyond Spain: Modernity, Literary History, and National Identity*. Lewisburg: Bucknell University Press, 2005.

Henseler, Christine. *Spanish Fiction in the Digital Age: Generation X Remixed*. New York: Palgrave, 2011.

Ihrie, Maureen, and Salvador A. Oropesa, eds. *World Literature in Spanish*. 3 volumes. Santa Barbara: ABC-CLIO, 2011.

Kallendorf, Hilaire. *A Companion to Early Modern Hispanic Theater*. Leiden: Brill, 2014.

Labanyi, Jo. *Spanish Literature: A Very Short Introduction*. Oxford: Oxford University Press, 2010.

Mackenzie, Ann L., and Jeremy Robbins. *Hesitancy and Experimentation in Enlightenment Spain and Latin America*. Hoboken: Taylor & Francis, 2013.

Martin-Estudillo, Luis, and Nicolás Spadaccini, eds. *New Spain, New Literatures*. Nashville: Vanderbilt University Press, 2010.

Mueller, Stephanie Ann. "Conflicting Identities in Spain's Peripheries: Centralist Spanish Nationalism in Contemporary Cultural Production of Catalonia and the Basque Country." Iowa: University of Iowa, 2013. [Thesis].

Sánchez, Francisco J. *An Early Bourgeois Literature in Golden Age Spain: Lazarillo de Tormes, Guzmán de Alfarache, and Baltasar Gracián*. Chapel Hill: University of North Carolina Press, 2003.

Schmidt, Rachel. *Critical Images: The Canonization of Don Quixote through Illustrated Editions of the Eighteenth Century*. Quebec: McGill-Queen's University Press, 1999.

Schurlknight, Donald E. *Power and Dissent: Larra and Democracy in Nineteenth-Century Spain*. Lewisburg: Bucknell University Press, 2009.

Smith, Colin. *Poema de mío Cid*. Madrid: Cátedra, 2011.

Walters, D. Gareth. *The Cambridge Introduction to Spanish Poetry*. Cambridge: Cambridge University Press, 2002.

ART AND ARCHITECTURE

Bou, Louis. *NYC-BCN Street Art Revolution*. New York: Collins Design, 2006.

Calvo Serraller, Francisco. *The Museo del Prado and the Contemporary Artists*. Barcelona: Fundación Amigos del Museo del Prado, 2013.

Daix, Pierre. *Picasso: Life and Art*. New York: Icon Editions, 1994.

Dodds, Jerrilynn Denise. *Al-Andalus: The Art of Islamic Spain*. New York: Metropolitan Museum of Art –H. N. Abrams, 1992.

Gil, Emilio. *Pioneers of Spanish Graphic Design*. New York: Mark Batty, 2009.

Helmstufler Di Dio, Kelley, and Rosario Coppel. *Sculpture Collections in Early Modern Spain*. Burlington: Ashgate, 2013.

Hunter, Garry. *Street Art from around the World*. London: Arcturus, 2012.

Hunter, Sam, and John M. Jacobus. *Modern Art: Painting, Sculpture, Architecture*. New York: H. N. Abrams, 1985.

Illán Martín, Magdalena. *Carmen Laffón. La poética de la realidad en el arte español contemporáneo*. Sevilla: Universidad de Sevilla, 2012.

Jake. *Mammoth Book of Street Art*. Philadelphia: Running Press Pub., 2012.

Jodidio, Philip. *Architecture in Spain*. Los Angeles: Taschen, 2007.

Kleihues, Jan, et al. *Spanish Architects Abroad / Arquitectos españoles en el extranjero*. Berlin: Jovis, 2011.

Lechado, José Manuel. *La movida: una crónica de los 80*. Madrid: Algaba, 2005.

Loeb Stepanek, Stephanie, et al. *Goya: Order & Disorder*. Boston: Museum of Fine Arts, 2014.

Mangini González, Shirley. *Maruja Mallo and the Spanish Avant-garde*. Burlington: Ashgate, 2010.

Martín, Luz A. *Textura: Valencia Street Art*. New York: Mark Batty, 2009.

Moffitt, John F. *The Arts in Spain*. New York: Thames & Hudson, 1999.

Museyon Guides. *Art + Travel Europe: Step into the Lives of Five Famous Painters*. New York: Museyon Guides, 2010.

Nichols, William J., and H. Rosi Song, eds. *Toward a Cultural Archive of La Movida: Back to the Future*. Madison: Fairleigh Dickinson University Press, 2014.

Pascual, Carlos. *Art in Spain*. Madrid: Egesa, 2005.

Payne, Laura, et al. *Essential History of Art*. Bath: Parragon Publishing, 2003.

Price, Bill. *Great Modern Architecture: The World's Most Spectacular Buildings*. London: Canary Press, 2009.

Richardson, John, and Marilyn McCully. *A Life of Picasso*. New York: Alfred A. Knopf, 2010.

Riera, Carme. *La Escuela de Barcelona*. Barcelona: Anagrama, 1988.

Robinson, William H., et al. *Barcelona and Modernity: Picasso, Gaudí, Miró, Dalí*. Cleveland: Cleveland Museum of Art in association with Yale University Press, 2006.

Rodgers, Eamonn, ed. *Encyclopedia of Contemporary Spanish Culture*. New York: Routledge, 1999.

Rosser-Owen, Mariam. *Islamic Arts from Spain*. New York: N. H. Abrams, 2010.

Schacter, Rafael, and John Fekner. *The World Atlas of Street Art and Graffiti*. New Haven: Yale University Press, 2013.

Schroth, Sarah, ed. *Art in Spain and the Hispanic World: Essays in Honor of Jonathan Brown*. London: Paul Holberton Publishing, 2010.

Sureda, Joan. *The Golden Age of Spain: Painting, Sculpture, Architecture*. New York: Vendome Press, 2006.

Tomlinson, Janis A. *From El Greco to Goya: Painting in Spain, 1561–1828*. New York: H. N. Abrams, 1997.

Vilches Fuentes, Gerardo. *Breve historia del cómic*. Madrid: Nowtilus, 2014.

MUSIC AND DANCE

Biddle, Ian, and Vanessa Knights, eds. *Music, National Identity and the Politics of Location: Between the Global and the Local*. Burlington: Ashgate, 2008.

Boyd, Malcom, and Juan José Carreras, eds. *Music in Spain during the Eighteenth Century*. Cambridge: Cambridge University Press, 1998.

Broughton, Simon, Mark Ellingham, and Jon Lusk, eds. *The Rough Guide to World Music: Europe, Asia and Pacific*. New York: Rough Guides, 2009.

Chase, Gilbert. *The Music of Spain*. 2nd rev. ed. New York: Dover Publications, 1976.

Hass, Ken, and Gwynne Edwards. *Flamenco!* New York: Thames & Hudson, 2000.

Holguín, Sandie. "Música y nacionalismo." In *Ser españoles*. Edited by Javier Moreno Luzón y Xosé M. Núñez Seixas. Barcelona: RBA, 2013 (497–529).

Kreitner, Kenneth. *The Church Music of Fifteenth-Century Spain*. Woodbridge: The Boydell Press, 2004.

Lechner, Ernesto. *Rock en español: The Latin Alternative Rock Explosion*. Chicago: Chicago Review Press, 2006.

Llano, Samuel. *Whose Spain? Negotiating "Spanish Music" in Paris, 1908–1929*. New York: Oxford University Press, 2013.

Marco, Tomas. *Spanish Music in the Twentieth Century*. Cambridge: Harvard University Press, 1993.

Martínez, Silvia, and Héctor Fouce, eds. *Made in Spain: Studies in Popular Music*. New York: Routledge, 2013.

Operé, Fernando,, and Carrie B. Douglass. *España y los españoles de hoy. Historia, sociedad y cultura*. New Jersey: Pearson, 2008.

Regev, Motti. *Pop-Rock Music*. Malden: Polity, 2013.

Ribera, Julian. *Music in Ancient Arabia and Spain*. Peterborough: Vincentpress, 2014.

Russell, Peter E. *Spain: A Companion to Spanish Studies*. New York: Routledge, 1989.

Rutherford-Johnson, Tim, ed. *The Oxford Dictionary of Music*. 6th ed. Oxford: Oxford University Press, 2012..

Washabaugh, William. *Flamenco Music and National Identity in Spain*. Burlington: Ashgate, 2012.

Webber, Christopher. *The Zarzuela Companion*. Lanham: Scarecrow Press, 2002.

Woods Peiró, Eva. *White Gypsies: Race and Stardom in Spanish Musicals*. Minneapolis: University of Minnesota Press, 2012.

FOOD

Andrews, Colman. *Ferran: The Inside Story of El Bulli and the Man who Reinvented Food*. New York: Gotham Books, 2010.

Aris, Pepita. *The Real Taste of Spain in 150 Traditional Dishes*. Wigston: Lorenz Books, 2013.

Balaguer, Oriol, et al. *Dessert Cuisine*. 2nd ed. Barcelona: Montagud Editors, 2006.

Batali, Mario. *Spain: A Culinary Road Trip*. New York: HarperCollins, 2008.

Camorra, Frank, and Richard Cornish. *MoVida Desserts & Pastries: Spanish Culinary Adventures*. Sydney: Murdoch Books, 2011.

Campbell Caruso, James, and Douglas Merriam. *España: Exploring the Flavors of Spain*. Layton: Gibbs Smith, 2012.

Christian, Rebecca. *Cooking the Spanish Way: Revised and Expanded to Include New Low-Fat and Vegetarian Recipes*. Minneapolis: Lerner Publications, 2002.

Escorial, José Manuel. *España y sus quesos: Spain and its Cheeses*. Spain: Akasa, 2006.

Evans, Polly. *It's Not about the Tapas*. New York: Bantam Dell, 2003.

Harráiz, Alberto. *Spain. Mediterranean Cuisine*. Cambridge: KÖNEMANN, 2006.

Koehler, Jeff. *Spain*. San Francisco: Chronicle Books, 2013.

Lawson, Jane, ed. *Cooking Spanish*. Vancouver: Whitecap, 2005.

Lewis, Emma. *200 Tapas & Spanish Dishes*. London: Hamlyn, 2013.

Michelin, Pneu (Firm). *España & Portugal 2013*. France: Michelin, 2013.

Radford, John, and Mario Sandoval. *Cook España, Drink España: A Culinary Journey around the Food and Drink of Spain*. New York: Hachette Book Group, 2009.

Read, Jan. *Wines of Spain*. London: Mitchell Beazley, 2005.

Richardson, Paul. *A Late Dinner: Discovering the Food of Spain*. New York: Scribner, 2009.

Trutter, Marion. *Culinaria Spain: Cuisine. Country. Culture*. Potsdam: h.f.ullmann, 2010.

Weinstein, Bruce, and Mark Scarbrough. *Ham: An Obsession with the Hindquarter*. New York: Stewart Tabori & Chang, 2010.

LEISURE AND SPORTS

Andreff, Wladimir, ed. *Contemporary Issues in Sports Economics*. Northampton: Edward Elgar Publishing, 2011.

Campbell, Polly, et al. *Focus on Spain*. Millwaukee: World Almanac Library, 2007.

Dickin, Schinas, Jill. *A Family Outing in the Atlantic*. London: Imperator Publishing, 2008.

Fallon, Lucy, and Adrian Bell. *Viva la Vuelta!* Norwich: Mousehold Press, 2005.

Galván, Javier A., ed. *They do What? A Cultural Encyclopedia of Extraordinary and Exotic Customs from around the World.* Santa Barbara: ABC-CLIO, 2014.

Gasol Sáez, Pau, and Lori Shepler. *Pau Gasol. Life = Vida.* Huntington Beach: CTK Productions LLC, 2013.

Green, Stewart M. *Rock Climbing Europe.* Guilford: Morris Book Publishing, 2006.

Hannan, Nicolette, and Michelle Williams. *Spanish Festivals and Traditions.* Bedfordshire: Brilliant Publications, 2011.

Hollander, Jim. *Run to the Sun: Pamplona's Fiesta de San Fermín.* Wilmington: Master Arts Press LLC, 2002.

Kennedy, Alison Louise. *On Bullfighting.* New York: Anchor Books, 2001.

Kuper, Simon, and Stephan Szymanski. *Soccernomics: Why England Loses, Why Spain, Germany, and Brazil Win, and Why the U.S., Japan, Australia—and Even Iraq—Are Destined to Become the Kings of the World's Most Popular Sport.* New York: Nation Books, 2014.

Lowe, Sid. *Fear and Loathing in La Liga: Barcelona vs Real Madrid.* New York: Nation Books, 2013.

McLenighan, Valjean. *Christmas in Spain.* Lincolnwood: Passport Books, 1995.

Medina, F. Xavier. *Food Culture in Spain.* Westport: Greenwood Press, 2005.

Muñoz, Pedro M., and Marcelino C. Marcos. *España. Ayer y hoy.* 2nd ed. London: Prentice Hall, 2010.

Nadal, Rafael, and John Carlin. *Rafa.* New York: Hyperion, 2011.

Nauright, John, and Charles Parrish, eds. *Sports around the World: History, Culture and Practice.* Santa Barbara: ABC-CLIO, 2012.

Núñez Florencio, Rafael. "Los toros, fiesta nacional." In *Ser españoles.* Edited by Javier Moreno Luzón and Xosé M. Núñez Seixas. Barcelona: RBA, 2013 (433–463).

Pérez de las Rozas, Emilio. *Marc Márquez: Dreams Come True: My Story.* London: Ebury Press, 2014.

Powell Kennedy, Brittany. *Between Distant Modernities: Performing Exceptionality in Francoist Spain and the Jim Crow South.* Jackson: University Press of Mississippi, 2015.

Quiroga, Alejandro. *Football and National Identities in Spain.* New York: Palgrave Macmillan, 2013.

Savater, Fernando. *Tauroética.* Madrid: Turpial, 2010.

Shubert, Adrian. *Death and Money in the Afternoon: A History of the Spanish Bullfight.* New York: Oxford University Press, 1999.

Suárez, Laureano. *Sports . . . in Spain.* Madrid: Turespaña, 1995.

Vaczi, Mariann. *Soccer, Culture and Society in Spain.* New York: Routledge, 2015.

Wertheim, L. Jon. *Strokes of Genius: Federer, Nadal, and the Greatest Match Ever Played.* Boston: Houghton Mifflin Harcourt, 2009.

MEDIA AND POPULAR CULTURE

Albarrán, Alan B., ed. *The Handbook of Spanish Language Media.* New York: Routledge, 2009.

Amago, Samuel. *Spanish Cinema in the Global Context.* New York: Routledge, 2013.

Benet, Vicente J. *El cine español. Una historia cultural*. Barcelona: Paidós, 2012.

Caparrós Lera, J. M. *Historia del cine español*. Madrid: T&B editores, 2007.

Carrión, Jorge. *Teleshakespeare*. Madrid: Errata Naturae, 2011.

Casablanca Migueles, Luis. *La moda como disciplina artística en España. Jesús del Pozo y la generación de los nuevos creadores*. Granada: Universidad de Granada, 2007.

Casas, Belén Ester. *En tierra de hombres. Mujeres y feminismo en el cine contemporáneo*. Madrid: Encuentro, 2015.

Castiella, Antxon Salvador. *Spanish Cinema: A Selection of 250 of the Best Spanish and Latin American Films from Sound Cinema to Today*. Rome: Gremese, 2013.

Centeno, Patrycia. *Política y moda. La imagen del poder*. Barcelona: Península, 2012.

Deltell Escolar, Luis et al. *Breve Historia del Cine*. Madrid: Editorial Fragua, 2009.

Deveny, Thomas G. *Migration in Contemporary Hispanic Cinema*. Lanham: Scarecrow Press, 2012.

Gentile, Alessandro, Anna Sanmartín Ortí, Ana Lucía Hernández Cordero. *La sombra de la crisis. La sociedad española en el horizonte de 2018*. Madrid: Centro Reina Sofía Sobre Adolescencia y Juventud. Fundación de Ayuda contra la Drogadicción (FAD), 2014.

Gubern, Roman, José Enrique Monterde, Julio Pérez Perucha, Esteve Riambau, and Casimiro Torreiro. *Historia del cine español*. 7th ed. Madrid: Cátedra, 2010.

Henseler, Christine, ed. *Generation X Goes Global: Mapping a Youth Culture in Motion*. New York: Routledge, 2013.

Labanji, Jo, and Tatjana Pavlovic, eds. *A Companion to Spanish Cinema*. Malden: Wiley-Blackwell, 2012.

Lomba, Modesto, ed. *Geography of Spanish Fashion*. Madrid: Artes Gráficas, 2009.

López de Zuazo Algar, Antonio. *The History of Spanish Newspapers*. Thornton Cleveleys: Ibertext, 2010.

Manzanera López, Laura. *Del corsé al tanga. 100 años de moda en España*. Barcelona: Ediciones Península, 2011.

Megías Quirós, Ignacio, and Elena Rodríguez San Julián. *Jóvenes y comunicación. La impronta de lo virtual*. Madrid: Centro Reina Sofía Sobre Adolescencia y Juventud. Fundación de Ayuda contra la Drogadicción (FAD), 2014.

Mira Nouselles, Alberto. *The A to Z of Spanish Cinema*. Lanham: Scarecrow Press, 2010.

Pavlović, Tatjana, Inmaculada Álvarez, Rosana Blanco-Cano, Anitra Grisales, Alejandra Osorio, and Alejandra Sánchez. *100 Years of Spanish Cinema*. Chichester: Wiley-Blackwell, 2009.

Pohl, Burkhard, and Jörg Türschmann, eds. *Miradas glocales. Cine español en el cambio de milenio*. Madrid: Iberoamericana, 2007.

Ramírez Nicolás, Inés. *Fashion, the Sweetheart of Electronic Commerce in Spain*. Madrid: eMarket Services Spain, 2013.

Richardson, Nathan E. *Constructing Spain: The Re-Imagination of Space and Place in Fiction and Film, 1953–2003*. Lanham: Bucknell University Press, 2012.

Rodríguez San Julián, I. Megías Quirós y T. Menéndez Hevia. *Consumo televisivo, series e Internet*. Madrid: Centro Reina Sofía Sobre Adolescencia y Juventud. Fundación de Ayuda contra la Drogadicción (FAD), 2012.

Rusiñol, Pere. "Introducción." In *Papel Mojado. Reality News/Mongolia*. Barcelona: Debate, 2013.

Sanmartín Ortí, Anna. *Indicadores Básicos de la Juventud*. Madrid: Centro Reina Sofía Sobre Adolescencia y Juventud. Fundación de Ayuda contra la Drogadicción (FAD), 2013.

Smith, Paul Julian. *Contemporary Spanish Culture: TV, Fashion, Art and Film*. Cambridge: Polity Press, 2003.

Sousa Congosto, Francisco de. *Introducción a la historia de la Indumentaria en España*. Madrid: ISTMO, 2007.

Stone, Rob. *Spanish Cinema*. London: Pearson, 2002.

Triana Toribio, Núria. *Spanish National Cinema*. London: Routledge, 2003.

INDEX

About the Author

Enrique Ávila López, PhD, is Cross-Appointed Associate Professor in the Departments of Humanities and General Education at Mount Royal University in Calgary, Canada. He received his master's degree in Latin American studies from the University of Liverpool and then completed his doctorate in contemporary Spanish Peninsular women's literature at Durham University in the United Kingdom. His published works include more than a dozen peer-reviewed articles in specialized international journals, book chapters, encyclopedia entries, and conference proceedings. His first book was a seminal work on the literature of Rosa Regàs, which received the Victoria Urbano Critical Award by the North American Hispanic Feminist Association AILCFH in 2007.